Lecture Notes in Computer Science 8619

Commenced Publication in 1973
Founding and Former Series Editors:
Gerhard Goos, Juris Hartmanis, and Jan van Leeuwen

More information about this series at http://www.springer.com/series/7409

Malika Auvray · Christian Duriez (Eds.)

Haptics: Neuroscience, Devices, Modeling, and Applications

9th International Conference, EuroHaptics 2014
Versailles, France, June 24–26, 2014
Proceedings, Part II

Springer

Editors
Malika Auvray
CNRS
Paris
France

Christian Duriez
Inria Lille
Villeneuve d'Ascq
France

ISSN 0302-9743
ISBN 978-3-662-44195-4
DOI 10.1007/978-3-662-44196-1

ISSN 1611-3349 (electronic)
ISBN 978-3-662-44196-1 (eBook)

Library of Congress Control Number: 2014949159

LNCS Sublibrary: SL3 – Information Systems and Applications, incl. Internet/Web, and HCI

Springer Heidelberg New York Dordrecht London

Printed on acid-free paper

Springer is part of Springer Science+Business Media (www.springer.com)

Preface

Welcome to the proceedings of the EuroHaptics 2014 conference. EuroHaptics is the primary European conference in the field of haptics and extends far beyond this frontier, attracting researchers from all over the world. This year, the authors represented 24 countries, with 42 % of them coming from Europe, 36 % from Asia, 17 % from America, and 5 % from Oceania.

EuroHaptics 2014 took place in Versailles, France, during June 24–27. We received a total of 183 submissions for the full-paper category. The review process led to 118 of these being accepted for publication. These papers were presented at the conference either as oral presentations (36) or as poster presentations (82). In the proceedings, the two types of presentation were considered as equal with no distinction being made between them. Furthermore, 27 demos were exhibited, each of them resulting in a short paper included in the proceedings. In addition, we are grateful to the three distinguished researchers who took part in the conference as keynote speakers: Aude Oliva, Karon McLean, and Jörg Sennheiser.

Conferences would not be possible without the challenging work conducted by the referees. This year the selection of papers was based on 627 reviews supervised by the 46 members of the Program Committee, aided by 321 external reviewers. On behalf of the EuroHaptics 2014 Organizing Committee, we would like to thank the members of the Program Committee and the reviewers for their remarkable effort. These proceedings reflect the multidisciplinary nature of Euro- Haptics with articles in human–computer interaction, human–robot interactions, neuroscience, perception and psychophysics, biomechanics and motor control, modelling and simulation, all involving a broad range of applications in medicine, rehabilitation, art, and design. This variety highlights that the field of haptics is of interest in many areas of science and technology all over the world. We hope that readers will enjoy the diversity of topics and disciplines linked to haptics present in the proceedings.

It is our pleasure to acknowledge all the people involved in the organization of this event, making EuroHaptics 2014 a memorable event. We would like to express our gratitude to the organizations that supported this event (the CNRS, the ISIR, the UPMC) and to our Platinum (Continental, Mercedes-Benz), Gold (CEA LIST, Technicolor), and Silver (Haption, Force Dimension, Immersion, Senseg, Elitac, Vibreight, Aito) sponsors. We also thank the organizing students for their precious help. Finally, we would like to acknowledge in particular General Chair Vincent Hayward, who spared no effort in the preparation of this conference and whose commitment and endless expertise in the field of haptics generated constant admiration throughout this adventure.

May 2014   Malika Auvray
                                                                           Christian Duriez

Organization

Program Committee

Mehdi Ammi	Laboratoire d'Informatique pour la Mécanique et les Sciences de l'Ingénieur, Orsay, France
Malika Auvray	Institut Jean Nicod, France
Wael Bachta	Université Pierre et Marie Curie, France
Gabriel Baud-Bovy	Istituto Italiano di Tecnologia, Italy
Bernard Bayle	Telecom Physique Strasbourg, France
Wouter Bergmann	Vrije Universiteit, Amsterdam, The Netherlands
Monica Bordegoni	Politecnico di Milano, Italy
Seungmoon Choi	Pohang University of Science and Technology, Republic of Korea
Sabine Coquillart	Institut National de Recherche en Informatique et en Automatique, France
Knut Drewing	Gießen Universität, Germany
Christian Duriez	Institut National de Recherche en Informatique et en Automatique, France
Antonio Frisoli	Scuola Superiore Sant'Anna, Italy
Alberto Gallace	Università degli Studi di Milano - Bicocca, Italy
Edouard Gentaz	Université de Genève, Switzerland
Gregory Gerling	University of Virginia, USA
Brent Gillespie	University of Michigan, USA
Frédéric Giraud	University of Lille, France
Martin Grunwald	Universität Leipzig, Germany
Moustapha Hafez	Commissariat à l'énergie atomique et aux énergies alternatives, France
Sylvain Hanneton	Université Paris-Descartes, France
Mathias Harders	Innsbruck University, Austria
Vanessa Harrar	Université de Montréal, Canada
Vincent Hayward	Université Pierre et Marie Curie, France
Ali Israr	Disney Research, USA
Hiroyuki Kajimoto	The University of Electro-Communications, Japan
Astrid Kappers	Vrije Universiteit, The Netherlands
Abderrahmane Kheddar	Centre National de la Recherche Scientifique, France
Katherine Kuchenbecker	University of Pennsylvania, USA
Anatole Lecuyer	Institut National de Recherche en Informatique et en Automatique, France
Vincent Levesque	Immersion Corporation Canada, Canada

Maud Marchal	Institut National de Recherche en Informatique et en Automatique, France
Marcia O'Malley	Rice University, USA
Ian Oakley	Ulsan National Institute of Science and Technology, Republic of Korea
Miguel Otaduy	Universidad Rey Juan Carlos, Spain
Sabrina Panëels	Commissariat à l'énergie atomique et aux énergies alternatives, France
Angelika Peer	Technische Universität München, Germany
Igor Peterlik	Institut Hospitalo-Universitaire Strasbourg, France
Thomas Pietrzak	Université Lille 1, France
Myrthe Plaisier	Vrije Universiteit, The Netherlands
Roope Raisemo	University of Tampere, Finland
Jean-Pierre Richard	Ecole centrale de Lille, France
Jee-Hwan Ruy	Korea University of Technology, Republic of Korea
Betty Semail	Université Lille 1, France
Jeroen Smeets	Vrije Universiteit, The Netherlands
Alexander Terekhov	Université Pierre et Marie Curie, France
Jean-Louis Thonnard	Université catholique de Louvain, Belgium
Jan Vanerp	Netherlands Organisation for Applied Scientific Research TNO, The Netherlands
Dangxiao Wang	Beihang University, China
Junji Watanabe	NTT Communication Science Laboratories, Japan
Mounia Ziat	Northern Michigan University, USA

Additional Reviewers

Achibet, Merwan
Adams, Richard
Ahmaniemi, Teemu
Akhtar, Aadeel
Aliakseyeu, Dzmitry
Altinsoy, Ercan
Ammi, Mehdi
Anastassova, Margarita
Argelaguet, Ferran
Arsicault, Marc
Artz, Edward
Avraham, Guy
Azanon, Elena
Ballesteros, Soledad
Barbic, Jernej
Barnett-Cowan, Michael
Barrea, Allan

Basdogan, Cagatay
Baud-Bovy, Gabriel
Bellan, Valeria
Bellik, Yacine
Bender, Jan
Berkelman, Peter
Berrezag, Amir
Bianchi, Andrea
Bianchi, Matteo
Blank, Amy
Bleuler, Hannes
Blum, Jeffrey
Bochereau, Serena
Bolzmacher, Christian
Bordegoni, Monica
Borst, Christoph
Boukallel, Mehdi

Bowthorpe, Meaghan
Brayda, Luca Giulio
Brock, Anke
Brown, Jeremy
Bueno, Marie-Ange
Cappadocia, David
Cha, Elizabeth
Changeon, Gwénaël
Choi, Kup-Sze
Cholewiak, Roger
Chun, Jaemin
Ciocarlie, Matei
Cirio, Gabriel
Colgate, J. Edward
Colledani, Frédéric
Cotin, Stéphane
Courtecuisse, Hadrien
Craig, James
Culbertson, Heather
Danieau, Fabien
Debats, Nienke
Delhaye, Benoit
Dequidt, Jeremie
Drewing, Knut
Eck, Ulrich
El Saddik, Abdulmotaleb
Erwin, Andrew
Esteves, Augusto
Etzi, Roberta
Fernando, Charith Lasantha
Ferre, Manuel
Ferrise, Francesco
Filatov, Anton
Filingeri, Davide
Fishel, Jeremy
Fitle, Kyle
Fleureau, Julien
Fontana, Federico
Friedl, Ken
Friedman, Jason
Frissen, Ilja
Fu, Michael
Fukumoto, Masaaki
Gapenne, Olivier
Gaponov, Igor
Garre, Carlos

Gatti, Elia
Gentaz, Edouard
Georges, Didier
Georges, Jean-Philippe
Gergondet, Pierre
Gerling, Gregory
Gilles, Benjamin
Giordano, Bruno
Giraud, Frédéric
Giraud-Audine, Christophe
Goldreich, Daniel
Gosselin, Florian
Gowrishankar, Ganesh
Grisoni, Laurent
Grunwald, Martin
Gueorguiev, David
Guest, Steve
Guiatni, Mohamed
Guinan, Ashley
Guéniat, Florimond
H, M
Hachisu, Taku
Hafez, Moustapha
Hagura, Nobuhiro
Hakulinen, Jaakko
Hartcher-O'Brien, Jess
Hasegawa, Shoichi
Hatzfeld, Christian
Hayward, Vincent
Heller, Morton
Henriques, Denise
Hetel, Laurentiu
Heylen, Dirk
Hirota, Koichi
Ho, Cristy
Howard, Thomas
Hughes, Barry
Huisman, Gijs
Hwang, Inwook
Hwang, Jung-Hoon
Isokoski, Poika
Israr, Ali
Jafari, Aghil
Jansen, Sander
Jenke, Robert
Jeon, Seokhee

Jones, Lynette
Jungers, Marc
Kaaresoja, Topi
Kaczmarek, Kurt
Kajimoto, Hiroyuki
Kashino, Makio
Katz, Brian
Keetels, Mirjam
Kim, Dongwon
Kim, Gerard Jounghyun
Kim, Kibum
Kim, Seung-Chan
Kim, Yeongmi
Kingma, Idsart
Kitada, Ryo
Klatzky, Roberta
Klöcker, Anne
Konyo, Masashi
Kruse, Onno
Kruszewski, Alexandre
Kuber, Ravi
Kucukyilmaz, Ayse
Kuling, Irene
Kurita, Yuichi
Kuroki, Scinob
Kyung, Ki-Uk
Laliberté, Thierry
Lang, Jochen
Latash, Marc
Lecuyer, Anatol
Lecuyer, Anatole
Lee, Chang-Gyu
Lee, Jaebong
Leib, Raz
Lenay, Charles
Levy-Tzedek, Shelly
Lezkan, Alexandra
Li, Jiting
Li, Zhenxing
Longo, Matthew
Lozada, José
Lozano, Cecil
Lylykangas, Jani
M., Manivannan
Maciel, Anderson
Magnusson, Charlotte

Maij, Femke
Majewicz, Ann
Makin, Tamar
Makino, Yasutoshi
Malacria, Sylvain
Marshall, Alan
Martin, Jean-Claude
Matsumiya, Kazumichi
Mcdonald, Craig
Mehdi, Boukallel
Menelas, Bob
Menelas, Bob-Antoine
Mersha, Abeje
Miki, Norihisa
Millet, Guillaume
Misztal, Marek
Miyaki, Takashi
Modarres, Ali
Mohamed, Bouri
Mohamed, Guiatni
Moscatelli, Alessandro
Mugge, Winfred
Mullenbach, Joe
Muller, Stefanie
Muller, Stephanie
Naceri, Abdeldjallil
Nadal, Clément
Nagakubo, Akihiko
Nakatani, Masashi
Niemeyer, Gunter
Nishida, Shinya
Nitsch, Verena
Nonomura, Yoshimune
O'Malley, Marcia
O'Modhrain, Sile
Ohmura, Yoshiyuki
Okamoto, Shogo
Okamura, Allison
Otaduy, Miguel
Ouarti, Nizar
Overvliet, Krista
Pakkanen, Toni
Palluel-Germain, Richard
Panday, Virjanand
Panzirsch, Michael
Parise, Cesare Valerio

Park, Young-Woo
Pawluk, Dianne
Payandeh, Shahram
Pehlivan, Ali Utku
Perez, Alvaro G.
Peshkin, Michael
Peterlik, Igor
Petit, Damien
Picard, Delphine
Picinali, Lorenzo
Pielot, Martin
Popov, Dmitry
Potier, Ludovic
Prattichizzo, Domenico
Pritchett, Lisa
Qiu, Zhaopeng
Rakkolainen, Ismo
Rantala, Jussi
Reinkensmeyer, David J.
Roberts, Jonathan
Rohde, Marieke
Romano, Daniele
Rose, Chad
Roudaut, Anne
Rovira, Katia
Ruffaldi, Emanuele
Russomanno, Alex
Ryu, Jeha
Saal, Hannes
Saboune, Jamal
Saga, Satoshi
Sahbani, Anis
Salargna, Fabrice
Salminen, Katri
Samur, Evren
Santangelo, Valerio
Sato, Katsunari
Schneegass, Stefan
Schneider, Oliver
Schuwerk, Clemens
Scilingo, Enzo Pasquale
Secchi, Cristian
Seizova-Cajic, Tatjana
Shin, Euncheon
Shull, Pete
Sinclair, Stephen

Sircoulomb, Vincent
Smeets, Jeroen
Solazzi, Massimiliano
Souvestre, Florent
Steinbach, Eckehard
Strachan, Steven
Tagliabue, Michele
Takamuku, Shinya
Takasaki, Masaya
Takemura, Kenjiro
Talbi, Abdelkrim
Talvas, Anthony
Tan, Hong
Tanaka, Yoshihiro
Tao, Zeng
Thonnard, Jean-Louis
Trejos, Ana Luisa
Tsalamlal, Yacine
Tsetserukou, Dzmitry
Tsuji, Toshiaki
Ursu, Daniel
van Beek, Femke E.
Van Dam, Loes
van den Dobbelsteen, John
Van Erp, Jan
van Polanen, Vonne
Vander Poorten, Emmanuel
Veit, Manuel
Velazquez, Ramiro
Vidal Verdu, Fernando
Vidal, Franck
Visell, Yon
Vlachos, Kostas
Wagemans, Johan
Wall, Lorna
Wang, Dangxiao
Wang, Qi
Wang, Yuxiang
Wei, Lei
Weiss, Astrid
Wesslein, Ann-Katrin
Wiertlewski, Michael
Willaert, Bert
Winck, Ryder
Winter, Christophe
Wolf, Katrin

Wu, Jun
Yamamoto, Akio
Yang, Gi-Hun
Yang, Yi
Yazdian, Seiedmuhammad
Yim, Sunghoon
Yousef, Hanna
Yu, Bo

Zaad, Hashtrudi
Zemiti, Nabil
Zeng, Tao
Zhang, Yuru
Ziat, Mounia
Zoller, Ingo
Zophoniasson, Harald
Zorn, Lucile

Contents – Part II

Robotics or Medical Applications

Modeling and Simulation

Demo Papers

Contents – Part I

Human Computer Interaction

Surface or Texture Perception and Display

Haptic Illusion and Rehabilitation

Experimental Validation of a Rapid, Adaptive Robotic Assessment of the MCP Joint Angle Difference Threshold

Mike D. Rinderknecht[✉], Werner L. Popp, Olivier Lambercy,
and Roger Gassert

Rehabilitation Engineering Lab, ETH Zurich, Zurich, Switzerland
{miker,poppw,olambercy,gassertr}@ethz.ch

Abstract. This paper presents an experimental evaluation of a rapid, adaptive assessment of the difference threshold (DL) of passive metacarpophalangeal index finger joint flexion using a robotic device. Parameter Estimation by Sequential Testing (PEST) is compared to the method of constant stimuli (MOCS) using a two-alternative forced-choice paradigm. The pilot study with 13 healthy subjects provided DLs within similar ranges for MOCS and PEST, averaging at $2.15° \pm 0.77°$ and $1.73° \pm 0.78°$, respectively, in accordance with the literature. However, no significant correlation was found between the two methods ($r(11) = 0.09$, $p = 0.762$). The average number of trials required for PEST to converge was 58.7 ± 17.6, and significantly lower compared to 120 trials for MOCS ($p < 0.001$), leading to an assessment time of under 15 min. These results suggest that rapid, adaptive methods, such as PEST, could be successfully implemented in novel robotic tools for clinical assessment of sensory deficits.

Keywords: Robot-assisted assessment · Sensory function · Proprioception · Difference threshold · Psychophysics · Hand function

1 Introduction

Robotic tools have been proposed for a more objective evaluation of sensory thresholds. This approach bears a high potential for the assessment of sensory deficits, e.g., in neurologically impaired patients, addressing the many shortcomings of existing sensory assessment tests, which suffer from low sensitivity and high variability [1], flooring effects [2] and poor inter-rater reliability [3]. Previous studies determined difference thresholds (DLs) of finger position at the level of the metacarpophalangeal (MCP) joint as a measure of proprioception [4–6]. All of these employed the method of constant stimuli (MOCS) [7], which is known to be inefficient — in terms of the required number of stimulus presentations to reach a specified error variance — compared to adaptive stimulus placement methods [8]. This impedes its applicability in clinical settings, where short assessments are favored due to the busy and limited therapy schedule of

© Springer-Verlag Berlin Heidelberg 2014
M. Auvray and C. Duriez (Eds.): EuroHaptics 2014, Part II, LNCS 8619, pp. 3–10, 2014.
DOI: 10.1007/978-3-662-44196-1_1

patients. Moreover, the choice of experimental paradigm has a crucial effect on the DL estimate: while psychophysical paradigms such as Yes-No, Remainder and Same-Different provide quantitative results, they suffer from low performance and are contaminated by effects of the decision criterion, i.e., response bias [7,9].

The goal of this pilot study was to evaluate the possibility of reducing the number of required trials for the assessment of the DL of passive index finger displacements with the Robotic Sensory Trainer, a 1 degree-of-freedom (DOF) robot developed in earlier work by Lambercy et al. [6]. For this purpose, DLs were determined in 13 healthy subjects using an adaptive method named Parameter Estimation by Sequential Testing (PEST) [10], and were compared to the outcomes provided by MOCS. For both methods, a two-alternative forced-choice (2AFC) paradigm was employed, as it is expected to be a more objective, more sensitive and almost bias-free alternative to the previously used paradigms [9].

2   Methods

2.1   Subjects

Thirteen healthy subjects (S1-S13, 28.3 ± 3.2 years, 10 males, 12 right handed) participated in this pilot study. Handedness was assessed with the Edinburgh Handedness Inventory [11]. Exclusion criteria were any sensory or motor deficits in the hand, or any history of neurological or hand injury. The study was approved by the institutional ethics committee of the ETH Zurich (EK 2011-N-61). All subjects gave informed consent before participating in the experiment.

2.2   Apparatus

An improved version of the Robotic Sensory Trainer [6] was used in this study to provide well-controlled, passive index MCP joint angle displacements in flexion and extension (Fig. 1). The passive flexion and extension of the finger is achieved trough a remote center of motion mechanism driven by a geared DC motor (RE-max 29, planetary gearhead GD 32 A 111:1, Maxon Motor, Sachseln, Switzerland). The index finger is inserted and attached to an adjustable finger carriage, which is mounted on top of the remote center of motion mechanism. The major changes to the initial design are found in the ergonomics of the device, with the addition of 6DOF positioning structures for the forearm support and the hand module supporting finger and palm, ensuring a more comfortable placement of the subject's hand and finger on the device. These modifications should also allow stroke patients with pathological hand and arm postures to use the device.

2.3   Experimental Protocol

The experiment consisted of two randomized sessions in which stimulus levels of MCP joint angle displacement where defined by either the (i) MOCS, or (ii) the

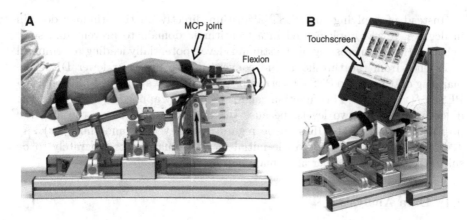

Fig. 1. (A) Side view of the improved version of the Robotic Sensory Trainer. (B) Experimental setup with a touchscreen, covering the tested hand, for instructions and subject feedback on perceived stimuli provided by the untested hand.

adaptive PEST procedure. In both sessions, subjects sat on a chair in front of the Robotic Sensory Trainer. The orientation of the forearm and palm supports were adjusted to ensure a comfortable posture. The right index finger as well as the hand and forearm were strapped to the device using Velcro® bands. Special care was taken to align the MCP joint with the remote center of motion of the Robotic Sensory Trainer. Only the index finger of the right hand was tested.

Regardless of the method, a trial consisted of two intervals, i.e., two successive passive finger movements to different MCP flexion angles applied by the Robotic Sensory Trainer, always starting from a rest position (all finger joints aligned). Each flexion movement lasted 1 s and the MCP flexion angle was maintained for a duration of 1.5 s. After the trial, subjects were asked which of the two angular movements was larger and provided their response directly on the touchscreen using their left hand. The two angles were presented in randomized order and always symmetrically arranged around a reference angle of 20° MCP flexion. The difference between the two angles was denoted $\Delta\theta$ (in the following referred to as stimulus level) and was always defined as positive and determined by either MOCS or PEST. In the case of MOCS, the angle differences $\Delta\theta \in \{0.5, 1.5, 3.5, 5.5\}°$ were presented 30× each in randomized order, resulting in 120 trials, similar to [6]. In the case of PEST, the stimulus levels are defined by a set of heuristic rules taking past stimuli and observer's responses into account [10]. The PEST algorithm was set to start at $\Delta\theta = 5.5°$ and the first step was defined to be ±2°. The PEST parameters $W = 1$ and $P_t = 0.75$ were used for the Wald sequential likelihood-ratio test, leading to a convergence of the PEST algorithm towards 75 % correct responses in a 2AFC experiment, at which we define the DL. The PEST session was terminated when either the minimum step of ±0.1°, a total of 120 trials or 20 consecutive trials at the same $\Delta\theta$ were reached.

Instead of applying the PEST algorithm directly on the stimulus domain in degrees, it was implemented in a logarithmic domain to prevent undesired behavior (i.e., zero crossing of the stimulus level, potentially leading to temporal divergence from the threshold, and convergence to upper or lower DL). The mapping of stimulus to PEST level can be performed by applying $f :$ Stimulus $\rightarrow$ PEST, $f(x) = \log x$. This function cannot be directly applied to a step, i.e., the difference between two levels, because the mapping depends on the absolute position. Instead, a step has to be regarded as a vector, and thus $f(x)$ and $f^{-1}(x)$ have to be applied to the initial and terminal points separately to be subtracted from each other after mapping.

2.4   Data Analysis

For both methods, the psychometric function $\psi(x)$ in Eq. (1) was fitted to the proportion of correct responses at stimulus levels x using a Maximum Likelihood criterion [12].

$$\psi(x; \alpha, \beta, \gamma, \lambda) = \gamma + (1 - \gamma - \lambda) F(x; \alpha, \beta) \tag{1}$$

The guessing rate γ was set to 0.5 (2AFC paradigm), while the lapse rate λ was kept at 0. Using a cumulative normal function for $F(x)$, α and β correspond to the inflection point and the slope at this point, respectively. The DL value was determined by $\psi^{-1}(x) = 0.75$. Mean and standard deviation, as well as the Weber fraction K (with a reference angle of $20°$), were calculated across subjects for the DL values given by the fitting procedures (DL^{fit}_{MOCS} and DL^{fit}_{PEST}) and the converged PEST sequences (DL^{convg}_{PEST}). Pearson's correlation was calculated between DL^{fit}_{PEST} and DL^{fit}_{MOCS}, as well as between DL^{fit}_{PEST} and DL^{convg}_{PEST} to validate the fitting procedure. Furthermore, a linear regression model was fitted to the latter pair. As the data was normally distributed, a one-sample t-test was performed to compare the required number of PEST trials to the 120 trials of the MOCS. All significance levels were set to $\alpha = 0.05$. Statistical analyses were performed in MATLAB 7.14 (MathWorks, Natick, MA) and SPSS 22.0 (IBM, Armonk, NY).

3   Results

The demographic characteristics of the subjects and the main outcome measures are summarized in Table 1. The difference thresholds were $\overline{DL}^{fit}_{MOCS} = 2.15° \pm 0.77°$ ($K = 10.8\% \pm 3.8\%$), $\overline{DL}^{fit}_{PEST} = 1.73° \pm 0.78°$ ($K = 8.6\% \pm 3.9\%$) and $\overline{DL}^{convg}_{PEST} = 1.59° \pm 0.77°$ ($K = 7.9\% \pm 3.9\%$).

The MOCS and PEST response and stimulus level sequences are shown in Fig. 2 for a representative subject (S5) together with the estimated DL, fitted after every trial using the data from the preceding trials. Given these responses at various stimulus differences, the percentage of correct responses is calculated in order to fit the psychometric function through those points (Fig. 3 *Left* illustrates this for subject S5).

Table 1. Demographic characteristics, estimated DLs and total number of required PEST trials.

Subject	Gender	Dominant hand	Age [years]	Finger length* [mm]	DL MOCS (fit) [°]	DL PEST (fit) [°]	DL PEST (convg) [°]	PEST trials
S1	F	right	35	105	1.80	1.41	0.90	72
S2	M	right	30	93	1.51	2.83	2.42	49
S3	M	right	31	96	2.82	1.30	1.20	72
S4	F	right	26	90	2.06	1.14	1.20	40
S5	M	right	22	95	2.01	1.04	0.95	81
S6	M	right	31	93	1.75	0.55	0.51	58
S7	M	right	26	96	2.46	2.10	2.17	66
S8	M	left	28	104	1.46	2.18	1.50	90
S9	M	right	28	84	1.73	1.21	1.20	29
S10	M	right	25	93	4.35	2.09	2.05	65
S11	M	right	29	87	1.63	2.37	2.29	53
S12	M	right	28	96	1.97	1.11	1.07	41
S13	F	right	29	85	2.40	3.17	3.22	47
Mean±SD			28.3±3.2	93.6±6.3	2.15±0.77	1.73±0.78	1.59±0.77	58.7±17.6

*measured from the MCP joint to the tip of the index finger.

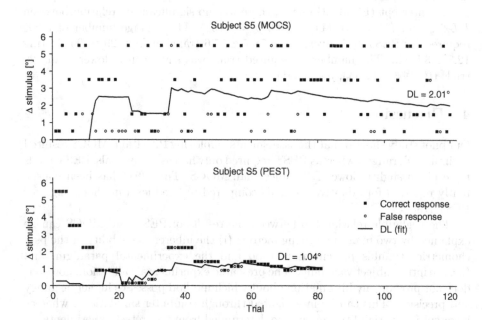

Fig. 2. *Top:* MOCS sequence of a representative subject (S5). The subject's responses are plotted for each trial at the corresponding presented stimulus difference. Correct and false responses are indicated by black squares and white circles, respectively. After every trial the fitting procedure was run based on the preceding trials to illustrate the evolution of the DL estimate. *Bottom:* PEST sequence from the same subject (S5).

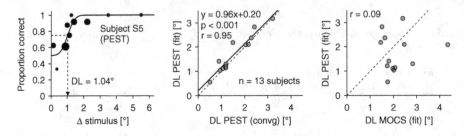

Fig. 3. *Left:* Psychometric function fitted to the PEST data of a representative subject (S5). The size of the black dots indicates the number of repetitions at same $\Delta\theta$. *Middle:* DL_{PEST}^{fit} plotted against DL_{PEST}^{convg} for each subject, showing strong correlation between the two. The bold black line indicates the fitted linear model. *Right:* DL_{PEST}^{fit} plotted against DL_{MOCS}^{fit}, showing moderate agreement between the two. The dashed lines indicate the diagonal where both methods would provide identical values.

At the group level, a strong positive correlation was found between DL_{PEST}^{fit} and DL_{PEST}^{convg}, which was statistically significant ($r(11) = 0.95$, $p < 0.001$). The coefficients (with 95 % confidence bounds) of the linear model fitted to the data were found to be 0.96 (0.76, 1.17) for the slope and 0.20 ($-0.16, 0.55$) for the intercept (Fig. 3). However, there was no significant correlation between DL_{MOCS}^{fit} and DL_{PEST}^{fit} ($r(11) = 0.09$, $p = 0.762$). The average number of trials required for PEST to converge was 58.7 ± 17.6 (ranging from 29 to 90) lasting 12.8 ± 3.5 min. The number of required trials was significantly lower than 120 trials ($t(12) = -12.533$, $p < 0.001$).

4   Discussion

Our pilot study showed that the assessments employing PEST and MOCS resulted in similar DL ranges, whereas PEST required only half as many trials. PEST tends to result in slightly lower DL values than MOCS. This effect has been consistently reported for adaptive methods compared to fixed-level methods, e.g., for PEST [13].

The negligible relationship between the results of PEST and MOCS can be explained by two main underlying factors: (i) the inherent variability of the psychometric stimulus placement method and the experimental paradigm, and (ii), the intra-subject variability. The presented experimental validation, however, does not provide any information about which method possesses higher accuracy and precision. This can be investigated through computer simulations, whereas intra-subject variability can only be determined from test-retest experiments.

As expected, the DL values from this pilot study ($\overline{DL_{MOCS}^{fit}} = 2.15°$, $\overline{DL_{PEST}^{fit}} = 1.73°$) lie in a similar range as the values reported in the literature, i.e., 2.46° [6], 2.3° [4], from 1.7° to 2.5° [5]. One reason for the tendency to lower values than reported in our previous work using the Robotic Sensory Trainer [6], is that 2AFC paradigms allow measurements of sensitivity to smaller thresholds compared to Same-Different implementations [9].

As it can be observed in Fig. 2, only a few false response at a large stimulus difference (trials 36 and 66 for subject S5) of the MOCS sequence can have a large impact on the estimated DL, due to the suboptimal placement of stimuli. This can lead to a long series of trials required to approach the DL again, as visible by the relatively constant descent of the DL estimate, which does not yet seem to have reached a steady state by the 120th trial. The DL estimate based on PEST may be less affected by erroneous trials, i.e., lapses, since the algorithm automatically tries to place the stimuli around the DL.

The fact that the DL values determined by the fitted PEST data correlate strongly with the DLs provided by the converged PEST sequences demonstrates that the fitting procedure works reliably. This offers the notable possibility to extract a DL from sequences where the PEST algorithm did not converge, e.g., due to an insufficient number of trials or late divergence because of attention loss. Moreover, methods such as PEST offer a major advantage: They can quickly adapt over a wide range in order to present stimuli at levels holding the most information, i.e., around the steeper part of the psychometric function. This feature is especially important in the context of assessments in patients, where there is no prior knowledge about the location of the DL.

This pilot study provides evidence that the assessment duration of the MCP joint angle DL can be reduced to below 15 min by using an adaptive robotic assessment tool, while providing more objective and sensitive measurements compared to previously presented approaches, e.g., by Lambercy et al. [6], and conventional assessments. The use of such fast, adaptive robot-assisted methods holds promise for successful implementation in novel clinical assessment tools of sensory deficits, providing better insights into the prevalence of post-stroke sensory deficits and allowing the design of prospective patient-tailored therapies.

Acknowledgments. The authors would like to thank J.-C. Metzger for inspiring and profitable discussions, as well as J. Liepert, M. Kaiser and V. Raible for their help in defining the clinical requirements for stroke patients. This research was supported by the National Center of Competence in Research on Neural Plasticity and Repair of the Swiss National Science Foundation, the Janggen-Pöhn Foundation and ETH Zurich.

References

1. Bell-Krotoski, J., Weinstein, S., Weinstein, C.: Testing sensibility, including touch-pressure, two-point discrimination, point localization, and vibration. J. Hand Ther. **6**(2), 114–123 (1993)
2. Jerosch-Herold, C.: A study of the relative responsiveness of five sensibility tests for assessment of recovery after median nerve injury and repair. J. Hand Surg.-Brit. Eur. **28**(3), 255–260 (2003)
3. Lincoln, N.B., Crow, J.L., Jackson, J.M., Waters, G.R., Adams, S.A., Hodgson, P.: The unreliability of sensory assessments. Clin. Rehabil. **5**(4), 273–282 (1991)
4. Brewer, B.R., Fagan, M., Klatzky, R.L., Matsuoka, Y.: Perceptual limits for a robotic rehabilitation environment using visual feedback distortion. IEEE Trans. Neural Syst. Rehabil. Eng. **13**(1), 1–11 (2005)

5. Tan, H.Z., Srinivasan, M.A., Reed, C.M., Durlach, N.I.: Discrimination and identification of finger joint-angle position using active motion. ACM Trans. Appl. Percept. (TAP) **4**(2), 10 (2007)
6. Lambercy, O., Juárez Robles, A., Kim, Y., Gassert, R.: Design of a robotic device for assessment and rehabilitation of hand sensory function. In: 2011 IEEE International Conference on Rehabilitation Robotics (ICORR), pp. 1–6, June 2011
7. Gescheider, G.: Psychophysics: Method, Theory, and Applications. Lawrence Erlbaum Associates, New Jersey (1985)
8. Watson, A.B., Fitzhugh, A.: The method of constant stimuli is inefficient. Percept. Psychophysics **47**(1), 87–91 (1990)
9. Macmillan, N.A., Douglas Creelman, C.: Detection Theory: A User's Guide. Lawrence Erlbaum Associates, New Jersey (2005)
10. Taylor, M.M., Douglas Creelman, C.: PEST: Efficient estimates on probability functions. J. Acoust. Soc. Am. **41**, 782 (1967)
11. Oldfield, R.C.: The assessment and analysis of handedness: the Edinburgh inventory. Neuropsychologia **9**(1), 97–113 (1971)
12. Prins, N., Kingdom, F.A.A.: Palamedes: matlab routines for analyzing psychophysical data (2009). http://www.palamedestoolbox.org
13. Taylor, M.M., Forbes, S.M., Douglas Creelman, C.: PEST reduces bias in forced choice psychophysics. J. Acoust. Soc. Am. **74**, 1367 (1983)

Friction Sensation Produced by Laterally Asymmetric Vibrotactile Stimulus

Akihiro Imaizumi, Shogo Okamoto[✉], and Yoji Yamada

Department of Mechanical Science and Engineering,
Nagoya University, Nagoya, Japan
okamoto-shogo@mech.nagoya-u.ac.jp

Abstract. Vibrotactile texture stimuli have commonly been used to produce sensations of roughness. The extension of such stimuli to other textural modalities enhances their applicability. We found that laterally asymmetric vibrotactile stimuli cause a sensation of friction rather than vibration. When a vibrotactile contactor moves in one direction, it sticks to the finger pad and induces lateral skin stretch. In contrast, when the contactor moves in the other direction, it slips because of its quick motion and induces little skin stretch. As a result, humans experience frictional sensations in scanning vibrating contactors with their fingertips. We examined participants' subjective responses and measured interactive forces between the finger pad and the contactor. Both perceptual and physical experiments corroborated the hypothesis of the production of a sensation of friction. Laterally asymmetric vibrotactile stimuli increased stretching of the finger pad skin and increased the sensation of friction.

Keywords: Texture display · Skin stretch · Friction · Vibrotactile

1 Introduction

Tactile texture displays have been extensively studied as a user interface technology that complements visual and auditory displays. Texture sensations consist of multiple modalities, including roughness, softness, friction, and thermal sensations. A texture display that addresses more modalities is considered to be more valuable. In the field of vibrotactile texture displays, which have been studied extensively because of their ease of use and commercial availability, many research groups have developed display techniques for roughness sensations. In addition, researchers have studied that the accurate representation of vibratory signals that are generated by rubbing materials impart their textures (e.g., [1]). If friction sensations can be conveyed in addition to these sensations, broader types of textures can be represented by vibrotactile stimuli.

This study was in part supported by KAKENHI Shitsukan (25135717).

© Springer-Verlag Berlin Heidelberg 2014
M. Auvray and C. Duriez (Eds.): EuroHaptics 2014, Part II, LNCS 8619, pp. 11–18, 2014.
DOI: 10.1007/978-3-662-44196-1_2

The objective of this study was to examine how to increase friction sensations using vibrotactile stimuli. Although many studies on frictional vibration between fingers and textures have been conducted [2–4], there has been little research on the production of the sensation of friction using vibrotactile stimuli. This is partly because a mechanism with an unlimited motion range is necessary to present friction sensations when the contactor of a tactile display is traced by a finger in one direction and a friction force works continuously in the opposite direction. Hence, spherical contactors that rotate infinitely in one direction [5] and skin stretchers that do not cause slippage between a finger pad and a stimulator [6,7] have been adopted in practice. In addition, the squeeze effect [8,9] and static electric friction [10] have been used to increase or decrease friction. A unique vibrotactile method was developed by Konyo et al., to convey friction sensations using vibratory stimuli normal to a finger pad and hence simulate high-frequency stick-slip vibration [11]. However, vibrotactile approaches to induce lateral skin stretching for conveying friction sensations have yet to be reported (see also the last paragraph in Sect. 2).

As described in Sect. 2, we asymmetrically vibrated a tactile contactor or stimulator in a direction tangential to a finger pad to induce the sensation of friction between the finger pad and the contactor. The effectiveness of this type of asymmetric vibrotactile stimulus in producing the sensation of friction was evaluated using a psychological test and friction force measurement.

2 Assumed Principle: Friction Sensations Produced by Laterally Asymmetric Vibrotactile Stimuli

Humans perceive friction from the shear deformation of the finger pad [6]: a larger shear deformation evokes a sensation of greater friction. We separated the frictional conditions of a finger pad moving across a contactor into two phases: sticking and slipping phases. Static and kinetic friction forces act during the sticking and slipping phases, respectively. Naturally, the finger pad stretches more in the sticking phase. We can also induce friction sensations by manipulating the finger pad stretch. In this section, we describe how laterally asymmetric vibration may preferentially cause stick or slippage.

As Fig. 1 shows, we assume that the contactor vibrates asymmetrically, moving more quickly to the right, and more slowly to the left, whereas the maximum displacements are the same in both directions. When the fingertip moves rightward across the contactor, and the contactor moves quickly, the relative velocity between the fingertip and the contactor is sufficiently large for them to slip and hardly stick (Fig. 2, Case A). In contrast, when the contactor moves slowly leftward, sticking frequently occurs because the relative velocity between the fingertip and the contactor is sufficiently small to cause sticking (Case B). Hence, humans feel more friction in Case B and less friction in Case A. As a result, a sensation of friction is induced rather than a sensation of vibration. We call these combinations of fingertip movements and asymmetric contactor motions "sticking conditions."

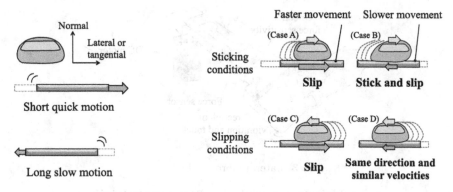

Fig. 1. Laterally asymmetric vibration

Fig. 2. Friction produced by rubbing asymmetrically vibrating contactor with fingertip

When the fingertip moves leftward, the shear deformation is moderate. When the contactor moves quickly, the finger pad deformation is small because the slipping phases is dominant owing to the largely relative velocity between the two bodies (Case C). When the contactor and the fingertip move in the same direction at similar velocities, the skin stretch is minimal because of the small relative displacement between the fingertip and the contactor (Case D). As a result, in these two cases, humans perceive weak friction sensations. We call these conditions "slipping condition."

Also, in cases A and D, the direction of finger deformation may become the same as the finger motion, which never happens in scanning still surfaces. Under such cases, the sense of friction is weakened [12]. Hence, we assume that the phenomenon reported in this article cannot be fully explained by physics but also by perceptual effects.

The overall idea is somewhat similar to the method developed by Chubb et al. [9]. They combined a tangential vibration and ultrasonic vibration to selectively produce shear forces in one direction. Although they used ultrasonic vibrations to reduce frictions when the contactor moves in one direction, we use fast lateral displacement of the contactor to reduce frictions. As a result, our method takes advantage of asymmetric lateral vibrations whereas the earlier study used symmetric ones. Asymmetric vibratory cues were also used for a different purpose in the field of haptics. They provide directional force sensations to a hand in which a vibratory source is grabbed [13, 14].

3 Experimental Setup

3.1 Tangential Vibrotactile Display

We used a vibrotactile display based on a DC motor (RE-40, Maxon) with an encoder (Type L, Maxon), as shown in Fig. 3. The contactor was made of finely

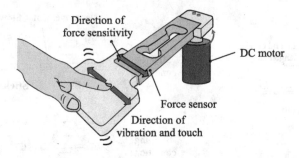

Fig. 3. Lateral vibrotactile display

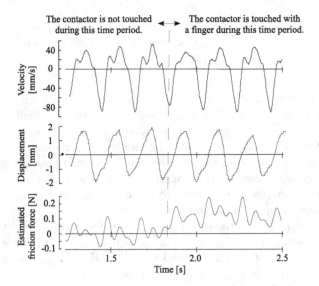

Fig. 4. Saw-toothed vibrotactile stimulus and estimated frictional forces between finger pad and contactor

polished ABS plastic that was fastened to the motor through a strain-gauge load cell (Model 1004, Tedea Huntleigh). This load cell measured the inertial force of the contactor and the frictional force between the contactor and a finger pad. We estimated the friction force by subtracting the inertial force, which is the product of the inertia of the contactor and its acceleration, from the measured force values.

3.2   Laterally Asymmetric Vibrotactile Stimuli

Figure 4 shows an example of the displacement and velocity of the asymmetric vibrotactile stimuli and the estimated friction force between the finger pad and the contactor. The displacement of the contactor was similar to a sawtooth profile with the contactor moving in one direction with a peak speed of

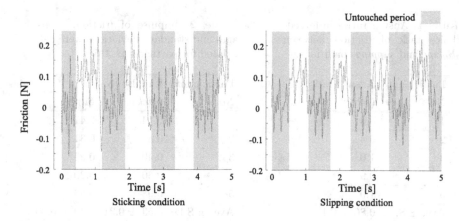

Fig. 5. Sample of friction forces

approximately 90 mm/s and in the other direction with a peak speed of 40 mm/s. The peak-to-peak displacement of the contactor was approximately 3.5 mm, and its frequency was set at 5 Hz. The motion of the contactor was feedback-controlled to maintain asymmetric motion even during contact with the finger pad. We determined the feedback gains using the linear quadratic integral design method. It should be noted that asymmetric motions are not necessarily ensured with large disturbance forces.

4   Experiment: Perceptual and Physical Measurement of Friction Under Laterally Asymmetric Vibrations

4.1   Methods

We tested the differences in the friction and frictional sensations between the *sticking* and *slipping* conditions in two types of experiments.

Five blindfolded and auditory-masked volunteers participated in paired comparison tasks. They were unaware of the objectives of the experiment. They scanned the contactor leftward and rightward for 10 s and identified the direction that corresponded to a stronger sensation of friction in a forced-choice manner. Ten trials were conducted for each volunteer, with the direction of asymmetric vibration randomly changed between trials.

After these tests were completed, we measured the frictional forces between the participants' finger pads and the contactor as each of the participants touched the contactor, using the load cell installed on the contactor. The participants slid their fingertips across the contactor in each of the two directions for 10 s.

Table 1. Answer ratios in forced-choice task of friction between *sticking* and *slipping* conditions.

Participant No.	Answer ratio (*stick* > *slip*)
1	0.6
2	0.8
3	1.0
4	0.9
5	1.0
Ave. ± S.D.	0.86 ± 0.17

Table 2. Impulse of friction. Averages and standard deviations were calculated for participants 2–5.

Participant No.	Impulse [N·s]	
	Stick	*Slip*
1	2.14	2.41
2	0.44	0.31
3	0.40	0.23
4	0.30	0.20
5	0.98	0.83
Ave. ± S.D.	0.53 ± 0.31	0.39 ± 0.30

4.2   Result: Differences in Perceived Friction Between the Two Conditions

Table 1 shows the ratios at which the participants felt that the *sticking* condition produced more friction than the *slipping* condition. Overall, the *sticking* condition was judged to produce more friction than the *slipping* condition ($t_0(4) = 4.81$, $p = 0.0085$, two-tailed paired t-test), except for participant 1. As described later, this participant experienced exceptionally substantial frictional forces for both conditions, potentially due to the large forces in the normal direction with which he pressed the contactor.

4.3   Result: Frictional Force

Figure 5 shows the estimated frictional forces measured during two trials for participant 2. The left and right figures correspond to the *sticking* and *slipping* conditions, respectively. During the masked periods, the frictional forces were small for a sustained period of time, which means that the participant's finger was not in contact with the contactor. The data for these periods were not used in the calculation of the statistics reported later.

Both the magnitude and duration of friction that the participants experienced may affect the participants' perception of friction; therefore, we calculated the impulse of friction forces (integral of friction over time) as a point of reference. Table 2 shows the impulses calculated for a single trial, typically eight strokes for 10 s, under the two conditions. These impulses were larger under the *sticking* condition than under the *slipping* condition, except for participant 1, for whom unusually large frictional forces were measured. We excluded the data for participant 1 from the statistics because of their inconsistency with the results for the other participants. Although conclusions drawn from the results should be viewed with caution because of the small number of participants, the trend observed was statistically valid ($t_0(3) = 7.98$, $p = 0.0021$, two-tailed paired t-test).

5   Conclusions

In this study, we examined the friction sensation caused by vibrotactile stimuli. We assumed that asymmetric vibrotactile stimuli cause anisotropic shear deformation of the finger pad and influence the perception of friction, although such mechanism should be discussed further. We controlled the motion of the contactor to ensure a saw-toothed-like displacement profile that produced an asymmetric vibrotactile stimulus. The participants felt stronger friction when scanning the contactor in one direction than in the other direction. In addition, the impulses of the friction forces between the participants' finger pads and the contactor were different between these two directions. This approach to producing the sensation of friction using vibrotactile stimuli broadens the applicability of vibrotactile texture displays.

References

1. Wiertlewski, M., Lozada, J., Hayward, V.: The spatial spectrum of tangential skin displacementcan encode tactual texture. IEEE Trans. Robot. **27**(3), 461–472 (2011)
2. Fagiani, R., Massi, F., Chatelet, E., Berthier, Y., Akay, A.: Tactile perception by friction induced vibrations. Tribol. Int. **44**(10), 1100–1110 (2011)
3. Nonomura, Y., Fujii, T., Arashi, Y., Miura, T., Maeno, T., Tashiro, K., Kamikawa, Y., Monchi, R.: Tactile impression and friction of water on human skin. Colloids Surf. B **69**(2), 264–267 (2009)
4. Smith, A.M., Chapman, C.E., Deslandes, M., Langlais, J.S., Thibodeau, M.P.: Role of friction and tangential force variation in the subjective scaling of tactile roughness. Exp. Brain Res. **144**(2), 211–223 (2002)
5. Murphy, T.E., Webster III, R.J., Okamura, A.M.: Design and performance of a two-dimensional tactile slip display. In: Proceedings of the EuroHaptics 2004, pp. 130–137 (2004)
6. Provancher, W.R., Sylvester, N.D.: Fingerpad skin stretch increases the perception of virtual friction. IEEE Trans. Haptics **2**(4), 212–223 (2009)
7. Prattichizzo, D., Pacchierotti, C., Rosati, G.: Cutaneous force feedback as a sensory subtraction technique in haptics. IEEE Trans. Haptics **5**, 289–300 (2012)
8. Watanabe, T., Fukui, S.: A method for controlling tactile sensation of surface roughness using ultrasonic vibration. In: Proceedings of the IEEE International Conference on Robotics and Automation, vol. 1, pp. 1134–1139 (1995)
9. Chubb, E.C., Colgate, J.E., Peshkin, M.A.: Shiverpad: a glass haptic surface that produces shear force on a bare finger. IEEE Trans. Haptics **3**(3), 189–198 (2010)
10. Yamamoto, A., Nagasawa, S., Yamamoto, H., Higuchi, T.: Electrostatic tactile display with thin film slider and its application to tactile telepresentation systems. IEEE Trans. Vis. Comput. Graph. **12**(2), 168–177 (2006)
11. Konyo, M., Yamada, H., Okamoto, S., Tadokoro, S.: Alternative display of friction represented by tactile stimulation without tangential force. In: Ferre, M. (ed.) EuroHaptics 2008. LNCS, vol. 5024, pp. 619–629. Springer, Heidelberg (2008)
12. Matsui, K., Okamoto, S., Yamada, Y.: Effects of presentation of shear deformation to finger pad on tracing movements. In: Proceedings of 2011 IEEE International Conference on Robotics and Biomimetics, pp. 2479–2485 (2011)

13. Tappeiner, H.W., Klatzky, R.L., Unger, B., Hollis, R.: Good vibrations: asymmetric vibrations for directional haptic cues. In: Proceedings of the 2009 IEEE World Haptics Conference, pp. 285–289 (2009)
14. Amemiya, T., Gomi, H.: Directional torque perception with brief, asymmetric net rotation of a flywheel. IEEE Trans. Haptics 6(3), 370–375 (2013)

Enhancing the Simulation of Boundaries by Coupling Tactile and Kinesthetic Feedback

Yi Yang[1,2(✉)], Yuru Zhang[1], Betty Lemaire-Semail[2], and Xiaowei Dai[1]

[1] State Key Lab of Virtual Reality Technology and Systems,
Beihang University, Beijing 100191, China
yuru@buaa.edu.cn, {eyang,daixw}@me.buaa.edu.cn
[2] L2EP-IRCICA, University Lille 1, 59650 Villeneuve d'Ascq, France
betty.semail@polytech-lille.fr

Abstract. Haptic enhanced boundaries are important for touch interaction. We quantify the amount of perceived force increment caused by adding variable friction tactile feedback to force feedback in simulating a boundary. We find that using a small lateral force feedback plus a tactile feedback can simulate a boundary which feels as stiff as that simulated by a large lateral force feedback. Moreover, the effect of the tactile feedback may be explained as a lateral force increment caused by increasing the friction coefficient of the touch surface.

Keywords: Squeeze film · Tactile feedback · Lateral force · Boundary simulation

1 Introduction

Boundaries are fundamental elements that distinguish one object from others. On a touch screen, the boundaries or edges of graphic user interfaces (GUIs) are basically presented by visual feedback. The lack of haptic feedback deteriorates users' performance in touch interactions [1]. On the contrary, haptic enhanced boundaries have been shown to be useful [2, 3]. They enable users to know when they are on a GUI element or moving between other GUI elements [4] so that they can make a right operation. Besides, haptic boundaries can also physically help users reach the target accurately and efficiently. For instance, this effect can be realized by modulating the friction coefficient of the target [5, 6]: low friction coefficient helps users to move smoothly and high friction coefficient rendered targets help users stop quickly when a target is encountered. The abrupt shift of friction coefficient enables users to feel a clear and sharp boundary. This improves users' performance not only in single-target task but also when distracters are presented [6]. However, the control of the friction coefficient itself may be not enough to provide an accurate boundary feeling. Particularly, if the change of friction coefficient is small, the feel of the boundary will be rather weak.

In this research, we intend to address this problem by combining force feedback with tactile feedback which is based on variable friction. We investigate whether the coupled haptic feedback will improve the simulation of boundary stiffness, and how much the improvement is. The coupled haptic feedback is compared with a series of

M. Auvray and C. Duriez (Eds.): EuroHaptics 2014, Part II, LNCS 8619, pp. 19–26, 2014.
DOI: 10.1007/978-3-662-44196-1_3

lateral force feedback. Our hypothesis is that, a variable friction feedback plus a small force feedback can produce a boundary as stiff as that simulated by a great lateral force. In this study, the tactile feedback is quantified to an amount of equivalent lateral force. Moreover, we also investigate if this perceived force increment (due to the tactile feedback) equals to the friction force increment produced by changing the friction coefficient of the touch surface. In the following sections, two experiments are presented. The first experiment measures the differential threshold of the stiffness of a boundary simulated solely by force feedback. The second experiment determines the added effect that variable friction has on the perceived force magnitude when presented in combination with force feedback. The second experiment realizes this by matching the coupled haptic feedback to an equivalent lateral force feedback. The increment of perceived force is then compared with the amount of friction force increment caused by increasing the friction coefficient.

2   Apparatus

The hardware used in the experiments consisted of a cable-driven force feedback device (FingViewer-I [7]) and a large STIMTAC tactile display (198 × 138 mm) [8] based on the squeeze film effect, as shown in Fig. 1(a). Users wore the ring of the FingViewer-I device at about their distal joints of the index finger. The position of the finger was tracked by the FingViewer-I while the cable tensions to exert force feedback were calculated accordingly. When the users touched on the large STIMTAC, the four force sensors on the four corners of the device [9] measured the normal force and thus identified if the finger was contacting with the touch surface. The vibration amplitude was then modulated to control the friction coefficient of the large STIMTAC.

We used a step function of resistant force to simulate a crisp and stiff boundary. Theoretically, the output of a step function of force requires infinite device rigidity, or

(a)The integrated haptic device   (b)Experiment setup

Fig. 1. The integrated haptic device (a) and the experiment setup (b): In the training session of the second experiment, a slider was shown on the monitor to represent the normal force. Participants were instructed to maintain the normal force in the green area which indicated the gauge output of 1–1.5 N. The slider was hidden when the experiment started.

the device will vibrate. In practice, we found that exerting a small force did not make our device vibrate. Therefore, the range of output force in this study was limited from 0.3 N to 1.2 N. Within this range, the force error was less than 5 %. Similarly, the output of the tactile device was also a step increase of friction coefficient for the simulation of a boundary. This was realized by reducing the friction coefficient of the touch surface through activating the squeeze film effect by a 52.2 KHz, 1.6 μm vibration before the user touched the boundary. When the user moved across the boundary, the vibration was stopped immediately restoring actual friction coefficient of the touch surface [10].

3 Experiment 1: Perception of a Boundary Simulated by a Step Function of Force Feedback Only

The first experiment is to establish the difference thresholds for the stiffness of a boundary simulated solely by a step function of resistant force feedback. The thresholds provide references for the second experiment to evaluate the adding effect of variable friction feedback on substituting a certain level of force feedback.

Task and Stimuli. We employed the method of constant stimuli with a paired-comparison, forced-choice test paradigm to obtain accurate differential thresholds [11]. The task requires participants to discriminate the stiffness of a pair of boundaries simulated solely by a step function of force feedback. The boundary was set at the center of the touch surface along the y-axis, as shown in Fig. 1(a). Once the finger moved across the boundary, the user could feel a constant resistant force feedback. Participants were asked to move the finger on the touch surface towards the boundary along the x-axis. They were instructed to 'tap' actively on the boundary to perceive its stiffness and retreat their finger as soon as they felt the boundary. This was designed to avoid vibration of the force feedback device and to obtain a precise stiffness discrimination threshold [12].

Nine right-handed volunteers (2 females and 7 males) between the ages of 24 and 30 attended the experiment. In each trial, two boundaries were presented in temporal order. Participants were asked to select the boundary which had a "greater" stiffness. During the experiment, Over-the-Head earmuffs were worn by all participants. There were three standard force levels: 0.6 N, 0.8 N and 1.0 N. For each standard stimulus, there were eight comparison stimulus values (four higher than the reference and four lower). The step change for the 0.6 N standard force was 8 % which was higher than step changes for the other two standard stimuli (5 %) because higher discrimination threshold was found for that level of force magnitude [13]. All combinations of standard and comparison stimulus were repeated 15 times. The three levels of force comparison were counterbalanced across participants with a Latin Square design. The order that the standard stimulus presented to the participants was randomized.

Results. The JND of each participant at each force level was calculated via methods outlined by Gescheider [11]. The average JND of the nine participants are summarized in Table 1. The average Weber's fractions were 10.3 %, 6.6 %, and 6.4 % for 0.6 N, 0.8 N and 1.0 N force levels respectively. The JND% in the 0.6 N level was higher than the other two levels ($p < 0.001$).

Table 1. Average JNDs for the three standard force levels.

Standard force (N)	Average JND	Standard deviation	Average JND %
0.6	0.064	0.008	10.3 %
0.8	0.053	0.008	6.6 %
1.0	0.063	0.012	6.4 %

4 Experiment 2: Perception of a Boundary Simulated by a Coupled Haptic Feedback

The second experiment compared the stiffness of a boundary simulated by a coupled haptic feedback to that simulated by a force feedback. The task in the second experiment was the same as in the first one. The participants were asked to judge which one of the paired stimuli was stiffer. The standard stimulus was the coupled haptic feedback: in addition to the step increase of resistant force, the participants perceived a step increase of friction coefficient once they moved across the boundary. The increase of friction coefficient was realized by reducing the vibration amplitude of the STIMTAC device from 1.6 μm to 0. In the training session, participants were trained to maintain their normal force within the range of 1–1.5 N, as shown in Fig. 1(b).

The comparison stimuli were rendered solely by the force feedback device as we described in the first experiment. The effect of the coupled haptic feedback was quantified by matching the boundary stiffness simulated by a smaller force feedback plus a variable friction feedback to that simulated by a greater force feedback. The force feedback in the standard stimuli was chosen to be 0.2 N smaller than the average force feedback in the comparison stimuli. The 0.2 N interval was chosen since it was much greater than the JND that we obtained in the first experiment. Moreover, we found that the amount of force that the variable friction feedback could substitute was approximate to 0.2 N in a pilot test. In this case, the distribution of the comparison stimuli should be symmetric to the standard stimuli. The stimuli in the second experiment are presented in Table 2. Six participants (2 female, 4 male aged between 24 and 29) took part in the second experiment.

Results and Discussion. Among the six participants, we found two groups of results. Three of the participants judged the stiffness of the boundaries solely on force

Table 2. Comparison stimuli for force levels in Experiment 2.

Standard stimuli	Comparison stimuli (N)								
0.4 N + T*	0.408	0.456	0.504	0.552	0.6	0.648	0.696	0.744	0.792
	(−32 %)	(−24 %)	(−16 %)	(−8 %)		(+8 %)	(+16 %)	(+24 %)	(+32 %)
0.6 N + T	0.64	0.68	0.72	0.76	0.8	0.84	0.88	0.92	0.96
	(−20 %)	(−15 %)	(−10 %)	(−5 %)		(+5 %)	(+10 %)	(+15 %)	(+20 %)
0.8 N + T	0.8	0.85	0.9	0.95	1.0	1.05	1.1	1.15	1.2
	(−20 %)	(−15 %)	(−10 %)	(−5 %)		(+5 %)	(+10 %)	(+15 %)	(+20 %)

* Tactile feedback: a step increase of friction coefficient. Accordingly, vibration amplitude was reduced from 1.6 μm to 0.

feedback: two reported that they did not feel the tactile feedback in the experiment; the other one reported that he could not combine the force feedback at the distal joint with the tactile feedback at the fingertip. There were two factors that might cause this result. The first, the two feedbacks were spatially separated. The force feedback was delivered through the ring which was worn on the distal joints of participants' index finger, while the tactile feedback was felt through the fingertips. Although previous research showed that the haptic integration with spatial separation could also improve user's perception of boundaries [14, 15] and shapes [16], the effect of spatial distance between the locations where the two feedbacks are applied needs to be further investigated. The second, the two feedbacks were temporally separated. In our experiment, the rising time of the friction coefficient was around 5 ms according to our previous measurement. However, the mean rising time for the force feedback was about 70 ms. The different rising time caused a sequential perception process. In combination with spatial separation, these two factors might cause the three participants failed to perceive the coupled haptic feedback. Therefore, the interaction between the two feedbacks and the effect of their spatial and temporal separation deserve further investigation.

The rest three participants took into account the tactile feedback in combination with force feedback to discriminate the boundary stiffness. Figure 2 shows the average subjective equality (PSE) obtained for the three participants over the three standard stimuli levels. The point of PSE indicates how much the comparison stimuli is perceived equal to the standard stimuli. According to Fig. 2, a variable friction feedback plus a small force feedback can produce a stiff boundary that requires a great force to simulate. Moreover, the amount of perceived force increment caused by tactile feedback was always greater than the JNDs of the corresponding force feedback in the standard stimuli (according to Table 1). This indicates that the tactile feedback was distinctively discriminated as a force increment.

To further investigate the effect of the tactile feedback, we compared the perceived force increment with the friction force increment caused by changing the friction coefficient. Ideally, we should measure the lateral force exerted by the participants in

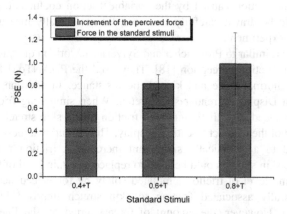

Fig. 2. The PSEs at the three standard stimuli levels. Error bars represent 95 % confidence interval. The force feedback in the standard stimuli are also plotted as a reference to indicate the increment of perceived force due to the addition of tactile feedback.

the experiment. However, the large STIMTAC was too big and heavy (due to the aluminum support) to be mounted on an accurate force sensor. Therefore, we used the maximum increment of friction to evaluate the adding effect of the tactile feedback. The maximum friction increment, f, was calculated according to the Coulomb's friction model $f = \Delta\mu N$. The normal force, N, was obtained by the force sensors on the large STIMTAC during the experiment. Assuming that the friction coefficient was reduced to zero by the squeeze film effect, the maximum friction coefficient reduction, $\Delta\mu$, would be equal to the dynamic friction coefficient of the touch surface when the device was static. The dynamic friction coefficients of the three participants were measured on a small plate with the same covering plastic film as the large STIMTAC. The small plate was fixed on a force sensor (ATI Nano 17). Each participant was asked to move his/her index finger back and forth on the plate as he/she did in the experiment. The average quotient between the lateral force and normal force was recorded as the friction coefficient. The perceived force increment and the maximum friction coefficient in the experiment are listed in Table 3.

Table 3. Perceived force increment and maximum friction force increment in the second experiment. Data are averaged across standard stimuli levels.

Perceived force increment (N)	Maximum friction force increment (N)	Normal force (N)
0.212 (SD = 0.062)	0.307 (SD = 0.096)	1.06 (SD = 0. 21)

The maximum friction force increment was about 0.1 N greater than the average perceived force increment. In fact, the squeeze film effect can reduce the friction coefficient to a very low level but not to 0. Current published minimum friction coefficient produced by the squeeze film effect was 0.1 [17]. The average normal force in the experiment was 1.06 N (SD = 0.21 N). The difference between the perceived force increment and the maximum friction force increment thus may be explained by the difference between the actual friction reduction limit (0.1) and the ideal friction reduction limit (0). In this case, the adding effect of tactile feedback may be explained by the increase of friction caused by the variable friction coefficient. However, this conclusion should be drawn carefully since we did not actually measure the friction increment in the experiment.

Our research is similar to Provancher and Sylvester's work on quantifying the effect of skin stretch on friction perception [18]. They used the PHANToM force feedback device to render normal force and kinesthetic resistance. In addition, they added a Contact Location Display to render skin stretch. When simulating friction, the integrated device produced kinesthetic rendered friction plus a skin stretch caused by the lateral movement of the Contact Location Display. They found that the small amount of skin stretch lead to a statistically significant increase in friction perception. This indicated that the skin stretch could be used to replace a certain level of force feedback to render the same level of friction simulated solely by force feedback device. This research successfully associated friction to skin stretch imposed by the Contact Location Display. However, the amount of force exerted by the linear actuator to produce the skin stretch was not quantified to the amount of perceived friction force increment caused by the skin stretch. In our research, we found that the perceived force increment might equal to the amount of friction force increment due to the increase of friction coefficient. This result indicated that the combination of the two types of haptic feedback was based on the resultant of lateral force. The effect of tactile feedback such as causing finger skin deformation was unlikely to boost the perception of lateral force so that the increment would be much more than the friction force increment.

5   Conclusion and Future Work

We have quantified the effect of coupling lateral force and variable friction tactile feedback in simulating a stiff and crisp boundary. We found that the tactile feedback produced a perceived force increment. Moreover, this amount of increment may equal to the amount of friction force increment caused by changing the friction coefficient. Therefore, the effect of tactile feedback can be treated as a certain level of force feedback in order to quantify the coupled haptic feedback in simulating boundaries. However, we still need to investigate why some participants could not combine the two types of feedback. The interactions between the two haptic feedbacks and the effect of their spatial separation need to be further understood.

Acknowledgment. This work has been carried out within the framework of the INRIA Mint Project, and the STIMTAC project of the IRCICA, France.

References

1. Banter, B.: Touch screens and touch surfaces are enriched by haptic force-feedback. Inf. Disp. **26**(3), 26–30 (2010)
2. Poupyrev, I., Maruyama, S., Rekimoto, J.: Ambient touch: designing tactile interfaces for handheld devices. In: Proceedings of UIST 2002, pp. 51–60 (2002)
3. Forlines, C., Balakrishnan, R.: Evaluating tactile feedback and direct vs. indirect stylus input in pointing and crossing selection tasks. In: Proceedings of CHI 2008, pp. 1563–1572 (2008)
4. Hoggan, E., Brewster, S.A., Johnston, J.: Investigating the effectiveness of tactile feedback for mobile touchscreens. In: Proceedings of CHI 2008, pp. 1573–1582 (2008)
5. Levesque, V., et al.: Enhancing physicality in touch interaction with variable friction. In: Proceedings of CHI 2011, pp. 2481–2490 (2011)
6. Casiez, G., et al.: Surfpad: riding towards targets on a squeeze film effect. In: Proceedings of the CHI 2011, pp. 2491–2500 (2011)
7. Yang, Y., et al.: Adding haptic feedback to touch screens at the right time. In: Proceedings of ICMI 2011, pp. 73–80 (2011)
8. Yang, Y., et al.: Power analysis for design of a large area ultrasonic tactile touch panel. Submitted to IEEE Trans. Haptics (2013)
9. Giraud, F., et al.: Design of a transparent tactile stimulator. In: Proceedings of Haptics Symposium 2012, pp. 485–489 (2012)
10. Biet, M., et al.: Discrimination of virtual square gratings by dynamic touch on friction based tactile displays. In: Proceedings of Haptics Symposium 2008, pp. 41–48 (2008)
11. Gescheider, G.A.: Psychophysics: The Fundamentals. Lawrence Erlbaum Associates, New Jersey (1997)

12. LaMotte, R.H.: Softness discrimination with a tool. J. Neurophysiol. **83**(4), 1777–1786 (2000)
13. Brodie, E., Ross, H.: Sensorimotor mechanisms in weight discrimination. Percept. Psychophys. **36**(5), 477–481 (1984)
14. Kammermeier, P., et al.: Display of holistic haptic sensations by combined tactile and kinesthetic feedback. Presence: Teleoper. Virtual Environ. **13**(1), 1–15 (2004)
15. Khatchatourov, A., et al.: Integrating tactile and force feedback for highly dynamic tasks: technological, experimental and epistemological aspects. Interact. Comput. **21**(1–2), 26–37 (2009)
16. Frisoli, A., et al.: A fingertip haptic display for improving curvature discrimination. Presence: Teleoper. Virtual Environ. **17**(6), 550–561 (2008)
17. Samur, E., Colgate, J.E., Peshkin, M.A.: Psychophysical evaluation of a variable friction tactile interface. In: Proceedings of SPIE-IS&T 2009, pp. 72400J1–72400J7 (2009)
18. Provancher, W.R., Sylvester, N.D.: Fingerpad skin stretch increases the perception of virtual friction. IEEE Trans. Haptics **2**, 212–223 (2009)

Find the Missing Element! Haptic Identification of Incomplete Pictures by Sighted and Visually Impaired Children

Anaïs Mazella[1,2(✉)], Jean-Michel Albaret[1], and Delphine Picard[2,3]

[1] PRISSMH EA4561, Université Toulouse III Paul Sabatier, 31058
Toulouse, France
anais.mazella@gmail.com,
jean-michel.albaret@univ-tlse3.fr
[2] PSYCLE EA3273, Aix Marseille Université, 13621 Aix en Provence, France
delphine.picard@univ-amu.fr
[3] Institut Universitaire de France, Paris, France

Abstract. This study investigates the haptic identification of incomplete raised-line drawings (i.e., pictures with a missing element) by sighted and early visually impaired children aged 9–10 years. Incomplete pictures have already been used in the visual modality to assess perceptual reasoning in children, but not yet under the haptic modality. We found that success at identifying incomplete raised-line pictures (correct naming of object plus missing feature) concerned 32.65 % of children's responses, suggesting that the task was hard although not entirely impossible. Overall, the visually impaired children outperformed the sighted controls at this task. However, there was a large variation in responses across items, and the superiority of the visually impaired children over their sighted peers was not systematic. We concluded that adapting materials from the Wechsler' image completion subtest to the haptic modality may be relevant to investigate haptic perceptual reasoning in children with and without visual impairments.

Keywords: Haptic perception · Incomplete raised-line pictures · Visual impairment

1 Introduction

Haptics and vision differ greatly in how they process incoming information. Vision usually proceeds from global apprehension to more local understanding of a display. Unlike vision, haptics proceeds more analytically due to the inherent constraint of serial processing of information within a limited perceptual field [1, 2]. Local processing thus dominates in early stages of haptic perception; access to the global structure of a stimulus occurs later in the course of information processing as it requires a mental integration of sequentially and locally gathered information [3].

Incomplete pictures, that is to say pictures with a missing feature (e.g., the picture of a comb with a missing tooth), have already been used in the visual modality to assess perceptual reasoning in children. Indeed, a famous subtest of the Wechsler Intelligence

© Springer-Verlag Berlin Heidelberg 2014
M. Auvray and C. Duriez (Eds.): EuroHaptics 2014, Part II, LNCS 8619, pp. 27–33, 2014.
DOI: 10.1007/978-3-662-44196-1_4

Scale for Children ([4]; 4th French revised version) is that of "picture completion". This subtest presents children with a series of incomplete pictures of common objects and requires that children identify the missing part of familiar objects' drawings using their sense of vision. This nonverbal subtest assesses children's ability to perceive and organize a visual array, as well as their concentration and sense of detail. In the present study, we used incomplete raised-line pictures as a material for haptic identification purpose, so as to investigate children's perceptual reasoning under the haptic modality.

We tested haptic perception of incomplete raised-line drawings in sighted and visually impaired children aged 9–10 years, so as to examine (1) whether (and possibly how) children can identify incomplete raised-line pictures through haptics, and (2) how visually impaired children and age-matched sighted controls compare in such a task. Regarding issue 1, it is not clear as to whether a disruption (missing feature) in the configural properties of a stimulus (raised-line drawing) actually hinders the haptic processing and recognition of that stimulus. A recent study by Puspitawati, Jebrane and Vinter [5] suggests that children are attentive to local and small size units when exploring a raised-line configuration, and hardly come to a global coherent percept of the stimulus; accordingly, we may hypothesise that the (initial and predominant) local processing in haptic perception would not constitute a major handicap to perceive and make sense of incomplete stimuli. Regarding issue 2, previous studies have shown an advantage of visually impaired children over sighted controls when pictures depict complete objects (e.g., [6, 7]). The present study explores whether this advantage still holds true in case where pictures have a missing feature.

2 Method

2.1 Participants

Participants were 13 visually impaired children (10 boys, 3 girls; Mean age = 121 months, SD = 7), and 13 sighted children (7 boys, 6 girls; Mean age = 122 months, SD = 6). The visually impaired children all had an early visual impairment (i.e., either congenital or acquired during childhood); two were totally blind (light perception at best), five were legally blind (best corrected visual acuity below 1/10), and seven had low vision (best corrected visual acuity below 4/10). They attended French specialized care centres for the sensory disables (Alfred Peyrelongue, and Cival-Lestrade centres). They had a moderate practice with tactile pictures at home or school. The sighted controls were recruited from normal schools and matched for chronological age with the visually impaired children. None of the sighted children had used raised-line pictures before the study.

2.2 Material

The stimuli were 8 incomplete raised-line pictures depicting common objects, adapted from the image completion subtest of The Wechsler Intelligence Scale for Children (4th French revised version [4]). The picture set appears in Fig. 1.

None of the pictures contain any information about the third dimension. The raised-line pictures were produced on Swell paper with a heating machine (largest picture

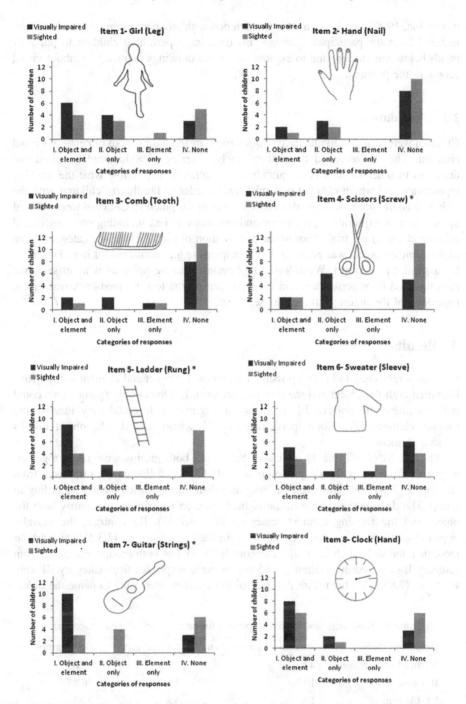

Fig. 1. Responses distribution by group for each item (* items for which response distribution varied significantly according to group).

dimension: 19 × 25 cm). We used a wooden box with an opaque curtain to hide the test material from the participants' view. This equipment permitted children to put their hands below the curtain, and to explore the tactile drawings haptically, without visual access to the pictures.

2.3 Procedure

Children were tested individually in a quiet room inside their school or centre for blind children. They were asked to explore freely a series of 8 incomplete raised-line drawings in order to identify as quickly and accurately as possible what the drawing represented and which element was missing. In order to familiarize children with the task, two additional raised-line drawings were used for practice. Children were allowed up to 2 min of exploration per picture and one answer (i.e., including both object and missing element) per trial. Prior to the presentation of each picture, the category name of the depicted object was given to the participants (e.g., instrument for item 7) (see [8] for a similar procedure). We selected this option because pre-tests without semantic cues revealed floor performance in children. During the test, no feed-back was given, regardless of the nature of the response.

3   Results

Children's responses fall into 4 possible categories: I. Object and element (participants identified both the object and the missing element); II. Object only (participants could only identified the object); III. Element only (participants could only identify the missing element); IV. None (participants could neither identify the object nor its missing element).

The results (see Table 1) indicated that, when both groups were taken together, responses from category IV predominated (47.65 %), followed by responses from category I (32.65 %). However, the response distribution varied clearly according to group. The dominant response of the sighted children was failure to identify both the object and the missing element (category IV: 58.7 %). By contrast, the visually impaired children succeeded frequently at the task (category I: 42.3 %), at least far more than the sighted children did (category I: 23 %). For both groups, responses from category II occurred quite often (16.85 %), whereas responses from category III were very rare (2.85 %). This meant that part of the children were able to name the object

Table 1. Responses distribution in percent for each group (all items together).

Response category	Visually impaired group	Sighted group	Both groups
I. Object and element	42.3	23	32.65
II. Object only	19.2	14.5	16.85
III. Element only	1.9	3.8	2.85
IV. None	36.6	58.7	47.65
Total	100	100	100

without identifying the missing element. By contrast, children rarely identified the missing element only. When we calculated a recognition score (0-8 points, with 0.5 point per picture when children found the expected name of the object, plus 0.5 point for the missing element), we found significant between-group difference with the visually impaired children scoring higher ($M = 4.23$, $SD = 1.98$) than the sighted children ($M = 2.50$, $SD = 1.54$), Mann-Whitney U-test, $p = 0.0333$.

When we look at the distribution of responses for each item separately (see Fig. 1), we observed a large variation in responses across items. Three different patterns emerged. In pattern 1, children's responses were fairly distributed among the 4 categories: this pattern concerned Item 1 (Girl), and Item 6 (Sweater). The distribution of responses did not vary significantly according to group for these two items (Girl: Fisher exact test, $p = 0.687$; Sweater: Fisher exact test, $p = 0.474$).

In pattern 2, children's dominant response was failure to identify both the object and the missing element: this pattern concerned Item 2 (Hand), Item 3 (Comb), and Item 4 (Scissors). For these three items, the failure rate was high in participants (69.5 % for Hand, 73 % for Comb, and 61.5 % for Scissors). The distribution of responses did not vary significantly according to group for Item 2 (Hand: Fisher exact test, $p = 0.719$), and Item 3 (Comb: Fisher exact test, $p = 0.573$). However, for Item 4 (Scissors), the distribution of responses varied significantly according to group (Fisher exact test, $p = 0.010$): failure to identify both the object and its missing element was the dominant response of the sighted children, but not that of the visually impaired children who could, for part of them, identify the object as scissors.

Finally, in pattern 3, children's dominant response was success to identify both the object and the missing element: this pattern concerned Item 5 (Ladder), Item 7 (Guitar), and Item 8 (Clock). For these three items, the identification rates were quite great in participants (50 % for Ladder and Guitar, and 53.8 % for Clock). The distribution of responses varied significantly according to group for Item 5 (Ladder: Fisher exact test, $p = 0.048$), and Item 7 (Guitar: Fisher exact test, $p = 0.011$), but not for Item 8 (Clock: Fisher exact test, $p = 0.532$). For Items 5 and 7, success to identify both the object and element was the dominant response of the visually impaired children, but not that of the sighted children who mainly failed to identify the object and its missing element.

4 Conclusion

Three main findings emerged from the study. First, success at identifying incomplete raised-line pictures through haptics (naming object plus missing feature) concerned 32.65 % of children's responses, suggesting that the task was hard although not entirely impossible (see [8, 9]). Interestingly, part of the children was able to identify the object without the missing feature, but the reverse quite never occurred. In line with our hypothesis, these findings suggest that a disruption (missing feature) in the configural properties of a stimulus (raised-line drawing) did not hinder the haptic processing and recognition of that stimulus in terms of object representation. It is likely that children paid attention to local and small size units when exploring the raised-line configurations; they may have guessed what a given picture could depict in terms of object representation, before they were able to identify the missing element through further analytical examination of the stimulus (see also [5]). To what extent children who succeeded at the task constructed an internal representation of raised-line pictures which integrated local parts into a coherent whole is however unknown, and may call for further investigations. Second, we found that overall the visually impaired children outperformed the sighted controls at the incomplete picture identification task. This finding confirms the overall superiority of visually impaired children over their sighted peers in haptic picture perception tasks (see [6, 7, 10]), and extents this observation to the haptic processing of incomplete pictures. Third, we found large variations in children's responses to incomplete pictures across items, and observed that the superiority of the visually impaired children over their sighted peers was not systematic, as it depended on the item to be processed.

In conclusion, findings from this study lead us to suggest that adapting materials from the Wechsler' image completion subtest to the haptic modality may be relevant to investigate haptic perceptual reasoning in children with and without visual impairments. The development and/or adaptation of tests for visually impaired children is still a challenge, as only a limited number of psychometric tools are currently available (see e.g., [11, 12] for a review). However, because the task was rather difficult, even for the visually impaired children, it would be worth completing these experimental results with scores obtained by older participants (sighted and visually impaired) in order to demonstrate that the task can be achieved with a rather good level of performance at the end of childhood. The next step of our research project therefore consists in collecting data with a larger sample of participants, including children, adolescents, and young adults, with and without visual impairment. Moreover, as suggested by several authors [13, 14], it might be necessary to proceed to separate standardizations in order to take the diversity inherent to the visually impaired people into account (associated disorders, visual status, individual's visual experience...).

Acknowledgments. This work was supported in part by a grant from the PRES of Toulouse and Région Midi-Pyrénées attributed to the first author for her Ph.D. Thesis. We thank Mélanie Labardin, Cival-Lestrade Centre, Sandra Mesnières, Alfred Peyrelongue Centre, and the children who took part in the study.

References

1. Berger, C., Hatwell, Y.: Dimensional and overall similarity classification in haptics: a developmental study. Cog. Dev. **8**, 495–516 (1993)
2. Lederman, S.J., Klatzky, R.L.: Haptic perception: a tutorial. Atten. Percept. Psychophys. **71**, 1439–1459 (2009)
3. Hatwell, Y., Streri, A., Gentaz, E.: Touching for Knowing. John Benjamins Publishing Company, Philadelphia (2003)
4. Wechsler, D.: WISC-IV, Echelle d'Intelligence de Wechsler pour Enfants et Adolescents. ECPA, Paris (2005)
5. Puspitawati, I., Jebrane, A., Vinter, A.: Local and global processing in blind and sighted children in a naming and drawing task. Child Dev. **85**(3), 1077–1090 (2014)
6. D'Angiulli, A., Kennedy, J.M., Heller, M.A.: Blind children recognizing tactile pictures respond like sighted children given guidance in exploration. Scand. J. Psychol. **39**, 187–190 (1998)

7. Pathak, K., Pring, L.: Tactual picture recognition in congenitally blind and sighted children. Appl. Cog. Psychol. **3**, 337–350 (1989)
8. Heller, M.A., Calcaterra, J.A., Burson, L.L., Tyler, L.A.: Tactual picture identification by blind and sighted people: effects of providing categorical information. Percept. Psychophys. **58**, 310–323 (1996)
9. Picard, D., Lebaz, S.: Identifying raised-line pictures by touch: a hard-but not impossible-task. J. Vis. Impair. Blind. **106**, 427–431 (2012)
10. Vinter, A., Fernandez, V., Orlandi, O., Morgan, P.: Exploratory procedures of tactile images in visually impaired and blindfolded sighted children: how they relate to their consequent performance in drawing. Res. Dev. Disabil. **33**, 1819–1831 (2012)
11. Ballesteros, S., Bardisa, D., Millar, S., Reales, J.M.: The haptic test battery: a new instrument to test tactual abilities in blind and visually impaired and sighted children. Brit. J. Vis. Impair. **23**, 11–24 (2005)
12. Mazella, A., Labardin, M., Mesnieres, S., Albaret, J.-M., Picard, D.: Construction of a 2D haptic tests battery for use with children and adolescents with and without visual impairment. In: Valente, D., Claudet, P. (eds.) Terra Haptica#4: Tactile Pictures, Cognition and Education, Issue 4, pp. 65–74 September 2014
13. Bonnardel, R., Baton, C., Thiebaut, E.: Test d'Intelligence Pratique pour Déficients Visuels: B101DV. Les Doigts Qui Revent, Talant (2010)
14. Dekker, R.: Visually impaired children and haptic intelligence test scores: intelligence test for visually impaired children (ITVIC). Dev. Med. Child Neurol. **35**, 478–489 (1993)

The Haptic Analog of the Visual Aubert-Fleischl Phenomenon

Alessando Moscatelli[✉], Meike Scheller, Gabriele Joanna Kowalski, and Marc Ernst

Cognitive Neuroscience and CITEC, Universität Bielefeld,
Universitätsstrassse 25, 33615 Bielefeld, Germany
{alessandro.moscatelli,meike.scheller,
g.kowalski,marc.erst}@uni-bielefeld.de
http://www.uni-bielefeld.de/(en)/biologie/cns/

Abstract. In vision, the perceived velocity of a moving stimulus is different depending on whether the image moves across the retina with the eyes immobile or whether the observer pursues the stimulus such that the stimulus is stationary on the moving retina. The effect is known as the Aubert-Fleischl phenomenon. Here, we reproduced the analog of this visual illusion in haptics. For this purpose, we asked our participants to estimate the speed of a moving belt either from tactile cues, by keeping the hand world stationary, or from proprioceptive cues by tracking the belt with a guided upper-limb movement. The participants overestimated the speed of the moving stimulus determined from tactile cues compared with proprioceptive cues, in analogy with the Aubert-Fleischl phenomenon. Reproducing the illusion in the haptic modality may help evaluating some of the general mechanisms of spatial constancy in perceptual systems.

Keywords: Velocity discrimination · Touch · Proprioception

1 Introduction

The retina, just like the skin, is a sensing surface that is movable with respect to the external space. This raises the question how the spatial constancy is achieved, that is how the velocity in the external world is perceived, given the non-stationary sensing surface [1]. In vision, the perceived velocity of a moving stimulus is different depending on whether the image moves across the retina with the eyes immobile, i.e. world-stationary, or whether the observer pursues the stimulus such that the stimulus is stationary on the moving retina (sensing surface). In the first case the velocity of the stimulus has to be estimated from the change of the luminance profile on the retina over time. In the latter case the velocity of the stimulus has to be estimated from the motion of the eye, that is from extra-retinal signals, such as the efferency copy to the eye-muscles. The stimulus is perceived as faster when it is estimated from the retinal signals

© Springer-Verlag Berlin Heidelberg 2014
M. Auvray and C. Duriez (Eds.): EuroHaptics 2014, Part II, LNCS 8619, pp. 34–40, 2014.
DOI: 10.1007/978-3-662-44196-1_5

compared to extra-retinal signals, that is when the eye is stationary compared to when it is pursuing the stimulus. The effect is known as the Aubert-Fleischl phenomenon [2, 3].

Three main hypotheses have been suggested to explain the illusion. First, it may be the consequence of an intrinsic difference between the retinal and extra retinal velocity signals, that is, the *gain* of the two signals would be intrinsically not unitary [4]. In a second hypothesis, the illusion would be the consequence of the bias induced in the retinal signal from the *temporal frequency* of the patterned stimulus [5, 6]. In accordance with this hypothesis, the illusion changes in magnitude and in sign depending on the frequency of the visual stimulus, and it even disappears when a single edge is used as stimulus [5, 7]. In a third hypothesis, the illusion would arise due to the difference in *precision* between the retinal and extra retinal signals [8]. The following Bayesian process would generate the illusion: First, the observer would measure independently the world-framed and the relative velocity of the object from the eye pursuit and retinal signals respectively. Each of the two measurements is combined with a static-world prior (sometimes called "slow motion" prior), reflecting the statistics that the world observed (inanimated objects) tends to be stationary or move slowly in the majority of all cases. The noisy sensory measurements (corresponding to the likelihood distribution in the Bayesian framework) and prior distributions are multiplied and the weighting between them depends on the relative variance of the distributions. The world-framed and the relative velocity measurements have different variance, hence are differently affected by the prior. Therefore, the sum of the two would generate the illusion.

Here, we aimed to reproduce the analog of this visual illusion in haptics. For this purpose, we asked our participants to estimate the speed of a moving belt either from tactile cues, by keeping the hand world stationary, or from proprioceptive cues by tracking the belt with a guided upper-limb movement. If the illusion were the same in touch as in vision, we expect the speed to be overestimated in the tactile-based estimates compared with the proprioceptive estimates. Reproducing the illusion in the haptic modality may help evaluating some of the general mechanisms of spatial constancy in perceptual systems.

2 Methods

2.1 Participants

Six healthy volunteers participated to the experiment (5 females, age range: 19–29 years). All participants were naïve to the purpose of the experiment, and gave informed consent prior to participation. The experiment was approved by the Ethical Committee of the University Clinics of Tübingen, Germany.

2.2 Apparatus

The device (Fig. 1) consists of a rubber belt (7.5×53.3 cm) actuated by a micro motor (Faulhaber 3564K024B CS). The belt has a uniformly-spaced ridged surface, each ridge is 1 mm high, the distance between different ridges being 3 mm.

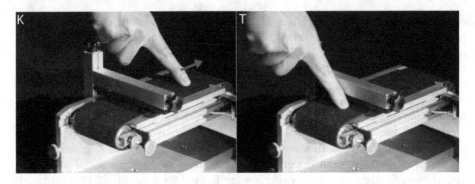

Fig. 1. Experimental procedure: The participants compared the speed of motion of the belt between the reference and the comparison stimulus. In K-stimuli, participants maintained the right index finger on a fixed spot of the moving belt (guided movement). In T-stimuli, participants kept the hand on the belt world-stationary; participants placed the finger adjacent to the right side of the handlebar, so as to prevent undesired hand motion. We generated four conditions from the combination of the two stimuli: KT, TK, TT, KK (the first in each condition is the reference stimulus).

The 3564K024B CS includes an electronically commutated DC-Servomotor, a high-resolution encoder (resolution 3000 Inc./turn) to determine the actual position, and a position and speed controller (recommended max speed: 12000 rpm; the speed ranged from 500 to 3000 rpm in the experiment). We used a custom-made Matlab code to send instructions to the motor. An L-shaped handlebar is attached to the device 60 mm apart from the right roll. There was no measurable slip of the belt during acceleration or when the finger pressed on the belt.

2.3 Stimulus and Procedure

Participants sat on an office chair in a dimly illuminated room. The tactile device was placed to the right of the participant; a black curtain hid the device from the participant's sight. Earplugs and headphones playing pink noise masked the noise generated by the device. In each stimulus interval, the belt moved leftward with respect to the participant, for a constant path length (10.7 cm). The speed of motion was constant within each stimulus, except for the short acceleration/deceleration ramp (duration ≈ 0.2 s) respectively at onset and at the offset of the stimulus.

The task consisted of a forced-choice speed discrimination task (Fig. 1). In each trial, participants compared the speed of the belt between the reference and the comparison stimulus (*inter-stimulus interval*: 2.5 s). Between one trial and the other, participants rested their arm on the handlebar. The plateau speed was equal to $6 \text{ cm} \cdot \text{s}^{-1}$ in the reference stimulus and was pseudo randomly chosen among seven possible values $(1.67, 3.11, 4.55, 6, 7.44, 8.88, 10.32 \text{ cm} \cdot \text{s}^{-1})$ in the comparison. Each participant performed four experimental blocks (140 trials each) testing the different experimental conditions. In the "kinaesthetic-tactile" condition (KT), participants estimated the reference speed using kinesthetic cues (K), by maintaining the right index finger on a fixed spot of the moving belt (see Fig. 1K). We did not constrain the upper limb movement in K, so as to restrict the tactile input to the index fingertip. Note that, as the task required a guided movement, the estimate of the reference stimulus is provided by both proprioceptive cues and the efferent copy of the motor command. In the comparison stimulus, participants kept the hand world-stationary with the finger in contact with the belt (see Fig. 1T) and estimated the speed of motion from tactile cues (T). The reference and the comparison stimuli were presented sequentially, the order of the two was counterbalanced between trials. Instructions on the computer monitor prompted the participant to perform either the K or the T task. After each trial, participants reported which of the two stimuli moved faster (either the first or the second interval presented), by pressing the right or the left button of a standard computer mouse. No feedback was provided during the experiment. The procedure was the same in the "tactile-kinaesthetic" condition (TK). The only difference was that participants estimated the reference stimulus from tactile cues, and the comparison out of the upper-limb kinematics. As a control, in two separate blocks we performed unimodal speed discrimination tasks (TT and KK); in each of the control tasks, the reference and the comparison stimulus were estimated from the same cues (tactile cues in TT and kinesthetic cues in KK).

2.4 Analysis

We modeled the responses of each participant using the psychometric function defined by Eq. 1:

$$\Phi^{-1}\left[P(Y_j = 1)\right] = \beta_0 + \beta_1 x \tag{1}$$

$Y_j = 1$ if in a given trial j, the participant reported that the speed was faster in the comparison than in the reference and $Y_j = 0$ otherwise. $P(Y_j = 1)$ is the probability of perceiving the comparison as faster and Φ^{-1} is the *probit* transform of this probability. On the right side of the equation, x is the physical speed of the belt in the comparison stimulus and β_0, β_1 are the intercept and the slope of the linearized equation, respectively. We applied the model separately in each experimental condition. The *point of subjective equality* $(PSE = -\beta_0/\beta_1)$ is an estimate for the accuracy of the response, while the *just noticeable difference* $(JND = 0.675/\beta_1$, where 0.675 is the 75 percentile of a standard normal distribution) is an estimate for the precision.

Next, we extended the analysis to the whole population (n = 6) by means of a *generalized linear mixed model* (GLMM; see [9,10]). The GLMM is similar to the psychometric function, with the advantage of allowing the analysis of clustered data—as in our case the collection of repeated responses in several participants. We estimated the two parameters (PSE and JND) and the related 95 % confidence interval using a bootstrap method, as explained in [9].

If the illusion holds in haptics the same way as in vision, then we expect a relative overestimation of the tactile-based perceived speed compared with

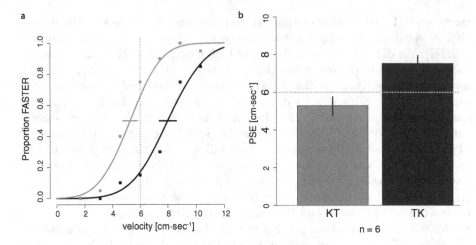

Fig. 2. (a) The psychometric functions for a representative participant, in the two experimental conditions (gray: KT; black: TK). The reference speed (6 cm · sec^{-1}) is indicated with a dashed line. (b) The *point-of-subjective-equality* (PSE) in the two experimental conditions (n = 6)

the proprioceptive-based perceived speed. Therefore, $PSE_{KT} < 6$ cm · s^{-1} < PSE_{TK}. Finally, we measured the JNDs in the two unimodal conditions, to verify that the discriminability of the stimuli was in accordance with the values reported in the related literature.

3   Results

Figure 2a shows the perceived speed of the stimulus for a representative participant in the two conditions KT (gray) and TK (black). The PSE is significantly different in the two experimental conditions ($PSE_{KT} = 5.3 \pm 0.3$, $PSE_{TK} = 8.0 \pm 0.3, Estimate \pm SE$). Notice that, in analogy to the visual illusion, $PSE_{KT} < 6$ cm · s^{-1} < PSE_{TK}.

We extended the analysis to all six participants using the GLMM (Fig. 2b). This analysis confirmed the response pattern from the single representative participant. The estimated PSE is 5.3 cm · s^{-1} in KT (95 % CI : 4.8 − 5.8 cm · s^{-1}), and 7.5 cm · s^{-1} in TK (95 % CI : 7.0 − 7.9 cm · s^{-1}). The 95 % *confidence intervals* are not overlapping between the two experimental conditions and they are significantly different from the speed of the reference stimulus.

The JNDs in the two unimodal conditions provide an estimate for the discriminability of the two cues. The JND is 1.05 in TT (95 % CI : 0.82 − 1.40) and 1.1 in KK (95 % CI : 0.84 − 1.48). This corresponds to a Weber fraction of 0.176 and 0.18, respectively. In both conditions, the discriminability of the stimuli was well in agreement with the values reported in the literature (e.g., see [11] for tactile- and [12] for proprioceptive-based discrimination).

4   Discussion

Here, we report a new haptic illusion which is the putative analogue of the Aubert-Fleischl phenomenon. In this experiment, participants overestimated the speed of the moving stimulus determined from tactile cues compared with proprioceptive cues. This result is in agreement with the general view of a weak spatial constancy in haptics [13,14]. Three hypotheses have been suggested to explain the visual phenomenon: The intrinsic gain, the frequency bias, and the static prior assumption. Testing these explanatory models is beyond the purpose of this study, however, the discussion of the current results may provide indications for future studies. In touch, as in vision, the perceived speed changes with the frequency of the patterned stimulus [6,15]. Therefore, the frequency bias hypothesis is at least qualitatively in agreement with the results in both modalities. On the other hand, the difference in precision between the tactile and the proprioceptive stimuli was rather small in the current experiment. However, a putative difference in the JND might have been masked by the extra cue provided by the duration of the stimuli (as the path length was constant in our protocol). The two variables that are supposed to generate the illusion (the spatial frequency and the relative reliability of the two cues) can be easily manipulated in haptics. This may offer the possibility to extend the proposed models to a different sensory modality, and, therefore, to test their limits.

Acknowledgments. This work is supported from the EU FP7/2007–2013 project no. 601165 WEARHAP (WEARable HAPtics for Humans and Robots) and project no. 248587 THE (The Hand Embodied).

References

1. Wurtz, R.H.: Neuronal mechanisms of visual stability. Vision. Res. **48**(20), 2070–2089 (2008)
2. Aubert, H.: Die Bewegungsempfindung. Pflugers Arch. **39**, 347–370 (1886)
3. Fleischl, E.V.: Physiologisch-optische Notizen, 2 Mitteilung. Sitzung Wiener Bereich der Akademie der Wissenschaften **3**, 7–25 (1882)
4. Dichgans, J., Körner, F., Voigt, K.: Vergleichende Skalierung des afferenten und efferenten Bewegungssehens beim Menschen: Lineare Funktionen mit verschiedener Anstiegssteilheit. Psychologische Forschung **32**(4), 277–295 (1969)
5. Dichgans, J., Wist, E., Diener, H.C., Brandt, T.: The Aubert-Fleischl phenomenon: a temporal frequency effect on perceived velocity in afferent motion perception. Exp. Brain Res. **23**(5), 529–533 (1975)
6. Diener, H.C., Wist, E.R., Dichgans, J., Brandt, T.: The spatial frequency effect on perceived velocity. Vision Res. **16**(2), 169–176 (1976)
7. Freeman, T.C., Banks, M.S., Crowell, J.: Extraretinal and retinal amplitude and phase errors during Filehne illusion and path perception. Percept. Psychophysics **62**(5), 900–909 (2000)
8. Freeman, T.C., Champion, R., Warren, P.: A Bayesian model of perceived head-centered velocity during smooth pursuit eye movement. Curr. Biol. **20**(8), 757–762 (2010)

9. Moscatelli, A., Mezzetti, M., Lacquaniti, F.: Modeling psychophysical data at the population-level: The generalized linear mixed model. J. Vision **12**(11):26, 1–17 (2012)

10. Knoblauch, K., Maloney, L.T.: Modeling psychophysical data in R. Springer, New York (2012)

11. Bensmaïa, S.J., Killebrew, J.H., Craig, J.C.: Influence of visual motion on tactile motion perception. J. Neurophysiol. **96**(3), 1625–1637 (2006)

12. Lönn, J., Djupsjöbacka, M.: Replication and discrimination of limb movement velocity. Somatosens. Mot. Res. **18**(1), 76–82 (2001)

13. Wexler, M., Hayward, V.: Weak spatial constancy in touch. in: Proceedings of 2011 IEEE World Haptics Conference, pp. 605–607 (2011)

14. Ziat, M., Hayward, V., Chapman, C.E., Ernst, M.O., Lenay, C.: Tactile suppression of displacement. Exp. Brain Res. **206**(3), 299–310 (2010)

15. Dépeault, A., Meftah, E.-M., Chapman, C.E.: Tactile speed scaling: contributions of time and space. J. Neurophysiol. **99**(3), 1422–1434 (2008)

Making Gestural Interaction Accessible to Visually Impaired People

Anke Brock$^{(\boxtimes)}$, Philippe Truillet, Bernard Oriola,
and Christophe Jouffrais

IRIT-UMR5505, CNRS and Université de Toulouse, Toulouse, France
{Anke.Brock,Philippe.Truillet,Bernard.Oriola,
Christophe.Jouffrais}@irit.fr

Abstract. As touch screens become widely spread, making them more accessible to visually impaired people is an important task. Touch displays possess a poor accessibility for visually impaired people. One possibility to make them more accessible without sight is through gestural interaction. Yet, there are still few studies on using gestural interaction for visually impaired people. In this paper we present a comprehensive summary of existing projects investigating accessible gestural interaction. We also highlight the limits of current approaches and propose future working directions. Then, we present the design of an interactive map prototype that includes both a raised-line map overlay and gestural interaction for accessing different types of information (e.g., opening hours, distances). Preliminary results of our project show that basic gestural interaction techniques can be successfully used in interactive maps for visually impaired people.

Keywords: Gestural interaction · Accessibility · Visual impairment · Interactive maps · Non-visual interaction

1 Introduction

The recent rise of multi-touch devices, has led to an increased use of those devices in daily life [1]. Yet, touch displays are poorly accessible without vision [2]. First, there is no cutaneous feedback. On touchscreens you cannot feel your way to an interactive component, whereas this is possible with a traditional button based interface. Second, it is hard to provide instructions for the next action to take (i.e. where to press on the screen). Third, in many applications the position of interactive elements on the screen is not fixed, while on button-based interfaces users can memorize the position of buttons [3]. Furthermore, visually impaired people fear accidentally activating features on touch screens [3]. Consequently, making multi-touch more accessible to visually impaired people is an important task. Kane, Morris, et al. [4] classified touch screen accessibility in three categories. First, "hardware-only" approaches apply hardware modifications on the touchscreen, such as gluing tactile dots and braille labels on the screen [5]. Second, "hybrid approaches" combine the use of hardware modifications, such as raised-line overlays, and audio output. Audio-tactile maps (interactive maps based on tactile maps and speech output [6]) are included in this category.

© Springer-Verlag Berlin Heidelberg 2014
M. Auvray and C. Duriez (Eds.): EuroHaptics 2014, Part II, LNCS 8619, pp. 41–48, 2014.
DOI: 10.1007/978-3-662-44196-1_6

Third, "software only" approaches make use of accessible gestural interaction combined with audio feedback. Indeed, gestural interaction might be a cheap and flexible way to improve accessibility of multi-touch technology. Yet, it has so far rarely been used in devices for visually impaired people and thus there is need for further investigations. We suggest that gestural interaction can augment "hybrid approaches", i.e. to combine gestural interaction with a raised-line overlay.

In this paper we focus on accessible gestural interaction. To our knowledge there is no comprehensive overview of existing research projects on accessible gestural interaction. Therefore, in the first section we investigate the current state of the art. We highlight existing solutions as well as their limits. Then, we present the design and preliminary evaluation of an accessible interactive map including both a raised-line map overlay and gestural interaction techniques. We conclude by opening up future research steps.

2 State of the Art on Accessible Gestural Interaction

Gestures are an integral part of human communication. In the context of Human-Computer Interaction, no standard definition exists but different authors have defined gestural interaction [7, 8]. The term "gesture" defines dynamic and intentional movements of certain body parts (likely the hands and arms). Because these movements follow a defined path they can be recognized by a computer and trigger a command.

Some research projects have developed accessible gestural interaction. Slide Rule [3] provided a set of accessible gestures for touch screen interfaces. Basic interaction techniques have been developed, as for instance a one-finger scan for browsing lists, a second finger to tap and select items, a multi-directional flick for additional actions and a L-shaped gesture for browsing hierarchical information. Slide Rule proved to be significantly faster than the use of a Pocket PC device, even if users made more errors and results concerning satisfaction were contradictory. Wolf, Dicke, and Grasset [9] studied gestural interaction for spatial auditory interfaces on smartphones without specifically targeting visually impaired people. The study included not only 2D but also 3D gestures measured by the embedded smartphone sensors (e.g. accelerometer or gyroscope). Participants mostly created gestures that were executed on the touch surface, some gestures that were based on 3D movements of the phone and only few gestures that combined both. To our knowledge, no project has studied the use of 3D gestures for visually impaired people even though it would be interesting. NavTouch [10] provided a text-entry method for blind users on a multi-touch device. The alphabet was navigated by performing directional gestures on the screen, while constant audio feedback was given. Other projects aimed at including gestural interaction in interactive maps. Zeng and Weber [11] implemented basic gestures such as panning and zooming. Yatani et al. [12] proposed the use of flick gestures for navigating lists or selecting items. Carroll et al. [13] suggested using common gestures but replacing the action that is associated in visual interfaces with these gestures. Performing a two-finger pinch would then not result in changing the zoom level of the map, but in changing the type of displayed content. Finally, commercial smartphones start to provide accessible gestural interaction. The most advanced accessible gestural interaction is provided by Apple with the VoiceOver Screen Reader [14].

2.1 Design Guidelines for Accessible Gestural Interaction

Only few guidelines for designing accessible gestural interaction exist. The Slide Rules project [3] led to the following design principles: prevent the risk of accidentally executing an action; provide a resolution adapted for the finger and not for the eye; reduce selection accuracy; provide quick browsing and navigation; make gestural mapping intuitive and enable a "return home" function. McGookin et al. [15] suggested not to use short impact related gestures—simple taps—as this led to unintended touch events; to avoid localized gestures or to provide a reference system; and to provide feedback for all actions. Kane, Wobbrock, and Ladner [16] proposed several guidelines for creating accessible gestures: avoid symbols and letters from print writing; position gestures in edges and on corners as cues for identifying one's position on the screen; expect low location accuracy; increase the time for executing gestures and use familiar layouts such as QWERTY keyboards.

2.2 Challenges of Accessible Gestural Interaction

As stated above, visually impaired users fear accidentally activating features by taping on the multi-touch screen [3]. Observations on unintended touch interaction of visually impaired participants have been made in different projects. El-Glaly, Quek, Smith-Jackson and Dhillon [17] proposed an application for allowing blind people to read books on an iPad. They observed unintended touch input from the palms resting on the touch surface, but also from other fingers unconsciously touching the surface while holding the device. The intended exploratory movement was a single finger moving over the surface in order to read the book. Because this movement was regular, they were able to track it and eliminate the unintended input. Furthermore, short impact related gestures, such as single taps, should be avoided because they are likely to occur accidentally [12, 15]. As described above, placing interactive zones in the edges or corners of a device, might reduce the likelihood to trigger this interaction accidentally [16]. Despite these first recommendations and solutions, it remains a challenge for the research domain of multi-touch to find adapted interaction techniques for visually impaired people that avoid accidental touch interaction. Furthermore it can be observed that so far very few studies put the focus on gestural interaction that is designed specifically for visually impaired people and evaluated in order to ensure usability. In the future, visually impaired people should thus be included throughout the design process from the creation of ideas to the evaluation.

3   Gestural Interaction for an Accessible Geographic Map

Traditionally, geographic maps for visually impaired people are hard-copy maps with raised lines. With the rise of new technologies, research projects have been devoted to the design of interactive maps for visually impaired people. The design of these maps varied in different aspects, such as content, devices and interaction techniques [18]. Many accessible interactive maps are based on the use of touch screens ranging from smartphones to large touch tables. Despite gestural interaction being usable by blind people [16], few of these projects made use of more complex gestures than tapping (see above). The information that accessible interactive maps provide is therefore often limited to basic information, such as street names [6].

Gestural interaction would provide the possibility to enrich interactive maps. First, gestures would enable the possibility to access important information, such as distances, directions, or itineraries. In the Talking TMAP prototype [19], which was based on a mono-touch display, the calculation of distances was executed with a combination of taps with a single finger. We suggest that using more than one finger could facilitate distance calculation. Second, it would be possible to present more complex information than names. Indeed, it is interesting for the user to choose the amount and type of information that is presented on the map and this possibility has been provided in prior maps. For instance, in the Talking TMAP project [19], different levels of information could be accessed through repeated tapping. This information included names of streets, spelling of the street name, address ranges and length of the street. Levesque et al. [20] compared three conditions for exploration of a tactile drawing by visually impaired people: (1) static content, (2) users could manually adapt the level of detail, (3) the level of detail was automatically determined from speed of exploratory movements. Although there was no significant difference in reading speed or error rate, users clearly preferred the mode in which they could manually toggle the amount of detail.

Taken together, this suggests the interest of providing access to more detailed information and of letting the user choose the level of detail that is displayed. Consequently, the aim of our project was to study how basic gestural interaction could be used to enrich a previously developed interactive map prototype (based on a multitouch device with raised-line overlay) [6] with extended functionality, such as adding supplementary audio output about opening hours, directions, etc.

3.1 Designing the Prototype

For the design of our interactive map prototypes we made use of participatory design methods and included visually impaired people throughout the design cycle [21]. Concretely for the design of gestural interaction, we conducted brainstorming sessions. The sessions took place between one blind expert and four sighted researchers. During the brainstorming sessions, we discussed how to make use of gestural interaction within the previously developed interactive map concept, i.e., touchscreen with raised-line overlay and audio output. We kept the idea of selecting different levels of information, as has been suggested in the literature. For instance with the same interactive map, it could be possible to switch between the audio output for basic points of interest, opening hours, or public transportation. We proposed the combined use of buttons and basic gestural interaction to access these different information levels, so that users could choose the content they were interested in. Also, we decided to explore how distance information could be provided, because users in our previous studies had stated that distance information was important.

3.2 Implementation of the Prototype

Our interactive map prototype consisted of a raised-line map overlay placed over a multi-touch screen, a computer connected to the screen and audio output [6].

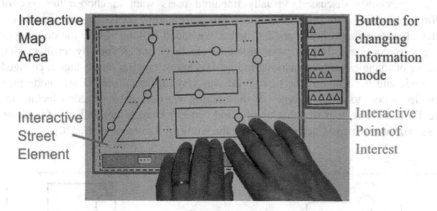

Interactive Map Area

Buttons for changing information mode

Interactive Street Element

Interactive Point of Interest

Fig. 1. The raised-line map drawing which is placed as an overlay on a multi-touch device (Color figure online).

The raised-line overlay (see Fig. 1) was based on the map drawing from previous studies [6] and included the geographical map (blue area in Fig. 1) as well as the button area (red zone in Fig. 1). We designed the map with Inkscape[1] in SVG format. SVG provides a text file that can be analyzed by an application as well as a visual representation. The visual view could then be printed as raised-line map. The SVG file was used by our application for extracting information on position and dimension of map elements. We came up with the idea of an additional configuration file that provided supplementary information on the map elements, such as opening hours, entry fees, length of a street, etc. This configuration file was written in XML. It was parsed by the application and then associated with the components in the SVG file.

Choice of Interaction Techniques. As stated before, the objective of this project was to test whether gestural interaction techniques were usable in interactive maps for visually impaired people. Interaction techniques comprised gestural input as well as audio output. For the latter we used the S.I. VOX /Vocalyze software.[2] We implemented gestural interaction with the MT4 J Gestural API [22], an open-source and cross-platform framework for developing multi-touch applications. Names of elements were announced when double tapping on interactive elements. Furthermore, we used basic gestural interaction techniques provided by the MT4 J API. Among these, MT4 J provided a lasso gesture, which means circling around a map element without lifting the finger (Fig. 2). Additionally, we implemented a tap and hold gesture. The user had

---

[1] http://inkscape.org/en [last accessed April 30th 2014].

[2] http://users.polytech.unice.fr/~helen/SERVER_SI_VOX/pages/index.php?page=Accueil [last accessed April 30th 2014].

to tap on a map element and maintain the finger pressed. A beep sound confirmed the activation. The user could then tap on a second map element and a second beep would confirm the activation (Fig. 2). The distance between both elements was then verbally announced.

As previously discussed, visually impaired users want to choose the type of information ([19]). We decided to make this information accessible via modes, i.e. different system states. For changing modes, we added buttons next to the drawing of the geographic map. Buttons were ordered from level one to four by an increasing number of triangles (see red marking in Fig. 1). Double tapping on the button changed the mode and the name of the new mode was verbally announced. Each mode then provided access to different types of information via different interaction techniques (see Table 1). The goal was that users could actively change the kind of information presented on the map in accordance with the study by Levesque et al. [20].

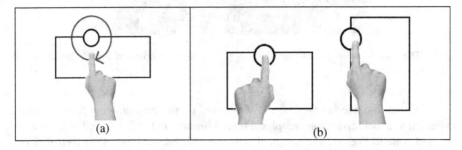

Fig. 2. Schema of the different gestural interaction techniques. (a) Lasso; (b) Tap and Hold

Table 1. Distribution of gestures and types of information in the current implementation.

Mode	1	2	3	4
Active gestures	Double Tap	Double Tap Lasso	Double Tap Tap and Hold	Double Tap
Type of information	Street Names Names of POI	Street Names Names of POI Detailed information about POI	Street Names Names of POI Distances between POI	Information on Public Transport

3.3   Evaluation

The present prototype is a proof-of-concept and currently only pretests have been done. The tests have been conducted with one blind researcher to check the functioning of different map features. This person had also tested the previous map prototype [6] and was thus familiar with the interactive map concept. The preliminary study showed that audio output was comprehensible, even if the voice was not perceived as pleasant. We detected that the user needed time to familiarize with the new gestures, but he was then able to use them for accessing different levels of information. The lasso gesture seemed to be challenging as it demanded to first identify a map element by following the raised lines and then circle around it. This is indeed more difficult without visual cues. There were no problems with accessing the different information levels by using the different buttons. Also the tap-and-hold gesture for the distance was usable and much appreciated.

4 Discussion and Conclusion

In this paper, we presented a state of the art of non-visual gestural interaction. Analysis of the literature shows different approaches to make gestural interaction accessible. It also reveals challenges that need to be addressed in the future, such as unintended touch input. Furthermore, we showed an example of how gestural interaction techniques can be used in interactive maps for visually impaired people. We checked that it was possible for a blind user to access distances and different types of information. Furthermore, our observations suggest that gestural interaction should be picked carefully. Gestures that are easy for sighted people may be less evident for visually impaired people (e.g., the lasso). This is in line with previous studies on accessible gestural interaction [16]. The present work only presented a proof-of-concept. A more advanced design process would be necessary, as well as extended evaluations with several visually impaired users. In the future, it would be interesting to go beyond the basic gestural interaction provided by the API, and to design specific gestural interaction. To sum up, we believe that thoroughly designed gestural interaction would open up new interaction possibilities in research and commercial prototype. However, it remains a challenge for the research domain of multi-touch to find interaction techniques that are usable without sight. We suggest that future studies should address the design of specific gestures for visually impaired people by including them throughout the design process from the creation of ideas to the evaluation.

Acknowledgments. We thank Alexis Paoleschi who developed the prototype presented in this paper and our blind participants.

References

1. Schöning, J.: Touch the future: the recent rise of multi-touch interaction. J. Eur. Comm. Futur. Emerg. Technol. Proactive Initiat. Pervasive Adapt. **5531**, 1–2 (2010)
2. Buxton, W.: Multi-touch systems that i have known and loved (2007)
3. Kane, S.K., Bigham, J.P., Wobbrock, J.O.: Slide rule: making mobile touch screens accessible to blind people using multi-touch interaction techniques. In: ASSETS'08, New York, NY, USA, pp. 73–80. ACM Press (2008)
4. Kane, S.K., Morris, M.R., Wobbrock, J.O.: Touchplates: low-cost tactile overlays for visually impaired touch screen users. In: ASSETS'13, Bellevue, Washington, USA. ACM (2013)
5. Xu, S., Bailey, K.: Design touch feedback for blind users. In: Stephanidis, C. (ed.) HCII 2013, Part I. CCIS, vol. 373, pp. 281–285. Springer, Heidelberg (2013)

6. Brock, A., Truillet, P., Oriola, B., Picard, D., Jouffrais, C.: Design and user satisfaction of interactive maps for visually impaired people. In: Miesenberger, K., Karshmer, A., Penaz, P., Zagler, W. (eds.) ICCHP 2012, Part II. LNCS, vol. 7383, pp. 544–551. Springer, Heidelberg (2012)

7. Pavlovic, V.I., Sharma, R., Huang, T.S.: Visual interpretation of hand gestures for human-computer interaction: a review. IEEE Trans. Pattern Anal. Mach. Intell. **19**, 677–695 (1997)

8. Kamber, Y.: Empirical investigation of the memorability of gesture sets (2011)

9. Wolf, K., Dicke, C., Grasset, R.: Touching the void: gestures for auditory interfaces. In: TEI'11, New York, NY, USA, pp. 305–308. ACM Press (2011)

10. Guerreiro, T., Lagoá, P., Nicolau, H., Gonçalves, D., Jorge, J.A.: From tapping to touching: making touch screens accessible to blind users. IEEE Multimed. **15**, 48–50 (2008)

11. Zeng, L., Weber, G.: Audio-haptic browser for a geographical information system. In: Miesenberger, K., Klaus, J., Zagler, W., Karshmer, A. (eds.) ICCHP 2010, Part II. LNCS, vol. 6180, pp. 466–473. Springer, Heidelberg (2010)

12. Yatani, K., Banovic, N., Truong, K.: SpaceSense: representing geographical information to visually impaired people using spatial tactile feedback. In: CHI'12, New York, NY, USA, pp. 415–424. ACM Press (2012)

13. Carroll, D., Chakraborty, S., Lazar, J.: Designing accessible visualizations: the case of designing a weather map for blind users. In: Stephanidis, C., Antona, M. (eds.) UAHCI 2013, Part I. LNCS, vol. 8009, pp. 436–445. Springer, Heidelberg (2013)

14. Apple: Apple - Accessibility - OS X - VoiceOver. http://www.apple.com/accessibility/osx/voiceover/

15. McGookin, D., Brewster, S.A., Jiang, W.W.: Investigating touchscreen accessibility for people with visual impairments. In: NordiCHI, pp. 298–307. ACM (2008)

16. Kane, S.K., Wobbrock, J.O., Ladner, R.E.: Usable gestures for blind people. In: CHI'11, Vancouver, BC, Canada, pp. 413–422. ACM Press (2011)

17. El-Glaly, Y., Quek, F., Smith-Jackson, T., Dhillon, G.: Audible rendering of text documents controlled by multi-touch interaction. In: ICMI'12, New York, NY, USA, pp. 401–408. ACM Press (2012)

18. Brock, A.M., Oriola, B., Truillet, P., Jouffrais, C., Picard, D.: Map design for visually impaired people: past, present, and future research. Médiation Inf. - Handicap Commun. **36**, 117–129 (2013)

19. Miele, J., Landau, S., Gilden, D.: Talking TMAP: automated generation of audio-tactile maps using Smith-Kettlewell's TMAP software. Br. J. Vis. Impair. **24**, 93–100 (2006)

20. Lévesque, V., Petit, G., Dufresne, A., Hayward, V.: Adaptive level of detail in dynamic, refreshable tactile graphics. In: IEEE Haptics Symposium, pp. 1–5 (2012)

21. Brock, A.M., Vinot, J.-L., Oriola, B., Kammoun, S., Truillet, P., Jouffrais, C.: Méthodes et outils de conception participative avec des utilisateurs non-voyants. In: IHM'10, Luxembourg, NY, USA, pp. 65–72. ACM Press (2010)

22. Laufs, U., Ruff, C., Weisbecker, A.: MT4j - an open source platform for multi-touch software development. VIMation J. **1**, 58–64 (2010)

Collaborative Pseudo-Haptics: Two-User Stiffness Discrimination Based on Visual Feedback

Ferran Argelaguet[1](✉), Takuya Sato[2], Thierry Duval[3], Yoshifumi Kitamura[2], and Anatole Lécuyer[1]

[1] Inria Rennes, Rennes, France
{fernando.argelaguet_sanz,anatole.lecuyer}@inria.fr
[2] Tohoku University Research Institute of Electrical Communication, Sendai, Japan
{takuyas6,kitamura}@riec.tohoku.ac.jp
[3] Université de Rennes 1, IRISA, Rennes, France
thierry.duval@irisa.fr

Abstract. Pseudo-Haptic feedback has been the object of several studies exploring how haptic illusions can be generated when interacting with virtual environments using visual feedback. In this work we explore how the concept of pseudo-haptic feedback can be introduced in a collaborative scenario. A remote collaborative scenario in which two users interact with a deformable object is presented. Each user, through touch-based input, is able to interact with a deformable virtual object displayed in a standard display screen. The visual deformation of the virtual object is driven by a pseudo-haptic approach taking into account both the user input and the simulated physical properties. Particularly, we investigated stiffness perception. In order to validate our approach, we tested our system in a single and two-user configuration. The results showed that users were able to discriminate the stiffness of the virtual object in both conditions with a comparable performance. Thus, pseudo-haptic feedback seems a promising tool for providing multiple users with physical information related to other users' interactions.

Keywords: Pseudo-haptics · User interfaces · Multi-user interaction

1 Introduction

Collaborative interaction has a wide range of applications such as virtual prototyping, training environments, project reviews and video games. In such applications, it is critical to ensure the communication between users (user awareness). All users must have knowledge about the state of the system and the actions performed by other users. In this work we explore how the concept of pseudo-haptic feedback can be introduced in such multi-user scenarios. Specifically, how the perception of physical properties of objects can be enhanced during of co-exploration and co-manipulation.

© Springer-Verlag Berlin Heidelberg 2014
M. Auvray and C. Duriez (Eds.): EuroHaptics 2014, Part II, LNCS 8619, pp. 49–54, 2014.
DOI: 10.1007/978-3-662-44196-1_7

Pseudo-haptic research has been conducted in order to explore how physical properties of virtual objects (e.g. stiffness, friction, mass) can be simulated without the need of dedicated haptic devices [5]. By delivering appropriate visual feedback accounting for users' actions and the simulated physical properties, some kind of "haptic illusions" can be induced [6]. Among them, the first pseudo-haptic paper focused on stiffness perception [5]. Users, by interacting with an isometric input device manipulated a virtual piston displayed on a computer string. The user could displace the virtual piston according to simulated stiffness. Varying the degrees of visual compression of the virtual piston leaded to different levels of perceived stiffness. However, pseudo-haptic studies have not only considered the simulation of physical parameter (e.g. stiffness, torque, friction). For example, Lécuyer et al. [4] explored how the relief of textures could be simulated by adjusting the Control/Display (CD) ratio of the mouse cursor based on the underlying texture information. Other studies have focused on the perception of the shape of 3D objects [1] or on graphical user interfaces [7].

In this research, in contrast to existing pseudo-haptic research on stiffness perception [5], we investigate the stiffness perception when two users interact in a non-collocated setup with deformable objects. The proposed setup enables two users to interact through a tactile interface with a deformable object. The feedback provided to the user is only visual, which is expected to enable stiffness discrimination [2]. The interaction with the deformable object is dependent on the users' actions and its physical properties. The results showed that participants were able to perceive the stiffness of virtual objects during co-manipulation through pseudo-haptic feedback. From this, we conclude that pseudo-haptic feedback can be introduced in collaborative environments. The remaining of the paper details the interaction model and its evaluation.

2   Concept of Pseudo-Haptic Stiffness Simulation in a Two-User Collaborative Scenario

The virtual environment considered is composed by a deformable object (cube), and two actuators at each side (see Fig. 1 left). In our two-user scheme, each user is able to manipulate one actuator in order to interact with the deformable object. For simplicity, the actuators only have one degree of freedom (horizontal axis). The system is designed in a way that users, in order to deform the object, have to work in a coordinate way. For example, if only one user is pushing, it results only in the translation of the cube without any deformation. In such a system, we have to determine (1) how the user input determines the force exerted by the actuator, and (2) how the forces applied by both actuators modify the state of the deformable object.

Regarding the user input, in our prototype, each user interacts with one of the actuators by moving his finger along a touch surface (see Fig. 1 right). The force (F) delivered by the actuator is linked with the amount of displacement accumulated is $F = \Delta x_f/a$. Where Δx_f is the displacement of the user's finger in the touch surface and a is a scaling factor. Each actuator is manipulated

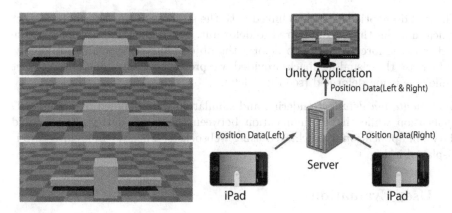

Fig. 1. (Left) the virtual environment considered is composed by one interactive object (center object) and two actuators. The deformation of the virtual object is only triggered when both users interact synchronously. (Right) System's architecture. Each user controls one actuator by swiping his finger on a touch device.

independently. When the user removes the finger from the tactile surface the actuator will no longer exert any force ($F = 0$).

Considering the environment and the user interaction, the system presents five different cases. They are characterized by the force delivered by each actuator (left F_l and right F_r) and whether the actuators are in contact with the deformable object or not:

1. The actuator is not in contact with the interactive object. The movement of the actuator is mapped directly with the user's input.
2. Only one actuator is pushing the interactive object. The actuator displaces the object along the horizontal axis with a 1:1 CD ratio.
3. Both actuators are in contact with the interactive object but one of them does not deliver any force. The behavior is the same as case 2 but the actuator with $F = 0$ is also displaced.
4. Both actuators are in contact with the interactive object, and $F_l > 0$ and $F_r > 0$. In this case, the force is transmitted to the deformable object which is deformed based on Hooke's law $x_d = F/k$. k determines the stiffness of the virtual cube and x_d is the compression of the cube in the x-axis. The force applied is $F = min(F_l, F_r)$. The exceeding force will displace the object and the actuator delivering less force.
5. The virtual object is compressed and $F = 0$. The virtual object will recover its original size (elastic deformation). If an actuator is in contact with the virtual object and their force is equal to zero, it will be displaced. The recovery time was not dependent on the cube's stiffness.

The simulation requires participants to interact synchronously when interacting with the virtual object. If both users do not deliver a similar force it will result in the displacement of the virtual object without any deformation.

The pseudo-haptic feedback is linked with the stiffness of the deformable object which modifies the force required to deform it. The higher the value of k is, the higher is the force required to deform the object and vice-versa. Additionally, to increase the visual feedback provided, we preserved the volume of the object while it is being deformed (see Fig. 1 left).

Implementation details. Rendering and simulation were handled by a Unity 3D application while the communication between the touch devices (iPads) and the main application was achieved using websockets. The system architecture is displayed in Fig. 1.

3   User Evaluation

A user evaluation of the system was conducted in order to explore its usability and explore the effects of the user collaboration on the perception of the pseudo-haptic feedback. The questions posed in the evaluation were the computation of the Just Noticeable Differences (JND) of the virtual stiffness and whether the fact that both users had to interact synchronously influenced their perception or not. These results are needed both to validate our approach and to provide guidelines to the integration of the proposed effect in a real application.

Design and Procedure. The evaluation followed a 2AFC (two alternative forced choice) procedure with two main conditions: single-user (S) and multi-user (M). For each trial, participants were presented with two virtual cubes (one after another) with different stiffness coefficients (k). Participants had to determine which one was the stiffest. While for the multi-user condition we used the system described in Sect. 2, for the single-user condition, the user interacted with two iPads at the same time with his two index fingers. For the 2AFC task, the comparisons were based on one reference value ($k_f = 4$) and six comparison values ($\pm30\,\%, \pm20\,\%, \pm10\,\%$). The order of the conditions (single vs multi) was balanced and the comparisons randomized. For each combination, users performed ten repetitions, resulting in a total of $2 \times 6 \times 10$ (120) trials. Regarding the procedure, for each trial, users were presented with a discrimination task. They had five seconds to interact with each virtual cube and then, they had to answer which cube was the stiffest. Users were able to answer the question through a GUI displayed on their iPads. For each trial, we recorded the answer for the question "Which virtual cube is the stiffest?". Furthermore, we also recorded the displacement of the virtual cube and the difference between the force applied by each effector, which are measures of the users' synchronization. Our hypotheses were [**H1**]: Stiffness discrimination accuracy will be higher for the single user condition and [**H2**]: The synchronization between both effectors will be higher for the single-user condition.

Participants. 16 users aged from 21 to 31 (11 male and 5 female) took part in the experiment. All users had no known perception disorders, and used their dominant hand to perform the task.

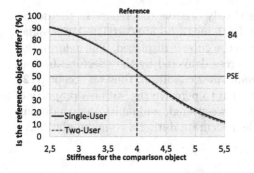

Fig. 2. Left, psychometric curves obtained for the single-user ($\alpha = 4.113, \beta = 0.711$) and multi-user ($\alpha = 4.098, \beta = 0.681$) conditions. Right, experimental setup.

Apparatus. The evaluation was conducted using two displays of 20" (see Fig. 2 right). Users interacted with the application sitting down, at 50 cm from the display. In the multi-user condition, users were not able to see neither the others user's display nor the others interface. Oral exchange was not allowed.

Results. The analysis of the results followed a classical psychophysical analysis as described in [3]. First, we consider the answers in which the reference is considered to be stiffer (see Fig. 2 left). The JND threshold is computed as the difference between the reference value and the value of the psychophysical curve ($f(x) = 1/(1 + e^{\frac{x-\alpha}{\beta}})$) at the 84 % ordinate. Multi-user: $\Delta I_M = 4 - 2.93 = 1.07$ and single-user: $\Delta I_S = 4 - 2.96 = 1.04$. With this information, we compute the Weber fraction as $k = \Delta I / I$ where I is the value of the reference stiffness. This computation results in $k_M = 0.267$ and $k_S = 0.26$.

The two-way ANOVA of Condition (multi,single) and Comparison ($\pm 30\%$, $\pm 20\%$, $\pm 10\%$) versus Accuracy showed a significant difference for Comparison ($F_{5,75} = 26.12; p < 0.001$) but no significant difference was found between conditions ($F_{1,75} = 0.49; p = 0.494$). The fact that there are no significant differences on the user accuracy is consistent with the fact that the Weber fractions for each condition are similar. In contrast, when analyzing the data regarding the synchronization between both actuators the two-way ANOVA for the cube displacement showed a main effect for Condition ($F_{1,15} = 712.43; p < 0.001$). Post-hoc tests (Bonferroni) showed that the cube displacement was significantly lower ($p < 0.05$) for the singe-user condition (38 % smaller). Regarding the force difference, there is also a significant effect on Condition ($F_{1,15} = 411.93; p < 0.001$). Post-hoc (Bonferroni) tests showed that the difference was significantly higher ($p < 0.05$) for the multi-user condition (29 % higher).

Discussion. The results show that users were able to perceive differences of stiffness with a comparable performance for single and multi-user conditions (similar Weber fractions and no significant differences in accuracy). Although we expected a reduced discrimination for the multi-user condition, this was not the case, thus we reject [**H1**]. Nevertheless, considering the results on cube displacement and force difference, we clearly observe differences in the degree of synchronization between conditions. Both measures are correlated, the higher is the difference between forces the more the cube is displaced. The deformation is determined by the minimum of the forces delivered by the effectors. In both cases, the values were higher for the multi-user condition, thus we accept [H2]. Hence, for the given simulation, users seem to perceive the stiffness property of the deformable object at the same level between single and multi-user conditions, although their motions are naturally less accurate during a co-manipulation.

4   Conclusion

In this work, we have studied the introduction of pseudo-haptic feedback in a collaborative perceptive task: two-user stiffness discrimination task based on visual feedback and tactile input. We have proposed and evaluated the interaction model. In the proposed simulation, two users could feel the stiffness of a deformable cube in a collaborative task. The evaluation conducted investigated the effects of the collaborative interaction in terms of user perception and synchronization. Although we expected a decrease in performance of stiffness discrimination for the collaborative task, the results surprisingly showed that it was not the case. The Weber fraction for single-user was 0.267 and 0.26 for the multi-user scenario. This result could be applied in various applications such as future remote co-exploration, assembly/maintenance simulations or multi-player video games.

References

1. Ban, Y., Kajinami, T., Narumi, T., Tanikawa, T., Hirose, M.: Modifying an identified curved surface shape using pseudo-haptic effect. In: IEEE Haptics Symposium, pp. 211–216, March 2012
2. Drewing, K., Ramisch, A., Bayer, F.: Haptic, visual and visuo-haptic softness judgments for objects with deformable surfaces. In: World Haptics, pp. 640–645, IEEE (2009)
3. Gescheider, G.A.: Psychophysics: Method, Theory, and Application. Lawrence Erlbaum Associates, Hillsdale (1985)
4. Lécuyer, A., Burkhardt, J.-M., Etienne, L.: Feeling bumps and holes without a haptic interface. In: Proceedings of the 2004 Conference on Human Factors in Computing Systems - CHI '04, New York, pp. 239–246 (2004)
5. Lecuyer, A., Coquillart, S., Kheddar, A., Richard, P., Coiffet, P.: Pseudo-haptic feedback: can isometric input devices simulate force feedback? In: IEEE Virtual Reality, pp. 83–90 (2000)
6. Pusch, A., Lécuyer, A.: Pseudo-haptics: from the theoretical foundationsto practical system design guidelines. In: 13th International Conference on Multimodal Interfaces, p. 57 (2011)
7. Rodgers, M.E., Mandryk, R.L., Inkpen, K.M.: Smart sticky widgets: pseudo-haptic enhancements for multi-monitor displays. In: Butz, A., Fisher, B., Krüger, A., Olivier, P. (eds.) SG 2006. LNCS, vol. 4073, pp. 194–205. Springer, Heidelberg (2006)

Centralizing Bias and the Vibrotactile Funneling Illusion on the Forehead

Hamideh Kerdegari[1]([⊠]), Yeongmi Kim[2], Tom Stafford[1],
and Tony J. Prescott[1]

[1] Sheffield Center for Robotics (SCentRo), University of Sheffield, Sheffield, UK
{h.kerdegari, t.stafford, t.j.prescott}@sheffield.ac.uk
[2] Interactive Graphics and Simulation Lab, University of Innsbruck,
Innsbruck, Austria
Yeongmi.kim@uibk.ac.at

Abstract. This paper provides a novel psychophysical investigation of head-mounted vibrotactile interfaces for sensory augmentation. A 1-by-7 headband vibrotactile display was used to provide stimuli on each participant's forehead. Experiment I investigated the ability to identify the location of a vibrotactile stimulus presented to a single tactor in the display; results indicated that localization error is uniform but biased towards the forehead midline. In Experiment II, two tactors were activated simultaneously, and participants were asked to indicate whether they experienced one or two stimulus locations. Participants reported the funneling illusion—experiencing one stimulus when two tactors were activated—mainly for the shortest inter-tactor difference. We discuss the significance of these results for the design of head-mounted vibrotactile displays and in relation to research on localization and funneling on different body surfaces.

Keywords: Head-mounted vibrotactile display · Localization · Funneling illusion

1 Introduction

Tactile displays provide an alternative way of communicating various kind of information and may be particularly useful when other communication channels, such as vision and hearing, are overloaded or compromised [1]. Consequently, tactile displays have been utilized to support a variety of applications including sensory substitution [2], sensory augmentation [3, 4], spatial orientation and navigation [5, 6] and exploration of virtual environments [7].

In several of these applications [3, 4], activation of vibrotactile stimulators at specific locations on the body provides a spatial cue to the location of an object or event in the environment or to show the navigation direction [5]. The number and configuration of the vibrotactile stimulators in the tactile display is known to play an important role in vibrotactile localization ability [8] although increasing array granularity does not necessarily improve localization ability [9, 10].

An important factor to consider in the design of tactile displays is the phenomenon known as the "funneling" illusion [11]. Funneling describes the experience of a single

© Springer-Verlag Berlin Heidelberg 2014
M. Auvray and C. Duriez (Eds.): EuroHaptics 2014, Part II, LNCS 8619, pp. 55–62, 2014.
DOI: 10.1007/978-3-662-44196-1_8

phantom sensation when multiple stimuli are presented simultaneously at nearby locations on the skin. If two nearby stimuli have the same intensity the phantom sensation is created in the middle of them, however, if they have different intensities, the sensation is "funneled" towards the actuator with higher intensity [12]. The separation distance between the tactors, their relative amplitudes, their temporal order, and their location on the body surface, have all been shown to effect the funneling illusion [11–13], moreover varying stimulation parameters at the two nearby sites can induce an experience of continuous apparent motion of the phantom stimulus [12, 14]. Hence when multiple vibrotactile actuators are activated in a tactile display the funneling effect influences the perceived pattern of stimulus in a complex manner, allowing various ways of communication direction or navigation information, whose control is still to be adequately understood.

The current paper arose from research aimed at the development of a vibrotactile headband display for fire fighter navigation. In an initial prototype ([4] and Fig. 1) we connected a 1-by-4 tactor display to an external array of ultrasound sensors, converting ultrasound distance signals to nearby surfaces, such as walls, into a vibrotactile display pattern on the area of the head closest to the nearest surface. We selected a head-based display as this allows rapid reactions to unexpected obstacles (tactile response latencies are linear in distance from the brain [15]), is intuitive for navigation, protects a critical part of the body, and leaves the fire fighter's hands free for tool use or for tactile exploration of objects and surfaces (see also [3]). In order to further optimize this design, and improve the usefulness of the low resolution tactile display, we need to better understand how simultaneous stimulation of multiple sites on the forehead is experienced and how best to configure our tactile display in order to relay effective information about object location. To this end, the current paper investigated vibrotactile localization accuracy on the forehead and the dependency of the forehead funneling illusion on inter-tactor spacing. The results of this study should help formulate guidelines for head-mounted vibrotactile displays and will also inform the wider understanding of the tactile funneling illusion.

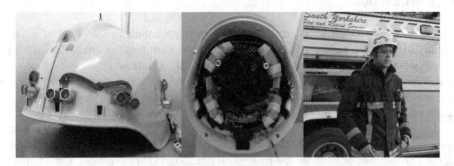

Fig. 1. The tactile helmet: a prototype sensory augmentation device developed to assist fire-fighters navigating in smoke-filled buildings [4].

2 Experimental Overview

The experimental was in accordance with University of Sheffield Ethical guidelines and conducted with approval of the local Ethics committee.

2.1 Participants

Ten participants—7 women and 3 men, average age 24—participated in each experiment; none of the participants reported any known abnormalities with haptic perception.

2.2 Apparatus

An easy-to-wear, lightweight tactile headband display was designed to provide stimuli on the user's forehead. The tactile headband consists of seven vibrating motors with 2.5 cm inter-tactor spacing that are attached to a Velcro strip that can easily be worn as a headband and that can be adjusted according to head size. The tactors used in the experiments were pancake-type vibration motors (Fig. 2 left) model 310–113 by Precision Microdrives with 10 mm diameter, 3.4 mm thickness, 3 V operating voltage and 220 Hz operating frequency at 3 V.

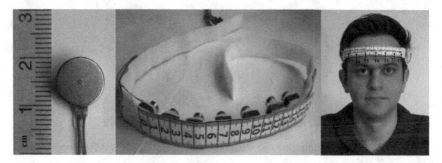

Fig. 2. Left: Pancake type vibration motor, Center: Tactile headband interface, Right: A participant wearing the tactile headband interface.

A paper ruler was attached on the outer side of the headband to aid accurate measurement of the stimulus position. The seven tactors were attached at positions 0, 2.5, 5, 7.5, 10, 12.5 and 15 cm relative to the ruler and are referred as tactors 1 (0 cm) to 7 (15 cm). Figure 2 (center) shows the headband, and (right) a participant wearing the array such that tactor 1 is on the far left of the forehead and tactor 4 is aligned with the forehead midline. In order to control the intensity of the vibrotactile actuators, a microcontroller, ATmega32u4 was used to generate pulse width modulation (PWM) signals. The microcontroller was connected to a PC through a RS232 serial port to transfer the command data to the vibration motors. The tactors have the highest intensity that could be produced using the system's PWM. A mirror was positioned so that participants were able to see the headband, and a mouse button and foot-switch were provided for participants to initiate each trial and trigger data capture, by inter-acting with a graphical user interface (GUI) displayed on the computer monitor.

2.3 Procedure

Participants were seated comfortably in front of the computer screen, camera, mirror, mouse and foot switch while the tactile display was worn on the forehead. A short practice session was provided to allow some familiarity with the experimental set-up. Once the participant felt comfortable, the trial phase was started. During the experi-ment, participants wore headphone playing white noise to mask any sounds from the vibrating motors.

Each trial consists of the participant clicking the GUI start button. After experi-encing a vibration stimulus (experiment I), or two simultaneous stimuli (experiment II), the participant was asked to respond by pointing to the perceived location(s) of stimulation on their forehead using one or two thin pointers and while looking into the mirror as illustrated in Fig. 3. By clicking again in the GUI a snapshot was captured with the digital camera recording the indicated position. A shutter sound played after image capture to indicate to that the trial was complete, and that the next trial was ready to commence. Participants interacted with the GUI using a mouse, in experiment I, and with a foot-switch in Experiment II (since both hands were needed for pointing).

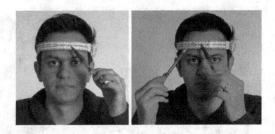

Fig. 3. Left: pointing on one location, Right: pointing on two locations

3 Experiment I: Vibrotactile Localization

The objective of Experiment I was to determine localization mean error for vibrotactile stimuli on the forehead. Each trial consisted of a vibration being displayed in a pseudo-random order to each tactor for 1000 ms. During the experimental session, a total of 105 trials were presented in a random order to each subject, 15 for each tactor. A practice session consisting of 5 randomly trials per tactor were provided before starting the experimental phase.

Localization mean error with standard deviation for each of the seven tactor positions is shown in Fig. 4 (left). As can be seen, this varies from 0.51 cm for tactor 4 to 0.76 cm for tactor 3. An ANOVA showed no significant difference in localization mean error across the seven positions ($F_{(6, 63)} = 0.882$, $p = 0.513$), although the data indicate that the lowest error occurs above midline. Figure 4 (right) shows the mean

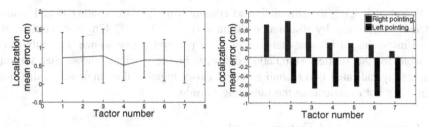

Fig. 4. Left: Localization mean error and its standard deviation, Right: Localization mean error for left and right sides.

error for left and right side pointing for each tactor. Moving from position 1 to 7 (from left to right), the error shifts from being strongly biased to the right to being strongly biased to the left. In other words, the perceived location of stimulation is biased towards the forehead midline for the outermost tactor locations.

4 Experiment II: Dependency of Funneling Illusion on Distance

Experiment II was designed to evaluate the dependency of the funneling illusion on the distance between tactors. Each trial consisted of vibration stimuli being displayed at one of the following tactor combination {(1, 4),(2, 3),(4, 7),(5, 6),(2, 6),(3, 5)} with both tactors activated simultaneously with 255 PWM intensity at 3 V for 1000 ms. The tactor combinations were chosen in a symmetric form to cover possible distances on the forehead. After displaying the vibration, subjects indicated whether they perceived one or two vibration stimulation on the forehead. During the experimental session, a total of 90 trials were presented in a pseudo-random order, 15 for each tactor combination. Before the experimental session there was a practice session consisting of 5 trials per tactor combination in random order.

Figure 5 (left) shows that by increasing the distance between tactors the percentage of pointing to one location decreases while the percentage of pointing to two locations increases. Tactor combinations with inter-tactor spacing of 2.5 cm showed highest rate of pointing to one location while tactor combination with inter-tactor spacing of 10 cm revealed highest rate of pointing to two locations. An ANOVA showed that the

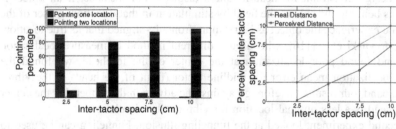

Fig. 5. Left: Percentage of pointing to one and two locations for different inter-tactor spacing, Right: Perceived and actual inter-tactor spacing

likelihood of judging the stimulation as coming from 2 sources rather than 1 source differed significantly by stimulation distance (F $(3, 27) = 92.426$, p < 0.0001). By visual inspection, it is clear that likelihood of perceiving one source was only more probable for the shortest stimulation distance. Figure 5 (right) shows that subjects consistently indicated two stimuli as being closer together than their actual distance, even when not experiencing the funneling illusion.

5 Conclusion and Future Work

The forehead is a promising location for vibrotactile displays for navigation since a display can easily fit inside the headband of a hat or helmet, signals reach the brain quickly allowing quick responses, and an intuitive mapping can be created between sensed objects (such as obstacles) and stimulation of the head in the direction of the object. One of the first devices to explore the use of a head-mounted interface was the "haptic radar" [3]. In this device, a one-to-one mapping was created between an infrared distance sensor and a tactor mounted directly beneath it. Users intuitively responded to objects moving close to the sensor by tilting or ducting away from the direction of the stimulus—indicating that the device could be useful for avoiding collisions. In the design for the "tactile helmet" ([4] and Fig. 1), a prototype sensory augmentation device for fire-fighters, we decoupled the configuration of an array of ultrasonic distance detectors from the arrangement of the tactors—in that case having eight detectors on the outside of a safety helmet and four tactors inside a head-band. However, in principle, the sensor array can have many more elements, and so be capable of building up a rich representation of the local scene. For this situation the optimal mapping of this representation onto patterns of vibrotactile stimulation has yet to be determined; signals should be intuitive and the tactile sensory channels not overloaded. Key constraints for display design will be the number and location of the tactors and appropriate use of tactile perceptual phenomena such as the funneling illusion and apparent motion.

To aid the design of head-mounted displays, such as that used in the tactile helmet, experiment I of the current study set out to explore localization accuracy on the forehead. Whereas mean error seems uniform across the forehead, somewhat to our surprise we found a bias towards the midline in localizing actuators that were away from the center of the forehead. Further testing is required to establish if this tactile saltation on the forehead is a robust effect, but if confirmed this would appear to be an important design constraint for head-mounted displays. For instance, if an object is displayed as being to the side of the head by stimulation in that direction, a user of the device could experience the object as being more frontally-aligned that its true location. Unlike Dobrzynski et al. [16], who used a different method to measure localization accuracy and found poor localization at the center of the forehead, we found the minimum localization mean error for midline tactor (front of the head) in the vibro-tactile headband, our results therefore go against the advice in that paper that the center of the forehead is a less optimal location for vibrotactile stimulation.

Our second experiment looked at the funneling illusion. Funneling can be used to increase localization accuracy [17] for a sparse array of actuators, or to communicate change of position [13] or movement [12, 14]. On the other hand, if used in an uncontrolled way, it could reduce localization accuracy or produce illusory signals that are misleading. The extent to which signals are "funneled" varies with many stimulus properties including amplitude, frequency, and onset/offset asynchrony [11–13]. The local mechanical properties of the skin, and underlying skeletal tissues are also important [18]. From the current study it would appear that funneling effects may occur primarily over fairly short distances on the forehead—we found only a small number of reports of funneling for inter-tactor distances of 5 cm or greater, whereas funneling was consistently reported (∼90 %) for the smallest distance of 2.5 cm. In contrast, on the surface of the arm a strong experience of funneling has been reported as occurring in the range 4–8 cm [17]. Further research is needed to explore the extent to which funneling on the forehead varies with stimulus parameters. For instance, an important avenue for future work is stimulus synchrony; systematic tests of asynchronous but overlapping stimuli should show to what extent timing is critical. Nevertheless our initial results do suggest that funneling could be a more localized effect on the forehead than elsewhere on the body. One possible explanation is that, compared to the arm, the skin of the forehead is stretched relatively tightly across the smooth surface of the skull with relatively little intervening fat/muscle. In [16], Dobrzynski et al. looked at the accuracy of reporting the correct number of stimuli for up to six tactors that were evenly distributed around the circumference of the head, finding success rates of 40 % or lower for two or more tactors. The current study suggests that this result may not have been specifically due to the funneling effect, since the tactors used in [16] were quite widely spaced; factors such as short-term memory and attention limitations could also be playing a role.

In experiment II, participants reported experiencing simultaneous stimuli at two locations as consistently closer to each other than their actual distance. In experiment I we found a saltation effect whereby single stimuli are experienced as closer to the midline which could partly explain the consistent under-estimating of inter-tactor distance in the second study, however, further experimentation will be required to dissect the contribution of a centralizing bias to this result.

A critical characteristic of devices such the haptic radar and the tactile helmet is that they are under user control, allowing the wearer to use them as active sensing devices [19]. Indeed, movement of the head is one of the most natural means through which to explore the local scene. Our future experiments will compare how a given pattern of stimulation on the skin is experienced when passively presented (as in the current study) and when induced by self-movement while wearing a sensory augmentation device. It seems plausible that the user experience in the latter case will be very different due to the 'sensorimotor contingencies' [20] created by the interaction between self-movement, environment structure and the vibrotactile signals delivered by the device.

Acknowledgment. This work was supported by the University of Sheffield Search and Rescue 2020 project and in parts by the EU project BEAMING 248620.

References

1. Geldard, F.A.: Some neglected possibilities of communication. Science **131**(3413), 1583–1588 (1960)
2. Kaczmarek, K.A., Bach-Y-Rita, P.: Tactile displays. In: Barfield, W., Furness, T. (eds.) Virtual environments and advanced interface design, pp. 349–414. Oxford University Press, New York (1995)
3. Cassinelli, A., Reynolds, C., Ishikawa, M.: Augmenting spatial awareness with haptic radar. In: 10th IEEE International Symposium on Wearable Computers (2006)
4. Bertram, C., Evans, M.H., Javaid, M., Stafford, T., Prescott, T.: Sensory augmentation with distal touch: the tactile helmet project. In: Lepora, N.F., Mura, A., Krapp, H.G., Verschure, P.F., Prescott, T.J. (eds.) Living Machines 2013. LNCS, vol. 8064, pp. 24–35. Springer, Heidelberg (2013)
5. Van Erp, J.B.: Presenting directions with a vibrotactile torso display. Ergonomics **48**(3), 302–313 (2005)
6. Jones, L.A., Lockyer, B., Piateski, E.: Tactile display and vibrotactile recognition on the torso. Adv. Robot. **20**, 1359–1374 (2006)
7. Lindeman, R.W., Yanagida, Y.: Empirical studies for effective near-field haptics in virtual environments. In: Proceedings of the IEEE Virtual Reality Conference, pp. 287–288. IEEE Computer Society, Los Alamitos, CA (2003)
8. Jones, L.A., Held, D., Hunter, I.: Surface waves and spatial localization in vibrotactile displays. In: IEEE Haptics Symposium, pp. 91–94 (2010)
9. Cholewiak, R.W., Brill, J.C., Schwab, A.: Vibrotactile localization on the abdomen: Effects of place and space. Percept. Psychophys. **66**(6), 970–987 (2004)
10. Jones, L.A., Ray, K.: Localization and pattern recognition with tactile displays. In: Haptic Interfaces for Virtual Environment and Teleoperator Systems, IEEE Symposium on Haptics, pp. 33–39 (2008)
11. Bekesy, G.V.: Funneling in the nervous system and its role in loudness and sensation intensity on the skin. J. Acoust. Soc. Am. **30**(5), 399–412 (1958)
12. Cha, J., Rahal, L., El Saddik, A.: A pilot study on simulating continuous sensation with two vibrating motors. In: Proceedings of HAVE, pp. 143–147 (2008)
13. Alles, D.S.: Information transmission by phantom sensations. IEEE Trans. Man-Mach. Syst. **11**(1), 85–91 (1970)
14. Rahal, L., Cha, J., El Saddik, A.: Continuous tactile perception for vibrotactile displays. In: IEEE International Workshop on Robotic and Sensors Environments (ROSE), pp. 86–91 (2009)
15. Stafford, T., Javaid, M., Mitchinson, B., Galloway, A.M.J., Prescott, T.J.: Integrating augmented senses into active perception: a framework. In: Poster Presented at Royal Society meeting on Active Touch Sensing, 31 Jan–02 Feb 2011 (2011)
16. Dobrzynski, M.K., et al.: Quantifying information transfer through a head-attached vibrotactile display: principles for design and control. IEEE Trans. Biomed. Eng. **59**(7), 2011–2018 (2012)
17. Barghout, A., et al.: Spatial resolution of vibrotactile perception on the human forearm when exploiting funneling illusion. In: IEEE International Workshop on Haptic Audiovisual Environments and Games (HAVE), pp. 19–23 (2009)
18. Sofia, K.O., Jones, L.A.: Mechanical and psychophysical studies of surface wave propagation during vibrotactile stimulation. IEEE Trans. Haptics **6**, 320–329 (2013)
19. Prescott, T.J., Wing, A.M.: Active touch sensing. Philoshipcal Trans. R. Soci. B. Biol. Sci. **366**(1581), 2989–2995 (2011)
20. O'Regan, K., Noë, A.: A sensorimotor account of vision and visual consciousness. Behav. Brain Sci. **24**(5), 939–973 (2001)

Haptic Rendering for Under-Actuated 6/3-DOF Haptic Devices

Petr Kadleček[✉], Petr Kmoch, and Jaroslav Křivánek

Faculty of Mathematics and Physics, Charles University in Prague,
Prague, Czech Republic
petr.kadlecek@gmail.com

Abstract. Under-actuated 6/3-DOF haptic devices are mostly used for simple 3-DOF point-based haptic interaction because of missing torque feedback. In this work, we present a system involving sensory substitution and pseudo-haptic feedback that effectively simulate torque feedback using visuo-tactile cues. The proposed system was implemented into a 6-DOF haptic rendering algorithm and tested on an under-actuated haptic device in a user study. We found that by applying our torque simulation system, the torque perception increases significantly and that 6/3-DOF devices can be used in complex tasks involving 6-DOF interactions.

Keywords: Haptic rendering · 6/3 Degrees of freedom · Under-actuated

1 Introduction

Although there are many types of 6-DOF (degrees of freedom) haptic devices, inexpensive devices are still limited to 3-DOF force feedback. Including 6-DOF sensors to a 3-DOF device does not substantially increase the complexity of device design and thus many of todays devices that fall into the group of 6-DOF sensing devices are limited to force-only feedback and do not provide torque feedback. Such devices with more sensors than actuators, i.e. 6/3-DOF, are called asymmetric or under-actuated devices [1].

The most common way of using 6/3-DOF haptic device is to implement a 3-DOF haptic rendering algorithm for a sphere-shaped tip of a 6-DOF controlled haptic probe where the rest of the probe simply penetrates the scene without reflecting any force feedback. While this approach ensures stability of the system, the overall haptic feedback impression is not realistic [2].

The aim of this paper is to improve the haptic feedback plausibility for under-actuated 6/3-DOF haptic devices. We propose to adjust a 6-DOF haptic rendering algorithm to 6/3-DOF haptic devices so that it eliminates instability and unnatural behavior when the virtual probe is subjected to torque due to the interaction with the scene.

We introduce the use of a sensory substitution and pseudo-haptic system [3] to create an illusion and a cue of missing torque feedback by using a combination

© Springer-Verlag Berlin Heidelberg 2014
M. Auvray and C. Duriez (Eds.): EuroHaptics 2014, Part II, LNCS 8619, pp. 63–71, 2014.
DOI: 10.1007/978-3-662-44196-1_9

of perceptual information obtained from different modalities. An experimental study was carried out in order to determine the benefit of our system. The results show that the proposed torque simulation system significantly increases task performance in interaction scenarios when torque perception is important and that 6/3-DOF haptic devices are suitable even for complex 6-DOF manipulation tasks.

2   Related Work

Barbagli et al. [1] formally defined the problem of sensor/actuator asymmetry and provided a framework for under-actuated haptic device analysis. Two 2-DOF examples showed that it is possible to correctly perceive a missing degree of freedom to some extent. Several studies examined the benefit of 6-DOF over 3-DOF manipulation in various tasks [2,4,5]. Forsslund et al. [6] compare task performance in virtual surgical environments using 3-DOF haptic rendering and 6-DOF haptic rendering on under-actuated 6/3-DOF and fully-actuated 6-DOF haptic devices. Results showed that for a 6-DOF controlled haptic probe, utilization of a 6-DOF haptic rendering algorithm with discarded torque feedback on an under-actuated device significantly increases task performance over the 3-DOF feedback of a sphere-shaped tip of the probe. Nevertheless, completely discarding the torque feedback from a 6-DOF haptic rendering often creates instability of the system and some interactions utilizing the torque become non-intuitive and confusing for the user.

Pseudo-haptic systems can be defined as "systems providing haptic information generated, augmented or modified, by the influence of another sensory modality" [7]. Most of the current research in pseudo-haptic feedback is focused on simulating haptic properties on passive devices with no force feedback [8]. Lécuyer et al. [9] showed that a passive apparatus (such as a 6-DOF Space-Ball device) can simulate haptic information and that haptic sense is blurred by visual feedback. Pseudo-haptically simulated haptic properties are currently applied in graphical user interfaces, tactile images, video games and include friction, stiffness, mass or haptic textures [8]. However, no work has attempted to address the problem of 6/3-DOF haptic rendering using pseudo-haptic feedback and sensory substitution.

Despite the conclusion of several studies that asymmetric devices have limited usability for certain situations demanding a realistic haptic feedback, propositions of future work in haptic rendering that would alleviate limitations of asymmetric devices were mentioned mainly due to the broad use of such devices.

3   6/3-DOF Haptic Rendering

The key concept of 6/3-DOF haptic rendering is to extend existing 6-DOF haptic rendering algorithms by applying methods that restrain instability and provide alternative means of torque simulation. The problem with instability lies within the full controllability and partial observability [1] of the haptic probe.

The discarded torque feedback enables a haptic stylus to rotate freely in situations where the haptic probe movement is restricted, such as wrenching or prying. The user has no information about the magnitude of the exerted torque and the virtual energy that is unintentionally generated in the virtual environment. This can lead to unwanted haptic probe penetration or even pop-through effects when using penalty-based (repulsive force field) methods without proper constraints for collision response, such as the popular voxel sampling method [10].

3.1   Simulation of Torque

To overcome the problem with the observability of the haptic probe, we propose to use sensory substitution and pseudo-haptic systems to simulate and create an illusion of the torque. We apply the following methods and criteria:

1. *Prevent scene penetration* by the haptic probe when exerting excessive torque.
2. Simulate a *torque feedback via a vibration effect* proportional to a measure of magnitude of the exerted torque to effectively stimulate the user.
3. Show a visually distinctive model of the haptic probe (e.g. wireframe model) having the actual position and *orientation of the haptic stylus* so the user can perceive and correct the discrepancies between the two.

Penetration Prevention. Precise and robust collision detection that prevents penetration provides an effective way of modifying the user's perception of the haptic stylus orientation. A sensory conflict is presented to the user when the visual information of the orientation of the haptic probe differs from kinesthetic (proprioceptive) information of the haptic stylus. Dominance of the visual modality over the haptic modality [7,8] provides the illusion of torque feedback when the haptic probe rotation is restricted.

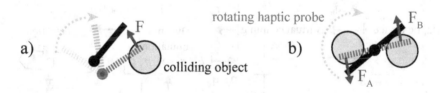

Fig. 1. a) The *"good torque"* scenario. b) The *"bad torque"* scenario.

Torque Feedback via a Vibration Effect. The sensory conflict as such does not provide enough information about the magnitude of the exerted torque in all situations. During experiments, we made one important observation that the torque exertion can be categorized into two general scenarios:

(a) Force F applied at a point distant from the center of mass of the rotating haptic probe, causing the probe to both translate and rotate. We call this the *"good torque"* scenario (see Fig. 1-a).

(b) Forces F_A, F_B applied at two different points causing only rotation and no translation (i.e. $F_A + F_B = 0$) of the rotating probe, such as wrenching or prying. We call this the *"bad torque"* scenario (see Fig. 1-b).

In spite of the fact that the classification based on the "good torque"/"bad torque" is not exhaustive, we found that it is sufficient for typical haptic probes.

In the *"good torque"* scenario, a translational force restricts the probe from penetrating the scene and provides instant contact resolution just using force feedback. The level of realism of this contact resolution depends on the distance of the applied force from the center of mass and on the shape of the haptic probe. In most typical cases, people do not even notice the omitted torque and we do not apply any cue informing the user about the exerted torque as it can be rather distracting.

In the *"bad torque"* scenario, however, there is no natural contact resolution for under-actuated devices and hence it is necessary to provide the required information using a different modality. We propose to provide users with a non-visual stimulus that alerts them in a tactile manner using a *vibration* generated by the haptic device.

Orientation of the Haptic Stylus. In situations when the haptic probe rotation is limited and the task demands highly accurate motion, the vibration that informs the user about the magnitude of the exerted torque may not be sufficient. To prevent orientation difficulties, a wireframe model of the haptic probe with the stylus orientation (i.e. an orientation not constrained by surrounding objects in the virtual scene) can be optionally shown when the magnitude of the torque exceeds a certain threshold. To prevent distractive blinking, we apply hysteresis thresholding.

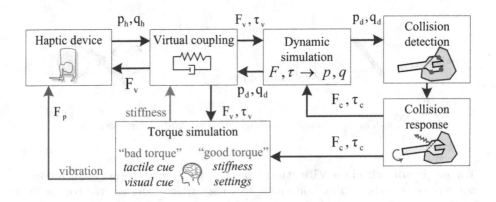

Fig. 2. 6/3-DOF Haptic rendering pipeline

3.2   Algorithm Description

We extended a 6-DOF haptic rendering algorithm by McNeely et al. [10]. We chose the method for its simplicity and wide use, and implemented the algorithm using the CHAI 3D library set [11]. The original 6-DOF haptic rendering algorithm uses volumetric representation for collision detection (voxelized meshes) and a penalty-based method for collision response. Stabilization and force filtering is performed using a simulation-based method known as virtual coupling.

The haptic rendering pipeline including our torque simulation extension is shown in Fig. 2. The haptic loop starts with a position and orientation (p_h, q_h) of the stylus sent to the virtual coupling unit. Collisions of the dynamic haptic probe are detected and a contact force and torque (F_c, τ_c) are computed and applied together with the coupling force and torque (F_v, τ_v) on the dynamic probe. A new position and orientation (p_d, q_d) of the dynamic probe are computed using semi-implicit numerical integration. The new coupling force (F_v) is then sent to the device.

Torque Simulation Extension. The first step of our torque simulation extension is a determination of the torque type. In the *"good torque"* case, we just need to ensure that the virtual coupling torque stiffness is high enough to achieve the best coupling transparency. However, the high torque stiffness of the coupling may result in scene penetrations of the haptic probe in the *"bad torque"* case. That is because users may unintentionally generate excessive torque by rotating the stylus in a situation when the physical torque feedback would not allow it. Therefore, in the *"bad torque"* case, we limit the virtual coupling torque stiffness to prevent penetration. Furthermore, we apply the vibration feedback and the optional visual cue.

Determining the Torque Type. To distinguish between the *"good torque"* and *"bad torque"* scenarios, the algorithm analyzes correlation of force and torque magnitude. For the *"bad torque"* scenario, torque magnitude is significantly higher than the magnitude of forces that could have affected the torque. Such forces are directed perpendicularly to the torque vector (as shown in the figure on the right). To filter these forces, we

Torque vector

project the coupling force (F_v) to a plane perpendicular to the torque vector and determine the *"bad torque"* using the following equations:

$$F_{proj} = F_v - \frac{\tau_v}{|\tau_v|}(F_v \cdot \tau_v) \tag{1}$$

$$"badtorque" = \begin{cases} true & \text{if} |\tau_c| > 0 \ \wedge \ |\tau_v| > T_{min} \ \wedge \ |\tau_v| > R_d |F_{proj}| \\ false & \text{otherwise} \end{cases} \tag{2}$$

where T_{min} is a minimal torque threshold and R_d is the radius of the probe.

Vibration Pattern. The vibration pattern for the *"bad torque"* scenario was chosen to be non-distractive, yet stimulative, for users. Experiments showed that the pattern of a constant frequency of 200 Hz is suitable for this purpose. We set the magnitude of the vibration force to be logarithmically proportional to the magnitude of the coupling torque: $|F_p| \propto log(|\tau_v|)$ and the generated vibration force (F_p) is sent directly to the haptic device so that it does not affect the virtual coupling (see Fig. 2).

4   User Study

An experimental study was designed to assess the influence of our torque sim-ulation system on perceiving the missing physical torque feedback when using an under-actuated 6/3-DOF haptic device. We expand on the results from the study of Forsslund et al. [6] who showed that there is a significant improvement in a task performance when using a 6-DOF haptic rendering algorithm even with discarded torque feedback. In our study, we measured the effect of the tac-tile (vibration) and visuo-tactile (vibration and wireframe model) cues on the perception of torque feedback.

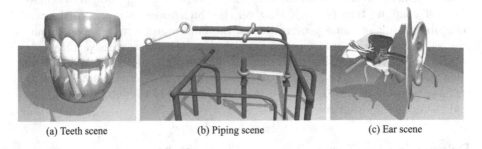

(a) Teeth scene   (b) Piping scene   (c) Ear scene

Fig. 3. Experimental scenes used in the study.

Experiment Design. We designed three scenes presenting different interaction scenarios, as shown in Fig. 3: Teeth, Piping and Ear scene. In each scene, the participant's task was to use the haptic probe to touch a visible checkpoint for 3 s until it disappeared and a next checkpoint became visible.

In the Teeth scene, the haptic probe represented a dental instrument. Check-points were located on hard-to-access locations such as interdental spaces to force the participant to manipulate the haptic probe in a non-trivial manner so that both force and torque feedback are employed. The Piping scene represented a virtual assembly scenario using a wrench with the shape of a ring spanner as the haptic probe. The participant had to move the ring spanner through the piping while being constrained by two pipes at both sides of the spanner as shown in Fig. 3-b. In the Ear scene, a needle insertion procedure was simulated. Careful manipulation with rolling of the bent needle was needed to complete the task.

Procedure. Three variants of torque simulation were tested on each subject. The first variant (A) did not use any tactile or visuo-tactile cue. It was included to provide comparison with a stable (i.e. meets criterion 1 in Sect. 3.1) 6-DOF haptic rendering algorithm when its torque output is simply discarded. The second variant (B) employed the vibration effect proportional to the exerted torque magnitude. The third variant (C) used both the vibration effect and visual help (the wireframe model). In total, participants performed all three tasks six times. In order to minimize the learning effect, we presented torque simulation variants (i.e. A, B, C) in random order and participants performed the task for all variants two times with no time limit. Before the measurement, we let participants familiarize themselves with the vibration effect as long as they needed to adopt the perception.

The study was conducted with the 6/3-DOF Sensable Phantom Desktop haptic device and Dell U2713HM 27" non-stereo monitor placed 80 cm in front of the participants. Fifteen subjects (8 male, 7 female) volunteered to participate in the experiment. Most of them had no or little experience with haptic devices. They ranged in age between 21 and 63 years, one of the subjects was left-handed. The procedure took 30 to 60 min for each participant.

Measurements. During each trial, we recorded information about the haptic probe interaction and analyzed the following factors: torque error E_τ, force error E_F and task completion time t_c:

$$E_\tau = \int_0^{t_c} \tau_v \, dt \qquad E_F = \int_0^{t_c} F_v \, dt \qquad (3)$$

Torque error and force error factors were derived to estimate a possible structural damage of the virtual scene by incautious manipulation of the haptic probe.

Analysis. Every subject had different manipulation skills and spatial orientation abilities. Therefore, we used within-subjects repeated measures analysis of variance (ANOVA) using three torque simulations variants (A, B, C) as independent variables. To determine which variants significantly differed from each other, Bonferroni pairwise comparisons were performed with significance level 0.05.

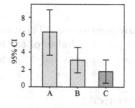

Fig. 4. Torque error mean estimates.

For the torque error factor E_τ, a significant difference was observed between the three variants $[F(2, 14) = 13.589; p < 0.001]$. Measured means and 95 % confidence interval limits of three variants (A, B, C) are shown in Fig. 4. The results showed that the tactile feedback (i.e. variant B) and visuo-tactile feedback (variant C) significantly decreased the torque error factor. According to Bonferroni pairwise comparisons, a significant difference was observed between the variant A and B ($p = 0.012 < 0.05$), and between A and C

($p < 0.001$), while no significant difference was observed between variants B and C ($p = 0.098 > 0.05$).

The ANOVA for force error E_F and task completion time t_c factors revealed statistically non-significant difference between measured torque simulation variants. Despite the completion time between subjects being considerably different, the within subject completion time was approximately the same for all three variants. This was mainly due to the fact that subjects were less aware of the produced torque error in the variant A.

One of the surprising results is that all participants were able to naturally discriminate between a vibration effect and forces generated by the virtual simulation. All participants agreed that they did not perceive the vibration effect as distractive, but they rather linked the effect with the torque feedback. They also agreed that the tactile cue as such provided an instant stimulation which can be used even for situations where the haptic probe is obscured by other objects and is not visible.

5   Conclusion

In this paper, we presented a new method to address the problem of haptic rendering for the widely used 6/3-DOF under-actuated haptic devices. To overcome the problem of limited observability of the haptic probe, we proposed and implemented torque simulation system involving visuo-tactile feedback. The user study showed that the proposed sensory substitution and pseudo-haptic system significantly increases torque perception and it is therefore possible to apply presented 6/3-DOF haptic rendering algorithm even for more complex tasks requiring a 6-DOF haptic probe interaction using under-actuated device.

In future work, we will examine the performance of torque simulation systems for advanced haptic rendering algorithms including surface materials, dynamic models or deformable models. We will also experiment with other pseudo-haptic systems and sensory substitution approaches, such as sound rendering.

Acknowledgments. The work was supported by the GA UK 2062214 and SVV-2014-260103 grants. Models of teeth and the ear used in the user study were downloaded from animium.com and 3dmodelfree.com.

References

1. Barbagli, F., Salisbury, K.: The effect of sensor/actuator asymmetries in haptic interfaces. In: Proceedings of 11th Symposium on Haptic Interfaces for Virtual Environment and Teleoperator Systems, HAPTICS 2003, pp. 140–147. IEEE (2003)
2. Wang, S., Srinivasan, M.A.: The role of torque in haptic perception of object location in virtual environments. In: Proceedings of 11th Symposium on Haptic Interfaces for Virtual Environment and Teleoperator Systems, HAPTICS 2003, pp. 302–309. IEEE (2003)

3. Pusch, A., Lécuyer, A.: Pseudo-haptics: from the theoretical foundations to practical system design guidelines. In: Proceedings of the 13th International Conference on Multimodal Interfaces, pp. 57–64. ACM (2011)
4. Verner, L.N., Okamura, A.M.: Force & torque feedback vs force only feedback. In: Third Joint EuroHaptics Conference and Symposium on Haptic Interfaces for Virtual Environment and Teleoperator Systems, World Haptics 2009, pp. 406–410. IEEE (2009)
5. Weller, R., Zachmann, G.: User performance in complex bi-manual haptic manipulation with 3 dofs vs. 6 dofs. In: Haptics Symposium (HAPTICS), pp. 315–322. IEEE (2012)
6. Forsslund, J., Chan, S., Selesnick, J., Salisbury, K., Silva, R.G., Blevins, N.H., et al.: The effect of haptic degrees of freedom on task performance in virtual surgical environments. Stud. Health Technol. Inform. **184**, 129–135 (2013)
7. Lécuyer, A., Burkhardt, J.M., Coquillart, S., Coiffet, P.: Boundary of illusion: an experiment of sensory integration with a pseudo-haptic system. In: Proceedings of IEEE Virtual Reality, pp. 115–122. IEEE (2001)
8. Lécuyer, A.: Simulating haptic feedback using vision: a survey of research and applications of pseudo-haptic feedback. Presence: Teleoper. Virtual Environ. **18**(1), 39–53 (2009)
9. Lécuyer, A., Coquillart, S., Kheddar, A., Richard, P., Coiffet, P.: Pseudo-haptic feedback: Can isometric input devices simulate force feedback? In: Proceedings of IEEE Virtual Reality, pp. 83–90. IEEE (2000)
10. McNeely, W.A., Puterbaugh, K.D., Troy, J.J.: Voxel-based 6-dof haptic rendering improvements. Haptics-e **3**(7), 56 (2006)
11. Conti, F., Morris, D., Barbagli, F., Sewell, C.: Chai 3d. http://www.chai3d.org (2006)

A Change in the Fingertip Contact Area Induces an Illusory Displacement of the Finger

Alessandro Moscatelli[3](✉), Matteo Bianchi[1,2], Alessandro Serio[1,2],
Omar Al Atassi[2], Simone Fani[2], Alexander Terekhov[4], Vincent Hayward[4],
Marc Ernst[3], and Antonio Bicchi[1,2]

[1] Advanced Robotics Department, Istituto Italiano di Tecnologia, Genova, Italy
matteo.bianchi@iit.it
[2] Universitá di Pisa, Centro di Ricerca E. Piaggio, Pisa, Italy
{bicchi,alessandro.serio,omar.atassi,simone.fani}@centropiaggio.unipi.it
[3] Universität Bielefeld, Cognitive Neuroscience and CITEC, Bielefeld, Germany
{alessandro.moscatelli,marc.ernst}@uni-bielefeld.de
[4] Sorbonne Universités, UPMC Univ Paris 06, UMR 7222, ISIR, 75005 Paris, France
{hayward,terekhov}@isir.upmc.fr

Abstract. Imagine you are pushing your finger against a deformable, compliant object. The change in the area of contact can provide an estimate of the relative displacement of the finger, such that the larger is the area of contact, the larger is the displacement. Does the human haptic system use this as a cue for estimating the displacement of the finger with respect to the external object? Here we conducted a psychophysical experiment to test this hypothesis. Participants compared the passive displacement of the index finger between a reference and a comparison stimulus. The compliance of the contacted object changed between the two stimuli, thus producing a different area-displacement relationship. In accordance with the hypothesis, the modulation of the area-displacement relationship produced a bias in the perceived displacement of the finger.

Keywords: Area of contact · Proprioception · Finger displacement

1 Introduction

Imagine you are pushing your finger against a deformable, compliant object, such as the sponge in Fig. 1a. Due to the deformation of the object and the skin, the area of contact (A) between them increases as the finger keeps pushing toward the center of the object, until it reaches a plateau. The change in the area of contact can provide an estimate of the *relative* displacement of the finger (Δx) among two instances t_1 and t_2, such that if $A_1 > A_2$, then $x_1 > x_2$. The area of contact would also provide an estimate of the *absolute* finger position x

---

Alessandro Moscatelli and Matteo Bianchi—These authors contributed equally to this work.

M. Auvray and C. Duriez (Eds.): EuroHaptics 2014, Part II, LNCS 8619, pp. 72–79, 2014.
DOI: 10.1007/978-3-662-44196-1_10

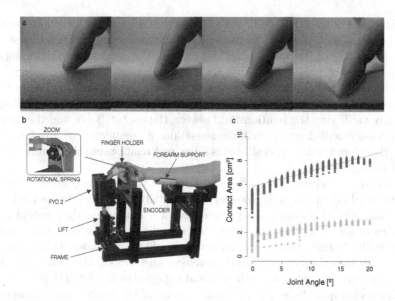

Fig. 1. (a) The area of contact between the skin and the sponge (marked in red in the figure) increases as the finger moves towards the bottom edge of the object. (b) The setup including the lift, the FYD-2 device and the angle encoder. (c) The area of contact changes as a function of the displacement of the finger and of the stretching state of the fabric, i.e. the rotation angle of the FYD-2 motors (in red $\theta = 10°$ and in grey $\theta = 80°$; results from a representative participant) (Color figure online).

(i.e., an estimate in units of lengths), if the perceptual system can internalize the relationship between A and other intrinsically absolute cues, such as the proprioceptive-based estimate $\tilde{x}_p$:

$$\tilde{x}_p = f(A)$$

Where $f(\cdot)$ is the relationship between the two cues, and $\tilde{x}_p$ provides an absolute estimate of x. To clarify the issue, the change in the contact area in haptics can be considered as a counterpart of the perspective cue in visual depth perception. The perspective cue is a relative depth cue, since it provides the observer with the depth relationships, and not with an absolute estimate (in units of lengths) of the distance with the object. In order to estimate the absolute depth, the perceptual system needs a scaling factor (e.g. from accommodation) to promote the relative depth cue into an absolute depth cue. This mechanism is known as *cue promotion* [1]. Whether relative or absolute, the evolution of the area of contact would provide a fair estimate of the displacement only assuming that the compliance of the object does not change over time. This leads to our experimental questions: Does the human haptic system use the change in the area of contact as a cue for estimating the displacement of the finger with respect to an external object?

The deformation of the contact surface and the ratio between the applied force and the displacement of the finger are the two major cues to discriminate the compliance of an object [2,3]. The tactile cue is responsible for a large part of this perceptual acuity; under the assumption of optimal combination of the two cues, nearly 90 % of the information depends on the local surface deformation [3]. The spread of the contact area conveys important information about the deformation of a compliant surface. There is a strong empirical evidence that the central nervous system decodes the contact area information [4]. Accordingly, artificially modifying the relationship between the contact force and the overall contact area is sufficient to elicit the sensation of compliance of a deformable object. Bicchi and colleagues called this force-area relationship the Contact Area Spread Rate (CASR) [2,5,6].

In the studies cited above, the compliance is the unknown quantity varying between different stimuli. However, in our daily experience we can reliably assume that the compliance of a given object will remain nearly constant over time. Reasoning along this line, when the compliance of the contacted object unexpectedly changes, the perceptual system could misestimate the indentation of the finger into the object — and therefore, misestimate the position of the finger. Here we conducted a psychophysical experiment to test this hypothesis. Participants compared the passive displacement of the index finger between a reference and a comparison stimulus. The compliance of the contacted object changed unexpectedly between the two stimuli, thus producing a different area-displacement relationship (i.e., a different indentation of the finger into the object). If participants rely on the cutaneous cue $f(A)$, this would induce a bias in the perceived finger displacement, such that the wider would be the contact area, the larger the perceived displacement.

2   Methods

2.1   Participants

Six healthy volunteers participated to the experiment (2 Females and 4 Males, Age: 26 ± 4, $mean \pm SD$). All participants were naie to the purpose of the experiment and they gave informed consent prior to participating. The experiment was approved by the Ethical Committee of the Universitá di Pisa.

2.2   Apparatus

The apparatus (Fig. 1b) simulates the interaction between the fingertip and a deformable, compliant object. It consists of three components: The *FYD-2 device* [7], a *vertically-moving platform* and a *hand-and-finger holder*.

The FYD-2 mimics the compliance of the surface by changing the stretching state of an elastic fabric in contact with the fingertip. The extremities of the fabric are connected to two rollers, which are rotated independently by two motors. Rotating the motors in opposite directions, it produces a stretching of the fabric, and thus increases its stiffness [7]. The contact area, the normal force were recorded, while the indentation of the finger was obtained through the force measurement and relying on device characterization [7].

As showed in Fig. 1b, the FYD-2 is placed on a platform, which is moved upward and downward with constant velocity of 10 mm/s using a linear actuator (Firgelli L16, Victoria, BC Canada). The fingerpad of the user is placed in a finger-holder, which restricts the movements to the flexo-extension of the metacarpo-phalangeal (MCP) joint. An absolute magnetic encoders (12 bit magnetic encoder by Austria Microsystems - Unterpremstaetten, Austria - AS5045 with a resolution of 0.0875 degree) placed on the finger-holder is used to read the extension of the MCP joint. During the lifting phase, the FYD-2 contacts the fingerpad of the user. When the MCP angle reaches the desired value, the linear actuator stops to lift up the FYD-2 and hence the finger, and it starts to move down, while MCP joint angle begins to decrease, i.e. to flex. Both the signal reading and control phases were performed using a custom made electronic board (PSoC-based electronic board with RS485 communication protocol).

A rotational spring (elastic constant of 5 N/deg; see zoom of Fig. 1b) is used to connect the finger-holder and the frame of the structure. In this manner, the force that the finger produces over the FYD-2 surface increases linearly with the MCP joint angle thus producing an increase in the contact area (Fig. 1c). Note that, without this spring, the contact area would increase only at the very beginning of the lift movement and immediately saturate as soon as the reaction force of the fabric deformed by the finger would reach an equilibrium with the weight of the finger. The area-angle relationship changes with the stretching state of the fabric of the FYD-2, which depends on the angular position of the two motors θ. The larger is the value of θ, the stiffer is the fabric.

2.3   Stimulus and Procedure

Participants were blindfolded and sat on an office chair, placing the right arm on an arm rest in front of the device. Headphones playing pink noise prevented the noise generated by the device to be used as a cue. In a *forced-choice procedure*, participants performed a finger-displacement discrimination task. The device displaced the finger up-and-down twice, in subsequent intervals corresponding to the reference and comparison stimulus. The rotation of the finger joint was equal to 12° in the reference stimulus. It was chosen pseudo-randomly between 5 possible values (range: 4°–20°) in the comparison. The order of presentation of the reference and the comparison varied in a pseudo-random fashion between trials. After the presentation of the stimuli, participants reported in which of the two intervals the displacement of the finger was larger. Participants received no information about the compliance of the contacted object.

The position of the rollers θ was always equal to 50° in the reference stimulus — this value is approximately in the middle of the compliance range that the device is capable to mimic. In the comparison stimulus, the device simulated an object that was either more ($\theta = 10°$) or less ($\theta = 80°$) compliant than the reference. No information about the compliance of the contacted surface were provided to the participants. The two compliance conditions were tested in two different blocks; each one consisting of 100 trials. The order of the two blocks was counterbalanced among participants.

2.4   Analysis

We modeled the responses of each participant using psychometric functions. We applied the following model, separately in the two experimental conditions:

$$\Phi^{-1}\left[P(Y_j = 1)\right] = \beta_0 + \beta_1 x \tag{1}$$

In a given trial j, $Y_j = 1$ if the participant reports that the displacement was larger in the comparison than in the reference and $Y_j = 0$ otherwise. $P(Y_j = 1)$ is the probability of perceiving a larger displacement in the comparison and Φ^{-1} is the *probit* transform of this probability. On the right side of the equation, x is the physical displacement of the finger in the comparison stimulus. β_0 and β_1 are the intercept and the slope of the linearized equation, respectively. The *point of subjective equality* $(PSE = -\beta_0/\beta_1)$ is an estimate for the accuracy of the percept. Next, we extended the analysis to the whole population (n = 6) by means of a *generalized linear mixed model* (GLMM; see [8,9]). The GLMM is similar to the psychometric function, with the advantage of allowing the analysis of clustered data—as in our case the collection of repeated responses in several participants. As described in [8] we estimated the PSE and the 95 % confidence interval in the two experimental conditions. If the difference in the *spread of the contact area* would affect the perceived displacement of the finger, then the PSE would be significantly different between the two compliance conditions. In particular, we expected that a simulated softer object (i.e. $\theta = 10°$) would increase the perceived finger displacement compared to the reference stimulus. This would predict that $PSE_{\theta 10} < 12°$ (the PSE would be smaller than the finger displacement of the reference stimulus). Similarly we expect that $PSE_{\theta 80} > 12°$.

3   Results

Figure 2 shows the perceived finger displacement in a representative participant, for the stretching state of the comparison $\theta = 10°$ (in red) and $\theta = 80°$ (in grey). The PSE is significantly different in the two experimental conditions $(PSE_{\theta 10} = 9.7 \pm 0.5, PSE_{\theta 80} = 12.8 \pm 0.6; Estimate \pm SE)$. Note that, in accordance with our predictions for a mimicked soft object $(\theta = 10°)$ the estimated PSE is smaller than the reference finger displacement. *Vice versa*, for $\theta = 80°$ the PSE was larger than the reference. We extended the analysis to the whole population (n = 6) with the GLMM. The analysis confirmed the same response pattern as in the representative participant. The estimated PSE is equal to 10.5 for $\theta = 10°$ (95 % $CI : 9.9 - 11.1$), and 12.8 for $\theta = 80°$ (95 % $CI : 12.1 - 13.6$). The 95 % *confidence intervals* are not overlapping between the two experimental conditions and significantly different from the value of the reference displacement.

4   Model

In this study we showed that a modulation of the spread of the contact area produces a bias in the perceived displacement of the finger. The result is consistent

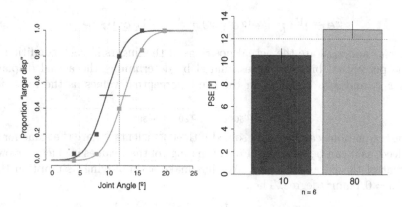

Fig. 2. (a) The psychometric functions for a representative participant, in the two experimental conditions (red: $\theta = 10$; gray: $\theta = 80$). The reference finger displacement (12°) is indicated with a dashed blue line. (b) The *point-of-subjective-equality* (PSE) in the two experimental conditions (n = 6) (Color figure online).

with a weighted sum of the tactile and proprioceptive cues. That is, we assume a linear relationship between the contact area A and the finger angular displacement x.

$$A = k(x - \bar{x}) + \bar{A},$$

where $\bar{x} = 12°$ is the reference displacement used in the current study. The parameters k and $\bar{A}$ depend on the stiffness of the display (angle θ) and on the finger properties of the individual subjects. The average values of these parameters and their standard deviations were computed across subjects from the experimental data

$$
\begin{array}{llll}
\bar{A}_{10°} = 4.8 \pm 0.8 & \bar{A}_{50°} = 2.8 \pm 1.0 & \bar{A}_{80°} = 2.2 \pm 0.9 & \text{(mm}^2) \\
k_{10°} = 0.16 \pm 0.05 & k_{50°} = 0.10 \pm 0.03 & k_{80°} = 0.09 \pm 0.02 & \text{(mm}^2/°)
\end{array}
\quad (2)
$$

Then the unimodal, cutaneous-based estimate of the displacement is:

$$x_A = \frac{1}{k_\theta}(A - \bar{A}_\theta) + \bar{x},$$

and the perceived finger movement is:

$$\tilde{x} = W_A[(A - A_\theta)/k_\theta] + W_x x,$$

where A_θ, k_θ are the priors on the parameters of interaction with the surface and W_A, W_x are the tactile and proprioceptive weight terms, respectively.

The cutaneous-based estimate x_A would introduce a bias, if the participant would assume *a priori* that the two coefficients A_θ, k_θ were the same among different stimuli. For the parameters $\Theta = 10°, 50°, 80°$ of the device (position of the FYD-2 motors) and the actual finger position x_Θ, the perceived finger position $\tilde{x}_\Theta$ is:

$$\tilde{x}_\Theta = W_A \frac{1}{k_\theta} [k_\Theta(x_\Theta - \bar{x}) + A_\Theta - A_\theta] + W_x x_\Theta.$$

where x_{10° and x_{80° are the actual positions of the fingers in each condition.

The perceptual bias can be estimated by determining the actual displacements x_{10° and x_{80° resulting in the same perceptual values as the reference, i.e.

$$\tilde{x}_{10^\circ} = \tilde{x}_{50^\circ}, \qquad \tilde{x}_{80^\circ} = \tilde{x}_{50^\circ}.$$

These equations can be easily solved if the coefficients k_Θ are the same for all Θ. Indeed, as it can be seen from Eq. 2, the range of their values is much narrower that that of the parameters $\bar{A}_\Theta$. We thus make a simplifying assumption that $k_\Theta = k_\theta = 0.1 \, \text{mm}^2/\text{degree}$. Then,

$$x_{50^\circ} - x_{10^\circ} = W_A/k_\theta[\bar{A}_{10^\circ} - \bar{A}_{50^\circ}],$$
$$x_{50^\circ} - x_{80^\circ} = W_A/k_\theta[\bar{A}_{80^\circ} - \bar{A}_{50^\circ}].$$

From these equations immediately follows the prediction on the sign of the bias: positive for $\Theta = 10^\circ$ (since $\bar{A}_{10^\circ} > \bar{A}_{50^\circ}$) and negative for $\Theta = 80^\circ$ (since $\bar{A}_{80^\circ} > \bar{A}_{50^\circ}$), in accordance with the empirical data. Moreover, the model predicts the magnitudes of the bias to be proportional to $|\bar{A}_{10^\circ} - \bar{A}_{50^\circ}|$ and $|\bar{A}_{80^\circ} - \bar{A}_{50^\circ}|$, respectively. For the estimated values of parameters, the model predicts the magnitude of the bias for $\Theta = 10^\circ$ to be approximately 3.9 times greater than for $\Theta = 80^\circ$. In the experimental measurements the bias magnitudes differ by the factor of 1.9. The weight W_A can be estimated from the bias magnitudes. It equals to 0.07 when computed using the bias for $\Theta = 10^\circ$ and 0.15 for $\Theta = 80^\circ$, respectively.

5   Conclusion

In this study, we showed that a modulation of the spread of the contact area produces a bias in the perceived displacement of the finger. In our setup, the normal force did not vary with the compliance of the surface, that is, it was the same between the two experimental conditions. Due to the change in the contact area, it follows that the normal pressure was different between conditions. However, it is unlikely that this produced the effect, since the tactile system is relatively insensitive to change in pressure [10].

The model relies on the assumption that the compliance of a contacted objects is roughly constant over time. For most of the daily-life objects, the change in compliance due, for example, to the viscoelastic properties of the surface is negligible, at least in a short time window (see for example the silicones characterized and used in softness discrimination studies with humans in [11]). In [12], the participants accurately reported the relative displacement between the finger and a surface in an horizontal plane. The present new findings complement the previous study along the third, vertical dimension, thus reinforcing the possibility that cutaneous cues contribute to proprioception. These findings may provide guidelines to reduce the working space in haptic devices, substituting partially the kinesthetic with tactile cues.

Acknowledgments. This work is supported by the European Research Council under the ERC Advanced Grant no. 291166 SoftHands (A Theory of Soft Synergies for a New Generation of Artificial Hands). This work has received funding from the EU FP7/2007-2013 project no. 601165 WEARHAP (WEARable HAPtics for Humans and Robots) and project no. 248587 THE (The Hand Embodied).

References

1. Landy, M.S., Maloney, L.T., Johnston, E.B., Young, M.: Measurement and modeling of depth cue combination: in defense of weak fusion. Vis. Res. **35**(3), 389–412 (1995)
2. Bicchi, A., De Rossi, D.E., Scilingo, E.P.: The role of the contact area spread rate in haptic discrimination of softness. IEEE Trans. Robot. Autom. **16**(5), 496–504 (2000)
3. Bergmann Tiest, W.M., Kappers, A.: Cues for haptic perception of compliance. IEEE Trans. Haptics **2**(4), 189–199 (2009)
4. Hayward, V., Terekhov, A.V., Wong, S.-C., Geborek, P., Bengtsson, F., Jörntell, H.: Spatio-temporal skin strain distributions evoke low variability spike responses in cuneate neurons. J. Royal Soc. Interface. **11**(93), 20131015 (2014)
5. Bicchi, A., Scilingo, E.P., Ricciardi, E., Pietrini, P.: Tactile flow explains haptic counterparts of common visual illusions. Brain Res. Bull. **75**(6), 737–741 (2008)
6. Bianchi, M., Serio, A., Scilingo, E.P., Bicchi, A.: A new fabric-based softness display. In: IEEE Haptics Symposium, 2010, pp. 105–112 (2010)
7. Serio, A., Bianchi, M., Bicchi, A.: A device for mimicking the contact force/contact area relationship of different materials with applications to softness rendering. In: IEEE/RSJ International Conference on Intelligent Robots and Systems (IROS), pp. 4484–4490 (2013)
8. Moscatelli, A., Mezzetti, M., Lacquaniti, F.: Modeling psychophysical data at the population-level: the generalized linear mixed model. J. Vis. **12**(11):26, 1–17 (2012)
9. Knoblauch, K., Maloney, L.T.: Modeling Psychophysical Data in R, vol. 32. Springer, New York (2012)
10. Hayward, V.: Is there a "plenhaptic" function? Philos. Trans. Royal Soc. B: Biol. Sci. **366**(1581), 3115–3122 (2011)
11. Scilingo, E.P., Bianchi, M., Grioli, G., Bicchi, A.: Rendering softness: integration of kinesthetic and cutaneous information in a haptic device. IEEE Trans. Haptics **3**(2), 109–118 (2010)
12. Moscatelli, A., Naceri, A., Ernst, M.: Navigation in the fingertip. In: IEEE World Haptics Conference (WHC), pp. 519–523 (2013)

Illusory Rotations in the Haptic Perception of Moving Spheres and Planes

Astrid M.L. Kappers$^{(\boxtimes)}$ and Wouter M. Bergmann Tiest

Move Research Institute, VU University Amsterdam, Amsterdam, The Netherlands
{a.m.l.kappers,w.m.bergmanntiest}@vu.nl

Abstract. Recently, we have shown that a translating bar on which blindfolded participants position their hand is perceived as also rotating. Here, we investigated whether such an illusory rotation would also be found if a sphere or a plane (i.e. a stimulus without a clear orientation) was used as translating stimulus. We indeed found similar rotation biases: on average a stimulus that translates over a distance of 60 cm has to rotate 25° to be perceived as non-rotating. An additional research question was whether the biases were caused by the same underlying biasing egocentric reference frame. To our surprise, the correlations between the sizes of the biases of the individual participants in the various conditions were not high and mostly not even significant. This was possibly due to day-to-day variations, but clearly, more research is needed to answer this second research question.

Keywords: Spatial perception · Rotation bias · Parallel · Psychophysics

1 Introduction

Recently, we reported that when blindfolded participants touch a bar translating to the right, this bar is perceived as also rotating counterclockwise [1]. If this same bar translates from the right of the participant to directly in front of the participant, a clockwise rotation is perceived (see Fig. 1 for a picture of the set-up). This illusory rotation was predicted from results of a parallelity experiment: if participants have to make a test bar located to their right parallel to a reference bar located to their left, the test bar is always rotated clockwise with respect to the reference bar, e.g. [2–6] (see also Fig. 1). Kappers showed that this rotation gradually and systematically increased with distance [7]. Therefore, the logical consequence of this mismatched parallelity was that a translating bar had to rotate in order to be perceived as non-rotating.

The explanation for these results is that although participants are instructed to make their judgements in a reference frame connected to the outside world (i.e. an allocentric reference frame), they are biased by their own egocentric reference frame (i.e. a hand-centred and/or body-centred reference frame [8]). When their hand moves from a location to their left to a location to their right, this involves also a clockwise rotation. If what is "parallel" were judged with respect

© Springer-Verlag Berlin Heidelberg 2014
M. Auvray and C. Duriez (Eds.): EuroHaptics 2014, Part II, LNCS 8619, pp. 80–87, 2014.
DOI: 10.1007/978-3-662-44196-1_11

to this egocentric hand reference frame, a test bar on the right has to be rotated clockwise in order to be perceived as parallel and a rightward translating bar has to rotate clockwise in order to be perceived as non-rotating. The deviations and biases found are indeed in a direction consistent with this egocentric reference frame, but they are less extreme. Thus, the deviations can be understood as originating from a biasing influence of an egocentric reference frame [8]. Interestingly, the biases are strongly participant-dependent [5], suggesting that the strength with which participants rely on their egocentric reference frame varies.

The current research addressed two questions. The first question was whether the illusory rotation depended on the presence of an object with a clear orientation. Would a participant also perceive a translating plane or sphere as rotating? In the previous study with the rotating bar, some participants tried to align their hand with the bar but because of the rotation, this was not always possible. This may have induced a greater awareness of the actual rotation resulting in smaller rotation biases. On the other hand, the changing position and orientation of the bar in combination with their moving hand that also changed in orientation, might have caused confusion resulting in larger biases. In that study, the use of a bar was motivated by the use of bars in the parallelity studies, but of course, for an illusory rotation study, a bar is not essential. In order to make the results more general, in the current study we investigated the existence of an illusory rotation in conditions where no orientation cue is present.

The second question addressed the generality of the egocentric reference frame in similar haptic tasks. We know that in different tasks different egocentric reference frames play a role [13]. In a previous study on the haptic and visual matching of the orientation of bars, it was found that whereas both haptic and visual deviations were significant, systematic and participant-dependent, the correlation between the visual and haptic deviations was only small [9]. The explained variance due to a common factor (i.e. the use of the same egocentric reference frame) was only 20 %. It was therefore of interest to investigate whether the correlations between deviations in several haptic tasks would be higher.

To answer the two research questions, we set up an experiment consisting of four conditions. In the first condition, a baseline condition termed "parallel", we measured the deviation in a parallelity task as in many of the previous experiments, e.g. [5]. The second condition was identical to the earlier illusory rotation study and was termed "bar" condition [1]. The third and fourth conditions were new and consisted of a translating and rotating sphere and plane and these were termed "sphere" and "plane" conditions, respectively.

2   Methods

2.1   Participants

Twelve participants (8 females and 4 males) took part in the experiment. All of them were right-handed as assessed by means of a questionnaire [10]. Nine of them received a monetary compensation for their efforts; the others were colleagues from another group. None of the participants were familiar with the

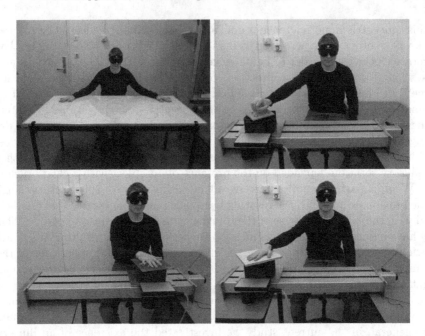

Fig. 1. Participant in the various experimental conditions. Top left: "parallel"; bottom left: "bar"; top right: "sphere"; bottom right: "plane". In "bar" the position of the stimulus is in its leftmost position, and in "sphere" and "plane" in the rightmost position.

research questions or the set-ups. Their ages ranged from 20 to 28 years. One of the original participants was replaced because at least in one condition it became clear that she was not performing the requested task. All participants signed for informed consent. The experiments were approved by the Ethical Committee of the Human Movement Sciences Faculty.

2.2   Set-Ups

The set-up for the parallellity task was used in many earlier studies and consisted of a table on which two aluminium bars were placed (see [5] for more details and Fig. 1 for a picture of the set-up). For the "sphere", "plane" and "bar" conditions the same rotation set-up as in [1] was used. The stimulus (either a wooden sphere, wooden board or aluminium bar) was fixed onto an Isel Automation linear and rotary positioning unit, which was attached to an Isel C142-1 CNC controller. The stimulus could translate back and forth over a distance of 60 cm with a velocity of 15 cm/s while also rotating in either clockwise or counterclockwise direction (for details see [1]). The movement range of the stimulus was from directly in front of the participant to 60 cm to the right of the participant. Illustrations of a participant in the set-ups of the various conditions are shown Fig. 1.

2.3   Procedure

Half of the participants started with "sphere" followed by "plane", whereas the other half did this in opposite order. The third and fourth conditions of all participants were always "parallel" and "bar", respectively. The motivation for this choice was that the "sphere" and "plane" conditions were new and we did not want to bias our participants in these conditions in any way. Moreover, since the "bar" condition might strengthen awareness that hand orientation changes during the trials, we preferred to have this condition after the "parallel" condition.

"Parallel" Condition. After checking whether the participant correctly understood the meaning of the word "parallel", the participant blindfolded her- or himself. Next, the experimenter placed the reference bar in a fixed orientation (20, 40, 60, 80, 100, 120, 140 or 160°) and the test bar in a random orientation. One of the bars (either the reference or the test) was placed 60 cm to the right of the participant and touched by the right hand, and the other 60 cm to the left and touched by the left hand (see Fig. 1). All reference orientations were presented once on the left and once on the right; left and right trials were interchanged with the reference orientations in random order. The task of the participants was to rotate the test bar so that it felt parallel to the reference bar. It took participants just a few seconds to perform one trial. The deviation, defined as the orientation of the left bar minus that of the right bar, was averaged over the 16 trials. We have chosen for this particular version of the "parallel" condition, because it has been the baseline throughout many previous studies.

"Sphere", "plane" and "bar" Conditions. To explain the task and make the participants familiar with the rotation set-up and the noise it produced, two trials of the first condition (either "sphere" or "plane") were shown to the participant. At this stage, the participant was not yet blindfolded and not allowed to touch the stimulus. Subsequently, the participant seated her- or himself on a stool, blindfolded her- or himself and the experiment started without any further instructions.

In the "sphere" condition, the participant was asked to grasp the sphere from above. In the "plane" condition, they had to place their hand centred on the board. If they misplaced their hand (because they could not see the centre), the experimenter gave verbal instructions to replace the hand. In the "bar" condition, they placed their flat hand on the bar without touching the plate on which this bar was fixed. They were explicitly told that as the rotation would sometimes be substantial, it would not always be possible to keep their hand aligned with the bar. The task was to decide on each trial (i.e. a translation to the right or a translation to the left) whether the translating stimulus (sphere, plane or bar) rotated clockwise or counterclockwise. All participants used their right hand. The start orientation of the stimulus (only relevant for the bar) was random.

Within a condition, four interleaved one-up-one-down staircases of 15 trials each were run to determine the rotation bias of a participant (see left panels

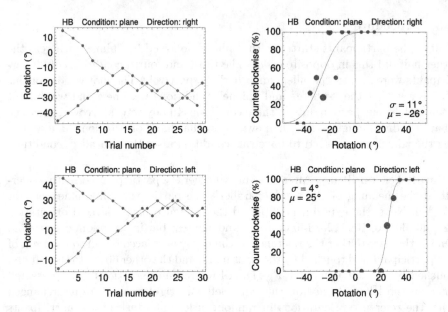

Fig. 2. Examples of the staircases and the derived psychometric curves for one partici-pant in the "plane" condition. Upper (lower) plots are for translation to the right (left). It can be seen that for each direction, two staircases, starting from opposite rotations, converge to the rotation that is necessary to perceive the stimulus as non-rotating. The size of the plot points in the right plots gives an indication of the number of times a certain value has been presented during the staircase procedure.

of Fig. 2. Two of these staircases belonged to the rightward translation, and the other two to the leftward translation. Based on previous research [1], the staircases started at -45 and $15°$ for the rightward trials and at -15 and $45°$ for the leftward trials, with step sizes of $5°$. Positive rotations are counterclockwise. A rotation of $0°$ (i.e. no rotation) was avoided as lack of vibrations due to rotation might trigger awareness of a "special" kind of trial. As all rotation biases were far from zero, this did not cause any problems.

From the staircase data, the percentages "counterclockwise" were determined for each rotation and each participant for both the rightward and the leftward translations (see right panels of Fig. 2). Psychometric curves were fitted to these data, using the following cumulative Gaussion function:

$$f(x) = 50 + 50 \operatorname{erf}\left(\frac{x - \mu}{\sqrt{2}\sigma}\right), \tag{1}$$

where μ is the bias (i.e. the rotation needed to perceive the stimulus as non-rotating) and σ a measure of the steepness of the curve (more precisely, the dif-ference between the values of 50 and 84 %). The overall rotation bias is defined as:

$$\frac{1}{2}(\mu_{\text{left}} - \mu_{\text{right}}), \tag{2}$$

where the subscripts indicate the translation directions.

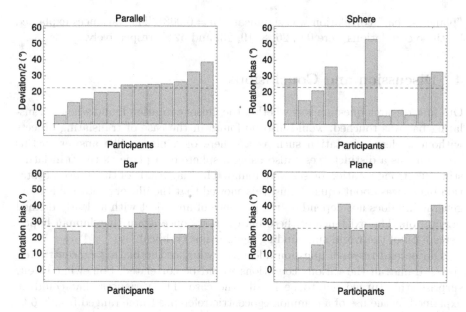

Fig. 3. Deviations found in the various conditions for the 12 participants, ordered by the deviation obtained in the "parallel" condition. Top left: "parallel"; bottom left: "bar"; top right: "sphere"; bottom right: "plane". The missing value in the "sphere" graph is due to one participant who did not show convergence in that condition. The dashed lines indicate the average over all participants within a condition.

3   Results

The deviation and rotation biases are shown in Fig. 3 for all participants and all four conditions. As the distance between the bars in the "parallel" condition was 120 cm, whereas the translation distance in the other conditions was only 60 cm, for proper comparison we divided this deviation by 2 in the graph and the analyses. In all four graphs, the participants are ordered according to the size of their deviation in the "parallel" condition. The average deviation in the "parallel" condition was 45° (not yet divided by 2) with an average standard deviation of 14°. The average rotation biases in the "sphere", "plane" and "bar" conditions were 23, 26 and 27°, respectively. These values were highly significantly different from 0 (all $ps < 0.0005$) as determined with one-sided t-tests. In all cases, the difference between μ_{left} and μ_{right} was significantly larger than the corresponding σ averaged over the two curves (all $ps < 0.005$), which is another indication of the significance of the biases.

The deviations and the rotation biases in the various conditions were of about the same size (see Fig. 3), which was confirmed by paired two-sided t-tests; none of these gave a significant result. The correlations between the deviation/rotation biases obtained in the various conditions are the following: "parallel" - "sphere": $R = 0.07$, "parallel" - "plane": $R = 0.5$, "parallel" - "bar": $R = 0.3$, "sphere" - "plane": $R = 0.4$, "sphere" - "bar": $R = 0.5$, "plane" - "bar": $R = 0.7$. Only the "plane" - "bar" correlation was significant ($p = 0.008$). The variances explained by these correlations were 0.6, 26, 8, 19, 23, and 52 %, respectively.

4   Discussion and Conclusions

Our first research question was whether the illusory rotation found when a translating bar was touched, would also be found in the case of translating objects without a clear orientation such as a sphere or a plane. The answer to this question was a distinct "yes": also using a sphere or a plane as the translating stimulus strong rotation biases were found. The magnitude of these several rotation biases was about equal. Thus, this showed that the illusory rotation is more general and does not depend on the presence of an object with a clearly defined orientation. The existence of these biases shows once again that human haptic perception of the world surrounding them is not veridical.

Our second research question addressed whether the biasing egocentric reference frames in the various conditions would be correlated. Somewhat to our surprise, this turned out to be hardly the case. The variances that could be explained by the use of a common egocentric reference frame ranged from 0.6 to 52 %. Although the 52 % explained variance between the "plane" and "bar" conditions is quite substantial and significant, the other values were much smaller and not significant. In a previous study [9] the correlations between visual and haptic judgements of parallel were also relatively small (explained variance 20 %). Although the bimanual "parallel" condition was somewhat different from the other three unimanual conditions with a translation over 60 cm, it has been shown that unimanual and bimanual deviations are very similar and that the deviations vary more or less linearly with distance [4]. Therefore, we do not expect that lack of correlation was caused by this particular choice of baseline condition.

The question now is why these correlations are so small. One possibility is that the model of the biasing influence of an egocentric reference frame is incorrect and that therefore there is no reason to expect high correlations. We think it unlikely that the model would be incorrect, as its validity has been shown in many earlier studies, e.g. [8]. However, it could be the case that participants use a different egocentric reference frame for every task. Tasks in daily life differ widely and many different egocentric reference frames are known, such as retinotopic, head-centred and body-centred reference frames, e.g. [11–13]. However, these different reference frames are used in tasks that are inherently different, whereas the tasks in the current experiment, especially those in the conditions "sphere", "bar" and "plane", are quite similar. Still, the stimuli are touched/grasped differently in the various conditions, so such an explanation of using different egocentric reference frames cannot be excluded. A final consideration is that although the overall biases obtained in these conditions are indeed of about the same size, there were quite some interindividual differences. If this spread in the data is caused by day-to-day variations in the biases of the individual participants, then a lack of correlation can be understood. Therefore, it seems important to focus a future study on this possible day-to-day variation of the rotation biases and not just on the existence thereof. With more data from the same participants and a larger number of participants it will be possible to really answer the question whether biases in the various condition do or do not correlate.

To summarize, we can say that the existence of illusory rotation biases does not depend on the presence of an object with a distinct orientation: planes and spheres without such a clear orientation lead to similar biases. Whether these biases are caused by the same underlying biasing egocentric reference frame still remains to seen.

Acknowledgments. This work has been supported by the European Commission with the Collaborative Project no. 248587, THE Hand Embodied, within the FP7-ICT- 2009-4-2-1 program Cognitive Systems and Robotics.

References

1. Kappers, A.M.L., Bergmann Tiest, W.M.: Illusory rotation in the haptic perception of a moving bar. Exp. Brain Res. **231**, 325–329 (2013)
2. Fernández-Díaz, M., Travieso, D.: Performance in haptic geometrical matching tasks depends on movement and position of the arms. Acta Psychol. **136**, 382–389 (2011)
3. Kaas, A.L., Van Mier, H.I.: Haptic spatial matching in near peripersonal space. Exp. Brain Res. **170**, 403–413 (2006)
4. Kappers, A.M.L.: Large systematic deviations in the haptic perception of parallelity. Perception **28**, 1001–1012 (1999)
5. Kappers, A.M.L.: Large systematic deviations in a bimanual parallelity task: further analysis of contributing factors. Acta Psychol. **114**, 131–145 (2003)
6. Van Mier, H.I.: Effects of visual information regarding allocentric processing in haptic parallelity matching. Acta Psychol. **144**, 352–360 (2013)
7. Kappers, A.M.L.: Intermediate frames of reference in haptically perceived parallelity. In: 1st Joint EuroHaptics Conference and Symposium on Haptic Interfaces for Virtual Environment and Teleoperator Systems, pp. 3–11. IEEE Computer Society (2005)
8. Kappers, A.M.L.: Haptic space processing - allocentric and egocentric reference frames. Can. J. Exp. Psychol. **61**(3), 208–218 (2007)
9. Kappers, A.M.L., Schakel, W.B.: Comparison of the haptic and visual deviations in a parallelity task. Exp. Brain Res. **208**, 467–473 (2011)
10. Coren, S.: The Left-Hander Syndrome. Vintage Books, New York (1993)
11. Cohen, Y.E., Andersen, R.A.: A common reference frame for movement plans in the posterior parietal cortex. Nat. Rev. Neurosci. **3**, 553–562 (2002)
12. Flanders, M., Soechting, J.F.: Frames of reference for hand orientation. J. Cogn. Neurosci. **7**, 182–195 (1995)
13. Paillard, J.: Motor and representational framing of space. In: Paillard, J. (ed.) Brain and Space, pp. 163–182. Oxford University Press, Oxford (1991)

Distinct Pseudo-Attraction Force Sensation by a Thumb-Sized Vibrator that Oscillates Asymmetrically

Tomohiro Amemiya[✉] and Hiroaki Gomi

NTT Communication Science Laboratories, NTT Corporation,
3-1 Morinosato-Wakamiya, Kanagawa, Atsugi 243-0198, Japan
amemiya.tomohiro@lab.ntt.co.jp
http://www.brl.ntt.co.jp/people/t-amemiya/

Abstract. This paper describes the development of a thumb-sized force display for experiencing a kinesthetic illusory sensation of being continuously pushed or pulled. We previously succeeded in creating a sensation of being pulled with a prototype based on a crank-slider mechanism, but recently we did so with a thumb-sized actuator that oscillates asymmetrically. With this tiny and light force display, the directed force sensation is perceived just as strongly as with the previous larger prototypes. We conducted a user study using the method of paired comparisons. The results show that a specific vibrator with a 7-ms pulse at 40 Hz induces the sensation most clearly and effectively.

Keywords: Sensory illusion · Perception · Asymmetric oscillation · Mobile device · Vibration

1 Introduction

The increase in mobile and wearable devices equipped with global positioning sensors has boosted their use for pedestrian navigation or city wayfinding. However, displays for pedestrian navigation are currently constrained to providing audiovisual and simple vibrotactile cues. Therefore, users usually have to fixate on a small map on the screens of their mobile devices to obtain helpful information. One of the easiest and most intuitive ways to give directions without the need to pay attention to a map is to help users turn in the direction they should be facing. A display creating a directed force sensation enables the user to promptly understand the presented direction since haptic stimuli are fundamentally directional.

Over the past years, we have been refining a method to create a sensory illusion of being pulled and have developed various ungrounded force displays to create a sensation. Since it is impossible to create a continuous translational force sensation without an external fulcrum, our method of exploiting the characteristics of human perception is the only way to create a translational force

M. Auvray and C. Duriez (Eds.): EuroHaptics 2014, Part II, LNCS 8619, pp. 88–95, 2014.
DOI: 10.1007/978-3-662-44196-1_12

sensation in mobile devices. The user does not feel the discrete simple vibrating sensation that is so common in conventional mobile devices today. Instead, the user feels a smooth sensation of being pulled, akin to what we feel when someone leads us by the hand. However, since our previous prototypes were based on mechanical linkages, they were too large and heavy to be applied to mobile devices.

In this paper, we introduce a new tiny but mighty force display. For all users, the haptic or somatosensory cues created by the developed force display are, like lead-by-hand navigation, intuitive in indicating a certain direction.

2   Our Approach

We have been developing translational force displays utilizing the nonlinearity of human perception since 2004 [1], and since then many approaches have been proposed and aggressively studied [6,9–11,13]. Our approach to creating a sensation of being pulled exploits the characteristics of human perception, using different acceleration patterns for the two directions to create a perceived force imbalance. A brief and strong force is generated in a desired direction (e.g., leftward), while a weaker one is generated over a longer period of time in the reverse direction (e.g., rightward). Although the average magnitudes of the two forces are the same, reducing the magnitude of the longer and weaker force to below a sensory threshold makes the holders feel as if they are being pulled to the desired direction (e.g., leftward). This force perception would be determined by a complex sensory input from the skin, joints and muscles. We fabricated a prototype consisting of a crank-slider mechanism to create an illusory sensation of force.

Nakamura and Fukui proposed an actuator, consisting of two eccentric masses attached to two motors' shafts, to generate an illusory sensation of force [9]. Rekimoto proposed a similar device using a commercially available vibrator (Force Reactor L-type; ALPS Inc.) [10]. Rekimoto used the cycle of 2 ms (ON) and 6 ms (OFF) for producing a force sensation, whose net cycle is virtually 125 Hz, or the pulse width corresponds to 250 Hz. Although a complex sensory input from not only cutaneous corpuscles but also those in tendons and muscles would creates the force perception as we address above, these frequency ranges maximize the response of Pacinian corpuscles on the glabrous skin [8]. The Pacinian corpuscles are sensitive to vibration at 100–300 Hz and are thought to detect vibration. In contrast, Meissner corpuscles, which detect slip, are most sensitive in the frequency range of from approximately 5 to 40 Hz [7,12], which is thought to detect vibration. The strong response of Pacinian corpuscles may make it difficult to discriminate differences in the symmetric vibration and the asymmetric acceleration change. If we use asymmetrically oscillating stimuli that selectively stimulate the Meissner corpuscles, not the Pacinian, the force sensation of being pulled will be more clearly perceived.

In this paper, we compare the perceptual characteristics using asymmetrically oscillating stimuli whose net frequency and pulse width are different.

Fig. 1. (a) Two different actuators covered with cylinders having the same shape used in the experiment. (b) How the cylinder was pinched in the experiment.

3   Evaluation

3.1   Method

Participants. Participants: We conducted an evaluation to compare combinations of pulse durations and actuators. Nine volunteer right-handed subjects, ranging from 25 to 49 years of age (seven males and two females, average 33.8 years, SD 7.1 years), participated in the experiment. They had no known tactile or kinesthetic sensory system abnormalities. This research was approved by the local ethics committee.

Apparatus and Stimulus. Here, we selected two linearly vibrating actuators (Force Reactor L-type, ALPS; Haptuator, Tactile Labs.). Each actuator was covered with a cylinder whose size is ϕ 40 mm × 17 mm (Fig. 1), which are made of ABS resin. A piece of a sand paper (#1000 grit) was pasted on its surface to control the surface roughness. The pulse duration cycle was 2 ms: 6 ms or 7 ms: 18 ms. The combination of 2 ms: 6 ms and the Force Reactor is identical to that in a previous report [10]. The duration cycle of 7 ms: 18 ms was selected from the result of a pilot study, which maximized the perceptual amplitude of the force sensation of being pulled. We used the same amplifier gain.

A stimulus was created by pairing a pulse duration cycle with an actuator. Figures 2 and 3 show acceleration patterns of the four combinations used in the experiment. Vibrations of the force display when an experimenter held it were recorded with a laser sensor (LK-G150, Keyence Inc.) at 20 kHz and smoothed using a fifth-order, zero phase lag, low-pass Butterworth filter with a cutoff frequency of 1 kHz. We then calculated the acceleration from the acquired position data.

The direction of the stimulus was lateral to the body (left-right direction) and switched every one second in a trial. The stimulus was presented for four seconds. The order of the pulse duration was also randomized.

Procedure. A trial consisted of two four-second stimulus intervals presented sequentially. An experimenter handed one of the two cylinders to a seated participant. The participants pinched the cylinder on the top and bottom using the

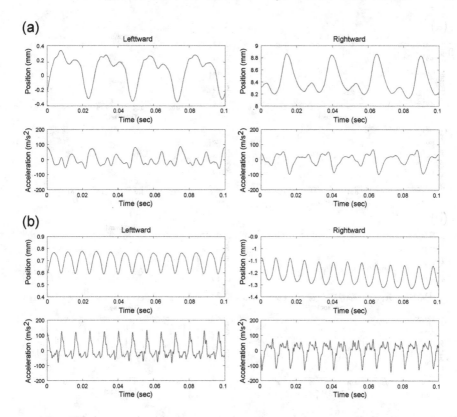

Fig. 2. Acceleration pattern of the four combinations used in the experiment. (a) Haptuator with 7 ms: 18 ms (the net cycle is virtually 40 Hz). (b) Haptuator with 2 ms: 6 ms (the net cycle is 125 Hz).

thumb and index finger of the dominant hand (right hand). They were allowed to move their arms and hands freely. After they had received instructions from the experimenter, the participants felt a vibration for four seconds. Then, the cylinder was changed by the experimenter. The participants pinched it and felt a vibration in the second interval. Participants reported which of the two intervals contained the stimulus inducing a clearer force sensation. In other words, we adopted the Thurstone's method of paired comparisons to find the stimulus that induces the force sensation the most clearly.

They experienced 2 actuators × 2 pulse duration cycle × 2 times (counterbalanced order). The participant was given about a 30-second break after every trial to reduce the effect of fatigue or sensory adaptation due to vibration. No feedback was given regarding their judgments. Visual input was suppressed by having the participants close their eyes during the experiment.

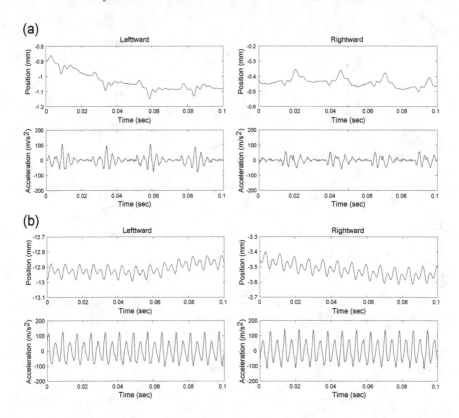

Fig. 3. Acceleration pattern of the four combinations used in the experiment. (a) Force Reactor L-type with 7 ms: 18 ms (the net cycle is virtually 40 Hz). (b) Force Reactor L-type with 2 ms: 6 ms (the net cycle is 125 Hz).

3.2 Result and Discussion

Figure 4 shows the scale values of the clarity of the force sensation. In this scale, on the basis of the average proportion of times a combination was chosen as the stimulus inducing a clearer force sensation, the combinations were ordered along a continuum to represent the degree of clarity of force sensation. For all four combinations (2 actuators × 2 pulse duration cycle), the combination of the Haptuator and the pulse duration of 7 ms: 18 ms was judged to create the clearest force sensation. In contrast, there were no differences between the Force Reactor with 2 ms: 6 ms [10] and Haptuator with 2 ms: 6 ms, both of which induced less clear force sensation than the Haptuator with 7 ms: 18 ms. Finally, the Force Reactor with 7 ms: 18 ms created the least clear sensation.

Interestingly, the conditions with the duration of 7 ms: 18 ms were judged to be both the best and the worst, indicating that the combination of the actuator and duration seems to be an important factor for inducing a clear force sensation. We speculate that this is due to the natural frequency of the actuators. The natural frequency of the Haptuator is about 60 Hz [14], and that of the Force

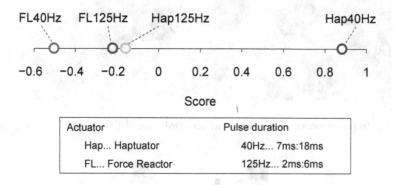

Fig. 4. Result of paired comparison.

Reactor is about 250 Hz, albeit both of them were not the resonant one of the system including two fingers. On the other hand, the half cycle of 70 Hz is close to 7 ms and that of 250 Hz is close to 2 ms. Therefore, the results for the Haptuator with a 7-ms pulse and the Force Reactor with a 2-ms pulse were better than for the other combinations.

All participants reported that they felt a strong illusory force sensation of being pulled in both directions with the Haptuator in the 7 ms: 18 ms condition. Some participants pointed out that only one direction (e.g., only rightward) was clear with the Haptuator in the 2 ms: 6 ms condition. There were no significant differences among the tendency of the participants' judges ($\chi^2(40) = 25.5$, $p = 0.96$).

4   Implementation

4.1   Thumb-Sized Force Display

On the basis of the results of the experiment, we fabricated two prototypes: a one-DoF force display [Fig. 5(a)] and a two-DoF force display [Fig. 5(b)]. The size of the one-DoF force display is greatly decreased by 95 % (to $18 \times 18 \times 37\,\mathrm{mm}^3$) compared to the earlier one [2,4], and its weight is greatly decreased by 90 % (to 25 g). With this tiny and light force display, almost all people who have experienced subjectively reported that the directed force sensation is perceived just as strongly as with the previous larger prototypes [3,5].

We have adopted the Haptuator as the actuator, and a microcontroller board (PIC18F2550) is connected to an amplifier unit to drive the actuators.

4.2   Application

Figure 6 shows examples of applications using the thumb-sized force display. With a motion tracking system, the amplitude and direction of the force sensation are altered according to the user's hand position while the user pinches the

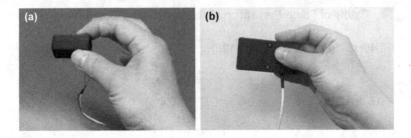

Fig. 5. Proposed novel thumb-sized (a) one-DoF and (b) two-DoF force displays.

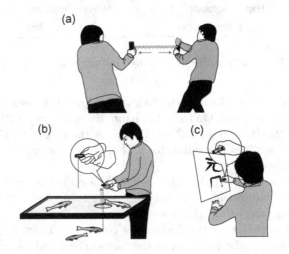

Fig. 6. Application examples using thumb-sized mobile force display. (a) Tug-of-war. (b) Angling game. (c) Calligraphy guidance.

thumb-sized force display. If we use two or more force displays, multiple users can experience the tug-of-war application together [Fig. 6(a)]. In the angling game, users can feel a sensation of a nibble on the hook and being pulled with no fishing lines [Fig. 6(b)]. In addition, users can learn calligraphy with the thumb-sized force display [Fig. 6(c)]. These devices can of course be used to support visually impaired people in finding their way [5,6].

5   Conclusion

We reported a novel approach for creating the sensation of being pulled or pushed, and we examined the pulse pattern that is clearly felt for participants using two vibrators. We have shown experimentally that the combination of a Haptuator with 7 ms: 18 ms pulse duration cycle induced the clearest sensation. On the basis of the results of the experiment, we developed a thumb-sized force display for experiencing a kinesthetic illusory sensation of being continuously pushed or pulled. These findings can provide valuable insights into the design of mobile force displays.

References

1. Amemiya, T., Ando, H., Maeda, T.: Development of direction guidance device using biased acceleration in periodic motion. In: Proceedings the 9th Virtual Reality Society of Japan Annual Conference, pp. 215–218 (2004, in Japanese)
2. Amemiya, T., Ando, H., Maeda, T.: Virtual force display: direction guidance using asymmetric acceleration via periodic translational motion. In: Proceedings of World Haptics Conference, pp. 619–622. IEEE Computer Society (2005)
3. Amemiya, T., Gomi, H.: Active touch sensing of being pulled illusion for pedestrian route navigation. In: Proceedings of ACM SIGGRAPH 2012 Poster. No. 68. ACM Press (2012)
4. Amemiya, T., Maeda, T.: Asymmetric oscillation distorts the perceived heaviness of handheld objects. IEEE Trans. Haptics 1(1), 9–18 (2008)
5. Amemiya, T., Sugiyama, H.: Orienting kinesthetically: a haptic handheld wayfinder for people with visual impairments. ACM Trans. Access. Comput. 3(2), 6:1–6:23 (2010)
6. Ando, T., Tsukahara, R., Seki, M., Fujie, M.: A haptic interface "force blinker 2"; for navigation of the visually impaired. IEEE Trans. Ind. Electron. 59(11), 4112–4119 (2012)
7. Johansson, R., Landstrom, U., Lundstrom, R.: Responses of mechanoreceptive afferent units in the glabrous skin of the human hand to sinusoidal skin displacements. Brain Res. 244, 17–25 (1982)
8. Johnson, K.O.: The roles and functions of cutaneous mechanoreceptors. Curr. Opin. Neurobiol. 11(4), 455–461 (2001)
9. Nakamura, N., Fukui, Y.: Development of a force and torque hybrid display "gyrocubestick". In: Proceedings of World Haptics Conference, pp. 633–634. IEEE Computer Society (2005)
10. Rekimoto, J.: Traxion: a tactile interaction device with virtual force sensation. In: Proceedings of ACM Symposium on User Interface Software and Technology, pp. 427–431 (2013)
11. Shima, T., Takemura, K.: An ungrounded pulling force feedback device using periodical vibration-impact. In: Isokoski, P., Springare, J. (eds.) EuroHaptics 2012, Part I. LNCS, vol. 7282, pp. 481–492. Springer, Heidelberg (2012)
12. Talbot, W.H., Smith, I.D., Kornhuber, H.H., Mountcastle, V.B.: The sense of flutter-vibration: comparison of the human capacity with response patterns of mechanoreceptive afferents from the monkey hand. J. Neurophysiol. 31, 301–334 (1967)
13. Tappeiner, H.W., Klatzky, R.L., Unger, B., Hollis, R.: Good vibrations: asymmetric vibrations for directional haptic cues. In: Proceedings of World Haptics Conference, pp. 285–289. IEEE Computer Society (2009)
14. Yao, H.Y., Hayward, V.: Design and analysis of a recoil-type vibrotactile transducer. J. Acoust. Soc. Am. 128(2), 619–627 (2010)

Obstacle Identification and Avoidance Using the 'EyeCane': a Tactile Sensory Substitution Device for Blind Individuals

Galit Buchs[1], Shachar Maidenbaum[2], and Amir Amedi[1,2,3(✉)]

[1] Department of Cognitive Science, Faculty of Humanities,
Hebrew University of Jerusalem, Hadassah Ein-Kerem, Jerusalem, Israel
galit.buchs@mail.huji.ac.il
[2] Department of Medical Neurobiology, Faculty of Medicine,
Institute for Medical Research Israel-Canada, Hebrew University of Jerusalem,
Hadassah Ein-Kerem, Jerusalem, Israel
shachar.maidenbaum@mail.huji.ac.il
[3] The Edmond and Lily Safra Center for Brain Research,
Hebrew University of Jerusalem, Edmond and Lily Safra Campus,
Jerusalem, Israel
amira@ekmd.huji.ac.il
http://brain.huji.ac.il

Abstract. One of the main challenges facing the blind and visually impaired is independent mobility without being obtrusive to their environment. We developed a tactile low-cost finger-size sensory substitution device, the EyeCane, to aid the Blind in obstacle identification and avoidance in an unobtrusive manner. A simplified version of the EyeCane was tested on 6 sighted blindfolded participants who were naïve to the device. After a short (2–3 min) training period they were asked to identify and avoid knee-to-waist-high (Side) and sidewalk-height (Floor) obstacles using the EyeCane. Avoidance included walking around or stepping over the obstacles. We show that in the fifth trial, participants correctly identified 87 ± 13.6 % (mean $\pm$ SD) and correctly avoided 63 ± 15 % of the side obstacles compared to 14 % in the control condition ($p < 4E\text{-}10$ and $p < 1.1E\text{-}05$ respectively). For Floor obstacles, participants correctly identified 79 ± 18.8 % and correctly avoided $41 \pm \%37.6$ compared to the control's 10 % ($p < 0.002$ and $p < 0.06$ respectively).

Keywords: Sensory substitution · Obstacle avoidance · Mobility · Blind · Assistive technology

1 Introduction

Mobility is crucial in numerous everyday situations. As vision is a leading factor in facilitating this ability the Blind and visually impaired are disadvantaged in this respect.

Galit Buchs and Shachar Maidenbaum: equal contribution.

© Springer-Verlag Berlin Heidelberg 2014
M. Auvray and C. Duriez (Eds.): EuroHaptics 2014, Part II, LNCS 8619, pp. 96–103, 2014.
DOI: 10.1007/978-3-662-44196-1_13

The most common means adopted by the Blind to overcome this problem is the white-cane, which significantly increases the mobility skills of this population. However this device is not used by many of the Blind, and especially not by the visually impaired [1–3]. One of the main reasons for this is the inherent obtrusiveness of the white-cane which by definition will often come into contact with people or fragile objects in the users' vicinity, especially in cluttered environments.

One approach for avoiding this inherent obtrusiveness would be a mobility aid which replaced the physical cane with a sensor beam. Several devices have been developed in an attempt to implement this approach (for some examples see [4, 5], for review see [6, 7]) but so far have not been adopted by the Blind community. While the reasons for this are not fully clear, common reasons cited include availability, cost, weight, reliability, complexity and length of required training and problems with the information received about the environments such as over estimating the location and size of obstacles [7].

We developed the EyeCane (see also [8]) in an attempt to deal with these issues. The EyeCane transforms information about the distance from objects through haptic cues, such that the closer the user is to an object the stronger the vibration. The EyeCane is light-weighted, finger-sized and low-cost. It has a very quick learning curve (can be used successfully after several minutes), and uses a narrow-beam approach to provide the user with accurate information about his environment.

In this study we begin testing the functionality of the EyeCane in identification and avoidance of different types of obstacles in an unobtrusive manner while navigating a cluttered environment.

2 Methods

2.1 Equipment

We developed the "EyeCane" which translates point-distance information into tactile cues. The device provides the user with distance information for detecting nearby ground level obstacles (0–1 m).

The distance is detected via a narrow infra-red (IR) beam (<5°) in the direction at which the device is pointed. This sensor (GP2Y0A02YK0F) was tested on different surfaces and in various lighting conditions. It was found that the sensor works also with transparent obstacles, such as glass, with decreased accuracy [9]. The signal modifies the baseline voltage in the electrical circuit, translating the distance from the detected object into a DC voltage signal. This DC-voltage signal is translated in real-time (>50 Hz) into vibration amplitudes and frequencies enabling instantaneous feedback to the user such that the closer an object is to the user the stronger and higher the frequency of vibration (Fig. 1).

2.2 Participants

A total of 6 blindfolded sighted individuals participated (4 female, age 24 ± 2.13 years (mean ± SD)) in this experiment. All participants were naïve to the device.

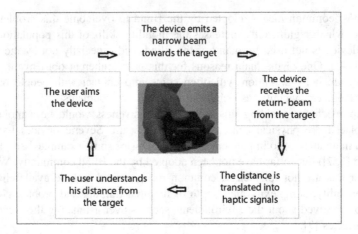

Fig. 1. Device function diagram

2.3 Ethics

The experiment was approved by the ethical committee of the Hebrew university. All participants signed their informed consent.

2.4 Stimuli

The experiment included 14 obstacles in different heights. For 10 of the obstacles, cardboard boxes of knee-to-waist-high (5–1 m high, 2–0.8 and 3–0.45 m) where used. The additional 4 obstacles where cut out of cardboard in the height of 0.2 m, similar to that of a sidewalk.

2.5 Procedure

This experiment included three parts; training and two tests. In both tests the participants needed to detect obstacles and to avoid them. The tests varied in the avoidance method they required of the participants; walking around the obstacle, or stepping over it. In both tests, the participants did not know the number of obstacles, but were told which avoidance method would be required.

In both tests the participants were asked to state when they detected an obstacle and only then try to avoid it. Additionally, they were requested to focus on completing the test as accurately (noticing as many obstacles as they could without touching them or any walls) as possible. Location of obstacles varied between trials and participants.

Each test included 5 trials with the device and as a control, an additional trial without it. This paradigm was chosen over that of direct comparison to a white-cane, as a control, because by definition, identification with the white-cane is achieved through its collision with the obstacles so that the user can then avoid them, and indeed due to the size of obstacles and corridor such contact with both obstacles and walls would be unavoidable. This defines early unobtrusive identification and full avoidance with the white-cane as 0 %, rendering such a control irrelevant.

Training. Participants received a basic explanation about how the device works and how to use it. They then walked towards and away from a wall, while pointing the device at it, to get a feeling of how the different distances are translated into vibration frequencies. They also identified the location of objects that were brought nearer to them in their vicinity while they remained stationary. Training duration was 2–3 min.

Test 1. The participants needed to walk down a straight corridor while walking around 10 knee-to-waist-high obstacles on their right and left (Fig. 2a). This corridor has large windows, thus lighting it up with sunlight.

Test 2. Participants were required to walk down the same straight corridor while stepping over 4 obstacles in the height of the sidewalk (Fig. 2b).

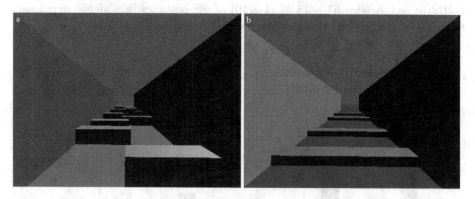

Fig. 2. Virtual recreation of the experimental setup for illustration: a. Corridor with knee-to-waist-high obstacles. b. Corridor with obstacles in the height of the sidewalk

2.6 Scoring

The avoidance score, for both tests and controls, was defined by the number of obstacles the participant did not collide with. Identification was considered successful if the participants both discerned the presence of an obstacle before attempting to avoid collision and also whenever they actually avoided it.

In the control trial, only collision or avoidance played a meaningful part in the assessment of participants' success, as they have no way of detecting the obstacles without collision. Due to technical reasons, one participant did not participate in a control trial.

3 Results

All participants were able to successfully navigate to the end of the corridor in all of the trials in both tests.

Scores are given in the format of "mean% ± SD% (worst-best/total)". For each test we added details about the actual range of obstacles that the participants avoided or identified. E.g., the notation (3–8/10) indicates that the participant with lowest success identified/avoided 3 obstacles, and the participant with the highest success identified/avoided 8 obstacles out of 10.

3.1   Test 1

In the control experiment participants reached an average success rate of 14 % (0–3/10).

Participants performed in a highly significant level above control already from the first trial (two-tailed T-test, Identification: p < 3.1E-07, Avoidance: p < 2.7E-05) with an average correct identification of 68 ± 21.3 % (3–9/10) and avoidance of 53 ± 19.6 % (2–7/10). This improved even further in their final trial when they identified 87 ± 13.6 % (7–10/10) and avoided 63 ± 15 % (4–8/10) of the obstacles in a highly significant manner (two-tailed T-test, Identification: p < 4E-10, Avoidance: p < 1.1E-05) (Fig. 3a).

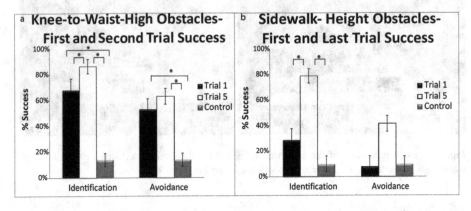

Fig. 3. Results. a: participants' success in the first and last trial of test 1 compared to control. b: participants' success in the first and second trial of test 2 compared to control.

When comparing the obstacle identification results of the participants' 1st and 5th trials, a highly significant improvement was found (two-tailed paired T-test, p < 1.2E-2) from 68 ± 21.3 % (3–9/10) to 87 ± 13.6 % (7–10/10). Looking at the scores for proper obstacle avoidance a non-statistically-significant improvement of 10 % was found (two-tailed paired T-test, p = 0.23) from 53 ± 19.6 % (2–7/10) to 63 ± 15 % (4–8/10) (Fig. 3a).

3.2   Test 2

In the control experiment participants reached an average success rate of only 10 % (0–1/4).

Already at their first attempt subject's ability to correctly identify obstacles (29 ± 36.7 % (0–3/4)) was higher with the device than without it (two-tailed T-test, p = 0.03), but at their last trial (79 ± 18.8 % (2–4/4)) they improved to a significantly higher level (two-tailed T-test, p < 0.002) than that of control (Fig. 3b). Avoiding the obstacles proved far more difficult to all participants. In the first trial, participants avoided only 8 ± 20.4 % (0–2/4) of the obstacles. By the fifth trial, this improved to 41 ± 37.6 % (1–4/4), but still was not significantly higher than that achieved by the control (p = 0.05) due to large variability between participants.

When comparing the obstacle identification results of the participants' 1st and 5th trials, a highly significant improvement was found (two-tailed paired T-test, p < 0.007). Looking at the scores for proper obstacle avoidance a similar, though smaller and not statistically significant, improvement (two-tailed paired T-test, p < 0.07) was found (Fig. 3b).

4 Discussion

We presented the "EyeCane" and showed that it can be used successfully for detecting and avoiding obstacles in an unobtrusive manner and with very short training. For the first test, where obstacles were knee-to-waist-high, participants succeeded in noticing and avoiding them after less than five minutes of practice. In the second test, in which obstacles where lower, participants needed more experience (e.g. the earlier trials in the test were not as good as subsequent ones) to achieve better scores than control in detection. Also, avoidance of obstacles was harder in the second task because, in addition to finding the obstacle, participants also needed to perceive its distance from their foot in order to be able to step over it. This required the users to not only observe the location of an obstacle but to learn to sense its actual distance. The major advantage of the EyeCane over the commonly-used white-cane is in its feature of unobtrusiveness. This benefit comes at the "cost" of a decreased sense of security reached when using a device that is stable, independent of battery power and provides information about the different contours of the walking surfaces such as the white-cane [10, 11]. Thus, for many users the EyeCane might mainly be useful in specific scenarios such as cluttered environments while using the traditional white-cane in others according to the tool that fits his or her needs in different circumstances.

The EyeCane uses a focused-beam. This approach differs conceptually from most previous assistive devices which use wide-beam sensors, for example, the Sonic Pathfinder [4] and the UltraCane [5]. Wide beams are easy to use passively, but come at the cost of a reduced accuracy which leads mainly to many false positives (i.e. identifying a door as an obstacle due to detection of its sides). Our approach adopts an active sensing "spotlight" method for obstacle detection and forces the user to constantly scan his environment, but in return allows him to locate obstacles with greater accuracy and gain more information about them. This choice was made following many accumulating results in recent years emphasizing the importance of active sensing for perceiving one's environment and the objects within it [12–14]. As part of this approach the EyeCane was also optimized for speedy accuracy (refresh rate of >50 Hz) and decreased size and weight to facilitate easy scanning [15].

Chebat and colleges confronted obstacle avoidance with the use of a sensory substitution device called the Tongue Display Unit (TDU) [16] and found that the Blind's performance exceeded that of sighted participants. This finding leads us to believe that blind participants will succeed in this task using the EyeCane, a hypothesis which will be tested in the next stage of this research. Our results here are in compliance with their findings that step-over obstacles were harder to avoid.

An alternative explanation for the increase in success rates as trials advances is due to the fixed size of the step-over obstacles and the motor learning of the proper step to take. Based on our empirical observation of the experiment we do not believe this to be the case, and feel that the difficulty was centered in perceiving its location and not its size. Furthermore, we believe that with additional training success in this avoidance task will continue to improve and exceed control in a significant manner, both in this specific task and also with varying sizes of floor obstacles.

5   Conclusions

The EyeCane device was found to be helpful in identifying and avoiding obstacles in a discrete and unobtrusive manner after a very short training. This device has the potential to aid the Blind in numerous everyday circumstances and thereby become a useful tool in the assistive devices toolbox available for them.

Acknowledgements. We would like to thank Shlomi Hannasy for help in developing the EyeCane and in running the experiments. This work was supported by a European Research Council grant to AA (grant number 310809); The Charitable Gatsby Foundation; The James S. McDonnell Foundation scholar award (to AA; grant number 220020284); The Israel Science Foundation (grant number ISF 1684/08).

References

1. Christy, B., Nirmalan, P.K.: Acceptance of the long cane by persons who are blind in south india. J. Vis. Impair. Blind. **100**(2), 115–119 (2006)
2. Gold, D., Simson, H.: identifying the needs of people in canada who are blind or visually impaired preliminary results of a nation widestudy. Int. Congr. Ser. **1282**, 139–142 (2005)
3. Russell, J.N., Hendershot, G.E., LeClere, F., Howie, L.J., Adler, M.: Trends and differential use of assistive technology devices: United States, 1994. Adv. Data **292**, 1–9 (1997)
4. La Graw, S.: The use of sonic pathfinder as a secondary mobility aid for travel in buisness environments: a single- subject design. J. Rehabil. Res. Dev. **36**(4), 333–340 (1999)
5. Penrod, W., Corbett, M.D., Blasch, B.: A master trainer class for professionals in teaching the ultracane electronic travel device. J. Vis. Impair. Blind. **99**(11), 696–706 (2005)
6. Dakopoulos, D., Bourbakis, N.G.: Wearable obstacle avoidance electronic travel aids for blind: A survey. IEEE Trans. **40**(1), 25–35 (2010)
7. Roentgen, U.R., Gelderblom, G.J., Soede, M., De Witte, L.P.: Inventory of electronic mobility aids for persons with visual impairments: A literature review. J. Vis. Impair. Blind. **102**(11), 702–724 (2008)

8. Maidenbaum, S., Levy-Tzedek, S., Chebat, D.-R., Amedi, A.: Increasing accessibility to the blind of virtual environments, using a virtual mobility aid based on the 'EyeCane': feasibility study. PLoS ONE **8**(8), e72555 (2013)
9. Innet, S., Ritnoom, N.: An application of infrared sensors for electronic white stick. In: International Symposium on Intelligent Signal Processing and Communication Systems, pp. 1–4 (2009)
10. Rodgers, M.D., Emerson, R.W.: Materials testing in long cane design: sensitivity, flexibility, and transmission of vibration. J. Vis. Impair. Blind. **99**(11), 696–706 (2005)
11. Koutsoklenis, A., Papadopoulos, K.: Haptic cues used for outdoor wayfinding by individuals. J. Vis. Impair. Blind. **108**(1), 43–53 (2014)
12. Lenay, C., Gapenne, O., Hanneton, S., Marque, C., Genouell, C.: Sensory substitution: Limits and perspectives. In: Hatwell, Y. (ed.) Touching for Knowing, pp. 275–292. John Benjamins, Paris (2003)
13. Auvray, M., Lenay, C., Stewart, J.: Perceptual interactions in a minimalist virtual environment. New Ideas Psychol. **27**(1), 32–47 (2009)
14. Horev, G., Saig, A., Knutsen, P.M., Pietr, M., Yu, C., Ahissar, E.: Motor-sensory convergence in object localization: a comparative study in rats and humans. Philos. Trans. R. Soc. Lond. B Biol. Sci. **366**(1581), 3070–3076 (2011)
15. Amedi, A., Hanassy, S.: Infra Red based devices for guiding blind and visually impaired persons. *WO Patent* 2,012,090,114 (2012)
16. Chebat, D.-R., Schneider, F.C., Kupers, R., Ptito, M.: Navigation with a sensory substitution device in congenitally blind individuals. NeuroReport **22**(7), 342–347 (2011)

Assessment of Tactile Languages as Navigation Aid in 3D Environments

Victor Adriel de J. Oliveira and Anderson Maciel[⊠]

Instituto de Informática (INF), Universidade Federal do Rio Grande do Sul
(UFRGS), Porto Alegre, RS PO. Box 15064, CEP 91501-970, Brazil
{vajoliveira,amaciel}@inf.ufrgs.br

Abstract. In this paper we present the design and evaluate alternative tactile vocabularies to support navigation in 3D environments. We have focused on the tactile communication expressiveness by applying a prefixation approach in the construction of the tactile icons. We conducted user experiments to analyze the effects of both prefixation and the use of tactile sequences on the user's performance in a navigation task. Results show that, even if tactile sequences are more difficult to process during the navigation task, the prefixed patterns were easier to learn in all assessed vocabularies.

Keywords: Vibrotactile communication · 3D navigation · User study

1 Introduction

Usually, the design of simple tactile vocabularies follows an approach known as "tap-on-shoulders" [6]. This approach can be exemplified by a tactile sensation printed on the side of the user's body that is facing a particular target or obstacle, for example. This approach adds an iconic factor on the tactile language because the sensation directly evokes the behavior [16]. However, other approaches work on arbitrary tactile patterns as a way to enhance the vocabulary expressiveness [4]. In order to create tactile languages with more expressivity we formalized the concept of Modifier Tactile Pattern for vibrotactile displays [12]. In vibrotactile displays it is possible to vary hardware parameters (e.g. frequency, amplitude, rhythm) to create different patterns. However, arbitrary variations may result in vocabularies that are difficult to memorize and process. The use of prefixation with modifier patterns could enhance the tactile vocabulary expressiveness keeping it easier to learn.

Prefixation is not a novel approach for tactile languages. In Braille, some signs are reserved to work as prefixes. Each prefix can be attached to a basic sign modifying its meaning. A modifier pattern however modifies the meaning of an entire tactile sequence or several sequences at once. The modifier tactile pattern on vibrotactile vocabularies should act as a flag. When activated, the user must comprehend other tactons in a different way. Such pattern can be displayed simultaneously with the basic tacton or sequence, following a compound approach, or can be attached at the beginning of the sequence as an ordinary prefix.

© Springer-Verlag Berlin Heidelberg 2014
M. Auvray and C. Duriez (Eds.): EuroHaptics 2014, Part II, LNCS 8619, pp. 104–111, 2014.
DOI: 10.1007/978-3-662-44196-1_14

In this paper, we present a user study we conducted to assess the differences between tactile vocabularies made by a prefixation and a non-prefixation approach. Fifty eight users were split in three distinct groups for a between-groups analysis. Results show how each vocabulary affects the performance of each group in a navigation task.

2 Related Works

Tactile displays are commonly made for a specific purpose. In mobility and navigation tasks, there are tactile vocabularies made to display instructions and directions for astronauts [15], militaries [9], drivers [1] and visually impaired pedestrians [3]. In all those works, only one set of tactile icons was designed and refined to a specific application. In this paper, we rather built three different set of tactons, so we could assess how the different choices affect the navigation task.

The parameters used in the construction of tactile patterns were presented earlier in the literature as haptic phonemes. According to Enriquez and Maclean [5], they represent the smallest unit of a constructed haptic signal to which a meaning can be assigned. We have explored the design of vibrotactile languages through a morphological point of view. Even without using the term "prefix", its possible to find it in the methods for syntax development proposed by Brewster and Brown [2]. It is also used for construction of tactile messages in the Terne's [14] research about the use and effects of rhythm. In this work, more than present a tactile vocabulary made by prefixation, we compare prefixed and non-prefixed vocabularies in order to assess the value of this approach in the user's performance.

3 Methods

3.1 The Tactile Display

Concerning navigation, the perception we have about the location of our own body in the three-dimensional space is often referenced to the orientation and location of the relatively stable trunk of the body. Therefore, we designed a tactile display made as a belt (see Fig. 1).

Our belt was constructed with eight electromechanical tactors $ROB - 08449$ (Amplitude Vibration: $0.8G$; Voltage Range: $2.5V \sim 3.8V$), each with $3.4\,mm$ and positioned at equidistant locations. Other studies also presented vibrotactile displays made with eight motors for mobility and navigation tasks [1,11].

3.2 The Tactile Vocabularies

We designed three different vocabularies to aid in a 3D navigation task. We designed them to transmit five different kinds of information: Destination, Obstacle, Course, Warning and Itinerary. The availability of such amount of information allows us to observe to what extent they are essential for the navigation

Fig. 1. The vibrotactile belt. In the middle, a participant using the belt to navigate. In the right, a top view of a humanoid showing the vibrators positioned at equidistant locations around the waist.

task and also how each information helps a person to follow a better route. The five-step methodology of Riddle and Chapman [13] was used to design the tactile icons on three different vocabularies.

The *First Vocabulary* was designed following a conventional approach, based only on metaphors; the *Second Vocabulary* was designed following a Modifier-based approach, with patterns made by juxtaposition of tactons in sequence; the *Third Vocabulary* was also designed as a Modifier-based vocabulary, this time with patterns made by superposition in order to isolate sequence as an independent variable. Figure 2 shows a representation of tactons in each vocabulary. Only motors that can be used to compose the pattern are exhibited in each tacton.

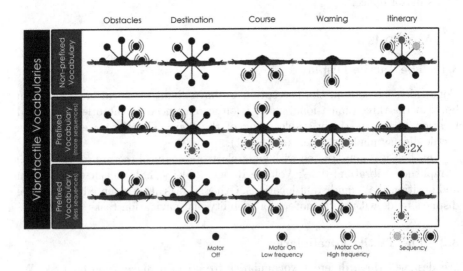

Fig. 2. Example of tactons in each vocabulary.

3.3   User Study

A population of 58 individuals have volunteered to participate in the tests; 47 are male and 11 females. The participants are students, covering an age range of 19–32 years. Testing was done in a dedicated room where just remained the volunteer and the researcher to best avoid distractions.

For a between-groups experiment, we divided our population into three distinct user groups that performed the same tasks but using a different vocabulary. The overall experiment took between 18 to 30 min for each participant.

After filling a pre-test characterization form, each participant was invited to wear the tactile belt and use a tutorial app. The tutorial is a step-by-step visual description of the vibrotactile language and the experiment. Then, each individual was exposed to tasks that evaluated their *perception* of the motors and their *interpretation* of tactons displayed by the belt. Finally, each user *navigated* through four different scenarios using the tactile belt. At the end they filled an evaluation form to give their opinions on the tactile vocabulary.

4   Results

In the preliminary *perception* test, many occurrences have been left unanswered for those patterns that were exhibited in sets of two and three motors. One-way ANOVA showed that there is a significant loss in the hits for patterns with many motors ($F(3.88) = 27.99$, $p < 0.00003$). As expected, in this task, the locations around the navel and spine provided the best correspondences. In a study about the perception of vibration across the body in mobile contexts, the stimuli delivered on the spine also was the one with the best results [10].

The results of the *interpretation* test have not presented significant difference between the vocabularies. However, the percentage of correct answers was lower for the second vocabulary (see Fig. 3).

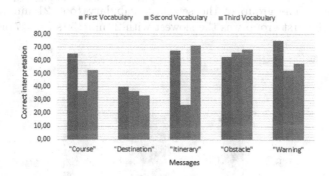

Fig. 3. Interpretation of messages by three different vocabularies.

In the *navigation* test, eleven users have shown to be outliers and were removed from the analysis. Ten of them reported to have felt significant nausea and dizziness during navigation, spending more than 2 standard deviations above the average or not being able to complete the task. The 11th outlier is one that spent more than an hour to complete the experiment.

In this test, each user navigated through four distinct scenarios that worked as levels of a game. The participants took a mean of 20 min to complete the whole task. The scenarios were displayed in a different order for each user, eliminating the effect of the scenario over the results. It is possible to observe the improvement of the three groups along the levels as their times and number of collisions decrease (see Fig. 4, left). With all vocabularies, users go faster at each subsequent level (see Fig. 4, right).

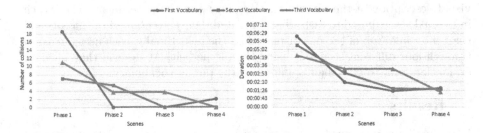

Fig. 4. User performance. Left: number of collisions in each level/scenario. Right: duration of the navigation in each level/scenario.

During this experiment, conflicts were observed between visual and tactile feedback. Most of the collisions occurred in the darkest part of the first scenario where the users could see the target very close ahead which encouraged them to anxiously ignore the tactile feedback and collide.

Figure 5 shows the mean time of each group. The group of the third vocabulary was the fastest, with a mean of 20 min (σ = 5 min : 31 s) to complete the whole task. The group of the second vocabulary took 21 min : 32 s (σ = 7 min : 35 s); the first group was the slowest with 22 min : 50 s (σ = 7 min : 03 s).

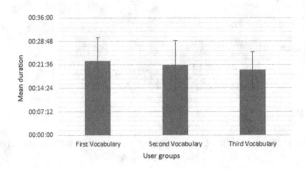

Fig. 5. Mean time to complete the task with each vocabulary.

The performance of the group with the second vocabulary in navigation was slightly better than the first group, even with more messages displayed as sequences. The users felt that the patterns in sequence were the most difficult to understand during navigation (see Fig. 6).

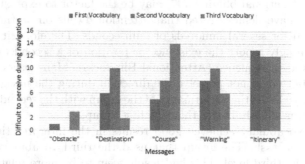

Fig. 6. Users opinion about patterns that were the most difficult to process during the navigation task.

Considering the duration and number of collisions during navigation, it can be seen that the group of the second vocabulary obtained the best results in some levels. The group that used the third vocabulary was the slowest at the third level and also the one that collided more at the third level. However, the third vocabulary had a great improvement at the last level.

5   Discussion

We proposed three different approaches to build a tactile vocabulary for navigation aid in VE. Our first vocabulary was made by varying hardware parameters as the metaphors to navigation. The other vocabularies were made with a pre-fixation approach. The prefixation was chosen to create tactons by the concatenation of a smallest set of tactons. The second vocabulary was made by printing one modifier pattern before the iconic representation of the information. And the third vocabulary was made by joining the sign to the prefix in order to make one single pattern for each information (except for the itinerary, that was made as a tactile sequence).

Hirsh and Sherrick [8] suggested that temporal processing can be broken down into two processes: the ability to correctly perceive that two events occurred (i.e. two strokes); and the ability to accurately judge which of two events occurred first. Thus, we know that at least two main issues are present in the tactile language processing: the processing of multiple stimuli at a time; and the processing of sequence of stimuli. Our first vocabulary is the one with more elements to recall. However, the first vocabulary is also the one with tactons made by composition of fewer motors at the same time. The second vocabulary was the one to address the sequence issue. The third vocabulary was the one with tactons made by the vibration of many motors at the same time.

In the second vocabulary four messages were displayed as sequences. The users felt that the patterns in sequence were the most difficult to understand during navigation. Sometimes the users did not even perceive the tacton during the task. The attentional blindness [7] may be the factor to explain this result. Several studies have demonstrated that attention dwells on a stimuli (visual, aural or tactile) for several hundreds of milliseconds. Therefore, it is common a person to wrongly report the existence or position of a second target of two targets displayed in sequence (Attentional Blindness). Many users understood the modifier, but could not perceive the direction during the navigation. Even with the sequence issue, the performance of the group with the second vocabulary in navigation was slightly better than the first group.

The third vocabulary achieved good results in the interpretation test and in the navigation task. The group that used the third vocabulary was especially slow at the third level. This bad result seem to be more related with the number of tactors activated simultaneously. In fact, the first task of the user experiment showed that the worst results were obtained from the perception of several motors at the same time. In the first task the users did not have to understand the meaning of the tacton; they had only to report the number and position of the active tactors. However, many users comprehended well the meaning of the tactons as seen in the second test.

6   Conclusion

We have studied three different choices in the design of a tactile language for 3D navigation. Analyzing the users performance we observed how it is influenced by tactile sequences and larger number of stimuli at same time. Even if the difference between the performances of the three groups was not statisticaly significant, the modifier-based vocabularies afforded the best results. Results show that, even if the processing of multiple stimuli at a time is more difficult, the way that the information was split into prefixation elements and iconic elements seemed to help the memorization. The results suggest a great potential for the modifier approach to be applied in the design of tactile interfaces.

The tactile language designed for navigation in virtual environments could also be used for navigation in physical environments. Therefore, our prefixal approach can be applied to render supplemental information when sight and hearing cannot be used, e.g., for orientation support in dark environments, as underground mines, or for the visually impaired, first person games for the blind and many others.

Acknowledgments. Thanks are due to the people that volunteered for the tests. We also acknowledge CAPES, CNPq-Brazil (305071/2012-2) and AES Sul for the financial support.

References

1. Boll, S., Asif, A., Heuten, W.: Feel your route: a tactile display for car navigation. IEEE Pervasive Comput. **10**(3), 35–42 (2011)
2. Brewster, S., Brown, L.M.,: Tactons: structured tactile messages for non-visual information display. In: Proceedings of the Fifth Conference on Australasian user interface, AUIC '04, vol. 28, pp. 15–23. Australian Computer Society Inc. Darlinghurst (2004)
3. Dakopoulos, D., Bourbakis, N.: Towards a 2D tactile vocabulary for navigation of blind and visually impaired. In: IEEE International Conference on Systems, Man and Cybernetics, SMC 2009, pp. 45–51. IEEE (2009)
4. Enriquez, M., MacLean, K.: The role of choice in longitudinal recall of meaningful tactile signals. In: Symposium on Haptic interfaces for virtual environment and teleoperator systems, Haptics 2008, pp. 49–56. IEEE (2008)
5. Enriquez, M., Maclean, K., Chita, C.: Haptic phonemes: basic building blocks of haptic communication. In: Proceedings of 8th International Conference on Multimodal Interfaces, ICMI 2006, ACM Press (2006)
6. Hao, F., guo Song, A.: Design of a wearable vibrotactile display waist belt. In: 2010 8th World Congress on Intelligent Control and Automation (WCICA), pp. 5014–5017. July 2010
7. Hillstrom, A.P., Shapiro, K.L., Spence, C.: Attentional limitations in processing sequentially presented vibrotactile targets. Percept. Psychophysics **64**(7), 1068–1082 (2002)
8. Hirsh, I.J., Sherrick Jr, C.E.: Perceived order in different sense modalities. J. Exp. Psychol. **62**(5), 423–432 (1961)
9. Jones, L.A., Kunkel, J., Torres, E.: Tactile vocabulary for tactile displays. In: EuroHaptics Conference, 2007 and Symposium on Haptic Interfaces for Virtual Environment and Teleoperator Systems, World Haptics 2007, Second Joint, pp. 574–575. IEEE (2007)
10. Karuei, I., MacLean, K. E., Foley-Fisher, Z., MacKenzie, R., Koch, S., El-Zohairy, M.: Detecting vibrations across the body in mobile contexts. In: Proceedings of the SIGCHI Conference on Human Factors in Computing Systems, pp. 3267–3276. ACM (2011)
11. Lindeman, R., Yanagida, Y., Noma, H., Hosaka, K.: Wearable vibrotactile systems for virtual contact and information display. Virtual Reality **9**, 203–213 (2006)
12. Oliveira. V. A. d. J., Maciel, A.: Introducing the modifier tactile pattern for vibrotactile communication. In: Proceedings of EuroHaptics (2014)
13. Riddle, D.L., Chapman, R.J.: Tactile language design. In: Proceedings of the Human Factors and Ergonomics Society Annual Meeting, pp. 478–482 (2012)
14. Ternes, David, MacLean, Karon E.: Designing large sets of haptic icons with rhythm. In: Ferre, Manuel (ed.) EuroHaptics 2008. LNCS, vol. 5024, pp. 199–208. Springer, Heidelberg (2008)
15. van Erp, J.B., Van Veen, H.: A multi-purpose tactile vest for astronauts in the international space station. In: Proceedings of EuroHaptics, pp. 405–408. ACM Press, Dublin (2003)
16. van Erp, J.B., Werkhoven, P.: Validation of principles for tactile navigation displays. In: Proceedings of the Human Factors and Ergonomics Society Annual Meeting, vol. 50, pp. 1687–1691. SAGE Publications (2006)

Altering Distance Perception from Hitting with a Stick by Superimposing Vibration to Holding Hand

Ryuta Okazaki[1,2(✉)] and Hiroyuki Kajimoto[1,3]

[1] The University of Electro-Communications, Chofu, Japan
{okazaki,kajimoto}@kaji-lab.jp
[2] JSPS Research Fellow, Tokyo, Japan
[3] Japan Science and Technology Agency, Tokyo, Japan

Abstract. Distance perception by hitting objects with a handheld stick is an important cue for people with visual impairments who use a white cane in daily life. In a previous paper, we found that adding vibration to the thumb side of the cane shortened the perceived collision distance more than adding vibration to the little-finger side, which partly agrees with our hypothetical model. In this paper, we conducted a similar experiment, changing the real distance between the palm and the object to explore the robustness of our hypothetical model. The experimental results showed that perceived collision distance shortened regardless of the real distance, but may be easily induced when the object is placed far from the palm.

Keywords: Distance perception · Hitting · Stick · Vibrotactile

1 Introduction

Most people have experience of perceiving distance by hitting objects with a stick. This perception is quite important, especially for the visually impaired who use white canes to guide them in daily life. Therefore, understanding the perception mechanism underlying this phenomenon might help in the development of supporting devices, such as an electric white cane that consists of a range sensor and a haptic display [1].

The mechanical characteristics of held objects can be perceived by haptic cues even if the objects are visually occluded [2]. This exploratory behavior is known as dynamic touch, and has mainly been studied as part of ecological psychology [3]. The length of a handheld rod can be estimated from cues such as its density, diameter, center of gravity, the user's swing, and grasping posture [4, 5, 6]. The "sweet spot" of a handheld tennis racket can be estimated before the actual hit [7]. In recent years, researchers have succeeded in producing the illusion of length, weight, or center of gravity of a virtual object by using haptic devices [8].

However, most studies have dealt with estimating the mechanical characteristics of the handheld object itself and have not directly considered distance perception from percussing objects with a handheld stick. Yao and Hayward [9] found that "rolling" a small object inside the rod can be expressed by simple vibration, but they did not

© Springer-Verlag Berlin Heidelberg 2014
M. Auvray and C. Duriez (Eds.): EuroHaptics 2014, Part II, LNCS 8619, pp. 112–119, 2014.
DOI: 10.1007/978-3-662-44196-1_15

directly deal with distance perception from hitting an object. The contribution of the rotational moment was considered but not fully explored [10]. Sreng et al. proposed that transient frequency components after hitting with a stick may play a role in perception [11]. However, the vibration frequency is easily affected by the material and length of the stick, which leads to frequency cues not being robust. We presume therefore that simpler yet more robust cutaneous cues play a role in this perception.

In our previous study [12], we advanced the hypothesis that the distance information obtained from hitting with a stick can be retrieved by the "center of gravity" of vibration in the palm, and tried to verify this hypothesis by superimposing external vibrations onto the real vibrations caused while percussing. In this paper, we conducted an experiment with various real distance conditions between the palm and the object, to explore the relationship between the effect of artificial vibrations from actuators and the real distance between the palm and the object.

2 Hypothetical Model of Distance Perception by Cutaneous Cues

Figure 1 shows a simplified mechanical model for percussing an object with a handheld rod. P_1, P_2, and P_3 indicate the positions of the object, thumb, and little finger, respectively. We assumed that the hand only contacts the rod with the thumb and little finger to simply the model, although in real-world cases the rod is held with the whole palm. F_1, F_2, and F_3 represent the generated forces by percussion, and L_1 and L_2 indicate the distances between P_1 and P_2 and P_2 and P_3, respectively.

As the handheld rod stops after the contact, the total rotational moment and translational force must be zero, which leads to the following equations.

$$F_1 + F_2 + F_3 = 0 \tag{1}$$

$$F_1 \cdot L_1 = F_3 \cdot L_2 \tag{2}$$

From these equations of balance, distance L_1 is obtained as follows:

$$L_1 = \frac{F_3 \cdot L_2}{F_1} = \frac{-F_3 \cdot L_2}{F_2 + F_3}. \tag{3}$$

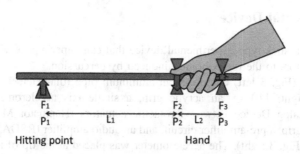

Fig. 1. Hypothetical model for distance perception of percussion with handheld rod.

As L_2 (distance between the thumb and little finger) is constant, this equation means that the distance of the percussed object L_1 is directly related to the ratio of F_2 and F_3, which are perceived as cutaneous sensations at the thumb side and little-finger side.

For instance, when the object is quite close, L_1 is nearly equal to zero, which gives $F_3 = 0$ in the equation. This means that the transmitted vibration at the thumb (P_2) is greater than that at the little finger (P_3) (Fig. 2, left). In contrast, when the position of the percussed object P_1 is far away, L_1 is infinite, which gives the solution $F_2 = -F_3$. Therefore, the intensities of the transmitted vibrations to the thumb and little finger become equal (Fig. 2, right).

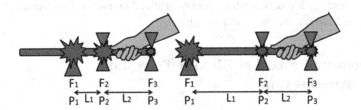

Fig. 2. Hypothesis of distance perception with cutaneous cue. Hitting a closer point induces a stronger vibration at the thumb side (left). Hitting farther induces equally distributed vibrations (right).

This simple model shows that the position of the percussed object P_1 can be estimated from the ratio of transmitted vibrations to the thumb (F_2) and little finger (F_3). This model is not completely accurate because we usually grasp the rod with the whole palm, but it shows that we may estimate the position of the percussed object by perceiving the position of the "center of gravity" of vibration in the palm. Presenting vibration at multiple sites is known to elicit the perception of a center of gravity, which is called a funneling or phantom sensation [13].

Based on this hypothesis, we fabricated an experimental device embedded with two actuators located at the bases of the thumb and little finger. We conducted an experiment to determine whether changing the center of gravity of the vibration that is transmitted to the palm modifies the perception of the percussed object's position.

3   Experimental Device

We developed a stick-type experimental device that can superimpose vibrations generated by actuators to the real vibration induced by percussion.

The device (Fig. 3 left) comprises an aluminum pipe (diameter: 15 mm, length: 1000 mm, weight: 110 g), an acrylic grip, a single-axis accelerometer ($\pm$250 g, ADXL193, Analog Devices), two vibrotactile actuators (Haptuator Mark II, TactileLabs) on the grip, a pre-amplifier circuit, and an audio amplifier (RSDA202, Rasteme Systems Inc.) (Fig. 3 right). The accelerometer was placed at the tip of the aluminum pipe to record the real contact (Fig. 4), and its analog output was connected to the two

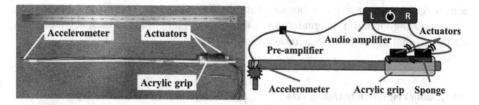

Fig. 3. (left) Stick-type experimental device. (right) The system configuration.

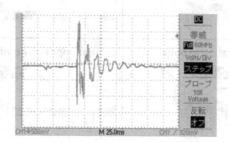

Fig. 4. The waveform of the hitting measured by the accelerometer.

actuators through the pre-amplifier circuit and audio amplifier. The two actuators were mounted on the grip beneath the bases of the thumb and little finger. They directly touched the skin surface when the device was grasped. A sponge was installed between the acrylic grip and actuators to avoid possible howling caused by the actuators and accelerometer. The total weight of the device was about 250 g.

Thanks to the simplicity of the implementation, the time delay between the actual contact to the replayed vibration became imperceptible. Each actuator was connected to the right and left channels of the audio amplifier; the amplitude ratio of the two actuators could be controlled by the balance control knob of the audio amplifier.

We prepared an object made of acrylic plate (height: 100 mm, width: 200 mm, thickness: 5 mm). It was attached vertically to the linear servomotor (F14-20-200-5L, Yamaha Motor Co., Ltd.) with a vice. To avoid possible damage to the stick and object, a rubber sheet (thickness: 5 mm) was attached on top of the object. This rubber sheet also helped mute the percussive sound, which can act as a cue for distance estimation.

4   Experiment

We conducted an experiment to verify the hypothesis of percussion distance perception. We assumed that participants would misjudge the position of the percussed object when vibration was superimposed, since this would alter the vibration center of gravity in the palm.

4.1   Experimental Conditions

Four pairs of vibration conditions were prepared: (a) superimposing vibration from the thumb-side actuator to the real collision, (b) superimposing vibration from both actuators, (c) superimposing vibration from the little-finger side actuator, (d) without superimposing vibration. In condition (b), the vibration amplitude of each actuator was set to half that of the other conditions (Fig. 5).

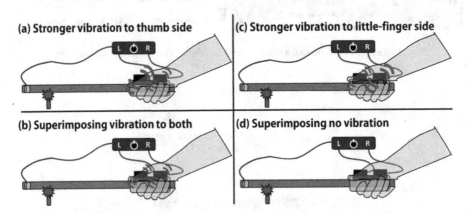

Fig. 5. Four pairs of vibrations were prepared for the experimental conditions.

To investigate the relationship between the effect of artificial vibrations from the actuators and the real distance between the palm and the object, we also prepared three different distance conditions: (1) the distance between the end tail of the device and the object was set to 500 mm, (2) 600 mm, and (3) 700 mm. The distance was controlled by the linear servomotor via computer.

4.2   Experiment Procedure

We recruited seven participants (all males, 21–29 years old, no reported tactile impairments). The participants sat on a chair and grasped the stick-type device with their right hands. To avoid visual and aural estimation of the collision distance [14], a black wall was installed on the right side of the participants, and they wore active noise-canceling headphones (QuietComfort, BOSE) and listened to white noise at a maximum pleasant volume. A 1000 mm scale ruler was placed in front of the partic- ipants to determine the visually and aurally occluded collision position (Fig. 6).

On each trial, participants percussed the object using the stick-device. Each trial had no time limit or limit on the number of percussions. The participants were instructed to keep their right hand at the same height so that they could not estimate the distance from the stick angle at the moment of percussion. Similarly, they were instructed to keep the end tail of the stick-device at the same position so that the collision position was only decided by the position of the linear servomotor (500, 600, or 700 mm). Also, an armrest was installed on the participants' right sides to allow them to maintain the position of their arms and to prevent fatigue. After percussion, participants estimated the perceived distance using the scale of the ruler. No feedback about correct distance was provided during the experiment. Each vibration condition was presented ten times, at three

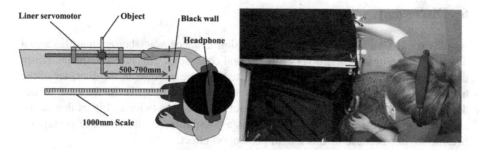

Fig. 6. Top view of experimental setup.

different distances randomized across trials; each participant performed 120 trials. To prevent fatigue, participants rested at least once every ten trials.

5   Results and Discussion

To verify the difference among conditions, a one-way repeated measures ANOVA and multiple comparisons (Ryan's method) were performed. Through all vibration and distance conditions, all participants tended to perceive the collision distance as shorter than the actual distance (500, 600, or 700 mm), including condition (d) (the natural condition).

Results at the distance of 700 mm are shown in Fig. 7 (A). The vertical axis represents the average results of the perceived collision distance among all participants. The horizontal axis represents the conditions. The error bars indicate the standard deviation. There were significant differences between conditions (a) and (b), (a) and (c), and (a) and (d) ($p < 0.05$). Results at the distance of 600 mm are shown in Fig. 7 (B). Similar to the 700 mm case, there were significant differences between conditions (a) and (b), (a) and (c), and (a) and (d) ($p < 0.05$). Results at the distance of 500 mm are shown in Fig. 7 (C). Different from the other two results, there were significant differences only between conditions (a) and (c), and (b) and (c) ($p < 0.05$).

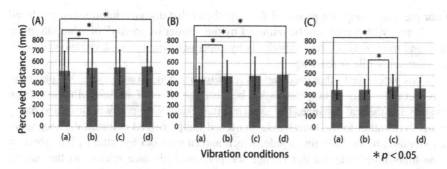

Fig. 7. Results for different vibration conditions at a distance of (A) 700 mm, (B) 600 mm, (C) 500 mm.

6 Discussion

As an overall tendency, the perceived collision distance was shorter than the actual distance, including for condition (d) (the natural condition). This can be explained from the viewpoint of dynamic touch. Chan reported that the increase in the diameter of the hand-held stick shortens the perception of the stick's length [4]. In the case of our device, the diameter of the acrylic grip (about 33 mm) was twice as big as that of the aluminum pipe (15 mm). Therefore, there is a possibility that the distance perception became shorter because of this length perception effect.

Then, we compared each statistical result with our proposed hypothetical model. As there was a significant difference between conditions (a) (vibration added to thumb side) and (d) (the natural condition), superimposing vibration onto the thumb side shortened the perceived collision distance compared with the natural condition at the 600 mm and 700 mm distances. Furthermore, there was also a significant difference between conditions (a) and (c) (vibration added to little-finger side), indicating that presenting the vibration to the thumb side shortened the perceived collision distance more than vibration to the little-finger side in all distance conditions. These results agreed with our proposed hypothesis.

On the other hand, there was no significant difference between condition (c) and (d) in all conditions. If we only perceive the distance by the vibration center of gravity in the palm, condition (c) should be perceived as longer than condition (d). Therefore, the results of condition (c) do not fully support our hypothesis. Thus, our hypothesis and device setup may need to be reconsidered, and we may need to include other factors such as the contribution of kinetic sensation or the resonance characteristics of the rod.

In sum, the perceived collision distance was altered by providing additional vibration, and increasing the vibration ratio on the thumb side significantly shortened the perceived collision distance compared to doing so on the little-finger side (which we consider counterintuitive). Also, this tendency was observed regardless of the real distance between palm and object, but may be easily induced when the object is placed far from the palm.

7 Conclusion

In our previous study, we proposed the hypothesis that distance information produced when hitting with a stick can be retrieved by the "center of gravity" of vibration in the palm, and tried to verify this hypothesis by superimposing external vibration onto the real vibration while percussing.

In this paper, we further used various real distance conditions between the palm and the object to investigate the relationship between the effect of artificial vibrations from actuators and the real distance. The experimental results were partly positive and partly negative: vibration to the thumb side shortened the perceived collision distance more than vibration to the little-finger side, which agreed with our hypothesis, but vibration to the little-finger side did not change the perceived distance relative to the natural condition, which did not agree with our hypothesis. These tendencies were observed regardless of the real distance between palm and object, but may be easily induced when the object is placed far from the palm.

In the present study, we superimposed external vibration onto the real vibration from percussion. In future work, we will investigate the reason why the vibration to the little-finger side did not affect the perceived distance by further developing our hypothesis, including other factors such as the contribution of kinetic sensation or the resonance characteristics of the rod, and determine how to intuitively present positional information from the collision.

References

1. Vera, P., Zenteno, D., Salas, J.: A smartphone-based virtual white cane. Pattern Anal. Appl. (2013)
2. Solomon, H.Y., Turvey, M.T.: Haptically perceiving the distances reachable with handheld objects. J. Exp. Psychol.-Hum. Percept. Perform. **14**, 404–427 (1988)
3. Gibson, J.J.: The Senses Considered as Perceptual Systems. Houghton Mifflin, Oxford (1966)
4. Chan, T.-C.: The effect of density and diameter on haptic perception of rod length. Percept. Psychophys. **57**, 778–786 (1995)
5. Carello, C., Fitzpatrick, P., Flascher, I., Turvey, M.T.: Inertial eigenvalues, rod density, and rod diameter in length perception by dynamic touch. Percept. Psychophys. **60**, 89–100 (1998)
6. Idsart, K., Langenberg, R., Beek, P.J.: Which mechanical invariants are associated with the perception of length and heaviness of a nonvisible handheld rod? Testing the inertia tensor hypothesis. J. Exp. Psychol.-Hum. Percept. Perform. **30**, 346–354 (2004)
7. Carello, C., Thuot, S., Anderson, K.L., Turvey, M.T.: Perceiving the sweet spot. Perception **28**, 307–320 (1999)
8. Minamizawa, K., Fukamachi, S., Kajimoto, H., Kawakami, N., Tachi, S.: Gravity grabber: wearable haptic display to present virtual mass sensation. In: Proceedings of ACM SIGGRAPH 2007, California, USA, 5–9 August 2007
9. Yao, H.-Y., Hayward, V.: An experiment on length perception with a virtual rolling stone. In: Proceedings of Eurohaptics, pp. 325–330 (2006)
10. Felicia, W., Zelek, J.S.: Tactile & inertial patterns from a long white cane. In: Proceedings of Biomedical Robotics and Biomechatronics, pp. 519–524 (2006)
11. Sreng, J., et al.: Spatialized haptic rendering: providing impact position information in 6DOF haptic simulations using vibrations. In: Proceedings of Virtual Reality Conference, pp. 3–9 (2009)
12. Okazaki, R., Kajimoto, H.: Perceived distance from hitting with a stick is altered by overlapping vibration to holding hand. In: Proceedings of ACM CHI 2014 (in press)
13. Bekesy, G.: Neural funneling along the skin and between the inner and outer hair cells of the cochlea. J. Acoust. Soc. Am. **31**, 1236–1249 (1959)
14. Carello, C., et al.: Perception of object length by sound. Psychol. Sci. **9**, 211–214 (1998)

Passive Mechanical Skin Stretch for Multiple Degree-of-Freedom Proprioception in a Hand Prosthesis

Aadeel Akhtar[1]([⊠]), Mary Nguyen[2], Logan Wan[3], Brandon Boyce[2],
Patrick Slade[3], and Timothy Bretl[2]

[1] Neuroscience Program, Medical Scholars Program, University of Illinois at
Urbana-Champaign, Urbana, IL 61801, USA
aakhta3@illinois.edu
[2] Department of Aerospace Engineering, University of Illinois at Urbana-Champaign,
Urbana, IL 61801, USA
[3] Department of Mechanical Engineering, University of Illinois at
Urbana-Champaign, Urbana, IL 61801, USA
{hnguyn10,wan14,boyce4,pslade2,tbretl}@illinois.edu

Abstract. In this paper, we present a passive linear skin stretch device that can provide proprioceptive feedback for multiple degrees of freedom (DOF) in a prosthetic hand. In a 1-DOF virtual targeting task, subjects performed as well with our device as with a vibrotactile array, and significantly better ($p < 0.05$) than having no feedback at all. In a 3-DOF grip recognition task, subjects were able to classify six different grips with 88.0 % accuracy. Training took 6 min and the average time to classification was 5.2 s. Subjects were also able to match a set of target grip apertures with 11.1 % error on average.

Keywords: Proprioception · Myoelectric prostheses · Skin stretch

1 Introduction

While major advancements have been made in the functionality of upper limb myoelectric prostheses, commercial devices still lack the ability to provide users with proprioceptive feedback. As a result, users have had to rely primarily on vision to know the position and orientation of their prosthesis. Surveys have reported that this over-dependence on vision is one of the largest contributors to prosthesis abandonment [1]. Various sensory substitution techniques have been used by research groups in order to provide proprioceptive feedback for use with upper limb myoelectric prostheses. Witteveen et al. used a vibrotactile array on the forearm to relay grip aperture to unimpaired subjects controlling a single degree-of-freedom (DOF) virtual hand with a mouse wheel [2]. Wheeler et al. developed a rotational skin stretch device that provided elbow angle feedback to unimpaired subjects controlling a single-DOF virtual arm with electromyography

© Springer-Verlag Berlin Heidelberg 2014
M. Auvray and C. Duriez (Eds.): EuroHaptics 2014, Part II, LNCS 8619, pp. 120–128, 2014.
DOI: 10.1007/978-3-662-44196-1_16

(EMG) [3]. While these devices were effective in improving accuracy when controlling a single-DOF virtual prosthesis, most users perform tasks which require controlling multiple DOFs on their prostheses, for example, in selecting between different grips for a specific task [4]. Furthermore, a large amount of surface area is required by both the vibrotactile array and the rotational skin stretch device. In addition, the rotational skin stretch device consumes a great deal of power and adds a considerable amount of weight (see Sect. 4.3).

Initial work to relay multiple DOF information was done by Cheng et al., who used vibrotactile patterns presented on a belt around the waist to convey the configuration of a virtual hand performing various grips [5]. While they achieved 79.7 % accuracy in grip recognition, these results were marred by a long training time (30 min) and slow average time to classification (29.4 s).

To alleviate power, weight, and space issues, as well as easily provide multiple-DOF proprioceptive feedback for a prosthetic hand, we developed a passive mechanical linear skin stretch device (Fig. 1). The device cost less than \$2 in raw materials. We compared our skin stretch device to a vibrotactile array and to a case where no feedback was given in a single-DOF virtual finger targeting task with myoelectric control. Our results show that the vibrotactile array and skin stretch device performed better than with no feedback given and that there was no statistical difference in performance between the two feedback methods.

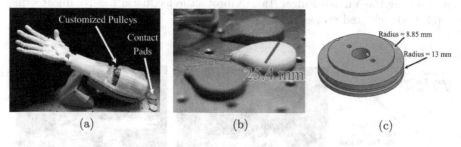

Fig. 1. Passive linear skin stretch device attached to prosthesis. The InMoov hand used in our study (a) had custom pulleys pulling both the tendons driving the fingers and the lines to the contact pads (b). A schematic of one of the pulleys is shown in (c).

Extending our experiment to three DOFs, we assessed how well the user could recognize grips involving different configurations of the thumb, index, and middle fingers. Subjects identified six different grips with 88.0 % accuracy. Training took 6 min per subject and the average classification time was 5.2 s. Finally, subjects also performed a task in which they were asked to match different levels of aperture for a pre-selected grip among the six used in the study. On average, the subjects were able to match the grip aperture (0–100 %) with 11.1 % error.

2   Methods

Five unimpaired subjects, four male, one female (ages: 19–27), volunteered for these experiments. The subjects were asked to participate in two experiments, one testing single-DOF proprioception, and the other testing multiple-DOF proprioception. During each experiment, six electrodes were placed over the finger flexor and extensor muscle groups located radially around the right forearm, with three electrodes being placed over each muscle group. A 16-channel Delsys Bagnoli system (Delsys, Inc., Natick, MA) was used to record the EMG signals measured across these muscles. All data were collected and processed using the MATLAB DAQ Toolbox (Mathworks, Natick, MA).

2.1 Single-DOF Virtual Finger Task

In the first experiment, subjects were asked to move an onscreen virtual finger in a single-DOF task (Fig. 2a) based on [3,6]. The virtual finger was constrained to move between 0–90°. Meanwhile, the subject's metacarpophalangeal (MCP) joints on the right hand were restrained to 45° in order to remove any of the subject's own proprioceptive cues in controlling the arm. Flexing or extending the MCP joints against the restraint (Fig. 2b) would generate EMG signals. Linear discriminant analysis was used to classify these EMG signals to virtual finger movements every 0.1 s, following the procedure outlined in [7]. In order to have subjects rely more on feedback than timing-based open loop control strategies [2], the angular velocity was changed by a random walk bounded between 5–20°/s with a random initial velocity. Three feedback conditions were tested during the Virtual Finger Task: vibrotactile feedback, passive linear skin stretch feedback, and no feedback.

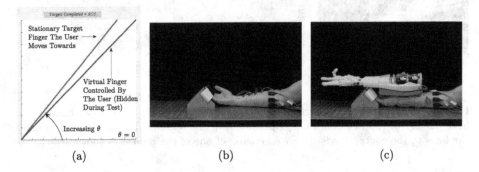

(a)   (b)   (c)

Fig. 2. (a) MATLAB GUI used for the single-DOF virtual finger task. (b) Vibrotactile array placement. (c) Passive linear skin stretch setup. A third contact pad was adhered to the skin on the radial side of the forearm. The orange triangular block restrained the subjects' hand in order to remove intrinsic proprioceptive cues.

Vibrotactile Array. We used a vibrotactile array based on [2] to provide proprioceptive feedback of the angle of the virtual finger. It consisted of eight standard ERM motors placed longitudinally along the forearm, with each tactor spaced 29 mm apart (Fig. 2b). The joint angle range of the virtual finger was divided into eight intervals, each successively mapped to one of the vibrotactile motors.

Passive Linear Skin Stretch. To use passive skin stretch to provide proprioceptive feedback, we constructed a prosthetic hand that pulled contact pads adhered to the forearm. The hand was modified from InMoov, an open source 3D-printed robotics project [8]. MG946R servo motors (TowerPro, Taiwan) mounted in the forearm of the prosthesis drove the tendon-actuated fingers. We seated the hand in a rigid plastic interface, which was then attached to a wrist brace. Guide holes at the proximal end of the interface kept the lines to the contact pads as horizontal as possible to maximize shear forces on the skin. For the single-DOF task, we adhered only the white contact pad to the skin (Fig. 2c).

We designed custom 3D-printed pulleys and mounted them onto the servos for the thumb, index, and middle fingers. A pulley had one channel to pull a tendon actuating a finger and a second to pull the line to a contact pad on the subject's arm. We set the ratio of the radii of these channels so that the displacement of the contact pad was 13 mm with respect to the finger's range of motion (Fig. 1c). In addition, we 3D-printed each contact pad to have a circular contact area of 507 mm^2 and a hole to connect to the line from the pulley (Fig. 1b). Contact pads were adhered to the skin using BMTT-A adhesives (Garland Beauty Products, Hawthorne, CA) with roughly 1.5 N of initial tension.

Training and Evaluation. A trial consisted of a training and evaluation phase for a particular feedback condition. During training, each subject used EMG to freely control the virtual finger for 60 s. Next, the subject was given five practice target angles from the evaluation phase. They were asked to move the virtual finger, now invisible, until it matched a series of displayed targets (Fig. 2a). Once the subject believed he was at the target angle, he would press a button and would be shown the actual angle to which he moved. Following the five practice angles, the subject was evaluated using 20 more targets. The mean absolute error between the target angle and the subject's estimate were recorded.

Subjects participated in two sessions consisting of a trial for each of the three feedback conditions, with each condition presented in a random order. Two sessions were conducted in order to evaluate whether performance improved over time. To help ensure subjects relied only on the feedback method under consideration, they wore headphones playing pink noise throughout the experiment. Additionally, when evaluating linear skin stretch, the prosthesis and contact pads were occluded from view.

2.2 Multiple-DOF Tasks

To extend the single-DOF skin stretch feedback to multiple-DOFs, we introduced two additional contact pads to either side of the right forearm. We placed a contact pad on the ulnar side for the middle finger, the middle for the index finger as before, and the radial side for the thumb (Fig. 2c). Two tasks were performed with skin stretch feedback: a grip recognition task and a grip aperture targeting task. For the grip aperture targeting task, subjects were also evaluated with no feedback. As before, subjects listened to pink noise through headphones and the prosthesis and contact pads were hidden from view during evaluation.

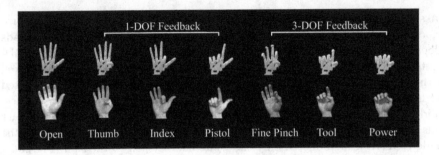

Fig. 3. Grips used for multiple-DOF experiments. The thumb, index, and pistol grips displace one contact pad; while the power, tool, and fine pinch grips displace multiple contact pads. The 1- and 3-DOF grips are shown at 100 % grip aperture.

The multiple-DOF tasks involved six grips plus a starting reference configuration (open hand) (Fig. 3). To examine whether single-DOF grips could be distinguished from multiple-DOF grips, half of the grips chosen displaced a single contact pad: the thumb, index, and pistol grips. The other three grips displaced multiple contact pads simultaneously: power, fine pinch, and tool grips. The amount of skin stretch per contact pad was proportional to each corresponding joint angle for each grip. These specific multiple-DOF grips were chosen because they are commonly implemented in upper limb myoelectric prostheses [4].

Grip Recognition Task. This task was modified from [5]. In this task, grips were presented starting from the open hand reference configuration, transitioning over about 4 s to the completed grip. During the first of two training periods, subjects were shown an image of the grip while also being provided with the appropriate skin stretch feedback. Once the grip had completed moving, it was held for 3 s. The order of the grips were randomized and each grip occurred twice. In the second training period, subjects were asked to identify grips within 3 s after grip completion and were told the actual grip. Again, the order of the grips was randomized, except each grip occurred three times. The combined total training time across both periods took 6 min.

During evaluation, subjects had to identify a series of 30 grips, with each grip being presented five times in random order. This time, subjects were not told the correct grip after their selection. No time limit was imposed on the subjects when selecting a grip, and they were allowed to select a grip before the grip reached completion. The proportion of correct selections and the time from grip onset to selection was recorded.

Grip Aperture Targeting Task. This task extended the single-DOF virtual finger task to incorporate the six grips from the grip recognition task. The aperture of each grip was normalized from 0 % (open hand) to 100 % (completed grip). Subjects had to match target apertures at 25 %, 50 %, and 75 % grip completion using EMG control.

To decouple EMG pattern recognition from matching a percent aperture for a grip, the grips were pre-selected. Subjects flexed or extended the same muscles from the single-DOF task to control the aperture for all grips. During training, the subject was prompted to close a grip to within ±5 % of a target percent aperture and stay in the zone for 2 s. This was repeated for each of the six grips at each of the three target apertures, presented in a randomized order.

Evaluation consisted of 30 random targets in which the subject tried to match percent aperture after starting from a random percentage between 0–100 %. In order to reduce the completion time of the experiment, a random subset of all the combinations of grip and percent aperture were presented to each subject. Subjects repeated the task twice for both no feedback and skin stretch feedback conditions, with the order of conditions randomized. The mean absolute error between the target percent and subject's estimate was recorded.

3 Results

For the single-DOF virtual finger task, the no feedback, vibrotactile, and skin stretch conditions had $(17.75 \pm 5.17°)$, $(8.58 \pm 2.12°)$, and $(9.79 \pm 2.68°)$ of mean absolute error, respectively. We ran a two-way repeated measures ANOVA, where the within-subject factors were session number and feedback condition. We found a significant difference between the no feedback and vibrotactile conditions ($p < 0.01$) as well as the no feedback and skin stretch conditions ($p < 0.05$) (Fig. 4a). However, there were no significant differences between skin stretch and vibrotactile or between sessions for any feedback condition.

Over the course of the multiple-DOF grip recognition task, subjects correctly selected $88.0 \pm 5.6\%$ of the presented grips on average. Figure 4b shows the confusion matrix, which depicts the absolute number of correct and incorrect selections for a presented grip. The average time for grip selection was 5.2 ± 0.6 s,

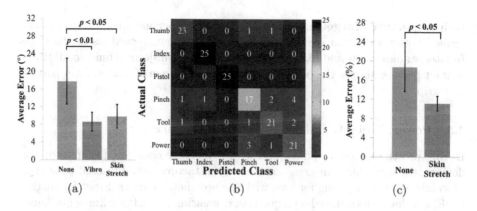

Fig. 4. (a) Average mean absolute error for the single-DOF virtual finger task. (b) Confusion matrix for grip recognition task. (c) Average percent grip aperture error for the grip aperture targeting task.

where time was measured from the start of when the reference began moving toward the closed grip. For the multiple-DOF grip aperture task, Fig. 4c shows that the error in percent aperture for the skin stretch condition ($11.1 \pm 1.5\%$) was significantly lower ($p < 0.05$) than the no feedback condition ($18.7 \pm 5.1\%$).

4   Discussion

4.1   Single-DOF Virtual Finger Task

In the single-DOF virtual finger task, subjects had lower average error when given either linear skin stretch or vibrotactile feedback than when they were given no feedback. There was no significant difference between either form of feedback. However, users of prostheses have reported that vibrotactile feedback becomes distracting after prolonged periods of time [9], though constant proprioceptive feedback may be desired. Subjects in this study reported skin stretch remained comfortable throughout the experiments, which could make it more desirable than vibrotactile stimulation at providing proprioceptive feedback.

4.2   Multiple-DOF Tasks

Grip Recognition Task. Subjects in this study distinguished between six different grips in an average of 5.2 s with 88.0 % accuracy across subjects, while those in Cheng et al. distinguished between five different grips in an average of 29.4 s with 79.7 % accuracy [5]. Though the grips used in this study differ from those used by Cheng et al., the similar success rates suggest that our passive linear skin stretch device is a viable system to use for multiple-DOF tasks.

Refinements will be made to the linear skin stretch system to further improve grip recognition accuracy. One possible improvement to the system would involve creating maximally distinct contact pad trajectories for each grip.

Grip Aperture Targeting Task. In the grip aperture task, subjects performed better with skin stretch feedback than without, regardless of the grip. In later studies, we would like to determine whether subjects attend to all three contact pads or simply the one with the maximum range of stretch for a particular grip.

4.3   Power, Weight, and Surface Area Comparisons

During prosthesis design, power and weight must be considered. For feedback devices, the available skin area and size of the tactors are additional concerns, especially when competing for area with the prosthesis' sensors. First, for single-DOF, our device introduced a torque loss, decreasing the battery life of our hand by 1 %. Our device would be even more efficient in prostheses that produce more torque. Assuming a 7.4 V, 2400 mA h battery, the vibrotactile array used in this study would decrease battery life by 2 %, while the 3.2 W motor for the rotational skin stretch device by Wheeler et al. [3] would decrease it by 9 % if the device ran constantly. Second, our device, the vibrotactile array, and Wheeler et al.'s device would add 2 g, 6 g, and 82 g to the prosthesis, respectively. Compared to the weight of commercially available prostheses, our device and the vibrotactile array were negligibly light. Finally, the area used by our device over the full range of stretch was 975 mm^2, while vibrotactile used 2380 mm^2, and Wheeler et al.'s device used 2800 mm^2. Thus, our passive skin stretch device used the least surface area of these three devices, drains little power, and is lightweight.

5   Conclusion

We have shown that for a single-DOF virtual finger targeting task, linear skin stretch is comparable to vibrotactile feedback and better than no feedback. In the multiple-DOF grip recognition task, our results are comparable to those attained in a previous study [5] that used a vibrotactile array. However, subjects in our study were able to achieve similar classification accuracy (88.0 % vs. 79.7 %) after a shorter training period (6 min vs. 30 min), requiring less time to make classifications (5.2 s vs. 30 s). In the grip aperture targeting task, subjects matched target grip apertures with 11.1 % error on average. Finally, the simplicity, low cost, low power consumption, light weight, small contact area, and overall comfort make our passive linear skin stretch device well-suited for multiple-DOF proprioceptive tasks.

Acknowledgments. The authors would like to thank Elizabeth Hsiao-Wecksler for the EMG system, and Anusha Nagabandi and David Jun for help with the vibrotactile array. This work is supported in part by National Science Foundation Grant No. 0903622.

References

1. Peerdeman, B., Boere, D., Witteveen, H., Hermens, H., Stramigioli, S., Rietman, H., Veltink, P., Misra, S., et al.: Myoelectric forearm prostheses: state of the art from a user-centered perspective. J. Rehabil. Res. Dev. **48**, 719–738 (2011)
2. Witteveen, H., Droog, E., Rietman, J., Veltink, P.: Vibro- and electrotactile user feedback on hand opening for myoelectric forearm prostheses. IEEE Trans. Biomed. Eng. **59**, 2219–2226 (2012)
3. Wheeler, J., Bark, K., Savall, J., Cutkosky, M.: Investigation of rotational skin stretch for proprioceptive feedback with application to myoelectric systems. IEEE Trans. Neural Syst. Rehabil. Eng. **18**, 58–66 (2010)
4. Kuiken, T.A., Li, G., Lock, B.A., Lipschutz, R.D., Miller, L.A., Stubblefield, K.A., Englehart, K.B.: Targeted muscle reinnervation for real-time myoelectric control of multifunction artificial arms. J. Am. Med. Assoc. **301**, 619–628 (2009)
5. Cheng, A., Nichols, K.A., Weeks, H.M., Gurari, N., Okamura, A.M.: Conveying the configuration of a virtual human hand using vibrotactile feedback. In: IEEE HAPTICS 2012, pp. 155–162. IEEE (2012)

6. Blank, A., Okamura, A.M., Kuchenbecker, K.J.: Identifying the role of proprioception in upper-limb prosthesis control: studies on targeted motion. ACM Trans. Appl. Percept. **7**, 15 (2010)
7. Jeong, J.W., Yeo, W.H., Akhtar, A., Norton, J.J., Kwack, Y.J., Li, S., Jung, S.Y., Su, Y., Lee, W., Xia, J., et al.: Materials and optimized designs for human-machine interfaces via epidermal electronics. Adv. Mater. **25**, 6839–6846 (2013)
8. Langevin, G.: InMoov - Open source 3D printed life size robot (2014). http://inmoov.fr, License: http://creativecommons.org/licenses/by-nc/3.0/legalcode
9. Jimenez, M.C., Fishel, J.A.: Evaulation of force, vibration and thermal tactile feedback in prosthetic limbs. In: IEEE HAPTICS 2014, pp. 437–441. IEEE (2014)

Robotics or Medical Applications

A Visual-Haptic Multiplexing Scheme for Teleoperation Over Constant-Bitrate Communication Links

Burak Cizmeci[⊠], Rahul Chaudhari,
Xiao Xu, Nicolas Alt, and Eckehard Steinbach

Institute for Media Technology, Technische Universität München,
Munich, Germany
burak.cizmeci@tum.de
http://www.lmt.ei.tum.de/

Abstract. We propose a novel multiplexing scheme for teleoperation over constant bitrate (CBR) communication links. The proposed approach uniformly divides the channel into 1 ms resource buckets and controls the size of the transmitted video packets as a function of the irregular haptic transmission events generated by a perceptual haptic data reduction approach. The performance of the proposed multiplexing scheme is measured objectively in terms of delay-jitter and packet rates. The results show that acceptable multiplexing delays on both the visual and haptic streams are achieved. Our evaluation shows that the proposed approach can provide a guaranteed constant delay for the time-critical force signal, while introducing acceptable video delay.

Keywords: Teleoperation · Haptic communication · Multi-modal multiplexing · Human-robot interactions over network

1 Introduction

Telepresence and teleaction (TPTA) systems allow us to immerse ourselves into and to operate within environments that are remote or inaccessible to human beings. Regarding manipulative ability in the remote environment, TPTA systems are often referred to as telemanipulation/teleoperation systems. In addition to acoustic and visual feedback, the exchange of haptic information enables physical interaction between the human operator and remote objects. A TPTA system consists of the human system interface (HSI) as master, the teleoperator (TOP) as slave, and a communication link connecting them [1]. The HSI is composed of a haptic device for position-orientation input and for force feedback output, a video display for visual feedback, and headphones for acoustic feedback. The TOP is a robotic system equipped with force/torque sensors, a

This work has been supported by the European Research Council under the European Union's 7th Framework Programme (FP7/2007–2013)/ERC Grant no. 258941.

© Springer-Verlag Berlin Heidelberg 2014
M. Auvray and C. Duriez (Eds.): EuroHaptics 2014, Part II, LNCS 8619, pp. 131–138, 2014.
DOI: 10.1007/978-3-662-44196-1_17

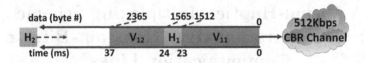

Fig. 1. Transmission hold-up for haptic information caused by a large video packet.

video camera and a microphone. The remote environment is sensed by the TOP, and the multi-modal information is sent to the human operator (OP) over the communication network. In this context, network-related issues can be divided into three subcategories: *transmission capacity, delay-jitter* and *packet loss*. In this paper, we focus on the multiplexing of haptic and visual signals for CBR communication links with severely constrained communication capacity. Such links exist in earth-to-space communication and satellite-internet connection in rural areas. We illustrate the main challenge in Fig. 1 using the example of a 512 kbps CBR link. In Fig. 1, a video packet V_{11} is in front of a haptic packet in the transmission queue, blocking the haptic packet H_1 for 23 ms as it occupies the CBR channel. Consequently, varying video packet sizes impose variable delay (jitter) on the force signal, which causes instability problems in TPTA systems. Additionally, jitter distorts the force signal which may lead to misperception of the remote environment. To avoid this, a jitter buffer can be employed to keep the end-to-end delay constant, or a passive control scheme [2] can be used to compensate time-varying communication delay. In the following, we propose a resource allocation solution to tackle the aforementioned delay-jitter problem for CBR channels. The packet delay d as a function of the transmission rate (TR) of the CBR link can be modelled as shown in Eq. (1).

$$d(n) = \frac{\sum_{i=0}^{n-1} P_i + P_n}{TR} \qquad (1)$$

Where P_i is the size of the ith packet already in the channel and P_n is the size of the current packet n waiting to be injected into the channel [3]. If the TR is known and constant over time, it is possible to control the delay for the currently enqueued packet by controlling the size of packets P_i before injecting them into the channel. With this approach, a constant delay service can be provided for time-critical closed-loop force/torque signals. In the literature, the transmission protocols for video and force have been studied under the name of multi-modal signal multiplexing, but the TR capacity problem in Fig. 1 has not been addressed so far. First steps towards a standard transport protocol for multi-modal streaming can be found in [4]. Recently, Eid et al. proposed a scheme for application-layer statistical multiplexing for a teleconference system involving passive haptic interaction [5]. Their approach doesn't consider the problem in Fig. 1 and instead allocates the resources to video and audio streams until the delay constraint of the force signal is violated. Contrary to their approach, our proposed scheme always assigns the force signal the highest priority to achieve the desired constant end-to-end delay. In order

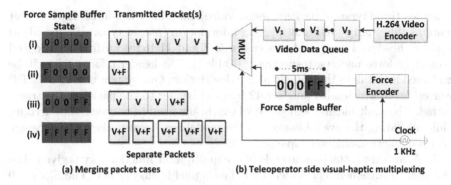

Fig. 2. Visual-haptic multiplexing on the feedback channel from the TOP to the OP.

to reduce the packet rate for the force transmission (from the TOP to the OP), the haptic data reduction scheme in [6] is used. This perceptual deadband (PD) based haptic data reduction scheme generates irregular sample transmission events as only perceivable signal changes are transmitted. To monitor the force transmission state, a watch buffer is placed between the force encoder and the multiplexer (see Fig. 2(b)). Depending on the buffer state, the multiplexer decides the rate allocation between the two modalities (see Fig. 2(a)). When few force updates need to be sent, the video can benefit from the unused transmission capacity. When the force needs to be updated frequently, the video can only use the remaining resources after the force signal is served. The next section introduces the proposed visual-haptic multiplexing framework and presents the experimental results.

2 Visual-Haptic Multiplexing

As shown in Fig. 2(b), the data-processing blocks are connected via media data queues. The haptic (force) encoder block utilizes the PD force data reduction scheme in [6] with a Zero-Order-Hold strategy. The only tuning parameter for this encoder is the constant Weber factor k, which determines the transmit/ non-transmit states on the force signal. $k = 10\%$ has been found to be the perceptual threshold of force [6]. When the current force signal value exceeds the perceptual threshold defined by the previously sent sample, the encoder marks the current force sample for transmission and enqueues it in the force sample buffer which holds N force samples ($N = 5$ in Fig. 2(b)) and monitors the transmit state of the upcoming samples. The haptic encoder and multiplexer blocks operate at a clock rate of 1 kHz which is also the sampling frequency of the force signal. At every clock tick, the haptic encoder updates the force buffer and the multiplexer dequeues a force sample from the head of the buffer. According to the transmission flag ("0" or "F") of the force sample, the multiplexer either discards or sends it, respectively. The user can configure the buffer size N before the session starts. According to the state of the system, the multiplexer generates three types of packets: force, video and joint video-force. Each packet contains timestamps and multiplexing information (packet type, size and id) as a packet header. These header sizes are 5, 7 and 11 bytes for force, video and joint video-force packets, respectively (Table 1). The header information will be explained in detail in the demultiplexer description. Our system uses IPv4/UDP over ethernet which adds another 42 bytes of header to the packet to be transmitted. The multiplexing and protocol overheads need to be taken into account while allocating the available slots to the modalities because they also consume the available transmission capacity.

In Algorithm 1, the pseudo code of the multiplexer functionality is given. The first control statement checks whether the channel is busy or not. The $Slots = 0$ condition indicates that the channel is free to transmit data and $Slots > 0$ means that the channel is still busy transmitting the previous packet. During the busy channel periods, a new packet cannot be injected into the channel and the multiplexer waits until the channel becomes free. When the channel is free, the multiplexer monitors the queued elements in the force buffer and counts the free slots either up to a planned-force transmission or reaching the tail of the buffer. According to the waiting data in the queues, the multiplexer decides what type of packet to send and updates the used number of $Slots$ if the multiplexed data size is smaller than the resource available. In the following, *CheckAvailableSlots()* function in Algorithm 1 is explained with possible force buffer examples given in Fig. 2(a). These examples are given for a 5 ms buffer size but the algorithm can work with different buffer sizes. The rectangular blocks on the left show the current state of the force buffer. The head of the buffer is on the left and the tail is on the right. The light gray square blocks on the right represent the allocated channel resource buckets for 1 ms time period. For 1 ms transmission segments, the size of a bucket is 512 bits (512 Kbit/s channel). *Case i:* If no important force sample has been identified for the past 5 ms, the available rate of the channel is allocated completely to the video data waiting in the video queue. A single combined video packet using 5 resource buckets (320 bytes) is pushed to the channel. *Case ii:* If the data reduction scheme marks the haptic sample at the head of the force buffer for transmission, it should be transmitted immediately within a single resource bucket. In this case, a joint video-force packet which uses 1 resource bucket is generated. *Case iii:* The algorithm counts the available slots up to the first flag in the force buffer. The multiplexer identifies a force sample to be transmitted at the 4th slot. Currently, this sample is delayed for 1 ms by the buffer and we are allowed to delay the sample for a further 4 ms in order to keep the multiplexing delay at 5 ms. At this point, the force sample is combined with the video data and transmitted as a joint packet extending over 4 transmission slots. With this, the remaining 4 ms delay for the force sample is introduced by the transmission delay of the joint packet. *Case iv:* The most critical case happens if the haptic encoder marks consecutive samples for transmission. The multiplexer generates separate packets including both video and force data and sends them at every clock tick. With this strategy, the transmission delay for the adjacent force updates is kept at 1 ms so that they don't block each other on the channel.

Algorithm 1. Multiplexer Thread

---

if $Slots == 0$ **then**

  $Slots = CheckAvailableSlots(ForceBuffer);$

  if $Force.Transmit == 1\ \&\&\ VideoBytes > 0$ **then**

    $Slots = MergeAndSend(Force, Video, Slots);$

  end if

  if $Force.Transmit == 1\ \&\&\ VideoBytes == 0\ \&\&\ Slots == 1$ **then**

    $Slots = SendForce(Force, Slots);$ // A critical force update

  end if

  if $Force.Transmit == 1\ \&\&\ VideoBytes == 0\ \&\&\ Slots > 1$ **then**

    $Slots = 0$ // wait one more clock cycle

  end if

  if $Force.Transmit == 0\ \&\&\ VideoBytes > 0$ **then**

    $Slots = SendVideo(Video, Slots);$

  end if

  if $Force.Transmit == 0\ \&\&\ VideoBytes == 0$ **then**

    $Slots = 0;$ // Reset and check queued streams

  end if

else

  if $Slots > 0$ **then**

    $Slots - -;$ // Wait for the packet transmission to finish

  end if

end if

2.1 Demultiplexing

When the demultiplexer receives a packet, firstly it parses the header which is the first byte of the received packet (Table 1). The header has the structure shown in Fig. 3. The first 3 bits marked with *"M"* represent the packet type. With 3 bits, 8 different packet types can be signalled which is sufficient for the current multiplexing scheme sending 3 different packet types. The remaining 5 cases are reserved for additional modalities. Currently, bits 3, 4, 5 and 6 tagged as *"N"* are reserved for future use. If the packet type includes video data, bit 7 tagged as *"L"* is used to signal the video frame completion which means the last fragment of the frame is received and it is ready to be decoded and displayed. Until the arrival of the last video fragment, the demultiplexer buffers the received fragments according to their frame and fragment numbers which are sent along with the packet header.

In Table 1, the overall packet structures for each packet type is explained. The demultiplexer is aware of this structure and parses the packets accordingly. When the demultiplexer receives a packet containing a force sample, it calculates

Table 1. Packet structures in the application layer

Packet type	Packet structure	Size (bytes)
F	$H(1) - TS(4) - FPL(6)$	11
V	$H(1) - FN(2) - FGN(2) - VPLL(2) - VPL(Y)$	$7+Y$
VF	$H(1) - TS(4) - FPL(6) - FN(2) - FGN(2) - VPLL(2) - VPL(Y)$	$17+Y$

H: multiplexing header, **TS:** timestamp, **FPL:** force payload,
FN: frame number, **FGN:** fragment number,
VPLL: video payload length, **VPL:** video payload, **Y:** video payload size

the current delay on the force sample. The delay can be lower than the target value set by the multiplexing buffer when video data doesn't fill in the available resources completely. In this case, the display of the force sample is delayed until the planned playout time comes. The force payload is a fixed size of 6 bytes which contains a 3 DoF force sample (2 bytes per sample). When the demultiplexer receives a video packet, it buffers the video data based on the side information containing its frame and fragment numbers. Since the video data sizes are variable based on the multiplexing algorithm, a video payload length information is needed to read the video data from the packet structure. When the demultiplexer receives a joint video-force packet, firstly it parses the force data and passes it to the force display to be displayed at the planned deadline. Similar to video-only packets, the video information is parsed afterwards. If the packets contain video information and the end of frame flag in the multiplexing header is set, the demultiplexer passes the buffered video frame to the decoder and display queue.

2.2 Experimental Setup and Results

To evaluate the system, a teleoperation setup is built using a KUKA Light Weight Robot arm, JR3 force/torque sensor and Force Dimension Omega 6 haptic device. The multiplexer (TOP side) and demultiplexer (OP side) are separated by a network emulator hardware which can impose precise channel capacity limitation [7]. A real-time linux PC is used to synchronize the clocks of test-PCs in order to measure signal latencies accurately. The video (640 × 480, 30 fps) is encoded by a GPU accelerated H.264 encoder [8] and the encoder parameters are set to constant bitrate mode at 440 kbps. The GOP structure

Fig. 3. Multiplexing header structure

is (IPPP..I) with an I frame period of 50. In order to keep the visual delay
as small as possible, B frames are not used. The average force stream rate is
around 3 kbps. The channel rate is set to 528 kbps which is the expected required
transmission rate for video and force transmission and it is calculated as the
size of the video rate plus 20 percent (based on interactive video requirements
specified in [9]). The force sample buffer size has an inverse relation with packet
rate and bandwidth usage. The smaller the buffer size the higher the packet
rate. For small buffer sizes, the multiplexer can not combine big packets which
leads to more overhead. The system is tested with increasing buffer sizes from
5 ms to 25 ms. The results show that for buffer sizes larger than 15 ms, significant
packet rate reduction cannot be observed. According to this observation, a buffer
of 15 ms was chosen for our experiments. The task is a peg-in-hole task where
the user moves stiff wooden toys with a single point contact tool to fill in the
correct holes. The proposed multiplexing scheme is compared with a first come
first serve (FCFS) strategy which is the case when no multiplexing scheme is
applied and the modalities are served according to their order of arrival.

In Table 2, the delay-jitter and average packet rate performances are given.
The proposed approach can guarantee constant and controllable delay on the
force signal by trading off a tolerable video quality degradation. Under real
conditions, a 2 ms buffer is needed at the demultiplexer side to compensate the
intrinsic jitter caused by the network devices. Consequently, this buffer delay is
added to the 15 ms multiplexing buffer delay. When we compare the packet rates,
the merging scheme reduces the overall packet rate of the system and almost all
of the force packets are transmitted together with the video information.

Table 2. The delay-jitter in ms and average packet rates with respect to packet types
and overall packet rate of the system, (PR: packet rate)

Mode	Video (ms)		Force (ms)		Packet Rates (packets/sec)			
	Delay	Jitter	Delay	Jitter	Force PR	Video PR	Joint PR	Total PR
MUX	65.07	50.23	**17**	**0**	0.33	55.72	38.36	**94.41**
FCFS	55.21	32.58	44.11	36.07	47	59.21	0	106.21

3   Conclusion and Future Work

In this paper, we propose a novel visual-haptic multiplexing scheme for teleoperation over CBR channels. With the help of the proposed algorithm, the delay-
jitter on the force signal can be controlled and a guaranteed constant delay can
be achieved. A demo video of the system can be accessed at[1]. In future work, we
will investigate the effects of visual-haptic asynchrony on the task completion

---

[1] Video illustrating the proposed visual-haptic multiplexing scheme for teleoperation
over CBR links, http://youtu.be/aMJVsAPy708, 2014.

and improve the system based on user experiences. Implementation of the time delay compensation architecture in [2] will be an essential extension to perform user experience and task performance experiments in the presence of time delay. Currently, the multiplexer is not resilient to packet losses. In order to reach an error resilient haptic interaction, we will use the error resilient version of the perceptual coder in [10]. Additionally, we observed that the rate assignment of the real-time video encoder [8] is not constant over frames which yields higher jitter (see Table 2) and demands more transmission capacity. However, this problem did not interrupt the motion of the operator because the movements are not fast in a peg-in-hole task. For fast interaction scenarios which can not tolerate visual jitter, we will implement a real-time H.264 encoder with a better rate control scheme.

Acknowledgment. The first author gratefully acknowledges the support of the TUM Graduate School's Faculty Graduate Center (Electrical Engineering and Information Technology) at the TU München.

References

1. Steinbach, E., Hirche, S., Kammerl, J., Vittorias, I., Chaudhari, R.: Haptic data compression and communication for telepresence and teleaction. IEEE Signal Process. Mag. **28**(1), 87–96 (2011)
2. Ryu, J.-H., Artigas, J., Preusche, C.: A passive bilateral control scheme for a teleoperator with time-varying communication delay. Mechatronics **20**(7), 812–823 (2010)
3. Paredes Farrera, M., Fleury, M., Ghanbari, M.: Accurate packet-by-packet measurement and analysis of video streams across an internet tight link. Signal Process. Image Commun. **22**, 69–85 (2007). (Elsevier Science Inc.)
4. Cha, J., Seo, Y., Kim, Y., Ryu, J.: An authoring/editing framework for haptic broadcasting: passive haptic interactions using mpeg-4 bifs. In: Proceedings of the 2nd Joint EuroHaptics Conference and Symposium, pp. 274–279 (2007)
5. Eid, M.A., Cha, J., El-Saddik, A.: Admux: an adaptive multiplexer for haptic-audio-visual data communication. IEEE Trans. Instrum. Measur. **60**(1), 21–31 (2011)
6. Hinterseer, P., Hirche, S., Chaudhuri, S., Steinbach, E., Buss, M.: Perception-based data reduction and transmission of haptic data in telepresence and teleaction systems. IEEE Trans. Signal Proc. **56**, 588–597 (2008)
7. Apposite-Technologies, Netropy n60 network emulation hardware. http://www.apposite-tech.com/products/netropy-N60.html
8. NVIDIA-CUDA-DEVELOPER-ZONE, Nvidia cuda video encode/decode c api (2010). http://developer.nvidia.com/cuda-cc-sdk-code-samples
9. Szigeti, T., Hattingh, C.: End-to-End QoS Network Design: Quality of Service in LANs, WANs, and VPNs (Networking Technology). Cisco Press (2004)
10. Brandi, F., Kammerl, J., Steinbach, E.: Error-resilient perceptual coding for networked haptic interaction. In: Proceedings of ACM Multimedia (Full Paper), (Firenze, Italy), October 2010

Low-Cost 5-DOF Haptic Stylus Interaction Using Two Phantom Omni Devices

Mats Isaksson[1], Ben Horan[2(✉)], and Saeid Nahavandi[1]

[1] Centre for Intelligent Systems Research, Deakin University,
75 Pigdons Road, Waurn Ponds, VIC 3216, Australia
[2] School of Engineering, Deakin University,
75 Pigdons Road, Waurn Ponds, VIC 3216, Australia
{mats.isaksson,ben.horan,saeid.nahavandi}@deakin.edu.au

Abstract. This paper introduces a haptic interface providing 5-DOF stylus interaction for applications requiring 3-DOF force and 2-DOF torque feedback. The interface employs two coupled Phantom Omni devices each offering 3-DOF force feedback and 6-DOF position sensing. The interface uses an inexpensive lightweight coupling and no additional actuators enabling the interface to maintain low inertia and stylus interaction, both similar to the original Phantom Omni device. The interface also maintains unconstrained rotation about the stylus' longitudinal axis aiding in handheld manipulation. Kinematic analysis of the 5-DOF interface is presented and the usable workspace of the device is demonstrated.

Keywords: 5-DOF haptic interaction · Phantom Omni · 5-DOF stylus

1 Introduction

Haptic interaction occurs bilaterally with the human user through their haptic sensory modality and offers potential benefits to a wide range of applications. The ability to utilise haptic interaction depends on the availability of suitable haptic devices or interfaces. There are various commercially available haptic devices each offering different characteristics including cost, workspace, DOFs (Degrees of Freedom), force range and inertia. Haptic device design is an area of increasing research interest and a variety of prototype research devices have been proposed.

Two popular lower end commercial haptic devices are the Novint Falcon and the Phantom Omni. The Novint Falcon utilises a parallel kinematic structure similar to the delta robot and provides 3-DOF force feedback. The device is low cost and offers a relatively high force output (>8.9N) as applied to a handle of fixed orientation. The Phantom Omni is the base model of the Phantom range of haptic devices and utilises a serial kinematic structure to provide 3-DOF force feedback as well 6-DOF positional measurement.

While both devices provide a single HIP (Haptic Interaction Point), the Phantom Omni utilises a stylus which is held by the user to interact with the

© Springer-Verlag Berlin Heidelberg 2014
M. Auvray and C. Duriez (Eds.): EuroHaptics 2014, Part II, LNCS 8619, pp. 139–149, 2014.
DOI: 10.1007/978-3-662-44196-1_18

device. The stylus aids in probing type interaction using the single HIP, however is passive about the 3-DOF of the device's spherical wrist and not designed to provide torque feedback to the user's hand. Stylus-type interaction offers an effective method to interact with the haptic device and is commonly employed in research prototype and commercial devices [1].

Applications of haptic interaction are diverse and include surgical training, robotic assisted surgery, teleoperation, rehabilitation and entertainment. In applications where force and torque feedback are required, commercially available 6-DOF devices such as the Phantom Premium and Haption Virtuose can be utilised. These devices however, remain relatively expensive and may be cost prohibitive for certain applications. In applications requiring force and torque feedback it is sometimes possible to achieve adequate haptic interaction through 3-DOF force and 2-DOF torque feedback. Such applications may include tool tasks where torque feedback about the tool's drilling axis is not required such as in the works by Boschetti et al. (surgical screw insertion) [2] and Zhu et al. (machining) [3].

One approach to achieving additional DOFs is to combine multiple haptic devices [1, 4–9]. In the recent work by Shah et al. a novel inexpensive 5-DOF haptic device was achieved using two 3-DOF Novint Falcons [10]. In order to interact with the device the user can hold a rod connected at each end by a ball joint. To address limited angular movement the rod can be reconfigured to be either vertical or horizontal when the device is in the home position.

To interact with a standard Phantom Omni device, the user grasps the stylus which is attached by one end to the unactuated spherical wrist which represents the device's HIP. This arrangement is beneficial in allowing the user to face the device front on and to grasp the stylus with different configurations. The approach presented in this paper focuses on the addition of 2-DOF torque feedback while maintaining similar user interaction with the Phantom Omni's stylus. This includes the ability to measure and provide unconstrained rotation about the stylus' longitudinal axis. It is suggested that by achieving similar stylus interaction, the 5-DOF interface can replace standard Phantom Omni devices in applications where torque feedback is required.

The approach employs two Phantom Omni devices and an inexpensive rigid coupling which exploits the existing passive DOF in the devices' spherical wrists. This enables the 5-DOF interface to be easily reproduced by other researchers. The forward and inverse kinematics of the 5-DOF haptic interface are derived. Workspace analysis and simulations are presented demonstrating the usable workspace of the interface. The following section introduces the haptic interface providing 5-DOF stylus interaction.

2   The 5-DOF Interface

The 5-DOF interface is achieved by coupling two Phantom Omni haptic devices which each offer 3-DOF force feedback and 6-DOF position sensing, as shown in Fig. 1. The interface uses an inexpensive lightweight coupling and no additional

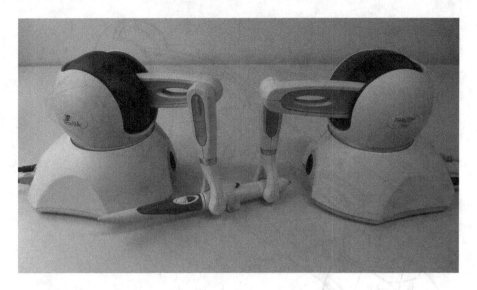

Fig. 1. The 5-DOF haptic interface.

actuators enabling the interface to maintain desirable characteristics similar to the original Phantom Omni device. These include low friction, low backlash, low inertia and good backdrivability which are important to a haptic interface [11]. Using a simple and inexpensive coupling also makes it straightforward for researchers to reproduce the 5-DOF interface for their research.

The following section derives expressions for the inverse and forward kinematics of the 5-DOF interface. The inverse kinematics is used to plot the workspace of the device while the expressions for the forward kinematics can be differentiated to give the Jacobian matrix, necessary to convert ordered force and torque in task space to torques for the three joints in each participating device.

3   Kinematics

3.1   Kinematics for the Two Devices

The coordinate systems, vectors, lengths and parameters necessary to describe the kinematics of each device are shown in Fig. 2.

The base coordinate systems of the two Phantom Omni devices are $\mathbf{F}_{0a}$ and $\mathbf{F}_{0b}$. The angles θ_{1a}, θ_{2a}, θ_{3a} and θ_{1b}, θ_{2b}, θ_{3b} represent rotation of the actuated joints in the coordinate systems $\mathbf{F}_{0a}$, $\mathbf{F}_{1a}$, $\mathbf{F}_{2a}$ and $\mathbf{F}_{0b}$, $\mathbf{F}_{1b}$, $\mathbf{F}_{2b}$ respectively. Each rotation is around the corresponding positive z-axis measured from the positive x-axis. Each Phantom Omni has a passive 3-DOF spherical wrist, however to aid in readability the corresponding wrist angles θ_{4a}, θ_{5a}, θ_{6a} and θ_{4b}, θ_{5b}, θ_{6b} are not included in Fig. 2. The wrist angles are not actuated and their working ranges limit the working range of the 5-DOF interface. The origin of coordinate system $\mathbf{F}_{6a}$ represents the HIP of the 5-DOF interface and is specified

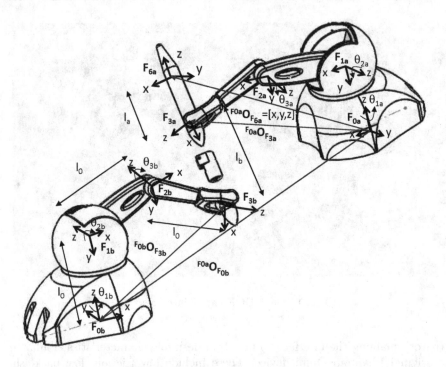

Fig. 2. The 5-DOF interface is established by connecting two Phantom Omni devices. The parameters and coordinate systems necessary to describe the kinematics are included

at an appropriate location on the stylus as depicted by Fig. 2. The coordinate system $\mathbf{F}_{6b}$ has the same origin as $\mathbf{F}_{3a}$ but is not shown in Fig. 2.

The origin of $\mathbf{F}_{3a}$ relative to $\mathbf{F}_{0a}$ is given by the position vector $^{F_{0a}}\mathbf{O}_{\mathbf{F}_{3a}}$ and the origin of $\mathbf{F}_{3b}$ in $\mathbf{F}_{0b}$ is given by $^{F_{0b}}\mathbf{O}_{\mathbf{F}_{3b}}$. The vector $^{F_{0a}}\mathbf{O}_{\mathbf{F}_{3a}}$ is a function of $(\theta_{1a}, \theta_{2a}, \theta_{3a})$ while the vector $^{F_{0b}}\mathbf{O}_{\mathbf{F}_{3b}}$ is a function of $(\theta_{1b}, \theta_{2b}, \theta_{3b})$. The origin of $\mathbf{F}_{6a}$ relative to $\mathbf{F}_{3a}$ is given by the position vector $^{F_{3a}}\mathbf{O}_{\mathbf{F}_{6a}}$ and the origin of $\mathbf{F}_{6b}$ in $\mathbf{F}_{3b}$ is given by $^{F_{3b}}\mathbf{O}_{\mathbf{F}_{6b}}$. The vector $^{F_{3a}}\mathbf{O}_{\mathbf{F}_{6a}}$ is a function of $(\theta_{4a}, \theta_{5a})$ while the vector $^{F_{3b}}\mathbf{O}_{\mathbf{F}_{6b}}$ is a function of $(\theta_{4b}, \theta_{5b})$. The forward kinematics of the individual Phantom Omni devices are given by

$$^{F_{0a}}\mathbf{O}_{\mathbf{F}_{3a}} = [o_{0a3ax}, o_{0a3ay}, o_{0a3az}]^{\mathrm{T}}, \tag{1}$$

$$^{F_{0b}}\mathbf{O}_{\mathbf{F}_{3b}} = [o_{0b3bx}, o_{0b3by}, o_{0b3bz}]^{\mathrm{T}}, \tag{2}$$

$$^{F_{3a}}\mathbf{O}_{\mathbf{F}_{6a}} = [o_{3a6ax}, o_{3a6ay}, o_{3a6az}]^{\mathrm{T}}, \tag{3}$$

$$^{F_{3b}}\mathbf{O}_{\mathbf{F}_{6b}} = [o_{3b6bx}, o_{3b6by}, o_{3b6bz}]^{\mathrm{T}}, \tag{4}$$

where

$$l_0 = 0.13335 \text{ m},$$
$$l_a = 0.065 \text{ m},$$
$$l_b = 0.073 \text{ m},$$
$$o_{0a3ax} = l_0 \cos(\theta_{1a})(\cos(\theta_{2a}) + \cos(\theta_{2a} + \theta_{3a})),$$
$$o_{0a3ay} = l_0 \sin(\theta_{1a})(\cos(\theta_{2a}) + \cos(\theta_{2a} + \theta_{3a})),$$
$$o_{0a3az} = l_0(1 - \sin(\theta_{2a}) - \sin(\theta_{2a} + \theta_{3a})), \tag{5}$$
$$o_{3a6ax} = l_a \cos(\theta_{4a}) \sin(\theta_{5a}),$$
$$o_{3a6ay} = l_a \sin(\theta_{4a}) \sin(\theta_{5a}),$$
$$o_{3a6az} = l_a \cos(\theta_{5a}).$$

The expressions for o_{0b3bx}, o_{0b3by}, o_{0b3bz}, o_{3b6bx}, o_{3b6by} and o_{3b6bz} are the same as in (5) where all θ_{ia} are replaced with θ_{ib} and l_a with l_b.

The orientation of the coordinate system $\mathbf{F}_{3a}$ in $\mathbf{F}_{0a}$ is given by a 3×3 rotation matrix $^{\mathbf{F}_{0a}}\mathbf{R}_{\mathbf{F}_{3a}}(\theta_{1a}, \theta_{2a}, \theta_{3a})$ while the rotation matrix for $\mathbf{F}_{3b}$ in $\mathbf{F}_{0b}$ is $^{\mathbf{F}_{0b}}\mathbf{R}_{\mathbf{F}_{3b}}(\theta_{1b}, \theta_{2b}, \theta_{3b})$. The orientation of the coordinate system $\mathbf{F}_{6a}$ in $\mathbf{F}_{3a}$ is given by a 3×3 rotation matrix $^{\mathbf{F}_{3a}}\mathbf{R}_{\mathbf{F}_{6a}}(\theta_{4a}, \theta_{5a}, \theta_{6a})$ while the rotation matrix for $\mathbf{F}_{6b}$ in $\mathbf{F}_{3b}$ is $^{\mathbf{F}_{3b}}\mathbf{R}_{\mathbf{F}_{6b}}(\theta_{4b}, \theta_{5b}, \theta_{6b})$. $^{\mathbf{F}_{3a}}\mathbf{R}_{\mathbf{F}_{6a}}$ and $^{\mathbf{F}_{3b}}\mathbf{R}_{\mathbf{F}_{6b}}$ are not used in the transforms between the actuated joints and the HIP of the 5-DOF interface but are necessary to calculate the angles of the passive wrist joints to verify if a configuration of the 5-DOF interface is possible due to collisions or joint limitations.

The expressions for the rotation matrices $^{\mathbf{F}_{0a}}\mathbf{R}_{\mathbf{F}_{3a}}$ and $^{\mathbf{F}_{3a}}\mathbf{R}_{\mathbf{F}_{6a}}$ are

$$^{\mathbf{F}_{0a}}\mathbf{R}_{\mathbf{F}_{3a}} = \begin{pmatrix} -c_1c_2s_3 - c_1s_2c_3 & -s_1 & c_1c_2c_3 - c_1s_2s_3 \\ -s_1c_2s_3 - s_1s_2c_3 & c_1 & s_1c_2c_3 - s_1s_2s_3 \\ s_2s_3 - c_2c_3 & 0 & -c_2s_3 - s_2c_3 \end{pmatrix}, \tag{6}$$

$$^{\mathbf{F}_{3a}}\mathbf{R}_{\mathbf{F}_{6a}} = \begin{pmatrix} c_4c_5c_6 - s_4s_6 & -c_4c_5s_6 - s_4c_6 & c_4s_5 \\ s_4c_5c_6 + c_4s_6 & -s_4c_5s_6 + c_4c_6 & s_4s_5 \\ -s_5c_6 & s_5s_6 & c_5 \end{pmatrix}, \tag{7}$$

where the short form $s_i = \sin(\theta_{ia})$ and $c_i = \cos(\theta_{ia})$ have been used to preserve space. The expressions for $^{\mathbf{F}_{0b}}\mathbf{R}_{\mathbf{F}_{3b}}$ and $^{\mathbf{F}_{3b}}\mathbf{R}_{\mathbf{F}_{6b}}$ are the same as in (6) and (7) where all θ_{ia} are replaced with θ_{ib}. The inverse kinematics of the Phantom Omni devices are determined using basic trigonometry in Fig. 2.

$$\theta_{1a} = \arctan2(o_{0a3ay}, o_{0a3ax}),$$
$$\theta_{2a} = \arctan2\left(l_0 - o_{0a3az}, \sqrt{o_{0a3ax}^2 + o_{0a3ay}^2}\right)$$
$$- \arccos\left(\frac{\sqrt{o_{0a3ax}^2 + o_{0a3ay}^2 + o_{0a3az}^2 - 2l_0o_{0a3az} + l_0^2}}{2l_0}\right), \tag{8}$$

$$\theta_{3a} = \arccos\left(\frac{o_{0a3ax}^2 + o_{0a3ay}^2 + o_{0a3az}^2 - 2l_0 o_{0a3az} - l_0^2}{2l_0^2}\right).$$

The expressions for θ_{1b}, θ_{2b}, θ_{3b} are the same as in (8) where o_{0a3ax}, o_{0a3ay}, o_{0a3az} are replaced with o_{0b3bx}, o_{0b3by}, o_{0b3bz}.

3.2   Base Coordinate System of the 5-DOF Interface

The coordinate system $\mathbf{F}_{0a}$ is chosen as the base coordinate system for the 5-DOF interface. The origin of the coordinate system $\mathbf{F}_{0b}$ relative to $\mathbf{F}_{0a}$ is given by position vector $^{F_{0a}}\mathbf{O}_{\mathbf{F}_{0b}}$. The orientation of $\mathbf{F}_{0b}$ relative to $\mathbf{F}_{0a}$ is given by XYZ Euler rotations $r_{0a0b\phi}$, $r_{0a0b\theta}$ and $r_{0a0b\psi}$. Using these definitions the origin of $\mathbf{F}_{3b}$ can be represented in $\mathbf{F}_{0a}$ according to

$$^{F_{0a}}\mathbf{O}_{\mathbf{F}_{3b}} = [o_{0a3bx}, o_{0a3by}, o_{0a3bz}]^T = {}^{F_{0a}}\mathbf{O}_{\mathbf{F}_{0b}} + {}^{F_{0a}}\mathbf{R}_{\mathbf{F}_{0b}}{}^{F_{0b}}\mathbf{O}_{\mathbf{F}_{3b}}, \qquad (9)$$

where

$$^{F_{0a}}\mathbf{O}_{\mathbf{F}_{0b}} = [o_{0a0bx}, o_{0a0by}, o_{0a0bz}]^T,$$
$$^{F_{0a}}\mathbf{R}_{\mathbf{F}_{0b}} = \mathbf{R}_x(r_{0a0b\phi})\mathbf{R}_y(r_{0a0b\theta})\mathbf{R}_z(r_{0a0b\psi}). \qquad (10)$$

The matrices $\mathbf{R}_i$ are Euler rotation matrices.

3.3   Coordinate System for the HIP of the 5-DOF Interface

The coordinate system $\mathbf{F}_{6a}$ for the HIP of the 5-DOF interface is specified at an appropriate location to apply forces and torques to the user's hand while grasping the stylus. The z-axis of this coordinate system represents the direction between the origins of the coordinate systems $\mathbf{F}_{3a}$ and $\mathbf{F}_{3b}$. Rotation of the stylus around this axis is not an active DOF but is subject to the joint limitations of the original Phantom Omni device.

The origins of coordinate systems $\mathbf{F}_{3a}$ and $\mathbf{F}_{3b}$ expressed in $\mathbf{F}_{6a}$ are given by

$$^{F_{6a}}\mathbf{O}_{\mathbf{F}_{3a}} = [0, 0, -l_a]^T, \qquad (11)$$
$$^{F_{6a}}\mathbf{O}_{\mathbf{F}_{3b}} = [0, 0, -(l_a + l_b)]^T. \qquad (12)$$

The origin of the coordinate system $\mathbf{F}_{6a}$ in the base coordinate system $\mathbf{F}_{0a}$ is given by three translations x, y, z. The orientation of $\mathbf{F}_{6a}$ relative to $\mathbf{F}_{0a}$ is given by XYZ Euler rotations ϕ, θ and ψ. The origins of the coordinate systems $\mathbf{F}_{3a}$ and $\mathbf{F}_{3b}$ are expressed in $\mathbf{F}_{0a}$ as

$$^{F_{0a}}\mathbf{O}_{\mathbf{F}_{3a}} = {}^{F_{0a}}\mathbf{O}_{\mathbf{F}_{6a}} + {}^{F_{0a}}\mathbf{R}_{\mathbf{F}_{6a}}{}^{F_{6a}}\mathbf{O}_{\mathbf{F}_{3a}}, \qquad (13)$$
$$^{F_{0a}}\mathbf{O}_{\mathbf{F}_{3b}} = {}^{F_{0a}}\mathbf{O}_{\mathbf{F}_{6a}} + {}^{F_{0a}}\mathbf{R}_{\mathbf{F}_{6a}}{}^{F_{6a}}\mathbf{O}_{\mathbf{F}_{3b}}, \qquad (14)$$

where

$$\mathbf{^{F_{0a}}O_{F_{6a}}} = [x, y, z]^{\mathrm{T}},$$
$$\mathbf{^{F_{0a}}R_{F_{6a}}} = \mathbf{R_x}(\phi)\mathbf{R_y}(\theta)\mathbf{R_z}(\psi). \tag{15}$$

Expanding (13) and (14) gives

$$\mathbf{^{F_{0a}}O_{F_{3a}}} = [x - l_a s_\theta, y + l_a c_\theta s_\phi, z - l_a c_\phi c_\theta]^{\mathrm{T}}, \tag{16}$$
$$\mathbf{^{F_{0a}}O_{F_{3b}}} = [x - (l_a + l_b)s_\theta, y + (l_a + l_b)c_\theta s_\phi, z - (l_a + l_b)c_\phi c_\theta]^{\mathrm{T}}, \tag{17}$$

where $c_\phi = \cos(\phi)$, $c_\theta = \cos(\theta)$, $s_\phi = \sin(\phi)$ and $s_\theta = \sin(\theta)$. As expected the expressions (16) and (17) are not dependent on the rotation ψ which does not need to be considered.

3.4   Inverse Kinematics

The centres of both spherical wrists relative to the base coordinate system of the 5-DOF interface ($\mathbf{^{F_{0a}}O_{F_{3a}}}$ and $\mathbf{^{F_{0a}}O_{F_{3b}}}$) are determined from (16) and (17) using known x, y, z, ϕ and θ. The expression $\mathbf{^{F_{0a}}O_{F_{3b}}}$ is transformed to the base coordinate system of that device ($\mathbf{F_{0b}}$) by rewriting (9) as

$$\mathbf{^{F_{0b}}O_{F_{3b}}} = [o_{0b3bx}, o_{0b3by}, o_{0b3bz}]^{\mathrm{T}} = \mathbf{^{F_{0a}}R^T_{F_{0b}}}(\mathbf{^{F_{0a}}O_{F_{3b}}} - \mathbf{^{F_{0a}}O_{F_{0b}}}). \tag{18}$$

By evaluating the expressions (16) and (18) and inserting them in (8) all actuated joint angles can be determined.

3.5   Forward Kinematics

The forward kinematics are solved by setting the two different expressions (1) and (16) for $\mathbf{^{F_{0a}}O_{F_{3a}}}$ and the two different expressions (9) and (17) for $\mathbf{^{F_{0a}}O_{F_{3b}}}$ to be equal which gives

$$\begin{aligned}
x - l_a \sin(\theta) &= o_{0a3ax}, \\
y + l_a \cos(\theta) \sin(\phi) &= o_{0a3ay}, \\
z - l_a \cos(\theta) \cos(\phi) &= o_{0a3az}, \\
x - (l_a + l_b) \sin(\theta) &= o_{0a3bx}, \\
y + (l_a + l_b) \cos(\theta) \sin(\phi) &= o_{0a3by}, \\
z - (l_a + l_b) \cos(\theta) \cos(\phi) &= o_{0a3bz}.
\end{aligned} \tag{19}$$

The right side of (19) is determined from known joint angles using (5) and (9). The solution to (19) is

$$x = \frac{(l_a + l_b)o_{0a3ax} - l_a o_{0a3bx}}{l_b},$$

$$y = \frac{(l_a + l_b)o_{0a3ay} - l_a o_{0a3by}}{l_b},$$

$$z = \frac{(l_a + l_b)o_{0a3az} - l_a o_{0a3bz}}{l_b},\tag{20}$$

$$\phi = \arctan2\left(o_{0a3by} - y, z - o_{0a3bz}\right),$$

$$\theta = \arcsin\left(\frac{o_{0a3ax} - o_{0a3bx}}{l_b}\right).$$

3.6 Joint Limitations

The limits of the actuated joint angles θ_{1a}, θ_{2a} and θ_{3a} are

$$-56 \text{ deg.} < \theta_{1a} < 56\text{deg.},$$

$$-103 \text{ deg.} < \theta_{2a} < 0 \text{ deg.},\tag{21}$$

$$\begin{cases} (-25 - \theta_{2a}) \text{ deg.} < \theta_{3a} < 139 \text{ deg.} &: \theta_{2a} \leq -45 \text{ deg.},\\ 20 \text{ deg.} < \theta_{3a} < 139 \text{ deg.} &: \theta_{2a} \geq -45 \text{ deg.} \end{cases}$$

The limits for all actuated joint angles θ_{ib} are the same as for the corresponding angles θ_{ia}. These joint limitations have been estimated using the devices' built-in encoders. The wrist angles θ_{4a}, θ_{4b}, θ_{5a} and θ_{5b} are determined by first calculating the vectors $^{F_{3a}}\mathbf{O}_{\mathbf{F}_{6a}}$ and $^{F_{3b}}\mathbf{O}_{\mathbf{F}_{6b}}$ according to

$$^{F_{3a}}\mathbf{O}_{\mathbf{F}_{6a}} = {}^{F_{0a}}\mathbf{R}_{\mathbf{F}_{3a}}^{\mathrm{T}}\left({}^{F_{0a}}\mathbf{O}_{\mathbf{F}_{6a}} - {}^{F_{0a}}\mathbf{O}_{\mathbf{F}_{3a}}\right),\tag{22}$$

$$^{F_{3b}}\mathbf{O}_{\mathbf{F}_{6b}} = {}^{F_{0b}}\mathbf{R}_{\mathbf{F}_{3b}}^{\mathrm{T}}\left({}^{F_{0b}}\mathbf{O}_{\mathbf{F}_{6b}} - {}^{F_{0b}}\mathbf{O}_{\mathbf{F}_{3b}}\right).$$

Utilising the expressions (5) the joint angles are determined from the elements of $^{F_{3a}}\mathbf{O}_{\mathbf{F}_{6a}}$ and $^{F_{3b}}\mathbf{O}_{\mathbf{F}_{6b}}$ according to

$$\theta_{4a} = \arctan2\left(o_{3a6ay}, o_{3a6ax}\right) + 180 \text{ deg.},$$

$$\theta_{4b} = \arctan2\left(o_{3b6by}, o_{3b6bx}\right) - 180 \text{ deg.},$$

$$\theta_{5a} = -\arccos\left(\frac{o_{3a6az}}{l_a}\right),\tag{23}$$

$$\theta_{5b} = -\arccos\left(\frac{o_{3b6bz}}{l_b}\right).$$

The corresponding joint limits are

$$-143 \text{ deg.} < \theta_{4a} < 143 \text{ deg.},$$

$$-143 \text{ deg.} < \theta_{4b} < 143 \text{ deg.},$$

$$-148 \text{ deg.} < \theta_{5a} < -41 \text{ deg.},\tag{24}$$

$$-135 \text{ deg.} < \theta_{5b} < -14 \text{ deg.}$$

The limits of the fifth joint for an unconnected haptic device are -148 deg. $< \theta_{5a}, \theta_{5b} < -14$ deg., however, due to the configuration of the coupling, the limits become slightly different as in (24).

When the devices are connected the rotation θ_{6a} is only controlled by the user, as is the case for an independent device, and does not normally limit the workspace. The rotation θ_{6b} however is dependent on the position and orientation of the stylus and the working range of this joint restricts the workspace of the 5-DOF interface.

Given the configuration of the coupling, the rotations θ_{6a} and θ_{6b} are about a common z-axis. The configuration of the coupling also means that it remains fixed with respect to coordinate system $\mathbf{F}_{5a}$ but rotates by θ_{6b} with respect to $\mathbf{F}_{5b}$, and when $\theta_{6b} = 0$ the y-axes of $\mathbf{F}_{5a}$ and $\mathbf{F}_{5b}$ are aligned. As such, θ_{6b} can be determined by the angular difference between the y-axes of $\mathbf{F}_{5a}$ and $\mathbf{F}_{5b}$ about the common z-axis:

$$\theta_{6b} = \arccos\left({}^{\mathbf{F}_{0a}}\mathbf{y}_{\mathbf{F}_{5a}} \cdot {}^{\mathbf{F}_{0a}}\mathbf{y}_{\mathbf{F}_{5b}}\right), \tag{25}$$

where $\cdot$ denotes the vector dot product and ${}^{\mathbf{F}_{0a}}\mathbf{y}_{\mathbf{F}_{5a}}$ and ${}^{\mathbf{F}_{0a}}\mathbf{y}_{\mathbf{F}_{5b}}$ are the y-axes of the coordinate systems $\mathbf{F}_{5a}$ and $\mathbf{F}_{5b}$ expressed in $\mathbf{F}_{0a}$. ${}^{\mathbf{F}_{0a}}\mathbf{y}_{\mathbf{F}_{5a}}$ is identical to the second column vector in ${}^{\mathbf{F}_{0a}}\mathbf{R}_{\mathbf{F}_{6a}}$ when $\theta_{6a} = 0$ and similar for ${}^{\mathbf{F}_{0a}}\mathbf{y}_{\mathbf{F}_{5b}}$. The necessary rotation matrices are calculated according to

$$\begin{aligned}{}^{\mathbf{F}_{0a}}\mathbf{R}_{\mathbf{F}_{6a}} &= {}^{\mathbf{F}_{0a}}\mathbf{R}_{\mathbf{F}_{3a}}{}^{\mathbf{F}_{3a}}\mathbf{R}_{\mathbf{F}_{6a}}, \\ {}^{\mathbf{F}_{0a}}\mathbf{R}_{\mathbf{F}_{6b}} &= {}^{\mathbf{F}_{0a}}\mathbf{R}_{\mathbf{F}_{0b}}{}^{\mathbf{F}_{0b}}\mathbf{R}_{\mathbf{F}_{3b}}{}^{\mathbf{F}_{3b}}\mathbf{R}_{\mathbf{F}_{6b}}. \end{aligned} \tag{26}$$

The corresponding joint limit is

$$\theta_{6b} < 146 \text{ deg}. \tag{27}$$

4   Simulations and Workspace Analysis

In this section the derived inverse kinematics is used to plot the positional and rotational workspace of the 5-DOF interface. Simplified drawings are also presented to illustrate configurations at the edge of the reachable workspace. For the simulations the Phantom Omni devices are facing each other with a distance of 0.33 m between the origins of their base coordinate systems:

$$\begin{aligned}{}^{\mathbf{F}_{0a}}\mathbf{O}_{\mathbf{F}_{0b}} &= [o_{0a0bx}, o_{0a0by}, o_{0a0bz}]^{\mathrm{T}} = [0.33 \text{ m}, 0 \text{ m}, 0 \text{ m}]^{\mathrm{T}}, \tag{28} \\ r_{0a0b\phi} &= 0 \text{ deg}., r_{0a0b\theta} = 0 \text{ deg}., r_{0a0b\psi} = 180 \text{ deg}. \tag{29}\end{aligned}$$

Figure 3(a) illustrates the reachable positional workspace for a fixed orientation ($\phi = 90$ deg., $\theta = 0$ deg.) of the stylus while Fig. 3(b) shows a configuration ($x = 0.165$ m, $y = -0.245$ m, $z = 0.16$ m, $\phi = 90$ deg., $\theta = 0$ deg.) immediately inside the border of the reachable workspace. In this case further movement in the negative y-direction is limited by θ_{5a} according to (24). Figure 3(c) illustrates the rotational workspace for a central position ($x = 0.165$ m, $y = -0.105$ m, $z = 0.16$ m). The reachable workspace is coloured white. The other colours signify different limitations of the device. Black signifies a joint 2 limitation, blue a joint 3 limitation, red a joint 4 limitation, green a joint 5 limitation and yellow a joint 6 limitation. In case multiple limitations are present the limitation for the lowest joint number is plotted. Figure 3(d) shows a configuration at the border of the rotational workspace ($\phi = 41$ deg., $\theta = 0$ deg.) where reduced positive pitch of the stylus is limited by θ_{5b} according to (24). As can be observed from the simulations, the 5-DOF interface provides positional and rotational workspaces adequate for the intended applications.

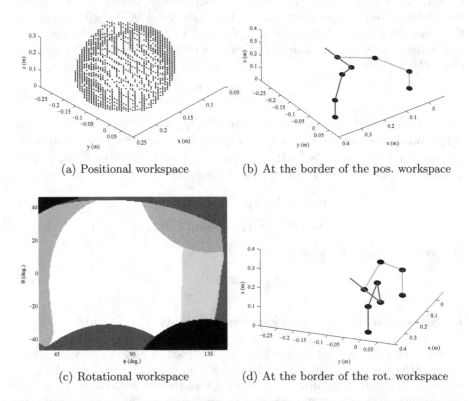

(a) Positional workspace   (b) At the border of the pos. workspace

(c) Rotational workspace   (d) At the border of the rot. workspace

Fig. 3. Workspace and configurations of the 5-DOF interface. (a) illustrates the positional workspace for constant orientation of the stylus while (c) shows the rotational workspace for a central position. (b) illustrates a configuration immediately inside the border of the reachable positional workspace while (d) shows a configuration immediate inside the border of the reachable rotational workspace. In (b) and (d) all joints are marked with spheres. (a) Positional workspace, (b) At the border of the pos. workspace, (c) Rotational workspace, (d) At the border of the rot. workspace

5   Conclusion and Future Work

This paper introduced an interface achieving 5-DOF haptic interaction using two low-cost Phantom Omni haptic devices. The 5-DOF interaction was achieved using a simple low-cost coupling which utilises the passive DOF of the devices' spherical wrists and enables the interface to maintain stylus interaction similar to an original Phantom Omni device. Future work includes determining the optimal length of the connection between the participating haptic devices as well as the relative positions and orientations of the two devices. These parameters affect both the workspace as well as the forces and torques achievable by the 5-DOF interface. Future work also includes analysing the stiffness properties and perceived inertia of the 5-DOF device.

References

1. Martin, J., Savall, J.: Mechanisms for haptic torque feedback. In: First Joint Euro-haptics Conference and Symposium on Haptic Interfaces for Virtual Environment and Teleoperator Systems, pp. 611–614 (2005)
2. Boschetti, G., Rosati, G., Rossi, A.: A haptic system for robotic assisted spine surgery. In: 2005 IEEE Conference on Control Applications, pp. 19–24 (2005)
3. Zhu, W., Lee, Y.S.: Five-axis pencil-cut planning and virtual prototyping with 5-DOF haptic interface. Comput. Aided Des. **36**(13), 1295–1307 (2004)
4. Ho, C.-H., Basdogan, C., Srinivasan, M.A.: Ray-based haptic rendering: force and torque interactions between a line probe and 3D objects in virtual environments. Int. J. Robot. Res. **19**(7), 668–683 (2000)
5. Iwata, H.: Pen-based haptic virtual environment. In: IEEE Virtual Reality Annual International Symposium, Seattle, pp. 287–292 (1993)
6. Salcudean, S.E., Stocco, L.: Isotropy and actuator optimization in haptic inter-face design. In: IEEE International Conference on Robotics and Automation, San Francisco, USA (2000)
7. Stocco, L.J., Salcudean, S.E., Sassani, F.: Optimal kinematic design of a haptic pen. IEEE/ASME Trans. Mechatron. **6**(3), 210–220 (2001)
8. Gosselin, F., Bidard, C., Brisset, J.: Design of a high fidelity haptic device for telesurgery. In: IEEE International Conference on Robotics and Automation, Barcelona, Spain (2005)
9. Gosselin, F., Ferlay, C., Bouchigny, S., Megard, C., Taha, F.: Specification and design of a new haptic interface for maxillo facial surgery. In: IEEE International Conference on Robotics and Automation, Shanghai, China, (2011)
10. Shah, A.V., Teuscher, S., McClain, E.W., Abbott, J.J.: How to build an inexpensive 5-DOF haptic device using two novint falcons. In: Kappers, A.M.L., van Erp, J.B.F., Bergmann Tiest, W.M., van der Helm, F.C.T. (eds.) EuroHaptics 2010, Part I. LNCS, vol. 6191, pp. 136–143. Springer, Heidelberg (2010)
11. Massie, T.H., Salisbury, K.J.: The PHANToM haptic interface: a device for probing virtual objects. In: 1994 ASME International Mechanical Engineering Congress and Exhibition, vol. DSC 55–1, pp. 295–302 (1994)

The Effects of Force Feedback on Surgical Task Performance: A Meta-Analytical Integration

Bernhard Weber[(⊠)] and Sonja Schneider

German Aerospace Center, Robotics and Mechatronics Center,
Oberpfaffenhofen, Germany
Bernhard.Weber@dlr.de

Abstract. Since the introduction of surgical robots into clinical practice, there has been a lively debate about the potential benefits and the need to implement haptic feedback for the surgeon. In the current article, a quantitative review of empirical findings from 21 studies ($N = 332$ subjects) is provided. Using meta-analytical methods, we found moderate effects on task accuracy ($g = .61$), large effect sizes of additional force feedback on average forces ($g = .82$) and peak forces ($g = 1.09$) and no effect on task completion times ($g = -.05$) when performing surgical tasks. Moreover, the magnitude of the force feedback effect was attenuated when visual depth information was available.

Keywords: Haptics · Force feedback · Telesurgery · Surgical robots · Minimally invasive surgery · Depth information · 3D vision · Stereoscopy

1 Introduction

The major advantages of teleoperated surgical robots are a high degree of manipulative dexterity and precision, leading to improved surgical task performance compared to conventional procedures, e.g. in the case of minimally-invasive surgery [6]. Although surgical robots are rather frequently used nowadays, commercially available systems do not provide haptic feedback to the surgeon. Yet, eliminating all haptic (kinesthetic as well as tactile) information during robotic surgery might have a negative effect on surgical performance [30], because surgeons have to rely on visual information only.

Haptic information is crucial during tissue palpation, when trying to identify certain structures or tissue characteristics (e.g., distinguishing between tumorous and healthy tissue). Excessive forces applied during tissue manipulation might cause traumas to healthy tissue or breaking of fine sutures on the one hand [19]. Insufficient forces when grasping tissues or surgical material, on the other hand, might cause slippage, loose sutures, knots or clamps. When exploring tissue (e.g. palpation) tissue consistency or elasticity can only be assessed to a very limited extent. Surgeons are not aware of contacts or collisions of the surgical instruments with tissue or other instruments when occurring outside the field of endoscopic view.

In [16], the authors report 148 cases of cardiac surgeries performed with a surgical robot. They concluded that operations can be performed safely, but the main limitation

M. Auvray and C. Duriez (Eds.): EuroHaptics 2014, Part II, LNCS 8619, pp. 150–157, 2014.
DOI: 10.1007/978-3-662-44196-1_19

is the lack of haptic feedback. In line with this notion, it has been reported [29] that absence of haptic feedback in robot-assisted surgery increases errors, leading to a tripling of tissue damages. Although the majority of empirical results (see [27, 30] for reviews) indeed report positive effects of haptic feedback, there are also a number of studies showing no clear benefit (cf. [27]). It has been argued that surgeons are able to perform robot-assisted surgery successfully without haptic information. With high-definition, 3D displays of modern telesurgical systems the endoscopic image provides crucial visual cues like tissue tension, deformation and discoloration in a very high quality [12]. Thus, it is possible to compensate absent haptic information by using these visual cues to estimate the forces applied by the surgical instruments. Based on the results of their survey with 52 subjects performing a series of basic surgical tasks with the da Vinci© robot (Intuitive), Hagen and her colleagues [12] state that "haptic feedback might be a fairly unimportant feature".

In the present paper, we report the results of a meta-analysis, integrating primary studies investigating the effect of force (i.e. kinesthetic) feedback on surgical task performance in robot-assisted surgery and surgical virtual reality trainers. The main objective is the assessment of the overall effect of force feedback (FF) and the moderating influence of visual depth information (2D vs. 3D displays).

The following hypotheses were formulated:

Hypothesis 1: Surgical task performance is improved when force feedback is available.

Hypothesis 2: The positive effect of additional FF is smaller when visual depth information is provided.

2 Methods

Sample of Studies. We conducted a literature research using different combinations of key words ([haptics OR force OR force feedback] AND [surgery OR minimally invasive surgery OR laparoscopy OR virtual reality OR simulation OR robotic surgery OR telesurgery OR teleoperation]) in the PubMed, IEEE Xplore, ScienceDirect and Springer.com databases. Altogether, 75 primary studies were collected.

Next, the following inclusion criteria were applied: (1) direct empirical comparison of conditions with and without FF for the same task (omitting studies on haptic training), (2) availability of statistical data relevant for effect size computation (see next paragraph), (3) surgical experimental tasks, (4) telerobotic or VR training systems (omitting box trainers, laparoscopy, etc.), (5) methodological control of time effects (learning, fatigue). After application of the inclusion criteria, a sample of 21 studies with $N = 332$ subjects remained.

Effect Size Computation. As main measure for the effect of FF on performance we calculated the mean difference between the control (no FF) and experimental (FF) conditions standardized by the pooled standard deviation (i.e., Cohen's d; [7]):

$$d = \frac{\bar{x}_{No\ FF} - \bar{x}_{FF}}{s} \tag{1}$$

A correction factor was used and d was converted to Hedges' g (see [13] for the exact formulas), leading to a more conservative estimation of the true effect size, particularly when sample sizes are small. In case that necessary descriptive data were missing, effect sizes were calculated on basis of the p or t statistics. Conventionally, effect sizes of 0.2 to 0.5 are considered as small, from 0.5 to 0.8 as medium and from 0.8 to infinity as large effects [7].

For a more detailed analysis of potential moderators and to obtain an adequate number of analysis units, we calculated separate effect sizes for each level of the independent variables of a study and different outcome variables.

As main measure for task performance, task-specific criteria for accuracy (like tissue damage, penetration depths, quality of sutures or knots, asf.) were aggregated. In addition, the average and peak forces applied during task completion were analyzed. Please note that we do not equate force application with task performance. Provided that critical thresholds (e.g. for breaking a suture) are not exceeded, higher forces are not necessarily an indicator of low task performance [32]. Finally, we explored whether the use of additional FF has an impact on task completion times. Similar to the applied forces, completion times are not a direct measure for task performance, but might e.g. reflect the cognitive load when processing and interpreting visuo-haptic information.

Most of the studies only reported a subset of these outcome variables or only one of them. In sum, $k = 71$ units of analysis were available for meta-analytical integration.

Effect Size Aggregation and Moderator Analysis. Effect sizes were precision weighted and after aggregation of a class of effect sizes, the precision and reliability of the resulting mean effect size was quantified by calculating confidence intervals [13]. The range of the confidence interval depends on the variance of observed effect sizes, i.e. the wider the confidence interval, the less accurate is the estimation of the true effect size. A 95 % confidence interval e.g. indicates that there is a 95 % probability that the confidence range encompasses the true mean effect size. The robustness of a significant, aggregated effect size can be assessed computing the *fail-safe N*, i.e. the number of studies with smaller effects that would be necessary to have a non-significant overall effect. Heterogeneity within classes of k effect sizes was tested using the Q and the I^2 statistics [13]. Q is defined as the sum of squared differences between each study (i) effect size (Y_i) and the mean effect size (M) weighted by the inverse-variance ($W_i = 1/s_i^2$) of that study:

$$Q = \sum_{i=1}^{k} W_i (Y_i - M)^2 \tag{2}$$

The difference between the observed Q and the expected value of Q, which simply is the degrees of freedom ($df = k-1$), is tested on statistical significance. A significant difference indicates that the aggregated effect sizes do not share a common effect size, but that there are e.g. further moderating factors causing heterogeneity. Additionally, the I^2 statistic was calculated, indicating what proportion (ranging from 0–100 %) of the observed variance Q reflects real (rather than spurious) differences in effect sizes (for a detailed description see e.g. [3]):

$$I^2 = \left(\frac{Q - df}{Q}\right) * 100\% \tag{3}$$

Substantial heterogeneity within an effect sizes class indicates the influence of moderators. We tested the impact of moderators by ANOVAs (fixed effect model [13]) resulting in a between sub-classes effect Q_b and a within sub-classes effect Q_w. All analyses were performed using the CMA$^©$ software package (version 2.2; Biostat).

3 Results

Overall Effects. In a first step we analyzed the overall effects of additional FF on task accuracy and found a positive, moderate effect ($g = .61$; $k = 18$ units of analysis; 95 % confidence interval CI ranging from $g = .39$ to $.82$; $p < .001$), with an average improvement of 26.5 %.

Exploring the average forces applied during the experimental tasks revealed a positive, large effect of FF ($g = .82$; $k = 12$; $CI = .61, 1.04$; $p < .001$). The applied forces were reduced by a percentage of 23 % or 0.49 N, respectively. We also found a positive and large effect of FF on peak forces ($g = 1.09$; $k = 17$; $CI = .86, 1.30$; $p < .001$). The average peak force reduction was 35.6 % in relative or 1.09 N in absolute numbers. Finally, no significant effect was found for task completion time ($g = -.05$; please note, that minus means longer times in the FF condition; although not significant in this case, $p = .58$; $k = 24$; $CI = -.23, .13$). Duration times were increased by 9.5% in the FF compared to the no FF condition. All findings are summarized in Table 1.

The fail-safe number of the significant effects is $N = 166$ for task accuracy, $N = 158$ for average force and $N = 520$ for peak force. Furthermore, effect sizes were distributed normally for each of the four outcome variables (Kolmogorov-Smirnov $Z = .76$ for task accuracy, $Z = .86$ for average force, $Z = .87$ for peak force and $Z = .72$ for completion time, all being not statistically significant; *ns*) indicating no publication bias, but a high degree of external validity of findings.

Table 1. Overall Effects of Force Feedback

Outcome Variable	k	g	95 % CI (g)	Q	I^2
Task Accuracy	18	0.61^{***}	0.39–0.82	33.2^{*}	48.8
Average Force	12	0.82^{***}	0.61–1.04	35.2^{***}	68.7
Peak Force	17	1.09^{***}	0.86–1.30	51.6^{***}	69.0
Completion Time	24	-0.05	-0.23–0.13	51.4^{***}	55.2

Note. $^{*}p < .05$; $^{***}p < .001$; 95 % CI = upper and lower limit of the 95 % confidence interval.

Heterogeneity tests reached significance for all of the four outcome variables (Task accuracy: $Q = 33.2$; $p < .05$; $I^2 = 48.8$; Average force: $Q = 35.2$; $p < .001$; $I^2 = 68.7$; Peak force: $Q = 51.6$; $p < .001$; $I^2 = 69.0$; Completion time: $Q = 51.4$; $p < .001$; $I^2 = 55.2$), indicating a considerable amount of variability within the aggregated effect sizes. Consequently, further moderating analyses were conducted.

Moderator Analyses. In a next step of analysis, we explored the moderating influence of additional depth perception on the task accuracy effect of FF. Therefore, we compared analysis units from studies with 2D vs. 3D vision provided during the experimental tasks. We found a marginally significant moderating influence for task accuracy ($Q_b = 2.8$; $p < .10$; $g_{2D-3D} = .44$; see Table 2).

There was a significant and moderate FF effect with 2D vision (g = .63, p < .001) and only a small, non-significant FF effect with 3D vision (g = .19, ns). Further explorative analyses revealed no such effect for average and peak forces ($Q_b = 0.2$ and 0.6, respectively; ns), but a marginally significant effect for completion time ($Q_b = 3.5$; $p = .06$).

Table 2. Moderating Influence of Visual Depth Information (2D vs. 3D display)

Outcome variable	Q_b	k	g	95 % CI (g)	Q_w	I^2
Task accuracy						
2D	$2.8^\dagger$	9	0.63^{***}	0.32–0.93	20.9^{**}	61.7
3D		3	0.19	−0.23–0.71	4.0	49.4
Average force						
2D	0.2	5	0.91^{***}	0.39–1.42	27.1^{***}	85.2
3D		6	0.78^{***}	0.54–1.02	7.3	31.2
Peak force						
2D	0.6	11	1.17^{***}	0.81–1.52	48.2^{***}	79.3
3D		6	1.0^{***}	0.73–1.26	0.7	0
Completion time						
2D	$3.5^\dagger$	17	-0.28^*	−0.52––0.04	33.5^{**}	52.2
3D		3	0.19	−0.24– 0.62	4.1	51.6

Note. $^\dagger p < .10$; $^* p < .05$; $^{**} p < .01$; $^{***} p < .001$; CI = confidence interval.

When working with 2D vision, the addition of FF leads to longer task completion times ($g = -.28$, $p < .05$), while there is no significant effect of FF when 3D vision is available ($g = .19$, ns; $g_{2D-3D} = .47$).

4 Discussion

In the current paper, we provide a quantitative review of studies investigating the effect of kinesthetic force feedback on surgical task accuracy, force application and completion times. Integrating findings of 21 empirical studies confirmed H1, i.e. there is a positive, moderate effect of additional force feedback (FF) on task accuracy ($g = .61$)

with a relative improvement of 26.5 %. We also found large effects of FF on average and peak forces ($g = .81$ and $g = 1.09$), with an average force reduction of 23 % and peak force reduction of 35.6 %. Finally, overall analyses also indicated that the positive accuracy and force regulation effects do not come at the price of longer completion times ($g = -.05$).

In a meta-analysis on the effects of haptic feedback on teleoperation performance in general ([18]; with 22 studies investigating kinesthetic feedback), the authors also reported significant positive effects of FF on task accuracy ($g = .96$) and force application ($g = .59$). Moreover, a positive effect on completion times ($g = .69$) was documented. The partially divergent result patterns might be explained by the nature of experimental tasks. In [18], telerobotic tasks like moving a robot and basic manipulation tasks (pick-and-place, peg-in-hole, grasping) were mainly investigated. In the current review surgical tasks like suturing, knotting, dissection, needle insertion and palpation were exclusively analyzed.

Most teleoperation tasks are very well practiced everyday activities where haptic feedback is easy to interpret and mainly necessary to detect object collisions. During the more complex surgical tissue manipulation and exploration tasks, a higher degree of precision is required and exaggerated forces may cause tissue damage. As a consequence, smaller effects of FF on task accuracy occur, because task-related abilities are more relevant (surgical expertise, e.g.) and subjects perhaps try harder to avoid task errors independently from FF. When FF is enabled, forces are applied in a cautious manner (particularly by unexperienced subjects [32]) and complex visuo-haptic information has to be integrated. Thus, the effect of additional FF on force application is larger, but there is no positive effect on completion times during surgical tasks.

Investigating the moderating effect of depth information showed that there is no significant effect of FF on task accuracy when having depth information, but a significant and moderate effect when no such information is available. Although the moderation analysis did not reach the conventional level of significance (due to the small ks), there is at least initial evidence supporting H2. Similarly, we found first evidence for a moderating impact of depth information on task completion times, i.e. significantly longer times were required with than without FF when having no depth information. A non-significant, almost small effect size was evident when depth information was activated. With visual depth information, relative positions of the surgical tool, material and tissue as well as tissue deformations can be interpreted more precisely, resulting in improved spatial perception and awareness. As a consequence, surgical task accuracy is improved, partially cancelling out the beneficial effect of force feedback. Additionally, the source and meaning of force feedback might be easier to interpret when having depth information as reflected by similar completion times with and without FF (cf. [28]). Still, there is an independent and substantial effect of FF in terms of force regulation, i.e. visual depth information does not lead to an altered force application strategy, but rather helps understanding the spatial configuration and integrating visuo-haptic information. Nevertheless, force feedback is indispensable when visual information is not sufficient (e.g. in case of occlusions [10] or when pulling a thread during knotting) or when surgical tasks require fine regulation or detection of forces (e.g. during palpation).

Although depth information turned out to be a relevant moderator, the remaining variability of findings indicates further moderating influences like the technical setup, the quality and amount of FF, the specific task demands as well as subjects' surgical and system experience. Their joint impact on the FF effect has to be scrutinized in future research.

References

1. Arata, J., Takahashi, H., Yasunaka, S., Onda, K., Tanaka, K., Sugita, N., Hashizume, M., et al.: Impact of network time-delay and force feedback on tele-surgery. Int. J. Comput. Assist. Radiol. Surg. **3**(3–4), 371–378 (2008)
2. Bauernschmitt, R., Gaertner, C., Braun, E.U., Mayer, H., Knoll, A., Schreiber, U. Lange, R.: Improving the quality of robotic heart surgery: Evaluation in a new experimental system. In: Proceedings of the 4th Russian-Bavarian Conference on Biomedical Engineering at Moscow Institute of Electronic Technology, pp. 137–140. Technical University, Zelenograd, Moscow, Russia, 8/9 July 2008
3. Borenstein, M., Hedges, L.V., Higgins, J.P., Rothstein, H.R.: Introduction to Meta-Analysis. Wiley, Hoboken (2011)
4. Braun, E.U., Mayer, H., Knoll, A., Lange, R., Bauernschmitt, R.: The must-have in robotic heart surgery: haptic feedback. In: Medical Robotics, pp. 9–20. I-Tech Education and Publishing, Vienna, Austria (2008)
5. Braun, E.U., Gaertner, C., Mayer, H., Knoll, A., Lange, R., Bauernschmitt, R.: Haptic Aided Roboting for Heart Surgeons. In: Proceedings of the 4th European Conference of the International Federation for Medical and Biological Engineering, pp. 1695–1696. Springer Berlin Heidelberg (2009)
6. Cadiere, G.B., Himpens, J., Germay, O., Izizaw, R., Degueldre, M., Vandromme, J., et al.: Feasibility of robotic laparoscopic surgery: 146 cases. World J. Surg. **25**(11), 1467–1477 (2001)
7. Cohen, J.: Statistical power analysis for the behavioral sciences (2nd ed.). Hillsdale, NJ: Erlbaum (1988)
8. Debus, T., Becker, T., Dupont, P., Jang, T.J., Howe, R.: Multichannel vibrotactile display for sensory substitution during teleoperation. In: Proceedings of SPIE–The International Society for Optical Engineering, Vol. 4570, pp. 42–49 (2001)
9. Deml, B.: Telepräsenzsysteme - Gestaltung der Mensch-System Schnittstelle, Dissertation thesis, University of the Armed Forces. http://edok01.tib.uni-hannover.de/edoks/e01dd01/482342803l.pdf (2004). Accessed 16 Jan 2014
10. Gerovich, O., Marayong, P., Okamura, A.M.: The effect of visual and haptic feedback on computer-assisted needle insertion. Comput. Aided Surg. **9**(6), 243–249 (2004)
11. Gwilliam, J.C., Mahvash, M., Vagvolgyi, B., Vacharat, A., Yuh, D.D., Okamura, A.M.: Effects of haptic and graphical force feedback on teleoperated palpation. In: ICRA'09. IEEE International Conference on Robotics and Automation, 2009, pp. 677–682. IEEE (2009)
12. Hagen, M.E., Meehan, J.J., Inan, I., Morel, P.: Visual clues act as a substitute for haptic feedback in robotic surgery. Surg. Endosc. **22**(6), 1505–1508 (2008)
13. Hedges, L., Olkin, I.: Statistical Methods for Meta-Analysis. Academic Press, San Diego (1985)
14. Kazi, A.: Operator performance in surgical telemanipulation. Presence Teleoperators Virtual Environ. **10**(5), 495–510 (2001)

15. Mahvash, M., Gwilliam, J., Agarwal, R., Vagvolgyi, B., Su, L. M., Yuh, D. D., Okamura, A. M.: Force-feedback surgical teleoperator: Controller design and palpation experiments. In: Symposium on Haptic Interfaces for Virtual Environment and Teleoperator Systems, Haptics 2008, pp. 465–471. IEEE (2008)
16. Mohr, F.W., Falk, V., Diegeler, A., Walther, T., et al.: Computer-enhanced 'robotic' cardiac surgery: experience in 148 patients. J. Thorac. Cardiovasc. Surg. **121**, 842–853 (2001)
17. Moody, L., Baber, C., Arvanitis, T.N.: Objective surgical performance evaluation based on haptic feedback. Stud. Health Technol. Inf. **85**, 304–310 (2002)
18. Nitsch, V., Färber, B.: A meta-analysis of the effects of haptic interfaces on task performance with teleoperation systems. IEEE Trans. Hapt. **6**(4), 387–398 (2012)
19. Okamura, A.M.: Methods for haptic feedback in teleoperated robot-assisted surgery. Ind. Rob. Int. J. **31**(6), 499–508 (2004)
20. Panait, L., Akkary, E., Bell, R.L., Roberts, K.E., Dudrick, S.J., Duffy, A.J.: The role of haptic feedback in laparoscopic simulation training. J. Surg. Res. **156**(2), 312–316 (2009)
21. Paul, L., Cartiaux, O., Docquier, P.L., Banse, X.: Ergonomic evaluation of 3D plane positioning using a mouse and a haptic device. Int. J. Med. Rob. Comput. Assist. Surg. **5**(4), 435–443 (2009)
22. Santos-Carreras, L., Beira, R., Sengül, A., Gassert, R., Bleuler, H.: Influence of force and torque feedback on operator performance in a VR-based suturing task. Appl. Bion. Biomech. **7**(3), 217–230 (2010)
23. Salkini, M.W., Doarn, C.R., Kiehl, N., Broderick, T.J., Donovan, J.F., Gaitonde, K.: The role of haptic feedback in laparoscopic training using the LapMentor II. J. Endourol. **24**(1), 99–102 (2010)
24. Seibold, U.: An advanced force feedback tool design for minimally invasive robotic surgery. Dissertation Thesis, Technical University Munich (2013)
25. Talasaz, A., Trejos, A. L., Patel, R.V.: Effect of force feedback on performance of robotics-assisted suturing. In: Proceedings of the 4th IEEE RAS & EMBS International Conference on Biomedical Robotics and Biomechatronics (BioRob), pp. 823–828. IEEE (2012)
26. Tholey, G.: A teleoperative haptic feedback framework for computer-aided minimally invasive surgery. Doctoral Dissertation, Drexel University (2007)
27. Van der Meijden, O.A.J., Schijven, M.P.: The value of haptic feedback in conventional and robot-assisted minimal invasive surgery and virtual reality training: a current review. Surg. Endosc. **23**(6), 1180–1190 (2009)
28. Wagner, C.R., Howe, R.D.: Force feedback benefit depends on experience in multiple degree of freedom robotic surgery task. IEEE Trans. Rob. **23**(6), 1235–1240 (2007)
29. Wagner, C.R., Stylopoulos, N., Howe, R.D.: The role of force feedback in surgery: analysis of blunt dissection. In: Symposium on Haptic Interfaces for Virtual Environment and Teleoperator Systems, pp. 73–79 (2002)
30. Westebring-van der Putten, E.P., Goossens, R.H.M., Jakimowicz, J.J., Dankelman, J.: Haptics in minimally invasive surgery-a review. Minim. Invasive Ther. Allied Technol. **17** (1), 3–16 (2008)
31. Yiasemidou, M., Glassman, D., Vasas, P., Badiani, S., Patel, B.: Faster simulated laparoscopic cholecystectomy with haptic feedback technology. Open Access Surg. **4**, 39–44 (2011)
32. Zhou, M., Perreault, J., Schwaitzberg, S.D., Cao, C.G.L.: Effects of experience on force perception threshold in minimally invasive surgery. Surg. Endosc. **22**(2), 510–515 (2008)

Switching Robust Control Synthesis
for Teleoperation via Dwell Time Conditions

César A. López Martínez[✉], René van de Molengraft, and Maarten Steinbuch

Control Systems Technology, Department of Mechanical Engineering,
Eindhoven University of Technology, Eindhoven, The Netherlands
{c.lopez,m.j.g.v.d.molengraft,m.steinbuch}@tue.nl

Abstract. Control design for bilateral teleoperation is still an open
problem, given that it is desirable to meet a proper balance in the inherent trade-off between transparency and stability. We propose the use of
switching robust control, in which smooth switching among controllers is
achieved by the existence of multiple Lyapunov functions with a special
structure, linked by conditions of maximum average dwell time switching
among controllers. We show the advantage of the proposed method by
means of a control design synthesis for an 1-DoF teleoperation system,
and by means of simulations of the corresponding closed loop system.

Keywords: Switching robust control · Bilateral teleoperation · Linear
matrix inequalities · Control system synthesis · Dwell time

1 Introduction

Teleoperation systems are used to manipulate a remote environment by means
of a master and a slave device. It is desirable that the system presents high
performance, e.g. the operator feels as if he/she is manipulating the environment directly, in a stable fashion. Nonetheless, the inherent trade-off between
performance and stability represents a challenging problem in designing controllers that meet an appropriate balance [9]. During many years the focus of
the control design was only on stability, therefore passivity [8] based methods
have been widely used to design controllers that guarantee stability but performance is often not taken into account a priori. Moreover most of them are only
applicable to Linear Time Invariant (LTI) systems, however, in practice oper-
ator/environment dynamics are inherently time-varying and partially bounded.
In [5] they have included such properties during the control design process to
balance transparency and stability. However, the achieved robustness range of
environment stiffness is limited, not fully covering realistic conditions in applications hard contacts might be present for example during collision between
instruments.

To increase the region of performance, one can think of designing controllers
that adapts to the environment stiffness. Reference [1] use environment adaptation for bilateral teleoperation control, however they rely on unbiased, low noise

© Springer-Verlag Berlin Heidelberg 2014
M. Auvray and C. Duriez (Eds.): EuroHaptics 2014, Part II, LNCS 8619, pp. 158–166, 2014.
DOI: 10.1007/978-3-662-44196-1_20

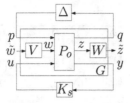

Fig. 1. Generalized plant with weighting filters.

and fast convergence of the estimated environment stiffness. More recently, [6] suggested the use of switching robust control. They account for uncertainty in the operator and environment dynamics as well as uncertainty and noise in the estimation of the environment stiffness. The controllers were designed such that they share a common quadratic Lyapunov function, which ensures smooth as well as arbitrary fast switching between them, which can still add conservatism. Therefore, to decrease such conservatism, an average switching dwell time concept [2] can be used. Such concept has been already used in [3] for robustness against time-varying delays, and also in [7] for LPV control of an aircraft. Based on the latter work, we propose an extension to the work of [6], such that the requirement of a common Lyapunov function is relaxed and we find conditions for control synthesis that reduces the conservatism in the achievable performance. We validate the proposed method by means of a control design synthesis for a 1-DoF teleoperation system and we present simulations showing transition and contact with different environments.

2   Methods

We used the same model as in our previous work [6] and here it is briefly discussed. The model's structure is shown in Fig. 1, where q and p are the signals interfacing the uncertainty block Δ, y the measured force and position signals, w the disturbances such as the noise on the measured signals and active operator and environment forces, u represents the actuation forces of master and slave and z the performance signals, including force and position error signals of operator and environment, and master/slave actuation signals to limit the actuation forces. P_0 contains all fixed parameters of operator, master and slave devices. The controller K_s in this case represents the switching robust control to be designed. Moreover, $\tilde{w}$ and $\tilde{z}$ are weighted versions of w and z by means of the filters V and W respectively, which are designed to achieved force and position tracking. In the model, the operator stiffness k_h and the environment stiffness k_e are assumed to be uncertain, bounded and they are also considered time-varying to account for more realistic behavior. Thus, the uncertainty block becomes $\Delta = \begin{bmatrix} k_h & 0 \\ 0 & k_e \end{bmatrix}$ such that $\Delta \in \mathbf{\Delta}$, where the class $\mathbf{\Delta} = \left\{ \begin{bmatrix} k_h & 0 \\ 0 & k_e \end{bmatrix} : k_h \in [\underline{k_h}, \bar{k}_h] \wedge k_e \in [\underline{k_e}, \bar{k}_e] \right\}$.

Next, [6] designed a switching robust controller for the 1-Dof teleoperation system. It consists of two controllers sharing a common quadratic Lyapunov

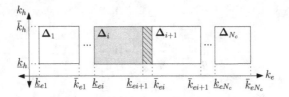

Fig. 2. Uncertainty regions $\mathbf{\Delta}_i$ of a switching robust controller.

function. They showed that it was possible to increase the range of environment stiffness for which robust performance is achieved. However, the requirement of a common Lyapunov function might limit the potential of the proposed multi-controller structure. Here we propose the use of multiple Lyapunov functions. Initially we discuss the main idea of switching robust control for bilateral tele-operation [6]. It consists of designing a specific number N_c of LTI controllers, in which the controller K_i, $i = 1, ..., N_c$ has an uncertainty region $\mathbf{\Delta}_i^{RP}$ of robust performance, such that all regions combined form a bigger region $\mathbf{\Delta}^{RP} \in \mathbf{\Delta}$, each K_i is then activated in its corresponding region $\mathbf{\Delta}_i^{RP}$ based on an estimate $\hat{k}_e$ of k_e with possibly uncertainty and noise.

Thus, $\mathbf{\Delta}$ is partitioned in $\mathbf{\Delta}_i = \left\{ \begin{bmatrix} k_h & 0 \\ 0 & k_{ei} \end{bmatrix} : k_h \in [\underline{k}_h, \bar{k}_h] \wedge k_{ei} \in [\underline{k}_{ei}, \bar{k}_{ei}] \right\}$ and $\mathbf{\Delta} \subseteq \mathbf{\Delta}_1 \cup ... \cup \mathbf{\Delta}_{N_c}$, for $i = 1, ..., N_c$ as illustrated in Fig. 2. We define also the uncertainty blocks $\Delta_i \in \mathbf{\Delta}_i$ such that $\Delta_i = diag(k_h, k_{ei})$. Note that although k_e is estimated, it is still an considered as an uncertainty on each sub-region $\mathbf{\Delta}_i$. There is overlapping between the regions to avoid chattering behavior due to noise and to avoid incorrect scheduling of controllers based on $\hat{k}_e$. Next, we would like to find the state space representation of the to be designed controllers $K_i = ss(A_{ci}, B_{ci}, C_{ci}, D_{ci})$, such that the robust performance region of each controller satisfies $\mathbf{\Delta}_i \subseteq \mathbf{\Delta}_i^{RP}$. Before going into details of the synthesis we present first the following equations taken and adapted from the work of [2, 10]. Let $\mathbf{P}_i$ be a family of symmetric matrices P_i which satisfies $\int_0^{T_0} \begin{pmatrix} \Delta_i(q)(t) \\ q(t) \end{pmatrix}^T P_i \begin{pmatrix} \Delta_i(q)(t) \\ q(t) \end{pmatrix} dt \geq 0$. Each matrix $P_i = \begin{pmatrix} Q_i & S_i \\ S_i^T & R_i \end{pmatrix} \in \mathbf{P}_i$ describes the corresponding uncertainty region $\mathbf{\Delta}_i$. Since all P_i are constant, they describe infinitely-fast time-varying uncertainty.

Moreover, consider matrices $\mathcal{X}_i = \mathcal{X}_i^T$ that satisfy: $\mathcal{X}_i \succ 0$

$$
(\star)^T \begin{pmatrix} 0 & \mathcal{X}_i & 0 & 0 & 0 \\ \mathcal{X}_i & 0 & 0 & 0 & 0 \\ 0 & 0 & \lambda_0 \mathcal{X}_i & 0 & 0 \\ \hline 0 & 0 & 0 & P_i & 0 \\ \hline 0 & 0 & 0 & 0 & P_p \end{pmatrix} \begin{pmatrix} I & 0 & 0 \\ A_i & B_{i1} & B_{i2} \\ I & 0 & 0 \\ 0 & I & 0 \\ \hline C_{i1} & D_{i11} & D_{i12} \\ 0 & 0 & I \\ \hline C_{i2} & D_{i21} & D_{i22} \end{pmatrix} \prec 0 \quad (1)
$$

where the performance index $P_p = \begin{pmatrix} -\gamma^2 I & 0 \\ 0 & I \end{pmatrix}$, represents the $\mathcal{L}_2$ gain γ from disturbances to performance signals, $(\star)$ is the same matrix in the right hand side of Eq. (1) and $i = 1, ..., N_c$. The matrices $\mathcal{A}_i$, $\mathcal{B}_{im}$, $\mathcal{C}_{in}$, $\mathcal{D}_{imn}$ correspond to the state space realization of the system G in closed loop with the controller K_i as in Fig. 1 (taking $K_s = K_i$), therefore the controller matrices A_{ci}, B_{ci}, C_{ci}, D_{ci}, are incorporated in the matrices $\mathcal{A}_i$, $\mathcal{B}_{im}$, $\mathcal{C}_{in}$, $\mathcal{D}_{imn}$.

Based on the robust control theory with Linear Matrix Inequalities (LMIs) of [10], [6] already presented a way to achieve overall robust performance of the system by using the concept of a common quadratic lypaunov function:

Theorem 1. *For $i = 1, ..., N_c$, consider Eq. (2) holds for all $q \in \mathcal{L}_2[0, T_0]$ $T_0 \geq 0$ and $\Delta_i \in \mathbf{\Delta}_i$. Then, the system after closing the loop with the controller $K_i = ss(A_{ci}, B_{ci}, C_{ci}, D_{ci})$, such that $u = K_i y$ when $\Delta_i \in \mathbf{\Delta}_i$, is robustly stable and has robust $\mathcal{L}_2$ gain performance smaller than γ if there exist a matrix $\mathcal{X} = \mathcal{X}^T \succ 0$, such that $\mathcal{X}_i = \mathcal{X}$ and Eqs. (1) hold, with $\lambda_0 = 0$.*

The fact that all controllers share a common quadratic Lyapunov function $V(x) = x^T \mathcal{X} x$, makes the overall switched system globally stable in case of arbitrary fast switching between all N_c controllers [4]. The disadvantage of such requirement is that it adds unnecessary conservatism. In real applications the slave devices might encounter sudden changes in the environment, however consecutive switching of environment is not expected to take place infinitely fast. Therefore, we might relax the requirement of a common Lyapunov function and allow a different one per controller, given that we guarantee specific conditions on how much they differ. In order to achieve this, we make use of the average dwell time concept by [2]. Such concept is used in combination with theorem 1 as follows.

Theorem 2. *For $i = 1, ..., N_c$, consider Eq. (2) holds for all $q \in \mathcal{L}_2[0, T_0]$ $T_0 \geq 0$ and $\Delta_i \in \mathbf{\Delta}_i$. Then, the system after closing the loop with the controller $K_i = ss(A_{ci}, B_{ci}, C_{ci}, D_{ci})$, such that $u = K_i y$ when $\Delta_i \in \mathbf{\Delta}_i$, is robustly stable and has robust $\mathcal{L}_2$ gain performance smaller than γ if the switch between regions $\mathbf{\Delta}_i$ and therefore between controllers K_i have an average dwell time $\tau_a > \frac{ln(\mu)}{\lambda_0}$ given that $\mu > 1$, $\lambda_0 > 0$ and there exist matrices $\mathcal{X}_i = \mathcal{X}_i^T \succ 0$, such that*

$$\frac{1}{\mu}\mathcal{X}_j \preceq \mathcal{X}_i \preceq \mu\mathcal{X}_j \tag{2}$$

for any $i, j = 1, ..., N_c$ and the matrix inequalities in Eq. (1) hold.

Conceptually, theorem 2 says that we allow a mismatch between the different Lyapunov functions $V_i(x) = x\mathcal{X}_i x^T$, such that

$$\frac{1}{\mu}V_j(x) \leq V_i(x) \leq \mu V_j(x) \tag{3}$$

and there is also a guarantee of a minimum rate of decay of such functions by means of $\lambda_0 > 0$. Thus when there is a switch of controllers, the new Lyapunov function might increase and because there is a guaranteed level of exponential decrease, the average dwell switching time is guaranteed as well. The reader can refer to the work of [2] and [4] for more discussion on that topic. Now, our goal is to find conditions for control synthesis. However, when translating conditions in Eq. (2) to the synthesis, non-linear terms appear in the equations. To illustrate this, we describe first how the controller synthesis based on Theorem 1 works.

Equation (1) is actually not a LMI when K_i, $\mathcal{X}$ and P_i are unkown and the synthesis procedure is non-convex. However if we iterate the design between controllers K_i and uncertainty multipliers P_i, it is possible to make Eq. (1) convex as follows. When the controllers K_i are known, Eq. (1) becomes already a LMI, i.e. linear in the unknowns parameters $\mathcal{X}_i$ and P_i. However, in the case when P_i is known, two additional steps are needed to transform Eq. (1) into a LMI. The details of these steps are found in the work of [10]. Here we will describe part of the first step, which is key to understand the control synthesis method here proposed. It consists of the congruence transformation of the Lyapunov functions $V_i(x) = x^T \mathcal{X}_i x$. Consider the next partition of the matrices $\mathcal{X}_i$,

$$\mathcal{X}_i = \begin{pmatrix} X_i & U_i \\ U_i^T & * \end{pmatrix} \text{ and } \mathcal{X}_i^{-1} = \begin{pmatrix} Y_i & V_i \\ V_i^T & * \end{pmatrix} \tag{4}$$

with $X_i Y_i + U_i V_i^T = I$. Next, if we apply a congruence transformation to condition $\mathcal{X}_i \succ 0$ with matrix $\mathcal{Y}_{Ai} = \begin{pmatrix} Y_i & I \\ V_i^T & 0 \end{pmatrix}$, it is transformed to $\mathbf{X}_i = \begin{pmatrix} Y_i & I \\ I & X_i \end{pmatrix} \succ 0$. thus $Y_i \succ 0$. In a similar way Eq. (1) is transformed with matrix $\mathcal{Y}_{Bi} = diag\{\mathcal{Y}_{Ai}, I, I\}$ to an equation that depends on $X_i, Y_i, J_i, L_i, M_i, N_i$, where the last four are new variables that represent the controller. By an additional step such equation can be made affine in its unknowns. Due to lack of space these equations are not included here but the reader can refer to the work of [10]. Now, the main inconvenience with theorem 2 to arrive at synthesis conditions comes from the fact that we can not apply a congruence transformation with $\mathcal{Y}_{Ai}$ to Eq. (2) because it involves different indexes i, j. To be able to still satisfy conditions (3), we use the same trick applied by [7]. One can show from Eq. (4) that $\mathcal{X}_i = \begin{pmatrix} X_i & U_i \\ U_i^T & -U_i^T Y_i V_i^{-T} \end{pmatrix}$, in which the non-linear lower-right term poses an issue to make the synthesis process solvable with LMI's. One way to solve the issue is as follows. First, one can select $V_i = Y_i$ and therefore $U_i = Y_i^{-1} - X_i$, thus $\mathcal{X}_i$ in Eq. (4) becomes

$$\mathcal{X}_i = \begin{pmatrix} X_i & Y_i^{-1} - X_i \\ Y_i^{-1} - X_i & X_i - Y_i^{-1} \end{pmatrix} \tag{5}$$

Therefore, partitioning the closed loop state vector as $x = [x_p, x_c]^T$, where x_p and x_c are the state vectors of the plant and controller respectively, we get:

$$V_i(x) = x_p^T Y_i^{-1} x_p + (x_c - x_p)^T (X_i - Y_i^{-1})(x_c - x_p) \tag{6}$$

Now, note that conditions in Eq. (3) are only necessary at the moment of switching. Therefore if at the switching moments the controller state vector is reset to $x_c = x_p$, the Lyapunov function at the switching instant becomes $V_i([x_p, x_p]^T) = x_p^T Y_i^{-1} x_p$, which in turns can be substituted in Eq. (3) to obtain $\frac{1}{\mu} Y_j^{-1} \preceq Y_i^{-1} \preceq \mu Y_j^{-1}$. Moreover, we can also conclude that including the switching instants, at all times $V_i(x) \geq x_p^T Y_i^{-1} x_p \geq 0$. Now, we know that $Y_i \succ 0$ and therefore $Y_i^{-1} \succ 0$. Thus, applying properties of positive definite matrices and because of interchangeability of subscripts i, j we arrive to conditions $\frac{1}{\mu} Y_j \preceq Y_i \preceq \mu Y_j$, which are also affine in Y_i, Y_j, allowing us to synthesize controllers K_i given that P_i is known and the controller state is reset to $x_c = x_p$ at the switching instants.

Next, to obtain P_i when K_i is known, we use the same structure as in Eq. (5), therefore we can infer the following theorem.

Theorem 3. *For $i = 1, ..., N_c$, consider controllers $K_i = ss(A_{ci}, B_{ci}, C_{ci}, D_{ci})$ with state vector size equal to that of the plant, consider also that Eq. (2) holds for all $q \in \mathcal{L}_2[0, T_0]$ $T_0 \geq 0$ and $\Delta_i \in \mathbf{\Delta}_i$. Then, the system after closing the loop with the controller K_i, such that $u = K_i y$ when $\Delta_i \in \mathbf{\Delta}_i$, and resetting the controller state vector to $x_c = x_p$ when a switching occurs, is robustly stable and has robust $\mathcal{L}_2$ gain performance smaller than γ if the switching between regions Δ_i and therefore between controllers K_i has an average dwell time as in Eq. (2) given that $\mu > 1$, $\lambda_0 > 0$ and there exist positive definite matrices $X_i \succ 0$, $Y_{Ii} = Y_i^{-1} \succ 0$, such that $\mathcal{X}_i = \begin{pmatrix} X_i & Y_{Ii} - X_i \\ Y_{Ii} - X_i & X_i - Y_{Ii} \end{pmatrix} \succ 0$ and*

$$\frac{1}{\mu} Y_{Ij} \preceq Y_{Ii} \preceq \mu Y_{Ij} \tag{7}$$

for any $i, j = 1, ..., N_c$ and the matrix inequalities in Eq. (1) hold.

We finally summarize the synthesis procedure as follows. We define each region Δ_i, transform it and scale in the same way as in the work by [5]. Then, without loss of generality, the uncertainty parameters can be transformed into new parameters $\check{k}_h \in [0, 1]$, $\check{k}_{ei} \in [0, 1]$ such that transformed uncertainty becomes $\check{\Delta}_i = \begin{bmatrix} \check{k}_h & 0 \\ 0 & \check{k}_{ei} \end{bmatrix}$. Then the new uncertainty block can be scaled by a real number such that $\tilde{\Delta}_i = r\check{\Delta}_i$ and $r \in [0, 1]$. Note that when $r = 0$, we end up with a nominal set of plants with no uncertainty. Then, we design first a nominal controller for $r = 0$, minimizing the performance γ.

Next, we iterate between the following three steps: (a) for fixed K_i, maximize r and get matrices P_i, while $\gamma < \bar{\gamma}$; (b) for fixed P_i, maximize r and get controllers K_i while $\gamma < \bar{\gamma}$, (c) Once $r = 1$ is achieved, we iterate between the two previous steps and on each the performance level γ is minimized.

Now, the reset conditions introduced here helped to relax the requirement of a common Lyapunov function. However, the actual implementation of such reset can be very difficult to achieved in practice. A solution can bes *not* to

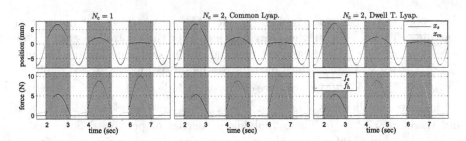

Fig. 3. Time domain response when using different control synthesis methods and environments. The gray areas show when the slave is in contact with the environment.

perform the controller state reset at the moment of switching. All we have to do is to perform a final analysis using theorem 2, take $r = 1$ and minimize γ. In fact even less conservative results are obtained in the analysis since we do not have to enforce a particularly structure in $\mathcal{X}_i$. Thus, the reset conditions are *only* used to be able to have a synthesis procedure based on LMI's that relax the requirement of a common Lyapunov function.

3   Simulation Results

To show the advantage of the proposed method with respect to our previous work [5], we perform the synthesis procedure using the same generalized plant model described there, i.e. weighting filters, master and slave parameters are similar. The next parameters are set to: $N_c = 2$, $k_e \in [80, 20000]\,\mathrm{N/m}$ to include soft and stiff environments, $\bar{k}_{e1} = 3900\,\mathrm{N/m}$, $\bar{\gamma} = 40$, $\mu = 1.2$, $\lambda_0 = 0.3$, $|\epsilon(k_e)| < 0.15 k_e$ and $\eta_c < 50\,\mathrm{N/m}$. The remaining parameters are then computed: $\tau_a = 0.608 sec$, $\underline{k}_{e1} = 80\,\mathrm{N/m}$, $\underline{k}_{e2} = 2350\,\mathrm{N/m}$ and $\bar{k}_{e2} = 20000\,\mathrm{N/m}$.

The LMIs involved in the controller synthesis procedure were solved using the solver Sedumi by [11]. We performed the synthesis procedure for three cases: a single controller, two controllers with a common Lyapunov function and two controllers with different Lyapunov functions with average dwell time conditions. For the first and second case we obtained $\gamma = 24.7$ and $\gamma = 19.64$ respectively, for the third case we obtained $\gamma = 14.95$ using theorem 3, and after performing analysis without controller state reset using theorem 2 we obtained $\gamma = 12.98$.

Next, we perform simulation using the three synthesized controllers. For the operator stiffness we used the nominal stiffness $k_h = 776.7\,\mathrm{N/m}$. For the environment, we used different virtual springs such that when the slave position changes from free air at $x_s < 0$ to $x_s \geq 0$, we test three different stiffness values consecutively on each transition to $x_s \geq 0$: $k_e = 800\,\mathrm{N/m}$, $k_e = 4000\,\mathrm{N/m}$ and $k_e = 20000\,\mathrm{N/m}$. To simulate the desired task we used the human active force $f_h^* = (0.2 - 0.6 cos(\pi t))N$. Moreover, because the implementation of the environment estimator is not on the focus of this work, we simulate the estimate $\hat{k}_e$ with added uncertainty and noise by taking $\epsilon(k_e) = 0.14 k_e\,\mathrm{N/m}$ and $\eta_c = 49\,\mathrm{N/m}$. The time domain responses are depicted in Fig. 3 for all three cases from left to right. For the last two cases there is a switch of controllers so that the corresponding controller K_2 is active when in contact with the springs $k_e = 4000\,\mathrm{N/m}$ and $k_e = 20000\,\mathrm{N/m}$. All cases achieve position and force tracking to some extent, the improvement can be better seen in the force signals. Moreover, when the slave device is in free air, the smaller the magnitude of the force felt by the operator, the better is the haptic feeling of free air, and it is improved by the last two controllers in comparison with the case where a single controller is used. Moreover, one can see that all the controllers can handle the transition from $k_e = 0\,\mathrm{N/m}$ to $k_e = 20000\,\mathrm{N/m}$, representing a hard contact.

In summary the proposed control method achieved the best performance out of the three cases, showing the effectiveness of relaxing the common Lyapunov function requirement, and showing its potential to move towards bridging the stability-performance gap in teleoperation.

4   Conclusion

In this paper, we have proposed a new methodology for control synthesis of a switching robust controller for bilateral teleoperation. It is not required to have a common Lyapunov function among its controllers but instead the controllers are linked with a condition based on average dwell time switching. The synthesis results showed already that we can achieve a lower $\mathcal{L}_2$ gain γ using the new relaxed conditions. Moreover, simulations confirmed the expected improvement in position and force tracking with respect to the case where a single controller and two controllers with a shared Lyapunov function are used.

Although the system is robust to average switching greater than τ_a, we still need to study the guarantees on such time, independent of the operator active force. Moreover, we will validate the proposed controller experimentally.

References

1. Cho, J.H., Lee, D.Y.: Gain-scheduling control of a teleoperation system. In: IEEE International Conference on Systems Man and Cybernetics, pp. 1489–1495 (2009)
2. Hespanha, J.P., Morse, A.S.: Stability of switched systems with average dwell-time. In: Proceedings of the 38th IEEE Conference on Decision and Control, 1999, vol. 3, pp. 2655–2660. IEEE (1999)
3. Kruszewski, A., et al.: A switched system approach to exponential stabilization through communication network. IEEE Trans. Control Syst. Technol **20**(4), 887–900 (2012)
4. Liberzon, D.: Switching in Systems and Control. Birkhäuser, Boston (2003)
5. López Martínez, C.A., Molengraft, R.V.D., Steinbuch, M.: High performance and stable teleoperation under bounded operator and environment dynamics. In: Proceedings of 10th International IFAC Symposium on Robot Control, Dubrovnik, Croatia, pp. 373–379. September 5–7 2012
6. López Martínez, C.A., Molengraft, R.V.D., Steinbuch, M.: High performance teleoperation using switching robust control. In: IEEE World Haptics Conference 2013, pp. 383–388. April 14–17 2013

7. Bei, Lu, Fen, Wu: Switching lpv control of an f-16 aircraft via controller state reset. IEEE Trans. Control Syst. Technol. **14**(2), 267–277 (2006)

8. Niemeyer, G., Slotine, J.-J.E.: Stable adaptive teleoperation. IEEE J. Oceanic Eng. **16**(1), 152–162 (1991)

9. Passenberg, Carolina, Peer, A., Martin, B.: A survey of environment-, operator-, and task-adapted controllers for teleoperation systems. Mechatronics **20**(7), 787–801 (2010)

10. Scherer, C.W., Weiland, S.: Linear matrix inequalities in control. Technical report 2010–56, SimTech Cluster of Excellence, 70569 Stuttgart (2010)

11. Sturm, J.F.: Using sedumi 1.02, a matlab toolbox for optimization over symmetric cones. Optim. Methods Softw. **11**(1), 625–653 (1999)

Performance Evaluation of a Surgical Telerobotic System Using Kinematic Indices of the Master Hand-Controller

Yaster Maddahi[✉], Michael Greene, Liu Shi Gan, Tomas Hirmer,
Rachael L'Orsa, Sanju Lama, Garnette Roy Sutherland, and Kourosh Zareinia

Project NeuroArm, University of Calgary, 3280 Hospital Dr NW,
Calgary, AB T2N 4Z6, Canada
{ymaddahi,mrgreene,lsgan,thirmer,ralorsa,slama,
garnette,kzareini}@ucalgary.ca
http://www.neuroArm.org

Abstract. This paper investigates how kinematics of the master hand-controller, in a teleoperated system, is related to performance of the entire system. Experimental validations are presented on a surgical robotic system by emulating a part of microsurgery procedure in a laboratory setting. Isotropy index is chosen as a quantitative kinematic tool. The performance of the system is evaluated using four measures: rates of slave and master actuators efforts as well as distances travelled by the slave end-effector and the haptic implement. Results indicate that when the haptic device moves within regions with higher isotropy index, the performance improves. In order to further enhance the performance, the master site is augmented by a clutch that is found helpful to increas the hand-controller dexterity.

Keywords: Haptics · Performance evaluation · Dexterity · Manipulability · Isotropy index · Robotic surgery

1 Introduction

In robot-assisted minimally invasive surgery (RMIS), enhanced surgeon dexterity may lead to improved surgical performance [1]. In a teleoperated RMIS, dexterity is a factor that limits the use of the master hand-controller (HC) [2]. A HC with high dexterity allows the surgeon to have better control of the master HC [3,4]. The first step to improve the dexterity is to find a tool by which the surgeon can recognize movement within a reasonable region of dexterity. The tool, employed in this study, is manipulability of the HC. Manipulability describes the degree to which a manipulator can freely apply forces and torques, or move in arbitrary directions [5]. Manipulability is a quantitative tool to determine the ease of arbitrarily changing kinematic and/or dynamic properties of the HC

An erratum to this chapter is available at 10.1007/978-3-662-44196-1_50

© Springer-Verlag Berlin Heidelberg 2014
M. Auvray and C. Duriez (Eds.): EuroHaptics 2014, Part II, LNCS 8619, pp. 167–175, 2014.
DOI: 10.1007/978-3-662-44196-1_21

implement. With the manipulability measure of HC, an intuitive visualization of movement directions or applying forces is available. Manipulability measures are considered as useful tools to analyze, design, and control a robotic manipulator [6]. The measure is also a useful tool to visualize how the HC can contribute to a task execution by considering its configuration. Some of manipulability measures, previously defined, are Yoshikawas measure of manipulability [6], condition number [6], isotropy index [7], and eccentricity measure of manipulability [8]. A manipulability measure does not give exact numerical information about velocity or force values, but rather, it suggests directions along which the HC can access or apply forces [9]. The manipulability measures are highly related to the structure and configuration of the HC [10]. For example, when the HC is located in a singular configuration, the surgeon's hand movement, in some directions, becomes difficult; while in other directions is optimal. Conversely, the HC may be placed in a configuration such that the surgeon has an identical accessibility in all directions, i.e. the isotropy index, for example, approaches 1.

A few studies have examined the enhancement of robotic surgery by increasing surgeon's dexterity through evaluating the dexterity of surgical tools or the slave manipulator [2,11,12]. The authors are unaware of any published work on investigating the effect of the master HC manipulability on performance of the teleoperated system used for conducting robotic surgery. Therefore, employing the concept of manipulability, for the HC, should assist surgeons move the HC within the working space with better dexterity. Indeed, by measuring the HC manipulability of HC, the surgeon can change the configuration of the HC in order to locate it in a better position in terms of dexterity.

In order to investigate the correlation between the HC manipulability and the teleoperated system performance, the manipulability velocity ellipsoid (MVE) is first explained. The MVE is the ease of arbitrarily changing the position and orientation of the tool located at the HC implement [13]. In fact, MVE is the geometric interpretation of the eigenvectors of Jacobian matrix which are obtained by using the singular value decomposition (SVD) technique [14]. Using SVD, the isotropy index of the HC is calculated. At the same time, the performance of the system is evaluated using four performance measures: (i) rate of slave manipulator effort, (ii), rate of master HC effort, (iii) distance travelled by the slave end-effector, and (iv) distance travelled by the haptic implement. There are two trajectories along which each performance measure and the isotropy index are computed. These values are then used to investigate the correlation between the HC manipulability and the task performance. In order to further enhance the system performance, a clutch is added to the master site. When the operator realizes that the HC is moving within the region with poor manipulability, she/he disengages the clutch, moves the HC implement to a region with better manipulability measures, and engages the clutch again to continue the surgical task.

The rest of this paper is organized as follows. The concept of manipulability and the manipulability velocity ellipsoid are described in Sect. 2, followed by defining the isotropy index. The experimental test rig is described in Sect. 3.

Experimental validations are presented in Sect. 4. Section 5 outlines the conclusion of this paper.

2 Kinematic Measures

Let $P^i = [x^i y^i z^i \phi^i_x \phi^i_y \phi^i_z]^T$ denotes posture (position and orientation) of the HC implement with respect to the reference frame, $\{x_R, y_R, z_R\}$. In each point of the HC's workspace, there are some limiting factors affecting the HC motion such as configuration and velocity/torque limitations. By increasing velocities or accelerations of the implement along a given trajectory or locating the manipulator in an improper configuration (e.g. close to singular configuration), effects of HC kinematics on dexterity increase, which may violate the workability of the HC. In this case, the quantitative tools can be used to design a control mechanism that can prevent the operator from moving along an improper trajectory.

Consider the HC's degree of freedom (DOF) is denoted by n, the implement's DOF in Cartesian space is shown by s. Assuming the HC is non-redundant, i.e. $n=s$, we have:

$$\dot{P}^i = J(q^i)\dot{Q}^i \tag{1}$$

where $J(q^i)$ is the Jacobian matrix of the HC. $Q^i = [q^i_1...q^i_n]^T \in R^n$ and $\dot{Q}^i = [\dot{q}^i_1...\dot{q}^i_n]^T \in R^n$ represent the vector of joint angular/linear displacement and velocity, respectively. Note that Q^i describes the relative displacement between two adjacent links. The HC implement linear/angular velocity is defined by $\dot{P}^i = (\dot{x}^i, \dot{y}^i, \dot{z}^i, \dot{\phi}^i_x, \dot{\phi}^i_y, \dot{\phi}^i_z)^T \in R^s$, when $s = 6$. Note that if $|J(q^i)| \neq 0$, the HC would be in non-singular condition. In this case, the system can kinematically be evaluated. Hereafter, $J(q^i)$ will be written as J for notational compactness.

In order to correlate the performance of the teleoperated system to the manipulability concept, an index is required to quantitatively measure the dexterity of the HC. To define this index, we employ the concept of the manipulability velocity ellipsoid (MVE). The MVE helps us visualize directions of the velocity at the HC implement. Definition of MVE will later be used to calculate the isotropy index. Using MVE, we are able to define some tools such as determinant, eigenvalues, and eigenvectors in order to analyze properties of the ellipsoid. In this study, the generalizations are captured by the singular value decomposition (SVD) of the mapping matrix in the manipulability ellipsoid [14].

In Eq. (1), if we map the unit circle $\{\dot{Q}^i \in R^n \mid \|\dot{Q}^i\| = \sum_{w=1}^{n} (\dot{q}^i_w)^2 = 1\}$ to the space of implement velocity, $\dot{P}^i$, the MVE is defined by $\{\dot{P}^i \in R^s : \dot{P}^i = J\dot{Q}^i \mid \|\dot{Q}^i\| = 1\}$. As seen, the mapping matrix of velocity is the Jacobian matrix. Using SVD, three sub-matrices of J are derived as follows:

$$J = U\Sigma V^T \tag{2}$$

where $U = [u_1...u_n] \in R^{n \times n}$ and $V = [v^T_1...v^T_n] \in R^{s \times s}$ are orthogonal matrices. $\Sigma \in R^{n \times s}$ is a combined matrix (a diagonal matrix and a zero matrix) with

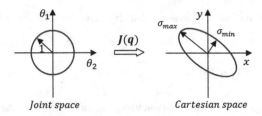

Joint space   Cartesian space

Fig. 1. Mapping the joint space into Cartesian space using MVE concept.

non-negative real numbers, and is written as:

$$\Sigma = [diag(\sigma_1\ \sigma_2\ ...\ \sigma_n)\ |\ 0\ ...\ 0] \tag{3}$$

In (3), $\sigma_1 > \sigma_2 > \cdots > \sigma_n$ are the eigenvalues of JJ^T. Note that the number of zeroes is equal to $n - s$. The length of each principal axis of MVE is given by eigenvectors of JJ^T. The principal axes are also shown by $\sigma_n u_n$. The major axis of the ellipsoid, $\sigma_1 u_1$, corresponds to the direction of the implement that can move most easily while the least easily happens at $\sigma_n u_n$ direction. For example, when the ellipsoid becomes a circle (in 2D), the implement can move with uniform ease in both directions, such configuration is called isotropic configuration. Geometrically, isotropy index (Σ_I) is the ratio of the length of minor semiaxis to the length of major semiaxis of the MVE ($\Sigma_I = \frac{\sigma_n}{\sigma_1}$). This is well-behaved because it remains bounded between 0 and 1. The isotropy index, which is defined by the reciprocal of the condition number of J, expresses the uniformity of manipulability. Note that the HC implement is able to move with uniform ease in all directions when isotropy value is close to 1 ($\Sigma_I \rightarrow 1$). For a 2-DOF planar robotic arm, for example, Fig. 1 shows how the Jacobian matrix maps the unit circle in joint space to the MVE in Cartesian space.

3   Description of the System

Figure 2 illustrates the developed experimental setup which composed of a KR6 Kuka manipulator (slave) and a PHANToM Desktop haptic device (master). The master and slave sites are connected through a Local Area Network (LAN) in which the time delay and the packet loss are negligible. This teleoperated system, which is part of neuroArm project [4], is designed to investigate effects of employing different control strategies, hand-controllers, and surgical tools on task performance. As observed in Fig. 2b, a bipolar forceps is attached to the slave end-effector to conduct the experiment. A 6-DOF force/torque sensor is mounted between the bipolar forceps and the manipulator end-effector to measure interaction forces. In this setup, the interaction forces are then transferred to the operator's hand using the master haptic device. In addition to the force feedback, the operator utilizes a real-time 3D visual feedback provided by two HD microscope cameras attached to a surgical microscope. Two sets of experiments are presented in which an operator was asked to pick up a piece of cotton

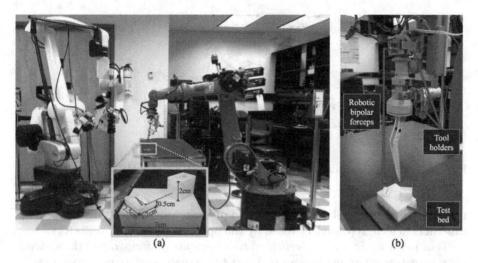

Fig. 2. Teleoperated surgical robotic system: (a) Kuka manipulator and microscope, and (b) roll and actuation mechanism for bipolar forceps. Master implement velocity is mapped into velocity of slave end-effector. Position of end-effector is then computed using integration techniques.

strips ($20\,\text{mm} \times 12\,\text{mm} \times 2\,\text{mm}$) and place it to another cube (see Fig. 2). In practice, cotton strips are often placed between brain pathology and adjacent brain as an aid to dissection.

The PHANToM Desktop haptic device is a linkage-based haptic device. The coordinate systems of the Desktop haptic device is shown in Fig. 3. With reference to Fig. 3, the Jacobian matrix, which will be used to measure the isotropy index, is defined as:

$$
J = \begin{bmatrix}
l_1 s_1 c_2 + l_2 s_{23} & l_2 s_2 c_2 + l_2 c_{23} & l_2 c_1 c_{23} & 0 & 0 & 0 \\
l_1 c_1 c_2 + l_2 s_{23} & l_2 s_1 c_{23} + l_1 s_1 s_2 & l_2 s_1 c_{23} & 0 & 0 & 0 \\
0 & l_1 c_2 + l_2 s_{23} & l_2(s_2 c_3 + c_2 s_3) & 0 & 0 & 0 \\
0 & s_1 & s_1 & c_1 s_{23} & J_{45} & J_{46} \\
0 & -c_1 & -c_1 & s_1 s_2 c_3 + c_2 s_3 & J_{55} & J_{56} \\
1 & 0 & 0 & -c_{23} & -s_4 s_{23} & J_{66}
\end{bmatrix} \quad (4)
$$

where $J_{45} = c_1 s_4 c_2 c_3 + c_1 s_4 s_2 s_3 + s_1 c_4$, $J_{46} = c_1 c_4 c_5 c_{23} - c_1 s_5 s_{23} + c_5 s_1 s_4$, $J_{55} = s_1 s_4 s_2 s_3 - s_1 s_4 c_2 c_3 - c_1 c_4$, $J_{56} = c_4 c_5 c_{23} - s_1 s_5 s_{23} - c_1 c_4 c_5$, and $J_{66} = c_4 c_5 s_{23} - s_5 c_{23}$.

4   Experimental Results

There were a total number of 2(paths) $\times$ 11(trials) $= 22$ trials collected. Each path represents particular mean values of isotropy indices (0.419 and 0.322). An operator was asked to hold the stylus of the haptic device in a pen holding fashion (similar to holding of a surgical tool) and complete the task along two

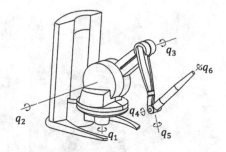

Fig. 3. Generalized coordinate systems attached to PHANToM Desktop haptic device.

paths (see Fig. 4a). Each path represented different value of isotropy index. The experiments were repeated 11 times by the operator along each trajectory.

Four performance indices were used to investigate performance of the system: slave actuators effort per second $(\hat{e}_s)$, master actuators effort per second $(\hat{e}_m)$, distance travelled by the slave end-effector (d_s), and distance travelled by the haptic implement (d_m). After comparing the performance along both Path I and Path II, a new measure was defined, HC measure: the ratio of HC isotropy index and rate of HC effort $(\Sigma_{HC} = \frac{\Sigma_I}{\hat{e}_m})$. As observed, the HC measure includes the properties of both operator's effort and HC isotropy index. Figure 4b illustrates a typical trajectory of the HC implement that was randomly chosen from trials completed along first path. The angular displacements of the HC actuator, for this typical task, are also depicted in Fig. 4c. As observed, although the operator was asked to move along straight lines, some deviations from trajectories were unavoidable.

Figure 5 shows the isotropy index (Σ_I) and the HC measure (Σ_{HC}) that were obtained for the trial depicted in Fig. 4b. Table 1 lists a summary of information obtained from all 22 trial runs. Each parameter, shown in Table 1 is obtained by averaging the mean value of that parameter in each trial. For example, in order to obtain Σ_I, the mean value of isotropy indices in each trial is calculated. Afterwards, the average of all 11 mean values is computed. Results, presented in Table 1, indicate that Path I exhibited higher values of isotropy index and HC measure as compared to Path II. Although the distances travelled by the HC implement (10.21 cm and 10.11 cm) and the slave end-effector (13.21 cm and 14.09 cm) were almost same, the slave and master efforts over time was less in Path I. Therefore, the operator could move the HC more easily along Path I than Path II. The values of the newly-defined HC measure confirm this result ($925\frac{sec}{rad}$ in Path I as opposed to $708\frac{sec}{rad}$ in Path II). The proposed HC measure has benefits of both isotropy index and operator's effort. The HC measure not only investigates the smoothness of the operator's motion, but also incorporates the role of the HC configuration. Therefore, using a single measure, effects of both operator and HC are investigated.

One way to improve the surgeon's dexterity, during robot-assisted surgery, is to find a technique by which the surgeon's hand is always kept within an

Table 1. Summary of quantitative performance measures, isotropy index, and HC measure.

Path	Σ_I	$\Sigma_{HC}(\frac{sec}{rad})$	$\hat{e}_s(\frac{rad}{sec})$	$\hat{e}_m(\frac{rad}{sec})$	$d_m(cm)$	$d_s(cm)$
I	0.419	925	0.103	0.025	10.21	13.21
II	0.322	708	0.153	0.032	10.11	14.09

acceptable HC isotropy index. The technique, proposed in this study, was to augment the master workstation by a clutch. Using clutch, when the surgeon feels that the HC falls within low isotropy index, the clutch is disengaged. The clutch stops sending information to the slave site; therefore, the slave motors do not actuate and stays fixed. Then, the surgeon can move the HC towards regions within higher index, and reengage the clutch to continue surgery. In order to investigate effects of the clutch on HC manipulability, three experiments were conducted, along Path II. Table 2 shows how the operator's performance is improved by employing the clutch. The operator engaged/disengaged the clutch for 2, 5, or 6 times during each trial in with-clutch mode. Results showed that by using the clutch, mean values of the isotropy index and the HC measure increased as compared to without-clutch mode. However, no conclusion could be established on the correlation between the number of clutches pressed and the value of the isotropy index.

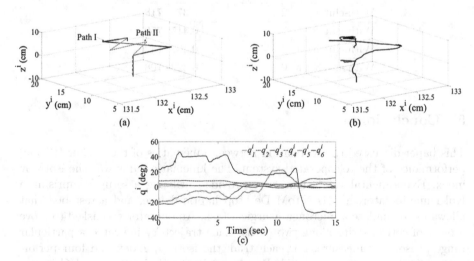

Fig. 4. (a) Desired task trajectories; (b) a typical experimental result along Path I, and (c) corresponding angular displacements of HC's joints. Both Path I and Path II have the same length

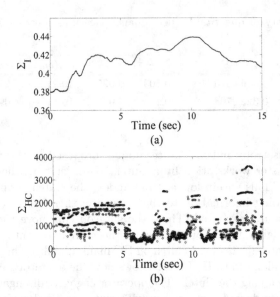

Fig. 5. (a) Isotropy index (Σ_I) and (b) HC measure (Σ_{HC}) for typical test shown in Fig. 4. Σ_{HC} is a function of Σ_I and $\hat{e}_m$.

Table 2. Effect of adding clutch on isotropy index and HC measure.

Clutch Mode	No. of Clutches	Σ_I	$\Sigma_{HC}(\frac{sec}{rad})$
With-clutch	2	0.372	718
With-clutch	5	0.415	750
With-clutch	6	0.402	742
Without-clutch	0	0.322	708

5   Conclusions

This paper discussed the correlation between kinematics of the master HC and performance of the teleoperated system. The kinematic index was the isotropy index. Experimental validations were provided utilizing a setup comprising a Kuka manipulator, a PHANToM Desktop haptic device, and a test bed that allows us to emulate a microneurosurgical task. An operator was asked to move a piece of cotton strips along two paths. Each trajectory indicated a particular range of isotropy measure. For each trial, the isotropy index and four performance measures were calculated. Results indicated that when the HC moved along a trajectory with higher isotropy measure, the performance of the system was improved. This shows that the surgeon's ability in moving the HC can effectively change the system performance. Finally, a new measure was proposed by which the isotropy index and the HC effort were evaluated by a single measure. The new measure is more useful when the aim is at comparing the performance of different HCs. The results suggest that the proposed measure can be a potential tool for evaluating the performance of teleoperated systems.

References

1. Berkelman, P., Ma, J.: A compact, modular, teleoperated robotic minimally invasive surgery system. In: IEEE International Conference on Biomedical Robotics and Biomechatronics, pp. 702–707 (2006)
2. Konietschke, R., Ortmaier, T., Weiss, H., Hirzinger, G., Engelke, R.: Manipulability and accuracy measures for a medical robot in minimally invasive surgery. In: International Conference on Advances in Robot Kinematics (2004)
3. Greer, A.D., Newhook, P., Sutherland, G.R.: Human-machine interface for robotic surgery and stereotaxy. Int. J. Comput. Assist. Radiol. Surg. 1, 295–297 (2006)
4. Sutherland, G.R., Lama, S., Gan, L.S., Wolfsberger, S., Zereinia, K.: Merging machines with microsurgery: clinical experience with neuroArm. J. Neurosurg. 118, 521–529 (2013)
5. Angeles, J., Park, F.C.: Performance evaluaion and design criteria. In: Siciliano, B., Khatib, O. (eds.) Handbook of Robotic, Chap. 10, pp. 229–244. Springer, Heidelberg (2008)
6. Yoshikawa, T.: Manipulability and redundancy control of robotic mechanisms. IEEE Int. Conf. Rob. Autom. 2, 1004–1009 (1985)
7. Balye, B., Fourquet, J.Y., Renaud, M.: Manipulability of wheeled mobile manipulators: application to motion generation. Int. J. Robot. Res. 22, 565–581 (2003)
8. Balye, B., Fourquet, J.Y., Renaud, M.: Nonholonomic mobile manipulators: kinematics, velocities and redundancies. J. Intell. Rob. Syst. 36, 45–63 (2003)
9. Melchiorri, C., Chiaccio, P., Chiaverini, S., Sciavicco, L., Siciliano, B.: Global task space manipulability ellipsoids for multiple-arm systems and further considerations (with reply). IEEE Trans. Rob. Autom. 9, 232–236 (1993)
10. Merlet, J.P.: Jacobian, manipulability, condition number and accuracy of parallel robots. J. Mech. Des. 28, 199–206 (2006)
11. Beasley, R.A.: Medical robots: Current systems and research directions. J. Robot. 2, 1–14 (2012)
12. Wortman, T., Meyer, A., Dolghi, O., et al.: Miniature surgical robot for laparoendoscopic single-incision colectomy. Surg. Endosc. 26, 727–731 (2012)
13. Yoshikawa, T.: Analysis and control of robot manipulators with redundancy, J. Robot. Res. pp. 735–747 (1984)
14. Gloub, G., Van Loan, C.: Matrix computation, Johns Hopkins University Press (1996)

Development of Two-Handed Multi-finger Haptic Interface SPIDAR-10

Lanhai Liu[(⊠)], Satoshi Miyake, Naoki Maruyama,
Katsuhito Akahane, and Makoto Sato

Precision and Intelligence Laboratory, Tokyo Institute of Technology,
4259 Nagatsuta, Midori-Ku, Yokohama 226-8503, Japan
{lanhai.liu,miyake.s.ac,naoki.maruyama,kakahane}
@hi.pi.titech.ac.jp, msato@pi.titech.ac.jp

Abstract. This article describes the development of a wire-driven multi-finger haptic interface named SPIDAR-10(Space Interface Device for Artificial Reality), which can render a 3 degree-of-freedom spatial force feedback for human fingers through 4 wires attached to each fingertip. SPIDAR-10 enables users to manipulate virtual objects in a VR world with ten fingers of both hands. With two rotary cylindrical frames, which motors are mounted on, the interference of the wires can be reduced. A method of frame control is also proposed. The experimental results of the performance of the basic SPIDAR system and rotary frame are also given.

Keywords: Haptic interface · Virtual reality · SPIDAR · Multi-finger device · Rotary frame

1 Introduction

1.1 Background

Nowadays, researchers have been focusing on real-time simulations. The demand of virtual reality simulations that requires complicated operations by human hands is also increasing. Multi-finger haptic interfaces [1] are widely studied. These devices allow users to interact with virtual objects directly through their hands, which make it possible for users to finish some complicated tasks.

In this article, we proposed and developed a wire-driven two-handed multi-finger haptic interface, which allows user to manipulate virtual objects with all of their ten fingers of both hands. The rotary frames are also proposed for the operations which need user to twist their hands, such as wringing a towel, opening the bottle cap or loosening bolts and nuts. The frames are designed to rotate with the user's hands to reduce the interference of the wires (Fig. 1).

1.2 Related Works

Various types of haptic interface have been developed, such as HIRO [2] developed by Kawasaki et al., Encounter-Type Haptic Device [3] developed by Nakagawara et al.,

© Springer-Verlag Berlin Heidelberg 2014
M. Auvray and C. Duriez (Eds.): EuroHaptics 2014, Part II, LNCS 8619, pp. 176–183, 2014.
DOI: 10.1007/978-3-662-44196-1_22

Fig. 1. Rotate a rubik's cube.

CyberForce [4] developed by CyberGlove-Systems company (immersion company in the past), MasterFinger [5, 6, 7] developed by Jorge Barrio et al., SPIDAR-8 [8] and SPIDAR-MF which are developed in our laboratory.

The HIRO provides a large force output and has a wide force direction output, but the operational space is relatively smaller and the gestures can be identified is limited because that the user must fit their fingertips into a robot hand which is opposed to human hand. The Encountered-type Haptic Device can only presents the sense of touch by moving plates which are located at the the position where user will touch the object in VR space. The CyberForce has a large workspace and provides more operational freedom, but there is a short delay in the force output and a limitation of the direction of forces. Also, user needs to wear the position sensing glove and the exoskeleton structures, which may make the user feel restrained and uncomfortable. MasterFinger is a modular device for manipulating the virtual objects with fingers. However, this device may restrict the gesture of user's hand because it has solid bars of serial-parallel mechanism.

SPIDAR-8 is a two-handed multi-finger device, which allows user to operate with 4 fingers of each hand. It has a better responsiveness and larger workspace, while the direction of force is limited, because it has only three wires attached to one finger. Also the wires may interfere with each other because of the movement of the fingers. SPIDAR-MF is a multi-finger haptic interface with a rotary frame. SPIDAR-MF allows user to do the tasks such as rotating his wrist to turn over an object to see the bottom surface of it. In addition, it is operated by 5 fingers of one hand. However, it is configured only for one hand, and the axis of rotation is parallel to the two circular planes of its cylindrical frame which makes it difficult for one user to do two-handed tasks by using two SPIDAR-MFs (Fig. 2).

2 Rotary Frame Haptic Device SPIDAR-10

2.1 Device Overview

SPIDAR-10 has two cylindrical rotary frames which are connected to the fixed frame by pulleys. It is possible to rotate the cylindrical frame by using a DC motor mounted

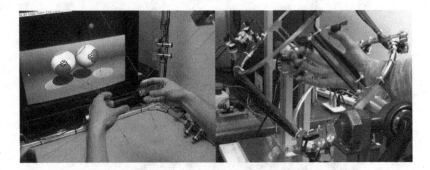

Fig. 2. SPIDAR-8(left) and SPIDAR-MF(right).

on the fixed frame. Therefore, SPIDAR-10 allows the movements of rotating or twisting virtual objects. 20 motors are arranged on each rotary frame. There are also 5 finger-caps for one frame and each finger-cap is connected to 4 wires (Fig. 3).

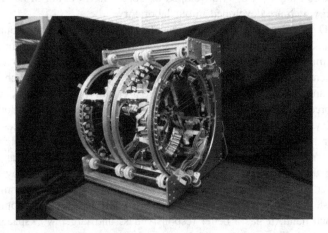

Fig. 3. Device overview.

2.2 Motor Arrangement

We specify the coordinate system of the rotary frame for the right hand, and the motors on the left frame are arranged symmetrically. The local coordinate system is shown in Fig. 4. The origin of local coordinate system is located at the center of this cylindrical frame. Also the direction of the rotational angle of the rotary frame is defined in the left figure.

The motors and wires are arranged at the proper position of the rotary frame, so that the interference of the wires is as little as possible and the force rendering space is as large as possible. These motors are numbered as in the right figure. Motor 1 to 4 are for thumb, 5 to 8 are for index finger, 9 to 12 are for middle finger, 13 to 16 are for ring finger and 17 to 20 are for little finger.

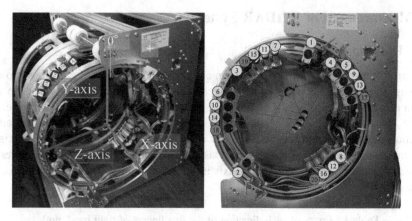

Fig. 4. The local coordinate system, rotation direction of the frame and the motor arrangement.

2.3   Frame Control

In the SPIDAR system, when the total length of the wires of one pointer(fingertip) is shorter, the fingertip is closer to the home position, and accuracy of position calculation and force rendering is relatively higher. It is also contemplated that when the length of the wire is short, interference of the wires is difficult to occur.

The Fig. 5 shows the position of the frame(thick line circle), the finger-cap(filled circles) and the 4 wires(thin line). As the fingertip moves, the total length of the 4 wires also changes. And by rotating the frame, we can reduce the total length of the wires.

Assume that the current rotational angle of the frame is θ, and d is a small rotational angle. The target angle of the frame ω is among θ, θ + d and θ − d which can minimize the total length of all wires. Thus, the frame will always rotate in order to reduce the total length of all wires.

$$\omega = \operatorname{argmin}\ \mathrm{TotalLen}\left(\theta'\right)\left(\theta' \in \{\theta, \theta + d, \theta - d\}\right) \tag{1}$$

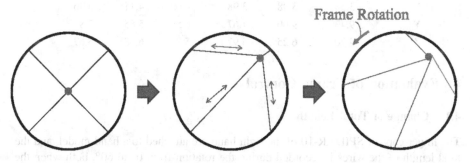

Fig. 5. Frame Rotation

3   Measurement of SPIDAR System

3.1   Fingertip Position

The errors between the calculated position and the actual position of each fingertip are shown in Table 1. Four wires of one fingertip are tied together and moved from the origin to a target position of 20 mm along a certain axis in the real space, and the error of the calculated position is recorded. It is repeated for both positive and negative direction of each axis of the five fingers of right hand. The average error of X-axis is 1.04 mm, which is larger than that of Y-axis 0.71 mm and Z-axis 0.84 mm. The result is mainly because that the space of X-axis in the rotary frame is narrower than that of Y-axis and Z-axis.

Table 1. Errors of each direction of the five fingers of right hand[mm].

Direction	Thumb	Index	Middle	Ring	Pinky
+X	1.00	1.41	1.20	1.29	1.10
−X	0.98	0.97	1.01	0.52	0.89
+Y	1.66	0.41	1.01	0.64	0.53
−Y	1.12	0.57	0.32	0.41	0.48
+Z	0.47	1.00	1.07	0.92	0.90
−Z	0.32	1.13	0.80	1.05	0.77

3.2   Output Force

We measured the magnitude of force output at the origin. In Table 2, the average force output of X-axis is smallest, and the force output of Y-axis is the largest. The angle between each wire of finger-caps and the X-axis is larger than that of Y and Z-axis. Thus the motors can only provide a smaller force output in the X-axis.

Table 2. Maximum force output[N].

Direction	Thumb	Index	Middle	Ring	Pinky	Average
X	3.58	3.98	3.98	4.09	4.15	3.96
Y	9.43	9.60	7.67	6.59	5.85	7.83
Z	4.20	6.25	5.97	5.85	6.08	5.67

4   Evaluation of Frame Control

4.1   Change of Total Length

The finger-caps of SPIDAR-10 of the right hand are attached to a hand model, and the total length of the wires is recorded during the rotation from 0° to 60°, both when the frame is fixed and controlled by the proposed method. This is repeated 5 times for all 3 kinds of hand models. The result and the used hand model are shown in Fig. 6.

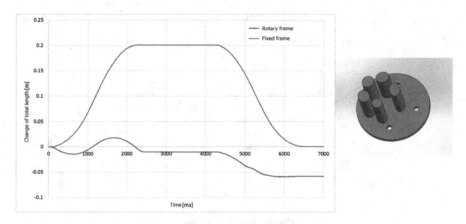

Fig. 6. The change of total length of all wires and the hand model.

With the consideration that when the frame is controlled by the proposed method, the total length of the wires is not minimized at 0 ms, the change of total length by our method during the rotation is actually reduced to about 0.05 m, while the total length is significantly increased to 0.2 m when the frame is fixed.

4.2 Fingertip Position Estimation When Rotating

The position of thumb of right hand is fixed at 20 mm and −20 mm along each axis, and the frame is rotated from −60° to 60°. The errors between the calculated position and the actual position are shown in the figures below. The errors of other fingers and left hand are similar (Figs. 7, 8 and 9).

The errors are caused by inaccuracy of wire length estimation and the position calibration. And because the wires cannot be accurately attached to just one point, there is also an error in the position of each fingertip.

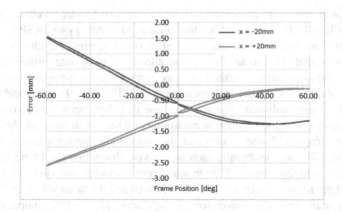

Fig. 7. Errors at x axis.

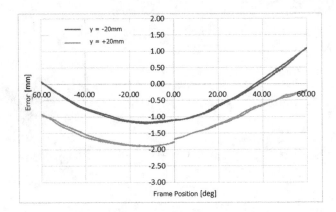

Fig. 8. Errors at y axis.

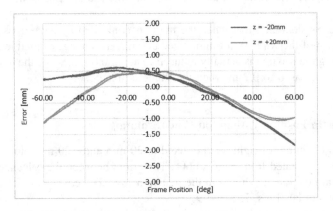

Fig. 9. Errors at z axis.

5 Conclusions and Future Works

We have proposed and developed a wire-driven two-handed multi-finger haptic interface SPIDAR-10. Compared to the former SPIDAR systems(SPIDAR-8 and SPIDAR-MF), as there are 4 wires attached to one fingertip, the direction of force output is not limited. Two rotary frames also allow user to operate virtual objects with two hands at the same time. A method of frame control is also proposed to minimize the total length of all wires. At last, performance of the SPIDAR-10 system and the frame control method are evaluated. The results show that the system can provide a two-handed multi-finger haptic interaction environment which is suitable for the rotational tasks and the proposed frame control can also reduce the interference of the wires.

There are still some problems, such as the vibration when the frame reaches the target position, and the remaining slight interference between the wires. Therefore, the algorithm of the frame control needs to be improved and the arrangement of the motors and the way of accurate calibration needs to be discussed. The force output during the process of rotating also needs to be evaluated in the future.

References

1. Galiana, I., Ferre, M.: Multi-finger Haptic Interaction. Springer, London (2013)
2. Endo, T., Kawasaki, H., Mouri, T., Ishigure, Y., Shimomura, H., Matsumura, M., Koketsu, K.: Five-Fingered Haptic Interface Robot:HIRO III. In: Proceedings of WorldHaptics 2009, pp. 458–463 (2009)
3. Nakagawara, S., Kajimoto, H., Kawakami, N., Tachi, S., Kawabuchi, I.: An encounter-type multi-fingered master hand using circuitous joints. In: ICRA2005 (2005)
4. CyberForce, CyberGlove-Systems. http://www.cyberglovesystems.com/products/cyberforce/overview
5. Gragera, J.B.: Control architecture for multifinger haptic devices applied to advanced manupilation. Ph.D. Thesis Technical University of Madrid (2011)
6. Monroy, M., Oyarzabal, M., Ferre, M., Campos, A., Barrio, J.: MasterFinger: Multi-finger haptic interface for collaborative environments. In: Ferre, M. (ed.) EuroHaptics 2008. LNCS, vol. 5024, pp. 411–419. Springer, Heidelberg (2008)
7. Brenosa, J., Cerrada, P., Ferre, M., Aracil, R.: Design of an ergonomic three-finger haptic device for advanced robotic hands control. In: Proceedings Of WorldHaptics 2011, pp. 257–262 (2011)
8. Walairacht, S., Koike, Y., Sato, M.: A new haptic display for both-hands-operation: SPIDAR-8. In: ISPACS'99 (1999)

A Human-Like Bilateral Tele-Handshake System: Preliminary Development

Sungjun Park, Sangsoo Park, Sang-Yun Baek, and Jeha Ryu[✉]

Gwangju Institute of Science and Technology, Gwangju, Republic of Korea
{psj,pss,sybaek,ryu}@gist.ac.kr

Abstract. While developing a new human-like bilateral tele-handshake system that can provide multimodal sensations including visual, kinesthetic, tactile, temperature, and auditory, this paper proposes a 4-channel energy-bounding bilateral tele-handshake framework for stable and transparent kinesthetic sensations. Instead of directly measured fore, this framework uses position-based force feedback along with position signals. Preliminary experimental results with the LTE network showed somewhat natural kinesthetic feeling while remote handshaking.

Keywords: Tele-handshake · Energy-bounding algorithm · Time delay

1 Introduction

Recently, tele-meeting systems are being widely used for tele-conference meetings with advanced wireless and 4G networks. In the tele-meeting, a bilateral tele-handshake that can provide haptic sensations can significantly increase tele-presence feelings. In this system, stability and transparency are two major requirements; The system must be stable and robust against any uncertainties in humans that have different dynamic properties and against uncertainties in any communication channels that contain significant delays, jitters, and losses. In the meantime, some degrees of transparency are needed to provide a realistic feeling as if the human shake hand with the other, directly. For this, a human-like haptic interface needs to be developed beyond the pen type interface such as a Phantom stylus [1]. Besides haptic sensations, visual and auditory information may also be provided for full immersion.

Previous investigations on the bilateral tele-handshake systems; Kunii and Hashimoto [2] created the first tele-handshake system providing the measured grasping forces. Instead of sending the handshake motion, a virtual human impedance model is used to generate a reference position of tele-handshake device. Later, Hashimoto and Manorotkul [3] extended the tele-handshake system in the real-internet. Systematic design of control parameters of the virtual model with human impedance may however be difficult to guarantee robust stability against any uncertainties in humans with very diverse impedance parameters. Moreover, providing the grasping force only without real arm movements may also lack in real handshaking feeling. Efforts in [4] and [5] provided kinesthetic sensation using a commercial haptic device with a stylus without investigating stability and transparency against any network conditions. Works in [6, 7]

M. Auvray and C. Duriez (Eds.): EuroHaptics 2014, Part II, LNCS 8619, pp. 184–190, 2014.
DOI: 10.1007/978-3-662-44196-1_23

between a human and a robot focused on the analysis and generation of the robot motion (trajectory) without considering communication time delays.

We are developing a new human-like bilateral tele-handshake system that can provide multimodal sensations including visual, kinesthetic, tactile, temperature, and auditory. The system must work reliably with anybody at anytime and anywhere as long as a communication network is working. This means that robust stability must be guaranteed against any uncertainties in humans and any networks such as wireless Internet, satellite, mobile communication. This paper proposes a 4-channel energy-bounding bilateral tele-handshake framework for stable and transparent kinesthetic sensations. Instead of directly measured fore, this framework uses position-based force feedback along with position signals. Some preliminary experimental results are presented on the quality of the force sensations in wrist/elbow joints. The hardware system includes a mannequin, camera, monitor, microphone, speaker, 1-dof haptic device, and human-like hand interface. To guarantee robust stability against any network delays and data losses, this paper proposes a position error-based energy-bounding approach (EBA) that is an extended version of [8]. The proposed algorithm only requires energy dissipation capability of the haptic interfaces. This can easily be identified offline and can thus be applied to any humans and networks.

2   A Human-Like Bilateral Tele-Handshake System

Two human-like bilateral tele-handshake systems are being developed in local and remote sites, as shown in Fig. 1; one for men and the other for women. Each is composed of a mannequin, a camera, a monitor, a microphone, a speaker, a 1-dof haptic device for the lower arm, and a hand. The mannequin is used as a human upper body, leg and left arm. The monitor located at the top of the mannequin is used as a human face to only display the other partner's face. The camera located at the top of the monitor is used as a human eye to capture only a human face that is transferred to the other site through Skype that can provide peers with voice, video, and instant messaging over the Internet. For kinesthetic feeling, a 1-dof haptic device is used as an elbow joint of a human right arm and is attached to the right arm of the mannequin as

Fig. 1. The human-like bilateral tele-handshake system

shown in Fig. 2 (a). It is actuated by a MAXON motor (RE-40) with 8000 pulse encoders and with a back-drivable torque-amplifying capstan mechanism. Specifications of the haptic device are: workspace of 160 mm; maximum force of 20 N and control rate has 1000 Hz. In addition, a spring-like passive joint is attached to the wrist joint for the more natural kinesthetic feeling as shown in Fig. 2 (b). For tactile, temperature, and visual sensation the human-like hand interface is used and is attached to the end of the right arm as shown in Fig. 2 (c). Inside a silicon hand, a urethane and wooden stick is inserted for simulating a stiffness of the hand skin and bone. In addition, heat rays are used to provide the sense of heat. Two tele-handshake systems may be connected through a communication channel such as Internet, satellite, mobile communication (WCDMA/LTE/LTE-A), and etc. We use the LTE as a communication channel showing a significant variation of time delay (82 ms average round trip delay (RTT), min. 28 ms & max. 130 ms, and 95 % data loss).

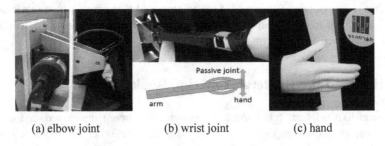

(a) elbow joint   (b) wrist joint   (c) hand

Fig. 2. The human-like arm and hand

3   A 4-Channel Bilateral Tele-Handshake Framework

According to [3], ideal control objectives of the tele-handshake system can be defined as follows; for stability, the system remains stable. For transparency, force sensation must be realized and there are no position differences between the master and slave positions. Therefore, the control objectives for transparency can mathematically be represented as

$$\text{Objective } 1 - F_d(t) \rightarrow F_{oh}(t - \tau) \tag{1}$$

$$\text{Objective } 2 - x_d(t) \rightarrow x_{oh}(t - \tau) \tag{2}$$

where F_d and F_{oh} are the forces exerted on the haptic device and by the other site human, respectively; x_d and x_{oh} are the positions of the haptic device and of the other site human, respectively; τ is a communication time delay.

In order to achieve the control objectives for kinesthetic sensation, this paper proposes the 4-channel bilateral tele-handshake framework shown in Fig. 3. In this framework, the local (block (A)) and remote sites (block (B)) each includes a 1-dof haptic device, position error-based position controller, and a stabilizing EBA. Force

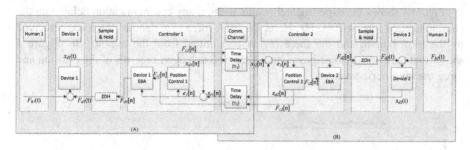

Fig. 3. A 4-channel bilateral tele-handshake framework

and position information are exchanged and the transmitted force and position from other site are used as an input to the position error-based EBA. Note that this is the indirect force display because the direct force display that reflects the measured force requires an expensive force/torque sensor. In the indirect force display mode, the force reflection is obtained as

$$F_c(n) = K_P(x_d(n) - x_r(n)) + K_D(\dot{x}_d(n) - \dot{x}_r(n)) \tag{3}$$

where K_P and K_D are proportional and derivative gains; x_d and x_r are the haptic device and reference positions (delayed haptic device position of other site (= $x_{oh}(t\text{-}\tau)$)), respectively.

The control law of the error-based EBA is defined as follow;

Control Law:

$$F_d(n) = F_d(n-1) + \beta(n)\Delta e(n) \tag{4}$$

$$\text{where } \beta(n) = \frac{F_i(n) - F_d(n-1)}{\Delta e(n)} \text{ for } \Delta e(n) \neq 0, \tag{5}$$

$\Delta e(n) = e(n) - e(n-1)$, $e(n) = x_d(n) - x_r(n)$; $F_t(n)$ is the delayed $F_c(n)$ through the communication channel. The parameter $\beta(n)$ may be bounded to guarantee stability against high stiffness and poor network conditions (delay, loss, or jitter). The bounding law for stability is similar to the slave site's bounding law in [8] and thus is omitted here.

4   Experiments

Preliminary experiments are conducted to evaluate the feasibility of the proposed bilateral tele-handshake system. In the experiments, a human (a leader) in the local site shakes the haptic device as naturally as possible and the remote site human (a follower) follows passively the motion of the haptic device while relaxing his/her arm. After gravity compensation, a proportional position controller gain of 0.5 kN/m is used for the realistic handshake feeling based on the repetitive handshake experiments.

Figure 4 shows the experimental results without any communication delay with the communication rate of 1000 Hz. Here, the EBA force (F_d) denotes the force perceived by the local human and the force (F_t) is transmitted from the remote site. Figure 4 shows that the control objectives 1 and 2 are well achieved in terms of the position and force tracking performance.

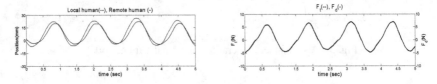

Fig. 4. The experimental results for no time delay

For the evaluation in any communication networks, a tethering function of mobile communication such as LTE communication channel is used. In this case, the communication rate is about 17–25 Hz. Since this low communication rate causes an abrupt variation of the transmitted information, the following low pass filter (LPF) is inserted after the communication channel to prevent the abrupt variation of the position and force information

$$Low\ Pass\ Filter = \frac{300}{s^2 + 50s + 300} \tag{6}$$

Note that the LPF causes 320 ms additional first order delay.

Figure 5 represents the experimental results for the LTE communication channel, which shows the stable operation regardless of the low communication rate. Without the LPF, an overshoot occurs due to the abrupt variation of the transmitted position (reference position), which causes uncomfortable feelings to the humans. On the other hand, with the LPF, the force (F_d) transmitted to the human became smooth as shown

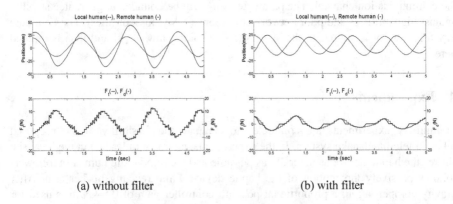

(a) without filter   (b) with filter

Fig. 5. The experimental results for LTE communication channel

in the solid line of Fig. 5 (b). So, both humans feel more naturally. However, the EBA force (F_d) did not fully display the transmitted force (F_t) due to the bounded $\beta(n)$ for stability against time delays. Note that despite shifted human motion as much as transmission delay plus filter delay, any severe unnaturalness is observed. This is because the human in each side does not know the real hand motion of the other human motion only with a face displayed in the screen.

5   Conclusion

The proposed system could provide stable and somewhat natural handshake feeling. The control bandwidth showed about 2 Hz and the proposed handshaking system showed stability for any humans, for any networks, and for any shaking frequencies. For better performance of the proposed tele-handshake system, future studies are planned for: (i) comprehensive experiments for the various handshake behavior, (ii) addition of the grasping force and gain tuning of position controller for the kinesthetic sensation based on the grasping force, (iv) more human-like appearance/ interface and evaluation of multimodal sensation such as visual, temperature, auditory, and etc. (v) evaluation of the human likeness using turing-like handshake test [9], etc.

Acknowledgements. This work was supported by the Micro Soft Research Asia (MSRA) and the "Basic Research Projects in High-tech Industrial Technology" Project through a grant provided by GIST in 2014.

References

1. Alhalabi, M.O., Horiguchi, S.: Tele-handshake: a cooperative shared haptic virtual environment. In: Proceedings of Eurohaptics, pp. 60–64 (2001)
2. Kunii, Y., Hashimoto, H.: Tele-handshake using HandShake Device. In: Proceedings of the IEEE 21st International Conference on Industrial Electronics, Control, and Instrumentation, pp. 179–182 (1995)
3. Hashimoto, H., Manorotkul, S.: Tele-Handshake through the internet. In: Proceedings of the IEEE International Workshop on Robot and Human Communication, pp. 90–95 (1996)
4. Wang, D., Tuer, K., Ni, L., Porciello, P.: Conducting a real-time remote handshake with haptics. In: Proceedings 12th International Symposium on Haptic Interfaces for Virtual Environment and Teleoperator Systems (2004)
5. Kwon, Y.-M., Park, K.-W.: Tnagible tele-meeting system with DV-ARPN (augmented reality peripheral network). In: Proceedings of the International Conference on Computational Science and its Applications, pp. 913–920 (2005)
6. Jindai, M., Watanabe, T.: Development of a handshake request motion model based on analysis of handshake motion between humans. In: Proceedings of the 2011 IEEE/ASME International Conference on Advanced Intelligent Mechatronics, pp. 560–565 (2011)
7. Wang, Z., Giannopoulos, E., Slater, M., Peer, A., Buss, M.: Handshake: realistic human-robot interaction in haptic enhanced virtual reality. Presence: Teleoperators and Virtual Environ. **20** (4), 371–392 (2011)

8. Seo, C., Kim, J.-P., Kim, J., Ahn, H.-S., Ryu, J.: Robustly stable bilateral teleoperation under time-varying delays and data losses: and enerby-bounding approach. J. Mech. Sci. Technol. **25**(8), 2089–2100 (2011)
9. Avraham, G., Nisky, I., Fernandes, H., Acuna, D., Kording, K., Loeb, G., Karniel, A.: Towards perceiving robots as humans: three handshake models face the turing-like handshake test. IEEE Trans. Haptics **5**(3), 196–207 (2012)

Evaluation of Stretchable Conductor
for Measuring Clothing Pressure

Katsunari Sato[1(✉)], Sayasa Otsubo[1], Teppei Araki[2], Tohru Sugahara[2],
and Katsuaki Suganuma[2]

[1] Nara Women's University, Kitauoya Nishi Machi, Nara, Japan
katsu-sato@cc.nara-wu.ac.jp, sayasa3838@gmail.com
[2] Osaka University, Mihogaoka 8-1, Ibaraki, Osaka 567-0047, Japan
teppei@eco.sanken.osaka-u.ac.jp,
{sugahara, suganuma}@sanken.osaka-u.ac.jp

Abstract. In this study, we developed a stretchable conductor and evaluated whether it is capable of measuring clothing pressure. The experimental relationship between electrical resistance and strain, and the results regarding the physical effects of the conductor on the textile showed that this device could be used to measure clothing pressure by being printed on the textile (with particular suitability when the textile is made from polyester). Furthermore, we clarify the current problems of the conductor such as the variation in the electrical resistance with time and the bending characteristics.

Keywords: Clothing pressure · Stretchable conductor · Strain sensor

1 Introduction

Clothing pressure, which humans perceive on their skin over their bodies when they wear garments or wearable interfaces, is an important factor when developing comfortable garments or wearable interfaces. Therefore, the evaluation of clothing pressure is an essential part of garment and wearable interface manufacturing technology. There are two main methods for evaluating clothing pressure [1, 2]: a direct method that measures clothing pressure by placing a sensor element, such as an air-pack-type pressure sensor, between the human body and the textile (in this study, we define the textile as the cloth of a garment or a wearable interface device); and an indirect method that models the clothing pressure based on the physical parameters of the textile and the human body on a computer. Currently, the direct method is commonly used because it remains difficult to estimate clothing pressure correctly using indirect methods, particularly in dynamic situations in which the wearer moves, although the simulation technology has improved. However, there are also difficulties in measuring clothing pressure using direct methods, particularly when trying to measure pressure at multiple points. For example, air-pack-type sensors (which are a commonly used measurement technology) require multiple air-packs to be placed between the human body and the textile. In this case, it becomes difficult to prepare the measurements, and the presence of the packs restricts the movement of the wearer. Furthermore, displacement of the packs owing to improper fixing results in measurement errors.

© Springer-Verlag Berlin Heidelberg 2014
M. Auvray and C. Duriez (Eds.): EuroHaptics 2014, Part II, LNCS 8619, pp. 191–197, 2014.
DOI: 10.1007/978-3-662-44196-1_24

We believe that sensor elements used for the direct measurement of clothing pressure should (1) be easy to affix to the textiles or the human body, (2) be as stretchable and flexible as the textile, and (3) be able to accurately detect the pressure distribution. Several sensor elements that are both stretchable and flexible have been developed [3–5]; however, affixing them to the textile or the human body becomes a problem. For the sensor element, we focused on a stretchable conductor that changes its electrical resistance as a function of strain. Because traditional stretchable conductors were developed for electrical wires, it is a difficult process to affix them to the textile and/or to measure the state of strain repetitively, even in currently available devices [6, 7]. On the other hand, the stretchable conductor that we have developed [8] has the potential to both be easily affixed to the textile and be used for repetitive measuring clothing pressure.

In this study, we evaluated the characteristics of our developed stretchable conductor to determine whether it can be used for measuring clothing pressure. Furthermore, we clarified the current problems of the conductor when used for this measurement.

2   Stretchable Conductor for Measuring Clothing Pressure

To create a sensor element for measuring clothing pressure, we used a stretchable conductor composed of silver flakes and polyurethane [8]. The developed stretchable conductor can be easily fabricated by printing it on various materials such as paper, cotton, polyimide, and polyvinyl chloride. This device has a positive correlation between electrical resistance and strain. On the basis of these characteristics, the conductor can be directly printed on textiles, forming a clothing pressure sensor.

In a practical implementation, we print a number of pieces of stretchable conductor on a piece of textile for which we want to evaluate the distribution of clothing pressure. When the clothing pressure increases between the wearer's body and the textile, the textile stretches; the extent of stretching is detected as changes in the electrical resistance of the conductors: the larger change in the resistance represents a larger value of clothing pressure. In this case, the preparation for measurement is simply to wear the sensor-affixed textiles and ensure that the sensor element is not displaced. If the conductor is more stretchable and flexible than the textile, it does not limit the wearer's movement during measurement.

3   Experiments

3.1   Purpose

We evaluated whether the stretchable conductor could be used for measuring clothing pressure considering the two following criteria:

1. The relationship between electrical resistance and strain including time variation to examine accuracy and stability.
2. The effect of printing the stretchable conductor on a textile to examine the change in the physical parameters of the textile.

3.2 Materials and Methods

Construction of Stretchable Conductor [8]. Silver pastes were prepared by uniformly dispersing silver flakes of 2 to 3 µm in size (Fukuda Metal Foil & Powder, AgC-239) in a water-based polyurethane emulsion (Bayer Material Science, Dispercoll U42). Uniform dispersions were obtained using a high-speed vacuum mixer (THINKY, ARV-310) operated at 2000 rpm for 3 min under vacuum conditions. The silver pastes were mask-printed onto either a polyurethane sheet or a textile and dried at 70 °C for 3 h. The width, length, and thickness of the stretchable conductor were 3, 30, and 0.3 mm (or 5, 30, and 0.3 mm for the textile), respectively. The stretchable conductors were fabricated with a silver content of approximately 56 vol.% (91 wt.%).

Relationship Between Electrical Resistance and Strain. Figure 1(a) shows the experimental arrangement used for measuring the electrical resistance, including the xy-stage (Chuoseiki, QT-CM2) and Kelvin clips. The electrical resistivity of the stretchable conductor was measured using the four-point probe method (Tsuruga Denki, Model3568). The conductor was stretched by the xy-stage at a test speed of 1 mm/s. The distance between the chucks was 20 mm before stretching. The room temperature was approximately 20 °C.

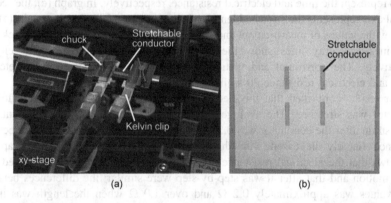

(a)   (b)

Fig. 1. Experimental conditions. (a) Settings for evaluating the relationship between electrical resistance and strain. (b) Textile (polyester) with stretchable conductors.

We first stretched the conductor 2.0 mm and recorded its electrical resistance six times over 25 s. Then, we changed the stretching length from 0.5 mm to 5.0 mm (in steps of 0.5 mm) and recorded the electrical resistance at each step for 25 s. In this case, we stretched the conductor directly from 0 mm to the target length. Finally, we stretched the conductor step-by-step, stretching 0.5 mm every 20 s up to a total length of 5.0 mm. The recording interval for electrical resistance was 1 s for all measurements.

Effects of Printing the Stretchable Conductor on the Textile. The textiles used in this experiment were cotton and polyester, which are typical materials in clothing. We printed four stretchable conductors on 200 mm × 200 mm sheets of the textiles, as shown in Fig. 1(b). The distance between the centers of the stretchable conductors was 50 mm. The long axis of the conductor was the warp direction of the textile. The room temperature was approximately 20 °C.

We evaluated the changes in the bending, tensile, and shear characteristics of the textile after printing the stretchable conductor using a KES system [9]. A KES system can electronically measure data about the texture sensation of the cloth. Regarding the bending characteristics, we measured stiffness (B) and hysteresis (2HB) with a KES-FB2-AUTO-A (Kato Tech Co.). We also measured the tensile characteristics—strain (EM), linearity (LT), energy (WT), and resilience (RT)—and the shear characteristics—stiffness (G) and hysteresis (2HG and 2HG5) —with a KES-FB1-AUTO-A (Kato Tech Co.). These nine characteristics were important factors when we considered both the evaluation of the clothing pressure caused by stretching of the textile and the lack of restriction to the movement of the wearer.

3.3 Results

Relationship Between Electrical Resistance and Strain. The graphs in Fig. 2 present the results under each condition. The horizontal and primary vertical axes of graphs (a)–(c) represent the time and electrical resistance, respectively. In graph (c), the second vertical axis represents the stretched length of the conductor. The dots in graphs (a) and (b) show the values of measurement and stretching length, respectively. The black dots with lines and gray lines show the electrical resistance and stretching lengths, respectively. The horizontal and vertical axes in graph (d) represent the stretching length and electrical resistance 20 s after stretching, respectively.

Our results confirmed that the electrical resistance gradually decreased after the conductor was stretched. The averaged standard deviation of six measurements for 2 mm strain after the conductor was 0.32 Ω. The graph in (b) shows that the electrical resistance linearly increased with the stretch length. Furthermore, the graph in (d) shows that the electrical resistance at 20 s after the conductor was stretched in a single motion and that after it was step-by-step were similar: the differences between these values was approximately 0.2 Ω and over 1.0 Ω when the length was under 3.0 mm and over 3.5 mm, respectively.

Effect of Printing the Stretchable Conductor on a Textile. Table 1 lists the measurement physical parameters of the textile. The row "Dir." and "Cond." represent the direction of the textile and the existence of the conductor, respectively. The tensile characteristics of polyester in the weft direction were not measured because the textile was stretched too much to be measured by the measuring machine.

The dark gray and gray cells indicate that the physical parameters changed by more than 50 % and 25 % of the original value, respectively. We confirmed that the presence of the stretchable conductor has little effect on the tensile characteristics of both the textiles and that it shares the characteristics of the polyester.

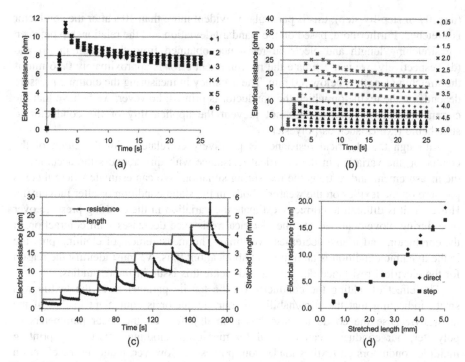

Fig. 2. Experimental results of the electrical resistance. (a) Six measurements for 2 mm stretch. (b) Measurement at different stretch lengths. (c) Measurement for increasing stretch length. (d) Electrical resistance 20 s after stretching to each length, directly or step-by-step.

Table 1. Physical parameters measured by KES system.
Dir.: direction of textile. Cond.: existence of the conductor.

Textile	Dir.	Cond.	B	2HB	EM	LT	WT	RT	G	2HG	2HG5
Cotton	Warp	Yes	0.031	0.015	4.55	0.39	4.40	60.23	0.49	0.60	1.00
		No	0.027	0.010	4.45	0.50	5.60	52.68	0.49	0.40	1.00
	Weft	Yes	0.072	0.026	9.10	0.68	15.45	34.95	0.44	0.60	1.00
		No	0.018	0.006	6.95	0.67	11.65	42.06	0.84	1.00	2.40
Polyes-ter	Warp	Yes	0.011	0.003	30.15	0.53	39.70	45.97	0.38	0.80	0.80
		No	0.007	0.002	24.80	0.56	34.75	47.77	0.33	0.60	1.00
	Weft	Yes	0.031	0.023	–	–	–	–	0.49	1.00	1.20
		No	0.063	0.033	–	–	–	–	0.49	1.00	1.30

4 Discussion

In this section, we discuss the experimental results in terms of whether our developed stretchable conductor is appropriate for measuring clothing pressure.

The results of the electrical resistance measurement confirmed that the electrical resistance is positively correlated with the strain, regardless of the stretching method (directly or step-by-step); this is particularly evident more than 10 s after the conductor is stretched. Furthermore, based on the standard deviation and the relationship between the stretching length and electrical resistance obtained from the graph in (a) and (d), respectively, we can estimate the measurement error is approximately 0.26 mm if the stretching length is below 3.0 mm. The accuracy in measuring the clothing pressure depends on the textile on which the conductor is printed; however, we believe that the current measurement error does not prevent the applicability of the conductor to stretchable textiles such as polyester.

Although the electrical resistance is positively correlated with the strain of the conductor, the variation in the electrical resistance with time reduces the accuracy of the measurement and restricts the measuring situation. We can estimate where there is pressure on the textiles on the wearer's body in the static condition or after movement. However, it is difficult to correctly estimate the variation in the clothing pressure over time during movement because the electrical resistance decreases with contraction of the conductor, and it also decreases over time. The measurement of clothing pressure in the dynamic condition is an important application; thus, we must identify the reason for the electrical resistance decreasing and tackle this issue in future studies.

The effect of adding the conductor on the tensile parameters of the textile was small, indicating that the stretchability of our conductor is equivalent to that of the textile. Because the conductor also has a small effect on the shear parameters of polyester, our conductor can be used for measuring clothing pressure by printing multiple conductors on textiles made from polyester. However, reducing the effect on the bending characteristics will be the subject of future research because it relates to the comfort of textiles when wearers move.

5   Conclusion and Future Works

We proposed a novel stretchable conductor for measuring clothing pressure; this conductor can be printed on textiles. We evaluated (1) the relationship between electrical resistance and strain, including time variation, and (2) the effect of printing the stretchable conductor on textiles. Our results confirmed that our conductor can be used for measuring clothing pressure when printed on textiles, and is particularly suited to use on textiles made from polyester. Furthermore, the results showed the current problems of the conductor, such as the variation in the electrical resistance over time and the effect of the bending characteristics.

In the future, we will investigate the reasons for (and methods of improvement of) the problems that we found in this study so as to decrease the limitations on the measurement of clothing pressure. Then, we will evaluate the accuracy of our conductor as a sensor of clothing pressure by printing it on several textiles and further evaluating the relationship between pressure and electrical resistance. In the present study, we did not consider several effects that should be evaluated in practice, such as temperature, hysteresis, and linearity. Therefore, we will further investigate the characteristics of the conductor using these criteria.

Acknowledgement. This work was performed under the Cooperative Research Program of "Network Joint Research Center for Materials and Devices" and supported by JSPS Grant-in-Aid for Young Scientists (Start-up) 25880014.

References

1. Dongsheng, C., Hong, L., Qiaoling, Z., Hongge, W.: Effects of mechanical properties of fabrics on clothing pressure. PRZEGLĄD ELEKTROTECHNICZNY **R.89**, 232–235 (2013)
2. Lee, Y., Hong, K.: Development of indirect method for clothing pressure measurement using three-dimensional imaging. Text. Res. J. **83**, 1594–1605 (2013)
3. Inoue, M., Kawahito, Y., Tada, Y., Hondo, T., Kawasaki, T., Suganuma, K., Ishiguro, H.: A super-flexible sensor system for humanoid robots and related applications. In: Proceedings of the International Conference on Electronics Packaging, pp. 114–119 (2007)
4. Lipomi, D.J., Vosgueritchian, M.B., Tee, C.-K., Hellstrom, S.L., Lee, J.A., Fox, C.H., Bao, Z.: Skin-like sensors of pressure and strain enabled by transparent, elastic films of carbon. Nanotub. Nat. Nanotechnol. **6**, 788–792 (2011)
5. Sugiura, Y., Inami, M., Igarashi, T.: A thin stretchable interface for tangential force measurement. In: Proceedings of ACM UIST 2012, pp. 529–536 (2012)
6. Ahn, B.Y., Yoon, J.: Omnidirectional printing of flexible, stretchable, and spanning silver microelectrodes. Science **323**, 1590–1593 (2009)
7. Tang, L.: A facile route for irreversible bonding of plastic-PDMS hybrid microdevices at room temperature. Lab Chip **10**, 1274–1280 (2010)
8. Araki, T., Sugahara, T., Nogi, M., Suganuma, K.: Effect of void volume and silver loading on strain response of electrical resistance in silver flakes/polyurethane composite for stretchable conductors. Jpn. J. Appl. Phys. **51**, 11PD01 (2012)
9. Kawabata, S.: Easy guide on the point of the hand evaluation and clothes. J. Text. Mach. Soc. Jpn. 33(2) (1980)

The LegoPress: A Rehabilitation, Performance Assessment and Training Device Mechanical Design and Control

Jeremy Olivier$^{(\boxtimes)}$, Maxime Jeanneret, Mohamed Bouri,
and Hannes Bleuler

Laboratory of Robotic Systems (LSRO),
Swiss Federal Institute of Technology Lausanne (EPFL), Lausanne, Switzerland
{jeremy.olivier,maxime.jeanneret,mohamed.bouri,
hannes.bleuler}@epfl.ch
http://lsro.epfl.ch/

Abstract. In this paper we present the LegoPress, a simple and cost-effective robotic device intended to be used for leg-press movements in rehabilitation and training. Basic adjustments can be done on the sitting position so as to maximize comfort and adapt the posture of the user depending on the desired training. The LegoPress has two motorized axes independently acting on the two legs. By means of force sensors positioned at the pedal level, a precise monitoring is possible. The force sensor is as well used to improve the impedance control, which enables to reproduce various behaviors. The device is not only able to mobilize the user's legs but also to interact with her/him.

Keywords: Rehabilitation · Leg press · Impedance control

1 Introduction

In the past decades, robotic devices have proven their efficiency in rehabilitation, performance assessment and in training [1, 2]. This is mainly due to their ability to perform repetitive tasks precisely (without fatigue, as opposed to human physiotherapists). Moreover robotic devices accurately monitor and record the user's progresses for on-line fine tuning and for later evaluation and optimization of a training program.

The Laboratory of Robotic Systems (LSRO) has contributed to that field notably with devices like the WalkTrainer [3], the MotionMaker [4] or with the Lambda [5]. While the WalkTrainer provides rehabilitation during over-ground walking, the MotionMaker and the Lambda are intended for sitting position. The two latter devices have three active degrees of freedom (DOF) per leg, which enables leg press movements, cycling or any other kind of trajectories in the sagittal plane. Their versatility is therefore optimal for various activities. However, their level of complexity being relatively high, there is a need for simpler systems conserving all the merits of robotic devices. Clinical trials with the MotionMaker have shown that leg press movements only can be used for rehabilitation [4, 6]. The typical velocity for such an exercise is usually smaller than 0.5 m/s. As the device is intended to be used in rehabilitation, the

© Springer-Verlag Berlin Heidelberg 2014
M. Auvray and C. Duriez (Eds.): EuroHaptics 2014, Part II, LNCS 8619, pp. 198–205, 2014.
DOI: 10.1007/978-3-662-44196-1_25

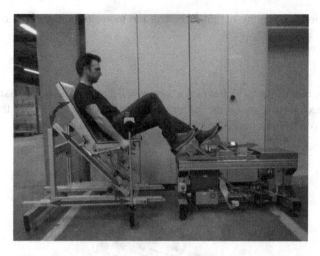

Fig. 1. The LegoPress. The red arrows represent the actuated degrees of freedom while the blue ones are the possible pre-defined settings on the chair (Color figure online).

maximal required force is assumed to be less than the force that a person applies on the ground with his/her feet. Therefore, 500 N per leg is enough for most rehabilitation strategies.

In this paper we present a simple and cost-effective device to train the flexion/extension movements (leg press): the LegoPress (see Fig. 1). This device has only one active DOF per leg in addition to pre-defined adjustments at the seat and at the ankle level. The characteristics and capabilities of the LegoPress and its control are presented in what follows. The LegoPress works as an interactive haptic device, with a wide range of potential interaction strategies going well beyond straight-forward mobilization.

2   Hardware

In this section, the mechanical specificities of the LegoPress are detailed. The two actuated axes are first described. Then, the different possible adjustments on the sitting position and on the pedal are explained. The force applied on the pedal being crucial, the force sensing system is as well detailed at the end of the section.

2.1   Actuated DOF

The main DOFs of the LegoPress are the translations along the horizontal axes, which enables the flexion/extension of the legs, i.e. the leg press movements. These axes are actuated with 400 W Maxon motors through a transmission composed by a reduction made of pulleys and a block and tackle mechanism as presented on Fig. 2 (the different variables used in the equations are also presented on Fig. 2). The stiffness of the belts being high, the approximation of a perfectly rigid system is considered. Indeed, the measured stiffness at the output when the motor is at a fixed position is bigger than 300 N/mm at any position in the workspace.

The equation linking the output force and the motor torque is given by:

$$F = \frac{\tau_m}{\frac{1}{2}n_{12}n_{34}R} \tag{1}$$

where F is the output force, τ_m the motor torque, n_{12} and n_{34} the transmission ratios of the pulleys mechanisms and R the radius of the pulley which transfers the rotational movement into a translation in the block and tackle mechanism.

(a)

(b)

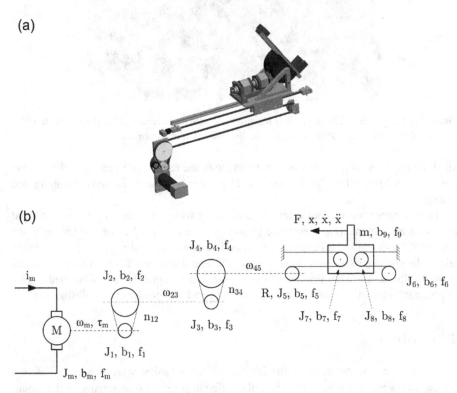

Fig. 2. One of the two motorized axes of the LegoPress. The reduction is composed by two stages of pulleys and by a block and tackle mechanism. (a) CAD view. (b) Schematic view of the different element composing the actuation. i_m is the current which is converted into a torque τ_m by the motor. ω_m is the velocity at the motor level. J, b and f are respectively the inertias, the viscous friction and the dry friction of the different elements composing the transmission. n corresponds to the reduction ratio between two consecutive stages. R is the radius of the pulley which transfers the rotational movement into a translation in the block and tackle mechanism. m is the mass of the parts moving in translation, F and x are the force and the translational displacement at the end effector.

The reduction ratio of this mechanism is thus 0.0012 m/rad. Therefore the maximum velocity at the end effector is about 0.6 m/s and the maximal force that can be generated is approximately 600 N, which corresponds to our requirements. The inertia and the friction of the different parts composing this mechanism generate additional forces at the end effector (see Fig. 2(b)). In order to calculate the maximal acceleration, the equation of motion is used:

$$F = m_{eq}\ddot{x} + b_{eq}\dot{x} + \text{sgn}(\dot{x}) \cdot F_{feq} \tag{2}$$

where m_{eq} b_{eq} and F_{feq} are the equivalent mass, viscous coefficient and dry friction. They are given by:

$$m_{eq} = \frac{J_m + J_1}{\left(\frac{1}{2}n_{12}n_{34}R\right)^2} + \frac{J_2 + J_3}{\left(\frac{1}{2}n_{34}R\right)^2} + \frac{J_4 + J_5 + J_6}{\left(\frac{1}{2}R\right)^2} + \frac{J_7 + J_8}{R^2} + m \tag{3}$$

$$b_{eq} = \frac{b_m + b_1}{\left(\frac{1}{2}n_{12}n_{34}R\right)^2} + \frac{b_2 + b_3}{\left(\frac{1}{2}n_{34}R\right)^2} + \frac{b_4 + b_5 + b_6}{\left(\frac{1}{2}R\right)^2} + \frac{b_7 + b_8}{R^2} + b_9 \tag{4}$$

$$F_{feq} = \frac{\tau_{fm} + \tau_{f1}}{\frac{1}{2}n_{12}n_{34}R} + \frac{\tau_{f2} + \tau_{f3}}{\frac{1}{2}n_{12}R} + \frac{\tau_{f4} + \tau_{f5} + \tau_{f6}}{\frac{1}{2}R} + \frac{\tau_{f7} + \tau_{f8}}{R} + F_{f9} \tag{5}$$

The theoretical maximal acceleration is therefore about 5 m/s^2, which is in most of the cases largely enough for such a device.

2.2 Settings on the Chair

The sitting position relatively to the motorized axes can be set so as to adjust the position of the hip. This may be useful to train different movement or to enhance the comfort during the training. The settings which can be done on the chair are presented on Fig. 1.

2.3 Settings on the Pedal

The angular equilibrium position of the pedal can as well be adjusted. A passive mechanism (spring-based) enables to set the equilibrium position. The stiffness is set differently in dorsiflexion and in plantar flexion. Moreover, the minimal force to induce a pedal angular movement can be adjusted.

2.4 Force Sensing

In order to be able to have a precise control on the force acting between the LegoPress and the user's foot, a force sensor is integrated on the pedal (as close as possible to the foot as shown on Fig. 3). As only the force acting along the direction of movement is of interest, a blade structure was designed so as to have an optimal measurement without perturbation coming from other transverse forces and torques. The force sensing mechanism is presented on Fig. 3.

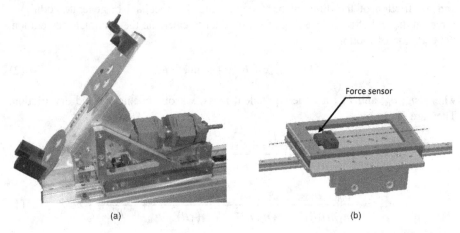

Fig. 3. Force measurement system. (a) Detail of the pedal with the force measurement system. The sensor itself is colored in red. (b) CAD of the force measurement system on the moving platform (pedal not shown). The blades (blue parts) enable only the displacement along the main axis (red axis) of the force sensor (red part), the parasitic forces and torques are therefore suppressed (Color figure online).

3   Control

The LegoPress runs on a PC-based open architecture which allows to easily modify the control algorithms. Rehabilitation not only requires mobilization but also necessitates a bidirectional interaction between the user and the robot. Position control is easy to implement with the LegoPress but it is also required that the user is able to lead the movement. In order to be able to render different behaviors, we decided to implement an impedance controller. To do so, we first evaluated the transparency capabilities of the device.

3.1   Transparency

The analytical model of the LegoPress was developed (based on the equation of motion) in order to compensate for its dynamical effects. The transparency was then evaluated with this compensation. Even though an important improvement could be achieved, the effect of the dry static friction was persistent due to the impossibility to compensate for it when the pedal is not moving. The force sensor was thus used in order to improve the behavior of the impedance controller as proposed in [7].

3.2   Impedance Controller

From the transparent mode, almost any impedance can be reproduced by superimposing the adequate motion to force relation. Figure 4 presents the block diagram of the implemented impedance controller. Its only limitation comes from the system's maximal performances in terms of velocities, accelerations and forces.

To demonstrate the capabilities of the LegoPress with an impedance controller, we implemented stiffness and friction (dry and viscous) behaviors. The output force was then measured as a function of position and velocity. The results are presented on Fig. 5.

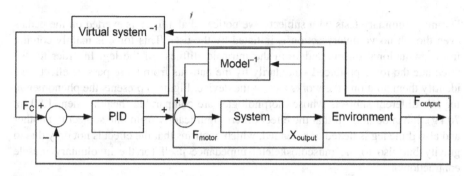

Fig. 4. Block diagram of the impedance controller. The system is compensated by means of a model based on Eq. 2 (red frame). In order to improve the transparency of the system, force measurement is used (blue frame). The desired impedance is superimposed to the transparent system (Color figure online).

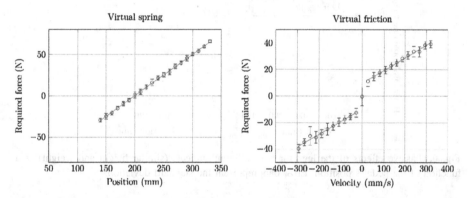

Fig. 5. Implemented impedances: spring (left), and friction (right). The error bars represent the standard deviation. For the virtual spring, the range of velocity during the measurement was $\pm$ 200 mm/s and the acceleration was $\pm$ 1000 mm/s^2. The PID gains are: K_p = 2 N/N, K_i = 300 N/(N·s), K_d = 0.05 N/(N/s). The parameters of the model are: F_{feq} = 20 N, b_{eq} = 0.09 N/(m/s), m_{eq} = 60 kg.

3.3 Safety

In order to guarantee a safe behavior, the LegoPress is equipped with redundant position sensors (potentiometers which enable absolute position measurement) in addition to the motor encoders, a watchdog timer and an emergency stop button. If the control variables (target and measure) exceed predefined limits or in case of unexpected events (e.g. redundancy errors), the winding of the motors are short-circuited in order to stop the pedals and limit the risk of injury.

4 Personalized Biomechanical Model

During preliminary tests with subjects, we noticed that a force is exerted on the pedals even though no voluntary action is initiated by the user. This force is mainly coming from gravitational effects and from the intrinsic stiffness of the leg. In order to differentiate the force produced voluntarily by the patients from these passive effects, we identify them all along the workspace of the device. Figure 6 presents the phenomenon for two different subjects whose morphologies are comparable (healthy men, 1.80 m, 70 kg). It can be noticed that the effect differs significantly from one subject to another and also if the leg is flexed or extended, which confirms that the effect is not only due to gravity but also to the musculoskeletal impedance itself (or the involuntary muscle contractions).

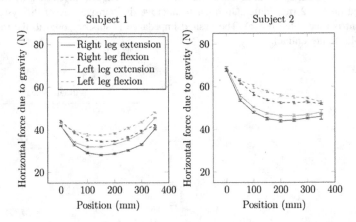

Fig. 6. Passive effects of the legs for two different subjects (similar height and weight) as a function of the pedal's position. Error bars represent the standard deviation.

5 Discussion

The LegoPress is a device intended to be used for rehabilitation, training and assessment. Thanks to its simple design, it can easily be produced at a decent cost. The redundancy of sensing (notably additional analog position sensors on the axes) ensures its safety and it is therefore ready to be used with subjects. The open architecture also enables to easily implement various strategies. Additional functionalities can therefore be considered in the future. As an example, electromyography can be used in addition to the force sensing and may even be used as input for the controller.

As the device possesses force sensors at the pedals' level, it is able to precisely monitor the interaction with the user. These force sensors are as well used for impedance control as the dry static friction is not optimally compensated otherwise. First tests with the device have demonstrated that various behaviors can be implemented appropriately.

Preliminary investigations were conducted with subjects and basic tests were ran notably to compensate for passive leg actions (mainly weight and intrinsic stiffness effects). It was observed that significant differences can be identified between subjects and even between the two legs of a person. These results confirm that the device is able to precisely measure the interaction forces and suggest that a personalized model should be established for each subject for an optimized rehabilitation strategy.

Future work will focus on conducting experiences with subjects in order to develop rehabilitation strategies in close collaboration with therapists.

Acknowledgments. This research was supported by the National Center of Competences in Research Robotics. We also would like to thank Sylvain Tozzini for his contribution to the mechanical design of the LegoPress.

References

1. Jezernik, S., Colombo, G., Keller, T., Frueh, H., Morari, M.: Robotic orthosis Lokomat: a rehabilitation and research tool. Neuromodulation Technol. Neural Interface **6**, 108–115 (2003)
2. Maffiuletti, N.A., Bizzini, M., Desbrosses, K., Babault, N., Munzinger, U.: Reliability of knee extension and flexion measurements using the Con-Trex isokinetic dynamometer. Clin. Physiol. Funct. Imaging **27**, 346–353 (2007)
3. Stauffer, Y., Allemand, Y., Bouri, M., Fournier, J., Clavel, R., Metrailler, P., Brodard, R., Reynard, F.: The WalkTrainer—a new generation of walking reeducation device combining orthoses and muscle stimulation. IEEE Trans. Neural Syst. Rehabil. Eng. **17**, 38–45 (2009)
4. Métrailler, P., Blanchard, V., Perrin, I., Brodard, R., Frischknecht, R., Schmitt, C., Fournier, J., Bouri, M., Clavel, R.: Improvement of rehabilitation possibilities with the MotionMaker TM. In: International Conference on Robotics and Biomimetics ROBIO, pp. 359–364. IEEE (2006)
5. Bouri, M., Le Gall, B., Clavel, R.: A new concept of parallel robot for rehabilitation and fitness: the Lambda. In: International Conference on Robotics and Biomimetics ROBIO, pp. 2503–2508. IEEE (2009)
6. Bouri, M., Abdi, E., Bleuler, H., Reynard, F., Deriaz, O.: Lower limbs robotic rehabilitation case study with clinical trials. In: Rodić, A., Pisla, D., Bleuler, H. (eds.) New Trends in Medical and Service Robots, pp. 31–44. Springer, Bern (2014)
7. Carignan, C.R., Cleary, K.R.: Closed-loop force control for haptic simulation of virtual environments. Haptics-e **1**, 1–14 (2000)

Receiver-Based Hybrid Sample Prediction for Error-Resilient Haptic Communication

Fernanda Brandi$^{(\boxtimes)}$ and Eckehard Steinbach

Institute for Media Technology, Technische Universität München,
Munich, Germany
{fernanda.brandi,eckehard.steinbach}@tum.de

Abstract. We propose the use of a hybrid predictor at the receiver side of a teleoperation system to mitigate haptic artifacts due to packet losses. We define maximum wait times based on prediction angles for the sender to trigger new updates and for the receiver to switch prediction methods. Results show robust minimization of signal distortion in the presence of adverse transmission conditions while preserving the data rate conveniently low.

Keywords: [Robotics and automation]: Teleoperators · [H.5.2.g]: Haptic I/O · [E.4.a]: Data compaction and compression · [C.2.1.g]: Network communications · [Information Theory]: Error compensation

1 Introduction

The core idea behind most haptic signal compression schemes is the omission of redundant or perceptually irrelevant data and predictive coding [1–3]. The correctness of the haptic sample prediction at the receiver is highly dependent on the data transmission success. For telemanipulation sessions over the internet, we must assume that some packets are bound to be lost or delayed. The resulting asynchronicity between sender and receiver can introduce severe artifacts to the haptic interaction posing a risk to the system's stability and transparency [4,5].

In order to mitigate undesirable side effects due to challenging channel conditions, a few sender-based error-resilient approaches for haptic communication were introduced in the last years [4,6–8]. Although executed in distinct ways, these schemes share the basic notion of estimating the state of the receiver and deciding whether to add redundancy into the system (i.e. selectively transmitting extra packets). However, since these schemes focus solely on artifact prevention by estimating the reconstructed signal, they cannot promptly be certain of which samples are successfully transmitted to the receiver, thus, not being aware of how the signal is being predicted and if artifacts are still be occurring.

As an alternative to the aforementioned schemes, a perception-aware error-resilient approach [9] was recently presented. This scheme proposes the use of two simultaneous prediction techniques, namely, zero-order linear predictor

M. Auvray and C. Duriez (Eds.): EuroHaptics 2014, Part II, LNCS 8619, pp. 206–214, 2014.
DOI: 10.1007/978-3-662-44196-1_26

(ZOLP) and the first-order linear predictor (FOLP), to determine sample estimates. Whenever one of these estimates is non-compliant to the haptic perception thresholds, a new packet is injected into the channel. As shown in [9] results, this scheme manages to lessen the signal distortion when packets are lost but has the drawback of also decreasing the efficiency of the haptic data reduction.

Furthermore, linear predictors (such as ZOLP and FOLP) and also linear regression techniques are studied and compared in [10]. The authors show that the steeper the prediction gradients are, the higher is the signal distortion in the event of packet losses since the incorrect predictions tend to significantly overshoot. As an example, it is observed that when the ZOLP (which has null gradient) is employed as the predictor in the deadband-based data reduction approach [1], the signal distortion is kept generally low even in the presence of packets losses (the drawback being a less efficient data reduction). Conversely, when the FOLP is employed, the data rate drops considerably while the loss-induced distortion quickly becomes critical in the absence of error-resilient schemes.

With such challenges in mind, a novel scheme to mitigate haptic artifacts due to packet losses is introduced in Sect. 2. The remainder of this manuscript is organized as follows: Sect. 3 details our experimental setup and we present and discuss the tests results in Sect. 4 before concluding this work in Sect. 5.

2 Proposed Error-Resilient Haptic Communication

The approach proposed in this paper has two main goals: (a) to significantly reduce the signal distortion at the receiver when haptic packets are lost (i.e. decrease the occurrence of artifacts) and (b) to keep the data reduction as efficient as possible. Our main idea revolves around allowing the receiver to employ an alternative predictor when deemed necessary to minimize deviation. Due to the ZOLP being the most conservative approach among the linear predictors yielding overall the lowest signal distortion as shown in [10], we reserve this method as the *secondary* predictor in our scheme.

As the *primary* prediction method, we propose the use of any linear prediction technique (besides the ZOLP) to estimate the samples which are dropped at the sender. When the next sample to be transmitted is selected, we analyze the respective prediction gradient angles. Based on the steepness of these angles, we define a *maximum wait time* that determines how long the system can go without a following update. In other words, the steeper the gradient angles are, the less time we allow until the next update sample is to be triggered. Therefore, a packet is injected into the channel either when the waiting time is up or when the data reduction approach triggers the next regular update.

This scheme has two main advantages over previous error-resilient approaches. Firstly, since the maximum wait time is also signaled to the receiver, the latter knows until when it should expect the arrival of a new update. In case no packet arrives until this time is over, the receiver can take the precaution measure of switching from the *primary* predictor to the *secondary* predictor. This action is able to avoid excessive prediction overshoot and, thus, undesirable artifacts. Secondly, this approach avoids having steep gradient prediction for too long since

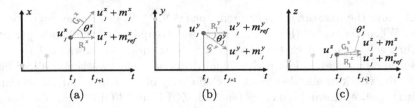

Fig. 1. Illustration of the prediction and reference vectors for dimensions x, y and z. The update sample u_j, the reference m_{ref} and the prediction increment m_j, and the angle θ_j between prediction vectors at the time instant t_j are also shown.

the sender must soon send a follow-up update when this occurs. So, the sender decides to trigger new packets not only when, for example, the perceptual dead-band is violated as in [1], but also because the prediction is deemed significantly steep and therefore excessively risky in the presence of packet losses. Therefore, the proposed scheme only sends additional packets to provide some information to the receiver about when a possible artifact could occur so the latter can act against it on its own.

The prediction gradient angles regarding each dimension are determined as illustrated in Fig. 1(a–c). Each update sample at the time t_j can be split in its three coordinates $[u_j^x, u_j^y, u_j^z]$ and the respective prediction gradient is also divided into three prediction vectors signaled as $[G_j^x, G_j^y, G_j^z]$. The angles $[\theta_j^x, \theta_j^y, \theta_j^z]$ between the prediction vectors G_j and the reference vectors R_j (i.e. the horizontal lines) are calculated using the scalar product between G_j and R_j in each coordinate. The general expression of such calculation is shown in Eq. 1.

$$\theta = acos\left(\frac{G \cdot R}{||G||\,||R||}\right) = acos\left(\frac{G_h R_h + G_v R_v}{\sqrt{G_h^2 + G_v^2}\sqrt{R_h^2 + R_v^2}}\right) \tag{1}$$

where the horizontal ($[.]_h$) and vertical ($[.]_v$) elements of each vector are

$$\begin{aligned}
G_h &= & t_{j+1} - t_j & = 1 \\
G_v &= u_j + m_j - u_j & = m_j \\
R_h &= & t_{j+1} - t_j & = 1 \\
R_v &= & u_j - u_j & = 0
\end{aligned} \tag{2}$$

which results in the angles $[\theta_j^x, \theta_j^y, \theta_j^z]$ being individually calculated as

$$\theta_j = acos\left(\frac{1}{\sqrt{1 + m_j^2}}\right) \tag{3}$$

Once the prediction angles are determined, a multiplier parameter q_j is calculated according to Eq. 4. Since $|\theta_{max}|$ symbolizes the maximum angle in the system, the parameter q_j assumes values from 0 to 1.

$$q_j = 1 - \frac{max(|\theta_j^x|, |\theta_j^y|, |\theta_j^z|)}{|\theta_{max}|} \tag{4}$$

The maximum wait time $tmax_j$ is then determined as

$$tmax_j = \alpha \cdot q_j \cdot Tmax \tag{5}$$

where $Tmax$ is a certain predefined maximum overall wait time and α is an adjustment parameter (usually set to 1). To avoid unnecessary triggering of packets when all prediction angles are zero (i.e. the signal is unchanged), we reset the parameter α to a number arbitrarily larger than 1, thus allowing more wait time in between updates while there is no contact or motion. Note that if $max(|\theta_j^x|, |\theta_j^y|, |\theta_j^z|) = |\theta_{max}|$ then $q_j = 0$ and, subsequently, $tmax_j$ is also null. That simply means that whenever the next sample is acquired, it is already flagged for transmission without any wait time.

Lastly, after the calculation of the maximum wait time, the sender must also transmit $tmax_j$ additionally to what is normally being transmitted to the receiver, namely, the update sample $\boldsymbol{u}_j$, the prediction gradient $\boldsymbol{m}_j$ and the time stamp t_j. With this slight modification in the packet payload, the receiver is made aware of when to employ the *primary* and the *secondary* predictors.

3 Experimental Setup

The experiment consists of recording both velocity and force signals (i.e. the data flowing, respectively, from the master to the slave, and vice-versa) from three 60-second haptic sessions with diverse object interactions, contact time duration and motion speeds. Diverse algorithms are then applied to the recorded sessions to be fairly compared and evaluated. We separate this experiment in two phases, the first one testing stand-alone approaches and the second phase testing combined approaches. The first phase compares five schemes: two deadband-based data reduction approaches [1] employing either the ZOLP ("DB+ZOLP") or the FOLP ("DB+FOLP"), two error-resilient data reduction approaches [6] employing either the ZOLP ("ER+ZOLP") or the FOLP ("ER+FOLP") and our proposed scheme ("Prop") employing the FOLP and the ZOLP, respectively, as the *primary* and the *secondary* prediction approaches. The second experimental phase shows our scheme being coupled with the error-resilient data reduction approach in [6] ("Prop+[6]") which means two error-resilient schemes being simultaneously employed (one at the sender and ours at the receiver).

In all phases our scheme is also further tested regarding different $Tmax$ which range from 5 to 50 ms. When $[\theta_j^x, \theta_j^y, \theta_j^z]$ is null, α is set to 10 (otherwise, $\alpha = 1$). Furthermore, θ_{max} is initialized with a considerably acute angle ($\pi/10000$) that automatically increases whenever a greater angle is found in the system (usually stabilizing within a few seconds into the session).

We evaluate all approaches in terms of data reduction (i.e. the resulting packet rate in percentage with relation to the original 1 kHz transmission rate) and also in terms of signal distortion. We employ the WMSE which is a distortion

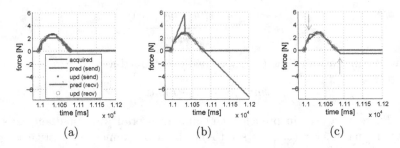

(a)   (b)   (c)

Fig. 2. Snippet of the reconstructed signal at the sender (blue) and at the receiver (purple) for DB+ZOLP (a), DB+FOLP (b) and the proposed approach (c). In the latter, note the saturation of the incorrect predicted signals at the receiver preventing overshoots (as in (b)). The two green arrows indicate the moments when the prediction mode is switched from the FOLP to the ZOLP (producing the horizontal lines) (color figure online).

metric that takes into account the human haptic perception limitations [10]. Note that such metric is not intended to replace subjective tests but yet can be useful as a guideline to compare the signal distortion among the tested approaches. The packet loss probability *ploss* is set to the following values 0 %, 2 %, 4 %, 6 %, 8 %, 10 %, 15 %, 20 %, 25 %, 30 %, 40 % and 50 % and all tests are repeated 25 times to avoid bias in the results.

4   Experimental Results

Phase One. An example of the immediate mitigation of artifacts can be seen in Fig. 2. In the three plots it can be observed the acquired signal (mostly hidden black curves), the reconstructed signal at the sender (blue curves), the reconstructed signal at the receiver (purple curves), the triggered update samples at the sender (red dots) and the successfully received update samples at the receiver (red circles). Note in Fig. 2(a) that, as expected, the use of the DB-ZOLP [1] achieves a rather low signal deviation since it has the most conservative prediction method. As discussed earlier, the cost of using such approach is the significant increase in the number of update samples (i.e. less efficient data rate reduction). On the other hand, if the DB-FOLP [1] is employed (Fig. 2(b)) the number of triggered packets is reduced if compared to the DB-ZOLP. However, in the occurrence of packet losses the reconstructed signal can seriously overshoot at the receiver causing highly impairing artifacts as discussed in [4,5]. These potential overshoots are quickly contained by our approach (Fig. 2(c)) wherein the incorrect predictions are cropped and stabilized still in its early stages preventing strong signal deviation and mitigating perceivable haptic artifacts.

Such improvements can also be reflected by the experimental rate-distortion curves in Fig. 3 showing that the distortion is kept low even at high packet loss probabilities. Note that, as expected, most of the curves have a purely vertical growth since neither [1] nor our proposed scheme take into account

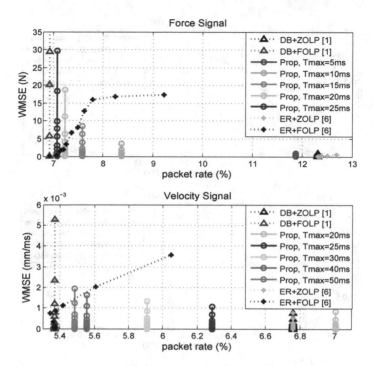

Fig. 3. Results for force (top) and velocity (bottom) signals. Each plot compares two data-reduction approaches (DB-ZOLP, DB-FOLP), two sender-based error-resilient approaches (ER-ZOLP, ER-FOLP) and our proposed scheme with changing $Tmax$ ranging from 5 ms to 50 ms (the five selected values for each plot reflect the best results). The packet loss probability (different points within each curve) ranges from 0 % to 50 %. Note that for better visualization the DB-FOLP curve in the top plot is cropped after $ploss$ reaches 6 % since the deviation results for this curve reaches four-digit numbers.

variations in $ploss$. Observe that even though the proposed scheme might slightly get behind in terms of data rate reduction if compared to the error-resilient approach in [6], the signal deviation is largely minimized. Furthermore, if $Tmax$ is properly selected, both deviation and data rate can be maintained conveniently low.

Phase Two. The proposed scheme allows customization and can be coupled with other prediction algorithms, data reduction approaches and error-resilient schemes which can potentially further improve the overall performance. As an example of such improvement, it is shown in Fig. 4 the results achieved when the proposed scheme is employed with the low-complexity error-resilient data reduction scheme in [6]. Note that the data rate reduction is comparable to the ones presented in Fig. 3 showing that both schemes complement each other without unnecessarily increasing the number of transmitted packets. Moreover, the signal deviation is considerably lower if compared to the stand-alone error-resilient schemes presented in Fig. 3. This shows how well a combination of a

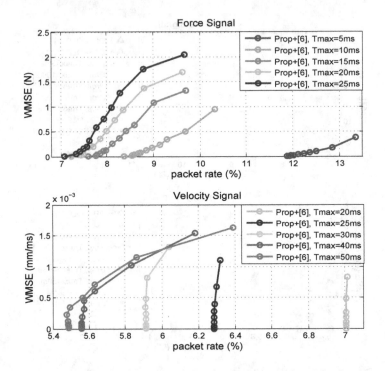

Fig. 4. Results for force (top) and velocity (bottom) signals with changing $Tmax$ ranging from 5 ms to 50 ms and changing packet loss probability (different points within each curve) ranging from 0 % to 50 %. These curves show the results when the proposed approach is employed with the low-complexity error-resilient data reduction approach in [6]. Note that the distortion is considerably lower than employing any of the schemes individually such as observed in the first experimental phase.

sender-based and our receiver-based error-resilient strategies can be to contain incorrect predictions and, ultimately, to reduce the occurrence of haptic artifacts due to packets being lost or abnormally delayed in the communication channel.

5   Conclusion

This work proposes a novel error-resilient scheme for haptic communication. The core idea is to allow the receiver side of a telemanipulation system to act on its own to prevent the occurrence of haptic artifacts induced by packet losses. To achieve that goal, our scheme analyzes the prediction gradient angles at the sender in order to determine the maximum wait time until the next update. The steeper the gradient is, the less time is allowed. The sender transmits this wait time to the receiver which is promptly made aware when to expect the next sample. In case no packets arrive until the signaled wait time is up, the receiver acts on its own switching the prediction technique to a more conservative predictor to prevent signal reconstruction overshoots and therefore quickly mitigating possible haptic artifacts. The proposed scheme also allows customization and can be employed with several types of predictors, haptic data reduction schemes and other error-resilient approaches.

We perform experiments to evaluate how our scheme works independently as well as coupled with another error-resilient algorithm. Based on experimental results, this scheme can successfully keep the signal distortion under control at the receiver when packets are lost while the data rate reduction efficiency is not compromised. Lastly, we observe the benefits of the simultaneous use of a sender-based and our receiver-based error-resilient approaches showing that they enhance each other effectiveness lowering even further the signal deviation while not significantly increasing the haptic data transmission rate.

Acknowledgment. This work has been supported by the European Research Council under the European Union's Seventh Framework Programme (FP7/2007–2013)/ERC Grant agreement no. 258941.

References

1. Hinterseer, P., Hirche, S., Chaudhuri, S., Steinbach, E., Buss, M.: Perception-based data reduction and transmission of haptic data in telepresence and teleaction systems. IEEE Trans. Sig. Proc. **56**(2), 588–597 (2008)
2. Shahabi, C., Ortega, A., Kolahdouzan, M.R.: A comparison of different haptic compression techniques. In: Proceedings of the IEEE International Conference on Multimedia & Expo., Lausanne, Switzerland, vol. 1, pp. 657–660, August 2002
3. Ortega, A., Liu, Y.: Lossy Compression of Haptic Data. Prentice Hall, Englewood Cliffs (2002)
4. Brandi, F., Kammerl, J., Steinbach, E.: Error-resilient perceptual coding for networked haptic interaction. In: Proceedings of the ACM Multimedia, Firenze, Italy, pp. 351–360, October 2010
5. Brandi, F., Cizmeci, B., Steinbach, E.: On the perceptual artifacts introduced by packet losses on the forward channel of haptic telemanipulation sessions. In: Isokoski, P., Springare, J. (eds.) EuroHaptics 2012, Part I. LNCS, vol. 7282, pp. 67–78. Springer, Heidelberg (2012)
6. Brandi, F., Steinbach, E.: Low-complexity error-resilient data reduction approach for networked haptic sessions. In: Proceedings of the IEEE International Workshop on Haptic Audio Visual Environments and Games, Qinhuangdao, China, pp. 135–140, October 2011
7. Kammerl, J., Brandi, F., Schweiger, F., Steinbach, E.: Error-resilient perceptual haptic data communication based on probabilistic receiver state estimation. In: Isokoski, P., Springare, J. (eds.) EuroHaptics 2012, Part I. LNCS, vol. 7282, pp. 227–238. Springer, Heidelberg (2012)
8. Qin, J., Choi, K.S., Xu, R., Pang, W.M., Heng, P.A.: Packet-loss-resilient perception-based haptic data reduction and transmission using ACK packets. In: Proceedings of the International Conference on Signal Processing, Beijing, China, pp. 1165–1170, October 2012

9. Awed, J., Elhajj, I.H., Chehab, A., Kayssi, A.: Perception-aware packet-loss resilient compression for networked haptic systems. J. Comput. Commun. **36**(15–16), 1621–1628 (2013)

10. Brandi, F., Steinbach, E.: Prediction techniques for haptic communication and their vulnerability to packet losses. In: Proceedings of the IEEE International Workshop on Haptic Audio Visual Environments and Games, Istanbul, Turkey, pp. 63–68, October 2013

Multi-digit Softness: Development of a Tactile Display to Render Softness Feeling on Multiple Fingers

Toshiki Kitazawa[✉], Fuminobu Kimura, and Akio Yamamoto

The University of Tokyo, 7-3-1 Hongo, Bunkyo-ku, Tokyo, Japan
{kitazawa,fuminobu,akio}@aml.t.u-tokyo.ac.jp

Abstract. This paper describes a new tactile display that can present softness sensations to multiple phalanges on multiple fingers. Contact width control through sheet wrapping is adopted as a softness rendering method for each finger. Three separate mechanisms for contact width control for three fingers are integrated in one device. Passive mechanical linkages are employed to provide sensations to the whole fingers. The paper reports on the design of the developed device, as well as the result of psychophysical experiment that investigated the contributions of each phalange and finger in softness perception on this display.

Keywords: Softness display · Artificial softness · Remote palpation · Multi-digit

1 Introduction

Recently, techniques to render softness sensations on a bare finger have been actively explored in the field of haptics. On a bare finger, softness is perceived through two different senses: one is kinesthetic and the other is cutaneous. It has been revealed that the cutaneous sense plays a dominant role in softness perception [1–3]. Thus for realistic softness rendering, providing appropriate stimuli to the cutaneous sense is quite important. Several studies have developed methods to provide softness to the cutaneous sense, which typically focus on the contact area between a fingertip and a device. Bicchi et al. developed a softness display, in which the change rate of the contact area is controlled based on the contact force, using multiple co-axial cylinders [4]. Another device developed by Fujita et al. controlled contact area by wrapping a thin rubber sheet around the fingertip using a hydraulic actuator [1]. Kimura and Yamamoto developed a softness display, which controls contact width by wrapping a thin sheet using electric motors [5]. A display developed by Yazdian et al. also controlled contact width by using tilting plates [6]. Kimura and Yamamoto also reported that the device can render sensations of lumps or hard contents in virtual soft bodies, by controlling the tension given to the wrapping sheet [7]. It is also reported that, in addition to softness, viscosity of materials can be rendered by adjusting the controller temporal response [8]. This softness rendering technology focusing on contact [7, 8] is thus expected to be utilized in medical applications, such as remote palpation or training, as it can render the sensations such as lump sensation or viscoelastic sensation [9] that would be imperative to describe a human body in palpation.

© Springer-Verlag Berlin Heidelberg 2014

M. Auvray and C. Duriez (Eds.): EuroHaptics 2014, Part II, LNCS 8619, pp. 215–222, 2014.

DOI: 10.1007/978-3-662-44196-1_27

The previously developed softness displays render the softness sensations only to a single fingertip. In real medical procedures, however, palpations are typically done using multiple fingers [10]. In addition, real palpation utilizes whole fingers, not just fingertips. Therefore, for intuitive remote palpation, it is necessary to develop a new technology that allows us to render softness feelings to multiple fingers. In literatures, Daniulaitis et al. developed multi-fingered palpation simulator [11], but the sensation provided is limited to kinesthetic one given to fingertips. In this paper, we propose a new device that is able to render cutaneous softness feelings to multiple phalanges on three fingers at the same time.

The rest of the paper is composed of four sections. The next section discusses the concept of the multi-digit softness display. The third section describes the developed device in details. The forth section reports on the results of the softness rendering experiments, in which we compared the effect of the number of fingers in softness perception. The final section concludes the paper.

2   Concept of the Device

To render softness sensation, this paper focuses on the method proposed in [5]. The method, which is based on contact area control originally proposed in [1], controls the contact width between a fingertip and the display by wrapping a flexible sheet around the fingertip as shown in Fig. 1 (a). This paper extends the method to multiple phalanges on multiple fingers. As the first trial, this paper focuses on three fingers: index, middle, and ring fingers.

There are several possibilities to extend the method for multiple fingers. The most direct extension is depicted in Fig. 1(b), where a single sheet wraps all the three fingers by raising both ends of the sheet. For the closed posture, this approach might be a better choice. This simplest extension, however, would have limited softness rendering performance; it would be able to simulate relatively hard materials only because the surface deformation between the fingers would be neglected. Another possible extension is to have a separate mechanism for each finger, as illustrated in Fig. 1(c). This would suffer from mechanical complexity, but would have better softness rendering performance. This work, therefore, utilizes the latter method.

Figure 2 shows a conceptual illustration of the device. As the medical palpation often utilizes whole fingers, not just fingertips, it is also imperative to extend the area of the softness rendering to the whole finger. As each finger has three phalanges, which may not

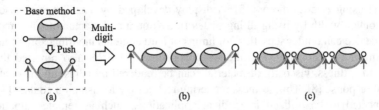

Fig. 1. Contact width control by sheet wrapping. (a) Single-digit display. (b) Multi-digit single-surface (sheet) display for closed-finger posture. (c) Multi-digit multi-surface display.

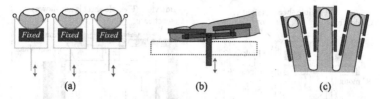

(a)   (b)   (c)

Fig. 2. Concept of the multi-digit softness display. (a) Each set of sheets is actuated independently to wrap around each finger. (b) A sheet is segmented into two parts to comply with a finger shape by a mechanical linkage. (c) The mechanical parts require the hand to be opened.

align in a perfect straight line, the sheets that wrap around the fingers should comply with the finger shapes. For better contact to the multiple phalanges, a sheet should be segmented into several parts. In this particular work, we utilize two sheets for one finger, one of which is exclusively used for distal phalanx, considering the importance of the fingertip, and the other covers middle phalanx and a part of proximal phalanx.

The segmentation of the wrapping sheet increases the number of the motors to control the sheet wrapping. If we use one motor to control each sheet, total six motors will be required, for this particular design. To reduce the number of motors, we utilize a mechanical linkage that complies with the finger shape, as shown in Fig. 2(b). A motor drives the supporting rod, which then pushes two shafts for sheet height control, so that they comply with a finger shape.

One drawback of the above approach would be that mechanical components exist between fingers, as illustrated in Fig. 2(c). Due to the size of the mechanical components, a user must open his or her finger to use the device (Fig. 2(c)).

3 Prototype Device

The prototype of the multi-digit softness display is presented in Fig. 3. The structure is schematically illustrated in Fig. 4. In this prototype, only contact width control was implemented, as softness rendering can be performed without elaborate tension control, as reported in [1, 4, 5]. Sheet tension was simply provided using springs; tension control concept, demonstrated in [7] for lump sensations, was not implemented.

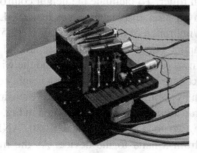

Fig. 3. Appearance of the prototype device.

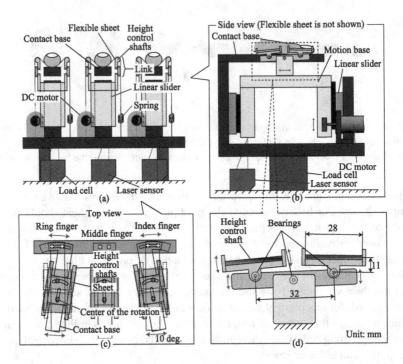

Fig. 4. Schematic illustrations of the prototype display. (a) Front view. (b) Side view illustrating the height control. (c) Top view illustrating contact bases. (d) Mechanical linkage for complying with finger shapes

On top of the display, there are three contact bases, each of which is 15 mm wide. (In the photos of Fig. 3, the bases are covered with polyimide sheets.) They are fixed to the device and their surfaces are flat. Their lengths are 74 mm for an index finger and a ring finger, and 82 mm for a middle finger. The orientations of the bases for an index finger and a ring finger can be adjusted to fit a shape of an open hand as illustrated in Fig. 4(c).

Height control shafts on both sides of each contact base are supported by mechanical linkages, as shown in Fig. 4(d). The mechanical linkages for each finger are connected in the bottom to a motion base, the height of which is controlled by a dc motor (A-max 22, Maxon) through a friction roller. To facilitate the height control, the height of each motion base is monitored by a laser displacement sensor (ZX-LD40, Omron) whose resolution is 2 μm. The moving range of the motion bases is 12.5 mm.

Six polyimide sheets (Kapton 200H, Dupont-Toray) are used to wrap around three fingers (two sheets for one finger). The thickness of each sheet is 50 μm and the width is 25 mm. Initially, each sheet covers the contact base and the corresponding height control shafts. The ends of the sheets are pulled down by springs which give adequate tensions to the sheets. As the shafts rise up, the sheets wrap around a finger as illustrated in Fig. 4 (a).

On the bottom of the device, there are two load cells (LC1205-K020, AND) to measure the vertical pushing force given from a hand to the device. As the motion bases are actuated, their inertial force will be added to the measurement of the load cell [8]. This effect, however, was ignored since we focused on quasi-static rendering. The two load cells facilitate the estimation of the center of pushing force distribution, although this function is not actively used in this paper.

The target heights of the motion bases and, in turn, the height control shafts, are calculated by a force-height model that accepts the pushing force measured by the load cells and outputs target heights. This particular work uses the simplest force-height model, in which the height is proportional to the pushing force. The heights of the motion bases are then controlled by PID feedback controllers.

The photo in Fig. 5 shows how well the height control shafts, and in turn the wrapping sheets, comply with shapes of fingers when the sheets are lifted up. The photo shows that the shafts and the sheets successfully comply with the finger shape owing to the passive mechanical linkage. With this passive mechanism, the user could feel the increased contact width on the whole fingers.

Fig. 5. The shafts and the sheets comply with the finger shape.

One problem found for the prototype was that when the sheets were lifted up, the shafts sometimes scratched the fingers, due to the proximity of the shafts to the fingers. Although the shafts were allocated to have enough margins against fingers in the original design, they were bent inside by the sheet tension when the sheets were lifted up. This should be improved in the future, e.g., by using more rigid material.

4 Experiment

In this prototype, the heights of the motion bases (which are almost equivalent with the wrapping heights of the sheets, but not exactly the same because of the passive mechanisms) are controlled in proportion to the pushing force provided by a hand. To investigate the relation between the proportional gain and perceived softness, psychophysical experiment was carried out. In the following experiment, the same height was used to control the three motion bases for the three fingers.

4.1 Procedure

Three subjects (one male and two females) in the lab, who are in their 20s, were recruited for the experiment. One of them had an experience on the previous softness display for a single fingertip [7]. However, all of them had no experience on this multi-digit softness display. Before the main sessions described in the following, there was a training session in which the subjects practiced to push the device within the force range from 0 to 5 N, as we thought that the simplest force-height model used in the main experiments would not be effective in larger force region. For this practice, the measured force was provided to the subjects through a PC monitor in real-time.

For the main session, a variant of magnitude production method was used in the experiment. Instead of being given a numerical value, the subjects were given a real soft object and then adjusted the sensation rendered on the device to match the softness of the given object. For the adjustment, subjects are requested to touch both the real sample and the device freely, within the force range from 0 to 5 N. The subjects were provided a twisting knob, through which they can change the height/force gain within the range from 0 to 1.5 mm/N, with a resolution of about 0.003 mm/N. They could change the gain even while they were pushing the device. Only one real sample was used as the reference, which was a block of sponge (PUF-06, WAKI) which has dimensions of 300 × 300 × 20 mm and Young's modulus of about 100 kPa.

To reveal the effect of the number of fingers in softness perception, the experiments were carried out in four different conditions: (a) push by fingertip of an index finger, (b) push by a whole index finger (using all the three phalanges), (c) push by two whole fingers (index and middle fingers), and (d) push by three whole fingers (index, middle, and ring fingers). For the condition (a), the mechanical linkage was fixed by a tape so that the two sheets are lifted up in the same amount, even in the absence of the middle and proximal phalanges. In the conditions that involve more than two fingers, the subjects were asked to apply roughly equal force on all the fingers involved. The procedure for height/force gain adjustment was repeated three times for each condition. Auditory cue was blocked by a head-phone, on which white noise was played. During the explorations of the real sample and the display, the subjects were asked to close their eyes to shut out visual cues.

4.2   Results and Discussions

Figure 6 shows the results. As the subject used more fingers or more phalanges (in other words, the larger contact area), the height/force gain became smaller. However, the obtained gain is not simply inversely-proportional to the contact area used. Focusing on the first two conditions, the height/force gain is at most twice as large in the fingertip condition though the contact area seems roughly one third of that for the whole finger. This seems to indicate the importance of the fingertip in softness perception.

In conditions (b) and (c), the height/force gain is roughly half in condition (c), which seems to indicate that the index and middle finger have almost the same impact on the softness perception. On the other hand, in condition (d), the height/force gain was almost the same with that for condition (c), despite that the contact area is almost three halves. This might be suggesting the less importance of the ring finger, as reported in [12].

The comments of the subjects revealed some problems of the device. One of the subjects commented that the subject sometimes recognized wrinkle of the sheets. Using another flexible material, such as rubber sheet, would be the solution for this problem. Another comment points out that the subject felt the fingertip was lifted up more than

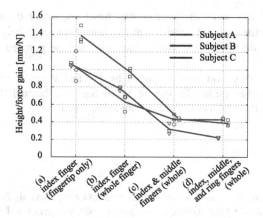

Fig. 6. The results of the height/force gain adjustment.

the other phalanges, which indicates the linkage mechanism has some effects that we did not intend. It should be investigated more in details in the future work. Some users commented on the difficulty to apply equal force on all the three fingers, especially on ring finger, for condition (d).

The obtained results cannot be fully attributed to human perception characteristics. Although the subjects were instructed to explore the device and the target within 0 to 5 N of pushing force, the actual pushing force sometimes exceeded 5 N, especially when more fingers were involved; pushing force tended to be smaller with less number of fingers. The difference of the pushing force among the conditions possibly affected the result.

5 Conclusions

This paper proposed a new tactile display that provides softness sensations for multiple phalanges on multiple fingers. The display is based on contact width control, in which the contact width of the finger and the display is controlled by wrapping a flexible sheet. To comply with finger shapes, the flexible sheets were segmented and supported by mechanical linkages.

In this particular work, the wrapping height of the sheet was controlled in proportion to the pushing force. The height/force gain was experimentally identified for several conditions that differ in the number of phalanges or fingers used to perceive the softness. The result, although still preliminary, seems to suggest the importance of fingertip, as well as the less importance of ring finger in softness perception.

Although not demonstrated, the device can independently control the wrapping heights for the three fingers. By providing different heights for the three fingers, the device is expected to render distributed softness, or a large lump. Also, a relatively small lump (in mm order, as in [7]) would be rendered by implementing sheet tension control. Their combination would allow us to render wide variety of lumps, which is imperative for medical palpation. One limitation of the current device is that it can render only flat surfaces, as all the three contact bases are arranged on the same height. By introducing another motion mechanism to control the base heights, rendering of curved surfaces would be realized. Such extensions will be pursued in a future work.

Acknowledgements. This work was supported by Funding Program for Next Generation World-Leading Researchers (#LR013), Grant-in-Aid for Scientific Research (B) (No. 26280069), and Grant-in-Aid for JSPS fellows (24.8552) from JSPS, Japan.

References

1. Fujita, K., Ohmori, H.: A new softness display interface by dynamic fingertip contact area control. In: 5th World Multiconference on Systemics, Cybernetics and Informatics (2001)
2. Bergmann Tiest, W.M., Kappers, A.M.: Kinaesthetic and cutaneous contributions to the perception of compressibility. In: Ferre, M. (ed.) EuroHaptics 2008. LNCS, vol. 5024, pp. 255–264. Springer, Heidelberg (2008)
3. Srinivasan, M.A., LaMotte, R.H.: Tactual discrimination of softness. J. Neurophysiol. **73**(1), 88–101 (1995)
4. Bicchi, A., Scilingo, E.P., De Rossi, D.: Haptic discrimination of softness in teleoperation: the role of the contact area spread rate. IEEE Trans. Robot. Autom. **16**(5), 496–504 (2000)
5. Kimura, F., Yamamoto, A., Higuchi, T.: Development of a contact width sensor for tactile tele-presentation of softness. In: 18th IEEE International Symposium on the Robot and Human Interactive Communication, pp. 34–39. IEEE (2009)
6. Yazdian, S., Doxon, A.J., Johnson, D.E., Tan, H.Z., Provancher, W.R.: Compliance display using a tilting-plate tactile feedback device. In: 2014 IEEE Haptics Symposium (HAPTICS), pp. 13–18. IEEE (2014)
7. Kimura, F., Yamamoto, A.: Rendering variable-sized lump sensations on a softness tactile display. In: 2013 World Haptics Conference (WHC), pp. 97–102. IEEE (2013)
8. Kimura, F., Yamamoto, A.: Effect of delays in softness display using contact area control: rendering of surface viscoelasticity. Adv. Robot. **27**(7), 553–566 (2013)
9. Widmer, A., Hu, Y.: A viscoelastic model of a breast phantom for real-time palpation. In: 2011 Annual International Conference of the IEEE Engineering in Medicine and Biology Society, EMBC, pp. 4546–4549. IEEE (2011)
10. Walker, H.K., Hall, W.D., Hurst, J.W.: Clinical Methods: The History, Physical, and Laboratory Examinations, 3rd edn. Butterworths, Boston (1990)
11. Daniulaitis, V., Alhalabi, M.O., Kawasaki, H., Tanaka, Y.: Medical palpation of deformable tissue using physics-based model for Haptic Interface RObot (HIRO). In: Proceedings of the 2004 IEEE/RSJ International Conference on Intelligent Robots and Systems, (IROS 2004), vol. 4, pp. 3907–3911. IEEE (2004)
12. King, H.H., Donlin, R., Hannaford, B.: Perceptual thresholds for single vs. multi-finger haptic interaction. In: 2010 IEEE Haptics Symposium, pp. 95–99. IEEE (2010)

Haptic Rendering on Deformable Anatomical Tissues with Strong Heterogeneities

Guillaume Kazmitcheff[1,2,3]($\boxtimes$), Hadrien Courtecuisse[1], Yann Nguyen[2,3,4],
Mathieu Miroir[2,3], Alexis Bozorg Grayeli[5], Stéphane Cotin[1],
Olivier Sterkers[2,3,4], and Christian Duriez[1]

[1] Shacra, INRIA, Université Lille 1, 59650 Villeneuve d'Ascq, France
`guillaume.kazmitcheff@inserm.fr`
[2] Sorbonne Universités, UPMC (University of Paris 06), UMR_S 1159,
75005 Paris, France
[3] INSERM, UMR_S 1159, 75005 Paris, France
[4] AP-HP, Hôpital Pitié-Salpétrière, service ORL, 75013 Paris, France
[5] CHU Dijon, service ORL, 21000 Dijon, France

Abstract. This paper is focus on the development of a haptic rendering method to simulate interactions with heterogeneous deformable materials, such as anatomical components. Indeed, the strong heterogeneities of the biological tissues involves numerical and real-time issues to simulate the deformations and the mechanical interactions between the organs and the surgical tools. In this paper, we propose a new haptic algorithm adapted to the modeling of heterogeneous biological tissues, based on non-linear finite element model. The central contribution is the use of a triple asynchronous approach: one loop at low rate, which computes a preconditionner that solves the numerical conditioning problems; a second at intermediate rate, to update the model of the biological simulation; and the haptic loop which provides the feedback to the user at high rate. Despite of the desynchronization, we show that the calculation of haptic forces remains accurate compared to the model. We apply our method to a challenging microsurgical intervention of the human middle ear. This surgery requires a delicate gesture in order to master the applied forces.

1 Introduction

The haptic rendering in a real-time simulation of deformable objects composed of non-homogeneous materials is still a challenging scientific issue. Recent studies propose to use non-linear Finite Element Models (FEM) computed on the Graphics Processing Unit (GPU) to reach the required computing performance for real-time simulation. But the modeling of heterogeneities using FEM leads to ill-conditioned and non-linear systems of equations. This restrains the development of realistic surgical simulations dedicated to education and training.

Several haptic rendering approaches are introduced to handle with the simulation of soft deformable tissues. In [1], a method based on the Signorini's contact

© Springer-Verlag Berlin Heidelberg 2014
M. Auvray and C. Duriez (Eds.): EuroHaptics 2014, Part II, LNCS 8619, pp. 223–231, 2014.
DOI: 10.1007/978-3-662-44196-1_28

law [2] and a Linear Complementary Problems (LCP) formulation is developed to solve contacts between deformable objects. This method works on linear models. An extension to non-linear deformations is proposed in [3]. This one is based on a desynchronized approach and an intermediate model of the LCP. This approach is exported to other types of mechanical interactions in [4]. However, with this method, the calculation of deformations is not compatible with ill-conditioned models, like heterogeneous materials with a high mass/stiffness ratio. Indeed, the deformable model is calculated in the simulation loop at low frequency (less than 30 Hz) using a Conjugate Gradient (CG). But, the CG does not converge if the problem is ill-conditioned. One solution to this issue, proposed in [5], is to use an asynchronous preconditioner based on the Graphics Processing Unit (GPU). Therefore, our paper focuses on the adaptation of this preconditioner to apply it for the computation of the haptic rendering.

In this paper, a simulation of a middle ear microsurgical intervention is used to illustrate our haptic rendering method. Our objective is to provide a training simulator for these procedures. Thus, it is essential to provide a realistic haptic rendering in order to learn and master the forces applied to the anatomical structures. The middle ear is mainly composed of the ossicles (malleus, incus, stapes) and their ligaments (Fig. 1(a)). Those components involve a large mass/stiffness ratio, heterogeneous tissues with non-linear deformations. Surgeons have to manipulate bones of less than 4 mm high localized inside a maximized 16 × 16 mm cavity size at 34 mm depth, through the external ear canal with a diameter between 4 to 8 mm. The ossicles are very sensitive to injury, such

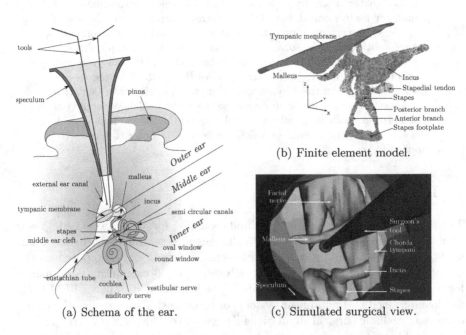

(a) Schema of the ear.

(b) Finite element model.

(c) Simulated surgical view.

Fig. 1. Anatomy of the human ear and its modeling.

as forces upper $1N$ [6]. To perform a non-traumatic intervention submillimetric motion inside a narrow workspace is required. However, the surgeons evaluate the state of the ossicles by a simple palpation using a micro-instrument. This palpation allows, firstly to determine the stiffness of the ossicles before the surgery to evaluate the fixation level of the stapes, and secondly to assess the stability and the flexibility of the ossicles after the intervention. Therefore, a realistic rendering of contact forces is required to provide relevant information to the surgeons, since some surgical choices and outcomes depend on this palpation.

Today, there is no system that allows such a simulation. The Visible Ear (Denmark) and the Voxel-Man (Germany) are currently available to simulate only the mastoidectomy surgery. This procedure consists in the drilling of the temporal bone and doesn't involve interaction with the ossicles. Several FEM of the human middle ear are developed, but their goals are to analyze and reproduce the mechanical behavior of the anatomical structures [7,8]. They are not suitable for real-time simulation and haptic interactions.

To our best knowledge, there is currently no method that can provide a physics based haptic rendering of deformable tissues with strong heterogeneities. This is the central focus and contribution of this paper. Particularly, we propose a method that faces the numerical issues related to the ill-conditioned FEM formulation, while allowing a high refresh rate of the haptic loop. Therefore, the main contribution of this article is to introduce and evaluate a method that allows an accurate haptic rendering and realistic interactions between tools and organs, which are composed of non-linear deformable elements, and heterogeneous materials. This method is based on a triple asynchronous approach: one loop solves the numerical problems at low rate; a second, at intermediate rate, updates the model of the biological simulation; and finally the haptic loop provides the feedback to the user at high rate. The additional contribution discussed in this paper is the demonstration that our approach can be applied to a concrete problem that have no solution up to now: the haptic rendering for a surgical simulation of the middle ear. A FEM of the middle ear was previously developed and validated by comparison with experimental observations in [9]. The aim of our method is to preserve the same level of accuracy for the haptic rendering. Moreover, several experimental data about the applied forces during a surgical palpation of the middle ear structures are available in literatures, allowing a comparison with our simulation.

First, a description of our FEM of the middle ear is presented. Then, we provide some details about the haptic rendering approach based on a triple desynchronisation method. Finally, we discuss the results of our desynchronisation approach on our FEM of the middle ear, by comparing the forces obtained during a simulation offline (without real-time constraints), then by real-time haptic interactions.

2   Methods

Validated deformation model: A FEM of the human middle ear including the three ossicles and their ligaments is implemented in the Simulation Open

Framework Architecture (SOFA, www.sofa-framework.org), a real-time medical simulation project. The geometry is provided by a micro-magnetic resonance imaging acquisition and by a manual reconstruction according to published literatures. The structures are meshed by 4361 tetrahedral elements (Fig. 1(b)). The ligaments connected to the middle ear cavity represent our boundaries conditions. The Young's modulus and the density parameters of all the components are set according to published data on human ear or by cross-calibration process and are reported in our previous publication [9]. In Fig. 1(b), the non-homogenous elements of the model are represented with different colors: the blue tetrahedrons correspond to soft tissues and the red to stiffer ones (Young Moduli from 4.90×10^4 to 1.41×10^{10} N.m^{-2}). The behavior of our model is validated by comparison with experimental measurements on human temporal bones in dynamic and in static [9]. The method presented in the paper aims at computing the haptic rendering without simplification of the FEM using a multi-rate approach.

Numerical resolution: The nonlinearities are managed by a corotational approach [10]. For time integration, a backward Euler scheme is used. At each step, a linearization of the model is computed. It leads to the following equation:

$$\underbrace{\left(\frac{\mathbf{M}}{h^2} + \frac{\mathbf{B(q)}}{h} + \mathbf{K(q)}\right)}_{\mathbf{A}} \underbrace{d\mathbf{q}}_{\mathbf{x}} = \underbrace{\mathbf{r}}_{\mathbf{b}} + \mathbf{H}^T(\mathbf{q})\lambda \qquad (1)$$

where h is the time step, $\mathbf{M}$ and $\mathbf{B}$ are the mass and the damping matrices of the FEM, $\mathbf{K}$ is the tangent matrix, which corresponds to a local linearization of the FEM internal forces $\mathbf{f(q)}$ (i.e. $\mathbf{K} = \frac{\partial \mathbf{f}}{\partial \mathbf{q}}$), $d\mathbf{q}$ is the displacement vector of the nodes of the FEM between two simulation steps. $\mathbf{r}$ is the residual of forces (difference between external and internal forces and some remaining forces from the temporal integration). $\mathbf{H(q)}$ corresponds to the direction of constraints, when a contact is created between the FEM model and a surgical instrument. λ is the value of the Lagrange multipliers that correspond to the solution of the constraints (see, for instance, [3,4] for more details).

In the simulation, the first step consists in the simulation of all bodies without contact $\lambda = 0$ and it's called the free motion. During the free motion, a CG is called to solve Eq. (1) but if $\mathbf{A}$ is ill-conditioned, the CG does not converge. To improve the convergence, a preconditioning method can be used to enhance the conditioning. For that, the idea is to define a matrix $\mathbf{P}$, "close to $\mathbf{A}$", so that $\mathbf{P}^{-1}\mathbf{A}$ is similar to the identity matrix $\mathbb{I}$. This enhancement is the aim of the paper presented in [5]. The next simulation step consists in the detection of the contact with the creation of the matrix $\mathbf{H}$ that gathers the contact directions. The collision response is computed based on a LCP formulation. The LCP matrix is obtained by computing $\mathbf{HA}^{-1}\mathbf{H}^T$. However, the computation of $\mathbf{A}^{-1}$ (similar to the compliance matrix) in real-time is a real issue, because it is a very time consuming problem. Again, a preconditioning approach can be used to estimate the compliance matrix: $\mathbf{P}^{-1} \approx \mathbf{A}^{-1}$, in order to reduce the computation time of finding the exact solution. Yet, in [5], there is no solution provided for the haptic rendering. In the existing solution for haptic: [3] use the rest shape configuration, A_0^{-1} to compute the LCP matrix, and a CG without preconditioning for the free motion. Because of the bad conditioning of the model, related to non-homogeneous tissues, the method in [3] does not converge. However, we keep from this paper the idea of the multi-thread approach for the haptic rendering.

The originality of our method is to use a multi-threaded approach on three different update frequencies: a low rate loop that updates the factorization of the preconditioner to solve the ill-conditioning issues; a medium rate loop (at visual interactive rates) that computes the FEM, the collision and the LCP matrix; and a high rate loop that calculate the haptic rendering (see Fig. 2). The low rate loop assumption is that the matrix A does not undergo drastic change between each time step. Thus, the validity of the preconditioner is assumed to be satisfactory during several consecutive time steps. If necessary, the temporal coherency could be reinforced using a warping technique (see [3,5]). The update of the preconditioner can be performed in another thread. Therefore, there is sufficient time (N time steps) to compute a $\mathbf{LDL}^T$ factorization of $\mathbf{P}$, with $\mathbf{L}$ a lower triangular matrix and $\mathbf{D}$ a diagonal matrix. This factorized matrix $\mathbf{P}$, which is very similar to $\mathbf{A}$, can be used for preconditioning of the CG allowing its convergence. But more importantly, this factorized matrix can also be used to compute the matrix of the LCP, $\mathbf{HP}^{-1}\mathbf{H}^T$, while using the GPU to improve the computation time. We show now that this approach can be extended to haptic rendering.

Haptic rendering: The high rate loop approach extends the idea proposed in [4]. The LCP is used as an intermediate model between the simulation and the haptic loops. Indeed, once the LCP matrix with the preconditioner is obtained, it is solved in the simulation thread and it is shared for use in the haptic loop. Thus, we differentiate the simulation loop refreshed at low frequency (typically below 60 Hz), and the haptic loop computed at high frequency (1 kHz) (Fig. 2). During the latter one, the haptic constraints are updated according to the last position of the haptic device. The advantage of our extension is that, now, the computation is based on an asynchronous update of $\mathbf{P}^{-1}$, which is close to the compliance matrix $\mathbf{A}^{-1}$ of the FEM. Thus, we obtain an accurate calculation of the contact forces for the haptic rendering. Indeed, the haptic loop uses the best possible estimation of the compliance matrix. This one is directly based on our validated mechanical model of the middle ear structures. We can therefore expect to maintain the same level of accuracy of our FEM when running a multithreaded haptic rendering. To evaluate this, we propose two tests: a numerical assessment and a real-time simulation in a surgical context.

Evaluation: The relevance of the haptic rendering is evaluated with one contact interaction between the ossicular chain model and a virtual instrument representing the haptic device. A scheduled motion of the haptic interface is performed in order to reproduce similar displacement between the different simulations. The

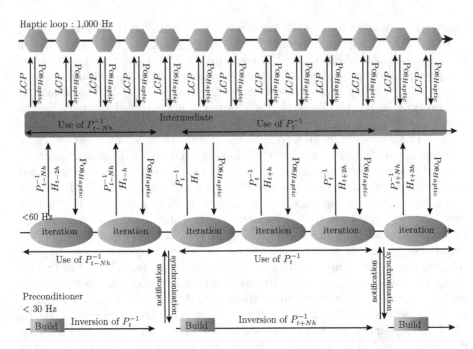

Fig. 2. Haptic rendering process using a preconditioner updated asynchronously at low frequency and a multithreaded haptic rendering approach computed at high rate.

force feedback is refreshed at 1 kHz. Several simulations are performed, with different time steps: from 1 ms for a synchronization between the haptic and the simulation computation, to 40 ms for a multithreading computation of the force feedback. The reference is the simulation computed at 1ms (no real-time), that is compared with the multithreaded approaches and the real-time simulation calculated at 40 ms.

Surgical simulation application: A second test is performed using a haptic device in real-time condition on the FEM of the middle ear. The palpation of the ossicles is simulated. For that, the surgeons manipulate a virtual micro-instrument with a haptic device. The mechanical interactions with instruments, and especially the contact response, are treated using constraint-based approaches presented above. A phantom Omni device (Sensable, Wilmington, MA) with 6 degrees of freedom for positioning and 3 for force feedback is used to interact with the simulation. All our simulations are performed on a conventional workstation, with a backward Euler scheme and a time step set at 40 ms. The 3D rendering of the virtual scene is ensured with a 3D viewer HMZ-T2 (Sony, San Diego, CA).

3 Results

The bad conditioning of matrix **A** in the simulation clearly justifies our method. Indeed, very low convergence of the CG is observed for our model when solving

Table 1. Contact forces (N) computed in the simulation and in the haptic loops for simulations with different time step (noted dt).

Computation	dt = 1 ms	4 ms	10 ms	40 ms
Simulation	0.276	0.253	0.333	0.234
Haptic	0.281	0.273	0.291	0.233

Eq. (1) without preconditioning. In the best cases, it takes 1 s to compute the thousands of iterations required by the CG to converge. And in the worst cases, there is no convergence at all, due to the accumulation of numerical errors. When we use the asynchronous update of the preconditioner, a stable refresh rate of the simulation loop at 60 Hz is observed. This frequency falls to 48 Hz when the instrument collides with our model. The contacts forces computed in the simulation and in the haptic loop are reported in the Table 1.

During palpation of the incus, a stable refresh rate of 47 Hz is observed. The convergence of the CG associated with the preconditioner is achieved in a maximum of 7 iterations. When the surgical instrument is in contact with the ossicles, the forces are calculated and returned to the user *via* the haptic device. Again, we observe that the forces calculated in the simulation loop and the haptic forces are similar, although they have different update rates (47 Hz for the simulation *vs* 1 kHz for the haptic rendering).

4   Discussion and Conclusions

Results show that the methods presented in [3,4] cannot be applied to our simulation. This is due to the bad conditioning of our model related to high mass/stiffness ratio, strong non-homogeneous materials and non-linear tissues. Coupling the haptic rendering algorithm to the asynchronous precomputation of the compliance system on GPU presents many advantages. First, a fast convergence of our model is reached with a refresh rate compatible with real-time computation (above 30 Hz). This method proposes a fast estimation of the inverse of the compliance system computed asynchronously at low rate. Second, the haptic forces, computed from the compliance matrix of our heterogeneous FEM at high frequency, are coherent with forces calculated at low frequency, with different time steps. This guarantees the accuracy level of our model, which is validated. Our approach is successfully applied to an interactive simulation in real-time of a challenging microsurgical intervention. Haptic interactions are also performed on our ill-conditioned FEM. In addition, forces computed in our simulations (Table 1) using the asynchronous computation of the compliance system are consistent with forces reported in literature on human temporal bones experiments [6,11,12]. In [12] the authors report forces ranging from 0.098 to 0.655 N during the palpation of the incus depending on the experience of the surgeons. The presented haptic rendering methods coupled to the asynchronous computation of the compliant matrix will be used in our surgical simulator. However, the computed force feedback is within the backdrive friction of our Phantom Omni haptic device (0.26 N). As, the goal of the simulator is to provide a training and a rehearsal tool for the surgical team, it is important to offer a more realistic haptic rendering using a more efficient device.

Haptic rendering is stable and realistic compared to forces computed at low rates and within forces measurements on human specimens. We assess that the method is able to compute and reproduce accurately the forces during interactions with non-linear and non-homogeneous objects. Adaption of the presented method to hyperelastic materials will constitute our further work. In addition, a new haptic device with 6 degrees of freedom for force feedback and a low backdrive friction will be implemented in our simulation to enhance the quality of the force perceived by the user.

Acknowledgements. The authors would like to thank Collin Ltd. (Bagneux, France) for financial support.

References

1. Duriez, C., Dubois, F., Kheddar, A., Andriot, C.: Realistic haptic rendering of interacting deformable objects in virtual environments. IEEE Trans. Vis. Comput. Graph. **12**(1), 36–47 (2006)
2. Signorini, A.: Sopra alcune questioni di elastostatica. Atti della Società Italiana per il Progresso delle Scienze (1933)
3. Saupin, G., Duriez, C., Cotin, S.: Contact model for haptic medical simulations. In: Bello, F., Edwards, E. (eds.) ISBMS 2008. LNCS, vol. 5104, pp. 157–165. Springer, Heidelberg (2008)
4. Peterlik, I., Nouicer, M., Duriez, C., Cotin, S., Kheddar, A.: Constraint-based haptic rendering of multirate compliant mechanisms. IEEE Trans. Haptics **4**(3), 175–187 (2011)
5. Courtecuisse, H., Allard, J., Kerfriden, P., Bordas, S.P.A., Cotin, S., Duriez, C.: Real-time simulation of contact and cutting of heterogeneous soft-tissues. Med. Image Anal. **18**(2), 394–410 (2013)
6. Lauxmann, M., Heckeler, C., Beutner, D., Lüers, J.C., Hüttenbrink, K.B., Chatzimichalis, M., Huber, A., Eiber, A.: Experimental study on admissible forces at the incudomalleolar joint. Otol. Neurotology **33**(6), 1077–1084 (2012)
7. Gan, R.Z., Feng, B., Sun, Q.: Three-dimensional finite element modeling of human ear for sound transmission. Ann. Biomed. Eng. **32**(6), 847–859 (2004)
8. Kelly, D.J., Prendergast, P.J., Blayney, A.W.: The effect of prosthesis design on vibration of the reconstructed ossicular chain: a comparative finite element analysis of four prostheses. Otol. Neurotology **24**(1), 11–19 (2003)
9. Kazmitcheff, G., Miroir, M., Nguyen, Y., Ferrary, E., Sterkers, O., Cotin, S., Duriez, C., Grayeli, A.B.: Validation method of a middle ear mechanical model to develop a surgical simulator. Audiol. Neuro-otology **19**(2), 73–84 (2014)
10. Felippa, C.A., Haugen, B.: A unified formulation of small-strain corotational finite elements: I. Theory. Comput. Meth. Appl. Mech. Eng. **194**(21–24), 2285–2335 (2005)

11. Miroir, M., Szewczyk, J., Nguyen, Y., Mazalaigue, S., Sterkers, O.: Design of a robotic system for minimally invasive surgery of the middle ear. In: IEEE RAS & EMBS BioRob, pp. 747–752. IEEE (2008)

12. Bergin, M., Sheedy, M., Ross, P., Wylie, G., Bird, P.: Measuring the forces of middle ear surgery; evaluating a novel force-detection instrument. Otol. Neurotology **35**(2), e77–e83 (2014)

Grasping Control in Three-Fingered Robot Hand Teleoperation Using Desktop Haptic Device

Lingzhi Liu, Guanyang Liu[✉], and Yuru Zhang

State Key Lab of Virtual Reality Technology and Systems,
Beihang University, Beijing, China
gyliu@me.buaa.edu.cn

Abstract. This paper presents a three-fingered robot hand teleoperation system using desktop haptic device as the master manipulator. The grasp mapping and force feedback methods are developed for the system. Grasp forces of the robot hand are transformed to proper feedback force in master side. Operator controls the robot hand to grasp and hold different objects depending on the force feedback rather than visual feedback. We demonstrated that a wide range of objects, whose properties are well known by operator, were safely and stably grasped and the force based grasping control was more reliable than visual feedback based control. The intuitive and easy-to-realize system raises a new control scheme in robot hand teleoperation.

1 Introduction

Multi-fingered robot hands are favored end effectors of slave robot enabling the tele-operation systems interacting with remote environment flexibly. However, because of the multiple degrees of freedom in fingers, robot hand manipulation in unknown environments becomes a challenge [1–3]. Haptic glove (Fig. 1) is mostly chosen as a master device to control a robot hand and to provide force feedback to operator. While, most robot hand used in engineering is not humanoid hand, so the kinematic structures of haptic glove and robot hand are different, it is required to find intuitive grasp and force mapping methods [4, 5]. And there is still a design bottleneck for a reliable haptic glove that it is hard to find the ideal small actuator placed in limited human hand space [6]. Besides, many sensors and actuators in the haptic glove reduce the transmission rate of system which lowers the force feedback available to the operator [7]. Desktop haptic device is rarely used for robot hand manipulation although it is usually the master device for robot arm control in many teleoperation systems. In [8], the haptic device is used to position final desired grasp poses in the virtual environment for real robot to execute.

This paper presents a three-fingered robot hand teleoperation system based on desktop haptic device. The haptic device in the system is a parallel mechanism device with a ball handle (Fig. 1). It has similar kinematic structure with three-fingered robot hand and can provide stable and high frequency force feedback to operator. The three-dimensional device motions are intuitively mapped to the fingers and spread motion of

© Springer-Verlag Berlin Heidelberg 2014
M. Auvray and C. Duriez (Eds.): EuroHaptics 2014, Part II, LNCS 8619, pp. 232–240, 2014.
DOI: 10.1007/978-3-662-44196-1_29

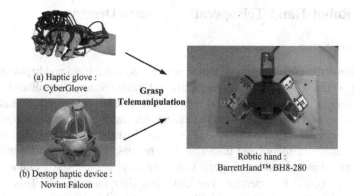

(a) Haptic glove :
CyberGlove   **Grasp**
            Telemanipulation

(b) Destop haptic device :
Novint Falcon

Robtic hand :
BarrettHand™ BH8-280

Fig. 1. Different haptic devices (a) and (b) used in three-fingered robot hand teleoperation.

robot hand. When operator grasping the handle of haptic device, it is just like the robot hand grasping objects.

During robot hand grasping, proper grasp force is critical for a safe and stable grasp (Fig. 2). Insufficient grasp force causes repeated pre-grasps. And excessive grasp force may deform even damage the objects. This problem is addressed in laparoscopic grasp control [9]. In order to control the grasp force of robot hand in teleoperation system, force feedback is necessary since the visual feedback is unreliable when grasping objects of different properties. In our system, the grasp forces of the robot hand are transformed to proper feedback force in haptic device. Operators control the three-fingered robot hand to safely grasp and hold different objects depending on the feedback force.

We raise two hypotheses related to the proposed system: (1) the operator can control the robot hand to grasp a wide range of objects based on the feedback force, (2) the proposed force feedback based grasping control is more reliable and effective than vision feedback control.

Excessive grasping   Insufficient grasping   Safe grasping

Fig. 2. The effects of different grasp forces.

The main contribution of this paper is that we present an intuitive three-fingered robot hand teleoperation system by using desktop haptic device as a master device and propose a simple force feedback method to realize safe and stable robotic hand grasping. And the following section introduces our system design. Section 3 describes our experiment for the system and its results analysis. Section 4 presents our conclusion and future work.

2   The Robot Hand Teleoperation System Design

2.1   System Setup

Figure 3 shows the teleoperation system structure. The robot hand and haptic device are connected to networked computers respectively. Communication is realized by a UDP/IP connection in a local area network where time delay is neglected. The slave side receives the motion commands from the master side and sends the finger position and grasping force information back. A USB webcam is installed in slave side to capture video information of robot hand transmitted to the master side. The video information and a virtual robot hand simulating the real robot hand are displayed in the Graphical User Interface (GUI) for operator. The Graphical User Interface (GUI) is developed using VC++ and OpenGL library. The frequency of the haptic rendering and network transmission are both 1 KHz.

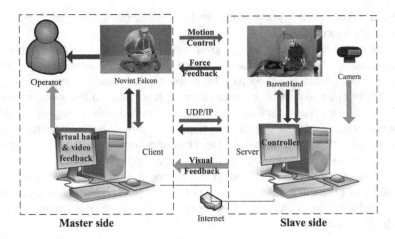

Fig. 3. The three-fingered robot hand teleoperation system.

The three-fingered robot hand used in the system is BarrettHand^{TM} BH8-280 (Barrett Technology Inc.). A strain gage installed about the distal joint of each finger measures the torque applied at the fingertip over a range of ±1 N-m. The maximum load at the tip of each finger is 2 kg. The haptic device used in the system is Novint Falcon (Novint Technologies Inc.) with the maximum Force Capabilities of 2 lbs.

2.2   Grasp Mapping

The kinematic structure of Falcon and BarrettHand are similar to some extent. When operator grasps the handle, it is just like the robot hand grasping objects. So we develop the grasp mapping between these two devices with the principle that the operation should be as simple and intuitive as feasible. There are only two kinds of basic motions for BarrettHand: fingers and spread close or open. Therefore, z direction movement of Falcon maps to the finger's motion. Three of the four buttons on the handle represent three fingers respectively. Spread motion is mapped to y direction movements from intuition point of view (Fig. 4). Operators take control of the fingers or spread by pressing the corresponding buttons.

Repeated calibration is used in our mapping method to solve the problem of different workspaces. Operator releases the control of robot hand by pressing the button again and relocates Falcon device just like using computer mouse. However, in order to guarantee the continuity of the feedback force, this operation is invalid when the hand is contacting with objects.

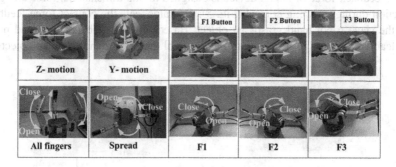

Fig. 4. Motion mapping of Falcon and BarrettHand.

The mapping relation of the haptic device position and the robot hand joint angle is as follows:

$$P_{RHi}(k) = k_p \sum_{t=0}^{k} \Delta P_{Falcon\_z} + P_{RHi}(0) \tag{1}$$

where $P_{RHi}(k)$ is the current robot hand position of the finger i ($i = 1, 2, 3$, spread) at k moment and $P_{RHi}(0)$ is the initial position of the finger. $\Delta P_{Falcaon\_z}$ is the z position (or y position for spread) difference of haptic device between current moment and previous moment. k_p is the mapping coefficient which is 14.65 rad/m in our system. This value is calculated based on the workspace of haptic device and the robot hand. It is adjusted according to precision requirement of robot hand grasp.

2.3 Force Feedback

The strain gage properties of BarrettHand represent the torques applied on the fingers. The grasp force is calculated by these properties. The grasp force on the fingertip F_{RHi} is calculated using the strain gage value S_{sgi} (2), assuming the contact point is exactly at the fingertip. All the grasps in the experiment are fingertip grasps that only the fingertip can contact the object.

$$F_{RHi} = k_f S_{sgi} \tag{2}$$

where i ($i = 1, 2, 3$) represents the fingers of BarrettHand. The unit of strain gage value obtained from the BarrettHand is count. The value ranges from 0 to 4000 and the initial value for each finger without load is about 2000. k_f is a coefficient which converts the count number of strain gage value to grasp force.

The feedback force F_Z in master side is calculated by averaging the grasp forces of three fingers.

$$F_z = \frac{1}{3}\sum_i F_{RHi} \tag{3}$$

The feedback force of haptic device is designed to one-dimensional force along the z direction during grasping control (Fig. 5). Operator feels the contact force feedback when the slave robot hand grasps an object. Based on the feedback force and previously learned knowledge in grasping, they control the robot hand to grasp objects.

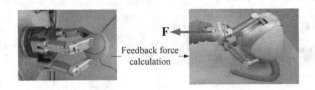

Fig. 5. One-dimensional feedback forces.

3   Experiment

User experiment compares the proposed force feedback based grasping with visual feedback based grasping in robot hand teleoperation (Fig. 6).

Fig. 6. The experimental scene.

3.1   Participants and Task

Ten students, 6 male and 4 female in the laboratory, aged from 21 to 30, were invited to participant in the experiment. They are all right handed and familiar with the haptic device. All the participants never controlled a robot hand to grasp objects by using glove or haptic device before.

There are ten objects need to be grasped in the experiment for each participant (Fig. 7). These objects are common things in our daily life and their properties vary in a wide range. Their properties are well known by participants. Each participant needs to grasp the same object twice based on different feedback information.

1. plastic bottle
2. paper cup
3. foam rubber
4. tennis ball
5. book
6. porcelain doll
7. iron box
8. aluminum sheet
9. orange
10. apple

Fig. 7. Objects in the experiment.

The experimental task is using the haptic device to control the robot hand to grasp and hold the objects. All the grasps are fingertip grasp where the objects could not contact with the palm of the hand. Participants should first adjust the robot hand to a proper pre-grasp pose according to the video feedback. Then, they begin to grasp the object to find a proper grasp force to hold the object based on force feedback (F mode, no visual feedback) and visual feedback (V mode, no force feedback) respectively in random order. Finally, the robot hand is moved up and down to see if the object is stably grasped. During the process, any drops are not allowed. Because the robot hand has not been connected to the arm yet, we cannot change its position to reach an object. So we manually put the object close to the hand where it can grasp it through pose adjusting based on visual feedback.

3.2 Evaluation

After each grasp, the grasp force is recorded. The performance of grasp is evaluated by relative grasp force. Relative grasp force is calculated as follows:

$$p_{relative\_gf} = \frac{F_g - F_{\min\_obj}}{F_{\min\_obj}} \times 100\% \tag{4}$$

where F_g is the grasp force recorded each trail which equals to F_z. F_{min_obj} is the minimum grasp force necessary for robot hand to grasp the object. F_{min_obj} of each object is obtained before experiment through increasing grasp force until no slippery is happened. The relative grasp force reflects the level of safety grasp and 10–30 % is regarded as safety margin for bare hand grasp [10].

3.3 Results and Discussion

Figure 8 shows the results of participants' grasp forces based on visual and force feedback (Fig. 8). It can be seen that the force feedback based grasping shows a much smaller variance in grasping force for most objects. It can be concluded that the force feedback based grasping is more stable than visual feedback based grasping. We remove the outliers in our dataset and calculate the relative grasp forces for each grasp and the average relative grasp forces of each participant.

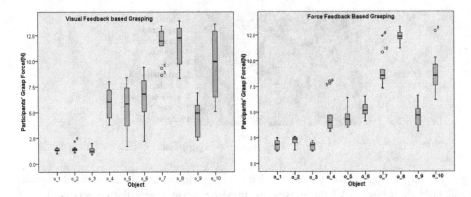

Fig. 8. Grasp forces based on visual feedback (a) and force feedback (b).

Figure 9 shows the average relative grasp forces of each participant based on force feedback and visual feedback. The ANOVA results show that the differences of relative grasp force between force and visual feedback based grasping are significant ($p = 0.00 < 0.05$). Most of the relative grasp forces in force feedback based grasping control are smaller than the forces in visual feedback control. But it is the opposite results when grasping light and flexible objects (plastic bottle, paper cup, foam rubber) whose minimum grasp forces are lower than about 1 N. The reason is that the grasp forces for these objects are too small for operator to be perceived at the beginning in force feedback mode. But the object deformation can be easily noticed by participants through visual feedback.

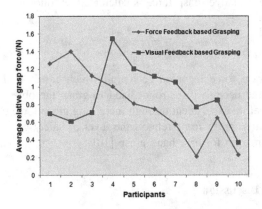

Fig. 9. Average relative grasp forces for each participant.

From the experiment results we get the conclusion that operator grasped a wide range of objects by using the proposed three-fingered robot hand teleoperation system. For most objects grasping, the force feedback based grasping control was proved more reliable and effective compared with visual feedback based control. These results demonstrated the hypotheses proposed in Sect. 1.

However, there is no participant who can successfully grasp all the objects in the experiment. For force feedback based grasping control, it is hard to grasp plastic bottle without deformation. The grasp force in robot hand is calculated by the strain gage properties. Since the finger itself has gravity, this torque value is not zero when the fingers close or open without load. So the grasp force cannot be distinguished when grasping materials of large elasticity in our system. When participant felt the force, the objects already had deformation. This also explained why the average of grasp forces for the flexible objects using force feedback based control are larger than the forces using visual feedback based control. For visual feedback based grasping control, the problem of excessive grasp force is inevitable especially grasping stiff objects. Operator relies more on the force feedback to control the robot hand grasp force which is similar with human hand grasp. So the force feedback based control is necessary. For engineering application, the two feedback modes can be combined to complement each other.

4 Conclusion and Future Work

This paper presents a three-fingered robot hand teleoperation system to grasp objects in unstructured environment based on force feedback, by using desktop haptic device as the master manipulator. The grasp mapping and force feedback methods are developed for this system. In particular, we transform the grasp forces of the robot hand to one-dimensional feedback force in master side. The system is intuitive and easy-to-realize for robot hand teleoperation application.

To evaluate the effectiveness of our system, an experiment was conducted in which subjects were instructed to grasp 10 objects of different stiffness, based on force feedback and visual feedback respectively. Our results demonstrated that the subjects grasped a wide range of objects with a proper grasp force without slippage or damage by using the proposed three-fingered robot hand teleoperation system. The force feedback based grasping control was proved more reliable and effective compared with visual feedback based control. However, the results also showed that not all objects in the experiment can be safely grasped because of the effect of force feedback accuracy.

In future work, we will further evaluate the system on the effectiveness of distinguishing the objects with different materials and weights, and how difficult it is for operator to adapt this kind of force feedback. Furthermore, we are interested in the difference of grasp forces when people grasp objects with teleoperated robot hand and the bare hand. This will be an important basis to design proper force feedback to improve the transparence of robot hand teleoperation.

Acknowledgment. This research was supported by China domestic research project for International Thermonuclear Experimental Reactor (ITER) program under grant 2012GB102006, 2012GB102008 and supported by the Innovation Foundation of BUAA for PhD Graduates.

References

1. Yoshikawa, T.: Multi-fingered robot hands: control for grasping and manipulation. Ann. Rev. Control **34**(2), 199–208 (2010)
2. Okamura, A.M., Smaby, N., Cutkosk, M.R.: An overview of dexterous manipulation. In: Proceedings of 2000 IEEE International Conference on Robotic and Automation, vol. 1, pp. 255–262 (2000)
3. Pelossof, R., Miller, A., Allen, P., Jebara, T.: An SVM learning approach to robotic grasping. In: Proceedings of 2004 IEEE International Conference on Robotic and Automation, vol. 4, April 26–May 1, pp. 3512–3518 (2004)
4. Peer, A., Einenkel, S., Buss, M.: Multi-fingered telemanipulation - mapping of a human hand to a three finger gripper. In: Proceedings of the 17th IEEE International Symposium on Robot and Human Interactive Communication, 1–3 August 2008, pp. 465–470 (2008)
5. Geng, T., Lee, M., Hülse, M.: Transferring human grasping synergies to a robot. Mechatronics **21**, 272–284 (2011)
6. Blake, J., Gurocak, H.B..: Haptic glove with MR brakes for virtual reality. In: IEEE/ASME Trans. Mechatron. **14**(5), 606–615 (2009)
7. Lii, N.Y., Chen, Z., Pleintinger, B., Borst, C.H., Hirzinger, G., Schiele, A.: Toward understanding the effects of visual- and force-feedback on robotic hand grasping performance for space teleoperation. In: The 2010 IEEE/RSJ International Conference on Intelligent Robots and Systems, 18–22 October 2010, pp. 3745–3752 (2010)
8. Leeper, A., Chan, S., Hsiao, K., Ciocarlie, M., Salisbury, K.: Constraint-based haptic rendering of point data for teleoperated robot grasping. In: IEEE Haptics Symposium 2012, Vancouver, BC, Canada, 4–7 March 2012, pp. 377–383 (2012)
9. Westebring-van der Putten, E.P., van den Dobbelsteen, J.J., Goossens, R.H.M., Jakimowicz, J.J., Dankelman, J.: The effect of augmented feedback on grasp force in laparoscopic grasp control. IEEE Trans. Haptics **3**(4), 280–291 (2010)
10. Griffin, W.B., Provancher, W.R., Cutkosky, M.R.: Feedback strategies for telemanipulation with shared control of object handling forces. Presence **14**(6), 720–731 (2005)

A High-Fidelity Surface-Haptic Device for Texture Rendering on Bare Finger

Michaël Wiertlewski[1]([⊠]), Daniele Leonardis[1,2], David J. Meyer[1],
Michael A. Peshkin[1], and J. Edward Colgate[1]

[1] Department of Mechanical Engineering, Northwestern University,
Evanston, Il 60208, USA
{wiertlewski,peshkin,colgate}@northwestern.edu,
meyerdj@u.northwestern.edu
[2] PERCRO Laboratory, Scuola Superiore SantAnna, 56127 Pisa, Italy
d.leonardis@ssup.it

Abstract. We present the design and evaluation of a high fidelity surface-haptic device. The user slides a finger along a glass plate while friction is controlled via the amplitude modulation of ultrasonic vibrations of the plate. A non-contact finger position sensor and low latency rendering scheme allow for the reproduction of fine textures directly on the bare finger. The device can reproduce features as small as 25 µm while maintaining an update rate of 5 kHz. Signal attenuation, inherent to resonant devices, is compensated with a feedforward filter, enabling an artifact-free rendering of virtual textures on a glass plate.

Keywords: Surface-haptics · Texture rendering · Finger friction · Feedforward filtering · High fidelity haptics

1 Introduction

The tactile perception of texture is influenced by a wide set of physical properties including roughness at multiple length scales, skin-surface adhesion, and surface deformability [1]. Each of these properties, along with the mechanics of the finger itself, contribute to frictional losses which relate to the perception of slipperiness and stickiness [2], as well as vibrations which relate to perceived roughness [3]. A challenge that faces the designers of haptic interfaces is emulating a wide range of tactile experiences with control over a substantially reduced set of physical variables.

Rendering Tactile Texture on a Bare Fingertip. One variable that lends itself to control is the net force acting on a fingertip. Thus, a large body of work has been devoted to the reproduction of texture using force-feedback devices [4]. While these allow for complex simulations, they are often poorly suited to the very fine temporal and spatial scales of texture [5]. These limitations can be circumvented with vibrotactile actuators. The reproduction of the friction force

© Springer-Verlag Berlin Heidelberg 2014
M. Auvray and C. Duriez (Eds.): EuroHaptics 2014, Part II, LNCS 8619, pp. 241–248, 2014.
DOI: 10.1007/978-3-662-44196-1_30

as a vibration correlated with the motion of the fingers allows the rendering of complex roughness profiles. However, because vibrotactile actuation is limited to frequencies higher than 20 Hz, the quasi-static content is not represented which implies that the stickiness dimension of the texture cannot be controlled [6].

Ultrasonic Modulation of Friction. The friction reduction effect was first described by Watanabe et Fukui [7]. They noticed that, when touching a plate excited by out-of-plane ultrasonic vibrations, users experienced reduced friction. Subsequently it has been shown that modulation of friction correlated with finger motion enables rendering of coarse gratings [8,9]. But the refresh rate and position resolution of previous devices has limited the fineness of spatial patterns that can be rendered. In addition, the physics of high-Q resonant systems limits the bandwidth at which the amplitude can be modulated [10,11].

Present Study. We address the previously-mentioned limits by implementing high performance hardware and a rendering scheme that achieve performance comparable to the known psychophysical threshold of human tactile perception. A custom-made non-contact position sensor and a fast rendering processor allow friction to be controlled with a 5 kHz refresh rate and 8 μm position resolution. The high-performance piezoelectric actuators used in this device allow for a high dynamic range of friction force. Lastly, the amplitude modulation dynamics is compensated using feedforward filters, providing a flat frequency response over the entire bandwidth of human tactile perception.

2   Human Factors

The ideal device has infinite bandwidth, spatial resolution and force resolution. We can approach this ideal by designing a device with enough quality that it will be indistinguishable from the ideal case. This section reviews the psychophysics and biomechanics involved in the perception of vibratory and frictional cues in order to draw specifications for a high-fidelity rendering device.

Temporal Resolution. It is well established that the maximum frequency that can be felt by the human somatosensory system is about 800 Hz [12]. In terms of latency between the user motion and the force rendering, a 30 ms delay has been reported as unnoticeable while exploring virtual vibrotactile surfaces [13].

Spatial Resolution. The smallest grating a human can perceive will depend on the speed of the exploration. Considering a slow exploration speed of 40 mm/s [14] and the previously-mentioned frequency limit of $f = 800$ Hz, we estimate that the smallest perceptible wavelength is on the order of $\lambda = v/f = 50$ μm. The estimate is consistent with [15].

Force Resolution and Dynamic Range. Millet et al. estimated the smallest static force that a human can perceive is 10^{-2} N [16]. However tactile perception is much more sensitive to transients than to static stimulation. Considering that the smallest displacement perceptible is in the order of 10^{-7} m at 300 Hz [17], and that the impedance of the finger pad at this frequency is approximately

3 N.s/m [18], the smallest dynamic forces that can be perceived should be closer to 5.10^{-4} N. Considering that texture exploration is usually achieved with normal force in the vicinity of 0.5 N [14], and that a typical coefficient of friction (before reduction) is unity, it is necessary to display a peak lateral force of 0.5 N. This suggests that a dynamic range of 10^3 is sufficient.

3 High-Speed High-Resolution Rendering

Figure 1a shows a picture of the device and Fig. 1b presents a schematic of its components. An optical sensor captures the position of the finger at a rate of 5 kHz and with a spatial resolution of 8 μm. From this position value, a command value is computed and output at the same rate, then mixed with a 30 kHz carrier. The signal is fed to the piezoelectric actuators that produce ultrasonic vibration of the glass touch surface. If we compare to the limits derived in Sect. 2, the current setup can render an 800 Hz temporal sine wave and a 50 μm spatial wavelength both with a margin of 6.25 samples per period. The high refresh rate allows for robust rendering even with exploration speeds up to 250 mm/s [5].

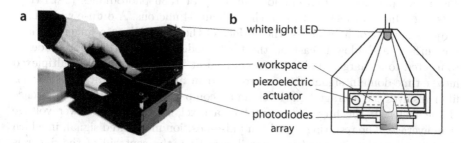

Fig. 1. a. Picture of the high-fidelity device. **b.** The internals of the device. The user touches the glass plate undergoing ultrasonic vibration. The finger casts a shadow on the photodiode array sensor.

3.1 Rendering Scheme

Texture rendering uses the process illustrated in Fig. 2. The texture signal is stored on a micro-controller (PIC32MX250, Microchip Inc., Itasca, IL, USA) as a force-position profile. Every 200 μs, the position of the finger, acquired by the optical sensor later described, is used to fetch the force value in the stored profile and after applying a correction filter, is converted to analog using a 12-bit digital-to-analog converter (MCP4922, Microchip Inc., Itasca, IL, USA). This signal modulates the carrier frequency using an analog multiplier (AD633, Analog Devices Inc., Northwood, MA, USA) and is then fed to a ±100 V amplifier (PDm200, PiezoDrive, Pty Ltd, Callaghan, Australia) which excites the piezoelectric actuators glued to the glass. This produces an amplitude-modulated

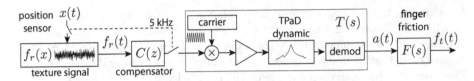

Fig. 2. Mixed analog/digital rendering scheme. From the position of the finger $x(t)$ and a stored texture waveform $f_r(x)$, a force command $f_r(t)$ is generated. This signal is then fed into a compensation filter $C(z)$ which corrects for the amplitude-modulation dynamics $T(s)$ and the fingertip interaction $F(s)$.

drive signal with a sine wave at the resonance frequency as carrier, and the texture waveform as modulation signal. The interaction between the finger and the vibrating glass creates a demodulation. The user experiences only changes in amplitude but has no perception of the ultrasonic carrier.

3.2   Non-contact Position Sensor

The finger position system employs an array of 1536 photodiodes (TSL1412S, AMS-TAOS Inc, TX, USA) with a pitch of about 64 microns. A diffuse white LED projects a sheet of light across the surface of the glass. When a finger contacts the surface, a shadow is cast on the photodiodes. Each of the photodiodes is connected to a charge amplifier and sampled at 5 kHz. The data is multiplexed into a time-domain signal that is processed in analog electronics. A low-pass filter resolves the average light level, and a comparator determines the presence of the finger. If the finger is in front of a pixel, it will read a lower voltage than average. The resulting signal is a pulse-position modulated signal, in which the finger position is encoded. After digitization, the centroid of the finger is determined with a resolution of $8\,\mu m$ and an update rate of 5 kHz.

3.3   Friction Modulation Device

The friction reduction device is based on a $135 \times 25 \times 3.2\,mm^3$ borosilicate substrate. The $f_0 = 30\,kHz$ resonant frequency corresponds to a $(0,1)$ normal mode with free boundaries, see Fig. 3a and b. Dimensions were calculated to cancel any standing wave in the longitudinal direction and thus offer constant friction reduction properties over the full length of the touch surface. Low-loss piezoelectric actuators (SMD19T03112S, Steminc and Martins Inc, Miami, FL, USA) are glued on the plate to provide actuation. At resonance, the assembly deforms up to $4.8\,\mu m$ under 50 V excitation and exhibits a quality factor of $Q = 300$ when unloaded. A measurement of quasi-static friction reduction is shown Fig. 3c. The high voltage-to-amplitude gain of this device allows feedforward compensation to be implemented without encountering saturation.

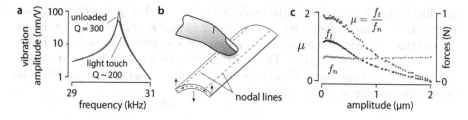

Fig. 3. a. Frequency response. **b.** Mode shape **c.** Friction modulation.

4   Compensation Filters

The resonant behavior of the plate limits the rate of change of the amplitude of the ultrasonic vibration. This has the effect of attenuating modulation frequencies above $\frac{f_0}{2Q}$. With a finger touching the surface (which reduces Q), this cutoff frequency is typically on the order of 75 Hz. The relatively large impedance of the glass plate dominates the impedance of the finger, as a result the frequency response is only slightly affected by the variation of finger stiffness or pressure applied. In addition, the frictional mechanics of the finger also introduces attenuation. In [11], we characterized the attenuation of the amplitude of vibration $a(t)$ and the magnitude of the friction force oscillations $f_t(t)$ with respect to a sinusoidal reference signal $f_r(t)$. The former is well described by a first order filter while the latter exhibits a non-trivial frequency response. Without correction, attenuation will cause the amplitude of spatial gratings to vary with scanning velocity, resulting in a perceptual inconsistency. This section presents two approaches to correct for attenuation, and to provide a uniform frequency response over a wide range of frequencies.

4.1   Lead-Lag Compensator

The first order attenuation of the vibration amplitude can be corrected with the help of a lead-lag controller. Ideally, the device should have a flat response between DC and 800 Hz, which translates into $C(s)\,T(s) = \frac{Q}{1+\tau_w s}$ with $\tau_w = 0.2$ ms. Uncompensated, the attenuation is well described by $T(s) = \frac{Q}{1+\tau_r s}$ with $\tau_r^{-1} = \frac{\omega_0}{2Q}$. Therefore the lead-lag controller in continuous time is $C(s) = \frac{1+\tau_r s}{1+\tau_w s}$. We implemented the controller in discrete time using Tustin's approximation.

4.2   Higher-Order Correction Filter

The lead-lag compensator provides a simple and effective way to enhance high-frequency content but is limited to correcting the amplitude attenuation, and does not address effects due to the frictional mechanics of the finger. Using a higher order filter, these effects can be addressed as well. The transfer function that relates the desired force f_r to the actual friction force f_t is $C(s)\,T(s)\,F(s)$, where $F(s)$ models the friction force as a function of the vibration amplitude. The identification of $F(s)$ and potential explanation for its behavior has been covered in [11]. Here, we used a swept-sine signal lasting 2 s to identify the behavior. From the identified transfer function of the system, the controller was designed to be $C(s) \propto ((1 + \tau_w) T(s) F(s))^{-1}$. The controller is estimated in discrete-time by a Yule-Walker optimization. Good agreement between ideal and actual filters is found using a bilinear filter of order 10 or above.

4.3   Experimental Results

We experimentally measure the frequency bandwidth of the force modulation using a stiff piezoelectric force sensor that can resolve 50 μN up to 800 Hz (9203, Kistler Instrumente AG, Winterthur, Switzerland). The ultrasonic vibration of the glass was measured using a piezoelectric pickup glued to the glass and calibrated with a laser Doppler vibrometer. The full bandwidth was measured using 3 s swept-sine signals covering a 10–800 Hz band. The first two authors participated in the experiment. Before the experiment, they trained to maintain a scanning velocity of 40 mm/s and a normal force of 0.5 N. They applied talc to the fingertip before each session to ensure consistent moisture levels and took ten measurements, five going from left to right and five going from right to left.

The amplitude-modulation frequency responses for the non-filtered, the lead-lag controller and the higher order filter cases are shown in Fig. 4a. Both average and standard deviation are shown for each case. Figure 4b shows the action of each controller. Figure 4c shows the friction force frequency response for each case. The high frequencies show a resonance that is attributed to the force sensing system. The high-order filter produces the flattest friction force response. However, despite its simplicity the lead-lag compensator also provides satisfactory results. The effectiveness of this system at displaying a feature in space is demonstrated using a Gaussian-shaped friction profile of 20 ms of width. The spatial tracking performance is shown in Fig. 4d.

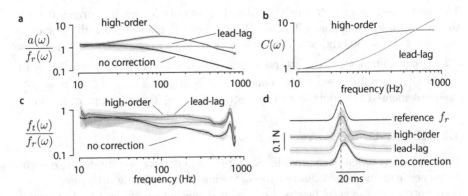

Fig. 4. a. Frequency response of amplitude modulation. **b.** Frequency response of compensators. **c.** Frequency response of the friction force acting on a sliding finger. **d.** Time domain performance.

5 Conclusion

We presented the design and implementation of a surface haptic display able to modulate friction on a bare fingertip with a high dynamic range and wide bandwidth. With the help of a novel non-contact position sensor, an efficient friction-reduction glass plate and correction filtering, the system provides high-fidelity in the rendering of rapid transient changes of friction. High-order filters achieve a better flatness of the force frequency response and a better time-domain tracking performance, at the expense of a more complex implementation. The lead-lag compensator provides good results with a lower performance footprint that makes it suitable for embedded implementation. A further refinement could include a feedback loop to control the amplitude, although this would require real-time monitoring of the vibration of the plate.

The resulting device can render features as small as 25 μm with high temporal accuracy. The high spatial resolution and low latency of the system gives the user a strong sense of the spatial persistence of tactile features that, to the best of our knowledge, has never been achieved before on surface haptic devices. The flatness of the frequency response enables a fine spatial grating to be consistently reproduced regardless of the scanning velocity. In the future we plan to perform a psychophysical evaluation of the perceived quality of the rendered textures.

Acknowledgements. This work has been supported by the National Science Foundation, grants No. IIS-0964075 and IIS-1302422. The authors acknowledge the help of Daniel Russman in the development of the experimental platform.

References

1. Bergmann-Tiest, W.M., Kappers, A.M.L.: Analysis of haptic perception of materials by multidimensional scaling and physical measurements of roughness and compressibility. Acta Psychol. **121**(1), 1–20 (2006)
2. Smith, A.M., Chapman, C.E., Deslandes, M., Langlais, J.S., Thibodeau, M.P.: Role of friction and tangential force variation in the subjective scaling of tactile roughness. Exp. Brain Res. **144**(2), 211–223 (2002)
3. Bensmaïa, S., Hollins, M.: The vibrations of texture. Somatosens. Mot. Res. **20**(1), 33–43 (2003)
4. Minsky, M., Lederman, S.: Simulated haptic textures: roughness. In: Proceedings of the ASME Dynamic Systems and Control Division, vol. 58, pp. 421–426 (1996)
5. Campion, G., Hayward, V.: Fundamental limits in the rendering of virtual haptic textures. In: IEEE World Haptics Conference, pp. 263–270 (2005)
6. Wiertlewski, M., Lozada, J., Hayward, V.: The spatial spectrum of tangential skin displacement can encode tactual texture. IEEE Trans. Robot. **27**(3), 461–472 (2011)
7. Watanabe, T., Fukui, S.: A method for controlling tactile sensation of surface roughness using ultrasonic vibration. In: IEEE ICRA, pp. 1134–1139, May 1995
8. Biet, M., Giraud, F., Lemaire-Semail, B.: Squeeze film effect for the design of an ultrasonic tactile plate. IEEE Trans. Ultrason. Ferroelectr. Freq. Contr. **54**(12), 2678–2688 (2007)

9. Winfield, L., Glassmire, J., Colgate, J.E., Peshkin, M.: T-pad: tactile pattern display through variable friction reduction. In: IEEE World Haptics Conference, pp. 421–426 (2007)
10. Giraud, F., Amberg, M., Lemaire-Semail, B.: Design and control of a haptic knob. Sens. Actuators, A Phys. **196**, 78–85 (2013)
11. Meyer, D.J., Wiertlewski, M., Peshkin, M., Colgate, J.E.: Dynamics of ultrasonic and electrostatic friction modulation for rendering texture on haptic surfaces. In: Proceedings of Haptic Symposium, pp. 218–226. IEEE (2014)
12. Bolanowski Jr, S.J., Gescheider, G.A., Verrillo, R.T., Checkosky, C.M.: Four channels mediate the mechanical aspects of touch. J. Acoust. Soc. Am. **84**, 1680 (1988)
13. Okamoto, S., Konyo, M., Saga, S., Tadokoro, S.: Detectability and perceptual consequences of delayed feedback in a vibrotactile texture display. IEEE Trans. Haptics **2**(2), 73–84 (2009)
14. Smith, A.M., Gosselin, G., Houde, B.: Deployment of fingertip forces in tactile exploration. Exp. Brain Res. **147**(2), 209–218 (2002)
15. Skedung, L., Arvidsson, M., Chung, J.Y., Stafford, C.M., Berglund, B., Rutland, M.W.: Feeling small: exploring the tactile perception limits. Sci. Rep. **3** (2013)
16. Millet, G., Haliyo, S., Regnier, S., Hayward, V.: The ultimate haptic device: first step. In: IEEE World Haptics Conference, pp. 273–278 (2009)
17. Verrillo, R.T.: Effect of contactor area on the vibrotactile threshold. J. Acoust. Soc. Am. **35**, 1962 (1963)
18. Wiertlewski, M., Hayward, V.: Mechanical behavior of the fingertip in the range of frequencies and displacements relevant to touch. J. Biomech. **45**(11), 1869–1874 (2012)

Task-Oriented Approach to Simulate a Grasping Action Through Underactuated Haptic Devices

Leonardo Meli[1,2](✉) and Domenico Prattichizzo[1,2]

[1] Department of Information Engineering and Mathematics,
University of Siena, Via Roma 56, 53100 Siena, Italy
[2] Department of Advanced Robotics, Istituto Italiano di Tecnologia,
Via Morego 30, 16163 Genova, Italy
{meli,prattichizzo}@dii.unisi.it

Abstract. Force rendering is important in underactuated haptic systems. Underactuation means that some force directions at the contacts cannot be rendered because of the lack of actuation. In this paper we propose to exploit the knowledge of the task to mitigate the effect of the underactuation. The simulation of a grasp is considered and two alternative algorithms are proposed to improve the sensitivity in the underactuated system. The basic idea is to exploit the actuated force direction, optimizing the force feedback according to the type of forces involved in the specific grasping task. These forces can be squeezing forces or forces able to move the grasped object. Experiments show that the proposed task–oriented force rendering considerably increases the ability of perceiving the properties of the grasped virtual object.

Keywords: Haptics · Underactuation · Grasping

1 Introduction

The first haptic interface has been designed to simulate a single point contact interaction with virtual environments [1] and this happens for many devices available out of the laboratories. Only recently, multi-contact haptic interfaces have been released, such as the CyberGlove&Grasp (CyberGlove Systems LLC, San Jose, CA) [2]. This complex device exploits the combination of two technologies, tendons and exoskeletons and it is provided with up to twenty sensors to retrieve the position of the hand, and five actuators, one for each finger. In [3], Giachritsis *et al.* present the MasterFinger-2, a novel multi-finger haptic interface that allows bimanual manipulation of virtual objects with precision grip.

The research leading to these results has received funding from the European Union Seventh Framework Programme FP7/2007–2013 with project "WEARHAP - WEARable HAPtics for humans and robots" and project "THE - The Hand Embodied".

M. Auvray and C. Duriez (Eds.): EuroHaptics 2014, Part II, LNCS 8619, pp. 249–257, 2014.
DOI: 10.1007/978-3-662-44196-1_31

Each arm has a serial-parallel structure with 6 DoF for movement and 3 DoF for force reflection, allowing grasping actions in any direction.

However simulating the interaction with multiple contacts can be difficult. Assume that each finger shares a contact point with an object; according to the Hard-Finger contact model (HF) [4], three actuators are needed to simulate the force interaction at each contact point, leading to more complex haptic devices.

When size and weight constraints arise in a haptic device, a simplification of its design is needed. A promising solution is to reduce the number of actuators, that leads to an underactuated haptic interface. For instance Iqbal et al. in [5] present a robotic exoskeleton, in which each finger is equipped with only one actuator. However, this lack in terms of actuation can introduce a discrepancy between what the user expects to feel and the forces actually fed back through such an interface. In the case of the Da Vinci surgical system advantages and disadvantages of the use of underactuation are under investigation. As stated in [6], in some circumstances, it may be effective for users to obtain force information along certain directions and not along others. For instance, while performing a teleoperated needle insertion, only the force feedback related to the shearing force, i.e. force parallel to the surface of the tissue, can be provided to the operator. Axial force feedback could lead to overshoot and vibrations of the telemanipulator, since the needle penetrates through tissues with different stiffness. Thus, in such a case, partial force feedback is beneficial for the operator. However, in [7], investigating upon the partial force rendering effects, it is pointed out that force rendering does influence the user's confidence in her/his perception of a remote environment during a telemanipulation task.

The focus of this paper is the development of force feedback algorithms for underactuated haptic devices. The main idea of our approach is to emphasize the more relevant forces, accordingly to the task at hand, and achieve a good perception even if the number of actuators is not sufficient to simulate the whole set of contact forces. Information lost due underactuation can be partially recovered exploiting some geometric properties of the task considered.

The paper is organized as follows: in Sect. 2 the haptic rendering is described, together with the geometric and mathematical bases underneath the proposed algorithms. In Sect. 3 two experiments are characterized and the performance, during a grasping and a lifting tasks, are analysed. Finally Sect. 4 addresses concluding remarks and perspectives of the work.

2   Modelling the Underactuation

To formalize the problem of underactuation, consider a haptic interface able to simulate a certain number of contact forces, grouped in a vector λ. Assume that not all the contact force components of vector λ can be independently actuated. In particular assume that the relationship between the real actuator action λ_a and the vector of contact forces λ is given by

$$\lambda = M_a \, \lambda_a \,, \tag{1}$$

where M_a is referred to as the *actuation matrix*, whose structure and size strictly depend on the number of contact points, the number of available actuators, and the geometry of the system. In this paper we assume that the set of contacts defines a certain grasp configuration, whose geometry is described by the grasp matrix G [4]. G is frequently used to asses the equilibrium of a grasp through the equation $w = G\lambda$, where w is the external wrench applied to the grasped object, and λ is the vector of all contact forces applied by the hand on the object. From the equilibrium equation, two important subspaces for contact forces can be defined. (1) The subspaces of internal forces, *i.e.* self balanced forces whose net wrench on the object is zero and that belong to the nullspace of the grasp matrix $\mathcal{N}(G)$ [8]. (2) The subspace of external forces, *i.e.* forces that cause a non zero net wrench on the object and belong to the complementary set of the nullspace of the grasp matrix $\mathcal{R}(G^T)$ [8]. Different solutions of the underactuated forces λ_a can thus benefit different components of the full contact forces λ. The straightforward solution to Eq. (1) is

$$\lambda_a = (M_a)^{\#}\,\lambda, \qquad\qquad (2)$$

where $(\cdot)^{\#}$ is the Moore-Penrose pseudoinverse operator. It minimizes the sum of the force squared residuals upon all the space [9], regardless of the task's aim. Taking into account the task at hand and projecting the Eq. (1) onto the subspace of interest, we can propose better solutions in terms of algorithms.

Internal Forces Algorithm (IF). The *IF Algorithm* projects the contact forces onto the nullspace of the grasp matrix $\mathcal{N}(G)$, solving the system of equation

$$\begin{cases} (N_G)^T\,\lambda = (N_G)^T\,M_a\,\lambda_a \\ \lambda = M_a\,\lambda_a \end{cases},$$

where N_G denotes a matrix whose columns form a basis for $\mathcal{N}(G)$. Forces exerted by the actuators can be expressed as

$$\lambda_a = \left[B^{\#}\,(N_G)^T\right]\,\lambda + \left[N_B\,(M_a\,N_B)^{\#}\,\left(I_{6\times 6} - M_a B^{\#}\,(N_G)^T\right)\right]\,\lambda,$$

where $B \triangleq (N_G)^T M_a$, N_B is a matrix whose columns form a basis for $\mathcal{N}(B)$, and $I_{6\times 6}$ is an identity matrix of size 6. Imagine to handle a regular object, e.g. a solid cube, with two fingers. We naturally grasp it placing our thumb and index on its opposite faces. The more relevant forces belong to the subspace described by $\mathcal{N}(G)$. The *IF Algorithm* can then be really convenient when it comes to deal with most of grasping tasks.

External Forces Algorithm (EF). The *EF Algorithm* is based on the same idea of the *Internal Forces* one, but, differently it takes advantage of the complementary space of $\mathcal{N}(G)$, the range of the transpose of the grasp matrix $\mathcal{R}(G^T)$, as follows

$$(R_{G^T})^T\,\lambda = (R_{G^T})^T\,M_a\,\lambda_a,$$

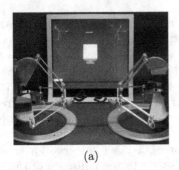 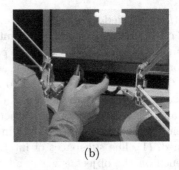

(a)   (b)

Fig. 1. The experimental setup, composed of two Omega 3 haptic interfaces with thimbles as end-effectors and a virtual environment to interact with. (a) General overview. (b) Detail of the thumb and index fingers placed inside the thimbles.

where R_{G^T} denotes a matrix whose columns form a basis for $\mathcal{R}(G^T)$. Since in this case we assume that $\mathcal{N}(G\,M_a) = \emptyset$, the forces exerted by the actuators can be simply computed as

$$\lambda_a = (G\,M_a)^{\#}G\,\lambda.$$

This time all the force components belonging to $\mathcal{N}(G)$ are disadvantaged despite of all the others that are not part of such a subspace. For instance the weight of an object does not usually belong to the nullspace of G during a common grasping task.

3   Experiments

In order to validate the feasibility of the proposed methods two experiments have been carried out. They basically consisted of two contact points pinch grasps, where underactuated forces were rendered through the different methods aforementioned. Force rendering performance has been evaluated in the different cases with a just noticeable difference (JND) analysis on the collected data [10]. Different properties of the virtual object have been tested during the two experiments, so then to give a greater role to internal forces rather than to external ones, and vice versa.

Two Omega 3 haptic interfaces, one for each contact point, were exploited. Since the Omega 3 can render a contact force vector with three independent components, we simulated an underactuated system via software, selecting two actuated directions according to a given geometry. This setup can indeed be used as an experimental testbed for rapid prototyping of underactuated solutions in haptics. We used two thimbles as end-effectors of the haptic interfaces to make the grasp more realistic for the operators during the trials proposed. The virtual environment was composed by a cube, the object aimed to interact with, and a black background (see Fig. 1). Virtual walls and a virtual ground limited the area of interaction. Two spheric grey cursors allowed the operator to locate their fingertips in the virtual world.

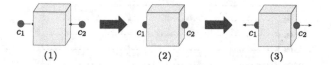

Fig. 2. Schematic overview of the first experiment, consisting of grasping a virtual cube with two fingers placed on its opposite side faces. Experiment steps: (1) grasp the cube, (2) 3 s exploration of the cube's stiffness, (3) release the cube.

3.1   Experiment 1: Grasping Task

The first task proposed consisted of grasping the cube, with two fingers on the opposite faces. Being interested in internal forces only, the dynamic of the object was not considered and the cube was fixed in the middle of the virtual workspace. This experiment aimed to compare the JND, when the stiffness of a virtual object was rendered through the *IF Algorithm* and the pseudoinverse of Eq. (2).

Five participants, four males, one female, age range 20–33, took part to the experiment, all of whom were right-handed. Four of them had previous experience with haptic interfaces. None of the participants reported any deficiencies in their perception abilities. Subjects were asked to suit the thimbles connected to the haptic devices on their thumb and index fingers of the same hand and complete the task proposed. It consisted of grasping the virtual cube for no more than 3 s. After the first exploration the user had to leave the grip to allow the change of the object's stiffness, then he could start a new interaction for 3 s again. When the time was over, he had to release the grip and state whether the second touched object was stiffer than the first one. All the experiment steps are summarized in Fig. 2. The comparison was between a *Standard stiffness* (Ss), constant for an entire series, and six *Comparison stiffnesses* (Cs), computed as different ratios of Ss and changing on each trial. Each Cs was proposed 10 times to the subject in a pseudo-random order. Once all the trials were considered, the standard stimulus was increased and a new series started with the same modality. Three series of 60 trials, one per standard stimulus in the set [30 60 90] N/m, were performed per subject under each of the considered force rendering conditions, i.e. *IF Algorithm* and pseudoinverse method. All the answers were collected to be elaborated and statistically analysed. A pink noise was continuously provided to participants through headphones throughout the experimental trials, in order to guarantee a better isolation from the surrounding world and keep the subjects more focused. The set of Ss provided and the relative Cs have been properly tuned during a preliminary testing session to obtain a significant evaluation and exploit at its best the sensitivity of the investigated algorithms.

From the collected responses three different psychometric curves were fitted for each subject, each corresponding to a specific standard stimulus. Thresholds computed for each curve were averaged over the whole dataset among each Ss and then plotted in Fig. 3. It shows that the *IF Algorithm* increases the sensitivity of the haptic feedback in an underactuated configuration and allows to better perceive the stiffness of a virtual object performing a grasping task. Comparison of

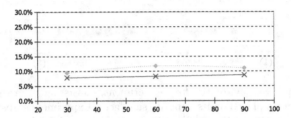

Fig. 3. JND ratio values when the pseudoinverse of Eq. (2) (dotted green line) and the *IF Algorithm* (red solid line) are used to render the stiffness of a virtual cube in a two fingers grasping simulation. The horizontal axis shows the range of stiffness expressed in N/m (color figure online).

the means among the two feedback modalities was tested using a paired samples t-test, which revealed significantly statistically differences between the means for the same values of Ss. t-values of 3.074, 6.169, 2.942 and relative p-values of 0.037, 0.040, 0.042 have been computed for the standard stimuli [30 60 90] N/m respectively.

Contrary as we expected, regarding both methods, the JND index does not decrease for higher stimuli, although the higher the Ss provided to the subject, the larger the gap between the minimum/maximum Cs and the Ss itself (Cs is a ratio of Ss). Hence the higher Ss, the more difficult the perception of the object's stiffness change.

3.2   Experiment 2: Lifting Task

The second conducted experiment consisted of lifting a cube with two fingers placed on its opposite side faces. Contrary to the first experiment of the previous section the cube was free to move in all the directions of the 3D space and the gravity force was rendered. Our purpose was to compare the JND when an external force, i.e. the gravity force, acting on a virtual object, was provided using the *EF Algorithm* and the pseudoinverse of Eq. (2). The same five participants of the first experiment took part to this one and the same experimental setup was used as well. The task consisted of grasping the cube and lifting it for no more than 3 s. Then the user had to leave the grip to allow the change of the object's weight, so he could start a new similar interaction for the same 3 s. When the time was over he had to release the grip again and state whether the second raised object was heavier than the first one. All the experiment steps are summarized in Fig. 4. The comparison was between a *Standard weight* (Sw), constant for an entire series, and six *Comparison weights* (Cw), computed as different ratios of Sw and changing on each trial. Each Cw was proposed 10 times to the subject in a pseudo-random order. Once all the trials were considered, the standard stimulus was increased and a new series started with the same modality. Three series of 60 trials, one per standard stimulus in the set [30 60 90] g, were performed per subject under each of the considered force rendering conditions, i.e. *EF Algorithm* and pseudoinverse method. All the answers were thus collected to be

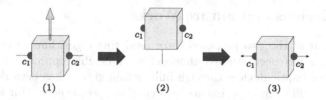

Fig. 4. Schematic overview of the second experiment, consisting of lifting a virtual cube with two fingers placed on its opposite side faces. Experiment steps: (1) grasp and lift the cube, (2) 3 s exploration of the cube's weight, (3) release the cube.

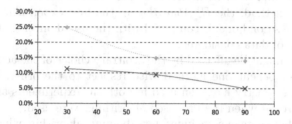

Fig. 5. JND ratio values when the pseudoinverse of Eq. (2) (dotted green line) and the *EF Algorithm* (blue solid line) are used to render the weight of a virtual cube in a lifting simulation. The horizontal axis shows the range of weights expressed in g (color figure online).

elaborated and statistically analysed. As for the first experiment throughout the simulation, a pink noise was continuously provided to the participants. The set of Sw provided and the relative Cw have been again properly tuned during a preliminary testing session to obtain a significant evaluation and exploit at its best the sensitivity of the investigated algorithms.

From the collected data regarding each subject three different psychometric curves were fitted, one for each standard weight. Thresholds computed for each curve were averaged over the whole dataset among each Sw and then plotted in Fig. 5. It shows that the *EF Algorithm* increases the sensitivity of the haptic feedback in an underactuated configuration and allows to better perceive the weight of a virtual object, i.e. an external force, while performing a lifting task.

Comparison of the means among the two feedback modalities was again tested using a paired samples t-test, which revealed significantly statistically differences between the means for the same values of Sw. t-values of 27.648, 3.650, 5.867 and relative p-values of < 0.001, 0.022, 0.004 have been computed for the standard stimuli [30 60 90] g respectively.

Note in Fig. 5 that the JND values decrease with the increase of the object's weight, probably because the difference between Sw and Cw becomes larger and the subjects can better perceive the gap (Cw is a ratio of Sw).

4 Conclusions and Future Works

The behaviour of the two proposed force rendering algorithms in an underactuated system has been studied thoroughly. A flexible approach to simulate underactuated haptic devices through fully actuated ones has been defined and applied in two different experiments involving five people each. Our idea allows to introduce an efficient way to distinguish between the two different categories of forces, internal and external, acting in grasping, and develop algorithms that privilege the rendering of one force type despite of the other. Both the experiments show an improvement in terms of performance, when the investigated force rendering method, the *IF Algorithm* in the first experiment and the *EF Algorithm* in the second one, is compared with the pseudoinverse of Eq. (2) over the entire range of data considered.

Performance might be affected by the arbitrary choice of the actuation directions, which can benefit one method with respect to the other. However the same actuation geometry has been used in both the experiments and the user's perception improved when the proposed algorithms were used.

Future developments may include a new dynamic algorithm, which can switch from rendering internal forces to external ones, according to the task being executed by the user. Benefits achieved by the different methods addressed in this work, can then be merged together to guarantee a better sensitivity to the operator while performing general tasks and using underactuated haptic devices. Moreover a larger number of participants should take part in further experiments to make the data analysis more accurate and reliable.

References

1. Salisbury, K., Brock, D., Massie, T., Swarup, N., Zilles, C.: Haptic rendering: programming touch interaction with virtual objects. In: Proceedings of the International Symposium on Interactive 3D Graphics, pp. 123–130 (1995)
2. Nikolaki, G., Tzovaras, D., Moustakidis, S., Strintzis, M.G.: Cybergrasp and phantom integration: enhanced haptic access for visually impaired users. In: Proceedings of the International Conference on Speech and Computer, pp. 507–513 (2004)
3. Giachritsis, C.D., Ferre, M., Barrio, J., Wing, A.M.: Unimanual and bimanual weight perception of virtual objects with a new multi-finger haptic interface. Brain Res. Bull. **85**(5), 271–275 (2011)
4. Prattichizzo, D., Trinkle, J.: Grasping. In: Siciliano, B., Kathib, O. (eds.) Handbook on Robotics, pp. 671–700. Springer, New York (2008)
5. Iqbal, J., Tsagarakis, N.G., Caldwell, D.G.: A multi-dof robotic exoskeleton interface for hand motion assistance. In: Proceedings of the IEEE International Conference on Engineering in Medicine and Biology Society, pp. 1575–1578 (2011)
6. Verner, L.N., Okamura, A.M.: Sensor/actuator asymmetries in telemanipulators: implications of partial force feedback. In: Proceedings of the IEEE International Symposium in Haptic Interfaces for Virtual Environment and Teleoperator Systems, pp. 309–314 (2006)
7. Verner, L.N., Okamura, A.M.: Effects of translational and gripping force feedback are decoupled in a 4-degree-of-freedom telemanipulator. In: Proceedings of the IEEE International Conference on World Haptics Conference, pp. 286–291 (2007)

8. Bicchi, A.: On the closure properties of robotic grasping. Int. J. Robot. Res. **14**(4), 319–334 (1995)
9. Peters, G., Wilkinson, J.H.: The least squares problem and pseudo-inverses. Comput. J. **13**(3), 309–316 (1970)
10. Stern, M.K., Johnson, J.H.: Just noticeable difference. Corsini Encyclopedia of Psychology (2010)

Integration of a Particle Jamming Tactile Display with a Cable-Driven Parallel Robot

Andrew A. Stanley[1]([⊠]), David Mayhew[2], Rikki Irwin[2],
and Allison M. Okamura[1]

[1] Department of Mechanical Engineering, Stanford University, Stanford, USA
{astan,aokamura}@stanford.edu
[2] Robotics and ElectroMechanical Systems,
Intelligent Automation, Inc., Rockville, USA
{dmayhew,rirwin}@i-a-i.com

Abstract. Integration of a tactile display onto the end effector of a robot allows free-hand exploration of an encountered-type environment that provides both kinesthetic and cutaneous feedback. A novel tactile display approach, called Haptic Jamming, uses a combination of particle jamming and pneumatics to control the stiffness and shape of a surface. The tactile display mounts to the cable-driven platform of a kinesthetic system for medical simulation, called KineSys MedSim. The parallel structure of the robot provides a high strength-to-weight ratio for kinesthetic feedback in combination with a spatially aligned visual display. Its controller uses hand tracking to move the platform to the portion of the workspace the user is reaching toward. Data from a lump localization simulation demonstrates that the integrated system successfully tracks the user's hand and reconfigures the tactile display according to the location of the end effector.

Keywords: Haptic device design · Haptic I/O · Particle jamming · Tactile display · Parallel cable robotics

1 Introduction

Realistic touch feedback in virtual environments requires both cutaneous tactile feedback and kinesthetic feedback to accurately recreate physical interactions. This involves rendering not only forces but also vibrations, skin deformation, and other tactile sensations. We present a novel medical simulation system that enables simultaneous programmable control of tactile and kinesthetic feedback.

Many medical procedures require a clinician to rely upon the sense of touch to make a diagnosis or treatment decision, so haptic feedback plays an important role in any simulator used to practice these procedures. Classic mannequins provide real physical environments for the trainee to explore directly with his or her hands, but do not permit significant changes in geometry or material properties to simulate a variety of scenarios. On the other end of the spectrum

© Springer-Verlag Berlin Heidelberg 2014
M. Auvray and C. Duriez (Eds.): EuroHaptics 2014, Part II, LNCS 8619, pp. 258–265, 2014.
DOI: 10.1007/978-3-662-44196-1_32

of haptic simulation, virtual environments can be reprogrammed to render a wide range of medical scenarios, from the contour of a skull to the compliance of a soft tissue.

Typically, virtual environments that provide haptic feedback apply resolved forces to a hand-held stylus, thimble, or other handle via a series of motors for the kinesthetic feedback. Programmable cutaneous feedback typically requires additional actuators or hardware built into the hand-held component to adjust the vibrotactile, skin deformation, or other cutaneous sensations that the user feels. With this setup, however, the user is constrained to hold onto the end effector of the device at all times and is no longer truly free to explore the physical environment directly with his or her own hands. Even when there is no programmed physical interaction in such a virtual environment, the user still feels the device that he or she is holding.

Bridging the gap between these two ends of the spectrum, tactile displays and shape rendering devices create programmable physical environments with variable shape and mechanical properties for a user to explore directly and freely. The complexity of these tactile displays often results in either a limited size of the explorable workspace or low tactile resolution. In this work, we address these limitations of haptic simulators by integrating a tactile display onto the end effector of a new six degree-of-freedom (DOF) cable-driven parallel robot developed specifically to create virtual environments for medical simulation. The tactile display can adjust both its mechanical and shape properties using particle jamming and pneumatics, as we explain in our previous work [2,14]. The robot uses eight motors connected to cables on each corner of the end effector to drive the platform in space below a visual display. Integrating these two new devices creates a freely explorable environment with a large workspace and both cutaneous and kinesthetic haptic feedback, a novel combination for medical simulators.

2 Background

In an effort to present users with programmable physical environments they can explore freely, researchers have developed number of tactile displays, shape rendering devices, and encountered-type haptic displays. Many tactile displays focus primarily on adjustable mechanical properties so that the forces and displacements a user feels while exploring a surface can change. For example, this can be accomplished via magnetorheological fluids [8] or electrorheological fluids [15], which adjust the stiffness or damping of the material with the application of a magnetic or electrical field, respectively. Other tactile displays focus on adjustable shape output properties. Implementations of displays with controllable geometries include shape memory alloy arrays [16] and other various arrays of pins [4,12] or balloons [6]. The concept of "Digital Clay" [13] represents an ideal for a tactile interface capable of both controllable geometry and stiffness for a deformable computer input and output, and recent displays using particle jamming [14] and pneumatics [3] aim to achieve these features.

The end effector of a 6-DOF robot can create a workspace larger than the typical tactile display, so many encountered-type haptic displays utilize this feature to allow users to explore environments more freely. Using computer vision to track a user's hand motion allows a robot to relocate a surface mounted to its end effector anywhere within its workspace to simulate a much larger surface with varying orientations [17]. Other shape rendering interfaces [7] have suggested mounting the display to a robot end effector to present different objects of varying shapes in different regions of the workspace.

Parallel robots, in contrast to serial manipulators, connect the end effector directly to the base through multiple links [10]. In cable-driven parallel robots where the end effector is suspended below the base and cable mass is minimal, the manipulator can be viewed as an upside-down version of the common Stewart-Gough platforms, which allows the calculation of their inverse kinematics in six degrees of freedom [11]. However, the cables can only support tensile forces and not compressive forces [1]. Parallel cable robots typically have a larger workspace and lower weight than serial robots of similar size and strength, features that have driven their use in applications ranging from shipping to neurorehabilitation [9].

3   KineSys MedSim Robot

The second generation of a kinesthetic system for medical simulation (KineSys MedSim), shown in Fig. 1, creates a hands-free haptic environment by moving a tactile display in three-dimensional space underneath a visual display of a virtual environment. The first generation of the KineSys MedSim robot is described in [5]. A user stands next to the robot and looks down at the reflection of a 3D display above his or her head on the semi-silvered mirror of a suspended particle device (SPD) that changes light transmission properties under the application of a voltage. Switches on the right side allow adjustment of the transparency of

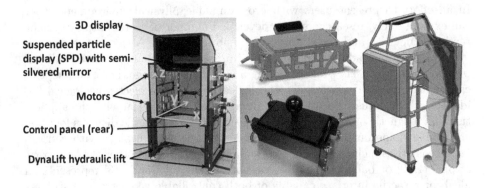

Fig. 1. Photos and CAD drawings of the Kinesys Medsim robot, its coordinate frame, and its end effector. The end effector configuration shown does not have a tactile display integrated but rather a handle for only kinesthetic haptic interaction.

Fig. 2. A video camera below the workspace is used in combination with the AR Tracking toolkit and fiducial markers on the bottom of the end effector to set the home position of the robot. A Leap Motion sensor tracks the user's fingers and palm (right).

the SPD display and of the robot height via a hydraulic lift. Thus, the visual display can sit just below the chin of anyone within the 10th percentile of female height to 90th percentile of male height and can range from fully mirroring the screen above to allowing some visibility of the user's hand below.

Beneath the visual display, eight cables drive the end effector platform around a 0.86 m × 0.76 m × 0.71 m workspace. The corners of the workspace each house a fairlead and a pulley to guide the cables around the shafts of eight brushless DC motors that extrude out of the sides of the robot with encoders for position tracking. The robot can generate up to 178 N of force with a maximum velocity and acceleration of 0.762 m/s and 2.54 m/s^2, respectively. As shown in Fig. 1, the end effector consists of a 0.22 m × 0.13 m × 0.075 m shell that holds a 0.19 m × 0.12 m × 0.043 m mounting frame on top of a 6-DOF ATI Gamma NET force-torque sensor. A Beckhoff Automation CX1030-0110 embedded PC serves as the central control unit for the Advanced Motion Controls EtherCAT drives that run the motors. The embedded PC enables a fixed 1000 Hz control loop rate as it communicates with the main GUI client PC. A Leap Motion controller mounts to the outside of the end effector to track the user's hand above the surface and a Logitech HD Webcam mounted below the workspace uses AR Tracking toolkit with the fiducial markers on the bottom of the end effector (Fig. 2) to automatically move the end effector to its home position and calibrate the motor encoders when the robot is first powered.

4   Haptic Jamming Display

The Haptic Jamming display provides simultaneous control of shape output and mechanical stiffness in a single interface. The underlying design concept, described in much greater detail in [14], relies on pneumatics and particle jamming. For integration with the KineSys MedSim robot described here, we use a single-cell version of the display, although we have prototyped several multi-cell arrays capable of creating more complex geometries [14].

Particle jamming allows an object to adjust its mechanical properties, typically by filling a flexible membrane with a granular material and applying varying levels of vacuum. In this particular application, we use a hollow silicone membrane with a 0.17 m × 0.10 m × 0.011 m internal volume filled with coffee grounds such that the grounds jam together and become rigid when the air is vacuumed from the inside of the silicone. We construct the silicone shell by gluing together two separate pieces, both cast from custom laser-cut molds. The bottom piece of silicone is a 3.2 m thick layer that spans the top surface of the mounting frame on the end effector of the KineSys MedSim robot with a nub that the vacuum line glues into. The top piece of silicone consists of a .013 m thick hollow shell that fills with coffee grounds with an internal silicone structure of thin, disconnected walls that help prevent the grounds from shifting around too much when the cell deforms. Without these internal walls, the granules would all shift towards the outside of the cell when it balloons outwards with an increase in air pressure beneath the cell, making the center of the lump less rigid with the application of vacuum to the inside of the cell. This top shell spans the bottom silicone except for a 0.013 m border on each side that allows a piece of acrylic to clamp the bottom silicone piece onto the edges of a pressure-regulated air chamber below. The air chamber sits inside the mounting frame of the end effector.

A Proportion Air QB3 pressure regulator controlled by a National Instruments X-Series DAQ sets the air pressure inside the chamber. Increasing the pressure in the air chamber while the surface is in its soft, non-vacuumed state balloons the silicone outward. Subsequently applying a vacuum to jam the cell allows it to hold a deformed state rigidly, as depicted in Fig. 3.

5   Integration of the Tactile Interface and Robot

We designed the single-cell version of the Haptic Jamming display in Sect. 4 to fit the dimensions of the end effector, in order to simplify mechanical integration with the KineSys MedSim robot and allow easy interchanging with alternate tactile displays or a handle for purely kinesthetic interaction. Four screws at the

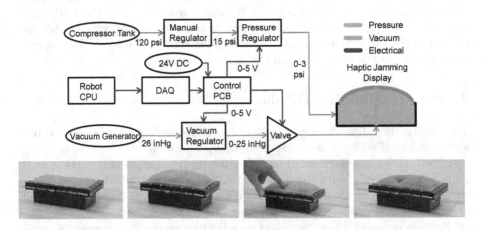

Fig. 3. The system architecture to control a single-cell Haptic Jamming display (top). The tactile display (bottom) consists of a thin particle jamming layer to adjust the stiffness of the surface laid over a pressurized air chamber to adjust its shape.

corners of the display hold it onto the mounting frame of the end effector such that the force-torque sensor below can register all interaction forces with the display. The pneumatic and vacuum lines feed into the control panel at the back of the robot and run from the electronic regulators and valves on the recessed panel of the workspace up to the end effector alongside the cables for the Leap controller and the force-torque sensor.

The robot can command a desired lump size and stiffness to the Haptic Jamming display and it will subsequently follow the sequence of timed steps necessary to create that configuration. The display controller updates the robot with a binary state of either reconfiguring or configured. For a preliminary demonstration based on the integrated system's original intent for medical simulation, the graphics use CHAI 3D to show a human torso with a faint sphere to mark the location of an embedded lump, as well as a green cursor that tracks the position of the end effector.

The system switches between two modes during operation. When the user is moving his or her hand freely above the display, the Leap controller tracks the hand position and moves the end effector in a plane below to track the measured X-Y position of the palm, which provides more reliable readings than the individual fingers, and aligns it with the front of the tactile display. If the end effector position aligns with the sphere indicating the embedded lump on the screen, the tactile display reconfigures from a flat, soft surface to a rigid lump, as shown in Fig. 4. When the user reaches down to touch the surface, as registered by the force-torque sensor under the tactile display, the system switches into an interactive mode, locking the configuration of the tactile display and using to an impedance controller to render kinesthetic interaction forces from the current position. Figure 5 shows a set of data collected during a sample interaction with the integrated system to demonstrate its functionality. When the end effector's X and Y coordinates fall within 0.013 m of the lump's coordinates, the soft, flat surface of the Haptic Jamming display converts to a rigid lump by commanding a higher pressure to the chamber beneath the surface to balloon it outward followed by commanding a higher vacuum to the interior of the cell to jam it into its rigid state.

Fig. 4. A single-cell Haptic Jamming display integrated onto the end effector of the KineSys MedSim robot. The graphics show a human torso with a lump location and a green cursor for the end effector position. The tactile display changes from a soft, flat surface to a rigid lump when the cursor aligns with the virtual lump.

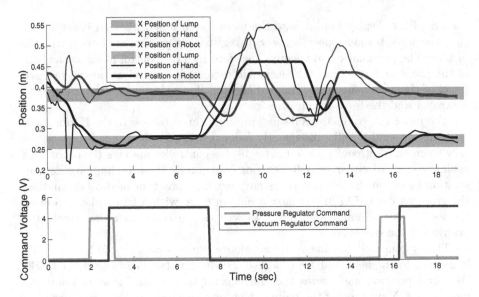

Fig. 5. Data showing the robot end effector tracking the hand as measured by the Leap controller, plateauing at the edge of its workspace. When the end effector reaches the location of the virtual lump, a sequence of commands to the pressure and vacuum regulators convert the Haptic Jamming display from a soft, flat surface to a rigid lump.

6   Conclusions and Future Work

This paper presents a novel framework for an encountered-type haptic display. The Haptic Jamming tactile display provides both controllable stiffness and shape in an environment that the user can explore directly with his or her hands. The KineSys MedSim cable-driven parallel robot not only provides more physical support for a tactile display than a serial robot, but also allows the platform to add underlying kinesthetic haptic feedback to the cutaneous feedback of the tactile display. A lump localization simulation demonstrates the integration of the graphics, hand tracking, and kinesthetic and cutaneous interaction in a medical simulation scenario. Future work will integrate a multi-cell Haptic Jamming display into the robot to present more complex surfaces, improve the control of the KineSys MedSim robot to utilize all six of its degrees of freedom, and test users in order to explore various control strategies for moving an encountered-type display during haptic interaction. Furthermore, experiments will test the relationship between the controllable kinesthetic stiffness of the robot and the adjustable stiffness of the tactile display and how users perceive these overlapping sensations.

Acknowledgments. This work was supported by U.S. Army Medical Research and Materiel Command (USAMRMC; W81XWH-11-C-0050) and by a National Science Foundation Graduate Research Fellowship. The views, opinions, and/or findings contained in this report are those of the authors and should not be construed as an official Department of the Army position, policy or decision unless so designated by other documentation. The authors thank Timothy Judkins and James Gwilliam for their work developing the robot and tactile display.

References

1. Dallej, T., Gouttefarde, M., Andreff, N., Dahmouche, R., Martinet, P.: Vision-based modeling and control of large-dimension cable-driven parallel robots. In: IEEE/RSJ Intelligent Robots and Systems, pp. 1581–1586 (2012)
2. Genecov, A.M., Stanley, A.A., Okamura, A.M.: Perception of a haptic jamming display: just noticeable differences in stiffness and geometry. In: IEEE Haptics Symposium, pp. 333–338 (2014)
3. Gwilliam, J.C., Bianchi, M., Su, L.K., Okamura, A.M.: Characterization and psychophysical studies of an air-jet lump display. IEEE Trans. Haptics **6**(2), 156–166 (2013)
4. Howe, R., Peine, W., Kantarinis, D., Son, J.: Remote palpation technology. IEEE Eng. Med. Biol. Mag. **14**(3), 318–323 (1995)
5. Judkins, T.N., Stevenson, M., Mayhew, D., Okamura, A.: Development of the KineSys MedSim: a novel hands-free haptic robot for medical simulation. In: Medicine Meets Virtual Reality (2011)
6. King, C.H., Culjat, M.O., Franco, M.L., Bisley, J.W., Dutson, E., Grundfest, W.S.: Optimization of a pneumatic balloon tactile display for robot-assisted surgery based on human perception. IEEE Trans. Biomed. Eng. **55**(11), 2593–2600 (2008)
7. Klare, S., Forssilow, D., Peer, A.: Formable object a new haptic interface for shape rendering. In: IEEE World Haptics Conference, pp. 61–66 (2013)
8. Liu, Y., Davidson, R., Taylor, P., Ngu, J., Zarraga, J.: Single cell magnetorheological fluid based tactile display. Displays **26**(1), 29–35 (2005)
9. Mayhew, D., Bachrach, B., Rymer, W., Beer, R.: Development of the MACARM - a novel cable robot for upper limb neurorehabilitation. In: Rehabilitation Robotics, pp. 299–302 (2005)
10. Merlet, J.P.: Parallel Robots, vol. 74. Springer, New York (2001)
11. Roberts, R.G., Graham, T., Lippitt, T.: On the inverse kinematics, statics, and fault tolerance of cable-suspended robots. J. Robot. Syst. **15**(10), 581–597 (1998)
12. Roke, C., Spiers, A., Pipe, T., Melhuish, C.: The effects of laterotactile information on lump localization through a teletaction system. In: IEEE World Haptics Conference, pp. 365–370 (2013)
13. Rossignac, J., Allen, M., Book, W., Glezer, A., Ebert-Uphoff, I., Shaw, C., Rosen, D., Askins, S., Bosscher, P., Gargus, J., Llamas, I., Nguyen, A.: Finger sculpting with Digital Clay: 3D shape input and output through a computer-controlled real surface. In: Shape Modeling International, pp. 229–231 (2003)
14. Stanley, A.A., Gwilliam, J.C., Okamura, A.M.: Haptic jamming: a deformable geometry, variable stiffness tactile display using pneumatics and particle jamming. In: IEEE World Haptics Conference, pp. 25–30 (2013)
15. Taylor, P.: Advances in an electrorheological fluid based tactile array. Displays **18**, 135–141 (1998)
16. Taylor, P., Moser, A., Creed, A.: A sixty-four element tactile display using shape memory alloy wires. Displays **18**, 163–168 (1998)
17. Yokokohji, Y., Hollis, R.L., Kanade, T.: What you can see is what you can feel-development of a visual/haptic interface to virtual environment. In: IEEE Virtual Reality Annual International Symposium, pp. 46–53 (1996)

Humanoid Robot Teleoperation with Vibrotactile Based Balancing Feedback

Anais Brygo[✉], Ioannis Sarakoglou,
Nadia Garcia-Hernandez, and Nikolaos Tsagarakis

Istituto Italiano di Tecnologia, Genova, Italy
anais.brgyo@gmail.com

Abstract. One of the main challenges while teleoperating a humanoid robot consists in maintaining the slave's balance while satisfying the operator's intention. The main goal of this work is to settle whether feeding back the robot's balance state to the operator by the mean of a vibrotactile belt can lead to an enhanced quality teleoperation. This study examines if an adequate cutaneous guidance can enable the operator to understand when the robot is approaching a loss-of-balance configuration, and use this information to adjust his teleoperation strategy. To achieve this objective, three different feedback patterns were compared during an initial experimental study. The evaluation focused on the subjects capacity to recognize the boundaries of a virtual workspace under each feedback mode and to adapt accordingly their teleoperated motions. The best suited feedback mode was selected and used during a second experiment which compared the performances obtained with and without tactile feedback during the teleoperation of the humanoid robot COMAN. Results clearly reveal that the cutaneous feedback of the slave's balance state leads towards an enhanced quality teleoperation combining an increased safety as well as an unrestrained use of the entire stable workspace.

1 Introduction

Due to their anthropomorphic structure, humanoid robots constitute a powerful tool to operate in a world designed by humans for humans. Although they have the technical capability to execute a large range of actions, the current progress in artificial intelligence is still far from providing adequate decision-making skills needed by a robot to evolve autonomously in an unstructured world. An elegant way to overcome this difficulty is to rely on the human intelligence and experience through teleoperation. It then becomes possible to safely perform highly complex tasks in hazardous and dynamically varying environments. Teleoperating a humanoid robot constitutes a real challenge for two main reasons. In first place their large number of DOFs make these systems complex to control. Moreover, as the slave represents a floating rather than a fixed-base system, balance has to be maintained while integrating the operator's intentions. Although different stabilizing strategies can be implemented to autonomously recover from

© Springer-Verlag Berlin Heidelberg 2014
M. Auvray and C. Duriez (Eds.): EuroHaptics 2014, Part II, LNCS 8619, pp. 266–275, 2014.
DOI: 10.1007/978-3-662-44196-1_33

external disturbances issued by the environment, they cannot compensate for a loss of balance due to an aggressive teleoperation without compromising the task completion. As a consequence operators can be exposed to stress and a heavy mental load that can rapidly become overwhelming. The objective of this work is to analyze the potential benefits of assisting operators to evaluate the balance state of the robot by the mean of a dedicated feedback. Such guidance could substantially improve the safety and the quality of the teleoperation by leading operators to adapt their teleoperation strategy in the same way humans constantly use their equilibrioception (or sense of balance) to carry out a task without falling.

We propose to present the balance information by the mean of a cutaneous feedback. Vibrotactile belts appear suitable since they can easily convey a directional information, through the activation of the adequate tactor, as well as an additional information through the modulation of the vibration signal. In previous studies [3,4], tactile feedback belts have been used as sensory substitution devices for displaying balance information to impaired patients. The vibrotactile feedback reflecting the body stance has shown to be effective in improving the postural stability of subjects with vestibular deficits during stationary tasks and during multi-axis perturbed stance. In the same way, we propose to feedback to the operator balance informations that cannot be perceived by his sensory system in order to generate a postural adjustment leading to a balance recovery. The proposed strategy consists in evaluating the balance state of the robot by monitoring in real time the position of its center of pressure (COP). Indeed the balance of a humanoid robot is maintained as long as its COP lies within the support polygon, i.e. the convex hull defined by all the points of contact between the floor and robot [1]. When the COP enters into the peripheral zone of the support polygon, a cutaneous signal is presented to the operator who is expected to rectify his stance and consequently - by the mean of the tracking system - the robot's posture, leading to a rectification of its COP. In order to generate an appropriate reaction from the operator, the tactile feedback signal has been designed such that the robot's balance state was properly perceived and effectively interpreted.

This paper is organized as follows: Sect. 2 presents the vibrotactile feedback signal design; Sect. 3 analyzes the benefits of the tactile feedback during the humanoid robot teleoperation; Sect. 4 presents the conclusions of this work.

2 Design of the Tactile Feedback

The objective is to provide a directional cutaneous feedback by the mean of a vibrotactile belt to indicate to operators the borders of the robot's stable workspace. In this section we compare three feedback patterns relating the COP position and the displayed vibration signal. They are evaluated considering their capacity to guide operators to the desired behavior.

2.1   Vibrotactile Feedback Belt

The vibrotactile feedback belt consists of four tactors mounted on a velcro strip as shown in Fig. 7. Each tactor, as represented Fig. 8, consists of a protection box which encloses an eccentric mass attached to the shaft of a motor. This belt has been designed to be easily adjusted to each operator's physiognomy thanks to the variable-size strip and the sliding tactors that can be positioned around the waist so as to cover the four cardinal directions. The activation of a tactor indicates which edge of the support polygon the COP is getting close to and thus the direction in which the robot is about to fall. In addition, the distance of the COP from the border of the support polygon, which indicates how critical the slave's balance is, can be transmitted to the operator by modulating the frequency or amplitude of the vibration signal.

2.2   Stimulation Signal Selection

The vibration signal displayed by the tactors is expected to stimulate the Pacinian corpuscle, one of the five types of mechanoreceptors of the human skin. These phasic tactile receptors are optimally stimulated by high frequency vibrations (around 200–400 Hz). Due to the vibration travel through the belt strip, a constant amplitude signal leads to a decreased perception of the spatial localization of the vibration source. Considering these two phenomenon we build the vibration signal as a variable high frequency sine wave carrier shaped by a constant low frequency sine wave signal.

On the basis of a pilot study, we chose to increase both the amplitude and the frequency of the envelope to indicate a rise of the risk corresponding to a decrease of the balance stability margin. We thus elaborated four vibration signals V_1 to V_4 of increasing frequency and amplitude. To evaluate the proper perception of these vibration levels, we conducted a preliminary experiment on 13 subjects. After a short training (less than two minutes) during which subjects got familiar with the signals, a 16-trials test has been performed. Signals of consecutive levels (V_1 to V_2, V_4 to V_3) were presented, and at each transition subjects were instructed to indicate if the new vibration signal was stronger or weaker than the previous one. Subjects were wearing noise canceling headset in order to ensure they couldn't rely on the noise level to identify the vibration signal. With a successful recognition rate of 99.5 %, we validated the vibration signals design for a further use.

2.3   Experimental Study: Evaluation of Three Balancing Feedback Modes

In order to allow operators to accurately recognize the boundaries of the workspace, one option consists in displaying a vibration signal whenever a border is reached. However observations show a delay between the activation of a tactor and the effective reaction since the cutaneous signal has to be sensed and recognized before triggering the motor response. The objective of this work is to

Fig. 1. Feedback type I. Feet of the robot with a colored representation of the vibration levels associated to each zone of the support polygon - yellow: V_1 - orange light: V_2 - orange dark: V_3 - red: V_4 (Color figure online)

Fig. 2. Feedback type II. Feet of the robot with a colored representation of the vibration levels associated to each zone of the support polygon - yellow: V_1 - orange light: V_2 - orange dark: V_3 - red: V_4 (Color figure online)

Fig. 3. Feedback type III. Feet of the robot with a colored representation of the vibration levels associated to each zone of the support polygon - yellow: V_1 - orange light: V_2 - orange dark: V_3 - red: V_4 (Color figure online)

study whether a warning signal could lead to enhanced performances by allowing operators to forecast their reaction. Moreover, we would like to determine if the addition of a distance information within the warning signal leads to better performances. To achieve this objective, we compare three feedback patterns characterized by a different warning signal.

To perform this experiment, we defined a virtual point representing the COP of an inverse pendulum of length 0.5 m with a point mass at its extremity. The spatial orientation of the pendulum is controlled by the torso orientation of the operator, which is measured using a vision-based motion tracking system. This COP evolves within a virtual rectangle oriented such that the operator drives the point towards the front edge of the rectangle by bending forwards and similarly for the other three cardinal directions. The rectangle is divided into three concentric zones corresponding, from the center to the periphery, to the free zone, the warning zone and the alarm zone. When the virtual COP lies in the free zone no vibration is displayed whereas the alarm zone is associated to the strongest vibration signal V_4. The vibrotactile signal associated to the warning zone varies according to the feedback type. Feedback I presents a gradual signal such that when the virtual COP travels from the free zone to the alarm zone the operator experiences successively V_1, V_2 and V_3 as illustrated Fig. 1. Feedback II presents a constant low warning signal using V_1 as illustrated Fig. 2. Feedback III doesn't present any vibration signal within the warning zone, as shown Fig. 3.

The experiment was performed on 13 subjects composed of 11 men and 2 women between 26 and 35 years old. Subjects were instructed to bend the torso forwards until perceiving the alarm signal, which enjoined them to stop bending with a minimum of overtaking and to straighten up the torso back to the vertical position. This operation was repeated in each cardinal direction. To increase the cognitive demand of subjects so as to get close to real teleoperation conditions, they were instructed to read a book without disruption. To ensure that subjects could not rely on aural cues to identify the vibration level, a brown noise [6] was displayed. Samples corresponding to the four directions were recorded 7 times for each feedback type, that have been presented in turn in order homogenize the learning impact among the feedback types, for a total number of 13*7*4=364 trials per feedback type for all subjects.

2.4   Results

The impact of each feedback mode is evaluated considering three parameters. The first one is the distance of the controlled point from the corresponding alarm border. The second one is the number of conservative trials, which are defined as cases where operators stop before experiencing the alarm signal. The third one is the attention level required to recognize the tactile feedback, which was rated on a scale from 1 to 5 by the subjects.

Distance of the Controlled Point from the Border. For each trial we retrieved the minimum distance between the virtual COP and the corresponding border of the alarm zone. The repartition of the average distance among subjects is shown on Fig. 4: Feedback I leads to the lowest average distance (3.66 cm), Feedback II shows intermediate results (3.96 cm) while Feedback III leads to the highest distance (4.10 cm). However a repeated measures ANOVA test revealed that in this experiment the feedback type has no significant effect on the average distance of the controlled point from the border of the alarm zone ($F(2,24)=2.703$, $p=0.0874$).

Number of Conservative Trials. Among the position error previously analyzed, the major part referred to the position overshot of the virtual point with respect to the alarm margin. However a small part corresponds to conservative errors: operators stopped before reaching the alarm border. The number of conservative trials represents 8 % of the trials for Feedback I, 1.4 % of the trials for Feedback II and 0.3 % of the trials for Feedback III. A repeated measures ANOVA test revealed that the feedback type has a significant effect on the number of conservative trials ($F(2,24)=6.610$, $p=0.0052$). A tukey's HSD post hoc analysis indicated that there was a significant difference between the number of conservative trials under Feedback I and II as well as under Feedback I and III but that the difference was not significant between Feedback II and III.

Level of Attention Required. In order to evaluate the cognitive load required to identify the vibrotactile feedback, we asked to subjects to rate each feedback according to the attention dedicated to the feedback on a scale from 1 (low attention) to 5 (high attention). The repartition of the results among subjects is presented Fig. 5. The highest average grade was assigned to Feedback I (4.15), the lowest one to Feedback III (2.62), close to Feedback II (2.85). A repeated measures ANOVA test revealed that in this experiment the feedback type has a significant effect on the required attention ($F(2,24)=5.355$, $p=0.0119$). A Tukey's HSD post hoc analysis indicated that there was a significant difference between the average attention required under Feedback I and II as well as between Feedback I and III but not between Feedback II and III.

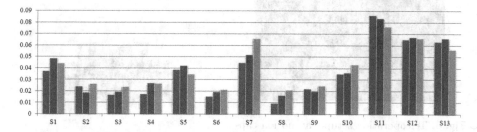

Fig. 4. Average distance of the COP from the alarm border (m). Comparative results for Feedback I (in blue), Feedback II (in red) and Feedback III (in green) (Color figure online)

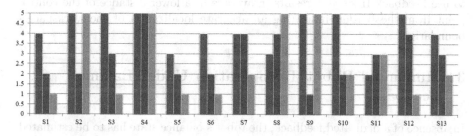

Fig. 5. Level of attention dedicated to the tactile feedback (1:low - 5:high). Comparative results for Feedback I (in blue), Feedback II (in red) and Feedback III (in green) (Color figure online)

The above results suggest that the different feedback patterns lead to equivalent performances regarding the positioning of the COP in the vicinity of a border. However, the significantly higher number of conservative trials under Feedback I suggest that this feedback introduces some confusion. Indeed subjects were explicitly instructed to bend until experiencing the alarm feedback; conservative trials indicate that the warning signal V_3 has been improperly identified as the alarm signal V_4. Such interpretation is correlated by the significantly higher attention dedicated to the tactile feedback recognition under Feedback I. These considerations led us to reject Feedback I. As no significant difference appears

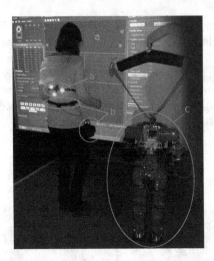

Fig. 7. Vibrotactile belt

Fig. 6. Teleoperation setup - a: motion capture tracker - b: vibrotactile belt and boards - c: humanoid robot COMAN

Fig. 8. Tactor

between Feedback II and III regarding the considered criteria, both of these feedbacks are considered to be eligible for the second experiment. We decided to use Feedback II since it results in average in a lower distance of the control point from the border, indicating an accurate localization of the workspace's boundaries.

3   Humanoid Robot Teleoperation Under Balance Feedback

In absence of a dedicated feedback, the robot's balance state has to be estimated from visual hints. In order to evaluate if the tactile feedback of the slave's balance state can lead to an enhanced quality of the teleoperation, we conducted a comparative study during the teleoperation of the 31-DOFs compliant humanoid robot COMAN.

3.1   Teleoperation Interface

In order to evaluate the benefits of the balance tactile feedback, we developed a simple and intuitive teleoperation interface, see Fig. 6.

A marker attached to the operator's back allows to monitor in real time his torso position and orientation X_{op} thanks to the vision-based motion capture system OptiTrack from NaturalPoint, Inc [5]. Retrieved at low rate (10 Hz) to filter parasite tremors, the raw data is then processed (frame change, scaling, spline interpolation) to generate a smooth trajectory of the desired cartesian

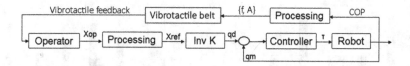

Fig. 9. Teleoperation control scheme

position and orientation of the robot's torso X_{ref}. All desired joints trajectories q_d are then computed through inverse kinematics from this low-dimensional input, see Fig. 9.

This intuitive interface allows to extend the reachable workspace in the vertical direction by bending the legs, as well as in the horizontal plane by adjusting the center of mass (COM) cartesian position and by bending the waist in any direction.

3.2 Experiment

In this experiment, 5 subjects were instructed to drive the robot in limit of stability by teleoperating its COM cartesian position and its torso orientation. Performances were evaluated considering the number of falls and the complete use of the robot's stable workspace under two feedback conditions: visual only and visual+tactile.

3.3 Results

Number of Falls. Five trials per feedback condition were performed by each subject. Each trial consisted in driving the COP in the four cardinal directions until perceiving the vibrotactile alarm signal (first feedback condition) or until estimating the imminence of a fall from visual hints (second feedback condition). The comparison between the percentage of falls with and without tactile feedback for each subject is represented in Fig. 10. A two-tail paired t-test revealed that the average percentage of falls is significantly lower under tactile+visual feedback than under visual feedback only (t(4)=3.207, p=0.0327).

Workspace Exploration. The use of the workspace was then analyzed considering only the trials during which the robot didn't fall. As two subjects made the robot fall 2 times out of 5, we randomly selected 3 trials for each feedback condition and for each subject so as to consider an equal number of samples in each case. We then computed the average minimum distance between the COP and the margin of the support polygon considering the front and back directions, which are predominantly used in order to increase the reachable workspace. Results are presented in Fig. 11. A two-tail paired t-test allowed to reject the null hypothesis of equal means (t(4)=2.835, p=0.047). The average error is thus

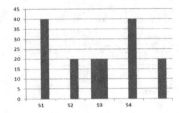

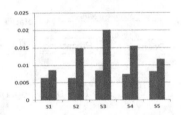

Fig. 10. Percentage of falls. Comparative results with tactile feedback (in blue) and without tactile feedback (in red) (Color figure online)

Fig. 11. Distance COP polygon border (m). Comparative results with tactile feedback (in blue) and without tactile feedback (in red) (Color figure online)

significantly lower under vibrotactile+visual feedback than under visual feedback only, which indicates that the use of the vibrotactile feedback leads to a less conservative teleoperation with a complete use of the COP workspace.

The above results show that the teleoperation under tactile feedback is characterized by a lower number of falls as well as a lower distance between the COP and the border of the support polygon. It is thus clear that the balance feedback leads towards a safer and less conservative teleoperation of the humanoid system.

4   Conclusion

Teleoperation constitutes a powerful tool to compensate for robots lack of decision-making skills required to operate in dynamical and uncertain environments. However teleoperating a humanoid robot can result very complex and demanding since the balance of the slave has to be maintained while performing the task. In order to assist the operator, we propose to provide a feedback of the robot's balance state by the mean of a vibrotactile belt. Based on the distance of the COP from the support polygon boundaries, a directional signal warns the operator when the stability margin of the robot drops. The operator is expected to modify his stance so as to reestablish the balance of the slave.

In a first study we compared three tactile feedback patterns relating the COP position to the displayed vibration signal. The evaluation focused on the capacity of operators to accurately locate the borders of a virtual workspace depicted by the cutaneous signal. The best suited feedback type has been selected and used during a second experiment that aimed at evaluating the benefits of the balance feedback during the teleoperation of the humanoid robot. Results show that the previously selected feedback pattern allows for a clear understanding of the slave's balance state and leads to enhanced teleoperation performances. Finally, feeding back the balance state of a humanoid robot by the mean of a vibrotactile belt leads towards a safer and less conservative teleoperation.

Acknowledgment. This work is supported by the EC project n 601165 WEARHAP - WEARable HAPtics for humans and robots.

References

1. Park, J., Haan, J., Park, F.C.: Convex optimization algorithms for active balancing of humanoid robots. IEEE Trans. Robot. **23**, 817–822 (2007)
2. Hasunuma, H., Harada, K., Hirukawa, H.: The tele-operation of the humanoid robot - whole body operation for humanoid robots in contact with environment. In: Proceedings, Humanoids (2006)
3. Sienko, K.H., Balkwill, M.D., Oddsson, L.I.E., Wall, C.: Effects of multi-directional vibrotactile feedback on vestibular-deficient postural performance during continuous multi-directional support surface perturbations. J. Vestib. Res. **18**, 273–285 (2008)
4. Sienko, K.H., Vichare, V.V., Balkwill, M.D., Wall, C.: Assessment of vibrotactile feedback on postural stability during pseudorandom multidirectional platform motion. IEEE Trans. Biomed. Eng. **57**, 944–952 (2010)
5. http://www.naturalpoint.com/optitrack/
6. http://www.simplynoise.com/

Comparison of Multimodal Notifications During Telesurgery

Rachael L'Orsa[1]([✉]), Kourosh Zareinia[2], Chris Macnab[1],
and Garnette Roy Sutherland[2]

[1] Department of Electrical and Computer Engineering, University of Calgary,
Calgary, Canada
{ralorsa,cmacnab}@ucalgary.ca
[2] Project neuroArm, Faculty of Medicine, University of Calgary, Calgary, Canada
{kzareini,garnette}@ucalgary.ca

Abstract. This paper examines the utility of multimodal feedback during telesurgery to notify surgeons of excessive force application. Average puncture forces were characterized for varied thicknesses of an artificial membrane, and human operators then attempted to apply a maximum force to the membranes without causing a puncture via an experimental telesurgical apparatus. Operators were notified via different sensory modalities when the force exerted by the tool-tip exceeded a pre-established force margin, defined as a set percentage of the average puncture force. Various combinations of auditory and vibrotactile notifications both with and without force feedback were compared in order to investigate the relationship between feedback modality, force margin, and puncture force. Factor screening results identify multiple two-factor interactions as having statistically significant effects on both the maximum applied force and task completion time, warranting further investigation. Notifications of any type decreased both response variables for operators who relied on them.

Keywords: Haptics · Multimodal feedback · Keyhole surgery · Teleoperation · Telesurgery

1 Introduction

Minimally invasive surgery (MIS) provides patients with improved outcomes compared to open surgery [1]. Robot-assisted minimally invasive surgery (RMIS) improves on the benefits of MIS by providing surgeons with augmented dexterity [2], flatter learning curves [3], the ability to scale inputs (force, position, and/or velocity), and superior integration with pre- and intra-operative tools such as path-planning software and imaging techniques [4]. The primary criticism for RMIS is that it may decouple surgeons from their sense of touch, which they routinely rely on to assess tissue condition and/or properties during procedures [5]. Many groups hypothesize that robotic telesurgery with force feedback will address this concern by restoring the sense of touch [6], which could ease surgeon

© Springer-Verlag Berlin Heidelberg 2014
M. Auvray and C. Duriez (Eds.): EuroHaptics 2014, Part II, LNCS 8619, pp. 276–284, 2014.
DOI: 10.1007/978-3-662-44196-1_34

workload and limit complications. However, there is very little conclusive data in the literature to support or refute this belief. While the inclusion of force feedback provides supplemental information regarding the interaction between patient and tool-tip, it does not necessarily provide an accurate gauge as to the amount of force applied to patient structures. Previously, we investigated the relationship between force feedback and applied force during a simple tool interaction task. We further incorporated a novel system of notifications during telesurgery, and found that operators were better able to avoid unintentional tissue punctures via a telesurgical apparatus both with notifications and force feedback. However, the use of force feedback significantly increased task completion times [7]. This paper expands on these results; the goal of this work is to perform an initial factor screening to determine what affects maximum force application and task completion time for telesurgery. It is hypothesized that by isolating these key factors we will enable a quantification of operator force application awareness during teleoperated tasks.

During surgery, it is important to restrict the application of forces to safe levels, particularly with respect to non-target structures. Existing real-time controls that do so during RMIS are mostly limited to virtual fixtures and system-wide force/position/velocity clipping. In a microneurosurgical context, the former is inadequate for procedures that cannot physically isolate target anatomy from delicate structures such as cranial nerves. Notifications may solve this issue by allowing operators to interact with delicate structures while improving their awareness of safe force application levels.

The use of notifications to alert operators of impending negative events during focus-intensive tasks is not new. Several groups have explored the utility of single-channel and multimodal notifications – primarily auditory and vibrotactile – to warn drivers of imminent collisions [8]. Another study used a combination of force feedback, visual feedback, and auditory warnings to help construction robot teleoperators improve performance with regards to grasping force [9], which is particularly important for telesurgical tasks such as suturing. There is no consensus as to which notification modality is preferred during these tasks, nor whether single-channel or multimodal notifications produce superior operator performance. Furthermore, it is unclear whether or not results gathered from vehicle or machinery operation tasks could be generalized to the operation of a telesurgical robot by a highly specialized professional. For this reason, we analyze the effects of factors such as notification modality, force margin, force level, and force feedback on the force applied via a telesurgical apparatus.

2 Experimental Design

Experiments utilize a custom prototype 7 degree of freedom (DOF) telesurgical system whose movement is restricted solely to the Z-axis to penetrate layers of translucent plastic fitted to a custom mount. The synthetic membranes are not comparable to real tissue, but rather allow for repeatable tool-tip interactions due to their nearly-static contact geometry. An average puncture force $F_{p.ave}$

for each thickness of synthetic membrane is established prior to trials, which is then used in conjunction with varied force margins for activation of notifications during teleoperation.

2.1 Apparatus

A SensAble Phantom Desktop 6 DOF haptic interface is used as the master, controlling a Kuka KR-6 slave robot for all experiments. A custom tool coupled with an ATI Gamma 6 DOF force/torque sensor attaches to the robot's end-effector. The custom tool-tip is machined to a dull point from a 28 mm length of solid 4.5 mm diameter cylindrical aluminium that allows for repeatable interactions with the synthetic membrane due to its symmetrical tip profile. The Desktop reproduces forces from the Gamma scaled by a factor of 0.2 when its amplifiers are activated.

An HP Compaq 6200 Pro with a 3.4 GHz Intel Core i7 processor running 64-bit Windows 7 Professional SP1 with 4 GB of RAM processes information for the master system, connecting the Desktop, an external speaker, and a 10 mm × 3.4 mm Polulu Shaftless Vibration Motor controlled via a Quanser Q2-USB data acquisition board (DAQ). The slave system uses a custom PC with a 3.3 GHz Intel CORE i5 processor running 32-bit Windows 7 Professional SP1 with 4 GB of RAM. The slave PC connects to the Kuka workstation and another Quanser Q2-USB DAQ, which interfaces with the force sensor and its accompanying hardware (a National Instruments DAQ and signal conditioning box provided by ATI). Matlab/Simulink R2011a with Quanser QUARC 2.2 blocks provides a real-time interface between hardware and the master and slave PCs respectively. Master and slave PCs communicate over a LAN via the TCP/IP protocol.

Also, a Leica M525 OH4 surgical microscope coupled with two Ikegami HDL 20D microscope camera systems, a Sony LMD2451MD LCD monitor, and RealD 3D glasses provides a magnified real-time 3D video feed of the tool-tip's interaction with the synthetic membrane. Figure 1 shows an overview of the experimental apparatus.

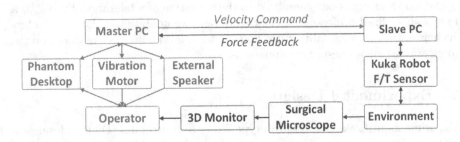

Fig. 1. System diagram

2.2 Design of Experiment

A simple 1DOF tool-tip interaction task is used for this experiment: participants (operators) are asked to apply a slow, steady, downwards force to a synthetic membrane via the telesurgical apparatus until they feel they've reached a maximum, then retract the tool to the starting position. Operators are informed that a puncture of the membrane is classified as a failed trial, whereupon the puncture conditions are stored and the trial is repeated. Experimenters instruct operators to observe the real-time 3D video feed from the surgical microscope closely for visual deformation cues to help gauge applied force. Operator performance is quantified based on the maximum force applied during each trial (F_{max}) and the task completion time (t_c), as bounded by the last zero crossing of force data before F_{max} and the first zero crossing after F_{max} (i.e. the task completion time is the period during which the tool-tip contacts the membrane). The task is performed with both single and double layers of the synthetic membrane ($f_{Level.1}$ and $f_{Level.2}$ respectively), both with and without force feedback (FF), and with a variety of notification modalities: auditory (audio, a), vibrotactile (haptic, h), auditory and vibrotactile (ah), or none at all (visual, v). When notifications are employed, they are triggered when an operator applies a force in excess of a predetermined force margin, defined as either 30 % or 70 % of the average puncture force $F_{p.ave}$ ($f_{Margin.1}$ and $f_{Margin.2}$ respectively).

Thus the notification feedback modality (audio, haptic), the inclusion of force feedback, the percentage of average puncture force at which notifications are applied (force margin), and the amount of average puncture force required (force level) are screened as primary factors affecting two response variables, F_{max} and t_c. These five factors were input into Minitab using a 2_V^{5-1} design with five replicates to produce the randomized trials for the experiment, which were then exported to Matlab via Excel and used to set experiment variables in Simulink for each individual trial. Table 1 summarizes the five main factors and the low/high levels defined for each.

2.3 Initialization, Calibration, and Training

The entire system undergoes a full initialization and recalibration process between operators to ensure the consistency of results. First, the slave robot initializes to

Table 1. Main factors and associated levels

Factor	Symbol	Low level	High level
Audio notification	a	off	on
Haptic notification	h	off	on
Force feedback	FF	off	on
Force margin	$f_{Margin-1,2}$	0.3	0.7
Force level	$f_{Level-1,2}$	1 layer	2 layers

the same pre-set home position. Second, an artificial membrane is fitted to a custom mount centred below the slave's tool-tip and clamped in position such that it is perpendicular to the tool-tip's linearly-restricted axis of motion. Third, the force sensor data at a negligible tool-tip velocity is zeroed to account for any bias. The tool-tip advances in the negative direction along the Z-axis until a maximum force is achieved or the membrane is punctured, and then the process is repeated for the next trial.

From 10–30 calibration trials are run by experimenters between each operator until $F_{p.ave}$ can be determined with a variance less than or equal to 0.1 N for $f_{Level.1}$ or 1 N for $f_{Level.2}$. Simulink multiplies this $F_{p.ave}$ for each operator by the force margin for each trial to set the threshold at which notifications are generated. When audio notifications are activated, the speaker emits a 60 dB, 0.05 sec 'beep' repeated at a frequency of 5 Hz. The vibrating motor, attached to the inside of the operator's non-dominant wrist, reproduces the same signal at an amplitude of 0.75 g when activated. The physical locations of both notification sources remain constant throughout all experiments.

Each operator performs two sets of four training trials prior to beginning the experiment: one with no notifications, one with an audio notification, one with a haptic notification, one with both audio and haptic notifications, and then all four repeated with force feedback. Given the 2_V^{5-1} experiment design with five puncture-free replicates per individual combination of factors, each operator performs 80 successful trials in random order and response variables are stored for both successful and unsuccessful trials. Experimenters inform operators which feedback modalities to expect prior to the commencement of each trial. Nine operators with varied levels of teleoperation experience in neuroArm's [4] Surgical Performance Laboratory perform the full experiment.

3 Results

The overall average puncture force from across all ten calibration trials was 11.4 N for $f_{Level.1}$ and 21.8 N for $f_{Level.2}$. Thus for a trial using a 30 % force margin with a single layer of the synthetic membrane, notifications are triggered when an operator applies 3.4 N to the membrane via the slave. As the average puncture force $F_{p.ave}$ varies between operators, the F_{max} for each trial is transformed into a percentage of the given operator's average puncture force, $F_{max.n}$, to allow for inter-operator comparisons:

$$F_{max.n} = \frac{F_{max}}{F_{p.ave}} \tag{1}$$

As task completion times also vary widely between operators, a normalized task completion time t_n is similarly calculated using the maximum task completion time across all trials for a given operator. The factor combinations, original response variables, and transformed response variables for all ten operators are imported back into Minitab for statistical analysis using a General Linear Model

Table 2. Analysis of variance results

Source	Norm. max applied force			Norm. task completion time		
	DF	F	P	DF	F	P
FF	1	24.79	0.000	1	72.91	< 0.001
fMargin	1	1020.71	0.000	1	206.72	< 0.001
Operator	9	67.65	0.000	9	209.59	< 0.001
fLevel	–	–	–	1	6.89	< 0.001
a*fMargin	1	153.92	0.000	1	13.75	< 0.001
h*fMargin	1	145.57	0.000	1	44.98	< 0.001
FF*fLevel	1	206.79	0.000	–	–	–
FF*Operator	9	2.54	0.010	9	7.79	< 0.001
a*h	–	–	–	1	6.16	< 0.001
a*Operator	–	–	–	9	4.17	< 0.001
fMargin* Operator	–	–	–	9	9.26	< 0.001

ANOVA that accounts for all main factor effects and two-factor interactions with $\alpha = 0.05$. It is assumed that higher order interactions are negligible.

Relevant results from Minitab are reproduced in Table 2, where DF is the number of degrees of freedom, F is the F-distribution value, and P is the P-value. Here we see that force feedback, force margin, and operator are all factors that produce statistically significant effects on the normalized maximum applied force. It is difficult to ascertain exactly what their effects are, however, given that all three are also subject to interaction effects. It seems intuitive that the force margin would impact the applied force, as a heightened awareness of any boundary could logically alter an operator's behaviour. That individual operators might apply different force magnitudes is also unsurprising, but will require follow-up experiments with a much larger number of participants in order to confirm. Similarly, the existence of effects from the way an operator handles force feedback or from the interplay between force feedback and the amount of puncture force required are interesting to note, but will require further investigation to clarify.

Table 2 illustrates an even more complex array of factor interactions that produce statistically significant effects on the normalized task completion time. The force level is the only factor providing a main effect without interactions. If an operator is applying force slowly and smoothly, it seems logical that it would take more time to apply more force. Again it is unsurprising that different operators react differently to audio notifications, force feedback, and the force margin, though operator effects will likely diminish with a larger number of participants. It also seems intuitive that there is an interplay between notification modality and force margin, as one might expect an increased awareness of notifications to be accompanied by a heightened sensitivity to notification modality. What is somewhat unexpected given that most participants reported no perceived difference between responses at different notification modalities, is that there is a statistically significant interaction between audio and haptic notification modalities. It would be appropriate to perform follow-up experiments in a surgical setting where participants are constantly bombarded by an overload of sensory information in order to confirm this interaction.

As the experiment progressed, a noticeable reliance on either notifications or visual feedback emerged, as measured by the proximity of F_{max} to either the force threshold at which a notification occurred or the average puncture force. This is quantified using two new variables, R_N for a normalized numerical representation of an operator's reliance on notifications and R_V for the visual equivalent. Note that in Eqs. 2 and 3, f_M is the force margin and $F_{p.ave}$ is specific to the number of synthetic membranes for the given trial:

$$R_N = \frac{|F_{p.ave} \cdot f_M - F_{max}|}{F_{p.ave} \cdot f_M} \tag{2}$$

$$R_V = \frac{|F_{p.ave} - F_{max}|}{F_{p.ave}} \tag{3}$$

By calculating individual values of R_N and R_V for each operator's 80 trials, we can determine a percentage representation of how much an operator relies on notifications or visual feedback overall. Table 3 shows this overall reliance per operator along with the total number of punctures they produced, listed according to the type of notification (visual - no notification, audio, haptic, audio and haptic) and feedback (no force feedback, force feedback) received. It is immediately apparent that operators 6, 7, and 8, who relied heavily on visual cues to judge force application, produced substantially more punctures than their notification-reliant counterparts.

Table 3. Overall operator reliance and puncture results

| Operator | Overall [%] | | Number of punctures | | | | | | |
	R_N	R_V	v	a	h	ah	No FF	FF	Total
1	90	10	1	0	0	0	0	1	1
2	76	24	5	2	0	0	5	2	7
3	86	14	1	1	0	1	3	0	3
4	73	27	0	0	2	0	2	0	2
5	71	29	2	0	1	0	3	0	3
6	18	82	7	3	3	1	7	7	14
7	21	79	4	6	7	6	13	10	23
8	18	82	0	2	2	3	6	1	7
9	75	25	1	2	1	1	0	5	5

Table 4. Average task completion time and puncture results based on operator reliance

Group	Ave. time	Average number of punctures						
		v	a	h	ah	No FF	FF	Total
N	6.0 sec	2	1	1	0.3	2.2	1	3.5
V	9.1 sec	4	4	4	3.3	8.7	6	14.7

This phenomenon is even more apparent in Table 4, which averages raw task completion times and column-wise puncture results within each of the two groups: notification-reliant operators (N) and visual feedback-reliant operators (V). Though larger sample sizes are required, these preliminary results imply that a reliance on visual feedback alone increases both an operator's task completion time and the number of times they apply excessive force, regardless of notification modality or force feedback inclusion.

4 Conclusion

Factor screening identifies multiple significant interaction effects. Preliminary results show that operators who rely on visual feedback more than on notifications apply higher forces more often on average during simple teleoperated tasks and take longer to complete them. This must be confirmed in a larger pool of participants, but may imply that properly optimized notifications could help surgeons consistently decrease both their task completion times and the frequency with which they apply excessive forces via RMIS. Future extensions of this work should focus on continued factor characterization, factor optimization, and the confirmation of results using natural tissues instead of synthetic membranes.

Acknowledgments. The authors wish to thank Kiran Grant for his assistance with this work.

References

1. Reisch, R., Stadie, A., Kockro, R.A., Hopf, N.: The keyhole concept in neurosurgery. World Neurosurgery. (2012). http://www.sciencedirect.com/science/article/pii/S187887501200157X
2. Ballantyne, G.: Telerobotic gastrointestinal surgery: phase 2 – safety and efficacy. Surg. End. **21**(7), 1054–1062 (2007)
3. Ahlering, T.E., Skarecky, D., Lee, D., Clayman, R.V.: Successful transfer of open surgical skills to a laparoscopic environment using a robotic interface: initial experience with laparoscopic radical prostatectomy. J. Urology. **170**(5), 1738–1741 (2003)
4. Lang, M.J., Greer, A.D., Sutherland, G.R.: Intra-operative robotics: NeuroArm. In: Necmettin Pamir, M., Seifert, V., Kiris, T. (eds.) Intraoperative Imaging Acta Neurochirurgica Supplementum, pp. 231–236. Springer, New York (2011)

5. Cuss, A., Abbott, J.: Complications of laparoscopic surgery. Obstet. Gynaecol. Reprod. Med. **22**(3), 59–62 (2012)
6. Okamura, A.M.: Haptic feedback in robot-assisted minimally invasive surgery. Curr. Opin. Urol. **19**(1), 102–107 (2009)
7. L'Orsa, R., Zareinia, K., Gan, L.S., Macnab, C., Sutherland, G.: Potential tissue puncture notification during telesurgery. In: Oakley, I., Brewster, S. (eds.) HAID 2013. LNCS, vol. 7989, pp. 30–39. Springer, Heidelberg (2013)
8. Spence, C., Ho, C.: Multisensory warning signals for event perception and safe driving. Theor. Issues Ergon. Sci. **9**(9), 523–554 (2008)
9. Yusof, A.A., Kawamura, T., Yamada, H.: Evaluation of construction robot telegrasping force perception using visual, auditory and force feedback integration. J. Rob. Mecha. **24**(6), 949–957 (2012)

A Multi-DOF Haptic Representation Using Suction Pressure Stimuli on Finger Pads

Daiki Maemori[✉], Lope Ben Porquis, Masashi Konyo, and Satoshi Tadokoro

Graduate School of Information Science, Tohoku University,
6-6-01 Aramaki Aza Aoba, Aoba-ku, Sendai, Miyagi, Japan
{maemori,lopeben,konyo,tadokoro}@rm.is.tohoku.ac.jp
http://www.rm.is.tohoku.ac.jp

Abstract. Humans can perceive external forces applied on a grasping tool based on skin pressure distribution at multiple contact areas during grasp. The authors have tried to represent external forces and torques by controlling the skin pressure distributions using suction stimuli and confirmed the potential but in a heuristic manner. In this paper, we investigate an improved method of skin stimulation based on a combination of psychophysical experiments and mechanical simulation. We focus on a simplification method of the complex strain energy density (SED) distribution at the contact areas with four quadrant values (SED index). The relationship between suction pressure and SED index was achieved by connecting the experiment and the mechanical simulation. We confirmed that a suitable SED index could represent the magnitudes of forces in multiple directions with a linear function. Experimental results also showed that the proposed method could represent arbitrary directions between pairs of the orthogonal axes.

Keywords: Haptic interfaces · Force illusion · Suction pressure · Skin deformation · Tool manipulation

1 Introduction

Humans can perceive external forces applied on a grasping tool even in indirect touch. We may feel that whatever action we did on the tool appears to be felt direct by our fingertips. This transparency of haptic information from indirect contact is an interesting topic for research. A possible cue of such capability is skin pressure distributions at multiple contact areas during grasp. For example, cutaneous sense has contributions to force perception [1,2]. However, the force extracting procedure from multiple contact points is still unclear.

The authors have tried to represent external forces and torques by controlling the skin pressure distributions using suction pressure stimuli at multiple contact points [3–5]. A special suction pressure vacuuming skin with a small hole can induce the similar activity of mechanoreceptors with an ordinary positive pressure stimulus [8]. Such stimulation method is useful for creating new interfaces

© Springer-Verlag Berlin Heidelberg 2014
M. Auvray and C. Duriez (Eds.): EuroHaptics 2014, Part II, LNCS 8619, pp. 285–294, 2014.
DOI: 10.1007/978-3-662-44196-1_35

because suction pressure makes skin contact stable with a simple hardware. The authors also demonstrated that suction pressure could represent virtual stiffness by enhancing force perception in response to the output from a force sensor as an augmented reality technology called TAKO-Pen [6]. However, the conventional control method of the suction pressure was based on heuristics, and the quality of the induced force was limited. In addition, we could not represent the force direction between pairs of the orthogonal axes.

The purpose of this paper is to investigate an improved method of skin stimulation by suction pressure for representing multi-DOF forces. We optimize the method by combining psychophysical experiments and mechanical simulation of skin deformations. Especially, we focus on a simplification method to represent the complex strain energy density (SED) distribution, which is associated with the activity of the mechanoreceptors, at the contact areas with a four quadrant values (SED index). The relationship between suction pressure and the SED index is achieved by connecting the experiment and the mechanical simulation. By finding a proper index, we will be able to control the on-target amount of perceived force and directions. In the experiments, we confirm the linearity between the applied force and the perceived force and capability of force direction between the orthogonal axes.

2   Overview of Suction Pressure Interface

Our previously developed suction pressure interface called the TAKO–Pen is shown in Fig. 1 [6]. The suction holes are arbitrarily arranged but these are grouped into four sections. Hole sizes ranged from 1.5 mm to 2 mm diameter, as recommended by [8]. The hole spacing is based from the two–point discrimination threshold at the fingertips. The pad area of the thumb is made larger than the index finger to maintain the natural occurrence of contact area of these two digits. The air pressure on each section of the contact pad can be controlled independently, a total of eight individually controllable pressure chambers allows a combination of pressure distribution to evoke a sense of force and torque up to six DoF. Vacuum pressure is generated from a piston pump actuated by servo motors.

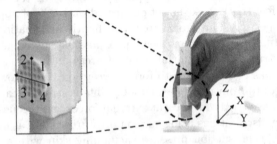

Fig. 1. Suction pressure interface: Tako-Pen

We assigned a reference coordinate system originating at the middle of the pinch grasp. The X–axis represents the tangential axis along the contact plane pinched by two fingers, the Y–axis represents the normal axis to the contact plane, and the Z–axis represents the long axis of the pen. Force and torque illusions can be expressed by a combination of pressurized sections. For example, pressurizing the Sects. 1 and 2 with the same amount represents upward force in the X–axis, or pressuring the Sects. 2 and 3 represent forwarding force in the X–axis. To express a pronation torque, for example, pressures are applied on the Sects. 1 and 2 on the thumb and the Sects. 3 and 4 on the index finger, which are symmetrical in the torque axis [4].

We had conducted initial psychophysical experiments to explore the relationships between the perceived forces and the suction pressure stimuli [5]. The results showed that the perceived force in Y–axis had a linear relationship, while those in X and Z–axes had non–linear trends. In this paper, we investigate the force representing method that can control the perceived force linearly not only in the X and Z–axes but also in the arbitral diagonal direction between the orthogonal axes.

3   Proposal of Four Quadrant Representing Method

3.1   Procedure

For investing the new force representing method, we associate the strain energy density (SED) distributions during pen grasp with the exerted force. The SED is known as an index associated with the activity of the SA I type receptors [7], which are obtained by the mechanical simulation of the finger deformation using the finite element analysis (FEA). It is also reported that suction pressure stimuli on the skin can produce the similar SED distributions when the skin is pushed [8]. However, the number of the pressure chambers is so limited that it is difficult to reproduce the actual SED distribution. Therefore, we propose a new simplified index (SED index) that represents the trend of the SED distribution under each section of the pressure chambers.

For associating with the perceived force, we use the psychophysical results in the Y–axis, which was conducted in the previous study [5]. Note, we cannot use the previous data in the X and Z–axes because the previous experiments just exerted pressures at the higher-pressure sides and the lower pressures in the whole contact area were not considered.

A flow diagram to achieve the formula that controls the suction pressures (P) to produce perceived forces (pF) linearly in the X and Z–axes is shown in Fig. 2. The first goal is to achieve the strategy to control the SED index by the suction pressure. The relationship between the suction pressure and the SED index is derived by associating the psychophysical data and the SED result in the Y–axis, where both psychophysical and FEA data had linear relationships against forces, if we assume that the exerted force to the force sensor by the subject in the psychophysical experiment [5] is equivalent to the applied force to

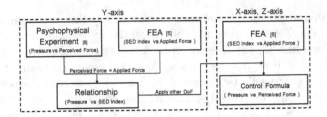

Fig. 2. Calculation flow of the suction pressure distribution based on SED index.

the pen simulated in the FEA. The second step is applying the relationship in the Y-axis achieved in the first step to the results of FEA in the X and Z–axes.

3.2 Recalibrating the Psychophysical Data

Referring to the psychophysical data of pF in the Y–axis [5], we can observe that there is an amount of pF at zero pressure stimuli. This is not an offset caused by perceived force, it is due to the subjects' initial grasp on the interface. If we remove this offset, the diagonal line intersects the x–axis at about 3 kPa. This value coincides with the minimum perception threshold of vacuum pressure that we obtained from an experiment using the method of limits. As a result, the relationship between P and pF is expressed as $pF = 0.044 \times P_{1,2,3,4} - 0.13$. The subscripts of P indicates the four independently controllable pressure section of each contact pad.

3.3 Investigation of SED Index from Finite Element Analysis

We simulated the distributions of SED inside the finger model when external forces in the X, Y, and Z–axes were applied to the pen (a rigid cylinder) contacting with the finger model using the FEA reported in [5]. In this paper, we simplified the SED distribution by dividing it into four sections, which corresponds to the four quadrants of the contact plane between the finger pad and the pen. Two contact pads for with four quadrants each gives us eight independent controllable pressure sections. This is the minimum number of quadrants needed to reproduce six DoF force and torque in the pinch grip configuration [5].

The simplified index (SED index) of each quadrant is defined as Four Quadrant Represent Values (4QRV). We assumed that a simple possible index representing SED distribution could be the average or the maximum of SED on each section. From the preliminary experiments, however, we found that these indexes were not suitable because the maximum was too strong and the average was too weak for producing forces. Thus, we need some intermediate.

In this paper, we define a new index as 4QVR to take an average for every quadrant after extracting with a certain offset value from the SED distribution. A problem is how to determine the appropriate offset value. After several preliminary investigations, we choose three possible offset values (A:0.0015, B:0.0020,

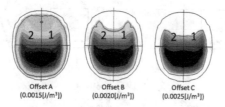

Fig. 3. Examples of the SED distribution extracted by each offset ($Fz = 0.6$ N).

C:0.0025 [J/m^3]). Figure 3 shows the examples of the extracted SED on each offset when the external force of 0.6 N is applied in the Z–axis. In the case of Offset B (0.0020 J/m^3), the formula of 4QRV and applied Force in FEA (aF) is shown $4QRV = 7.32 \times 10^{-5} \times aF + 2.43 \times 10^{-3}$. This intercept of the formula (2.43×10^{-3}) means 4QRV stored by giving grasp force (2 N in Y–axis).

3.4   Transformation to Suction Pressure from 4QRV

In this section, we show formulas for P and pF (in X and Z–axes) using the relationship between 4QRV and P (for Y–axis). These formulas are based on the offset value 0.0020 J/m^3. During transformation, we looked at two different viewpoints about Fy. One is the relationship of P and pF from psychophysical experiment, and the other is the relationship of 4QRV and aF from FEA. From the above relations, if assumed that applied force (aF) is equivalent to perceived force (pF), we can derive the relation between 4QRV and P for Y–axis. This is expressed as $4QRV = 3.35 \times 10^{-5} \times P + 2.33 \times 10^{-3}$. For X and Z–axes, the transformation is similar by using 4QRV–aF relationship from FEA. Thus, we can obtain a relation of suction pressure (P) and force (pF) by substituting the 4QRV of Fx and Fz to the above expression. But since x and z axes have nonlinear tendencies, we need to adapt a nonlinear function. In this case, we try to use a exponential function because the tendency of human perception is known to increase exponentially. Thus, we obtained a relationship between P and pF by substituting the 4QRV regarding to the X and Z–axes for as shown in Fig. 4.

3.5   Evaluation for Adequate Offset Value

In previous section, we derived the relation of P and pF for Fx and Fz–axes using an offset value 0.0020 [J/m^3]. Then we repeated deriving the same relation using two more offset values (0.0015, 0.0025 [J/m3]), for the purpose of exploring the most suitable offset. These new relationships were then evaluated using the method of adjustment. In the adjustment experiment, P was presented first, the subject responds by exerting force that was perceived equivalent in magnitude with SP. A force sensor measures the exerted force and the data was logged. Seven male students participated. They are all right-handed and have mean age of 20. Five discrete levels of calculated aF values, (1.1 N to 1.9 N for Fx and 0.7 N

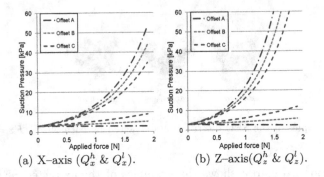

(a) X–axis $(Q_x^h \& Q_x^l)$.   (b) Z–axis$(Q_z^h \& Q_z^l)$.

Fig. 4. The relationships between applied forces and required suction pressure. The curve $(Q_x^h \& Q_z^h)$ having strong trend on each condition are applied for two high SED sections, which are quadrant 3 & 4 in Fig. 3. The weak curve $(Q_x^l \& Q_z^l)$ are applied for two low SED sections, which are quadrants 1 and 2 in Fig. 3.

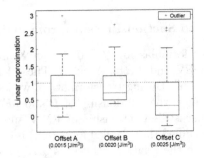

Fig. 5. Linear approximation of the relation between the applied force and the perceived force on each offset condition.

to 1.5 N for Fz) were seeded to the 4QRV rendering function to produce P along X and Z–axes. There are three types of 4QRV functions, each differ with offset adjustments (0.0015, 0.0020, 0.0025 [J/m3]). The stimuli were presented three times for each condition. We carry out linear approximation of the relations of P and pF, these are shown in Fig. 5. We consider the slope with Offset = 0.0020 is a good choice, because its value is near to 1.0 shown in Fig. 5. The relation of aF and pF at the Offset = 0.0020 is shown in Fig. 6.

4   Representation of Forces Between Orthogonal Axes

In the previous section, we derived a relation between P and pF based from the SED index (4QRV) for the translational forces along the X, Y, and Z–axes. In this section, we propose an extension method for repressing forces in the arbitral diagonal direction between the orthogonal axes based on the 4QRV.

We assume that 4QRV can represent diagonal forces if the 4QRV simulated in the FEA for the diagonal force is provided. However, it is not practical to

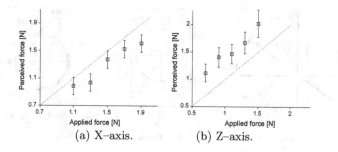

(a) X–axis.   (b) Z–axis.

Fig. 6. The relation of the applied force and the perceived force for Offset B (0.0020).

prepare many 4QRV for arbitral directions in advance. In this paper, we propose an approximate calculation method for 4QRV in the arbitral directions based on the equations of 4QRV determined for the translation forces along the X, Y, and Z–axes. We assume that the 4QRV for any applied forces can be expressed with a superposition of three 4QRV components in the X, Y, and Z–axes, which are calculated independently with the force components decomposed into the three axes. In a preliminary investigation, we confirmed that the approximated 4QRV accords with the actual 4QRV simulated in the FEA quantitatively. This result suggests that the superposition of the suction pressures calculated from 4QRV along the X, Y, and Z–axes independently will represent the arbitral force in the diagonal directions.

4.1   Derivation of Force Rendering Method Between Orthogonal Axes

Given a force vector f applied between three orthogonal axes, the force vector was decomposed into the three force components f_x, f_y, and f_z. Next, the decomposed force components are substituted with the pressure rendering formula derived in Sect. 3 to produce the suction pressure components (P_{x_i}, P_{y_i}, and P_{z_i}). Finally, the required pressures for the eight quadrant sections (for the two contact pads) are calculated as the summation P_i expressed in Eq. (1), where the index i indicates the number of the eight quadrant sections. P_{offset} is the adjustment pressure to let the offset pressure not exceed the detection threshold ($P_{\text{offset}} = 6$ kPa).

Pressures $P_{x_i}(f_x)$ for the eight quadrants corresponding to the force component f_x in the X–axis is delivered with Eq. (2). As shown in Fig. 4, there are two curves for representing the high (Q^h) and low (Q^l) pressures, which depend on the position of the quadrant section and the direction of the force. Selection of Q^h and Q^l is determined with the sign matrix H. Equation (4) shows the sign matrix for the X–axis. $P_{y_i}(f_y)$ and $P_{z_i}(f_z)$ are also delivered in the same manner.

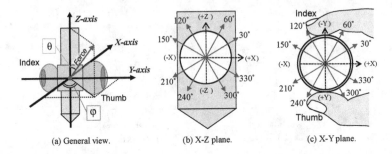

(a) General view.   (b) X-Z plane.   (c) X-Y plane.

Fig. 7. Experimental condition of representing Multi-DoF forces

$$P_i = P_{x_i} + P_{y_i} + P_{z_i} - P_{\text{offset}} \tag{1}$$

$$P_{x_i}(f_x) = \begin{cases} Q_x^h(f_x) & S_x(i) > 0 \\ Q_x^l(f_x) & S_x(i) < 0 \end{cases} \tag{2}$$

$$S_x(i) = \text{sign}(H(i)) , \text{ where } i = 1, 2, \cdots, 8 \tag{3}$$

$$H_x^{\mathrm{T}} = (+, -, -, +, +, -, -, +) \tag{4}$$

4.2   Psychophysical Evaluation of the Method

This section describes how the multi-degree-of-freedom force representing method was evaluated. First, P was presented to the participant. Then the participant was instructed to answer his/her closest estimate to one of the predefined force directions displayed on a chart. Next, the participant answers one of the directions in 30, 60, 120, 150, 210, 240, 300, 330 [deg] which is shown in Fig. 7. The current experiment was evaluated in two planes (X–Z, and X–Y planes) shown in Fig. 7(b),(c). The force vectors (8 patterns) were presented, each having 30 degrees apart. Because our goal was to evaluate the force direction between orthogonal axes we had to exclude the stimuli that renders along the X, Y, and Z–axes. Participants are 5 male students who are right-handed and the average age is 20 years old. Stimulus was presented five times for each condition. In total, there are 80 trials performed by each participant. The results shown in Fig. 8, is the summarized answer rates from 5 subjects. The accuracy of evaluating force vectors in the plane are: 59 % in X-Z plane and 58 % in X-Y plane. Moreover, if vectors to be next to correct vectors is regarded as correct one also, the rate of each planes become 90 %(X-Z plane) and 93 %(X-Y plane).

5   Discussions

The proposed method for representing forces between orthogonal axes was able to induce perceived force direction between axes. However, the adjacent force vector pose a problem that discrimination is difficult in Fig. 8. This problem is caused by the fine difference that is the similar tendency of adjacent force vectors. It maybe important to consider using higher resolution (more that 8 sections) to

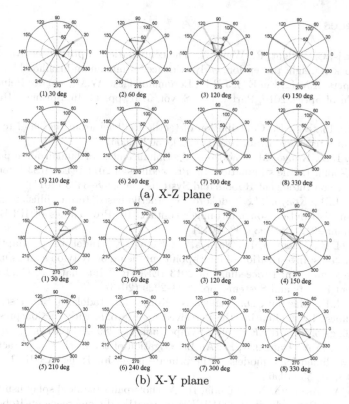

(a) X-Z plane

(b) X-Y plane

Fig. 8. Experimental results: answer rates against the presented force directions (The targeted directions are shown in blue lines) (color figure online).

render force between axes. We will be able to optimize the number of pressure rooms by using SED distribution. Moreover, given that adding to contact points from two finger or expanding contact area, the perception of directions improves precision.

6   Conclusions

In this paper, we proposed a representation method of multi-DoF forces by associating psychophysical experiment with FEA. The initial suction rendering approach based from intuition was improved using a analytical approach based on SED index. We had explored that it is possible to represent force between orthogonal axes using the new approach. In the future, we will examine the method that represent omnidirectional forces, and consider the effect of torque, and rotational sequences.

References

1. Giachritsis, C., Wright, R., Wing, A.: The contribution of proprioceptive and cutaneous cues in weight perception: early evidence for maximum-likelihood integration. In: Kappers, A.M.L., van Erp, J.B.F., Bergmann Tiest, W.M., van der Helm, F.C.T. (eds.) EuroHaptics 2010, Part I. LNCS, vol. 6191, pp. 11–16. Springer, Heidelberg (2010)
2. Jones, L., Piateski, E.: Contribution of tactile feedback from the hand to the perception of force. Exp. Brain Res. **168**, 298–302 (2006)
3. Porquis, L.B., Konyo, M., Tadokoro, S.: Enhancement of human force perception by multi-point tactile stimulation. In: Proceedings of 2011 IEEE/RSJ International Conference on Intelligent Robots and Systems, pp. 3488–3493 (2011)
4. Porquis, L.B., Konyo, M., Tadokoro, S.: Tactile-based torque illusion controlled by strain distributions on multi-finger contact. In: Proceedings of IEEE Haptics Symposium 2012, pp. 393–398 (2012)
5. Porquis, L.B., Maemori, D., Nagaya, N., Konyo, K., Tadokoro, S.: Haptic cue of forces on tools: Investigation of multi-point cutaneous activity on skin using suction pressure stimuli. In: Proceedings of 2013 IEEE/RSJ International Conference on Intelligent Robots and Systems, pp. 2023–2029 (2013)
6. Porquis, L.B., Maemori, D., Nagaya, N., Konyo, M., Tadokoro, S.: Presenting virtual stiffness by modulating the perceived force profile with suction pressure. In: Proceedings of 2014 IEEE Haptics Symposium, pp. 289–294 (2014)
7. Srinivasan, M.A., Dandekar, K.: An Investigation of the mechanics of tactile sense using two-dimensional models of the primate fingertip. Trans. ASME J. Biomech. Eng. **118**, 48–55 (1996)
8. Makino, Y., Asamura, N., Shinoda, H.: A whole palm tactile display using suction pressure. In: Proceedings of 2004 IEEE International Conference on Robotics and Automation, pp. 1524–1529 (2004)

Evaluating the BioTac's Ability to Detect and Characterize Lumps in Simulated Tissue

Jennifer C.T. Hui[1]([⊠]) and Katherine J. Kuchenbecker[1,2]

[1] Department of Computer and Information Science,
University of Pennsylvania, Philadelphia, PA, USA
jenhui@seas.upenn.edu
[2] Department of Mechanical Engineering and Applied Mechanics,
Haptics Group, GRASP Lab, University of Pennsylvania, Philadelphia, PA, USA
kuchenbe@seas.upenn.edu

Abstract. Surgeons can detect and characterize tumors in open surgery by palpating tissue with their fingertips, but palpation is not currently possible in minimally invasive surgery (MIS). Motivated by the goal of creating an automatic palpation tool for MIS, we evaluated the SynTouch BioTac sensor's ability to detect and characterize lumps in simulated tissue. Models were constructed from silicone rubber with rigid spheres of three sizes embedded at three depths, plus models without embedded lumps. Electrode impedance and DC pressure were recorded as each model was indented into the BioTac at sixteen indentation depths up to 4.0 mm. Support vector machine classifiers were trained on subsets of the data and tested on trials from withheld models for three tasks: lump detection, lump size characterization, and lump depth characterization. The lump detection and lump size classifiers achieved relatively high accuracies, especially at the deepest indentation depths, but the lump depth classifier performed no better than chance.

1 Introduction

Lump detection and characterization are critical in the diagnosis and treatment of cancers. Cancers such as those in the breast [1], prostate [2], and lung [3] manifest as stiff lumps in softer tissue. Palpation, the use of one's fingertips to detect features beneath the surface of tissues, is a primary skill for a physician [4]. During open surgery, surgeons palpate tissue to localize tumors in real time and guide the procedure. However they are unable to employ this skill in either laparoscopic or robot-assisted minimally invasive surgery (RMIS). In contrast with traditional open surgery, minimally invasive surgery (MIS) is performed using long slender tools inserted through small incisions in the patient's body. While the smaller incision size results in benefits such as reduced pain and scarring and faster recovery, the use of these tools eliminates the possibility of direct contact between the surgeon's hand and the tissue. This loss of haptic feedback is thought to hinder surgeons in providing their patients with the highest possible quality of care [5].

© Springer-Verlag Berlin Heidelberg 2014
M. Auvray and C. Duriez (Eds.): EuroHaptics 2014, Part II, LNCS 8619, pp. 295–302, 2014.
DOI: 10.1007/978-3-662-44196-1_36

Several different research groups have tested tactile sensors for the purpose of enabling palpation during minimally invasive procedures. Murayama et al. [6] developed a two-dimensional 64-element array of piezoelectric transducers to measure the stiffness of breast tissue. They demonstrated the device's ability to detect tumors in simulated tissue and clinical cases. Gwilliam et al. [7] compared the lump detection performance of a two-dimensional array of capacitive tactile sensors against the performance of human subjects using their index finger. They created tissue models with embedded lumps and used the sensor array to palpate the models using a motion perpendicular to the tissue surface. In addition to determining the minimum depth of reliable lump detection, Gwilliam et al. also evaluated the effects of lump size, lump depth, and surrounding tissue stiffness on detection. Jia et al. [8] evaluated the lump detection sensitivity of the GelSight sensor, which consists of clear elastomeric pad with a reflective membrane. They detected embedded lumps by optically measuring the membrane's deformations when pressed against simulated tissue. The GelSight sensor was shown to be more sensitive than humans at detecting lumps. More recently, Arian et al. [9] tested the ability of the BioTac (SynTouch LLC), a biomimetic tactile sensor, to detect artificial tumors in tissue models. Rather than using the perpendicular motion employed by Gwilliam et al. and Jia et al., they explored the models by moving the BioTac in a sweeping motion across the model's surface. They demonstrated that the BioTac was able to localize tumors when used in this manner, but it was unable to provide enough information to characterize lump size.

Despite the potential these tactile devices have shown in palpation and tumor detection, there has yet to be a commercially available automatic palpation system for surgeons to use in MIS. Instrument size is a major constraint. Minimally invasive instruments are usually between 5 mm and 10 mm in diameter. The tactile devices mentioned previously range in size from greater than 62 mm × 62 mm × 150 mm [8] to a cylinder 15 mm in diameter [9]. Another limitation of past research is that it has almost exclusively focused on lump detection, with little attention to characterizing the properties of a detected lump. Automatic palpation tools should be able to determine clinically relevant lump characteristics, such as stiffness, size, shape, and depth to adequately guide surgeons during an operation.

Doctors palpating tissue directly with their fingers are effective in detecting lumps in part due to the richness of sensations the human finger can capture. The BioTac is a multimodal tactile sensor designed to mimic the human finger. Its main physical structure consists of a solid core surrounded by incompressible conductive fluid and encapsulated by a rubber skin. With an array of 19 electrodes spatially distributed around the core directly below the finger pad, a fluid pressure sensor, and a temperature sensor, the BioTac can measure signals similar to the tactile sensations a human finger can feel. Its small size and multiple sensors make this tactile device a good candidate for MIS palpation. This paper sought to evaluate the BioTac's ability to detect and characterize embedded lumps when pressed perpendicularly into the surface of simulate tissue.

2 Methods

Our methods involved creating a set of rubber models with stiff embedded lumps, using the BioTac to passively touch these models, and training machine learning classifiers on the resulting data for the purposes of lump detection and lump size and depth characterization.

Model Set: Twenty-four simulated tissue models were constructed to match the palpation stimulus set of Gwilliam et al. [7]. Half of the models were made with soft Ecoflex 00-10 silicone rubber (Smooth-On Corp.) and the other with stiffer Ecoflex 00-30. In each set of twelve, three models have no embedded lump while the other nine contain a rigid sphere. As done by Gwilliam et al. [7], we created models in all combinations of three lump sizes (6.5 mm, 9.5 mm, and 12.5 mm diameter) and three lump depths (1.5 mm, 2.5 mm, and 3.5 mm from the top of the lump to the palpated surface).

Model Construction: Each cubic rubber model was cast in a 50.8 mm × 50.8 mm × 50.8 mm acrylic mold. Spheres of the specified diameters with thin conic stands of appropriate heights were 3D-printed in ABS plastic using a Stratasys Dimension Elite machine. The sphere-and-stand structure was attached to the center of the top face of the mold. Ecoflex was prepared and poured into the acrylic mold before installation of the top face containing the lump. Molds cured for 24 hours before the top face of the mold and the conic stand were removed, leaving the lump in place near the bottom face, which becomes the palpated surface of the model during data recording. The remaining conic hole was filled with Ecoflex, and the model cured for an additional 24 hours before being removed from the mold. To facilitate data recording, a stand made of a 150-mm-long standoff anchored to a 50.8-mm-square of ABS plastic was prepared and glued to the top face of each model.

Data Recording: A CNC milling machine was used to precisely indent the models into the BioTac. As in Fig. 1(a) the BioTac was placed in a rigid mounting block and clamped to the machine bed with the finger pad horizontal and facing upward. The cubic model was attached to the CNC machine's quill by clamping the chuck onto the model's stand. The bottom face of the model, which is the face closest to the embedded lump, was parallel to the bed. The bed was then moved to manually center the embedded lump over the middle of the BioTac finger pad. The quill was manually lowered until the model barely made contact with the BioTac, and the depth gauge was zeroed.

The horizontal location of the bed was held constant throughout the trials, and the model was moved vertically downward in a series of contact experiments while signals were recorded from the BioTac. As done in Gwilliam et al. [7], 16 unique indentation depths (ID) were tested for each model, ranging from 0.25 mm to 4.0 mm with a step size of 0.25 mm. In each trial, the model was indented into the BioTac at 50.8 mm/min until the desired ID was achieved. The model was held in place for one second before being removed at 3810 mm/min until contact with the BioTac ceased. This movement resulted in electrode and DC pressure

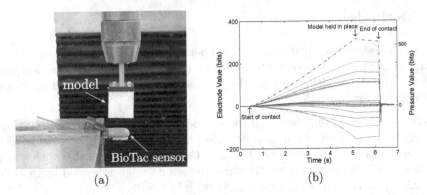

Fig. 1. (a) Experimental setup. (b) A sample single-trial recording of the BioTac's DC pressure (dash-dot) and 19 electrode impedances (solid lines) with baseline values removed. As expected, DC pressure increases to the plateau of stationary contact, stays approximately constant for one second, and then rapidly decreases. Electrode impedances increase where the skin indents and decrease where the skin bulges.

readings such as those in Fig. 1(b). 10 trials were recorded at each of the 16 ID for all 24 models, yielding 3840 trials.

Data Preprocessing: The data set includes 100 Hz readings from the BioTac's 19 electrodes and DC fluid pressure. The baseline values were separately removed from each recording by subtracting the mean of the first 50 data points from the rest of each signal. The 100 data points in the plateau section were then extracted and averaged, reducing each recording to an array of 20 values that represent how the model feels at a specific ID. Each of the 20 values was scaled by subtracting from it the respective mean and then dividing the result by the respective standard deviation. The mean and standard deviation of each value type was calculated from the 240 trials recorded at the same ID. Different labels were applied to the trials depending on the task of the classifier.

Support vector machine (SVM) classifiers were evaluated for the three tasks of lump detection, lump size characterization, and lump depth characterization. The SVM technique was selected because its decision boundaries are constructed based on the cross-class instances that are most similar. Because our models exhibited all combinations of two Ecoflex stiffnesses, three ball sizes, and three embedded depths, as well as no lump models, we anticipated that the BioTac recordings of the models would be similar and thus would benefit from the SVM classifier's attention to subtle differences. We also tested other machine learning techniques such as Naive Bayes, Decision Trees, Logistic Regression, and Discriminant Analysis and found that none performed as well as SVM's in all three tasks. We employed LIBSVM, a popular open-source machine-learning library for support vector machine implementations, to train and test the classifiers. The lump detection classifier is binary (does or does not contain an embedded lump), while the lump size and lump depth SVM's are both multi-class classifiers with four categories each (three finite diameters or depths and a fourth category of no embedded lump).

Each classifier was trained using data recorded at a single ID to enable us to study the influence of indentation depth on classifier accuracy. With this organization, models are classified based on what they felt like to the BioTac at the same ID. Following the accepted practice in machine learning, the data was split into a training set and testing set; examples in the testing set were excluded from the training set to prevent over-fitting of the classifier. Because the experimental setup was carefully controlled, the 10 trials of a single model were nearly identical. Each model that contains an embedded lump represents a unique combination of Ecoflex stiffness, lump size, and lump depth. Thus to prevent nearly identical trials from being used to train and test the classifier, all 10 trials of a model were placed in either the training set or the test set.

We performed leave-one-out cross-validation (LOOCV) to train all of our classifiers. In LOOCV, all 10 trials of a single model were set aside to be the testing set, while all trials of the remaining 23 models were grouped together as the training set. The classifier was trained with properly labeled training data and then used to make predictions on the unseen data in the test set. The proportion of correct predictions was taken to be the accuracy of that particular classifier. Since there were 24 models, 24 classifiers were trained for each combination of ID and task. The general accuracy of the classifier was then calculated as the mean accuracy of the 24 classifiers. This process was repeated for each of the 16 IDs for each of the three tasks. Classifier accuracy was plotted as a function of indentation depth.

3   Results

Figure 2 shows the accuracy achieved by each of the trained classifiers, organized by task and indentation depth.

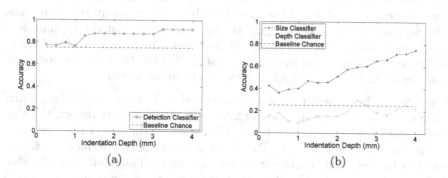

(a)   (b)

Fig. 2. Plot of accuracy as a function of indentation depth for (a) the lump detection classifier and (b) the lump size and lump depth classifiers. Because three out of four models contain a lump, we mark 0.75 as the baseline performance in lump detection. Discriminating between the four categories of lump size or lump depth has a baseline accuracy of 0.25.

Lump Detection: Because 18 of the 24 models have embedded lumps, the baseline accuracy is 0.75. Figure 2(a) shows that classifier accuracy was above the baseline for all 16 IDs. The accuracy generally increases with increasing ID and reaches its highest value, 0.917 (22/24), at the four deepest IDs. Perfect lump detection was not achieved. The two models mis-classified at the deepest IDs were Ecoflex-30 models, one no-lump model and one with the 6.5 mm diameter lump embedded at 3.5 mm.

Lump Size: The baseline accuracy for discerning lump size is 0.25 because there are four categories of lump size (no lump, 6.5 mm, 9.5 mm, and 12.5 mm diameter), each containing six models. Figure 2(b) shows that classifier accuracy was higher than the baseline accuracy for all 16 IDs. The accuracy plot exhibits an upward trend with increasing ID and reaches its highest value, 0.750, at the deepest ID. The accuracy curve does not plateau, and perfect classification was not achieved.

Lump Depth: The baseline accuracy for discerning lump depth is 0.25 because there are four categories of lump depth (no lump, 1.5 mm, 2.5 mm, and 3.5 mm depth), each containing six models. Figure 2(b) shows that classifier accuracy was generally below the baseline accuracy. Thus the trained lump depth classifier performs worse than random classification for this task. Increasing ID does not seem to improve classifier accuracy.

4   Discussion

Lump Detection: This set of classifiers achieved the highest accuracy of the three tested tasks. From IDs 0.25 mm to 1.0 mm, the classifier accuracy is just above the baseline, indicating that models with and without embedded lumps feel very similar at shallow IDs. The classifier accuracy increases between 1.0 mm and 1.5 mm, reaching a plateau at 0.875, corresponding to 210 correctly classified trials out of 240 total trials. From 3.25 mm to 4.0 mm, the classifier reaches its highest accuracy at 0.917, which corresponds to 220 correctly classified trials. The final increase in accuracy may be due to the fact that deeply embedded lumps are more difficult to perceive at shallower IDs. In general this classifier performed better than the baseline, suggesting that the BioTac's electrodes and pressure readings can detect most of the lumps in our model set.

Lump Size: This classifier achieved the second highest accuracy. The positive slope of the accuracy graph shows that as the model indents deeper, the electrodes and pressure sensor are better able to detect the size of the rigid lump within the compliant Ecoflex. The lump size classifier performed much better than baseline, but it was not as accurate as the lump detection classifier. Although the lump size classifier was most accurate at the deepest ID, it was not perfect. Indenting the models into the BioTac beyond 4.0 mm might have enabled even higher accuracy for this task.

Lump Depth: The consistently low accuracy of this set of classifiers showed that classifying lump depth was the most difficult of the three studied tasks. The classifier generally performed worse than random classification, suggesting that the BioTac's electrodes and pressure sensor readings at a single ID do not contain sufficient information to discern lump depth. Indenting the model further into the BioTac did not seem to improve accuracy much.

In general: The lump detection classifiers achieved the highest accuracy partially because detection is a simple binary task. Lump size classification is the multi-class version of the lump detection classifier, requiring the algorithm to learn finer distinctions between the stimuli; our lump size classifiers out-performed chance and showed better performance for higher IDs. Despite also being multi-class, the lump depth classifier was not nearly as accurate as the lump size classifier. The spatial distribution of the electrodes seems to enable the BioTac to measure differences felt across the finger pad, such as those that must be felt when determining lump size. Lump depth classification cannot take advantage of the electrodes' spatial arrangement, as the difference in sensation between lumps embedded at different depths is likely greatest along the axis perpendicular to the electrodes. The difficulty of lump depth classification was further increased because lump depths differed by only 1 or 2 mm. In contrast, lump size differed by at least 3 mm.

While retrospectively analyzing our dataset, we noticed that two different BioTacs were used in data collection. As evidenced by different baseline pressure readings, the fluid volume may have differed slightly between the two sensors, which may have altered their sensing ranges and introduced some variability in the collected data. Logically, the variability may have contributed to the difficulty of lump detection and characterization. The reported classifiers were thus re-trained and re-tested on subsets of the data from only one or the other BioTac. This additional testing achieved lower accuracy levels than were achieved on the entire dataset, indicating that the benefit of additional data outweighs the drawback of trial-to-trial variability. Indeed, the variability may have helped ensure that the learned models are invariant to sensor identity, as we would want for the envisioned use of lump detection and characterization during RMIS.

This preliminary study shows that the electrode and DC pressure readings from a BioTac biomimetic tactile sensor can be processed using SVMs to perform the tasks of lump detection and lump size characterization with accuracy levels far higher than chance, especially at the deepest IDs. In contrast, our approach was not able to discern lump depth. We plan to expand upon this work by using a wider variety of exploratory movements, just as a doctor often changes the finger position relative to the tissue, alters finger orientation, and applies lateral forces during palpation to gain more information about the tissue. We anticipate that using additional exploratory movements will allow the BioTac to record more information about how the models feel to improve the accuracy of lump detection and lump size and depth characterization.

Acknowledgements. The first author was supported by a research fellowship from the National Science Foundation Graduate Research Fellowship Program under Grant No. DGE-0822. The authors would like to thank the members of the Haptics Group, in particular John C. Nappo for his assistance in model manufacturing and Alexandre Miranda Añon and Claudio Pacchierotti for their assistance in preparing this manuscript.

References

1. Halsted, W.S.: The results of operations for the cure of cancer of the breast performed at the Johns Hopkins Hospital from June, 1889, to January 1894. Ann. Surg. **20**(5), 497–555 (1894)
2. Huggins, C., Johnson, M.A.: Cancer of the bladder and prostate. J. Am. Med. Assoc. **135**(17), 1146–1152 (1947)
3. Miller, A.P., Peine, W.J., Son, J.S., Hammoud, Z.T.: Tactile imaging system for localizing lung nodules during video assisted thoracoscopic surgery. In: Proceedings of the IEEE International Conference on Robotics and Automation, pp. 2996–3001 (2007)
4. Fletcher, S.W., O'Malley, M.S., Bunce, L.A.: Physicians' abilities to detect lumps in silicone breast models. J. Am. Med. Assoc. **253**(15), 2224–2228 (1985)
5. Howe, R.D., Peine, W.J., Kontarinis, D.A., Son, J.S.: Remote palpation technology. IEEE Eng. Med. Biol. Mag. **14**(3), 318–323 (1995)
6. Murayama, Y., Haruta, M., Hatakeyama, Y., Shiina, T., Sakuma, H., Takenoshita, S., Omata, S., Constantinou, C.E.: Development of a new instrument for examination of stiffness in the breast using haptic sensor technology. Sens. Actuators A **143**(2), 430–438 (2008)
7. Gwilliam, J.C., Pezzementi, Z., Jantho, E., Okamura, A.M., Hsiao, S.: Human vs. robotic tactile sensing: detecting lumps in soft tissue. In: Proceedings of the IEEE Haptics Symposium, pp. 21–28 (2010)
8. Jia, X.S., Li, R., Srinivasan, M.A., Adelson, E.H.: Lump detection with a GelSight sensor. In: Proceedings of the IEEE World Haptics Conference, pp. 175–179 (2013)
9. Arian, M.S., Blaine, C.A., Loeb, G.E., Fishel, J.A.: Using the BioTac as a tumor localization tool. In: Proceedings of the IEEE Haptics Symposium, pp. 443–448 (2014)

Modeling and Simulation

A Genetic Algorithm Approach to Identify Virtual Object Properties for Sharing the Feel from Virtual Environments

Yongyao Yan[1,2(✉)], Greg S. Ruthenbeck[1,2], and Karen J. Reynolds[1,2]

[1] The Medical Device Research Institute, Flinders University, Adelaide, Australia
[2] School of Computer Science, Engineering and Mathematics,
Flinders University, Adelaide, Australia
{yongyao.yan,greg.ruthenbeck,karen.reynolds}@flinders.edu.au

Abstract. Haptics has provided people with new computer interaction styles across a range of applications. However, it is difficult to share haptic experiences from haptic virtual environments (HVEs). In this paper, we introduce a genetic algorithm (GA) approach, which is used to identify the virtual object's properties (e.g. stiffness, friction coefficient and geometry parameters) based on haptic recordings, so that the haptic rendering can be reproduced without requiring the original HVE software to be deployed.

Keywords: Virtual environment · Haptic recording · Genetic algorithm

1 Introduction

Haptics is increasing in popularity as a way of enhancing the simulation experience. A HVE application controls the visual and haptic rendering in response to the user's haptic manipulation with objects in the virtual scene. However the haptic experience relies heavily on the computer hardware that is running the virtual environment software and it is difficult to share the haptic sensation. To address this issue, we proposed the Hapteo system in our previous work [9] to share the feel of rigid frictionless objects from a HVE. The system enables users to record visual-haptic information from a HVE by using the Hapteo Recorder software tool. Contact surface model and haptic force model are then reconstructed based on the recorded haptic data. By using the Hapteo Player software tool, users are able to actively replay the visual-haptic experience.

In this paper, we take a 2D rigid frictional circle as an example to introduce the GA approach to identify the virtual object's stiffness, friction coefficient and geometry parameters so as to reproduce the haptic rendering. Previous studies [4,6,8] can be found for simulating haptic feeling of real life objects, where the recorded haptic data is from the contact surface. However, when users touch the virtual object in a HVE, the position where users see the haptic stylus is not the position where the haptic interface point (HIP) is located. Generally a

M. Auvray and C. Duriez (Eds.): EuroHaptics 2014, Part II, LNCS 8619, pp. 305–312, 2014.
DOI: 10.1007/978-3-662-44196-1_37

HVE realizes the surface contact feeling by generating appropriate force feedback according to the virtual object's properties such as stiffness and friction, and the penetration of the HIP into the virtual object. For example, in Fig. 2 (left), the HIP is actually in the position P_1 when the user sees the haptic stylus on the virtual object's surface in the position $Proxy_1$ in visualization. Therefore the recorded haptic data (i.e. position and force) is from the position of HIP when users manipulate the virtual object. To the best of our knowledge, this is the first case to replay the feeling of virtual objects from HVEs.

2   Methods

2.1   The Genetic Algorithm

The GA [1,3] is a robust search and optimization strategy, which imitates biological evolution with the survival-of-the-fittest approach by applying genetic operations, such as selection, crossover and mutation, on chromosomes coded with solution parameters. Since the GA is a powerful global method for nonlinear optimization, it is adopted here to estimate the virtual object's geometrical and physical properties. We can therefore conceive the stiffness constant, friction coefficient and the virtual object's geometrical properties as the parameters of a haptic rendering model, which has the HIP position and haptic force feedback as the input and output respectively. In order to reproduce the haptic rendering for replaying the feel of the interaction in the original HVE, the parameters should be optimized based on the recorded haptic information (i.e. position and force data).

Assuming an user manipulates on a 2D rigid frictional circle surface using a point-based stylus in a HVE, we can code the parameters in a chromosome as below, which is to be evolved by GA:

$$\phi = \{s, \mu, a, b, r\}. \tag{1}$$

where s is the stiffness constant, μ is the friction coefficient, a and b are the x and y components of the circle center position and r is the contact radius (i.e. the total length of the circle radius and the haptic stylus radius). The flow diagram of the proposed GA is shown in Fig. 1. Initially, the first generation of random chromosomes is generated. Each chromosome is evaluated by calculating the fitness function and the best chromosome is used to compare the termination condition. If it meets the criteria of the termination condition, the GA stops and gets the optimized solution. Otherwise, the selection operation is used to choose two parents from the current chromosomes for creating a new child by applying crossover and mutation operations. The current generation is therefore transformed into a new generation which has the same population size of chromosomes as the initial one. This evolution process continues until the fittest chromosome is found and it meets the termination condition. Since the force feedback is the output of a haptic rendering model, it is naturally to use the root-mean-square (RMS) force error to define the fitness function and the termination condition.

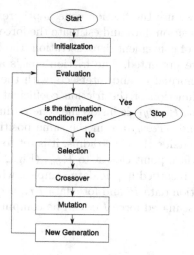

Fig. 1. The flow diagram of GA

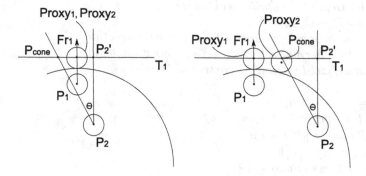

Fig. 2. The friction cone haptic rendering method [7] causing the proxy to stick (left) or slip (right)

2.2   The Fitness Function

A fitness function in GA is to determine the performance of each chromosome. In our proposed GA, the fitness function is defined as:

$$Fitness(\phi) = \frac{1}{RMS(\phi)}. \tag{2}$$

$$RMS(\phi) = \sqrt{\frac{1}{n}\sum_{i=1}^{n}\|Fr_i - Fe_i\|^2}. \tag{3}$$

where n is the number of samples, Fr_i and Fe_i are recorded and estimated force at sample i respectively. If the parameter set ϕ has the smallest force error, it has the best fitness function value.

As shown in Fig. 2, we use the friction cone haptic rendering method [7] to interpret the recorded position data and estimate the force Fe_i at each sampling period. For the purpose of convenient demonstration, the first two HIPs, P_1 and P_2, inside the object are presented. The friction cone's apex is at the new P_2 and the central axis is normal to and intersects with the last tangent line, T_1, at P_2'. The angle θ is function of the friction coefficient μ, $\theta = arctan(\mu)$. If the previous proxy point, $Proxy_1$, is inside the cone radius, $\|P_{cone}P_2'\|$, it sticks in place (e.g. $Proxy_1$ and $Proxy_2$ are in the same position as shown in Fig. 2 (left)). However if it is outside the cone radius, it is set to be the point, $Proxy_2$, which is the contact surface point closest to P_{cone} (Fig. 2 (right)).

Assuming we have n recorded haptic data samples, which penetrate into the object and contain position data P_i and fore data Fr_i, according to the relevant parameter set ϕ, each estimated force Fe_i can be computed as described in the following algorithm:

$C_{circle} = Point2D(a, b)$
$toCenterDistance = \|P_1 C_{circle}\|$
$penetrationDepth = r - toCenterDistance$
$direction = P_1 - C_{circle}$
$T_1 = the\ \ orthogonal\ \ vector\ \ of\ \ normalize(direction)$
$Proxy_1 = P_1 + normalize(direction) * penetrationDepth$
$Fe_1 = normalize(direction) * penetrationDepth * s$

$for\ \ (i = 2;\ \ i <= n;\ \ i++)\ \ \{$
$\quad P_i' = the\ \ projection\ \ point\ \ of\ \ P_i\ \ on\ \ T_{i-1}$
$\quad coneRadius = \|P_i' P_i\| * \mu$
$\quad len = \|Proxy_{i-1} P_i'\|$
$\quad if\ \ (len > coneRadius)\ \ \{$
$\quad\quad P_{cone} = P_i' + normalize(Proxy_{i-1} - P_i') * coneRadius$
$\quad\quad Proxy_i = getClosestContactSurfacePoint(P_{cone}, C_{circle}, r)$
$\quad\quad N_i = normalize(P_{cone} - Proxy_i)$
$\quad\quad T_i = the\ \ orthogonal\ \ vector\ \ of\ \ N_i$
$\quad\quad forceNormal = normalize(P_{cone} - P_i)$
$\quad\quad distance = \|P_{cone} P_i\|$
$\quad \}else\{$
$\quad\quad Proxy_i = Proxy_{i-1}$
$\quad\quad T_i = T_{i-1}$
$\quad\quad forceNormal = normalize(Proxy_{i-1} - P_i)$
$\quad\quad distance = \|Proxy_{i-1} P_i\|$
$\quad \}$
$\quad penetrationForceMagnitude = \|P_i' P_i\| * s$
$\quad cosin = \frac{\|P_i' P_i\|}{distance}$
$\quad forceMagnitude = \frac{penetrationForceMagnitude}{cosin}$
$\quad Fe_i = forceNormal * forceMagnitude$
$\}$

The function $getClosestContactSurfacePoint(P_{cone}, C_{circle}, r)$ in above algorithm is described as follows:

$Point2D \quad getClosestContactSurfacePoint(P_{cone}, C_{circle}, r)\{$
$\quad direction = P_{cone} - C_{circle}$
$\quad return \quad C_{circle} + normalize(direction) * r$
$\}$

2.3 The Value Range Estimation of the Parameters

In order to reduce the search space in GA, prediction of the value range (i.e. lower-bound and upper-bound) of each parameter is necessary. First of all, we can define the range of the angle θ, $1° \leq \theta \leq 89°$, the value range of the friction coefficient μ is $0.017 \leq \mu \leq 57.3$ (i.e. $\tan(1°) \leq \mu \leq \tan(89°)$).

We assume P_0 is the recorded HIP position before penetrating into the object and P_1 is the first HIP position penetrating into the object, the contact surface is somewhere between P_0 and P_1. We define the maximum penetration depth as $initMaxDepth = \|P_0P_1\|$. Since the haptic data is recorded at the high refresh-rate of the haptic rendering call-back which is normally at least 1 kHz, the distance between two sampling position is very small. We then define the reasonable minimum penetration depth as $initMinDepth = \frac{initMaxDepth}{100}$. According the Hooke's law, we can predict the value range of the stiffness constant s as $\frac{\|Fr_1\|}{initMaxDepth} \leq s \leq \frac{\|Fr_1\|}{initMinDepth}$.

As shown in Fig. 3, assuming the recorded force Fr_1 is normal to the circle surface, then the line L_c along this force direction must pass through the circle's center C. We assume P_n and P_{n+1} are the last HIP position inside and the first HIP position leaving the circle respectively. The surface point S_1 can locate in between P_0 and P_1 and the surface point S_2 can locate in between P_n and P_{n+1}. Therefore the circle will have two boundary cases which pass through P_0P_{n+1} and P_1P_n. Consequently two different circle centers correspondent to these two boundary cases will locate on the line L_c. Let's take the

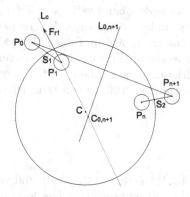

Fig. 3. Circle center position estimation

case of P_0P_{n+1} as an example. Since P_0P_{n+1} are points on an arc segment of a circle, the perpendicular line, $L_{0,n+1}$, which passes through the middle point between them must pass through the relevant circle center, $C_{0,n+1}$. By using the same method, we can get the relevant circle center $C_{1,n}$ correspondent to the case of P_1P_n. So we can get the value range of the circle center's x and y components, a and b, as $min(C_{0,n+1}^x, C_{1,n}^x) \leqq a \leqq max(C_{0,n+1}^x, C_{1,n}^x)$ and $min(C_{0,n+1}^y, C_{1,n}^y) \leqq b \leqq max(C_{0,n+1}^y, C_{1,n}^y)$, and the value range of the contact radius r as $min(\|P_1C_{0,n+1}\|, \|P_1C_{1,n}\|) \leqq r \leqq max(\|P_0C_{0,n+1}\|, \|P_0C_{1,n}\|)$.

2.4   Other GA Parameters

The GA is set to run with the population size of 100, the crossover rate fixed at half of the population size and the mutation rate of $\frac{1}{15}$. In the literature [2] the average user perception evaluation has good rating points, if the force deadband value is less than 5 %. The force deadband value $k = 2.5\%$ is therefore selected here to define the termination condition of the GA. We can get $\|Fr_i - Fe_i\| \leqq \|Fr_i\| * k$ based on the deadband principle. According to the Eq. (3), the termination condition is defined as $RMS(\phi) \leqq \sqrt{\frac{k^2}{n} \sum_{i=1}^{n} \|Fr_i\|^2}$.

3   Results

By using Microsoft XNA4.0 and the Novint Falcon haptic device, we set up a 2D HVE which allows users manipulate on a rigid frictional circle (center $(0, 0)$, radius 0.75, stiffness 5.0 and friction coefficient 0.3) with a point-based stylus (radius 0.08). The contact radius in this case is 0.83. We wrapped the original Novint Falcon's DLL file, hdl.dll, by using C++ to embed functions for intercepting the haptic position and force data at each haptic rendering call-back period. The Java Genetic Algorithms Package (JGAP) [5] is used to implement the proposed GA. Total 6067 interaction samples are recorded from the user's manipulation (i.e. touches, slips a short distance and keeps away from the surface). We use the force deadband value $k = 5\%$ to filter and reduce the data, and get finally 104 samples to feed the GA. The parameters optimization results of the GA's six runs are shown in Table 1. We take the mean values of the estimated parameters as the final results, which are very close to the original settings. Regarding the friction cone method [7], the haptic rendering can then be reproduced with the estimated stiffness constant, friction coefficient and the geometry parameters.

4   Discussion

The RMS force error in Table 1 is due to the deadband value setting $k = 2.5\%$, which is already within the setting range that has good user perception evaluation ratings [2]. It is possible to reduce the deadband value and further reduce

Table 1. Results of the GA runs

Parameters	Run 1	Run 2	Run 3	Run 4	Run 5	Run 6	Mean	Original value
s	5.0044	4.9725	5.0056	4.8602	5.0592	5.0806	4.9971	5.0
μ	0.2584	0.2629	0.2704	0.2660	0.2655	0.2653	0.2648	0.3
a	0.00005	0.0002	0.0002	0.00005	0.00005	0.0002	0.0001	0.0
b	0.0027	0.0004	0.0004	0.0027	0.0027	0.0005	0.0016	0.0
r	0.8285	0.8287	0.8303	0.8316	0.8270	0.8271	0.8289	0.83
RMS err.(N)	0.0218	0.0216	0.0218	0.0213	0.0216	0.0219	0.0217	-
Time spent (s)	15	4	14	11	3	6	8.83	-

the force error. The GA will therefore take more time to analyze the recorded data. Since the haptic data recording and replaying processes are separated and they are in the different software tools (i.e. the Hapteo Recorder and the Hapteo Player) of the Hapteo system [9], it is not necessary to consider the real-time performance.

Current proposed algorithms are limited to the friction cone haptic rendering method [7] and the 2D circle virtual object. There are various haptic rendering methods to simulate the haptic feeling for different purposes. One solution we are investigating is to consider multiple haptic rendering methods in the GA to find out the suitable optimization results.

5   Conclusion and Future Work

Regarding the haptic data recorded from the user manipulating a 2D rigid frictional circle in a HVE, it is proved that the feeling of virtual objects can be reproduced independently from the original HVE by using the proposed GA approach to identify the virtual object's properties. Future studies include user evaluation, extending the current solution to support 3D scenarios, high resolution and high degrees of freedom (DOF) haptic devices.

References

1. Goldberg, D.E.: Genetic Algorithms in Search, Optimization and Machine Learning, 1st edn. Addison-Wesley Longman Publishing Co., Inc., Boston (1989)
2. Hinterseer, P., Steinbach, E.: A psychophysically motivated compression approach for 3D haptic data. In: 2006 14th Symposium on Haptic Interfaces for Virtual Environment and Teleoperator Systems, pp. 35–41. IEEE (2006)
3. Holland, J.H.: Adaptation in Natural and Artificial Systems: An Introductory Analysis with Applications to Biology, Control, and Artificial Intelligence. University of Michigan Press, Ann Arbor (1975)

4. Kuchenbecker, K.J.: Haptography: capturing the feel of real objects to enable authentic haptic rendering. In: Proceedings of the 2008 Ambi-Sys workshop on Haptic user interfaces in ambient media systems, p. 3. ICST (Institute for Computer Sciences, Social-Informatics and Telecommunications Engineering) (2008)

5. Meffert, K.: JGAP - java genetic algorithms and genetic programming package (2014). http://jgap.sf.net

6. Pai, D.K., van den Doel, K., James, D.L., Lang, J., Lloyd, J.E., Richmond, J.L., Yau, S.H.: Scanning physical interaction behavior of 3D objects. In: Proceedings of the 28th Annual Conference on Computer Graphics and Interactive Techniques, pp. 87–96. ACM (2001)

7. Salisbury, K., Tarr, C.: Haptic rendering of surfaces defined by implicit functions. In: Proceedings of ASME Dynamic Systems and Control Division, vol. 61, pp. 61–67 (1997)

8. Vasudevan, H., Manivannan, M.: Recordable haptic textures. In: IEEE International Workshop on Haptic Audio Visual Environments and their Applications, HAVE 2006, pp. 130–133. IEEE (2006)

9. Yan, Y., Ruthenbeck, G.S., Reynolds, K.J.: Hapteo: sharing visual-haptic experiences from virtual environments. In: 2014 IEEE Haptics Symposium (HAPTICS). IEEE (2014)

Estimation of Finger Pad Deformation Based on Skin Deformation Transferred to the Radial Side

Yoichiro Matsuura, Shogo Okamoto[✉], and Yoji Yamada

Department of Mechanical Science and Engineering,
The Graduate School of Engineering, Nagoya University, Nagoya, Japan
okamoto-shogo@mech.nagoya-u.ac.jp

Abstract. Techniques to measure the deformation of finger pad when rubbing material surfaces are important for the analysis of textural sensations and development of tactile texture displays. However, such measurements are difficult because when the finger pad is in contact with the material surfaces, it is not exposed for measurement. We developed a technique to estimate finger pad shear deformation by using the skin deformation transferred to the side of the fingertip. Good agreement was shown between measured finger pad accelerations and those estimated by our method. The skin deformation of the finger side can be effectively used to estimate that of the finger pad with an average accuracy of 0.93.

Keywords: Accelerometer · Transfer function · Skin impedance

1 Introduction

Texture sensations are evoked during mechanical interaction between finger pads and material surfaces. Hence, measurement of finger pad deformation or shear force during rubbing motion is important for the analysis of tactile sensations and development of tactile texture displays. For example, as a representative display technique, the vibrotactile texture display presents the sense of materials by controlling the spectrum or frequency components of vibratory stimuli imparted to the finger pad [1]. Most of these techniques are based on the measurement of skin vibration or shear deformation of the finger pad during rubbing motion. However, such measurement during active touch is difficult and methods of direct measurement are limited.

The most successful measurement of finger pad slipping on materials appears to be recording with a camera through transparent materials [2], which is not applicable to general materials. Thus, many researchers have attempted or developed indirect measurements of finger pads. For example, Wiertlewski et al. measured the interaction forces between a fixed finger pad and materials moved laterally against the finger pad [3]. The shear displacement of a finger pad can be

---

This study is in part supported by KAKENHI Shitsukan (25135717).

M. Auvray and C. Duriez (Eds.): EuroHaptics 2014, Part II, LNCS 8619, pp. 313–319, 2014.
DOI: 10.1007/978-3-662-44196-1_38

determined from such force measurements, given that the finger pad's mechanical impedance is well specified. The neighboring skin parts reflect the mechanical deformation of the finger pad. Bensmaïa et al. analyzed fingertip vibration during tactile exploration of materials using a Hall effect transducer and magnet [4]. They also attempted to measure the displacement of the skin near the contact surface using a laser velocity sensor [5]. To estimate the load applied to the finger pad, Nakatani et al. measured the radial deformation of the fingertip that results from the Poisson effect when the finger pad is pressed [6]. Tanaka et al. measured the skin vibration propagated to the radial side of the fingertip during exploration of materials using the differential output of two accelerometers [7]. As demonstrated by these studies, it is effective to focus on the skin area close to the finger pad that transfers mechanical deformation to adjacent tissues. Accelerometers are suitable for measuring the fast and fine deformation of skin owing to their excellent frequency response [8]. In a completely different approach, some researchers embedded sensors in pseudo fingers to investigate the internal physics [9,10].

As described above, early studies were not adequate for measuring fast and fine finger pad deformation, or measured related quantities that are indirectly linked to finger pad deformation. In some studies, the attenuation of skin propagation was not considered. In this study, we have developed a fundamental technique to estimate the shear displacement of a finger pad from the displacement propagated to the radial side of the fingertip. Such a technique will lead to a wearable sensor for finger pad shear deformation caused by active exploration of material surfaces.

2 Operating Principle: Transfer Function Between the Side of the Fingertip and Finger Pad

As is shown in Fig. 1, deformation of the side of a fingertip accompanies the finger pad's shear deformation. Given the transfer characteristics between these two types of deformation, it is possible to estimate the shear deformation of the finger pad from the deformation of the side of the fingertip. With the physical model of the finger pad as shown in Fig. 1, the equations of motion of the finger pad and radial side point masses are:

$$m_{\mathrm{pad}}\ddot{x}_{\mathrm{pad}}(t) = k(x_{\mathrm{side}}(t) - x_{\mathrm{pad}}(t)) + c(\dot{x}_{\mathrm{side}}(t) - \dot{x}_{\mathrm{pad}}(t)) + f(t) \qquad (1)$$

$$m_{\mathrm{side}}\ddot{x}_{\mathrm{side}}(t) = -k(x_{\mathrm{side}}(t) - x_{\mathrm{pad}}(t)) - c(\dot{x}_{\mathrm{side}}(t) - \dot{x}_{\mathrm{pad}}(t)) \qquad (2)$$

where m_{pad} and m_{side} are the point masses of the finger pad and radial side, respectively; $x_{\mathrm{pad}}(t)$ and $x_{\mathrm{side}}(t)$ are the respective displacements of the finger pad and radial side; and $f(t)$ is the force that causes the displacement of the finger pad. The transfer function for which the input and output respectively are the displacements $x_{\mathrm{pad}}(t)$ and $x_{\mathrm{side}}(t)$ of the two point masses, is expressed by:

$$G(s) = \alpha \frac{(cs + k)}{m_{\mathrm{side}}s^2 + cs + k} \qquad (3)$$

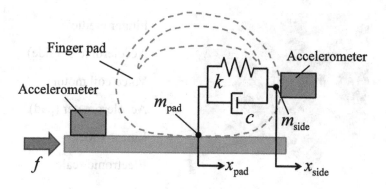

Fig. 1. Spring-mass-damper model of finger skin

where α is a constant value to indicate the transfer ratio between the two skin deformations, which is naturally smaller than 1.0. We use the inverse of this transfer function to estimate $x_{pad}(t)$ from $x_{side}(t)$. Note that the use of $G(s)^{-1}$ for high frequency bands is limited because $G(s)$ is a proper function. Eventually, these processes are similar to the specification of lump mechanical properties of the finger tip, which has been attempted by many research groups thus far (e.g. [11]).

3   Specification of Transfer Characteristics of the Fingertip

3.1   Measurement of the Skin Acceleration

Figure 2 shows an apparatus that generates and measures the acceleration of skin deformation. One accelerometer (2302B, Showa Sokki Co. Ltd., Japan, single degree of freedom) was taped to the radial side of the fingertip, and another was mounted on the vibration generator to which the finger pad was bonded. The vibration was produced by a voice coil motor and its motion was restrained along a low-frictional linear slider. The accelerometers recorded $\ddot{x}_{side}(t)$ and $\ddot{x}_{pad}(t)$, respectively, along the direction of vibration at 5 kHz. During the measurement, the proximal interphalangeal joint was fixed to the base through a clip. The contact force between the finger pad and vibration generator, or pressing force of the finger, was maintained at approximately 1 N by monitoring an electronic scale. Sinusoidal vibratory stimuli, swept across the frequency range of 10–500 Hz, were applied to the finger pad. This trial was repeated 10 times for each of the 5 male voluntary participants in their 20's.

3.2   Frequency Response Characteristics of the Finger Pad

Gain characteristics of the fingertip skin obtained from the five participants are shown in Fig. 3 with a dotted line. These values were computed using the

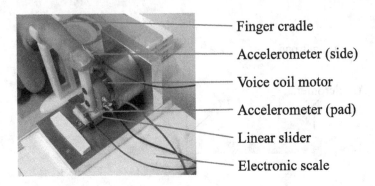

Fig. 2. Experimental apparatus for measuring acceleration of a fingertip

equation $G(f) = 20 \log_{10}(\ddot{x}_{\text{side}}(f)/\ddot{x}_{\text{pad}}(f))$, where f is the frequency. For this computation, the average gains of all of the trials were used for each individual. The peak of the gain characteristic was found in the frequency band of approximately 100–300 Hz. This value is similar to those reported in the literature referenced above [7,12].

3.3   Curve Fitting of the Transfer Function

We fitted transfer functions of (3) to the gain curves of each participant in order to identify the physical parameters m_{side}, k, c, and constant α. Transfer functions obtained from the gain curves are shown in Fig. 3 with a solid line. Identified values and R^2 values for the curve fits are listed in Table 1.

We cannot compare these parameters to those found in other studies because our dynamic model of the finger pad is different from those used by other researchers. However, computed values found in our study are not significantly different from those of other researches under similar conditions. Nakazawa et al. reported mean values of stiffness and damping coefficient of 4.80×10^2 N/m and 2.10 N·s/m, respectively, for the middle finger [13]. Wiertlewski et al. reported a point mass of 1.27×10^{-4} kg, stiffness of 9.13×10^2 N/m, and damping coefficient of 1.327 N· s/m as mean values.

4   Estimation of Finger Pad Deformation from that of the Side of the Fingertip

We validated the method for estimating the acceleration of finger pad deformation from that of the side of the fingertip using leave-one-out cross-validation. We computed how well the transfer function performed on the basis of the results of 9 of the 10 trials in Sect. 3.1 to estimate the output of the trial that was excluded. The computed mean and standard deviation of the goodness of estimation are shown in Table 2. The mean of the goodness of estimation was higher than 0.92, which is a high value for each participant.

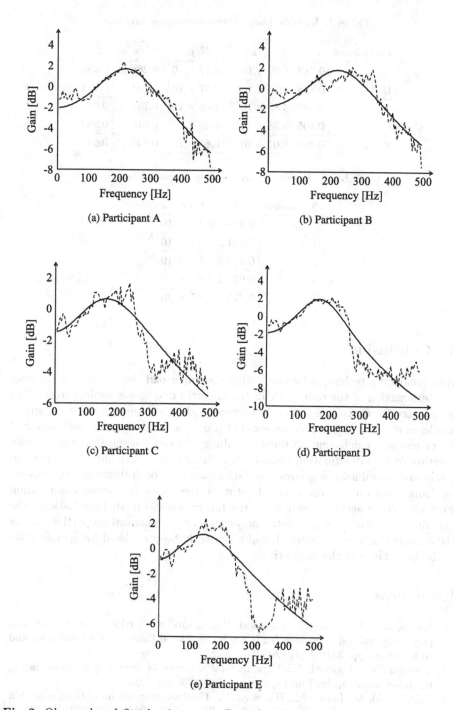

Fig. 3. Observed and fitted gain curves. Dotted and solid curves are observed and fitted characteristics, respectively.

Table 1. Identified parameters of transfer function

Participant	α	m_{side} kg	k N/m	c N·s/m	R^2
A	0.783	1.97×10^{-4}	5.17×10^2	0.288	0.937
B	0.818	1.76×10^{-4}	4.87×10^2	0.284	0.924
C	0.842	3.83×10^{-4}	7.09×10^2	0.731	0.946
D	0.805	5.38×10^{-4}	8.49×10^2	0.612	0.952
E	0.900	5.01×10^{-4}	6.85×10^2	0.845	0.924

Table 2. Result of leave-one-out cross-validation

Participant	Mean $R^2 \pm$ std. dev.
A	$0.938 \pm 2.14 \times 10^{-6}$
B	$0.924 \pm 2.52 \times 10^{-5}$
C	$0.946 \pm 8.09 \times 10^{-6}$
D	$0.952 \pm 1.93 \times 10^{-8}$
E	$0.925 \pm 4.47 \times 10^{-7}$

5   Conclusion

We developed a technique for estimating the finger pad shear deformation from the deformation of the radial side of the fingertip due to mechanical strain that propagates from the finger pad. Practically, this technique leads to a small, accelerometer-based wearable sensor that provides highly accurate estimation of finger pad shear deformation during rubbing motion. We specified the transfer function of skin deformation between the finger pad and radial side of the fingertip and examined the accuracy of estimation by cross-validation. As a result, we found that our approach could estimate the finger pad shear deformation with an average accuracy of 0.93. In the future, we will further sophisticate the experimental equipment and data analysis, and its mechanical properties such as the mass of the accelerometer should thoroughly be considered for specification of the impedance of the finger tip.

References

1. Konyo, M., Tadokoro, S., Takamori, T., Oguro, K.: Artificial tactile feel display using soft gel actuators. In: IEEE International Conference on Robotics and Automation, pp. 3416–3421 (2000)
2. Levesque, V., Hayward, V.: Experimental evidence of lateral skin strain during tactile exploration. In: Eurohaptics, pp. 261–275, July 2003
3. Wiertlewski, M., Losada, J., Hayward, V.: The spatial spectrum of tangential skin displacement can encode tactual texture. IEEE Trans. Robot. **27**, 461–472 (2011)
4. Bensmaïa, S., Hollins, M.: Pacinian representations of fine surface texture. Percept. Psychophys. **67**, 842–854 (2005)

5. Webera, A.I., Saala, H.P., Lieberb, J.D., Chenga, J.W., Manfredia, L.R., Dammann III, J.F., Bensmaïa, S.J.: Spatial and temporal codes mediate the tactile perception of natural textures. PNAS **110**, 17107–17112 (2013)
6. Nakatani, M., Shiojima, K., Kinoshita, S., Kawasoe, T., Koketsu, K., Wada, J.: Wearable contact force sensor system based on fingerpad deformation. In: IEEE World Haptics Conference, pp. 323–328 (2011)
7. Tanaka, Y., Horita, Y., Sano, A.: Finger-mounted skin vibration sensor for active touch. In: Isokoski, P., Springare, J. (eds.) EuroHaptics 2012, Part II. LNCS, vol. 7283, pp. 169–174. Springer, Heidelberg (2012)
8. Okamoto, S., Wiertlewski, M., Hayward, V.: Anticipatory vibrotactile cueing facilitates grip force adjustment. In: IEEE World Haptics Conference, pp. 525–530 (2013)
9. Tomimoto, M.: The frictional pattern of tactile sensations in anthropomorphic fingertip. Tribol. Int. **44**, 1340–1347 (2011)
10. Mukaibo, Y., Shirado, H., Konyo, M., Maeno, T.: Development of a texture sensor emulating the tissue structure and perceptual mechanism of human fingers. In: IEEE International Conference on Robotics and Automation, pp. 2565–2570 (2005)
11. Wang, Q., Hayward, V.: In vivo biomechanics of the fingerpad skin under local tangential traction. J. Biomech. **40**, 851–860 (2007)
12. Lundstrom, R.: Local vibrations-mechanical impedance of the human hands glabrous skin. Biomechanics **17**, 137–144 (1984)
13. Nakazawa, N., Ikeura, R., Inooka, H.: Characteristics of human fingertips in the shearing direction. Biol. Cybern. **82**, 207–214 (2000)

Haptic Rendering of Tissue Stiffness by the Haptic Enhanced Reality Method

Yoshihide Otsuru, Toshio Tsuji, and Yuichi Kurita(✉)

Hiroshima University, 1-4-1 Kagamiyama,
Higashihiroshima, Hiroshima 739-8527, Japan
{y-otsuru,tsuji,kurita}@bsys.hiroshima-u.ac.jp
http://www.bsys.hiroshima-u.ac.jp/

Abstract. We have developed a prototype medical simulator that uses the haptic enhanced reality (HER) method. In this method, the force from a haptic device overlaps the reaction force from a base object. The key idea is to use a base object that has a material property similar to that of the target and to combine the virtual force produced by the haptic device with the reaction force from the base object. To confirm the feasibility of the proposed method, we conducted an experiment in which the stiffness at different points on a target liver was rendered based on the observed luminance at each point.

Keywords: Haptic display · Surgical training simulator · Haptic enhanced reality

1 Introduction

During manual activities, tactile and haptic information is essential for controlling operations and completing tasks. Our research group has proposed the use of force rendering by augmentation to produce a realistic force response even when using a low-performance haptic device [1]. The key idea is to use an object that has a material property similar to that of the target object and to overlap the force produced by the haptic device onto the force of the base object. The haptic sensations produced by the proposed haptic enhanced reality (HER) method are improved because the base object compensates for a force response that is not perfectly modeled or that the device cannot completely produce [2]. Jeon et al. have proposed a method for placing a tumor virtually into silicon for applications to medical simulators by using a haptic augmented realty method [3].

In this study, we explore the feasibility of the HER method using a training simulator system for a minimally invasive surgery. To develop a surgical simulator with haptic feedback, it is necessary to display the force response of elastic tissue. We propose to use an elastic rubber sheet to generate the base stiffness, and enhance the force response of the elastic sheet using a haptic device based on color information from the target tissue.

© Springer-Verlag Berlin Heidelberg 2014
M. Auvray and C. Duriez (Eds.): EuroHaptics 2014, Part II, LNCS 8619, pp. 320–325, 2014.
DOI: 10.1007/978-3-662-44196-1_39

2   Method

2.1   Haptic Display System

Figure 1 shows an overview of the prototype developed for the surgical training system. The system is composed of a haptic device, an image projector, an elastic rubber sheet, and a box training system with a camera. Surgical forceps for a minimally invasive surgery were attached to the end of the manipulator of the haptic device (Geomagic Touch, 3D Co.,Ltd.). To monitor the force response, a force sensor (Nano5/4, BL Autotech Co.,Ltd.) was attached to the forceps. The mobile projector (M115HD, DELL Co.,Ltd.) displays an image of the target object on an elastic rubber sheet. The elastic rubber sheet was placed on the box training system for a minimally invasive surgery (EndWork Pro II, KYOTOKAGAKU Co.,Ltd.). A web camera (HD Pro Webcam C920T, Logicool Co.,Ltd.) captured the workspace of the forceps and displayed the image on a screen placed in front of the user.

In the HER method, the force generated by the haptic device F_{dev} is augmented by the reaction force of the base object F_{base}, and the total force $F_{\text{user}} = F_{\text{dev}} + F_{\text{base}}$ is displayed to the user. In this study, the reaction force of the elastic sheet was modeled by $F_{\text{base}} = K_{\text{sheet}}\, x$, where K_{sheet} is the stiffness constant of the elastic sheet and x is the penetration depth. The force generated by the haptic force was modeled by $F_{\text{dev}} = K_{\text{dev}}\, x$, where K_{dev} is the stiffness constant that changes depending on the endpoint position of the forceps. The penetration depth was determined by monitoring the endpoint position of the forceps, which was calculated by a coordinate transformation from the endpoint of the haptic device.

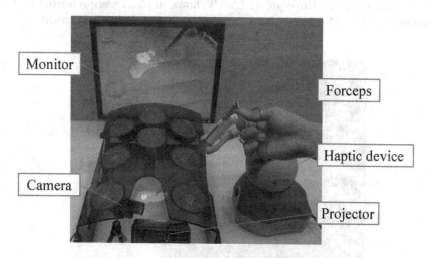

Fig. 1. Overview of the haptic display system.

2.2 Experiment

In this experiment, the force response of a human liver was rendered. It has been reported that the average Young's modulus of the normal human liver is 0.243 MPa [4] and that the average Young's modulus of a tumor (focal nodular hyperplasia) is approximately 2.5 times harder than that of a normal human liver [5]. Therefore, the Young's modulus of the abnormal tissue was set to 0.608 MPa. Based on these values, we defined the stiffness parameters of the normal and abnormal tissue as $K_{target}^{normal} = 0.102$ N/mm and $K_{target}^{abnormal} = 0.255$ N/mm, respectively. An elastic rubber sheet with a stiffness of $K_{sheet} = 0.061$ N/mm was used as the base object. To render the target force response, the haptic device generated a virtual force based on the difference in the stiffness parameters ($K_{dev} = K_{target} - K_{sheet}$).

Figure 2 shows an image of the human liver used in the experiment. The liver had a tumor, which is located by the box in Fig. 2. In the figure, the luminance of the abnormal tissue is higher than that of normal tissue. To display a realistic stiffness based on color information in the image, we defined the stiffness parameter K_{target} in terms of the luminance of the image. As shown in Fig. 3, K_{dev} was linearly interpolated from the representative luminance values of the normal and abnormal tissue. Figure 4 shows an overview of the experimental equipment. A linear actuator (SGAM26-105, SIGMAKOKI Co., Ltd.) was attached to the haptic device and provided vertical palpations. The palpation depth was 10 mm, and the palpation velocity was 10 mm/s.

3 Results and Discussion

Force responses at the three points (A–C) shown in Fig. 2 were rendered by the proposed method. Point A is hard (abnormal tissue), Point B is medium, and

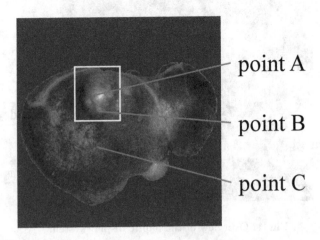

Fig. 2. Image of a human liver with a tumor at point A.

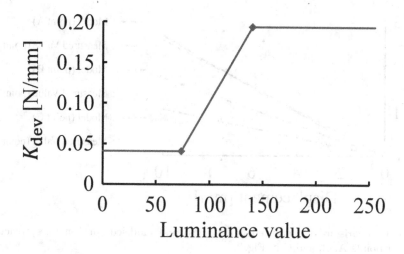

Fig. 3. Correlation of device stiffness constant, K_{dev}, with luminance of tissue.

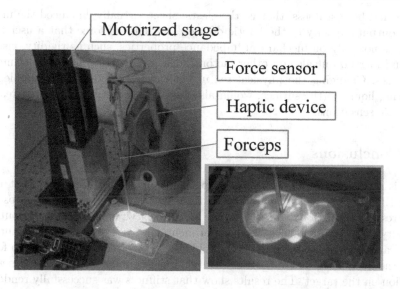

Fig. 4. Overview of the experimental equipment

Point C is soft (normal tissue). Figure 5 shows the desired force response (dashed lines) and the measured force response (solid lines). The desired force responses were determined based on luminance values at the positions where the endpoint of the forceps was located. The experimental results show that the proposed method successfully rendered target stiffness.

The proposed HER method can improve the performance of force rendering by using a base object. In this experiment, an elastic sheet provided the base stiffness, and the haptic device compensated for the difference between the

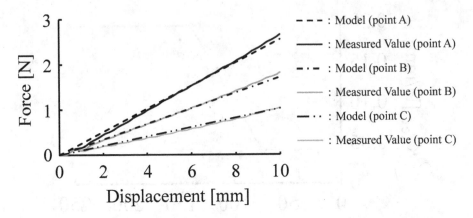

Fig. 5. Comparisons of measured (solid lines) and modeled (broken lines) reaction forces at points A, B, and C in Fig. 2.

target and base stiffness, that is, the elastic sheet virtually enhanced the maximum output capacity of the haptic device. The sense of force that a user feels depends not only on mechanical impedance properties, such as rigidity, viscosity, and inertia, but also on other factors, such as adherence and discontinuous responses. Changing the physical texture of the base object, for example, by applying liquid to the surface, would also be effective for enhancing the reality of haptic sensations.

4   Conclusions

In this study, we developed a prototype medical training simulator that uses the HER method. In this method, the force from a haptic device overlaps the force response from a base object, so the base object virtually extends the output capacity of the haptic device. In an experiment, the force response from a human liver was rendered by using an elastic rubber sheet to enhance the reaction force from the liver. Target stiffness was based on image luminance that changes with position on the target. The results show that stiffness was successfully rendered at three different points on the target tissue. In future work, we will upgrade the training simulator to learn the procedures to be followed in a minimally invasive surgery.

References

1. Ikeda, A., Kurita, Y., Tamaki, T., Nagata, K., Ogasawara, T.: Creating virtual stiffness by modifying force profile of base object. In: Kappers, A.M.L., van Erp, J.B.F., Bergmann Tiest, W.M., van der Helm, F.C.T. (eds.) EuroHaptics 2010, Part I. LNCS, vol. 6191, pp. 111–116. Springer, Heidelberg (2010)

2. Kurita, Y., Ikeda, A., Tamaki, T., Nagata, K., Ogasawara, T.: Haptic augmented reality interface using the real force response of an object. In: The 16th ACM Symposium on Virtual Reality Software and Technology, pp. 83–86 (2009)
3. Jeon, S., Choi, S., Harders, M.: Rendering virtual tumors in real tissue mock-up using haptic augmented reality. IEEE Trans. Haptics 5, 77–84 (1981)
4. Carter, F.J., Frank, T.G., Davies, P.J., McLean, D., Cuschieri, A.: Measurements and modeling of the compliance of human and porcineorgans. In: 10th IEEE International Symposium on High Performance Distributed Computing, pp. 231–236. IEEE Press, San Francisco (2001)
5. Yeh, W., Li, P., Jeng, Y., Hsu, H., Kuo, P., Li, M., Yang, P., Lee, P.H.: Elastic modulus measurements of human liver and correlation with pathology. Ultrasound Med. Biol. 28(4), 467–474 (2002)

Simulation of Soft Finger Contact Model with Rolling Effects in Point-Contact Haptic Interfaces

Gionata Salvietti[1](✉), Monica Malvezzi[2], and Domenico Prattichizzo[1,2]

[1] Department of Advanced Robotics, Istituto Italiano di Tecnologia,
Via Morego 30, Genoa, Italy
`gionata.salvietti@iit.it`
[2] Department of Information Engineering and Mathematics,
Università degli Studi di Siena, Siena, Italy
`{malvezzi,prattichizzo}@dii.unisi.it`

Abstract. Computation of contact point trajectories and forces exchanged between two bodies in contact are relevant to several disciplines. The solutions proposed in the literature are often too complex to be implemented in real time simulations, especially if rolling effects are considered. In this chapter, an algorithm for fast simulation of soft-finger contact model with rolling effects is proposed. The main idea is to use Euler angle decomposition algorithm to quantitatively describe the torque exchanged about the normal at the contact point and the motion of the contact point due to rolling. The proposed algorithm is validated with simulations and a preliminary application to point-contact haptic interface is proposed.

Keywords: Contact modeling · Soft finger model · Rolling effects

1 Introduction

One of the key features of the human fingertips is the ability to resist moments, up to a torsional friction limit, about contact normal. Considering friction between the finger and the object, forces can be exerted in any direction that is within the friction cone for the contact and moreover, a torque about the normal to the contact plane can be applied [1]. This model is usually known in literature as *soft finger contact model* [2]. It is worth nothing that human fingers are actually surfaces, and manipulation of an object by a set of fingers involves *rolling* of the fingers along the object surface. Rolling can be defined as an angular motion between two bodies in contact about an axis parallel to their common tangent plane [3].

In this chapter, we took inspiration from the interaction finger/object to simulate a soft-finger contact model with rolling effects in Haptics. Algorithms for contact simulation needs computation efficiency to guarantee to the user a correct perception of a stiff surface [5]. This makes usually intractable the

© Springer-Verlag Berlin Heidelberg 2014
M. Auvray and C. Duriez (Eds.): EuroHaptics 2014, Part II, LNCS 8619, pp. 326–333, 2014.
DOI: 10.1007/978-3-662-44196-1_40

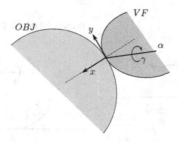

Fig. 1. Representation of the virtual finger touching a sphere

real-time solution of classical equation describing rolling effect [1]. Another issue in simulating soft contact is represented in Fig. 1. The contact model assumes that torque is exerted only about the normal to the contact surface [4,7], but in general, if only one finger is simulated to be in contact with an object, the exerted torque can be about a generic direction.

The contribution of this work is to extend the model of the soft-finger contact taking into account also possible rolling phenomena at the contact and keeping the same computational efficiency of point-based algorithm. The main idea is to use Euler angle decomposition algorithms to quantitatively describe the torque exchanged between the two bodies and the motion of the contact point due to rolling. We experimentally verified that our approach is more efficient in terms of computation time with respect to the integration of classical equation regulating rolling contacts. Moreover, we realized an application for Haptics, where we simulated the interaction between a fingertip and a plane.

The chapter is organized as it follows. In Sect. 2 the algorithm used is described in detail. In Sect. 3 validation of the method and experiment results on a simplified virtual environment are presented. Finally in Sect. 4 conclusion and future work are outlined.

2   Description of the Algorithm

The main target of this work is to find a computationally simple, but reliable algorithm for the simulation of the soft finger contact when rolling effects are considered. Although soft finger model implies a local deformation of the contact bodies, in this algorithm we do not evaluate the entity of such deformation, and the related stress distribution, and consider the contact bodies as undeformable. The effect of finger softness is represented only by the spin moment generated when the angular speed between the contact bodies have a component normal to the surfaces in the contact point.

The basic idea is to represent the relative displacement between contact bodies as a sequence of infinitesimal rotations. For each integration step, we use an Euler decomposition to get the rotational contribution along each axis of the reference frame built on the contact point.

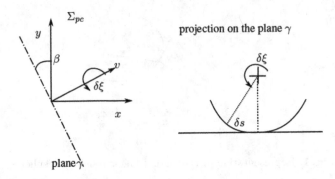

Fig. 2. Simplified model of the contact point evolution during rolling between a sphere and a plane with respect to a generic axis.

In the following we will assume that the contact forces fulfill the friction constraints, i.e. the contact force is inside the friction cone and then the contact surfaces have a relative rolling motion and no sliding is present at the contact point [9]. Let us assume that the relative rotation variation between the reference frames Σ_s and Σ_p can be represented by the Euler angles $\delta\phi$, $\delta\theta$ and $\delta\psi$, evaluated about the z, y and x axes, respectively.

The first component of the relative rotation $\delta\phi$ is adopted to evaluate the spin moment, that is reproduced by the haptic interface (HI)

$$\tau_n = k_z \delta\phi, \tag{1}$$

where k_z is a stiffness value that depends on surface properties and geometry.

The components $\delta\theta$ and $\delta\psi$ are employed to evaluate the contact point displacement, by means of the approximated method described below and shown in Fig. 2. Let γ be a plane, normal to the contact tangent plane, obtained by rotating the plane defined by the equation $x = 0$ by an angle β defined as

$$\beta = \text{atan2}\,(\delta\theta, \delta\psi)\,. \tag{2}$$

On each surface, the contact point will move along the intersection between the surface itself and the γ plane, the length of the contact point path is given by

$$\delta s = \frac{1}{k_\gamma}\delta\xi = \frac{1}{k_\gamma}\sqrt{\delta\theta^2 + \delta\psi^2} \tag{3}$$

where k_γ is the relative curvature between the contact surfaces, evaluated with respect to the plane γ. For instance, if the contact surfaces are two spheres, with radii R_1 and R_2 respectively, the curvature is constant: $k_\gamma = \frac{1}{R_1} + \frac{1}{R_2}$. In the example analysed in this paper, shown in Fig. 2, in which a sphere is rolling on a flat surface, we have $k_\gamma = \frac{1}{R}$, where R is the sphere radius. The main steps of the proposed algorithm used to evaluate the relative motion between rolling surfaces are summarized in the Algorithm 1.

```
1: for  each integration step  do
2:     compute frames at contact point
3:     compute rotation axis and angle
4:     compute Rotation Matrix using Rodriguez's formula
5:     compute Euler decomposition to get angles along contact frame δφ, δθ, δψ
6:     compute the Moment along the normal τₙ = k_z δφ
7:     compute contact point position on the plane
8:     update sphere position
9: end for
```

Algorithm 1: Computation of contact point position using Euler decomposition.

3   Application to Haptics

3.1   Validation of the Algorithm

In order to validate our method, we compared the obtained trajectories of the contact points with those obtained by directly integrating the equation of rolling reported in [1]. For the integration, a four-five order Runge-Kutta algorithm was adopted (ODE45). All the simulations were realized using Matlab R2009a over a 2.4 GHz Intel Core 2 Duo, 4 GB RAM.

We simulated a sphere rolling on a plane. The Euler angles were computed starting from the rotation unit vector α and the rotation angle γ (Fig. 1) as described in the following. First, the rotation matrix $R(\alpha, \gamma)$ was computed using the Rodriguez formula [1]

$$R(\alpha, \gamma) = \alpha \alpha^T + (I(3 \times 3) - \alpha \alpha^T) \cos \gamma + S(\alpha) \sin \gamma, \tag{4}$$

where the superscript T means the transpose matrix and $S()$ is the skew operator. Then, the Euler angles were computed using the Roll-Pitch-Yaw convention [6] as

$$\delta\theta = atan2 \left(\sqrt{r_{13}^2 + r_{23}^2}, r_{33} \right) \tag{5}$$

$$\delta\psi = atan2 \left(\frac{r_{31}}{\sin \delta\theta}, \frac{r_{32}}{\sin \delta\theta} \right) \tag{6}$$

$$\delta\phi = atan2 \left(\frac{r_{13}}{\sin \delta\theta}, \frac{-r_{23}}{\sin \delta\theta} \right), \tag{7}$$

where r_{ij} represents the components of the matrix $R(\alpha, \gamma)$. Note that the above representation has singularities in $\delta\theta = 0 \pm k\pi$. Moreover, equation (5) can be computed also as $\delta\theta = atan2(-\sqrt{r_{13}^2 + r_{23}^2}, r_{33})$. Anyway, we experimentally verified that this representation leads to a wrong approximation, so the solution proposed in (5) was always adopted.

In the sphere-plane simulation reported in Fig. 3 we considered, for each sampling step, $\delta\phi = 0.05$rad, $\delta\theta = 0.02$ rad, $\delta\psi = 0.03$ rad. The radius of the sphere was 10mm. The sampling time was 0.01 s, the simulation time was 1 s. The

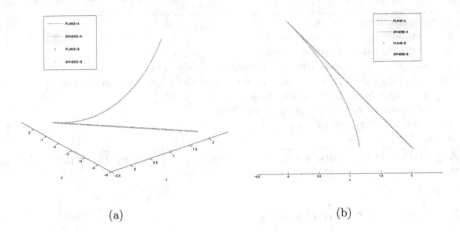

(a)   (b)

Fig. 3. (a) Trajectory of the contact point on the plane and on the sphere obtained with the classical formulation (A) and with the proposed algorithm (B); (b) Projection of the trajectories on the XY plane.

computation time necessary to perform the simulation using classic equations was 0.35 s, while using the proposed approach was 0.01 s. The maximum difference between the trajectories calculated with the two methods were 0.004 mm, 0.004 mm, 0.001 mm along the plane reference system axis x, y, z respectively.

3.2   Experiment with CHAI 3D

The proposed algorithm has been exploited in a haptic rendering application, due to the low computational load and to the simplicity of the implementation. We used an Omega.6 HI [10] with three active translation and 3 passive rotation. For this reason, in this first experiment the moment exerted on the haptic pointer, due to the soft finger model adopted for the contact point, can not be reproduced by the HI. The value of the friction torque above the contact normal direction is only visually shown. The whole application has been realized using the CHAI 3D library [11].

The contact detection and the force computation are important issues that have to be addressed during haptic simulations. We used a proxy-probe method [12] to generate the translational forces, while torque along the normal was computed as presented in Sect. 2. We reproduce the fingertip as a sphere and we simulate the interaction with a plane. The virtual reality scenario is shown in Fig. 4. Rolling conditions hold if the contact force comply with the friction constraints, and, in particular, if it is included in the friction cone. If the tangential component of the contact force exceed the friction limit, rolling conditions do not hold any more and the surfaces begin to slide each other. Different contact conditions have to be considered, and the contact mode transition is regulated by a Finite State Machine where the contact state can be one of the following: *rolling*, *contact breaking* or *sliding* [8]. The contact state transition can be pre-

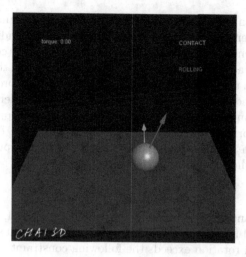

Fig. 4. Implementation with CHAI-3D. The white sphere represents the fingertip interacting with plane in the virtual reality.

dicted by the relative acceleration and contact forces that are computed from the measurements given by the HI. The condition are summarized as follows, where the subscripts R and S denote rolling and sliding contacts, N and T refer to the normal and tangential contact direction and μ_i is the coefficient of static friction and μ_{Si} is the coefficient of sliding friction and f if the force applied by the HI

- If $f_{i_N} = 0$ and $a_{i_N} > 0$, then contact is broken;
- If $f_{i_{NR}} > 0$, $\mu_i^2 f_{i_{NR}}^2 - f_{i_{TR}}^2 \geq 0$, $a_{i_{NR}} = 0$, $a_{i_{TR}} = 0$, then rolling is kept;
- If $f_{i_{NR}} > 0$, $\mu_i^2 f_{i_{NR}}^2 - f_{i_{TR}}^2 = 0$, $a_{i_{NR}} = 0$, $a_{i_{TR}}^2 \neq 0$, the rolling is switched to sliding;
- If $f_{i_{NS}} > 0$, $\mu_{Si}^2 f_{i_{NS}}^2 - f_{i_{TS}}^2 = 0$, $a_{i_{NS}} = 0$, then sliding is kept;
- If $f_{i_{NS}} > 0$, $\mu_{Si}^2 f_{i_{NS}}^2 - f_{i_{TS}}^2 \geq 0$, $a_{i_{NS}} = 0$, $v_{i_{TS}} = 0$, then sliding is switched to rolling.

In a real scenario, if the fingertip is rolled over the plane the contact point moves both on the finger and the plane. If we implement a classic proxy-probe method, only the contact point on the virtual finger moves, while that on the plane remain fixed. Practically, no rolling effect is considered and the finger slips over the plane. This phenomenon is typical in HI where there are three active DoFs displaying translational forces and three passive DoFs measuring the orientation of the device end–effector, such as the Omega.6. To overcome this effect and increase the realism in the haptic experience, we considered a spring-damper connection between the position computed through our algorithm and the actual position of the probe. This solution leads to a contact point velocity different from zero also when rolling state is detected. We solved this issue allowing sliding condition only when a force tangent to the contact plane is exerted having an arbitrary module but the sign concordant with the sign of the displacement generated by the rolling. In fact, rolling condition would never be detected if a generic tangential force was enough to switch to sliding since to update the contact point position in rolling we consider the spring-damper connection between the actual and computed position of the probe. When sliding condition is detected, no spring-damper connection is considered.

Sliding condition can be detected also when the torque applied to the probe is such that the corresponding contact force exits from the friction cone. The threshold condition between rolling and sliding can be computed equaling the applied torque to the tangential force exerted, i.e.

$$\Delta\theta \, r \, k_\tau = f_N \mu_s$$

where $\Delta\theta$ is the angular displacement measured by the HI, k_τ is the virtual stiffness considered for torque computation and r is the radius of the probe. So that, if the applied rotation exceeds the following constraint

$$\Delta\theta_{max} = \frac{f_N \mu_s}{k_\tau r},$$

rolling condition is switched to sliding.

4   Conclusions

This chapter presents a fast computation method for the simulation of soft finger contact model that considers also rolling effects. The algorithm is based on the Euler angle decomposition, used to quantitatively describe the torque exchanged about the normal at the contact and the motion of the contact point due to rolling and the evolution of contact point. The algorithm has been tested and validated with numerical simulations in which the sphere-plane rolling contact was considered. The results obtained with the simplified computation method were compared with those obtained by the integration of the classical rolling formulation, reported in [1]. The numerical results showed a consistent reduction of the computational time, while the precision in the contact point path during the simulation was not significantly affected. The availability of a fast method to simulate rolling effects and soft finger contact models could have different applications. In this paper we presented an example, in which the proposed model was adopted to simulate, by means of an haptic interface, the contact between a virtual fingertip and a plane. The application of the proposed algorithm to haptics is still going on, further validations will be analyzed, the limits of the computational method will be furthermore investigated and correction strategies, needed to avoid the drift of the predicted trajectories, will be assessed.

Acknowledgment. The research leading to these results has received funding from the European Union Seventh Framework Program FP7/2007-2013 under the grant agreement 601165 of the project "WEARHAP" and under the grant agreement 270460 of the project "ACTIVE".

References

1. Murray, R.M., Li, Z., Sastry, S.S.: A Mathematical Introduction to Robotic Manipulation. CRC, Boca Raton (1994)
2. Prattichizzo, D., Trinkle, J.C.: Grasping. In: Siciliano, B., Khatib, O. (eds.) Springer Handbook of Robotics. Springer, Heidelberg (2008)
3. Johnson, K.L.: Contact Mechanics. Cambridge University Press, Cambridge (1987)
4. Barbagli, F., Frisoli, A., Salisbury, K., Bergamasco, M.: Simulating human fingers: a soft finger proxy model and algorithm. In: Proceedings of the 12th International Symposium on HAPTICS '04, pp. 9–17 (2004)
5. Barbagli, F., Prattichizzo, D., Salisbury, J.K.: A multirate approach to haptic interaction with deformable objects single and multipoint contacts. Int. J. Robot. Res. **24**(9), 703–715 (2005)
6. Goldstein, H.: Classical Mechanics, 2nd edn. Addison-Wesley, Reading (1980)
7. Frisoli, A., Barbagli, F., Ruffaldi, E., Salisbury, K., Bergamasco, M.: A limit-curve based soft finger god-object algorithm. In: 14th Symposium on Haptic Interfaces for Virtual Environment and Teleoperator Systems, pp. 217–223 (2006)
8. Yin, Y., Sugimoto, T., Hosoe, S.: MLD modeling and MPC of hand manipulation. IEICE Trans. Fundam. Electron. Commun. Comput. Sci. **E-88-A**(11), 2999–3006 (2005)
9. Li, Z., Canny, J.: Motion of two rigid bodies with rolling constraint. IEEE Trans. Robot. Autom. **6**(1), 62–72 (1990)
10. On-line. http://www.forcedimension.com
11. On-line. http://www.chai3d.org
12. Ruspini, D.C., Kolarov, K., Khatib, O.: The haptic display of complex graphical environments. Comput. Graph. **31**(Annual Conference Series), 345–352 (1997)

Haptics Processing Unit Software Architecture for Transportable High Dynamics Force-Feedback Coupling

Annie Luciani[2], Nicolas Castagne[1(✉)], and James Leonard[1]

[1] ICA Laboratory, Grenoble INP, Grenoble, France
{nicolas.castagne,james.leonard}@imag.fr
[2] ACROE and ICA, Grenoble INP, Grenoble, France
annie.luciani@imag.fr

Abstract. This article is a contribution to today's stream of research studying the interests of employing a Haptics Coprocessing Unit (HPU) for force-feedback interaction, and possible core features and hardware/software architectures of such HPU. It introduces a force-feedback software framework, called CORDIS-In, powered by a DSP-based HPU. CORDIS-In's design was driven so as to obtain a transportable platform, however able to provide very high dynamics force-feedback coupling. It provides time deterministic synchronous computing of any mass-interaction physics-based network, possibly at high simulation rates, high precision and programmability in adjusting the mechanical coupling of the user and the simulation through the device, and generic communication protocols with the host.

Keywords: High dynamics force feedback · Time deterministic synchronous computing · Haptics processing unit · HPU features and software architecture

1 Introduction: Tendencies for Force-Feedback Architectures

Simulation platforms including force-feedback interaction have driven much research effort in the past 30 years. A number of hardware/software architectures have been proposed and experimented, with various general organizations and core features.

Three possible axes to support an analysis of this variety are: 1/ the qualities searched for the dynamics of the haptic interaction through the force-feedback device; 2/ the modeling/simulation principles employed; 3/ the positioning in regards to time determinism for the whole computations and to the synchronous or asynchronous nature of the algorithms' temporal skeleton. Though they may overlap in some cases, two main tendencies emerge when employing this analysis grid.

The first tendency mainly relates to cases when Haptics is approached from a Computer Graphics or Virtual Reality point of view. In this context, haptics is namely employed with the aims to add the sense of touch to previously visual-only solutions, by *"rendering"* deformable 3D scenes through the force-feedback device, and to enhance *interactivity* with such models. Primary tasks for the user are *exploring* 3D shapes spread over the 3D space by gesture, and *sensing* some mechanical properties

© Springer-Verlag Berlin Heidelberg 2014
M. Auvray and C. Duriez (Eds.): EuroHaptics 2014, Part II, LNCS 8619, pp. 334–342, 2014.
DOI: 10.1007/978-3-662-44196-1_41

and behaviors. Naturally, on the side of the modeling/simulation principles, emphasis remains first on 3D models and on graphics animation. Haptics is mainly tailored as an extension, by incrementing such models with additional parts dedicated to *haptics rendering*. A typical multi-core simulation architecture then consists in splitting the whole virtual scene into *various sub-systems* [1, 2] – possibly one per sensorial modality (Fig. 1). Each of the subsystems typically runs in its own thread, at an average and possibly varying frequency considered appropriate for the targeted modality – e.g. 500 Hz to 3 kHz for the part of the virtual object or environment directly related to the haptic probe, and less for the larger graphics part. All of the subsystems exchange information with each other through *asynchronous* protocols. Exemplary systems corresponding to this tendency are [3–5].

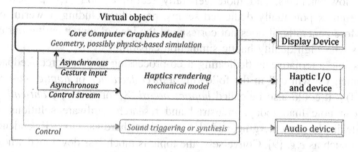

Fig. 1. A usual architecture for « haptics rendering » in VR-systems.

In comparison to the first, the second tendency puts the emphasis on the *dynamics qualities* of the force-feedback interaction, rather than on spatial qualities. Focus is on obtaining high quality *mechanical coupling* of the user with the full simulacra through the force-feedback device, and *coherent exchange of mechanical energy*, as defined for example through Cadoz' *instrumental interaction* paradigm [6]. In such contexts, the core simulation architecture ideally features a *unique* mechanical model, in charge of coherently generating all of the dynamic phenomena. Importantly, to reach coherent dynamics, the bandwidth of the simulation should consider the cut-off frequency of all the targeted phenomena. Also, low latencies, time determinism, and respect of a fully synchronous computing skeleton, are considered as key factors.

It should be noted that both of these two approaches can possibly lead to multi-sensory platforms, including graphics and audio along with force-feedback. However, and to further exemplify the importance of dynamics issues to differentiate between these two tendencies, one might with caution say that, in the usual VR-type approach, the general goal is achieving a "haptics rendering" of a core graphics 3D scene, whereas, in the instrumental approach, the general idea is rather providing a "graphics/audio output" of a core haptics/mechanical simulation.

2   Haptics Processing Units for High Dynamics Force-Feedback

When instrumental interaction and high dynamics haptics are searched (2nd tendency), one of the difficulties of hardware/software architecture design is providing haptics-specific computation means along with other services within a single computing platform. On the one hand, instrumental interaction calls for time-deterministic synchronous computing. On the other hand, such hard real time constraints should integrate seamlessly with many other computing tasks, possibly including audio and graphics outputs, and more generally with any sort of multi-task operating system services. Obtaining both is still a challenge.

A high power solution consists in employing a real-time operating system, so as to guarantee low latencies, and more generally real-time QoS [1, 7]. However, this solution requires potentially dedicated setups, possibly including powerful computer servers. More generally, it does not correspond the idea of incrementing our everyday computers with high quality haptic simulation capabilities.

A possible alternative is dedicating a co-processing unit to force-feedback interaction, which we will call in the following a *force-feedback* or *haptics co-processing unit* (HPU) – it could also be called *haptics board* [8], or *gesture front-end*.

One can note that, today, industrial and research hardware solutions aimed at vibrotactile display are emerging, and also sometimes hardware for VR-tendency force-feedback - such as *e.g.* [9]. Conversely, the topic is much less developed when aiming high dynamics force-feedback instrumental coupling. In this case, if any co-processing facility is used, they are usually servo or axis boards, inherited from Robotics. Indeed, the issue is still very open.

Obviously, it is hardly possible today to evaluate whether or not HPU hardware and software should and could become one day generic components of computer platforms - such as GPU and soundboards have now existed for many years for graphics and audio. Anyhow, from a theoretical viewpoint, the notion of HPU would make it possible to obtain a particularly high quality of reactive real time computing service for instrumental haptic loops, while freeing CPUs for other related or non related purposes, for example heavy graphics. Symmetrically, it would possibly enable incrementing any standard general-purpose hardware and operating system with high dynamics force-feedback, hence has potential to give birth to the concept of *transportable high dynamics force-feedback instrumental simulation platform*. Furthermore, system designers could be able to choose the HPU from a collection of possible co-processors, ranging from *e.g.* cheap micro-controllers to full CPU-powered co-processors, to adapt to the needs of the tasks at hand in regards to haptics interaction.

Globally speaking, HPU for high dynamics force-feedback should emphasize dynamics, hence time determinism – whereas, in comparison, GPU rather emphasize spatiality, geometry, and parallel computing. As a first rough overview of the needs, we propose that a HPU should at least provide high precision low latency input/output means on the side of the haptic device, computation means dedicated to in/out signal conditioning, communication with the host and, importantly, physics-based computation. This raises a range of technological and scientific challenges and questions, including: 1/ the categories of physics-based modeling and simulation methods that may, or should, be employed to express, then compute, the haptics/mechanical model; 2/ the software elements in charge of interconnecting the haptic device with the simulated model; 3/ the latencies, frequencies, temporal computing scheme, and computing power required; 4/ the categories of communication protocols needed to exchange data streams with the host, so as to inter-connect the haptics/mechanical simulation with other processes.

In the past years, in the framework of our ERGON_X force-feedback platforms, we have experimented with many hand-made implementations of numerous one-shot software for specific haptics scenes.

ERGON_X platforms are equipped with a specific HPU (TORO PCI board by Innovative Integration, equipped with a TMS320C6711 DSP and AD/DA converters), and with force-feedback devices from the ERGOS panoply.[1] ERGOS technology [10] enables having, on a single device, any number of independent one-dimensional force-feedback parallel axes – typically 4 to 12 high dynamics DoFs. *Mechanical morphologic adaptors* can then be mounted onto one, two, or several of these 1D independent DoFs, so as to provide various morphologies for the end effectors: piano-keyboard layouts, pliers, 3D and 6D joystick, 2D bow-like end effectors, etc. The current work integrates adaptation to such morphological variability, hence could adapt to most force-feedback platforms.

Recently, we started reshaping these many past experimental works into a generic software architecture, called CORDIS-In, spread over the HPU (haptics AD/DA transduction chains; fully synchronous, modular, high frequency physics-based computation; communication with the host…) and the host (loading and control of the DSP; communication with the DSP; graphics outputs…). The following reports on this new software architecture.

3 Software Architecture and Typical Usage Walk-Through

CORDIS-In software architecture consists in a series of C ++ packages spread over the host and the HPU. It globally behaves as a client/server system, where the HPU stands for a haptics simulation server, managed through a host proxy (Fig. 2).

The host proxy of CORDIS-In is in charge of HPU startup and monitoring. On the host, the CORDIS-In programming user first builds a full description of the whole model and parameters (*description phase*). This concerns: 1/ specifying the DSP's simulation loop properties, especially the simulation frequency; 2/ describing the transduction chain; 3/ specifying the physics-based model: structure, physical parameters, and initial state; 4/ setting up the chosen communication protocols that will stream data to the host during simulation. Then, these data are uploaded onto the HPU (*loading phase*); they are however also kept into the host's memory so as to help interpretation of the data streamed during simulation.

---

[1] http://ergostechnologies.com

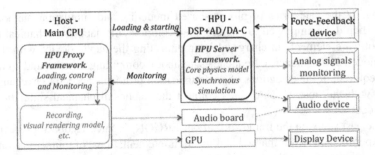

Fig. 2. General view of our Host/HPU architecture. Use of a GPU for graphics display of the simulated model, and of a soundboard, are possible. The HPU can optionally output through reserved DAC audio, and other analog control signals (e.g. to display on an oscilloscope).

Finally, the host starts the HPU synchronous real time loop (*simulation phase*). During simulation, data are streamed from the HPU to the host, to provide visual feedback and other monitoring, and save trace of the haptic interaction to drive.

On the HPU, the C ++ software structure features 3 main packages (Fig. 3).

Simulation steps are computed within a DSP software interruption, triggered by the HPU's hardware clock or an external clock. Depending on the model, our choice for the haptics simulation rate ranges from 1 kHz to the still-unique value of 44100 Hz.

Within each single strictly paced time step, computation goes through: 1/ acquisition of positions of each DoF of the haptics device on the ADC converters; 2/ calibration of the position; 3/ application of chosen real-to-virtual viewpoint laws on the positions, so as to adapt real-virtual impedances; 4/ computation of the position of the "virtual device", so as to invert the kinematics of the real morphologic adapters mounted on the device; 5/ computation of the physics-based mass-interaction model (new positions of each mass, then new forces of each interaction); 6/ spreading of the force onto each DoF of the device, by computation of the "virtual device", so as to

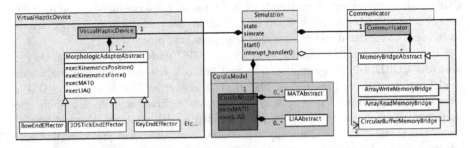

Fig. 3. Software architecture of CORDIS-In's HPU part. The main class, Simulation, manages the HPU's state automaton, the simulation frequency, the HPU's hardware clock, and the starting and organisation of the synchronous real time loop. The package CordisModel handles the physics-based mass-interaction model (Sect. 4). The package VirtualHapticDevice allows representing the haptic device; it manages ERGOS devices morphologic variability, and metrological adaptation of real-virtual correspondences (Sect. 5). The Communicator package implements the selected communication protocols with the host (Sect. 6).

retro-invert the kinematics of the real morphologic adapters mounted on the device; 7/ application of the chosen virtual-to-real viewpoint laws on the forces; 8/ calibration of the forces; 9/ DAC conversion of the forces; 10/ management of communication protocols with the host. 11/ optionally, the HPU's software can output audio and monitoring signals (to e.g. display on an oscilloscope) through reserved DAC channels.

4 Masses-Interactions Physics-Based Engine

The question of principles and methodology aimed at physics-based modeling for force-feedback interaction is still open. Most works, especially in the context of Virtual Reality or Computer Graphics (first "tendency" in the Introduction of this article) are rooted on solid or continuum mechanics to add physics-based behaviors on top of a geometric model. Employed techniques can then be, for example, collision detection algorithms, finite elements or diffuse elements methods, mass-spring meshes, possibly with adaptative resolution to provide higher cues around the position of the virtual haptic probe. Such methods have in common the facts that they rely on geometry, and are usually expensive to compute.

When searching for high dynamics mechanical coupling and instrumental force feedback interaction (second "tendency" in the Introduction of this article), mass-interaction mechanical modeling has proved to be a particularly relevant alternative, since it focuses more on dynamics of the phenomena than on their geometry, and enables synchronous and time deterministic computing. Indeed, CORDIS-In's physics-based engine relies on the concept of masses-interactions physical networks, as specified in the CORDIS-ANIMA formalism [11].

In this formalism, building a model consists in assembling masses, named MAT, and interaction functions, named LIA. MAT and LIA algorithms can consider a simulation space of 1 to 3 dimensions, allowing adapting the network to the dimensionality of the modeled phenomena. Interactions can be chosen among a large library of interaction profiles: linear or non-linear elasticity, linear or non-linear viscosity, cohesive Van der Waals interactions, plastic interactions, state-graph-defined interaction profiles, etc. The MAT-LIA assembly constitutes a computable *physics network*.

Starting from our standard CORDIS-ANIMA simulation engine, we tailored optimized releases for the DSP architecture. This included re-shaping of the major data structures, especially by aligning data into vectorized buffers, dedicated management of memory allocation, and redesign of some of the C-code of the modules' physical algorithms. The simulation engine now exists in two variants: one dedicated to 3D mass-interaction models, and one to 1D models. In comparison to the hand-made code previously employed for all of our haptic scenes on ERGON_X platforms, we have managed to provide a fully modular engine able to support any masses-interactions network, with any MAT-LIA topology, and with any category of mass and interaction elements, while maintaining 70 % to 90 % of the global efficiency. As a rough evaluation of the obtained efficiency, the 1D engine supports physics networks made of up to up to 140 MAT/LIA at audio rate (44100 Hz – see [12] for detail); and the 3D variant supports more than 330 MAT/LIA at 1050 Hz.

5 Coupling of the Simulacra with the Haptic Device

The package VirtualHapticDevice enables representing the real force-feedback device employed and providing precise management of the coupling of the user with the simulated model through the haptic device. On the one side, its instance lists the 1D DoFs used on the device's *base*, and describes each of the real *mechanical morphological adapters* actually mounted onto these DoF to provide specific ergonomics to the end effectors. On the other side, each of the employed end effectors is reflected in the mass-interaction physics-based model through one or several MAT elements. During simulation, this package's algorithms are in charge of:

1/ *rooting* of the various DoFs onto the appropriate virtual morphologic adapters;

2/ *inverse kinematics* for the employed morphologic adapters, so as to compute position of the corresponding MAT from the A/D positions acquired on the device, and reciprocally to spread the computed forces over these DoF. Each of the possible morphologic adapters (keyboard, stick, grasps...) corresponds to two specific algorithms.

3/ management of a series of calibration algorithms, on both directions of the transduction chain, so as to provide the user with metrological control of the real/ simulation correspondences of the user/simulation coupling, by performing impedance matching between the real world and the simulation, adapted with the physical models employed – see e.g. [12] for detail.

6 Host/HPU Communication Protocols

To provide flexible means for host/HPU data exchange, generic communication protocols are proposed on top of the host-post interface (HPI) of the DSP-powered HPU. Two basic means, handled through the Communicator class, enable passing commands from the host to the HPU, and sharing the state automaton of the HPU onto the host. Additionally, three communication protocols are provided: direct access to the HPU memory in write and in read mode, and HPU-to-host FIFO communication through circular buffers.

Two streams are proposed by default during simulation, both through the circular buffers protocol: 1/ the positions of all the MAT of the model are sent to the host, according to a chosen monitoring frequency that subdivides the simulation frequency, e.g. to enable graphics display of the model on the host; 2/ positions and forces exchanged through the AD/DA converters are sent to the host, to enable recording and later detailed analysis of the gesture interaction trace. In addition, the user can declare other communication streams, so as for example to upload debugging information on the host, or provide direct monitoring of other chosen model's state variables.

7 Exemplary Usages of CORDIS-in, and Conclusion

As a proof of concept, CORDIS-In was first employed to redesign each of the dozen haptic scenes that had been previously hand-crafted for ERGON_X platforms.[2]

---

[2] See our previous publications and http://aicreativity.eu/node/49.

These include for example various audio-graphics models for art installations, audio-haptics models – such as bowing models, various models designed for pedagogy of Nanophysics, research experiments, etc. Furthermore, the existence of a generic and self-pedagogical programming framework considerably reduced programming complexity, hence triggered new modeling possibilities by various non-expert programmers. Additionally, existence of a fully modular physics simulator made it possible to interconnect the ERGON_X platforms with mass-interaction modelers,[3] hence allowing to interactively design, then compute, any sort of mass-interaction models, with both high quality force feedback interaction, and visual/audio outputs [12].

More generally, we propose CORDIS-In as a contribution to the today's stream of research that questions the interests and the needed core features related to the concept of Haptic Processing Units. In this framework, this article has briefly, but widely, reviewed our recent proposals regarding HPU software: 1/ mass-interaction physics-based system to root physics-based modeling and DSP-based computation; 2/ modeling of the force-feedback device so as to adapt to the end effectors' morphology and manage the coupling of the user with the simulation through the device, with metrological performance; 3/ needs in terms of communication protocols with the host; and 4/ general host/HPU software architecture.

As a currently worked-on perspective, we are experimenting on extending CORDIS-In to standardize possibility of parallel computing of the physics-based simulation over the HPU and a dedicated host, powered with a real-time operating system, while strictly maintaining synchronous computing, such as experimentally proposed in [6]. This would dramatically increase the available computing power. Other perspectives include extending the temporal skeleton of the mass-interaction engine so as to enable physically rigorous multi-clock synchronous simulations, and incorporating support for many force-feedback devices into CORDIS-In.

Acknowledgments. This research was supported by the French Agence Nationale de la Recherche through the cooperative project DYNAMé - ANR-2009-CORD-007, the French Ministry of Culture and Grenoble Institute of Technology. We thank Jean-Loup Florens and Claude Cadoz for sharing with no reserve their high level of expertise through exiting discussions, and Stéphane Boeuf for the quality of his concepts and computer implementations.

References

1. Kern, T.A.: Engineering Haptic Devices: A Beginner's Guide for Engineers, 1st edn. Springer, Berlin (2009)
2. Salisbury, K., Conti, F., Barbagli, F.: Haptic rendering: introductory concepts. IEEE Comput. Graphics Appl. **24**(2), 24–32 (2004)
3. Conti, F., Barbagli, F., Morris, D., Sewell, C.: CHAI 3D: an open-source library for the rapid development of haptic scenes. In: IEEE World Haptics Proceedings, Pisa, Italy (2005)
4. Montgomery, K., et al.: Spring: a general framework for collaborative, real-time surgical simulation. Stud. Health Technol. Inform. **85**, 296–303 (2002). IOSPress

---

[3] Short description and references: http://aicreativity.eu/node/24; http://aicreativity.eu/node/25.

5. Jung, H., Cotin, S., Duriez, C., Allard, J., Lee, D.Y.: High fidelity haptic rendering for deformable objects undergoing topology changes. In: Kappers, A.M., van Erp, J.B., Bergmann Tiest, W.M., van der Helm, F.C. (eds.) EuroHaptics 2010, Part I. LNCS, vol. 6191, pp. 262–268. Springer, Heidelberg (2010)
6. Castet, J., Florens, J.-L.: A virtual reality simulator based on haptic hard constraints. In: Ferre, M. (ed.) EuroHaptics 2008. LNCS, vol. 5024, pp. 918–923. Springer, Heidelberg (2008)
7. Van der Linde, R.Q., Lammertse, P., Frederiksen, E., Ruiter, B.: The hapticMaster, a new high-performance haptic interface. In: Proceedings EuroHaptics, Ecosse, pp. 1–5 (2002)
8. Couroussé, D.: Haptic board. In: Enaction and Enactive Interfaces, a Handbook of Terms. In: Luciani, A., Cadoz, C. (eds.) Enactive System Books, pp. 126–127 (2007). ISBN 978-2-9530856-0-48
9. Akahane, K., Hamada, T., Yamaguchi, T., Sato, M.: Development of a high definition haptic rendering for stability and fidelity. In: Jacko, J.A. (ed.) Human-Computer Interaction, Part II, HCII 2011. LNCS, vol. 6762, pp. 3–12. Springer, Heidelberg (2011)
10. Florens, J.L., Luciani, A., Castagne, N., Cadoz, C.: ERGOS: a multi-degrees of freedom and versatile force-feedback panoply. In: Proceedings of EuroHaptics, pp. 356–360 (2004)
11. Cadoz, C., Luciani, A., Florens, J.L.: Responsive input devices and sound synthesis by simulation of instrumental mechanisms: the cordis system. Comput. Music J. **8**, 3 (1984)
12. Leonard, J., Florens, J-L., Cadoz, C., Castagné, N.: Exploring the role of dynamic audio-haptic coupling in musical gestures on simulated instruments. In: Auvray, M., Duriez, C. (Eds.): EuroHaptics 2014, Part I, LNCS, vol. 8618, pp. 469–477 (2014)

Geometrically Limited Constraints
for Physics-Based Haptic Rendering

Thomas Knott[(✉)] and Torsten Kuhlen

Virtual Reality Group - RWTH Aachen University, Aachen, Germany
{knott,kuhlen}@vr.rwth-aachen.de
http://www.vr.rwth-aachen.de

Abstract. In this paper a single-point haptic rendering technique is proposed which uses a constraint-based physics simulation approach. Geometries are sampled using point shell points, each associated with a small disk, that jointly result in a closed surface for the whole shell. The geometric information is incorporated into the constraint-based simulation using newly introduced geometrically limited contact constraints which are active in a restricted region corresponding to the disks in contact. The usage of disk constraints not only creates closed surfaces, which is important for single-point rendering, but also tackles the problem of over-constraint contact situations in convex geometric setups. Furthermore, an iterative solving scheme for dynamic problems under consideration of the proposed constraint type is proposed. Finally, an evaluation of the simulation approach shows the advantages compared to standard contact constraints regarding the quality of the rendered forces.

1 Introduction

The haptic sense is an important feedback channel in humans' everyday life interaction with objects. To transfer the benefits and possibilities of tactile and force cues to virtual environments, force and torque feedback have to be synthesized computationally; this is usually referred to as haptic rendering. If the interaction should be physically realistic, for instance, include inertia and frictional contact, the haptic rendering can try to emulate the correct dynamic behavior of the objects and their interactions. This is typically done by cycling between a collision detection and a time stepping component. The latter formulates a dynamic problem and updates the objects with an according solution. In this, the incorporated collision or contact information has a strong influence on the resulting dynamic problem and hence, the movements of objects. Corrective time stepping methods use only contacts which are already in a touching or penetrating state [2]. The drawback is that penetrations are unavoidable and that they depend on the length of the simulation time step and object velocities [7]. Preventive time stepping methods try to avoid this by also incorporating contacts that only possibly occur in the currently processed time step [10]. A problem then arises due to the contact model commonly used in time stepping algorithms

© Springer-Verlag Berlin Heidelberg 2014
M. Auvray and C. Duriez (Eds.): EuroHaptics 2014, Part II, LNCS 8619, pp. 343–351, 2014.
DOI: 10.1007/978-3-662-44196-1_42

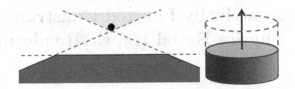

Fig. 1. (Left) An over-constrained configuration space. Dark gray depicts the geometry, light gray depicts the configuration space, and the dot depicts the valid position closest to the geometry. (Right) A limited contact constraint. The dark volume depicts the prohibited space.

for real time applications [2,6,10], where contact constraints are defined via infinite halfspaces which extend beyond the geometric features that the contact represents (see Fig. 1). Therefore, the configuration space, which describes the space objects can move to, is reduced more than necessary. This can directly influence the outcome of a timestep as depicted in Fig. 1. Here, the point would be trapped above the surface in a cone created by the over-constrained contact configuration space. The problem can be reduced by using collision detection methods that select a contact set on the basis of a good anticipation of the objects' movements. Nevertheless, this anticipation is always based on heuristics, for instance, the unconstrained movement of objects [5], and does not incorporate the full dynamics of the scene especially no collision response[1]. This can result in inappropriate contact sets. Therefore, some time stepping techniques employ a temporal back tracking to iteratively refine such contact sets considering intermediate dynamic problems [6]. As such a process is computationally expensive it is usually not employed for haptic simulations.

In this paper, a preventive time stepping method for single-point haptic rendering is proposed and evaluated which alleviates the problem using a different approach. Geometrically Limited contact constraints are introduced which are only active in a limited region that depends on the geometric features they represent (see Sect. 3.2). The used geometric features are disks (see Fig. 1) which are assembled into point shells to represent objects. In this, the configuration space is reduced only by a more appropriate amount better reflecting the actual geometry. Furthermore, an iterative solver is presented which is able to solve the dynamic problems created by the time stepping approach with consideration of the special constraint type (see Sect. 4).

2   Related Work

The term haptic rendering refers to algorithms that generate forces reflecting interaction with virtual objects; a good introduction and overview of different techniques can be found in [8]. Due to stability reasons, most approaches use a virtual coupling approach where a proxy object is coupled to the input of the

---

[1] Otherwise it would already solve the time stepping problem.

haptic device [1]. The behavior of the proxy object is determined by the rendering algorithms and is, in case of physically based methods, simulated with consideration of the laws of physics. In this, the proxy can be a single-point, like in [12], or more recently in [4] and the approach proposed in this paper. Other methods use rigid bodies [11] or deformable objects [5] as proxies. Some of the approaches are designed for static environments, for instance [11], others allow the interaction with deformable environments, e.g., [3], where friction is neglected or, e.g., [5], where it is included. Beside quasi-static approaches [3,11], all methods include a method to progress the simulation in time. This typically consists of a collision detection and a time stepping that updates the object states based on a temporal integration approach with consideration of contacts. For collision detection a multitude of approaches are available [6] which work with different geometric representations like triangles or voxels [6,8,11]. Another option is to sample surfaces using point shells, which is popular in haptic rendering due to its high performance [3,11], and therefore, also used in the approach described in this paper. Time stepping methods differ in the way collisions are handled [6], some use penalty forces [3,11] others bilateral [12] or unilateral [5,9] constraint-based approaches. The latter can be furthermore distinguished in reactive and preventive methods. reactive methods incorporate only contacts after they occur, for instance [2], and lead to penetrations by design, similar to penalty methods. Preventive methods alleviate this problem and consider also contacts that may occur in the following time step. This contact set can be generated using proximity instead of collision queries like in [10] and the approach presented in this paper, or, by performing a collision query with an object state calculated with a free motion without consideration of any contacts [5]. As described in the introduction, preventive methods can suffer from the problem of an over-constrained configuration space. This was tackled by [7] for polyhedral geometries, where contact constraints of neighboring convex polygons are combined using an intersection operation. By not applying the usual union, the configuration space is only reduced by a smaller more correct amount. In this paper, an approach with a similar goal that works on point shells instead of polygons and does not incorporate any neighborhood processing is presented.

3   Methods

In following section the chosen fundamental methods of dynamics and their integration into a time stepping approach are described for reasons of reproducibility and a better understanding of the proposed extension with limited constraints described in the following.

3.1   Dynamics and Time Stepping Fundamentals

The proposed simulation approach is based on the Newton-Euler equations to define the dynamic behavior of objects. All occurring degrees of freedom are stacked into state vectors q and v for generalized position and velocity.

$$M(q,t)\dot{v} = F(q,v,t), \ \dot{q} = Gv \tag{1}$$

M denotes the mass matrix, F the occurring forces, and G relates the velocities to the derivative of the positions. As commonly done, we use a virtual coupling approach and distinguish between the haptic interaction point (HIP), which directly corresponds to the input of the haptic device, and the virtual interaction point (VIP). In the approach described in this paper, the VIP is treated as a mass point which is coupled via a spring-damper to the HIP and its state is simulated according to the above mentioned equations of motion. The forces produced by the coupling to the HIP are defined as:

$$F_{VC}(q,v) = -k(q_{VIP} - q_{HIP}) - d(v_{VIP} - v_{HIP}), \tag{2}$$

where k and d are the device specific stiffness and damping parameters, and $q_{VIP}, q_{HIP}, v_{VIP}$, and v_{HIP} are positions and velocities of HIP and VIP.

Normal contact forces are based on the Signorini's contact model [8] and defined via a complementarity condition:

$$0 \leq \lambda \perp \psi(q,v,t) \geq 0, \tag{3}$$

where λ defines the magnitude of the contact force which is normal to the contact surface and ψ is a gap function describing the distance between the bodies with respect to the contact.

The simulation of friction is done similar to [9] using a 4-sided pyramid approximation of the Coulomb's friction cone defined by two tangential vectors t_1 and t_2. Although more directions would create a more accurate behavior, good results can also be achieved by aligning the friction pyramid to the current velocity projected into the contact space [9]. The according approximative Coulomb constraints are then:

$$\|\gamma_{t_i}\| \leq \mu\lambda \perp v_{t_i} \geq 0, \tag{4}$$

for each direction, where γ_{t_i} defines the friction force in the direction of tangent t_i and v_{t_i} is the velocity in the tangent direction, while the right inequality should prevent the friction forces to reverse the motion.

The method to simulate the progress in time builds upon the Stewart-Trinkle formulation [10]. A semi-implicit Euler integration step is performed with a fixed time step h and a linear approximation of the forces. Contact forces are integrated using the method of Lagrange multipliers enforcing the constraints at the end of the time step. The discrete equation of motion is formulated on a velocity level:

$$M dv = h(F_{t_i} + h\frac{\partial F}{\partial q}G dv + \frac{\partial F}{\partial v}dv + J^T\lambda + H^T\gamma), \tag{5}$$

$$0 \leq \lambda \ \perp \ J(v_{t_i} + dv) + \frac{\psi_{t_i}}{h} \geq 0, \tag{6}$$

$$\|\gamma\| \leq \lambda \ \perp \ H(v_{t_i} + dv) \geq 0, \tag{7}$$

where dv is the velocity change in the time step and v_{t_i}, F_{t_i}, and ψ_{t_i} are the values of the corresponding states or functions at the beginning of the time step. The contact forces λ and γ as well as the gap functions ψ are stacked into vectors. $J = \frac{\partial \psi}{\partial v}$ is the contact normal Jacobian which maps between configuration space and contact normal space. The matrix H is defined analogously for the friction constraints. For more details on the definition of J and H, we refer the interested reader to [6].

Equation 5 can be reformulated into the form $Ax = b$ and, combined with the constraints, describes a Mixed Linear Complementarity Problem (MLCP). Its solution $x = dv$ is used to update object velocities and positions.

3.2 Geometrically Limited Constraint Formulation

In the described approach above, each constraint reduces the configuration space by an infinite halfspace (see Fig. 1 left). In convex contact situations this over-constraines the configuration space to less than the actual available space defined by the geometries of the objects. This leads to the problem that the dynamics are simulated wrongly and that objects may get stuck at convex corners.

To tackle this problem, we propose a constraint type which reduces the configuration space only by a limited amount. The idea behind this approach is, that the contact constraints correspond to geometric features of the colliding objects, which only have a finite size, and therefore, the according constraints should also be restricted to a similar region. In case of geometries defined via point shells, this region can be defined by an extrusion of the surface area associated with the point shell point along its normal direction (see Fig. 1 right). To this end, a coordinate system around the contact point is defined using two tangential vectors t_1 and t_2. The tangential functions $\tau_1(q, v, t)$ and $\tau_2(q, v, t)$ describe the contact position with respect to these tangential directions and can be utilized to define constraints limited to specific regions:

$$0 \leq \lambda \perp (\psi \geq 0 \text{ or } \tau_1^2 + \tau_2^2 \geq r^2), \tag{8}$$

for a cylindrical region with r as its radius. The equation defines, that, if there is a gap between the objects or if the contact is outside the active region of the constraint, the contact forces need to be zero. Analogously, other constraint regions can be defined, for instance, for a box region.

Considering the semi-implicit nature of the time stepping method described in the previous section, the tangential functions τ_1 and τ_2 are approximated similarly to the gap function:

$$\tau \approx \frac{\tau_{t_i}}{h} + L_t(v_{t_i} + dv), \tag{9}$$

where τ contains both tangential functions of all contacts and $L_t = \frac{\partial \tau}{\partial v}$ is a mapping from the configuration space to the tangential contact space. Additionally, the constraint equations can be reformulated to match the standard complementarity format, therefore, the *or* operation can be expressed using a maximum function [7]:

$$0 \leq \lambda \perp max(\psi, \tau_1^2 + \tau_2^2 - r^2) \geq 0, \qquad (10)$$

In case of the box region constraint, it would be possible to reformulate the equation into a standard LCP using additional dummy variables [7]. As this increases the size of the problem which has to be solved and furthermore, is not applicable for the cylindrical region constraints, a different method to solve the arising problem is described in the next section.

4   Solver for Dynamic Problems with Limited-Constraints

In the following, a common way to solve the MLCPs arising in time stepping methods is described and then extended to handle the proposed limited constraints. In real-time applications the MLCPs are often solved using a Projected Gauss-Seidel (PGS) Method or similar methods based on other matrix splitting methods like Jacobi or Successive-over-Relaxation [6].

To this end, the MLCPs have to be reformulated into LCPs utilizing the Schur complement. The degrees of freedom of the resulting system are the contact forces λ and γ, thus, the equations to be solved have a reduced number of equations. The following linear complementarity problems can be formulated for the normal constraints using this technique:

$$0 \leq \lambda \perp \underbrace{\left[hJA^{-1}J^T \ hJA^{-1}H^T\right]}_{A_\lambda} \begin{bmatrix}\lambda \\ \gamma\end{bmatrix} + \underbrace{\left[J(v_{t_i} + hA^{-1}F_{t_i}) + \psi_{t_i}/h\right]}_{b_\lambda} \geq 0, \quad (11)$$

where every row of the system corresponds to one normal constraint. In this, the changes in the gap functions induced by constraint forces λ and γ are anticipated under consideration of the dynamics of the simulation objects A_λ. A similar LCP can be formulated for the frictional constraints:

$$\|\gamma\| \leq \mu\lambda \perp \underbrace{\left[hHA^{-1}J^T \ hHA^{-1}H^T\right]}_{A_\gamma} \begin{bmatrix}\lambda \\ \gamma\end{bmatrix} + \underbrace{\left[H(v_{t_i} + hA^{-1}F_{t_i})\right]}_{b_\gamma} \geq 0. \quad (12)$$

In general a Projected Gauss-Seidel method solves such equation system of type $Ax + b \geq 0 \perp x \geq 0$ by iterating over all rows of A. In this, for each row i, all variables are fixed beside the one in focus, x_i, for which a new value that leads to a zero residual for row i under consideration of the current values of all other variables is calculated. In case x_i should be constrained, the value is projected into the valid range. This process is performed several times for all contacts until the solution converges or a defined upper number of iterations is reached.

For the two LCPs described above, the computation of friction and normal forces can be done in an interlaced way as done e.g. by [8,9]. In this, one handles all constraints of one contact i, i.e., normal and friction, en block. At first a solution is calculated for the normal force λ_i then, the constraints for the friction LCP, which depend on the current λ_i, are updated and finally, the according solutions for the frictional forces $\gamma_i^{1,2}$ are calculated. Usually, this process is iterated for one contact several times before handling the next contact.

For the integration of the geometrically limited constraints, the Schur complement is again utilized to obtain a formulation of the approximative tangential functions solely depending on the contact forces λ and γ:

$$\tau \approx \underbrace{\left[hLA^{-1}J^T \ hLA^{-1}H^T\right]}_{A_\tau} \begin{bmatrix} \lambda \\ \gamma \end{bmatrix} + \underbrace{\left[L(v_{t_i} + hA^{-1}F_{t_i}) + \tau_{t_i}/h\right]}_{b_\tau} \quad (13)$$

In this, two consecutive rows define the values of the tangential functions τ_1 and τ_2 for each contact. These can be evaluated during the solving process described above and used to determine if a constraint should be active. The decision is made for a contact each time it is handled in the interlaced solving procedure. The full algorithm for solving the problem with geometrically limited frictional contacts proceeds as follows, where $A[i, .]$ refers to the ith row of A and x to a stacked version of the variables λ and γ:

```
algorithm Modified_Projected_Block_Gauss-Seidel
    λ = γ = 0
    for k iterations or until convergence of λ and γ
        for each contact i iterate 3 times²
            r_τ1 = Compute_Residual_Without_i(A_τ,x,b_τ,2i)
            r_τ2 = Compute_Residual_Without_i(A_τ,x,b_τ,2i + 1)
            if ( r²_τ1 + r²_τ2 <= (r/h)²)
                r_λ = Compute_Residual_Without_i(A_λ,x,b_λ,i)
                λ[i] = r_λ/A_λ[i,i]
                if λ[i] < 0 then λ[i] = 0
            else
                for j = 0 to number of friction directions−1
                    r_γj = Compute_Residual_Without_i(A_γ,x,b_γ,2i + j)
                    γ[2i + j] = r_γj/A_γ[2i + j, 2i + j]
                    Project ‖γ[2i + j]‖ ≤ μλ_i
    return x
function Compute_Residual_Without_i(A,x,b,i)
    return b − A[i,.] * x + A[i,i] * x[i]
```

5   Results

An experiment was performed to show the benefit of the proposed techniques using the scene depicted in Fig. 2. The introduced haptic rendering approach with geometrically limited constraints is compared to a rendering that uses infinite half planes as constraints. The environment collision geometry is modeled using a point shell which was sampled using a Poison-disk sampling with a radius of 7 mm.

---

[2] The iteration number is chosen similar to [9] and gives good results.

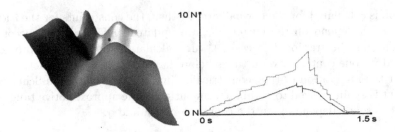

Fig. 2. (Left) Scene including the VIP as a blue sphere and the static environment. (Right) Coupling force magnitude plots. The blue plot corresponds to the simulation using the proposed limited constraints, red using infinite constraints (color figure online).

To prevent holes in the surface, the radius for the constraints was chosen conservatively 2 mm larger. The collision detection delivered a contact set of all point shell points in a radius of 20 mm around the VIP. The mass of the VIP was set to 20 g, the virtual coupling stiffness to 200 N/m, and the damping to 0.008 Ns/m. Measurements were performed on a common workstation with a 4 core Intel Xeon CPU with 2.53 GHz and 12 GB RAM using a Phantom Omni haptic device. The computation time of haptic simulation time steps stayed always below 1 ms.

For comparison, a HIP trajectory was recorded with a fast movement over the environment surface and then simulated with both methods. The magnitudes of the rendered forces are shown for both methods in Fig. 2. The plot of the simulation using infinite half planes as constraints shows jumps in the displayed forces. These artifacts result from temporally over-constraint configuration spaces in convex contact situations. Here the VIP is restricted to a position above the surface resulting in larger coupling forces, which then suddenly decrease when one of the over-constraining constraints gets out of the contact set and the VIP snaps closer again. The plot of the simulation using the proposed limited constraints is much smoother and lacks the discontinuities of the forces nearly completely.

6   Discussion and Conclusion

In this paper a haptic rendering approach that uses a newly introduced physics-based time stepping approach utilizing additional geometric information for a preventive collision response was presented. The proposed contact model uses constraint formulations which are restricted to regions reflecting the extend of the geometric features they correspond to. An experiment showed that the problem of over-constrained configuration spaces is alleviated by the presented technique. In this, the presented iterative solving scheme showed to solve the dynamic complementarity problems created by the proposed time stepping within the temporal bound implied by the haptic application.

Acknowledgments. This work received funding from the European Unions Seventh Framework Pro- gramme for research, technological development and demonstration under grant agreement no 610425.

References

1. Adams, R., Hannaford, B.: Stable haptic interaction with virtual environments. IEEE Trans. Robot. Autom. **15**(3), 465–474 (1999)
2. Anitescu, M., Potra, F.A.: Formulating dynamic multi-rigid-body contact problems with friction as solvable linear complementarity problems. Nonlinear Dyn. **14**, 231–247 (1997)
3. Barbic, J., James, D.: Six-DoF haptic rendering of contact between geometrically complex reduced deformable models. Trans. Haptics **1**(1), 39–52 (2008)
4. Chan, S., Blevins, N.H., Salisbury, K.: Deformable haptic rendering for volumetric medical image data. In: World Haptics Conference (WHC), 2013, pp.73–78, 14–17 April 2013
5. Duriez, C., Member, S., Dubois, F., Kheddar, A., Andriot, C.: Realistic haptic rendering of interacting deformable objects in virtual environments (2006)
6. Erleben, K., Sporring, J., Henriksen, K., Dohlman, K.: Physics-based Animation, June 2005
7. Nguyen, B., Trinkle, J.: Modeling non-convex configuration space using linear complementarity problems. In: International Conference on Robotics and Automation (2010)
8. Otaduy, M., Lin, M.: Haptic Rendering: Foundations, Algorithms, and Applications. AK Peters, Wellesley (2008)
9. Otaduy, M.A., Tamstorf, R., Steinemann, D., Gross, M.: Implicit contact handling for deformable objects. Comp. Graph. Forum **28**, 559–568 (2009)
10. Stewart, D., Trinkle, J.: An implicit timestepping scheme for rigid body dynamics with inelastic collisions and coulomb friction. Int. J. Numer. Methods Eng. **39**, 2673–2691 (1996)
11. Wan, M., McNeely, W.: Quasi-static approximation for 6 degrees-of-freedom haptic rendering. In: IEEE Vis. 2003, p. 34. IEEE Computer Society, Oct 2003
12. Zilles, C.B., Salisbury, J.K.: A constraint-based god-object method for haptic display. In: International Conference on Intelligent Robots and Systems (1995)

Vibration and Subsequent Collision Simulation of Finger and Object for Haptic Rendering

Shoichi Hasegawa$^{(\boxtimes)}$, Yukinobu Takehana, Alfonso Balandra,
Hironori Mitake, Katsuhito Akahane, and Makoto Sato

Tokyo Institute of Technology, R2-20, 4259 Nagatsuta-cho, Yokohama, Japan
{hase,takehana,poncho,mitake}@haselab.net,
{kakahane,msato}@hi.pi.titech.ac.jp
http://haselab.net

Abstract. Humans can discriminate object's materials [5,7,9] and tapping position [8] perceiving tapping vibrations. Susa *et al.* [4] proposed to simulate natural vibration of object to present arbitrary structured objects. However, the vibration of the tapping finger and subsequent collisions between the finger and the object are not simulated.

This paper proposes a simulation model for tapping, which considers finger's vibration motion and subsequent collisions between the object and the finger. Experimental results show that the proposed method renders realistic event based forces including impact impulse, decayed waves and subsequent collisions.

Keywords: Vibration haptic rendering · Simulation model for tapping · Subsequent collision

1 Introduction

Tactile perception of finger tip skin detects signals up to 1 kHz with the highest sensitivity around 250 Hz. These mechanoreceptors also differentiate some complex signals [2].

While the bandwidth of the haptic interaction systems remain limited, it is not easy to reproduce contact vibrations by a closed-loop-based haptic rendering. Akahane *et al.* [1] uses a 10 kHz control loop and a stiff virtual coupling to reproduce decayed sinusoidal contact vibration of around 50 Hz. A 10 kHz control loop requires special control circuits and local haptic renderings.

Therefore, rather than reproducing contacts by a closed loop, many researches present realistic contacts feeling by presenting event based open loop vibrations [5–7,9]. They measure the vibrations, and then present them by playback or mathematically fitted functions. Therefore, they do not reproduce the variation by the tapping positions.

On the other hand, Susa *et al.* proposed to simulate natural vibrations of the objects to present their arbitrary structure, in an event based manner [4]. However, they do not simulate the vibration of the tapping finger and subsequent

© Springer-Verlag Berlin Heidelberg 2014
M. Auvray and C. Duriez (Eds.): EuroHaptics 2014, Part II, LNCS 8619, pp. 352–359, 2014.
DOI: 10.1007/978-3-662-44196-1_43

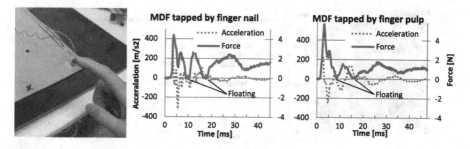

Fig. 1. Left: the measurement setup; An MDF plate is tapped by finger pulp and nail. Right: measured acceleration and force.

collisions between the finger and the object. Therefore, the rendered vibration is too simple and is not very realistic. This paper extends Susa *et al.*'s work [4] to simulate not only the object's vibration but also the finger's vibration and the subsequent collisions between the finger and the object.

2   Vibration Measurement

Structures and materials can be discriminated from simulated vibrations [4]. However, the vibration is not very realistic in some cases. Therefore, we measured the acceleration of a tapped plate and the force between the finger and the plate (Fig. 1). The accelerometer was *35 A* from *ENDEVCO* and the force sensor was *FlexiForce A201 1 lb* from *TekScan*. The weight of the accelerometer is small (1.1 g). The plate fixed by two screw on a heavy iron block is made of MDF (plywood like material) and the dimensions were $0.6 \times 0.6 \times 0.05$ m. The result shows that there are some periods when the finger floats from the plate.

In addition to the floating of the finger, the tapping feel is too soft when tapping happens around a fixed point. Therefore, Susa *et al.* [4] measured the vibration of user's finger when tapping objects and added some waveform to reflect the effect of the finger's vibration. Here, we measured finger's vibration when tapping non vibrating objects to observe the motion of the finger (Fig. 2). We attached the same accelerometer on the user's index fingernail using quick drying glue. The tapped objects are 6 mm $\times$ 30 mm $\times$ 300 mm aluminum and wooden bar. We test tapping by the finger pulp and the finger nail. The vibrations of the tapped bar were also measured by a laser displacement meter (*LK-G30* from *KEYENCE*) to confirm the order of the object's vibration. It was confirmed, that the plate's vibration is at least 100 times smaller than the finger's vibration. Figure 2 (right side) shows the measured acceleration of a tapping. All waveform showed strongly damped oscillations of 1.0 to 2.4 ms periods. In addition, the waveform depends both on the tapping ways and on the material of the tapped bar. The waveform tapped by finger nail might reflect the secondary collisions.

From the observations above, we were motivated to simulate the finger's motion on the vibrating objects.

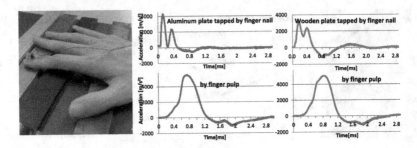

Fig. 2. Left: the measurement setup; Several bars fixed on a heavy weight iron plate are tapped by finger pulp and nail. The photo shows the aluminum bar tapped by finger pulp. Right: measured acceleration during a tapping.

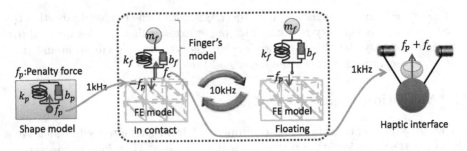

Fig. 3. Overview of the proposed simulation and haptic rendering

3   Proposed Method

The measurement result (Fig. 2) suggests that the vibration of the finger will be reproduced by a mass-spring-damper model with a large damping coefficient. Therefore, the finger dynamics were modelled by mass-spring-damper. In addition, when the normal force is smaller than 0, the tip of the spring-damper, which corresponds to finger's surface, will float from the object surface. Therefore, this phenomenon is also simulated. The object's vibration is simulated by a FE model with modal analysis [4]. To increase the stability of the finger's simulation, the update rate of the finger's simulation is set to 10 kHz, while object's FE model is simulated in 1 kHz (Fig. 3).

3.1   Object Shape Rendering

The penalty force f_p, used to present the object's shape, is calculated from a spring model between the God object [10] and the haptic pointer, whose position immediately reflects the haptic interface's position. This spring is far softer than the spring model for finger to ensure the stability of the haptic interaction. The God object's position is updated with the initial object shape and not regarding the deformation caused by the vibration, because the caused deformation is small and ignorable for the soft spring model between the God object. For the penalty force spring coefficient k_p, the haptic pointer position p_h and the god object position p_g, the penalty force f_p is given by:

$$f_p = -k_p(p_h - p_g).\tag{1}$$

3.2 Object's Vibration

The object's vibration is simulated by a FE model with modal analysis [4]. The first contact impulse is added to the FE model, while subsequent contact forces are not added to the FE model to ensure the stability (but added to the user's finger).

3.3 Finger's Vibration

This section describes the simulation of the finger's vibration and the subsequent collisions. The dynamics of the finger is modelled by a mass-spring-damper. In this model, both the spring and the damper are connected to the mass. The other free ends, which represent the finger's surface, may jump on the object.

Figure 4 shows the finger's mass-spring-damper model and the object's FE model in contact and floating state. This section describes the tapping simulation sequence. At the first contact, The length of the finger's spring-damper $l = x_f - x_t$ is set to 0 and the velocity of the finger's mass $\dot{x}_f$ is set to the velocity of the haptic pointer. The free end of the spring-damper is connected to the FE model's surface ($x_t = x_0, l = x_f - x_0$).

The equation of motion of the finger in the contact state is written as

$$m_f \ddot{x}_f = f_s + f_d = f_c.\tag{2}$$

Where, f_c corresponds to the input force for the object's FE model and the rendered force adding to the presenting force.

By discretizing the Eq. (5), we get two equations for the simulation:

$$x_f(t + \Delta t) = x_f(t) + \dot{x}_f(t)\Delta t, \quad \dot{x}_f(t + \Delta t) = \ddot{x}_f(t) + f_c\Delta t/m_f.\tag{3}$$

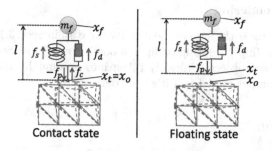

Fig. 4. Notation in contact and flying states

For the finger's impedance k_f and b_f, we calculate the contact force as

$$f_c = f_s + f_d = k_f l + b_f \dot{l}. \tag{4}$$

In addition to f_c, the finger gets f_p (normal component of the penalty force in Sect. 3.1). Therefore, when the total normal force given to the finger $f_c + f_p < 0$, the finger state is changed to the floating state.

In the floating state, $f_c = 0$, $x_t \neq x_0$ and $l = x_f - x_t \neq x_f - x_0$. Because, the penalty force f_p is also working on the finger, the equation of motion of the finger in the contact state changes to

$$m_f \ddot{x}_f = f_s + f_d + f_p = f_c + f_p. \tag{5}$$

In the contact state, f_p will also be working on the finger. However this force is received by the object directly. Therefore, the finger mass does not get f_p in the contact state.

In addition to the position of the finger's mass x_f, we have to simulate position of the free end of the spring-damper x_t. From $f_c = f_s + f_d = 0$, we get the following differential equation:

$$kl + d\dot{l} = 0. \tag{6}$$

By discretizing Eq. (6), we get the equation for the simulation:

$$kl + d\dot{l} = 0, \quad l(t + \Delta t) = l(t) - k/dl(t). \tag{7}$$

Then, we update the position of the free end x_t as $x_t = x_f - l$. When $x_t < x_0$, the finger state returns to the contact state.

The simulation frequency of the finger's mass-spring-damper is 10 kHz to keep the stability, while the simulation frequency of the object's FE model is 1 kHz. An average force of 10 steps is added to both the FE model and the presenting force. To ensure the stability, the average force is added to the FE model during the first 5 ms. The surface's position is updated in every 10 steps of the finger's simulation.

3.4   Haptic Rendering

The presenting force is the sum of the penalty force f_p in Sect. 3.1 and the vibration force, or the finger's spring-damper model's force f_c in Sect. 3.3, because the vibration of the object is already taken into account by the length of the finger's spring-damper model and it's time derivative.

4   Evaluation

For the evaluation, a haptic interaction environment was set up employing a PC (Windows 7, Intel(R) Core(TM) i7-2640M CPU 2.8 GHz) and the haptic

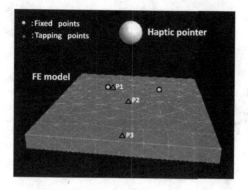

Fig. 5. The finite element model and the boundary conditions

Table 1. Parameter of the plate model

Plate size	$0.6 \times 0.6 \times 0.05\,\mathrm{m}$	Number of tets	443
Young's modulus	$1.0\,\mathrm{GPa}$	Density	$2.70 \times 10^3\,\mathrm{kg/m^3}$
Poisson's ratio	0.345	Rayleigh coeff.	α:100.8, β:1.50×10^{-5}

interface SPIDAR-G6 whose characteristics were evaluated in [3]. The haptic interface can present vibration of up to 300 Hz.

Figure 5 shows the finite element model for experiments, this image shows the finite element model vertices and edges. Table 1 shows the plate model's parameters. The material parameters are based on aluminium's physical properties. By comparing the feel of the tapping in real and the virtual environment, a finger's mass of 100 g and a spring-damper of 100 N/m and 130 Ns/m are chosen for finger's model.

4.1   Evaluation of the Vibration

Figure 6 shows the waveforms of the presenting forces when tapping on the points P1, P2 and P3 in Fig. 5. All waveforms start from the impulsive force of the first impact. Then, subsequent decaying vibrations, whose amplitude correspond to the tapping position, occur.

4.2   Evaluation of the Subsequent Collisions

To evaluate the simulation of subsequent collisions, we picked up one tapping where floating status occurs. Figure 7 shows the presented vibration force and the simulated vibration force and the penalty force. During the floating state, no vibration force was generated in the simulation (Fig. 7 below) as a result no vibration force was presented in addition to the penalty force. In addition the figure shows that long term floatings occur at the beginning of the tapping, while short term floatings remain until 27 ms.

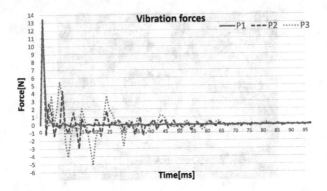

Fig. 6. Presented vibration forces after the tappings of the plate

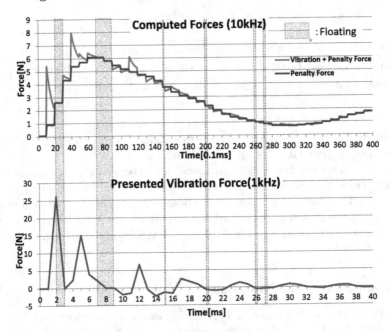

Fig. 7. Effect of finger floating on the presented and computed forces after a tapping

5   Conclusion

This paper proposed a method to simulate the tapping finger's motion and the object's vibration with a mass-spring-damper model for the finger and a FE model for the object. The contact force is taken from the finger's spring-damper model and it is presented to the user in addition to the penalty force to present the object's shape.

The experimental results showed that the proposed method renders realistic event based forces including impact impulse, decayed waves and the effect of the subsequent collisions. User studies and comparisons between rendered forces and real tapping forces are future works.

References

1. Akahane, K., Hasegawa, S., Koike, Y., Sato, M.: A proposal of a high definition haptic rendering for stability and fidelity. ICAT2006, pp. 162–167, Nov 2006
2. Bensmaïa, S.J., Hollins, M.: Complex tactile waveform discrimination. J. Acoust. Soc. Am. **108**(3), 1236–1245 (2000)
3. Ikeda, Y., Hasegawa, S.: Short paper: characteristics of perception of stiffness by varied tapping velocity and penetration in using event-based haptic. Joint Virtual Reality Conference EGVE-ICAT-EURO VR, pp. 113–116 (2009)
4. Susa, I., Takehana, Y., Balandra, A., Mitake, H., Hasegawa, S.: Haptic rendering based on finite element simulation of vibration. In: IEEE Haptics Symposium (2014)
5. Kuchenbecker, K.J., Fiene, J., Niemeyer, G.: Improving contact realism through event-based haptic feedback. IEEE Trans. Vis. Comput. Graph. **12**(2), 219–230 (2006)
6. Okamura, A.M., Cutkosky, M.R., Dennerlein, J.T.: Reality-based models for vibration feedback in virtual environments. IEEE/ASME Trans. Mechatron. **6**(3), 245–252 (2001)
7. Okamura, A.M., Dennerlein, J.T., Howe, R.D.: Vibration feedback models for virtual environments. In: Proceedings of the 1998 IEEE International Conference on Robotics and Automation, pp. 674–679, May 1998
8. Sreng, J., Lécuyer, A., Andriot, C.: Using vibration patterns to provide impact position information in haptic manipulation of virtual objects. In: Ferre, M. (ed.) EuroHaptics 2008. LNCS, vol. 5024, pp. 589–598. Springer, Heidelberg (2008)
9. Wellman, P., Howe, R.D.: Towards realistic vibrotactile display in virtual environments. In: Alberts, T. (ed.) Proceeding of the ASME Dynamics Systems and Control Division, Symposium on Haptic Interfaces for Virtual Environment and Teleoperator Systems, p. 57-2 (1995)
10. Zilles, C.B., Salisbury, J.: A constraint-based god-object method for haptic display. In: Proceedings of the 1995 IEEE/RSJ International Conference on Intelligent Robots and Systems 95. 'Human Robot Interaction and Cooperative Robots', vol. 3, pp. 146–151 (1995)

Computational Modeling Reinforces that Proprioceptive Cues May Augment Compliance Discrimination When Elasticity Is Decoupled from Radius of Curvature

Yuxiang Wang[1] and Gregory J. Gerling[2(✉)]

[1] Departments of Systems and Information Engineering, and Mechanical
and Aerospace Engineering, University of Virginia,
Charlottesville, VA 22903, USA
[2] Departments of Systems and Information Engineering, and Biomedical
Engineering, University of Virginia, Charlottesville, VA 22903, USA
{yw5aj,gg7h}@virginia.edu

Abstract. Our capability to discriminate object compliance is based on cues both tactile and proprioceptive, in addition to visual. To understand how the mechanics of the fingertip skin and bone might encode such information, we used finite element models to simulate the task of differentiating spherical indenters of radii (4, 6 and 8 mm) and elasticity (initial shear modulus of 10, 50 and 90 kPa). In particular, we considered two response variables, the strain energy density (SED) at the epidermal-dermal interface where Merkel cell endorgans of slowly adapting type I afferents reside, and the displacement of the fingertip bone necessary to achieve certain surface contact force. The former variable ties to tactile cues while the latter ties to proprioceptive cues. The results indicate that distributions of SED are clearly distinct for most combinations of object radii and elasticity. However, for certain combinations – e.g., between 4 mm spheres of 10 kPa and 8 mm of 90 kPa – spatial distributions of SED are nearly identical. In such cases where tactile-only cues are non-differentiable, we may rely on proprioceptive cues to discriminate compliance.

Keywords: Haptics · Softness · Compliance · Perception · Finite element analysis · Touch · Tactile · Proprioception · Mechanotransduction · Biomechanics

1 Introduction

In daily interactions with our environment, we classify the compliance of objects as soft or hard, or at levels in-between. The percept of compliance, despite its importance, is much less studied and understood than is the case for rigid bodies. It is also much less studied for bare finger interaction [1, 2] (e.g., palpation of cancerous nodules) than for probe-based interaction [3, 4] (e.g., simulation of detection of caries). Accordingly, work herein focuses upon bare finger interaction, and employs computational modeling to better understand the relative contributions of the fingertip skin and bone in encoding compliance.

To inform a percept of compliance, our somatosensory system senses, transforms and integrates various types of cues, both tactile and proprioceptive [1, 3], in addition

© Springer-Verlag Berlin Heidelberg 2014
M. Auvray and C. Duriez (Eds.): EuroHaptics 2014, Part II, LNCS 8619, pp. 360–368, 2014.
DOI: 10.1007/978-3-662-44196-1_44

to visual. Tactile cues arise from interactions between the fingertip skin and an object's surface whereby mechanosensitive afferents respond to spatial and temporal distributions of stress and strain fields in skin near their end organs. We rely almost exclusively upon tactile cues in passive touch. In contrast, in situations of active exploration, we augment tactile cues with proprioceptive cues from the movement of our fingers in space. Employing both systems together, in active touch, leads to peak performance. When finger movement cues are removed, our ability to discriminate compliance decreases [1]. Likewise, when tactile cues are removed (by an experimental setup that has the user grasp two rigid plates with the elastic substrate in-between), our ability to discriminate compliance decreases by more than three times [2].

To better understand the relative contributions of tactile and proprioceptive cues in discriminating compliance, stimulus elasticity needs to be decoupled from its radius of curvature. In specific, prior work has been conducted, but with stimuli whose properties were confounded as follows. First, stimulus compliance has been parameterized by its stiffness (force-displacement, units N/m) rather than its elastic modulus (stress-strain, units Pa) [1]. This is an issue because two stimuli can maintain equal stiffness yet differ in elasticity when accounting for size and surface geometry. Second, stimuli often employ a flat, rigid surface with a spring under the surface that controls compliance [2–4]. Such stimuli do not mimic the contact profile of an elastic object and the skin's surface. Third, others employ stimuli that correctly characterize compliance by elastic modulus and account for elastic-to-elastic surface contact, but only use stimuli of flat surface geometry. Finally and relatedly, single-nerve, electrophysiological recordings have recently been conducted in response to compliant stimuli [5, 6]. To fill the gap between single-unit recordings and psychophysical studies, computational models are required to decipher how a population of afferents encodes compliance. The modeling herein is a first step toward identifying parameters to be used to drive further, and more conclusive, psychophysical experiments.

We address this gap in the knowledge base by computationally modeling the mechanics of both the fingertip skin and bone and conducting numerical experiments where stimulus elasticity is decoupled from radius of curvature. We utilize control conditions that simulate active and passive touch and approximate tactile and proprioceptive cues. In the analysis of cutaneous tactile cues, we focus in this work upon the steady-state phase of the indentation, which is tied with the response of the slowly-adaptive type I afferent, as opposed to other afferent types.

2 Methods

Finite element analysis of the skin and bone of the distal fingertip was performed using both plane-strain and axisymmetric models. Their material properties were fitted to hyperelastic material constitutive laws, and optimized to predict known surface deflection and force-displacement relationships. Then, a series of numerical simulations were carried out with compliant spherical indenters of different radii (4, 6 and 8 mm) and elasticity (initial shear modulus of 10, 50 and 90 kPa). In two interaction cases, the fingertip and stimulus are moved and constrained in attempt to approximate active and passive touch. To help determine stimulus discriminability, two response variables were considered at steady-state fingertip-stimulus contact, the strain energy density (SED) at the epidermal-dermal interface where Merkel cell end-organs of slowly adapting type I afferents reside, and displacement of the fingertip bone necessary to achieve certain contact force. The first variable directly ties to cutaneous or tactile-only cues. The second variable ties to proprioceptive cues, where displacement of the bone in the normal direction is an approximate measure tied to change in muscle length, and force tied to muscle tension change.

2.1 Geometry of the Fingertip Model

Derived from the geometry of a 3D model of the human distal phalange [7], the two simplified 2D models with plane-strain elements (Fig. 1A) of a cross-sectional slice from proximal first digit to distal tip, to account for stimuli delivered across the width of the finger (e.g., bars), and with axisymmetric elements (Fig. 1B) revolved around the centerline of the fingerpad, to analyze stimuli normal to the contact surface (e.g., spherical and cylindrical indenters). Herein, the plane strain model was used to fit material properties to surface deflection data [8], while the axisymmetric model was used to fit force-displacement data [9] and perform simulations with compliant spherical objects. The simplified 2D models are of much less computational expense, necessary as the parametric study herein included a considerable number of model evaluations.

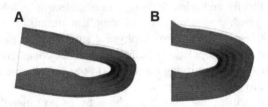

Fig. 1. (A) Plane-strain and (B) axisymmetric models, following the geometry of the human distal phalange [7].

The bones and fingernails in the models are analytic rigid bodies, as these structures are much stiffer than soft tissue. The fingernail is 0.46 mm thick and 13 mm long. Three layers of soft tissue were modeled as deformable bodies wrapped around the bone, namely epidermis, dermis and hypodermis. Layers interface were tied with no relative displacements.

Meshing was done with elements near the surface of the finest dimension, about 0.25 mm wide, with larger sizes gradually used closer to the bone. Triangular meshes were used throughout with 4,032 and 3,456 elements in the plane-strain and axisymmetric models.

2.2 Material Properties of the Fingertip Model

Hyperelastic material properties are used of the Neo-Hookean form of the strain energy function, Eq. 1. Specifically, Ψ is the strain energy term, $\bar{I}_1$ is the modified first strain invariant, J is the volume ratio known as Jacobian and C_{10}, D_1 are material constants [10].

$$\Psi = C_{10}(\bar{I}_1 - 3) + \frac{1}{D_1}(J - 1)^2 \tag{1}$$

The initial shear modulus G was first defined and then initial bulk modulus was set according to $K = G/10^3$. The relationship between parameters G, K and terms in strain energy function C_{10} and D_1 is $G = 2C_{10}$ and $K = \frac{2}{D_1}$.

We refer to material elasticity by its initial shear modulus (denoted as G), which fully defines the material. Though we specify elasticity only via the linear term G, the material is in fact nonlinearly hyperelastic. The purpose of choosing Neo-Hookean model is two-fold. First, only one parameter is needed (G) for each material, thereby simplifying the fitting procedure and leading to a more robust calibration. Second, instead of a linear Young's modulus, we use a hyperelastic form because we focus on soft objects, which deform in a finite-strain region.

In addition, a two-step model material calibration was conducted. First, the ratios between material elasticity of each layer were fitted to plane strain model to match observed spatial deflection of the fingertip surface to different displacements of different cylinders [8]. Second, the ratios were scaled in the axisymmetric model to match observed force-displacement relationships from four subjects [9]. The material parameters obtained from the fitting procedures are listed in Table 1. The final values of shear modulus G are epidermis 1.21 MPa, dermis 50.67 kPa and hypodermis 2.37 kPa. A friction coefficient between simulated skin and stimulus is set to 0.3 [11]. The models were constructed and analyzed using the commercial FE software package ABAQUS Standard, version 6.12 (Dassault Systèmes, Vélizy-Villacoublay, France).

Table 1. Material parameters from fitting

Subject	Initial shear modulus			R^2
	Epidermis (MPa)	Dermis (kPa)	Hypodermis (kPa)	
#1	1.74	72.74	3.40	0.99
#2	0.83	34.61	1.62	0.99
#3	1.31	54.96	2.57	0.99
#4	0.97	40.48	1.90	0.97
Mean	**1.21**	**50.67**	**2.37**	**0.99**
Std.	0.41	17.00	0.80	0.01

2.3 Modeled Indenter Tips

The set of compliant spherical indenters utilize three values of radii (4, 6 and 8 mm) and elasticity (initial shear modulus of 10, 50 and 90 kPa). The indenters are implemented as hemispheres, with the surface of their central section tied to a rigid plate. Their Poisson's ratio is set to 0.475 to mimic the nearly incompressible behavior of rubber. Triangular elements with 0.25 mm edge length are used because their size is comparable to elements used in the fingertip model in the region contacting its surface, for the purpose of suppressing stress concentrations near nodes. Larger elements of up to 1.0 mm are used to reduce computational cost in the region not directly contacting the skin.

2.4   Numerical Experiments

Nine numerical simulations (3 radii by 3 elasticity) were conducted on the 2D axisymmetric model. Two types of fingertip-stimulus contact and movement were simulated, tied to cases of active and passive touch. First, in the passive touch case (Fig. 2A), all compliant indenters regardless of size and material were loaded by 0.125, 0.25, 0.5 and 1 N force, while the fingertip bone was constrained. The response variables in the passive touch case were derived from tactile-only cues, indicated by the SED distributed on nodes at the simulated epidermal-dermal interface (470 μm beneath the skin's surface) calculated by averaging neighboring elements at each interface node. With the bone fixed, we assumed no proprioceptive cues as reaction force is provided by fixture instead of muscle activity. Second, in the active touch case (Fig. 2B), all compliant indenters were constrained at the center plate while the fingertip bone was loaded by the noted forces. The response variables in the active touch case were derived from both tactile and proprioceptive cues. The additional proprioceptive cues were derived from the translational displacement of the fingertip bone in the normal direction. This is a measure that ties to the change in the length of the muscle as detected by muscle spindles whereas the corresponding force indicates the muscle tension change of Golgi tendons [12]. Note that under both cases the SED distributions are identical due to the same loading magnitude.

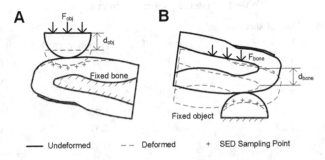

Fig. 2. Forces and constraints in simulated cases of passive touch (A) and active touch (B), with the undeformed fingertip and compliant hemisphere denoted by dark, thick solid lines, and the deformed fingertip and compliant hemisphere by grey, thin dashed lines. Tactile cues in both (A) and (B) are simulated by measuring the spatial distribution of SED at elements at the epidermal-dermal interface (marked as "+") and proprioceptive cues in B) only are simulated by measuring the displacement of the bone d_{bone}, given force load F_{bone} and the hyperelastic-to-hyperelastic contact interaction.

3   Result

At a first glance, the indenters deform the surface of the skin quite distinctly given changes in either radius or elasticity (Fig. 3).

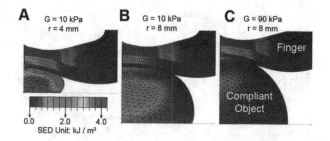

Fig. 3. Contour plot of the spatial distribution of SED in the axisymmetric fingertip model (upper) at steady-state for simulated contact with compliant spheres (lower) varying in radii r and elasticity G, with (A) smallest radius, most compliant, (B) largest radius, most compliant, and (C) largest radius, least compliant. Although the deformation of the spherical indenters differs vastly between (A) and (C), the surface deflection and the distribution of SED induced in the fingertip model are very similar.

For tactile-only cues, either a decrease in spherical radius or an increase in material elasticity (decrease in compliance) will significantly increase the concentration of SED near the contact centerline (Fig. 4). Therefore most differences of the indenter can be clearly captured and discriminated by comparing such curves. In certain cases, however, changes in elasticity may perfectly counteract changes in radius. In particular, the distribution of SED for the smallest radius, most compliant case (Fig. 4A) is nearly identical to that of the largest radius, least compliant case (Fig. 4E), as combined in Fig. 4F.

For proprioceptive cues, an increase in either indenter radius or elasticity will lead to a decrease in the displacement of the bone given the same force (Fig. 5). For example, in Fig. 5 the dotted line (G = 10 kPa, r = 4 mm) is clearly separable from the solid line with dot markers (G = 90 kPa, r = 8 mm). Also, curves differing by indenter radius (r = 4, 6, 8 mm) with the same elasticity (G = 10 kPa) yield a similar relationship. In contrast, curves differing by elasticity (G = 10, 50 kPa) the same radius (r = 8 mm) yield a much more distinct relationship.

4   Discussion

We computationally modeled the mechanics of both the fingertip skin and bone and conducted numerical experiments where stimulus elasticity was decoupled from radius of curvature. In two interaction cases, the fingertip and stimulus were moved and constrained in attempt to approximate active and passive touch. Response variables were tied to tactile and proprioceptive mechanisms of spatial distributions of SED and the displacement of the distal bone.

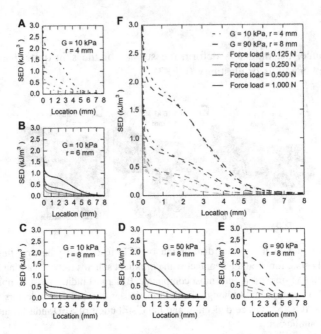

Fig. 4. Simulated spatial distribution of SED in the axisymmetric fingertip model for spherical indenters varying in radii r and elasticity G, where shown in sub-figures are (A–C) SED for indenter material G = 10 kPa and increasing radii from 4 mm to 8 mm, (C–E) SED for indenters with equal radii of 8 mm and increasing elasticity from G = 10 kPa to 90 kPa, and (F) the direct comparison of (A) and (E), demonstrating that the smallest radius, most compliant case in (A) may be confused with largest radius, least compliant case in (E) given SED distributions alone.

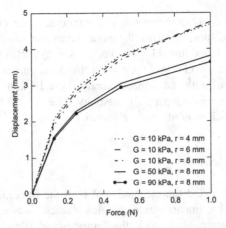

Fig. 5. Displacement-force relationships of the bone simulated in the axisymmetric model of the fingertip are given for five combinations of indenter radii and elasticity.

The results indicate that the tactile cues appear to more readily aid discriminating compliant objects, because of the clear separation of SED distributions (Fig. 4) compared to differences in the displacement of the bone in the normal direction, which we use to approximate proprioceptive cues (Fig. 5). In specific, the models predict that one might observe a tactile illusion in situations where proprioceptive cues are absent (e.g., in the passive touch case), when stimulating with spheres of 4 mm of 10 kPa versus 8 mm of 90 kPa, where one might be unable to differentiate the two spheres. However, adding the simulated proprioceptive cues enabled us to discriminate these cases. This result reinforces that, and provides a specific instance where, both tactile and proprioceptive cues might be jointly relied upon to discriminate compliant objects. This comes in general agreement with psychophysical studies where Bergmann Tiest et al. reported lower discrimination ability based on proprioceptive cues alone compared to tactile cues alone [2], and Srinivasan et al. reported that tactile cues encode more information than proprioceptive cues [1]. However, as we noted in the introduction those experiments were conducted in situations where stimulus compliance and/or surface contact were confounded together or ill defined.

While the effort here is a first attempt to decouple stimulus elasticity from radius of curvature, further work is needed to account for assumptions made herein. First, our FE analyses are done in steady-state and do not take material viscoelasticity into account. This time-varying information is likely to contribute to the response characteristics of both rapid-adapting and slowly-adapting type I afferents [5, 13], and it is likely that the timing of the action potentials in the stimulus ramp contribute to compliance discrimination [5]. Second, the spherical indenter used herein does not shed any light on how distinct spatial features, such as edges, might be encoded apart from material compliance. Third, several assumptions are made with respect to the proprioceptive cues we utilized. We use displacement and force in the normal direction as a first approximation, though cues might also be transferred to change in muscle length and tension. One may need to simulate the next phalange of the finger as well as consider the exact connectivity of the muscles and tendons to the bone at points in the finger digits. Fourth, an often-considered tactile cue for designing haptic displays [14], distinct from stress/strain at the locations of the SAI end organs, is the deflection of the skin's surface. Though less clearly tied to the neurophysiology, our preliminary analysis is similar to the spatial distribution of SED. Another prominent cue, the spread of the contact area, can be analyzed in detail by calculating the area on the finger where SED is observed to be greater than a certain threshold. Finally, further psychophysical experiments are required to validate the simulated results, in particular the hypothesized illusion, and the values of radii and elasticity provide a good starting point.

Acknowledgements. This work was supported by a grant from the National Institutes of Health (NIH NINDS R01NS073119). The content is solely the responsibility of the authors and does not necessarily represent the official views of the NIH.

References

1. Srinivasan, M.A., LaMotte, R.H.: Tactual discrimination of softness. J. Neurophysiol. **73**, 88–101 (1995)
2. Bergmann Tiest, W.M., Kappers, A.: Cues for haptic perception of compliance. IEEE Trans. Haptics **2**, 189–199 (2009). doi:10.1109/TOH.2009.16
3. Friedman, R.M., Hester, K.D., Green, B.G., LaMotte, R.H.: Magnitude estimation of softness. Exp. Brain Res. **191**, 133–142 (2008). doi:10.1007/s00221-008-1507-5
4. LaMotte, R.H.: Softness discrimination with a tool. J. Neurophysiol. **83**, 1777–1786 (2000)
5. Condon, M., Birznieks, I., Hudson, K., et al.: Differential sensitivity to surface compliance by tactile afferents in the human fingerpad. J. Neurophysiol. (2013). doi:10.1152/jn.00589. 2013
6. Gwilliam, J.C., Yoshioka, T., Okamura, A.M., Hsiao, S.S.: Neural coding of lump detection in compliant artificial tissue. J. Neurophysiol. (2014). doi:10.1152/jn.00032.2013
7. Gerling, G.J., Rivest II, Lesniak, D.R., et al.: Validating a population model of tactile mechanotransduction of slowly adapting type I afferents at levels of skin mechanics, single-unit response and psychophysics. IEEE Trans. Haptics 1–1 (2013). doi:10.1109/TOH.2013.36
8. Dandekar, K.: Role of mechanics in tactile sensing of shape (1995)
9. Gulati, R.J., Srinivasan, M.A.: Human fingerpad under indentation I: static and dynamic force response. ASME-Publications-Bed **29**, 261 (1995)
10. Holzapfel, G.: Nonlinear Solid Mechanics: A Continuum Approach for Engineering. Wiley, Chichester (2000)
11. Gitis, N., Sivamani, R.: Tribometrology of skin. Tribol. Trans. **47**, 461–469 (2004). doi:10. 1080/05698190490493355
12. Proske, U., Gandevia, S.C.: The proprioceptive senses: their roles in signaling body shape, body position and movement, and muscle force. Physiol. Rev. **92**, 1651–1697 (2012). doi:10.1152/physrev.00048.2011
13. Johnson, K.: The roles and functions of cutaneous mechanoreceptors. Curr. Opin. Neurobiol. **11**, 455–461 (2001). doi:10.1016/S0959-4388(00)00234-8
14. Bicchi, A., Scilingo, E.P., De Rossi, D.: Haptic discrimination of softness in teleoperation: the role of the contact area spread rate. IEEE Trans. Robot. Autom. **16**, 496–504 (2000). doi:10.1109/70.880800

Electrovibration Modeling Analysis

Eric Vezzoli$^{(\boxtimes)}$, Michel Amberg, Frédéric Giraud,
and Betty Lemaire-Semail

L2EP, University Lille1, F59650 Villeneuve d'Ascq, France
eric.vezzoli@ed.univ-lille1.fr,
Michel.Amberg@univ-lille1.fr,
{frederic.giraud,betty.semail}@polytech-lille.fr

Abstract. Electrostatic attraction may be used to modulate the apparent friction coefficient between two surfaces. Applied to the human finger and a polarized interface, the principle can modify the user perception of the interface surface. In this paper, the different steps towards the modeling of the electrovibration phenomenon are developed. An investigation on the current modeling will be carried out, with a focus on the temporal evolution and frequency dependence of the stimulus. Thus, an improvement of the modeling will be proposed to take into account this major effect, and then, it will be checked with an experimental set-up and compared with literature results.

Keywords: Electrovibration · Electrostatic force · Modeling · Haptic · Tactile · Friction

1 Introduction

The last few years have seen an increasing interest for haptic stimulation and simulation. Different technologies are available to provide a tactile feedback to a user by modifying his perception of a surface. In particular, it is possible to control the friction between a surface and a finger thanks to squeeze film effect or to electrovibration. This study is focused on the electrovibration effect: the modulation of the perceived friction coefficient due to the induced electrostatic force between a finger and a high voltage supplied plate [1]. The effect is known since the mid fifties [2], but the interest has raised only recently. Firstly, spatial division of electrode was developed to provide precise and complex stimulus pattern of conductive pads, but this solution suffered from its complexity and turned out difficult to apply [5]. Recently, electrovibration took advantage of technological improvements of fingertip's position sensor based on optical or resistive solutions. The possibility to track precisely the position of the finger leads to fine gratings simulation thanks to spatial-stimulus relation. With spatio-temporal transformation, the stimulator itself becomes easier to manufacture and it becomes possible to produce tactile feedback on transparent surfaces [1] or merge it with another tactile stimulation technique [3].

If the efficiency of the process to provide successful tactile feedback is clear, the physical modeling of the phenomenon involving the finger is not yet satisfactory. The aim of this paper is to investigate on the modeling proposed in the literature and to

© Springer-Verlag Berlin Heidelberg 2014
M. Auvray and C. Duriez (Eds.): EuroHaptics 2014, Part II, LNCS 8619, pp. 369–376, 2014.
DOI: 10.1007/978-3-662-44196-1_45

suggest a modification to take into account the frequency dependence of the effect. The work is organized as follows: first the experimental set up is presented, with a description of the working principle of the technology. Second, the electrostatic force applied on a finger will be described, and the different parameters included in the modeling will be discussed. Finally, a new modeling is proposed and the simulation results obtained will be compared with the experimental ones.

2 Electrostatic Force Analysis

2.1 Force Measurement

Electrovibration modifies the lateral force felt by the finger in motion by a modulation of the normal force. The modulation is due to electrostatic force and appears between the finger and the polarized surface (see Fig. 1a). The experimental set-up developed and detailed in this paper is able to detect these forces.

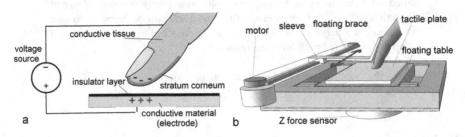

Fig. 1. (a) Schematic representation of electrovibration. (b) Representation of the measurement system, the finger is moved on the plate by the motor.

To measure the normal and lateral force felt by the finger, a tribometer has been developed, (see Fig. 1b). Past measurements indicate a value around 100 mN of the induced electrostatic force [3]. A high-bandwidth sensor is needed to measure this force due to its fast varying nature. A measurement of the normal force is also required. To achieve this goal, a force sensor (9217A, KISTLER, France) is used for the normal force measurements. On top of that, a floating table equipped with a force sensor (FSG, Honeywell, USA) coupled with a conditioner (max4209H, Maxim Integrated, USA) is mounted to ensure a fast acquisition of the lateral force.

To acquire the data, an oscilloscope (3014B, Tektronix, USA) is used providing both the acquisition and a visual feedback for the users. A waveform generator (33120A, Agilent, USA) provides waveforms to the high voltage amplifier supplying the tactile plate. The data are acquired and elaborated in a post-process. To provide electrostatic stimulation to the finger, an aluminum plate covered with a plastic insulator film has been used.

2.2 Electrostatic Force Expression

A finger approaching an electric field experiences an induced polarization. The polarized material interacts with an electric field generated by the electrode due to Coulomb interaction. The amplitude of this interaction is small, but is comparable with the amplitude of touch-sensing action [3]. A model of the phenomenon is deduced in [4], the expression of the electrostatic force, f_e, is the following:

$$f_e = \frac{\varepsilon_0 A v^2}{2\left(\frac{T_i}{\varepsilon_i} + \frac{T_{sc}}{\varepsilon_{sc}}\right)(T_{sc} + T_i)} \tag{1}$$

where ε_0 is the vacuum permittivity, A is the finger contact area, T_i and T_{sc} are the thicknesses of the insulator and the stratum corneum and ε_i and ε_{sc} are the relative permittivities of the insulator and stratum corneum. It may be noted that this expression gives as a result a constant force f_e if the applied voltage v is constant. Thanks to the experimental setup described in Sect. 2.1, we measured the force between a finger and the polarized plate, while there is no contact between the finger and the plate. In Fig. 2 is reported the normal force measured for a given voltage signal for a floating finger over the polarized plate. We can remark oscillations due to the difficulties to maintain the finger close to the plate without any contact. But the major behavior is in agreement with (1), that is roughly a constant force once the voltage applied is constant.

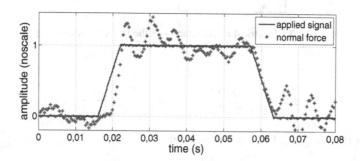

Fig. 2. Normal force for the finger suspended near the polarized plate

If we assume the force f_e is also given by the Eq. (1) once the finger touches the plate, we may define the tangential force f_t as $f_t = \mu(f_n + f_e)$ where f_n is the normal force applied by the finger and μ the dynamic friction coefficient of the plate. An increase of f_e would lead to an increase of the lateral force, creating a friction change feeling. Nevertheless, Giraud et al. [3] found an exponential reduction of the lateral force for an applied square signal when the finger is sliding on the plate. This phenomenon is unexplained by this static model.

3 Electrical Modeling Analysis

3.1 Frequency Dependence of the Parameters

Every human tissue exhibits specific electrical characteristics; in this case, it is interesting to investigate the properties of the stratum corneum for its relevant role in the
electrovibration force generation. The electrical properties of the stratum corneum were
investigated by Yamamoto et al. [6]. In their work, the strong frequency dependence of
the resistivity and permittivity is highlighted for this biological material due to its
intrinsic structural characteristics. In this modeling, the resistivity of deeper tissue is
neglected for its low value. On the basis of this assumption, it is possible to model the
interface of the finger and the insulator like in Fig. 3, with R_{sc} and C_{sc} the resistance
and the capacitance of the stratum corneum, C_i the capacitance of the insulator
and v the applied voltage. From electrical circuit theory it comes:

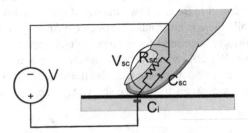

Fig. 3. Electrical representation of the stratum corneum

$$v_{sc} = \frac{R_{sc}C_i s}{1 + R_{sc}(C_{sc} + C_i)s} = \frac{C_i}{C_i + C_{sc}}\frac{\tau s}{1 + \tau s}v \tag{2}$$

where $\tau = (C_i + C_{sc})R_{sc}$. For a given material:

$$C = \frac{\varepsilon_0 \varepsilon_r A}{T} \quad \text{and} \quad R = \frac{\rho T}{A} \tag{3}$$

where ε_r is the material relative permittivity, r the material resistivity, A the area of the
electrode and T the material thickness. In this case, a plastic film has been used to
insulate the finger from the electrode, leading to $C_i = 32$ pF where $e_i = 3.35$, $T_i = 90$ μm
and the contact area between the finger and the plate is estimated as $A = 1$ cm^2. For the
stratum corneum, $C_{sc} = 6.9$ nF with $T_{sc} = 200$ μm [7] and $\varepsilon_{sc} = 1560$ [6]. It is possible to
assume $C_{sc} \gg C_i$ which leads, using (3), to $\tau = C_{sc}R_{sc} = \varepsilon_0\varepsilon_{sc}\rho_{sc}$. In Fig. 4, the frequency
dependence of the time constant t is represented; the parameters ε_{sc} and ρ_{sc} were
measured in function of the frequency in [6]. It may be noticed that there is a strong
frequency dependence of this time constant which substantially changes the behavior of
(2) from a pure first order high pass filter to a more complex frequency dependence.
It may be noted that this approach is valid for a static or moving finger.

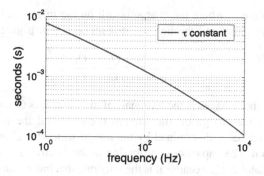

Fig. 4. τ constant frequency dependence, $\tau = \varepsilon_0 \varepsilon_{sc} \rho_{sc}$

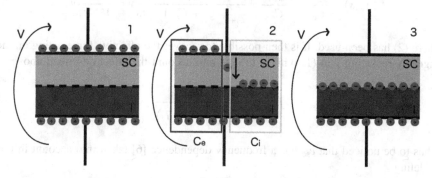

Fig. 5. Charge configuration at the border of the stratum corneum (SC) and insulator (I). The conductive part of the system is represented like the electrode of a capacitor. (1) Initial configuration on the charge when the voltage v is applied. (2) Discharge through the stratum corneum with the two equivalent capacitors. (3) Final configuration of the charges after the transient.

3.2 Loss of Charge During Contact

In addition with the previous phenomenon of frequency dependence, we have to consider in the modeling the charge lost through the stratum corneum. The lost charge is gathered on the surface of the insulator as free surface charge, for this reason it no longer participates to the generation of the force on the finger, and consequently, to the measured force. This happens because the charges on the surface of the insulator are no longer mechanically bounded to the finger and the insulator sustains the induced electrostatic force. Figure 5 illustrates three different moments of the discharge through the stratum corneum. The electrostatic force generated by v associated to the first configuration is described by (1), but in the third configuration the electrostatic force between the finger and the polarized plate is 0 for the reason explained before. During the transient period represented by the second case, it is possible to imagine the applied voltage v, distributed across two different perfect capacitances. These capacitances are

C_e formed by the case 1, where the charge is still on the finger, and C_i in the case 3, where the charge has migrated through the stratum corneum. It gives:

$$v = v_e + v_i = \frac{Q_{sc}}{C_e} + \frac{Q_i}{C_i} \tag{4}$$

where v_e and v_i are the voltages at the terminals of the capacitors C_e and C_i, and Q_{sc} and Q_i are respectively the charge on the stratum corneum and the insulator. The link between the two charges is determined by the rate at which the charge flows through the stratum corneum. The capacitor contributing to the electrostatic force between the finger and the insulator is C_e, because it is the only one that has a charge bounded to the finger. Then the effective part of the applied voltage contributing to the force is:

$$v_e(s) = \frac{Q_{sc}}{C_e} = \frac{C_{sc}v_{sc}}{C_e} = \frac{C_{sc}}{\frac{C_iC_{sc}}{C_i+C_{sc}}}\frac{C_i}{C_i + C_{sc}}\frac{\tau s}{1+\tau s}v = \frac{\tau s}{1+\tau s}v \tag{5}$$

where (2) has been used. It is then possible to recover the effective force acting on the finger by replacing v in (1) with v_e to take into account the effect described above:

$$f_e = \frac{\varepsilon_0 A v_e^2}{2\left(\frac{T_i}{\varepsilon_i} + \frac{T_s}{\varepsilon_{sc}}\right)(T_s + T_i)} \tag{6}$$

It has to be noticed that ε_{sc} has a frequency dependence [6] taken into account in this modeling.

4   Simulated and Experimental Results

From (6), it is possible to predict the time evolution of the lateral force f_t for a given applied voltage signal thanks to the relationship $f_t = \mu(f_n + f_e)$. The evolution of the measured lateral force compared to the predicted one is proposed in Fig. 6. The plate is polarized with a trapezium signal from 0 to 1000 V to investigate both the transient and the steady state. The signal is provided by an amplifier (HVA2 kV, Ultravolt, USA) with a safety system to avoid any electrical shock and to limit the current to $I_s = 250$ μA detailed in [3]. The mechanics of the finger and the measurement system has not been considered in this modeling.

The reported behavior has been observed on 8 different subjects, both male and female, aged from 22 to 29. Three of them were students and the other five were from the laboratory staff, all of them gave their informed consent to perform the experiment. We can remark a very close behavior between the proposed modeling and the experimental results on the rising steps, however on the discharging parts there is a difference between the modeled and the measured signal. One assumption to explain this phenomenon could be the measurements system that can show relaxation behavior. Nevertheless the modeling is able to take into account the discharge phenomenon of the finger. The absolute value of the measured force varies from 2 to 5 mN whereas the

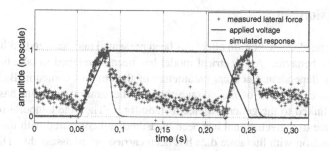

Fig. 6. Lateral force measured for the finger sliding at constant speed on the polarized plane (blue), in red is reported the modeled electrostatic force acting between the stratum corneum and the insulator (Color figure online).

model, for a thickness of the stratum corneum about 0.2 mm, predicts 2.5 mN. The variability of the force can be explained by the variability of the stratum corneum explained in [7]. It may be noticed that Giraud et al. [3] found a value of the decay of the lateral force, considering the mechanics of the measurements system, of $= 6$ ms for a square signal applied. The calculated value of τ with our modeling, considering their experimental situation, is 7.7 ms.

Another way to assess the relevance of this modeling is to compare with the experimental results from Meyer et al. [5]. In their paper, the authors investigated the frequency dependence of the electrostatic force from 100 to 10000 Hz. The inferred measured force had a noticeable dispersion between different subjects, but generally exhibited an increasing and a successive saturation for all the measure detailed in their article. The dispersion of the force is well explained by (6), considering the variability of the thickness of the stratum corneum in human fingers reported in [7]. The proposed model in comparison with one result from [5] is reported in Fig. 7. According to the different experimental situations described in the paper, the approximation of $\tau = C_{sc}R_{sc}$ is not valid anymore for the comparable value of C_i and C_{sc} and, in the shown simulation, we considered $\tau = (C_i + C_{sc})R_{sc}$.

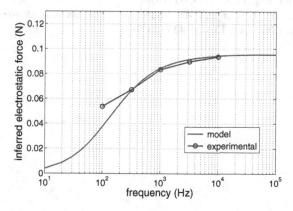

Fig. 7. Comparison of the model with experimental data taken from [5]

5 Conclusion

In this paper the electrovibration effect has been presented and analyzed on its temporal and frequency behavior. An electrical model has been developed to take into account the frequency dependent electrical parameters of the stratum corneum. Based on this data, the transfer function of the voltage through the stratum corneum has been calculated, and linked to the generated electrostatic force. Then the temporal response of the lateral force to a given signal has been measured and compared with the calculated one. A comparison with literature data has been carried out to assess the validity of the model.

Acknowledgement. This work was founded by the FP7 Marie Curie Initial Training Network PROTOTOUCH, grant agreement No. 317100. The authors would like to thank the IRCICA laboratory for hosting and Clement Nadal for the useful discussion.

References

1. Bau, O., Poupyrev, I., Israr, A., Harrison, C.: TeslaTouch: electrovibration for touch surfaces. In: Proceedings of the 23rd Annual ACM Symposium on User Interface Software and Technology, pp. 283–292 (2010)
2. Mallinckrodt, E., Hughes, A.L., Sleator, W.J.: Perception by the skin of electrically induced vibrations. Science **118**, 277–278 (1953)
3. Giraud, F., Amberg, M., Lemaire-Semail, B.: Merging two tactile stimulation principles: electrovibration and squeeze film effect. In: IEEE World Haptics Conference, pp. 199–203 (2013)
4. Kaczmarek, K.A., Nammi, K., Agarwal, A.K., Tyler, M.E., Haase, S.J., Beebe, D.J.: Polarity effect in electrovibration for tactile display. IEEE Trans. Biomed. Eng. **53**(10), 2047–2054 (2006)
5. Meyer, D.J., Peshkin, M.A., Colgate, J.E.: Fingertip friction modulation due to electrostatic attraction. In: IEEE World Haptics Conference, pp. 43–48 (2013)
6. Yamamoto, T., Yamamoto, Y.: Dielectric constant and resistivity of epidermal stratum corneum. Med. Biol. Eng. **14**(5), 494–500 (1976)
7. Fruhstorfer, H., Abel, U., Garthe, C.-D., Knuttel, A.: Thickness of the stratum corneum of the volar fingertips. Clin. Anat. **13**, 429–433 (2000)

Functional Microanatomical Model of Meissner Corpuscle

From Finite Element Model to Mechano-Transduction

Teja Vodlak[1,2], Zlatko Vidrih[1,2], Primoz Pirih[2], Ales Skorjanc[2],
Janez Presern[2], and Tomaz Rodic[2(✉)]

[1] College of Engineering, Zienkiewicz Centre for Computational Engineering,
Swansea University, Singleton Park, Swansea SA2 8PP, UK
[2] Faculty of Natural Sciences and Engineering,
Department of Materials and Metallurgy, University of Ljubljana,
Askerceva Cesta 12, 1000 Ljubljana, Slovenia
{t.vodlak,z.vidrih}@swansea.ac.uk,
tomaz.rodic@omm.ntf.uni-lj.si

Abstract. A multi-scale framework of human tactile sensation has been developed. The framework consists of two mechanical stages and a post-processing stage. In the first stage, a fingerpad and a stimulus are modelled. The second stage contains a slab of skin containing a Meissner corpuscle. The mechanical output of the second stage is processed by a mechanosensory channel activation model and a spike generator. To our knowledge, this is the first framework linking different levels of sensory processing from mechano-transduction to spike-train comparison. The results of the model are compared to the microneurographical data of a RA1 mechanosensory afferent fibre. The framework could be used as a tool for studying the finger pad-surface interaction in scientific and industrial communities related to touch.

Keywords: Meissner corpuscle · Multi-scale FEM · Touch · Tactile sensibility · Cutaneous mechanoreceptors · Mechano-transduction

1 Introduction

An overview of previous and on-going research of tactile sense modelling [1–5] reveals that biomechanical analyses of tactile scenarios cover mostly macroscopic and in some cases mesoscopic scales. The focus of these models is set on the evolution of stress-strain tensors at sampling points corresponding to the locations of mechanoreceptors, although it is not clear which combinations of stress and strain tensor components are relevant for mechano-transduction (MeT) at the mesoscopic level.

Little attention has been given to the multi-scale modelling of tactile sensations that could bridge the gap between the macroanatomical and the microanatomical or molecular scopes. The main aim of the research framework

© Springer-Verlag Berlin Heidelberg 2014
M. Auvray and C. Duriez (Eds.): EuroHaptics 2014, Part II, LNCS 8619, pp. 377–384, 2014.
DOI: 10.1007/978-3-662-44196-1_46

presented here is to integrate the micro-anatomic features of the mechanorecep-tors and surrounding skin tissues with cell bio-mechanics and the molecular basis of MeT. The proposed bottom-up approach to modelling of human tactile sen-sations is, to our knowledge, the first attempt to provide a complete multi-scale framework which is linking macroscopic tactile stimuli with spike generation taking into account the micromechanics of MeT.

The aim of this paper is to present the development of a finite element (FE) model of the Meissner corpuscle and to demonstrate the current capabilities of the tactile software framework in the case of a typical tactile scenario.

Meissner corpuscle (MC) is an oval-shaped structure situated in the dermis of the skin below the basal lamina, innervated by several types of afferent fibres of the dorsal root ganglion (DRG) neurones. The corpuscle has a relatively complex geometry, comprised of Collagen IV fibre network, the winding afferent fibres and the appendages of Schwann cells [6,7]. The mechanosensory input is conveyed through the unmyelinated endings of the $A\beta$ afferent fibres. Spikes are thought to be initiated outside the MC, at the first myelin sheath. The corresponding RA1 afferent fibres exhibit high sensitivity to mechanic stimulation and rapid adaptation [8].

The mechanosensory channels and gating mechanisms underlying MC MeT have not yet been characterised on the molecular or nanomechanical level. The literature overview [9–11] on the source of mechano-sensory characteristic pro-poses two possible direct gating types of mechanosensitive ionic channels: stretch-sensitive channels, gated by the forces in the membrane bilayer, and channels gated by tether linkage to the extracellular matrix. The density and possible clustering of mechano-sensitive channels in the membrane of the afferent fibres is also not known.

The presented model of MC was verified and calibrated against measure-ments performed in mechano-clamp *in vitro* experiments on DRG neurones [12] and compared with microneurography measurements from RA1 afferent fibres, performed at the University of Gothenburg, Institute of Neuroscience and Physiology.

2   Development of the Microanatomical Model of Meissner Corpuscle

The data on MC anatomical and physiological properties were collected from the literature [6,7]. A computer-aided design (CAD) model of MC was devel-oped (Fig. 1a), taking into consideration the putative positions of mechano-sensitive channels and the two postulated channel gating mechanisms (stretch and tethering).

MC was modelled as an ovoid structure, $50\,\mu m$ long and $20\,\mu m$ in diameter. The MC's collagen network was constructed as an envelope ($2\,\mu m$ thick) and four discoid septa ($3\,\mu m$ thick), which divide the envelope into five lumina. The afferent fibre ($3\,\mu m$ diameter, approx. $230\,\mu m$ long) pierces the septa and spirals around appendages of Schwann cells that fill the lumina. The space between the

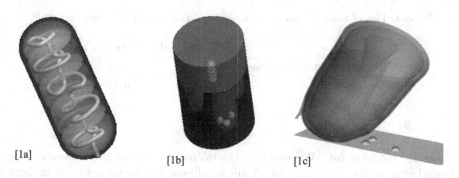

Fig. 1. [1a] CAD model of Meissner corpuscle. [1b] Representative volume of the skin with embedded mechano receptors: three Merkel cells and one Meissner corpuscle. [1c] Macro model of the finger with indicated location of representative volume (red) and mechanical stimulus (color figure online).

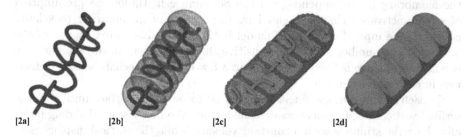

Fig. 2. The details of the micro anatomical FEM of MC. [2a] The afferent fibre. [2b] The fibre with the surrounding appendages of Schwann cells. [2c] Cross section of the envelope and appendages of Schwann cells with the fibre. [2d] Cross section of the envelope with appendages of Schwann cells and the fibre.

neurite and the appendages was set to 100 nm. The appendages were designed as firmly attached to the envelope, but not to the septa or the fibre [6]. As the membrane of living cells is closely associated with the underlying cortical cytoskeleton, the two materials were not modelled separately, but together as an elastic membrane-cytoskeleton adhesion.

The FE model of MC was developed from the CAD model (Fig. 1a). The envelope and membrane-cytoskeleton adhesion were modelled with shell elements, while the solid elements were used in the rest of the model. Separate domains of the FE model are presented in Fig. 2. The list of material properties used in MC model is presented in Table 1.

The FE model of MC was embedded into a micro-FE model of a representative volume within the skin ridges (Fig. 1b). An uncoupled multi-scale FE analysis was then performed in two stages: the mechanical deformations of the first stage were fed as the boundary conditions into the second stage. The macro-scale model consisted of the tip of the index finger and the stimulus surface (Fig. 1c), while the micro-scale model consisted of the skin ridge and the

Table 1. List of material parameters used in FE model of Meissner corpuscle.

Material	Elastic modulus	Poisson ratio
Membrane-cytoskeleton adhesion	339 kPa	0.30
Collagen IV	4 GPa	0.30
Cytosol, Cytoplasm	80 Pa	0.48

embedded model of MC. We note that the micro-scale model also contains three Merkel cells, which are related to SA afferent fibres, but we do not analyse them in this paper.

Under the presumption of the tether-gated mechano-sensitive channels, the proposed input parameter for the following MeT model is the change of distance between the selected spot on the fibre and a corresponding location on the membrane of the appendage of the Schwann cell. Under the presumption of stretch-activated channels, gated by the tension of membrane-cytoskeleton adhesion, the input for the MeT model is the local surface area change of the adhesion. The number of mechanosensitive channels present in the afferent fibre is not known; there is likely a few tens to a few hundred mechanosensitive channels in each sensory neurite.

In each model run, the finger was pressed towards the surface until the prescribed vertical displacement was reached. Then the finger started sliding laterally along the stimulus with a constant velocity, while the vertical displacement remained enforced.

A subset of triangular surface elements belonging to the membrane-cytoskeleton adhesion was randomly selected, representing the locations of the mechano-sensitive channels. The time courses of their distance to the element on the side of the membrane of the appendage, or the surface area change, were used as the mechanical parameters determining the channel activation (open probability).

The spike train output of the model was obtained using a two stage MeT model. In the first stage, mechanosensory currents in the afferent neurite were modelled as a channel inspired by the Hodgkin-Huxley-type sodium channel. In brief, the conductance of the mechanosensory channels is proportional to two gating probability parameters which correspond to channel activation and deactivation, respectively. Maximal activation and deactivation gating probabilities are related to the mechanical deformation via two Boltzmann sigmoid curves. The eight parameters of the model (two time constants, two pairs of parameters defining Boltzman sigmoids, and two parameters defining the inactivation shift) were obtained by fitting the modelled mechanosensory current time courses to the experimental data sets from DRG neurones [12]. The model will be fully described in a separate paper. In the second stage, a leaky integrate-and-fire neuron model of Izhikevich [13] was used to predict the neural spiking activity.

3   Application and Results

In the following section we present the results of the model with the stretch-activated channels. The numerical results were obtained by using a coarse grating as the mechanical stimulus. The width of the ridge is 0.4 mm, the width and the height of the gap is 1.2 mm. The oscillation frequency at sliding velocity 10 mm/s is 6.25 Hz. The indentation-sliding scenarios comprise of 0.2 s loading phase and 0.5 s sliding phase. The procedure was repeated with different final vertical displacements (0.25, 0.5 and 1.0 mm) and sliding velocities (10, 20 and 40 mm/s).

The time courses of surface area change of individual triangular elements of the neurite's membrane-cytoskeleton adhesion exhibit either a monotonic increase or decrease of the surface area during the initial loading phase, which is followed by the oscillations of the surface area during the sliding phase.

Interestingly, the surface area of individual elements oscillates either at the fundamental grating frequency (velocity divided by the period), or at a double frequency during the sliding phase.

The oscillation peaks which correspond to the passage of the grating edge remain roughly of the same amplitude throughout the sliding phase, while the peaks corresponding to the passage of the groove diminish. Higher velocities of sliding as well as larger indentations make this feature even more pronounced (Fig. 3).

The modelled spike trains were obtained by using 150 subsets consisting of 100 random neurite surface elements, which served as the input into the MeT model. The obtained spike trains were compared to the experimental results from microneurography (Fig. 4).

Comparison shows that the spikes produced by the model are roughly coinciding with the spikes obtained by the microneurography recordings from RA1 fibres. Experimentally obtained results have more spikes that seem not to be

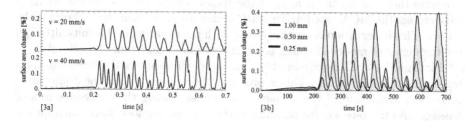

Fig. 3. Normalised surface area change for indentation-sliding scenario with coarse grating stimulus (width of the gap and height of the ridge 1.2 mm, width of the ridge 0.4 mm): loading phase for 0.2 s, followed by travelling phase for 0.5 s. [3a] Different travelling velocities of the finger, constant vertical displacement of 0.5 mm: 20 mm/s (upper plot) and 40 mm/s (lower plot). [3b] Different vertical displacement of the finger, constant travelling velocity of 20 mm/s: 0.25 mm (black), 0.50 mm (blue), 1.00 mm (purple) (color figure online).

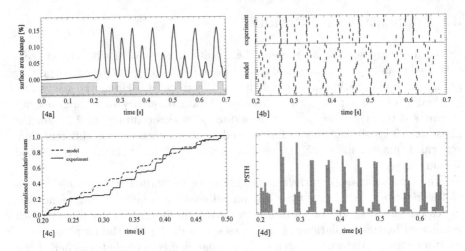

Fig. 4. Results for indentation-sliding scenario with coarse grating stimulus (width of the gap and height of the ridge 1.2 mm, width of the ridge 0.4 mm): loading phase for 0.2 s, followed by travelling phase for 0.5 s with travelling velocity 20 mm/s. [4a] Normalised surface area change over all the membrane-cytoskeleton adhesion elements over the time course. Gray step area: current position of the grating. [4b] Neural spiking activity from experimental results and a random set of predictions of the model during the sliding phase. [4c] The average absolute difference between the normalised cumulative sums of spikes from experimental and model sets is 0.05, while the average square root of quadratic differences is 0.003 at each time step. [4d] PST histogram of predicted spikes from 150 runs of mechano-transduction procedure during the sliding phase.

correlated to the stimulus while the modelled spikes tend to be more self-similar and show less dispersion in their occurrences.

In accordance with the surface area change and current activation of the neurones (not shown) the density of the spikes is the largest when the stimulus edge crosses the MC located underneath; spikes are rare when the MC passes the groove. This observation is roughly in line with the experimental results although the frequency of modelled spikes is larger and more consistent (Fig. 4b, c).

Plotting the PST histogram of the modelled spikes shows the decline in spiking during the time course. This is probably the consequence of the diminishing oscillation amplitude of the surface area change during the successive groove passages. As the peaks corresponding to the diminishing waves may be approximated with an exponential function, the cumulative sum of the modelled spikes is expected to show logarithmic shape when the simulation of the travelling phase is substantially extended (Fig. 4). A part of spike rate reduction may therefore be due to mechanical relaxation.

4   Discussion and Conclusions

In this paper we show a multi-scale framework for modelling human touch. Specifically we modelled the Meissner corpuscle which is innervated by RA1 afferent fibre. The deformations of the MC's sensory neurite membrane, obtained from a two stage mechanical model, are coupled to a two-stage electrophysiological model consisting of a mechanosensory channel model and an integrate-and-fire spike generator. The framework establishes a link between macroscopic tactile stimuli, the molecular basis of mechano-transduction and afferent spike trains of RA1 fibres.

Although the preliminary modelling results are in line with experimental neurographic data, the framework will need to be further optimised by calibration to additional experimental data. This optimisation will be done on both stages of the model. The material properties within the FE model and parameters used for spike prediction and generation will be further calibrated against new experimental results.

Since the FEM analysis is extremely time-consuming due to a large number of FE elements, the final stage of the optimisation of the framework will be employing a neural network. The neural network layer will work as an interpolator, speeding up the model predictions, and will optimally be able to generate spike trains instantly.

The presented framework may find use as a virtual tool in scientific or industrial applications related to neuroscience, haptics, prosthetics, virtual touch and packaging.

Acknowledgements. This work was supported by the European Union under the FP7 programs FP7-NMP-228844 NanoBioTouch and FP7-PEOPLE-317100 Prototouch. The FEM models were prepared in cooperation with Rockfield Software Ltd. and C3M d.o.o. Experimental results were kindly provided by prof. Johan Wessberg from Department of Physiology, University of Gothenburg, Sweden.

References

1. Dandekar, K., Raju, B.I., Srinivasan, M.A.: 3-D finite-element models of human and monkey fingertips to investigate the mechanics of tactile sense. J. Biomech. Eng. **125**(5), 682–691 (2003)
2. Wu, J.Z., Dong, R.G., Rakheja, S., Schopper, A.W., Smutz, W.P.: A structural fingertip model for simulating of the biomechanics of tactile sensation. Med. Eng. Phys. **26**(2), 165–175 (2004)
3. Adams, M., (Coordinator): Nano-engineering biomimetic tactile sensors. Specific targeted research project in Sixth Framework Programme, Priority NMP - Nanotechnologies and nano-sciences, knowledge-based multi-functional materials and new production processes and devices. University of Birmingham (2004)
4. Lesniak, D.R., Gerling, G.J.: Predicting SA-I mechanoreceptor spike times with a skin-neuron model. Math. Biosci. **220**(1), 15–23 (2009)

5. Wang, Z., Wang, L., Ho, V.A., Morikawa, S., Hirai, S.: A 3-D nonhomogeneous FE model of human fingertip based on MRI measurements. IEEE T. Instrum. Measur. **61**(12), 3147–3157 (2012)
6. Takahashi-Iwanaga, H., Shimoda, H.: The three-dimensional microanatomy of Meissner corpuscles in monkey palmar skin. J. Neurocytol. **32**(4), 363–371 (2003)
7. Par, M., Elde, R., Mazurkiewicz, J.E., Smith, A.M., Rice, F.L.: The meissner corpuscle revised: a multiafferented mechanoreceptor with nociceptor immunochemical properties. J. Neurosci. **21**(18), 7236–7246 (2001)
8. Johnson, K.O.: The roles and functions of cutaneous mechanoreceptors. Curr. Opin. Neurobiol. **11**(4), 455–461 (2001)
9. Lumpkin, E.A., Caterina, M.J.: Mechanisms of sensory transduction in the skin. Nature **445**(7130), 858–865 (2007)
10. van Netten, S.M., Kros, C.J.: Gating energies and forces of the mammalian hair cell transducer channel and related hair bundle mechanics. Proc. Biol. Sci. **267**(1455), 1915–1923 (2000)
11. Guharay, F., Sachs, F.: Stretch-activated single ion channel currents in tissue-cultured embryonic chick skeletal muscle. J. Physiol. **352**, 685–701 (1984)
12. Hao, J., Delmas, P.: Recording of mechanosensitive currents using piezoelectrically driven mechanostimulator. Nat. Protoc. **6**(7), 979–990 (2011)
13. Izhikevich, E.M.: Resonate-and-fire neurons. Neural Netw. **14**(6–7), 883–894 (2001)

Modeling Pneumatic Actuators
for a Refreshable Tactile Display

Alexander Russomanno[1]([⊠]), R. Brent Gillespie[1], Sile O'Modhrain[2],
and James Barber[1]

[1] University of Michigan, Mechanical Engineering, Ann Arbor, MI, USA
arussoma@umich.edu
[2] University of Michigan, School of Music, Theatre, and Dance,
Performing Arts Technology, Ann Arbor, MI, USA
{brentg,sileo,jbarber}@umich.edu

Abstract. In this paper, we develop a dynamic lumped parameter model of a pneumatic membrane actuator to inform the design of a shape display that meets force, speed and spatial density specifications for refreshable braille. A system identification experiment is undertaken to determine relevant system parameters that remain fixed under variation of the lengths of the connecting tubes and cavity volumes. Parameter values were found to fit a numerical solution to a step response in pressure for multiple line lengths. Two additional experiments were conducted using various applied pressures and actuator cavity volumes to validate the model. Extrapolation of the model to the dimensions of a first prototype scaled at 5/3 braille dot size and spacing predicts a 1.4 Hz bandwidth whereas experiments yield a 1.7 Hz bandwidth.

Keywords: Pneumatic actuators · Tactile graphics · Refreshable braille display

1 Introduction

Current braille display technology is based on long slender piezo bimorph actuators that can only render a single line of text at a time. Imagine viewing your computer screen one line at a time. Our goal is to address this problem head-on by developing new technology for a large-area refreshable tactile display based on tightly packed pneumatic actuators. Such a display would not only give braille readers access to a full-page display of braille text, but would also enable blind users to access spatially distributed information like maps, spreadsheets, and graphs that are otherwise impossible to access digitally.

Simple experiments involving a thimble on a finger exploring embossed braille will reveal that fine features within the distribution of forces across the finger contact patch are necessary for braille reading. Surface haptic technologies that modulate the resultant normal or tangential force across the contact patch without modulating the distribution of forces are not sufficient to render readable braille. Thus technologies based on electrostatics and electrovibration [1]

© Springer-Verlag Berlin Heidelberg 2014
M. Auvray and C. Duriez (Eds.): EuroHaptics 2014, Part II, LNCS 8619, pp. 385–393, 2014.
DOI: 10.1007/978-3-662-44196-1_47

or the squeeze-film effect [2] cannot be used to create a refreshable braille display. Further, the perceptual invariants arising from the constancy of shape and location of braille dots within a moving contact patch are likely important for readability. Thus we are pursuing the creation of a *shape display* technology, wherein densely spaced dots are individually actuated. Pneumatic displays offer the opportunity to provide the necessary modulated forces on the fingertip and are currently being explored for shape display for larger features such as buttons (for example, by Tactus Corp.). To the best of our knowledge, no one is currently addressing features at the scale of braille dots using pneumatic methods. Other shape displays have been built using piezo bimorphs (Metec "Hyperbraille"[1]) and shape-memory alloys [3]. The advantage of using pneumatics is that the power source is spatially separated from the actuator allowing many small tactile features to be tightly packed together. One disadvantage of using pneumatics is the complexity due to an independently controlled valve and pneumatic line for each tactile feature.

In the design proposed here, a tangible feature is created by pressurizing a cavity beneath a thin elastic membrane. This in turn drives a pin that interfaces with the reader's finger. The performance of these actuators is based on the properties of the elastic membrane, the pneumatic lines, cavities, and valves used in the pneumatic system. In this paper, a model is developed that considers the relevant actuator properties in order to provide insight for determining how to scale the design to meet force, speed and spatial density specifications for tactile features. Current specifications indicate that a refreshable braille display should have dots that are 0.5 mm high, with a spatial density (i.e. pitch) of 2.5 mm. This corresponds to the standard braille dot spacing within a single cell. Under a downward force of 50–150 mN applied by typical readers, the braille dot should maintain a height of at least 0.25 mm. For single line electronic braille devices, the desired line refresh rate is 10 Hz, but for a large-area multiple-line or full-page device, a rate on the order of 1 Hz may be tolerable [4].

2   Overview

Our actuator assembly consists of a thin polydimethylsiloxane (PDMS) membrane sandwiched between two layers of machined plastic, called the pin housing layer and the channel layer (see Fig. 1). Each pin occupies a cylindrical space in the pin housing layer and is driven upward based on the localized deflection of the membrane when the cavity below the membrane is pressurized. This configuration allows for a pin to return to its lowered position under the force of gravity once the cavity under the membrane returns to atmospheric pressure. The actuator membrane is very simple to realize. A 10:1 ratio of PDMS and curing agent (Sylgard 184, Dow Corning) is spun on a glass slide to create a thin film with a thickness of approximately 100–200 μm. The elastomer is cured in an oven at 75° C for 2.5 h. This long cure time allows any air bubbles to escape

---

[1] http://web.metec-ag.de/

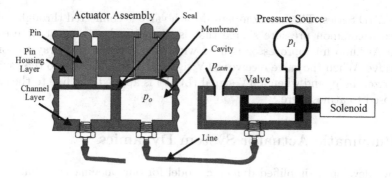

Fig. 1. Schematic of pneumatic actuator system.

from the polymer. Once the film cures, it is peeled away from the glass slide and placed between the pin housing layer and the channel layer.

The pins are designed to fit in the pin housing to achieve a maximum deflection of 0.5 mm corresponding to the desired maximum pin height for braille. Upon actuation, the pins move upward until the pin shoulder seats and the boss on the pin protrudes 0.5 mm. The bottom section of the pin housing is designed to allow for the largest possible diameter of the free membrane and thereby the largest membrane deflection. The diameter is limited by the standard separation between the braille dots, which is 2.5 mm [4]. The portions of the membrane that remain compressed between the stiff upper and lower layers act as a seal between the cavities; the membrane that is free to be deflected serves as the actuator. This simplifies the design, as both the actuators and the seal between them are made using a single PDMS membrane. The channel layer consists of cavities and routing channels that are patterned according to the separation of the pins in the pin housing layer. Hose barbs are used to individually connect thin elastic tubes ("PTFE 0.022 ID", Cole-Palmer) to each cavity.

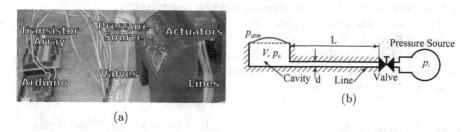

Fig. 2. (a) Picture of the pneumatic actuator setup. (b) Schematic of pneumatic actuator system.

A layout of our prototype system is shown in Fig. 2a. The pressure in each cavity is controlled by a 3-way, 24 V electronically-controlled pneumatic solenoid valve (LHD Series, The Lee Company). Each valve is connected through a manifold to a common pressure source that is maintained at a constant pressure p_i. An Arduino microprocessor is used with a 24 V transistor array to control each valve. When the valve receives 24 V signal (HIGH), the line to the cavity is pressurized by p_i and when a 0 V signal (LOW) is applied, the line to the cavity is exposed to atmosphere.

3   Pneumatic Actuator System Dynamics

Here we develop a simplified dynamic model for our pneumatic actuator, with the aim of describing how the speed of response depends on model parameters and scales with actuator packing density. The system consists of a constant pressure source p_i, a solenoid valve, a connecting line, and a cavity at a variable pressure p_o. A schematic of the actuator system is shown in Fig. 2b, with relevant variables and parameters indicated for each element.

The speed of response of the pneumatic actuator can be described as the *pressure response* of a pneumatic line-cavity system. Initially, the pressure p_o in the cavity is at atmospheric pressure p_{atm}. At time $t = 0$, the valve is opened and the gas in the line begins to move. The pressure in the cavity p_o increases over time until it reaches p_i. The system model is developed in two parts corresponding to the resistance of the line and the capacitance of the cavity.

3.1   Pneumatic Line and Valve Model

The resistance due to the line and orifices results in a pressure drop, decreasing the air flow rate into the cavity. There is also a time delay related to the speed at which the acoustic pressure wave travels the tube. The pressure losses and time delay in pneumatic elements have been studied in depth [5]. However, we seek a simple model to describe how tactile features can be scaled to meet the speed and spatial density specifications, and thus we assume the flow to be laminar and the time delay due to the pressure wave to be negligible.

The fluid in the line is modeled as incompressible so that a force due to the pressure differential will act to move the fluid through the line as a single lump. The forces due to acceleration of the flow are neglected. Equating the sum of the force due to the pressure differential $(p_i - p_o)$ with the force due to flow resistance F_{fr} yields:

$$A(p_i - p_o) = F_{fr} , \qquad (1)$$

where A is area of the pipe. The force of friction for steady pipe flow is related to the area of the pipe A, the sum of the distributed pressure loss ΔP_d (due to the line resistance) and localized pressure losses ΔP_ℓ (due to line fittings and the valve): $F_{fr} = A(\Delta P_d + \Delta P_\ell)$ [6]. The distributed pressure loss along a tube is given by the Darcy-Weisbach equation [7] as:

$$\Delta P_d = f\frac{\rho_\ell L}{d}\frac{v^2}{2} , \qquad (2)$$

where f is the friction factor, L is the length of pipe, d is the diameter of the pipe, v is the flow velocity, and ρ_ℓ is the density of the fluid in the pipe. For laminar flow, $f = 64/Re$, where Re is the Reynold's number equal to $\rho_\ell vd/\mu$. Keeping the physical parameters of the system and lumping the rest into a constant k_d, the distributed pressure loss becomes $\Delta P_d = k_d Lv/d^2$ [7]. The localized pressure losses for each element of the pneumatic system, i.e. the line fittings and the valve, are lumped together and defined as $\Delta P_\ell = k_\ell \rho_\ell v^2$. Substituting the distributed and localized losses into (1) yields the following relationship between fluid flow in a line and the pressure difference at the inlet and outlet:

$$(p_i - p_o) = k_d \frac{L}{d^2} v + k_\ell \rho_\ell v^2 . \tag{3}$$

3.2   Behavior in a Cavity

To develop a relationship between the air flow rate and the pressure change in the cavity, we apply conservation of mass, the ideal gas law, and an energy balance to a volume of gas. For this model, the gas is taken to obey the perfect gas law with $P = \rho_c RT$, where P is the absolute pressure of a gas, ρ_c is the density of the air within the cavity, R is the specific gas constant and T is the temperature measured in Kelvin. The continuity equation equates the mass flow into the cavity to the time variation of mass within the cavity and is given by

$$\rho_c v A = \frac{d}{dt}(\rho_c V) = \frac{d\rho_c}{dt} V + \rho_c \frac{dV}{dt} , \tag{4}$$

where V is the volume of the cavity. The membrane makes up the upper wall of the cavity and will deflect as the pressure in the cavity p_o increases, thereby increasing the cavity volume. The density within the cavity ρ_c changes with respect to the pressure p_o. This relationship, corresponding to the compression of the air within the cavity, is governed by a polytropic process defined by:

$$\frac{dp_o}{p_o} = n \frac{d\rho_c}{\rho_c} , \tag{5}$$

where p_o is the absolute pressure in the cavity and n is the polytropic exponent. Rearranging Eq. (4) and substituting in (5) results in

$$vA = \frac{dV}{dp_o} \frac{dp_o}{dt} + \frac{V}{np_o} \frac{dp_o}{dt} = \frac{dp_o}{dt} \left(\frac{dV}{dp_o} + \frac{V}{np_o} \right) \tag{6}$$

Based on our initial design of the pneumatic actuator, the membrane deflection is small compared to the size of the cavity, so we assume dV/dp_o is small and can be neglected. Applying the ideal gas law for p_o, Eq. (6) simplifies to

$$v = \frac{1}{nA} \frac{V}{\rho_c RT} \frac{dp_o}{dt} = \frac{C}{\rho_c A} \frac{dp_o}{dt} , \tag{7}$$

where we define C as the effective capacitance of the cavity equal to V/nRT. To find the governing equation for the combined line-cavity system, we substitute

Eq. (7) into (3). We consider the input of the system to be 0 for $t < 0$ and p_i for $t \geq 0$. The time-varying pressure p_o in the cavity is governed by a nonlinear 1st order ODE for $t \geq 0$:

$$k_\ell \rho_\ell \left(\frac{C}{\rho_c A} \frac{dp_o}{dt} \right)^2 + k_d \frac{L}{d^2} \frac{C}{\rho_c A} \frac{dp_o}{dt} + (p_o - p_i) = 0. \tag{8}$$

4   System Identification and Model Validation

The model of the pneumatic actuator system derived in the previous section includes geometric characteristics and parameters that cannot be found directly. We used a system identification process to determine the unknown parameters, k_d and k_ℓ, relating to the flow resistance. According to the model, k_d and k_ℓ remain constant for different lengths L of lines. A pressure transducer was fixed to a cavity with known volume V, and the pressure response of the cavity $p_o(t)$ to an applied constant external pressure p_i was recorded for different lengths of line. We used a forward Euler method to numerically solve Eq. (8) and a search algorithm to find the k_d and k_ℓ values that best fit the pressure response curves. Using the ideal gas law, the density of the air in the line ρ_ℓ is calculated at each time t from the average of $p_o(t)$ and p_i. The density of the air in the cavity ρ_c is calculated in the same manner from the measured cavity pressure $p_o(t)$. The values for the other parameters used in the calculations are listed in the table in Fig. 3. The best fit was determined using the built-in `fmincon` function in MATLAB to minimize the sum of the norm of errors between the experimental and theoretical curves for the different line lengths. The best fit k_d and k_ℓ values were found to be 4.31e-04 $Pa\ s$ and 20.80, respectively. The theoretical curves obtained match closely with the experimental data as shown in Fig. 3.

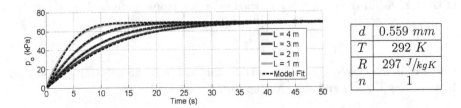

Fig. 3. The cavity pressure p_o over time for different lengths L of line an a table of the parameters used to find the theoretical curves using the model.

Two sets of experiments were performed to validate the model described by Eq. (8). In the first experiment, we varied the cavity volume and recorded the pressure response for a known applied pressure $p_i = 69\,kPag$ and line length $L = 2\,\mathrm{m}$. In the second experiment, we varied the applied pressure p_i for a known cavity volume $V = 61\,\mathrm{mL}$ and line length $L = 2\,\mathrm{m}$. Using the experimental flow resistance parameters $k_d = 4.31\mathrm{e}{-}04\ Pa\ s$ and $k_\ell = 20.80$ found from the system

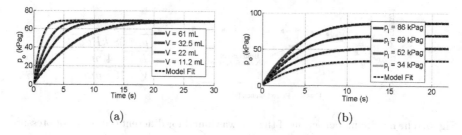

Fig. 4. Experimental data and a theoretical fits for the cavity pressure p_o over time for (a) different cavity volumes V and (b) applied pressures p_i.

identification and the relevant system parameters listed in the table in Fig. 3, the model described by Eq. (8) was solved numerically to find the theoretical pressure responses $p_o(t)$ for both experiments. The results in Fig. 4a and b show that the experimental data corresponds closely with the theoretical fit from the model.

5   Discussion

In this paper, we developed a simple model for the pressure response of the proposed pneumatic actuator design. The experimentation showed that the model scaled well for different applied pressures and cavity sizes. Based on the model, the time response curves for different sized cavities and line lengths can be extrapolated and scaled to the intended actuator size needed to meet the spacing specifications for refreshable braille.

To evaluate the predictive power of the model for an actuator near the desired scale, a pneumatic actuator scaled 5/3 to that of a standard braille cell was fabricated, shown in Fig. 2a. The actuator had a cavity volume of $153\,mm^3$, a line length of $4\,m$, and had the same fittings as used in the experiments described in Sect. 4. To test the pressure response of the actuator, a digital dial indicator (Fowler 54-562-777) was used to measure the maximum displacement of the pin. The indicator samples slowly, but advantageously has a mode wherein it registers the maximum displacement within a time period. A solenoid valve was used to apply $68\,kPag$ pressure pulses of various time durations to the cavity. We found the pulse duration at which the maximum deflection began to decrease to be $0.6\,s$ (see Fig. 5), corresponding to a bandwidth of $1.7\,Hz$. The pressure response time predicted by the model was calculated as the 0–95 % rise time. Using the relevant characteristics of the actuator listed in Fig. 5 and the resistance parameters found in Sect. 4, the pressure response was found to be $0.7\,s$, corresponding to a bandwidth of $1.4\,Hz$, which is on the order of the experimental value found.

According to the data sheet, the indicator measures with a downward force of 100 mN $\pm$15 %, which is in the range of the force typically applied by braille readers. The maximum deflection of the membrane under this load was about

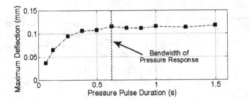

Fig. 5. The maximum deflection of the pin was found for different durations of pressure pulses.

0.1 mm. While this result for the scaled braille dot design is short of the desired 0.25 mm deflection for standard-sized braille dots under this load, the raised pins were perceivable by touch. An experienced braille reader was able to identify displayed letters of the alphabet without errors. An appropriately scaled version was also fabricated that can be read without difficultly.

Future work will focus on improving these devices by using a higher pressure source and changing the properties of the membrane so that the actuators can achieve larger deflections and sustain higher forces. Further, we will expand the model to include the mechanics of the membrane under the action of the load. In the model developed in this paper, the additional volume due to the displacing membrane was neglected. As revealed in the modeling, minimizing the cavity size results in faster actuator response. The proposed design allows the volume of the cavity beneath the free membrane to be reduced to zero. In this case, the volume due to membrane deflection would be significant. By including the mechanics of the membrane, the pressure response for the varying volume case can be found. We will also improve the model by considering the fluid in the line as compressible. For pneumatic lines with large pressure drops, the compressibility of the fluid makes a significant difference.

Future work will also focus on the interface that connects the pneumatic actuator to the human finger via the sliding pin. This work will include perceptual studies in order to quantify the limits of human perception in distinguishing the pins at different sizes and spatial densities. We will be scaling down the design even further to study how it may be used to create features that feel continuous or have textures.

Acknowledgements. The authors would like to acknowledge Bo Yu for his assistance with the modeling, simulation, and data analysis.

References

1. Bau, O., Poupyrev, I., Israr, A., Harrison, C.: TeslaTouch: electrovibration for touch surfaces. In: Proceedings of the 23nd Annual ACM Symposium on User Interface Software and Technology, UIST '10, pp. 283–292. ACM, New York (2010). http://doi.acm.org/10.1145/1866029.1866074

2. Winfield, L., Glassmire, J., Colgate, J.E., Peshkin, M.: T-PaD: tactile pattern display through variable friction reduction. In: Second Joint EuroHaptics Conference, 2007 and Symposium on Haptic Interfaces for Virtual Environment and Teleoperator Systems, World Haptics 2007, pp. 421–426. IEEE, Mar 2007
3. Howe, R.D.: The shape of things to come: pin-based tactile shape displays. In: Proceedings of the 4th International Conference Eurohaptics, pp. 2–11 (2004)
4. Runyan, N.H., Blazie, D.B.: The continuing quest for the 'holy braille' of tactile displays, pp. 81 070G–81 070G–17 (2011). http://dx.doi.org/10.1117/12.897382
5. Richer, E., Hurmuzlu, Y.: A high performance pneumatic force actuator system: Part i-nonlinear mathematical model. J. Dyn. Syst. Meas. Control 122(3), 416–425 (2000)
6. Barber, A.: Pneumatic Handbook. Elsevier, London (1997)
7. Munson, B., Young, D., Okiishi, T., Huebsch, W.: Fundamentals of Fluid Mechanics. John Wiley & Sons Inc., New York (2009)

Modeling the Weber Fraction of Vibrotactile Amplitudes Using Gain Control Through Global Feedforward Inhibition

Ken E. Friedl[✉], Yao Qin, Daniel Ostler, and Angelika Peer

Institute of Automatic Control Engineering, Technische Universität München,
Munich, Germany
{friedl,angelika.peer}@tum.de,
http://www.lsr.ei.tum.de

Abstract. Weber's law describes the linear drop of discriminative performance with increased base intensity of a stimulus. So far, this phenomenon has been modeled using multistable attractor decision networks based on the principle of biased competition between two mutually inhibiting recurrent neural populations. Due to the sensitive balance in a multistable fluctuation-driven regime, these decision models can only account for Weber's law in a narrow stimulus range. Psychophysical data shows though that the human exhibits this characteristic for a broad stimulus range. Recent neurophysiological evidence suggests that global feedforward inhibition expands the dynamic range of cortical neuron populations and acts as a gain control. In this paper, we introduce a computational model that exploits this type of inhibition and shows through a fit between simulation results and psychophysical data that it is a potential explanation for the principle mechanism behind Weber's law.

Keywords: Weber's law · Decision making · Attractor dynamics · Global inhibition

1 Introduction

A prominent psychopyhsical relationship was discovered by E.H. Weber in 1834 [3] for the differential perception of weights. He discovered that the just noticeable difference (jnd) for two relatively heavy weights is larger than for two relatively light weights. The derived Weber's law describes a linear relationship between stimulus intensity and its jnd: $\Delta\phi = c\phi$. Where $\Delta\phi$ is the just noticeable difference and c a constant fraction of the stimulus intensity ϕ [3].

So far Weber's law has been neurophysiologically modeled for vibrotactile frequency discrimination only [2]. The model is based on biased competition in a fluctuation-driven multistable regime of two competing mutually inhibiting neural populations. Due to the nature of sensitive attractor dynamics, this model has to be carefully tuned to exhibit Weber's law for a limited band of frequencies.

© Springer-Verlag Berlin Heidelberg 2014
M. Auvray and C. Duriez (Eds.): EuroHaptics 2014, Part II, LNCS 8619, pp. 394–402, 2014.
DOI: 10.1007/978-3-662-44196-1_48

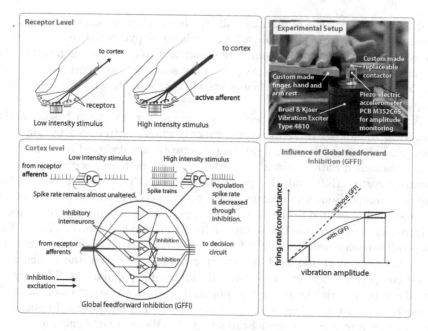

Fig. 1. Principle of global feedforward inhibition within the scope of vibrotactile amplitude discrimination

Psychophysical experiments show, however, that Weber's law holds for a wider range of frequencies of vibrotactile stimuli [13].

Vibrotactile amplitudes are encoded in the firing rate of individual receptor afferents, originating from the Pacinian and Meissner cells, and by the number of active afferents from these receptors as shown in Fig. 1.

In this paper, we address a potential neurophysiologically plausible computational model of Weber's law based on recent neurophysiological findings on GABAergic interneurons, which carry out global feedforward inhibition [17]. Additionally, we show that the model was matched to behavioral vibrotactile amplitude discrimination data.

2   Materials and Methods

2.1   Neurodynamical Model

The cortex is sensitive to weak stimuli but still responds to strong ones without saturating. While the complete mechanism is not fully understood yet, a certain subtype of inhibitory GABAergic interneurons carrying out global feedforward inhibition (GFFI) on pyramidal cells (PC) may play a crucial role in this process. These cell subtypes can perform distinct linear transformations and thus, increase the dynamic range of the cortex. The so-called parvalbumin-expressing (PV) neurons, for example, carry out division [17]. PV cells can represent up to 50 % of the GABAergic interneurons and have been found to inhibit compartments of cortical pyramidal cells [8]. Hence, they can control the spiking threshold and therefore the probability of spiking of pyramidal cells as a function of input strength [12]. PV-inhibition matched to excitation is possibly the reason for modulations in response gain in the somatosensory cortex [5,11] and therefore could explain Weber's law as we will demonstrate with the help of our computational model.

We modeled the dynamics behind perceptual discrimination based on the theoretical framework of attractor networks originally introduced by Machens *et al.* [9]. This two-node mutual inhibition network was designed to account for phenomenological data retrieved from the macaque monkey's secondary somatosensory cortex (S2) and the prefrontal cortex (PFC) during vibrotactile frequency comparison. The monkey's task was to perceive two successive vibrotactile stimuli presented to the same finger separated by a pause and to compare their frequency, the so-called two-interval discrimination using forced-choice. The two possible choices rate either the first or the second frequency higher than the other. Machens *et al.* modeled an attractor network based on the principle of biased competition between two mutually inhibiting populations. The sign of the difference in activities of the two populations after the comparison phase is considered the determining factor for correctly comparing the two frequencies. But in its current form the model cannot exhibit Weber's law behavior.

We applied the principle of Machens' frequency comparison model to vibrotactile amplitude comparison and incorporated GFFI to account for Weber's law. In the following, amplitudes are denoted as a_1 for the reference stimulus and a_2 for the comparison stimulus. The model is comprised of three distinct phases: loading, maintenance and comparison/decision (Fig. 2). During the loading and comparison/decision phase, stimuli evoked activity of S2 from the a_1-dependent

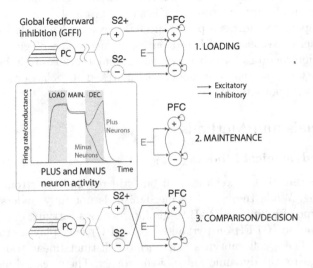

Fig. 2. Machens' model [9] with integrated global feedforward inhibition

reference and a_2-dependent comparison stimulus, respectively, is transferred to the PFC populations. No external input acts during maintenance in which the activity of PFC maintains for comparison.

The functional principle of this network is basically a transition between appropriate fixed points during each of the three phases of the task. During loading, an independent stable fixed point for amplitude a_1 is created, during maintenance a_1-dependent information is kept in a quasi-continuum of fixed points - a line attractor; and finally, an unstable fixed point depending on the value of amplitude a_2 carries out the comparison/decision. In the stationary mean-field approximation of this network, where population activity is averaged, the transition between attractor states is achieved by shifting the so-called i/o-function [9], which describes the relationship between inhibitory input and synaptic output for each of the two populations, to achieve mentioned attractor types. The dynamics of the network are described by the following equations:

$$\tau\dot{x} = -x + f(-\omega_I y + \lambda g_{E,x}(t)) + \xi \tag{1}$$

$$\tau\dot{y} = -y + f(-\omega_I x + \lambda g_{E,x}(t)) + \xi \tag{2}$$

Equation 1 describes the plus neuron and Eq. 2 the minus neuron population activity, where $\tau = 80\,\text{ms}$ denotes the time constant of the neuron population, x its activity, f characterizes the i/o function which is dependent on the inhibitory synaptic weights $\omega_I = 1.1575 \cdot 10^{-3}$. The activities of the opposite populations are denoted as x or y, the constant scaling factor is $\lambda = 2.5625$ and the external excitatory inputs are $g_{E,x}$ or $g_{E,y}$, respectively. The following values for $g_{E,x,..}$ and $g_{E,y,..}$ were applied:

$$g_{E,x,load} = 2 + 0.3 + \left(\frac{\alpha_{inh}a_1}{\beta_{inh}a_1} - k\right) \tag{3}$$

$$g_{E,y,load} = 2 + 0.3 - \left(\frac{\alpha_{inh}a_1}{\beta_{inh}a_1} - k\right) \tag{4}$$

$$g_{E,x,maintain} = g_{E,y,maintain} = 2 \tag{5}$$

$$g_{E,x,dec} = 2 - 0.5 + \left(\frac{\alpha_{inh}a_2}{\beta_{inh}a_2} - k\right) \tag{6}$$

$$g_{E,y,dec} = 2 - 0.5 - \left(\frac{\alpha_{inh}a_2}{\beta_{inh}a_2} - k\right) \tag{7}$$

where $\alpha_{inh} = 3 \cdot 1.05 \cdot 10^{-4}$ and $\beta_{inh} = 100$ are coefficients shaping the relationship between stimulus amplitude and conductance (Fig. 1), $k = 1.05 \cdot 10^{-4}$ is a constant scaling factor and a_1 and a_2 range from $40\,\mu\text{m}$ to $120\,\mu\text{m}$ in our particular case. The unit of all conductances $g_{E,..}$ is nS. All values for the parameters, except α_{inh}, β_{inh} and k, were taken from the original biologically realistic decision model [9]. α_{inh}, β_{inh} and k, which control GFFI were matched to fit the decision model to our psychophysical data, by maintaining a typical logarithmically shaped activation curve of GFFI found in [12].

Global feedforward inhibition (GFFI), see Fig. 1, leads to a behavior that is of divisive nature. The stronger the input stimulus, the stronger GFFI. With higher stimulus intensities more peripheral mechanoreceptor afferents are "active"; downstream, in the somatosensory cortex, each individual presynaptic neuron contributes less to the activation of the connected populations, because the excitatory postsynaptic activation threshold $EPSG$ is increased due to GFFI. Thus, this principle globally acts as cortical gain modulation of divisive nature on the pyramidal cells. Physical vibrotactile stimuli at comparatively high amplitudes (as opposed to lower amplitudes) activate more vibration sensitive receptors (Pacinian or Meissner corpuscles) and their afferents, since stimuli induced mechanical waves traveling through the skin tissue reach the critical absolute receptor activation threshold at a higher number of receptors. Additionally, the firing rate of each afferent is higher with more intensive stimuli. Since GFFI acts more intensively on stronger stimuli, distances between firing rates corresponding to physically equidistant vibration amplitudes decrease as a function of increasing base amplitude (Fig. 1). Therefore, differences in firing rate, which are being compared in the decision circuit, decrease with increasing stimulus base amplitudes. This principle alone does not account for the probabilistic nature of decisions. The important term here is the additive Gaussian noise $\xi = 0.3$ which leads to the necessary fluctuation to calculate the Weber fraction using the method of constant stimuli [6]. The mean field approximation as described by above mentioned equations was simulated using Matlab.

2.2 Psychophysical Experiments

Participants. Three human subjects (2 male, 1 female) volunteered for this study. They were right handed and reported normal tactile perception.

Apparatus. Vibrotactile stimuli were generated by a frequency generator (Agilent 33520B, 2-channel, 30 MHz) and triggered through a real-time Preemt-RT Simulink model on Ubuntu 12.04 and outputted through a DAQ card (MeCoVis DAQ board). The generated sine waves were transferred through an amplifier (Brüel&Kjær Power Amplifier Type 2718) to the vibration exciter (Measurement Exciter Type 4810). A custom made probe (ø 5 mm) contacted the distal pad of the right forefinger of a subject (Fig. 1). For vibration amplitude monitoring, it hosted a miniature accelerometer (Piezoelectronics PCB-M352C65) which was connected through a signal amplifier (Piezoelectronics PCB 482C) with an oscilloscope (HAMEG, Digital Storage oscilloscope HM205-s). For automatic calculation of the difference limen (DL), subjects had to confirm their decision using a custom made pair of buttons on a console connected to the DAQ card. To mask environmental and sounds generated through the stimulator, subjects wore headphones (Direct Sound Ex-29 Extreme Isolation) playing pink noise.

Procedure. The method of constant stimuli was applied and subjects were sequentially presented with vibrotactile stimuli pairs. Each stimulus had a duration

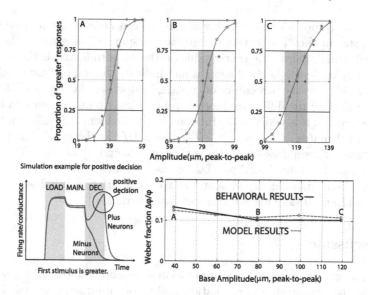

Fig. 3. Comparison of behavioral results and simulations using proposed computational model.

of 500 ms (base and comparison amplitude, randomized order, 500 ms interval between successive stimuli of a pair). Subjects were asked to press one of the two buttons on the console in their left hand, rating either the first or second stimulus as "greater". Three base vibration amplitudes (40, 80 and 120μm), representing a typical range from a relatively low to a relatively high amplitude, were presented within nine pairs (three higher and three lower amplitudes and in combination with an equal amplitude). Each pair was presented six times in a random fashion. The experiments were conducted under ethics committee approval No. 2925/10 from the Ethics committee of the Technische Universität München. The averaged results across subjects are shown in Fig. 3.

3   Results

Figure 3 illustrates the simulation results from the neurocomputational model and how the Weber fraction was calculated using the method of constant stimuli. The behavioral results to which the model parameters were fitted are displayed in the same figure. Weber fraction holds behaviorally and for the simulation, resulting in a constant between 0.11 and 0.12. The upper part shows mean-field population activity plots for plus (red circles) and minus (blue stars) neurons for the three phases: loading, maintenance and decision. Nine amplitude pairs around the base amplitudes (40, 60, 80, 100 and 120μm) were presented 6 times each to the model. The question was whether the first stimulus was greater than the second. Correct decisions were indicated by a higher population activity of plus in comparison to minus neurons for the case of a stronger reference stimulus

a_1 ("greater" response) and a higher minus neuron activity for a stronger a_2. One blue star in the "Proportion of "greater" responses" diagram is the result of 6 tested stimuli pairs. The center value on the amplitude axis is the reference stimulus amplitude. Higher and lower values indicate the comparison amplitude. The y axis indicates the percentage of "greater" responses. At 25 % and 75 %, the values to calculate the difference limen can be looked up on the amplitude axis. The less steep and less s-curved the function is, the smaller is the difference limen DL which calculates as $DL = \frac{DL_u - DL_l}{2}$, where DL_u is the upper boundary at 75 % of "greater" responses and DL_l is the lower boundary at 25 %. The Weber fraction results from dividing $\Delta\phi = DL$ by the reference stimulus $c = \frac{\Delta\phi}{\phi}$. In our amplitude discrimination experiment the Weber fraction is relatively constant between 0.11 and 0.12. This is consistent with literature [1].

4   Discussion

In this paper, we presented a computational neurophysiologically motivated model for the amplitude discrimination ability of vibrotactile stimuli capturing Weber's law. The crucial mechanism is based on cortical gain modulation by global feedforward inhibition (GFFI) leading to larger distances in postsynaptic firing rates of the globally inhibited pyramidal cell population between weaker stimuli than between stronger ones. Thus, decisions when comparing weaker stimuli are easier and less fluctuating as compared to decisions to be made comparing stronger stimuli. The decision model applied in this context [9] is a fine-tuned attractor network which shifts between fixed points and a quasi continuum line attractor state working as memory of the reference stimulus. An arbitrary linear relationship between the physical stimulus frequency and the corresponding conductances in S2 was assumed. Integrating GFFI, we applied a non-linear relationship between physical stimuli and the corresponding neural activity of S2. Additive Gaussian noise leads to fluctuations in decisions when firing rates of the stimuli pair are similar, accounting for the probabilitic nature of decisions. Using this combination, Weber's law for vibrotactile amplitude comparison was modeled with the psychophysical method of constant stimuli [6] and matched to behavioral data. Although the model by Machens *et al.* was originally designed for frequency discrimination, there is biological evidence that this decision principle is more generally applicable [15] to other decisions.

Weber's law by GFFI would, in principle, be applicable in combination with other types of decision models, such as other diffusion models by [15,18], where decision evidence is integrated over time until the decision boundary is reached, or phenomenological models with similar dynamics to a fixed boundary Ornstein-Uhlenbeck process [16]. The combination of GFFI with decision models could also account for other perceptual modalities. Besides the somatosensory cortex [4], there is accumulating biological evidence that GFFI plays a crucial role behind cortical gain control in the visual [14] and auditory cortex [10].

An important question is, if the principle of GFFI can be applied to frequency discrimination and thus, extend Deco's model [2]. Unlike amplitudes, which are coded in spike rates and number of active afferents, frequencies are encoded in a mixture of rate code and phase locked temporal firing patterns [7] in primary somatosensory cortex S1. Recordings from the macaque monkey's somatosensory cortex S2 exhibit non-linear distribution of firing rates for uniformly distributed frequencies [9]. This suggests that a non-linear scaling, such as through GFFI, happens in S2 or before.

References

1. Craig, J.C.: Difference threshold for intensity of tactile stimuli. Percept. Psychophys. **11**, 150–152 (1972). Springer
2. Deco, G., Scarano, L., Soto-Faraco, S.: Weber's law in decision making: integrating behavioral data in humans with a neurophysiological model. J. Neurosci. Soc. Neurosci. **27**, 11192–11200 (2007)
3. Fechner, G.T.: Elemente der Psychosophysik. vol. 2 (1860)
4. Gabernet, L., Jadhav, S.P., Feldman, D.E., Carandini, M., Scanziani, M.: Somatosensory integration controlled by dynamic thalamocortical feed-forward inhibition. Neuron **48**, 315–327 (2005). Elsevier
5. Gentet, L.J., Avermann, M., Matyas, F., Staiger, J.F., Petersen, C.C.: Membrane potential dynamics of GABAergic neurons in the barrel cortex of behaving mice. Neuron **65**, 422–435 (2010)
6. Gescheider, G.A.: Psychophysics: the fundamentals. Psychol. Press. **65**, 422–435 (1976)
7. Harvey, M.A., Saal, H.P., Dammann III, J.F., Bensmaia, S.J.: Multiplexing stimulus information through rate and temporal codes in primate somatosensory cortex. PLoS Biol. Pub. Lib. Sci. **11**, e1001558 (2013)
8. Kawaguchi, Y., Kubota, Y.: GABAergic cell subtypes and their synaptic connections in rat frontal cortex. Cerebral Cortex **7**, 476–486 (1997). Oxford Univ Press
9. Machens, C.K., Romo, R., Brody, C.D.: Flexible control of mutual inhibition: a neural model of two-interval discrimination. Science **307**, 1121–1124 (2005). American Association for the Advancement of Science
10. Moore, A.K., Wehr, M.: Parvalbumin-expressing inhibitory interneurons in auditory cortex are well-tuned for frequency. J. Neurosci. Soc. Neurosci. **33**, 13713–13723 (2013)
11. Okun, M., Lampl, I.: Instantaneous correlation of excitation and inhibition during ongoing and sensory-evoked activities. Nat. Neurosci. **11**, 535–537 (2008)
12. Pouille, F., Marin-Burgin, A., Adesnik, H., Atallah, B.V., Scanziani, M.: Input normalization by global feedforward inhibition expands cortical dynamic range. Nat. Neurosci. **12**, 1577–1585 (2009). Nature publishing group
13. Rothenberg, M., Verrillo, R.T., Zahorian, S.A., Brachman, M.L., Bolanowski Jr., S.J.: Vibrotactile frequency for encoding a speech parameter. Acoust. Soc. Am. **62**, 1003–1012 (1977)
14. Runyan, C.A., Sur, M.: Response selectivity is correlated to dendritic structure in parvalbumin-expressing inhibitory neurons in visual cortex. J. Neurosci. Soc. Neurosci. **33**, 11724–11733 (2013)
15. Smith, P.L., Ratcliff, R.: Psychology and neurobiology of simple decisions. Trends Neurosci. **27**, 161–168 (2004). Elsevier
16. Usher, M., McClelland, J.L.: The time course of perceptual choice: the leaky, competing accumulator model. Psychol. Revi. **108**, 550–592 (2001). American Psychological Association

17. Wilson, N.R., Runyan, C.A., Wang, F.L., Sur, M.: Division and subtraction by distinct cortical inhibitory networks in vivo. Nature **488**, 343–348 (2012)
18. Wong, K.-F., Wang, X.-J.: A recurrent network mechanism of time integration in perceptual decisions. J. Neurosci. **26**, 1314–1328 (2006)

Device for Estimation of Weight and Material of Contents by Shaking

Takeshi Yamamoto[(⊠)] and Koichi Hirota

Graduate School of Frontier Science, The University of Tokyo,
7-3-1 Hongo, Bunkyo-ku, Tokyo 113-8656, Japan
m126756@h.k.u-tokyo.ac.jp, k-hirota@k.u-tokyo.ac.jp

Abstract. Haptic stimuli rely mainly on interactive motion. When a person shakes a box, he or she can guess at the physical properties of its contents. This is often based on haptic stimuli. This paper describes the development of a haptic device and control system, as well as the modeling and simulation of a virtual box and its contents. It also discusses an investigation into differences in the manner of shaking depending on the properties of the model and the feedback conditions.

Keywords: Shaking operation · Estimation of properties · Haptic interaction

1 Introduction

It is possible for a person to guess the contents of a box by shaking it. This is, by shaking a box, it is possible to estimate the physical properties of the contents to some extent. The authors are proposing a device that virtually realizes this shaking interaction [1]. In a previous study, a prototype device that shakes a box by applying an inertial force was developed [2], and the feasibility of determining the physical properties of the solid contents of the box was proven [3].

Previous prototypes were only able to generate a small output force, and had only a short stroke. These features severely limited the model that can be represented by the device. Therefore, we redesigned the device and developed a new prototype. In addition, our research moved towards the investigation of mechanisms for recognizing the properties of an object by shaking interaction. This paper describes the design and implementation of the new device, as well as preliminary experiments that were undertaken using the device. The experiments focused on observing differences in the manner of shaking, according to the model of the object and the sensory feedback.

2 Related Research

Force feedback devices can be categorized into two types: grounded and non-grounded. Grounded devices generate force by using mechanical arms [4] or wires [5]. Most non-grounded devices have been developed for portable use. Some apply torque by using the inertial moment of a flywheel [6], whereas others make use of the gyroscopic effect [7]. In addition, a device that can apply a sense of continuous directional force by

© Springer-Verlag Berlin Heidelberg 2014
M. Auvray and C. Duriez (Eds.): EuroHaptics 2014, Part II, LNCS 8619, pp. 403–410, 2014.
DOI: 10.1007/978-3-662-44196-1_49

taking advantage of the non-linearity of human perception has been proposed [8]. Most of these studies have focused on the presentation of a sensation of force or torque. In contrast, our interests relate to the recognition of an object model through dynamic interaction. A non-grounded device is appropriate for shaking interaction, given the properties of objects.

Some studies have dealt with shaking interaction with a virtual object. Shoogle is a device that feeds back sound and vibration when it is shaken [9]. However, this device does not generate any force. Another study developed a device that applies normal and tangential forces to the fingertips and demonstrated the feasibility of presenting the sensation of weight and inertia by stimulating the skin without having to rely on deep sensations [10]. In addition, it was proven that the presentation of vibration together with physical phenomena is helpful to recognizing. A virtual rolling stone was used to demonstrate that the presentation of vibration can provide information on physical phenomena such as a rolling object [11]. Similarly, TECHTILE toolkit demonstrated that recording and reproducing vibration is helpful for haptically transmitting physical phenomena [12].

3 Shaking Device

3.1 Mechanism

In much the same way as our previous prototypes, the new device consists of a frame and a weight. The user grips the frame, and the device generates inertial forces by accelerating the weight relative to the frame (Fig. 1). In our new prototype, the mechanism was designed such that the stroke (i.e., the range through which the weight can be moved) is longer and the peak output force is higher. In the actual implementation, the masses of the weight and the frame were 400 g and 340 g, respectively, and the stroke was 57 mm.

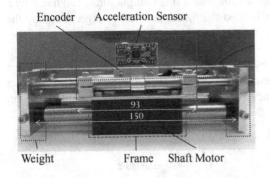

(a)   Implementation of prototype   (b)   Prototype as held by user

Fig. 1. Shaking device

The device consist of two shaft motors (S120D, GHC) arranged in parallel, an accelerometer (MM-2860, Sunhayato), an optical encoder (Ti-0020 and RGSZ20, RENISHAW), and a motor driver (MOVO2, Servan). The accelerometer measures the acceleration of the frame, and the optical encoder measures the displacement of the weight relative to the frame. The motor driver was operated in force-control mode, and it provides information about the actual force being output by means of a current monitoring function. The maximum total output force of the motors is 22 N.

3.2 Control System

The design of the control system is shown in Fig. 2. The basic control concept is the same as that of our previous prototypes [3]. The device outputs the acceleration of the frame $\ddot{X}_f$, the displacement of the weight D, and the actual output force (i.e., the force between the weight and the frame) f_{mon}. Based on this information, the external force acting on the frame (i.e. the force from the user) F is estimated by using a Kalman filter. In the virtual reality (VR) model, the motion of a box and its contents are computed. The model implemented for the experiment describes below simulates the one-dimensional motion of the solid contents of a box, based on the coulomb friction and energy dissipation caused by collision (Fig. 3). The mass of the contents m_m and the reflection coefficient e are varied in the experiment. The model takes external force F as its input, and then outputs the acceleration of the box $\ddot{x}_f$ as well as the position and velocity of the center of gravity of the model, this is, x_{cog} and $\dot{x}_{cog}$. The computation of the output force involves feed-forward and feedback components. For the feed-forward component f_f, the force that realizes the acceleration of $\ddot{x}_f$ on the frame is computed, whereas for the feedback component f_s, proportional derivative (PD) servo control is applied to ensure that the center of gravity of the device X_{cog} conforms to that of the VR model x_{cog}.

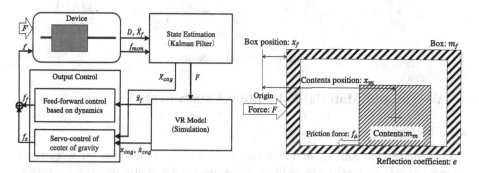

Fig. 2. Design of control system   **Fig. 3.** Structure of VR Model

3.3 Generation of Collision Sounds

To provide audible feedback, for the experiments described below, a simple sound generation algorithm was integrated into the control system. The algorithm generates a damped square wave; the base frequency was 1 kHz and the time constant was a decay of 0.11 s. The amplitude of the wave was reset to its maximum value whenever a new collision was detected in the model. Currently, the maximum amplitude is constant and independent of the velocity of the collision.

3.4 Verification of Operation

Figure 4 shows an example of the states of the model and the device during tilting and shaking; the positions of the centers of gravity of the model and the device, as well as the values of the actual and measured forces, are plotted. The actual force was measured using a force sensor (67M25, Nitta). The results show that the device closely follows both the motion of the center of gravity of the model and the interaction force.

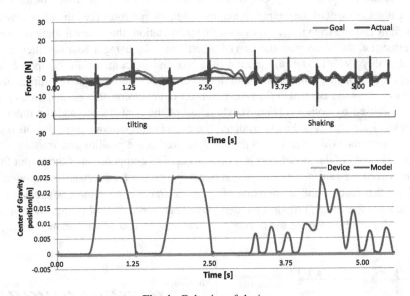

Fig. 4. Behavior of device

4 Weight and Material Estimation Experiment

4.1 Method

An experiment was carried out to evaluate a user's ability to estimate the weight and material of the contents of a virtual box. The experiment was also intended to observe the differences in the shaking depending on the modality of the feedback (i.e. sound or force). The experiment addressed two different modalities (sound and force- feedback), three values for the mass of the contents m_m (450 g, 350 g, and 250 g), and three values for the reflection coefficient e (0.0, 0.4, and 0.8). Moreover, the mass of the box was $m_f = 740 - m_m$, and the friction coefficient was $m = 0.10$. A set consisted of nine presentations, without any overlap, of nine random combinations of weight and reflection values. The subjects were four students (average age: 23), all of whom experienced three sets for each condition. A curtain was hung between the subject and the device to exclude visual information. Additionally, the subject wore earplugs and headphones generating traffic noise to exclude auditory information. To provide sound-feedback, the volume was adjusted so that the subject could hear the collision sounds. The subjects grasped the device with their dominant hand and shook it freely for 10 s. After this presentation, the subjects were asked to estimate the weight of the contents by pouring water into a cup so that the gross weight of the cup and water were equal to that of the contents. The subject was allowed to hold the cup to feel its weight. In addition, the subject was given a list of possible materials for the contents (clay, fabric, wood, stone, iron, plastic, rubber, glass, etc.) and was asked to select some of them, so as to verify the possibility of reliably expression the material by haptic stimuli.

4.2   Weight and Material Estimation Results

The weight estimation results are shown in Fig. 5. With sound- feedback, the weight of the contents was underestimated, with the average weight for all parameters being below 250 g, which was much smaller than the model parameter. In addition, the reflection coefficient tended to affect the estimation of the weight. However, regression analysis showed that there is no significant correlation between the estimated weight and reflection coefficient ($t = -1.8177, p = 0.0779$). With force-feedback, although the estimated values were very different from the actual weight of the contents in the model, the comparative difference in the weight could be recognized. This is indicated by the coefficient of the slope being other than 0, and there being a significant correlation between the estimated weight and weight of the contents, as determined by regression analysis ($t = 5.0772, p = 1.3641 \times 10^{-5}$). These results suggest that the sensation of force is more helpful than sound in recognizing the weight.

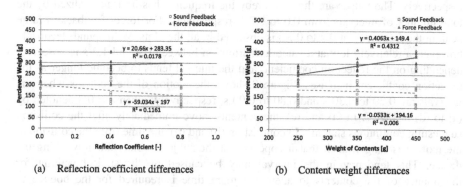

(a)   Reflection coefficient differences   (b)   Content weight differences

Fig. 5. Weight estimation results

The results for the material are shown in Fig. 6, in which the total choice counts for every material are plotted for both sound and force- feedback. With sound feedback, the most commonly chosen materials for all value of the reflection coefficient were different, while with force- feedback, the same material was chosen for $e = 0.0$ and 0.4. This result suggests that sound provides different and probably more detailed information about the contents. Moreover, there is no distinctive difference between the weight of the contents. As stated above, the subjects' auditory sense could perceive minor differences, but they were much less able to do so with their haptic sense.

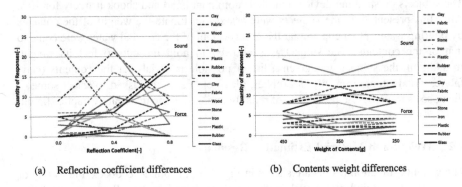

(a)   Reflection coefficient differences   (b)   Contents weight differences

Fig. 6. Material estimation results

4.3   Results: Shaking Form

The way in which the subjects shook the device was also analyzed. In the analysis, the sequence of the motion of the contents of the box was delimited by the collisions between them; the sequence was delimited at the first collision with a side of the box after the contents left the opposite side. In a cyclic shaking motion, the interval of the delimiters, or the duration of each delimited part, is considered to be half of the cycle time. Figure 7 shows a histogram of the interval, summarized in steps of 0.1 s, for a subjects' interaction under the conditions of the reflection coefficient and weight, respectively. The values are those whereby the frequency has been normalized by the total number of intervals from 0.0 to 0.2 s, respectively. For force- feedback, a large peak in the frequency at 0.2 to 0.3 s is observed in all the plots. With sound- feedback, however, a relatively low and smooth distribution between 0.4 and 1.2 s is observed, depending on the reflection coefficient, and the interval tends to become longer as the reflection coefficient increases. Figure 8 shows the motion of the contents when the intervals are 0.20 to 0.30 s and 0.80 to 0.90 s, respectively, when $e = 0.8$ denoted by (a) to (d) in Fig. 7. In (a) and (c), the contents move immediately after the collision, suggesting continuous shaking. In contrast, in (b) and (d), the time from the collision to the motion is longer, such that it appears that the subject is intermittently tilting the device. This tendency in the interval may be caused by the subject waiting for the bounce of the contents to attenuate; more time is required for the bounce to attenuate when the reflection coefficient is greater. There was no apparent difference between the histogram for the different weights, as shown in Fig. 7-(b).

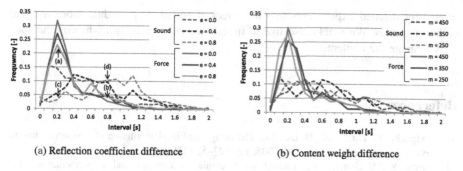

(a) Reflection coefficient difference   (b) Content weight difference

Fig. 7. Time distribution of collision in VR Model

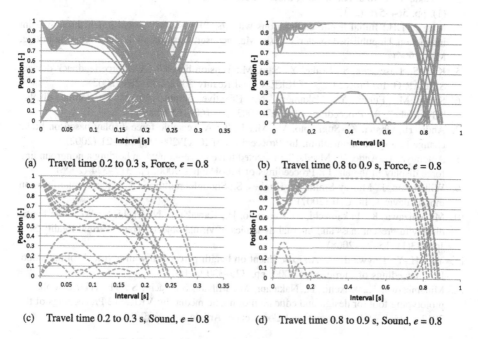

(a)   Travel time 0.2 to 0.3 s, Force, $e = 0.8$ (b)   Travel time 0.8 to 0.9 s, Force, $e = 0.8$

(c)   Travel time 0.2 to 0.3 s, Sound, $e = 0.8$ (d)   Travel time 0.8 to 0.9 s, Sound, $e = 0.8$

Fig. 8. Relationship between contents position and interval

5 Conclusion

This paper has described an approach for implementing a shaking device. An improved prototype device was developed and a control system was implemented. A box-and-contents model was implemented, and recognition of the model by the subjects through interaction with the device was examined. It was demonstrated that the manner of shaking differs depending on whether the subjects is provide with sound or force feedback. As a topic for future work, we will further investigate the users' shaking by comparing the interaction with that for a real box and contents. In addition, we will implement detailed experiments into the effect of sound by providing more realistic collision sounds. We would also like to investigate the mechanism whereby the subjects estimate the contents.

References

1. Sekiguchi, Y., Hirota, K., Hirose, M.: The design and implementation of ubiquitous haptic device. In: Proceedings of WHC 2005, pp. 527–528 (2005)
2. Hirota, K., Sekiguchi, Y.: Inertial force display - concept and implementation. In: Proceedings of ISUC 2008, pp. 281–284 (2008)
3. Tanaka, Y., Hirota, K.: Shaking a box to estimate the property of content. In: EuroHaptics (1), pp. 564–576 (2012)
4. Massie, T.H.: Initial haptic explorations with the PHANToM: virtual touch through point interaction. Unpublished master's thesis, Massachusetts Institute of Technology, Cambridge, MA (1996)
5. Kim, S., Hasegawa, S., Koike, Y., Sato, M.: Tension based 7-DOF force feedback device: SPIDAR-G. In: Proceedings of IEEE Virtual Reality 2002, 283–284 (2002)
6. Sakai, M., Fukui, Y., Nakamura, N.: Effective output patterns for torque display "GyroCube". In: Proceedings of ICAT 2003, pp. 160–165 (2003)
7. Ando, H., Obana, K., Sugimoto, M., Maeda, T.: A wearable force display based on brake change in angular momentum. In: Proceedings of ICAT 2002, pp. 16–21 (2002)
8. Amemiya, T., Ando, H., Maeda, T.: Directed force perception when holding a nongrounding force display in the air. In: Proceedings of EuroHaptics 2006, pp. 317–324 (2006)
9. Williamson, J., Murray-Smith, R., Hughes, S.: Shoogle: multimodal excitatory interfaces on mobile devices. In: CHI (2007)
10. Minamizawa, K., Fukamachi, S., Kajimoto, H., Kawakami, N., Tachi, S.: Wearable haptic display to present mass and internal dynamics of virtual objects. Trans. Virtual Reality Soc. Jpn. 13(1), 15–23 (2008)
11. Yao, H.-Y., Hayward, V.: An experiment on length perception with a virtual rolling stone. In: Proceedings of Eurohaptics 2006. pp. 325–330 (2006)
12. Minamizawa, K., Kakehi, Y., Nakatani, M., Mihara, S., Tachi, S.: TECHTILE toolkit: a prototyping tool for design and education of haptic media. In: VRIC '12 Proceedings of the 2012 Virtual Reality International Conference, Article No. 26 (2012)

Erratum to: Performance Evaluation of a Surgical Telerobotic System Using Kinematic Indices of the Master Hand-Controller

Yaser Maddahi[(⊠)], Michael Greene, Liu Shi Gan, Tomas Hirmer,
Rachael L'Orsa, Sanju Lama, Garnette Roy Sutherland,
and Kourosh Zareinia

Project NeuroArm, University of Calgary, 3280 Hospital Dr NW,
Calgary, AB T2N 4Z6, Canada
{ymaddahi,mrgreene,lsgan,thirmer,ralorsa,slama,
garnette,kzareini}@ucalgary.ca

Erratum to:
Chapter "Performance Evaluation of a Surgical Telerobotic System Using Kinematic Indices of the Master Hand-Controller" in: M. Auvray and C. Duriez (Eds.), Haptics: Neuroscience, Devices, Modeling, and Applications, DOI 10.1007/978-3-662-44196-1_21

In the original version, the name of the first author was spelled incorrectly by mistake. It should be Yaser Maddahi not Yaster Maddahi.

The online version of the original chapter can be found under DOI 10.1007/978-3-662-44196-1_21

M. Auvray and C. Duriez (Eds.): EuroHaptics 2014, Part II, LNCS 8619, p. E1, 2014.
DOI: 10.1007/978-3-662-44196-1_50

Demo Papers

Demonstration: Passive Mechanical Skin Stretch for Multiple Degree-of-Freedom Proprioception in a Hand Prosthesis

Aadeel Akhtar[1], Mary Nguyen[2], Logan Wan[3], Brandon Boyce[2], Patrick Slade[3], and Timothy Bretl[2]

[1] Neuroscience Program, Medical Scholars Program,
University of Illinois at Urbana-Champaign, Urbana IL, 61801, USA
aakhta3@illinois.edu
[2] Department of Aerospace Engineering,
University of Illinois at Urbana-Champaign, Urbana IL, 61801, USA
{hnguyn10, boyce4, tbretl}@illinois.edu
[3] Department of Mechanical Engineering,
University of Illinois at Urbana-Champaign, Urbana IL, 61801, USA
{wan14, pslade2}@illinois.edu

Abstract. In this demonstration, we present a passive linear skin stretch device that can provide proprioceptive feedback for multiple degrees-of-freedom (DOF) in a prosthetic hand. Participants can control various grips through electromyography and will perceive a proportional amount of skin stretch on the forearm corresponding to the grip aperture.

Keywords: Proprioception · Prosthetics · Skin Stretch

1 Introduction

While major advancements have been made in the functionality of upper limb myoelectric prostheses, commercial devices still lack the ability to provide users with proprioceptive feedback. As a result, users have had to rely primarily on vision to know the position and orientation of their prosthesis. Surveys have reported that this over-dependence on vision is one of the largest contributors to prosthesis abandonment [1]. While vibrotactile and rotational skin stretch devices have been effective in improving accuracy when controlling a single degree-of-freedom (DOF) for a prosthesis, most users perform tasks which require controlling multiple DOFs [2, 3]. Furthermore, these devices require a large amount of surface area, may consume a great deal of power, or may add considerable weight. To alleviate power, weight, and space issues, as well as easily provide multiple-DOF proprioceptive feedback for a prosthetic hand, we developed a passive mechanical linear skin stretch device (Fig. 1).

M. Auvray and C. Duriez (Eds.): EuroHaptics 2014, Part II, LNCS 8619, pp. 413–415, 2014.
DOI: 10.1007/978-3-662-44196-1

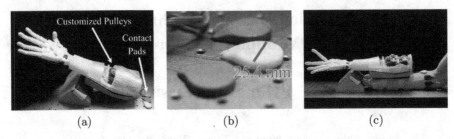

Fig. 1. The InMoov prosthetic hand used in our study (a) had custom pulleys pulling both the tendons driving the fingers and the lines to the contact pads (b). The device is shown attached to a participant in (c).

2 Demonstration

In this demonstration, participants will be asked to wear a wrist brace onto which a prosthetic hand will be attached. The hand was modified from InMoov, an open source 3D-printed robotics project [4]. The tendon-actuated fingers are driven by MG946R servo motors (TowerPro, Taiwan) mounted in the forearm of the prosthesis. The hand is seated in a rigid plastic interface, which is then attached to a wrist brace (Fig. 1c). Guide holes at the proximal end of the interface serve to keep the lines to the contact pads as horizontal as possible to maximize shear over normal forces on the skin. Up to three contact pads will be adhered to the skin of the proximal forearm using BMTT-A adhesives (Garland Beauty Products, Hawthorne, CA). The three contact pads provide skin stretch feedback for the thumb, index, and middle fingers.

Two to six electromyographic (EMG) electrodes will be placed over the flexor and extensor muscles located radially around the right forearm, with one to three electrodes being placed over each muscle group. All data will be processed using the MATLAB DAQ Toolbox (MathWorks, Natick, MA). The participant's metacarpophalangeal (MCP) joints on the right hand will be restrained to 45 degrees in order to remove any of his own proprioceptive cues in controlling the arm. Flexing or extending the MCP joints against the restraint will generate EMG signals. Pattern recognition algorithms will be used to recognize different grips being made by the participant. As the prosthesis actuates to perform a grip, the participant will simultaneously perceive a proportional amount of skin stretch on the forearm corresponding to the specific finger being actuated. The participant will be able to select among three to six different grips and will be able to control the aperture of the grip via EMG.

References

1. Peerdeman, B., Boere, D., Witteveen, H., Hermens, H., Stramigioli, S., Rietman, H., Veltink, P., Misra, S., et al.: Myoelectric forearm prostheses: state of the art from a user-centered perspective. J. Rehabil. Res. Dev. **48**, 719–738 (2011)

2. Witteveen, H., Droog, E., Rietman, J., Veltink, P.: Vibro- and electrotactile user feedback on hand opening for myoelectric forearm prostheses. IEEE Trans. Biomed. Eng. **59**, 2219–2226 (2012)
3. Bark, K., Wheeler, J., Lee, G., Savall, J., Cutkosky, M.: A wearable skin stretch device for haptic feedback. In: World Haptics 2009, pp. 464–469 (2009)
4. Langevin, G.: InMoov - Open source 3D printed life size robot (2014). URL: http://inmoov.fr, License: http://creativecommons.org/licenses/bync/3.0/legalcode

The PROTOTOUCH Project: An FP7 EU Marie Curie Initial Training Network

Mario Amante[1], Séréna Bochereau[2], Mariama Dione[1],
Brygida Maria Dzidek[3], David Gueorguiev[4], Andreas Heinrich[5],
Athanasia Moungon[4], Thomas Sednaoui[6], Eric Vezzoli[7],
Zlatko Vidrih[8], Teja Vodlak[8], and Michael Wand[5]

[1] University of Gothenburg, Gothenburg, Sweden
[2] UPMC Univ. Paris 6, Institut des Systèmes Intelligents et de Robotique,
Paris, France
[3] University of Birmingham, Birmingham, UK
[4] Université Catholique de Louvain, Louvain-la-Neuve, Belgium
[5] Instituto Dalle Molle di Studi sull'Intelligenza Artificiale, Manno, Switzerland
[6] ST Microelectronics, Grenoble, France
[7] L2EP/IRCICA Laboratory, Université de Lille 1, Villeneuve-d'Ascq, France
[8] Swansea University, Swansea, UK
b.m.dzidek@bham.ac.uk

Abstract. The main research goal of the PROTOTOUCH project is to exploit multiscale multiphysics simulation software, supported by neurophysiological measurements, for the virtual prototyping and optimisation of tactile displays. For the demonstration, the fellows of the project will introduce PROTOTOUCH, present key tactile devices, and explain the first results of the project.

Keywords: Tactile displays · Cognitive and Neural science · Psychophysics · Tribology · Computer simulation · Information processing

1 Introduction

PROTOTOUCH [1] is an EU funded FP7 Marie Curie Initial Training Network where 11 Early Stage Researchers (ESRs) and 4 Experienced Researchers (ERs) are being trained. With the associated research activities, the project will lead to a radical understanding of the underlying design principles and hence to the development of future generation devices. This will be achieved by the deployment of an interdisciplinary network involving experts in tactile displays, computer simulation, cognitive and neural science, psychophysics, information processing, materials science, tribology and medical rehabilitation.

M. Auvray and C. Duriez (Eds.): EuroHaptics 2014, Part II, LNCS 8619, pp. 416–418, 2014.
DOI: 10.1007/978-3-662-44196-1

2 Project Description

Devices. ST Microelectronics is involved to provide its expertise with industrial process and Thin-Film actuators, focusing on introducing friction modulation to commercial devices and exploring their new uses. At Université de Lille 1, a new model for electrovibration has been developed and the influence of various factor on the performance of both the electrovibration and squeeze-film effects is being exploited. A future goal is to couple the two stimulation effects into one device. At UPMC, a vibrotactile tile with finger stimulation through bulk broadband vibration of the plate is being developed.

Human Evaluation. At UCL, a new EEG approach to isolate and characterise the cortical activity elicited by the mechanical interaction between the contacting finger pad and tactile displays is being developed. Also, psychophysical methodologies, the most effective tools for quantifying tactile perception, are being used to modulate the touch of tactile stimuli (active touch, passive touch, normal force modulation, proprioceptive modulation). The aim is to understand how physical characteristics influence the perception of textures and to evaluate the performance of TDs at replicating these characteristics. At University of Gothenburg, single unit activity of afferent fibbers in response to a skin mechanical stimulation is recorded in awake human participants. This technique provides a direct way to compare the impulse activity in primary afferents to the sensation experienced and is used in combination with other relevant methods to identify the physiological (role of specific mechanoreceptors during active exploration) and psychophysical nature of the sensations elicited while using the different displays. Friction plays a role in the perception of roughness, slipperiness and warmth of the sliding contact between the finger pad and a product's surface. Hence, the tribological interactions of the finger pad and tactile displays is being investigated at University of Birmingham.

Computer Simulation and Machine Learning. At Swansea University, a finite element software framework for simulation of tactile scenarios is being developed. This software has the potential to become a useful tool for studying the finger pad surface interaction in scientific and industrial communities. At IDSIA, novel information processing techniques, including artificial neural networks, recurrent neural networks and reinforcement learning, are applied to assist in the design and simulation of tactile devices, as well as to extract meaningful information from large datasets from experiments.

3 Demonstration

All the results from the human evaluation, tribological measurements and computer simulation of the devices will help to optimise the second version of tactile displays. Aside from a few human evaluation tools, three first generation tactile displays will be presented. These include the UPMC Laterotactile display, the Univ. of Lille 1 SIMTAC and the ST Microelectronics Android platform.

Reference

1. Hynes, K.: Prototouch website (2014). http://www.prototouch.org

Distinct Pseudo-Attraction Force Sensation by a Thumb-Sized Vibrator that Oscillates Asymmetrically

Tomohiro Amemiya and Hiroaki Gomi

NTT Communication Science Laboratories, NTT Corporation,
3-1 Morinosato-Wakamiya, Atsugi Kanagawa, 243-0198, Japan
http://www.brl.ntt.co.jp/people/t-amemiya/
amemiya.tomohiro@lab.ntt.co.jp,

Abstract. In this presentation, we present a thumb-sized force display for experiencing a kinesthetic illusory sensation of being continuously pushed or pulled. We previously succeeded in creating a sensation of being pulled with a prototype based on a crank-slider mechanism, but recently we did so with a thumb-sized actuator that oscillates asymmetrically. With this tiny and light force display, the directed force sensation is perceived just as strongly as with the previous larger prototypes. We conducted a user study using the method of paired comparisons. The results show that a specific vibrator with a 7-ms pulse at 40 Hz induces the sensation most clearly and effectively.

Keywords: Sensory illusion · Perception · Asymmetric oscillation · Mobile device · Vibration

1 Introduction

Over the past years, we have been refining a method to create a sensory illusion of being pulled and have developed various ungrounded force displays to create a sensation. Since it is impossible to create a continuous translational force sensation without an external fulcrum, our method of exploiting the characteristics of human perception is the only way to create a translational force sensation in mobile devices. The user does not feel the discrete simple vibrating sensation that is so common in conventional mobile devices today. Instead, the user feels a smooth sensation of being pulled, akin to what we feel when someone leads us by the hand. However, since our previous prototypes were based on mechanical linkages, they were large and heavy to be applied to mobile devices.

In the demonstration, we introduce a new tiny but mighty force display in action. Although a complex sensory input from not only cutaneous corpuscles but also those in tendons and muscles would creates the force perception, we use asymmetrically oscillating stimuli that selectively stimulate the Meissner corpuscles, which are most sensitive in the frequency range of from approximately 5 to 40 Hz [4, 5] to create the force sensation of being pulled clearly. For all users, the haptic or somatosensory cues

© Springer-Verlag Berlin Heidelberg 2014
M. Auvray and C. Duriez (Eds.): EuroHaptics 2014, Part II, LNCS 8619, pp. 419–420, 2014.
DOI: 10.1007/978-3-662-44196-1

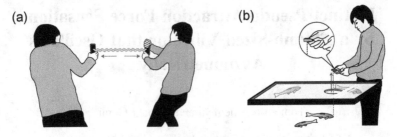

Fig. 1. Application examples using thumb-sized mobile force display. (a) Tug-of-war. (b) Angling game.

created by the developed force display are, like lead-by-hand navigation, intuitive in indicating a certain direction. The presented prototype will be compared directly with previous prototypes reported in [1–3] in terms of the effect of force sensation and their size and weight.

2 Demonstration

Figure 1 shows hands-on demo using the thumb-sized force display in our booth. Multiple participants can experience the tug-of-war application together by using two force displays (Fig. 1(a)). With a motion tracking system, the amplitude and direction of the force sensation are altered according to the participant's hand position and the distance of the participants while the participant pinches the thumb-sized force display.

In the angling game, participants can feel a sensation of a nibble on the hook and being pulled with no fishing lines [Fig. 1(b)]. We implemented the system with a tablet PC, the force display, and a motion tracking system.

References

1. Amemiya, T., Ando, H., Maeda, T.: Virtual force display: direction guidance using asymmetric acceleration via periodic translational motion. In: Proceeding of World Haptics Conference, pp. 619–622. IEEE Computer Society (2005)
2. Amemiya, T., Ando, H., Maeda, T.: Directed force perception when holding a nongrounding force display in the air. In: Proceedings of EuroHaptics, pp. 317–324 (2006)
3. Amemiya, T., Sugiyama, H.: Orienting kinesthetically: a haptic handheld wayfinder for people with visual impairments. ACM Trans. Access. Comput. 3(2), 6:1–6:23 (2010)
4. Johansson, R., Landstrom, U., Lundstrom, R.: Responses of mechanoreceptive afferent units in the glabrous skin of the human hand to sinusoidal skin displacements. Brain Res. 244, 17–25 (1982)
5. Talbot, W.H., Smith, I.D., Kornhuber, H.H., Mountcastle, V.B.: The sense of flutter-vibration: comparison of the human capacity with response patterns of mechanoreceptive afferents from the monkey hand. J. Neurophysiol. 31, 301–334 (1967)

Analysis of the Adapted Inclusive Haptic Rigs for Non-sighted People Using Duration and Collision Metrics

Lisa Bowers[1,2] and Farshid Amirabdollahian[1,2]

[1] Open University Gateshead, Gateshead, UK
[2] University of Hertfordshire, Hertfordshire, UK
f.amirabdollahian2@herts.ac.uk

Abstract. In this demonstration we present a haptic digital rig, which offers an inclusive adapted version of Wade's Nine Hole Peg Test (NHPT) [3]. After a manual NHPT, practice participants will be requested to complete a nine hole board with nine virtual pegs classed as a standard haptic assisted test, entitled 'Rig 1' (*refer to* Table 1). They will then be offered a greater level of haptic and multi modal assistance to enable them to complete the same nine hole board with nine pegs, at speed.

Keywords: Haptic · Inclusive design · Learning through touch · Multi-modal · Non-sighted · Sighted

1 Introduction

Learning through touch: Tactile sensory perception is often considered by the sighted world as the lesser dominant sense. The loss of a primary sense, usually termed as sight (ocular) can often mean that the sense of touch can become more efficiently utilised and, with practice, can become a very finely tuned acute transducer of the environment [1, 2].

This inclusive study has been previously conducted with congenitally blind individuals who, as applied art-makers, are well practiced at using their sense of touch and fine motor skills to craft artefacts from the germinal stage of creation to completion. As an inclusive study the haptic rigs have been designed to suit blind and visually impaired people's sensory perceptions to allow this group of people access to a digital system driven by touch.

2 Demonstration

Within this demonstration participants will be asked to operate a Phantom Omni offering 6 degrees of freedom (6 DOF). Initially participants will be requested to run through a short pre-trail test consisting of a shortened version of the nine hole peg board and they will be asked to place virtual pegs into the relevant holes, at this stage there will be very short bursts of verbal guidance from the demonstrator.

© Springer-Verlag Berlin Heidelberg 2014
M. Auvray and C. Duriez (Eds.): EuroHaptics 2014, Part II, LNCS 8619, pp. 421–422, 2014.
DOI: 10.1007/978-3-662-44196-1

2.1   Test Set Up

Participants can expect to see the rig set up in Fig. 1 but to also work through the test conditions laid out in Table 1.

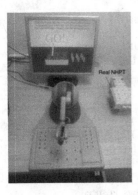

Fig. 1. The rig set up used in our study shows the wooden housing rig, the Phantom Omni, the real rig and a sample of a screen shot on the VDU.

Table 1. Different experiment conditions provided by the haptic rigs

Rig	Conditions
Rig 1 (Std)	Haptic forces, small virtual holes (3–5 mm), audio speech & non-speech sound
Rig 2	Haptic forces, larger virtual holes (5–9 mm), audio speech & non-speech sound
Rig 3	Very small haptic forces, decreased virtual target holes (1–3 mm), audio speech & non-speech sounds

Speech sounds – "well done" non-speech sounds –'ping'

2.2   Rig Test Conditions

After the pre-trial run, participants will be asked to work through three experimental rigs as seen in Table 1. Each separate rig requires participants to start on the haptic home cue, which feels rather like a rubber ball under the stylus tip, the haptic arm will then guide the user to the first hole, second hole and so forth until the final hole, hole nine. After each peg is placed correctly in the hole the users will receive a non-speech sound e.g. a ping, and after each line of three pegs are in place the user will receive a speech sound e.g. "well done". The user will be offered their personal time (seconds) of completion for each test when all three tests are fully finished.

References

1. White, B.Y., et al. Seeing with the skin. Percept. Psychophysics **7**, 23–27 (1970)
2. Loomis, J.M., Lederman, S.J.: Tactual perception. In: Boff, K., Kaufman, L., Thomas, J. (eds.) Handbook of Perception and Human Performance, pp. 31-1–31-41. Wiley, New York (1986)
3. Wade, D.T.: Measurement in neurological rehabilitation. Curr. Opin. Neurol. **5**(5), 682–686 (1992)

Haptic Music Player

Alfonso Balandra, Hironori Mitake, and Shoichi Hasegawa

Tokyo Institute of Technology, R2-20 Nagatsuta-cho, Yokohama 4259, Japan
{poncho,mitake,hase}@haselab.net
http://haselab.net

Abstract. This project aims to translate the basic music elements from a MIDI file into an enjoyable and coherent haptic vibration. To achieve this, an special kind of haptic music player was developed. This music player consists of 3 main parts: a MIDI player, a simple music structure animation and an event based haptic vibration. So, the complete system allows the user to focus his attention into an specific instrument, and then consequently understand the role of that instrument in the song.

Keywords: Haptic music ·Music vibration · Music haptic animation

1 Introduction

The main purpose of this project is to exchange the music listening experience though haptic vibration; giving the user the opportunity to enjoy the music with a different perspective. Currently, haptic vibration and the animation enables the user to find and focus on the notes played by a specific instrument. In addition, the combination of music, animation and vibration help the user to understand the general music structure and the role of an specific instrument in the complete song. Consequently, our efforts are focused on finding a novel way to represent coherently the note's pitch, timing and duration into a resemble a haptic vibration; to catch the user's attention.

2 Demonstration Description

This entertainment environment is composed of 3 modules synchronized in real time: a MIDI music player, a 3D music animation and a haptic vibration module.

2.1 MIDI Music Player

A simple MIDI player was developed to play the music. We used the MIDI file format because the song information is discrete, so an audio signal processing algorithm is not necessary to identify the song notes.

© Springer-Verlag Berlin Heidelberg 2014
M. Auvray and C. Duriez (Eds.): EuroHaptics 2014, Part II, LNCS 8619, pp. 423–424, 2014.
DOI: 10.1007/978-3-662-44196-1

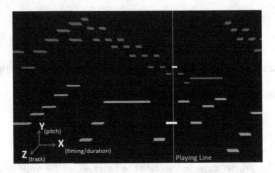

Fig. 1. Haptic music player animation.

2.2 3D Music Animation

The music animation used on this proposal is mostly based on the Kevin Kelly's project the *Music Animation Machine* [3]. Thus, we used 3D rectangles to represent the MIDI notes pitch, duration and timing. The rectangle position represent the note pitch (y axis) and timing (x axis), also the note's duration is represented with the rectangle length. To represent the time, the rectangles move from right to left accordingly to the music time. So when the notes are played, the rectangle that represent them change color and pass though the middle of the screen (see Fig. 1).

2.3 Haptic Rendering

This module computes and display an event haptic signal to the user. The haptic signal is computed using the note's pitch, duration and a sine damped function vibration. To compute the vibration signal we use Kuchenbecker [2] sine damping model. So, by using a simple direct proportion we map the notes' pitch to the sine wave frequency and amplitude of the damping function, and also using the notes' duration we calculate the sine wave decay. As a result, the notes with a low pitch will have a low frequency vibration, and the notes with a high pitch will have a high frequency. Finally, the resulting vibration rendering (using SPIDAR [1] as a haptic interface) is synchronized on real time with the music and the animation.

References

1. Akahane, K., Hasegawa, S., Koike, Y., Sato, M.: A proposal of a high definition haptic rendering for stability and fidelity. In: ICAT 2006, pp. 162–167, November 2006
2. Katherine, K.J.: Improving contact realism through event-based haptic feedback. IEEE Trans. Visual Comput. Graphics **12**(2), 219–230 (2006)
3. Kevin, K.: The music animation machine: music worth watching (1974). http://www. musanim.com/

Demonstration of the Vibration and Collision Between Finger and Object for Haptic Rendering

Alfonso Balandra, Shoichi Hasegawa, Yukinobu Takehana,
Hironori Mitake, Katsuhito Akahane, and Makoto Sato

Tokyo Institute of Technology, R2-20 Nagatsuta-cho, Yokohama 4259, Japan
{poncho,hase,takehana,mitake}@haselab.net,
{kakahane,msato}@hi.pi.titech.ac.jp
http://haselab.net

Abstract. This demonstration is focus on showing the audience a tapping vibration simulator, which considers the finger's vibration motion and the subsequent collision between the object and the finger. The participants can also compare the simulator vibration with a real model with the same size, shape and material.

Keywords: Vibration haptic rendering · Tapping finger Simulation · Sub-sequent collision · Vibration Simulation

1 Introduction

It is already known that humans can discriminate materials from objects [2, 3, 5] and the tapping position [4]; perceiving the vibrations when the object is tapped. Susa et al. [1] proposed to simulate the natural vibration of an arbitrary structured object. However, the vibration between the tapping finger and the subsequent collisions between the finger and the object were not simulated. So, we purpose a model that considers the finger vibration, the object vibration and the subsequent collisions between them.

2 Demonstration

To reproduce the finger vibration, we studied the finger's oscillations using different kinds of materials. We used an accelerometer and a laser displacement meter to measure the vibration on both finger and object. Then, we find that out the variation in the finger oscillations depending on the material. Therefore, we understood that this vibration variation must be simulated in order to display a more realistic haptic vibration.

Then using the measured finger's oscillation data, we built a simple mass-spring-damper model, to simulate the finger dynamics. In this model, when the normal force is

M. Auvray and C. Duriez (Eds.): EuroHaptics 2014, Part II, LNCS 8619, pp. 425–426, 2014.
DOI: 10.1007/978-3-662-44196-1

Fig. 1. Overview of the proposed simulation demonstration setup

smaller than 0, the spring-damper tip, which corresponds to the finger's surface, will float from the objects surface. Therefore, this phenomenon is also simulated. Finally, to increase the numeric stability, the update rate of the finger's simulation is set to 10 kHz, while the FE simulator, for the object vibration, runs at 1 kHz.

The software uses two modules: an FE simulator for the objects' vibration and the finger vibration model to reproduce the finger dynamics. In this system the user is able to fell the oscillations from the objects, where the finger vibration dynamics are also considered, consequently this upgrades the users' vibration sensation. The FE simulator enables us to present objects with different shapes, sizes and materials. The user interacts with the virtual environment using a haptic device that moves a haptic pointer (white sphere) inside the 3D environment. Also the participants can compare the simulator vibration with a real object, with the same size, shape and material. (See Fig. 1).

References

1. Ikumi, S., Yukinobu, T., Alfonso, B., Hironori, M., Hasegawa, S.: Haptic rendering based on finite element simulation of vibration. In: IEEE Haptics Symposium (2014)
2. Kuchenbecker, K.J., Fiene, J., Niemeyer, G.: Improving contact realism through event-based haptic feedback. IEEE Trans. Visual Comput. Graphics, **12**(2), 219–230 (2006)
3. Okamura, A.M., Dennerlein, J.T., Howe, R.D.: Vibration feedback models for virtual environments. In: Proceedings of the 1998 IEEE International Conference on Robotics and Automation, pp. 674–679, May 1998
4. Sreng, J., Lécuyer, A., Andriot, C.: Using vibration patterns to provide impact position information in haptic manipulation of virtual objects. In: Proceedings of the 6th international conference on Haptics: Perception, Devices and Scenarios, EuroHaptics '08, pp. 589–598. Berlin, Heidelberg (2008)
5. Wellman, P., Howe, R.D.: Towards realistic vibrotactile display in virtual environments. In: Alberts, T.(ed.) Proceeding of the ASME Dynamics System and Control Division, Symposium on Haptic Interfaces for Virtual Environment and Teleoperator System, pp. 657–662 (1995)

Transfer of Haptic Signals Between Hands

Lucile Dupin[1], Vincent Hayward[2], and Mark Wexler[1]

[1] Laboratoire Psychologie de la Perception,
CNRS and Université Paris Descartes, Paris, France
lucile.dupin@parisdescartes.fr
[2] ISIR, Université Pierre et Marie Curie, Paris, France

Abstract. When tactually exploring an object, kinesthetic and tactile information are fused and lead to the spatial perception of this object. In natural settings, the signals originate from the same source: when a fingertip moves and receives tactile signals, the kinesthetic signals come from the same hand. We explore the plasticity of tactile-kinesthetic combination by separating these signals between distinct body parts, directing the tactile signals to a stationary hand while the other hand moves. The demo is split in two parts. In the first one, kinesthetic and sensory information originate from the same hand. In the second one, kinesthetic information comes from one moving hand while the other hand feels the sensory consequence of this movement.

Keywords: Bimanual transfer · Spatial perception · Sensory-motor association

1 Introduction

Motor actions can profoundly affect the perceptual interpretation of tactile inputs [1, 2]. Haptic perceptions are built up of the integration of tactile sensations with kinesthetic or motor signals about the spatial position or velocity of the sensory surface, leading to the construction of spatiotopic rather than purely somatotopic perceptions. Can haptic shape perception still occur when sensory and kinesthetic information originates from different hands? In order answer this question, we had to separate tactile and kinesthetic cues to shape. Tactile signals simulated triangles felt through a slit, as in anorthoscopic perception in vision.

Fig. 1. Latero tactile display alone (left) and mounted on the slider (right).

M. Auvray and C. Duriez (Eds.): EuroHaptics 2014, Part II, LNCS 8619, pp. 427–429, 2014.
DOI: 10.1007/978-3-662-44196-1

2   Demonstration

The demo will consist in the presentation of a tactile stimulus. This stimulus is a line that expands or contracts on the index finger, delivered using a tactile display that can be mounted on a slider (Latero, Tactile Labs, Fig. 1) [3]. In the same condition (Fig. 2), the participant will push or pull the display using his/her index finger, with the tactile signals delivered to the tip of the same finger: thus, in this condition kinesthetic and sensory signals originate from the same hand. The participant will perceive a triangle. Its perceived orientation should depend on a combination of movement direction (backward or forward) and the stimulus (expansion or contraction) as illustrated in Fig. 3. Then, the participant will test the DIFF condition illustrated in Fig. 2. In this condition, the display is positioned beside the slider, with one stationary hand on the display, and the other hand moving the slider. In the latter condition, the perceived

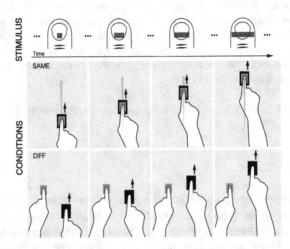

Fig. 2. Example of one trial, showing several snapshots of the temporal sequence. The tactile stimulus is an expanding line (in red). SAME condition: the hand is moving the tactile display (green) mounted on the slider (black). DIFF condition: the right hand is moving the slider forwards while the immobile left hand feels the tactile consequences of this movement (Color figure online).

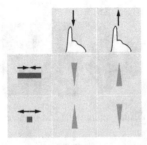

Fig. 3. Spatial orientation of the triangle as a function of the hand movement direction (forward or backward) and the tactile stimulus (expansion or contraction).

orientation results from the combination of movement direction and the stimulus illustrated in Fig. 3.

References

1. Heller, M.A.: Active and passive tactile braille recognition, Bull. Psychon. Soc. **24**(3), 201–202 (1986)
2. Smith, A.M., Chapman, E.C., Donati, F., Fortier-Poisson, P., Hayward, V.: Perception of simulated local shapes using active and passive touch. J. Neurophysiol. **102**(6) , 3519–3529 (2009)
3. Wang, Q., Hayward, V.: Biomechanically optimized distributed tactile transducer based on lateral skin deformation. Int. J. Robot. Res. **29**(4), 323–335 (2010)

Demonstration: A Digital Coach for Self-Tracking Athletes

Antoine Hogenboom[1], Iskander Smit[2], and Ben Kröse[1]

[1] CREATE-IT, Amsterdam University of Applied Sciences,
Amsterdam, The Netherlands
{a.w.hogenboom, b.j.a.kroseg}@hva.nl
[2] Info.nl, Amsterdam, The Netherlands
iskander@info.nl

Abstract. In this paper we present a digital coach for runners that provides feedback in an intuitive way, without interrupting the athletes running flow. This is done by giving vibration pulses in combination with visual led feedback. The digital coach is built into a wristband with GPS module, vibration motor and several LEDs. The digital coach is given a personality model according to the DISC coaching model. From the GPS data collected the digital coach should identify which style gives the best results for the athlete.

Keywords: Quantified Self · Coaching · Haptic feedback · Feedback loop · Self-learning systems · Running

1 Introduction

Self-tracking, lifelogging or the quantified self is the phenomenon by which people measure their own behavior or activities using tracking devices [1]. This way they are trying to get insights into their own lifestyle in order to be able to improve it. The most popular category of trackers is fitness and sports related.

The iterative process of measuring, analyzing data and modifying behavior is called a feedback loop [2]. All these measurements delivers a huge amount of data, but data is not necessarily equal to insights. Many existing fitness trackers, like the popular Fitbit and Nike Fuelband, only measure the performance of the athlete, but do not give any feedback. The user must interpret the data himself. Moreover, this data analysis is done only after an activity. Especially for athletes, it is desirable that they get immediate feedback on their performance during exercise. Therefore, we have developed a wearable coaching module for runners. Using a combination of tactile sensors and a GPS module, that is able to measure the performance of the athlete using GPS and can give feedback immediate feedback while running, using a vibration motor and LEDs. The digital coach can adapt its behavior to the athlete's personality by altering the frequency and intensity in which it gives feedback. The athlete's personality is determined by using the DISC coaching model.

© Springer-Verlag Berlin Heidelberg 2014
M. Auvray and C. Duriez (Eds.): EuroHaptics 2014, Part II, LNCS 8619, pp. 430–431, 2014.
DOI: 10.1007/978-3-662-44196-1

2   Demonstration

In this demonstration participants will experience the different styles of the digital coach. Participants are asked to wear a wristband (see Fig. 1), which is equipped with a GPS module, 8 RGB LEDs and a vibration motor. The wristband can provide feedback by vibration impulses, which can vary in intensity, length and frequency.

(a)   (b)

Fig. 1. The digital coach wristband we use in our study contains a GPS module, a vibration motor (a) and 8 RGB LEDs, of which four are white, two are red and two are green (b) (Color figure online)

Participants will also be asked to complete a digital questionnaire on a laptop to determine what kind of athlete they are. This questionnaire is part of the DISC coaching theory. This theory distinguishes four styles of personality, ranging from task-oriented to human-oriented, and from direct to indirect.

On the basis of this questionnaire the output of the digital coach is adjusted to that of the athlete. This means that the feedback of the wristband is tuned to the user. In the demonstration the participant is presented various scenarios that a runner might encounter, to which the digital coach will react accordingly.

References

1. Rivera-Pelayo, V., Zacharias, V., Müller, L., Braun, S.: Applying quantified self approaches to support reflective learning. In: Proceedings of the 2nd International Conference on Learning Analytics and Knowledge, Vancouver, British Columbia, Canada, pp. 111–114 (2012)
2. Clarke, F., Ekeland, I.: Harnessing the power of feedback loops. Wired Magazine, 19, 7 (2011)

Reconfigurable Multipurpose Haptic Interface

Ben Horan, Syafizwan Faroque, Mats Isaksson, and Quan-Zen Ang

Deakin University, Victoria, Australia
{ben.horan, smohdfar, mats.isaksson}@deakin.edu.au

Abstract. This paper presents a low-cost haptic interface providing four different kinematic configurations. The different configurations are achieved using two Phantom Omni haptic devices combined with a series of clip-on attachments. Aside from the flexibility to easily reconfigure the interface, three of the four configurations provide functionality which is either not readily available or is cost prohibitive for many applications.

Keywords: 5-DOF haptic stylus · Haptic gripper · Phantom omni

1 The Haptic Interface

The interface is achieved using two Phantom Omni haptic devices [1], a linear-rotary stage, and a series of low-cost attachments. To be able to connect the clip-on attachments, the Phantom Omnis require minor modification to remove the stylus jack. Changing between configurations is simply a matter of disconnecting the magnetic clip-on attachments and then reconnecting the required ones. Depending on the configuration it may also be necessary to slide and/or rotate the Phantom Omnis. To support portability and to reduce the amount of external ancillary hardware, a computer and power supply are installed within the base of the system. Therefore, to use the system, only a display, keyboard and mouse need to be connected. Figure 1 shows the four different configurations. The first is the two Phantom Omni haptic devices, able to be rotated and moved using the linear-rotary stage, suitable for bimanual 3-DOF haptic interaction. Second is a refined version of our earlier introduced haptic gripper providing independent 3-DOF cartesian forces to each finger [2]. Our 5-DOF wand configuration is then shown and was inspired by a similar approach using two Novint Falcon devices [3]. The final configuration is our 5-DOF stylus [4] which uses a similar approach to [5]. The 5-DOF stylus can be used in applications where haptic feedback about the stylus' longitudinal axis is not required.

© Springer-Verlag Berlin Heidelberg 2014
M. Auvray and C. Duriez (Eds.): EuroHaptics 2014, Part II, LNCS 8619, pp. 432–434, 2014.
DOI: 10.1007/978-3-662-44196-1

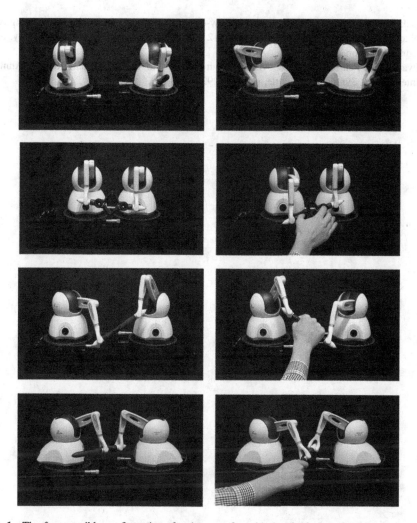

Fig. 1. The four possible configurations for the reconfigurable haptic device *(from top to bottom)*: Two 3-DOF Phantom Omnis, Dual-point Gripper, 5-DOF wand, and 5-DOF stylus.

References

1. Geomagic, http://geomagic.com/
2. Ang, Q-Z., Horan, B., Nahavandi, S.: Multipoint haptic mediator interface for robotic teleoperation. IEEE Syst. J. **PP**, 1–12 (2013)
3. Shah, A., Teuscher, S., McClain, E., Abbott, J.: How to build an inexpensive 5-DOF haptic device using two Novint Falcons. In: Kappers, A., van Erp, J., Tiest, W.B., van der Helm, F. (eds.) Haptics: Generating and Perceiving Tangible Sensations. LNCS, vol. 6191, pp. 136–143. Springer, Berlin/Heidelberg (2010)

4. Isaksson, M., Horan, B., Nahavandi, S.: Low-cost 5-DOF haptic stylus interaction using two phantom omni devices. In: Eurohaptics 2012 - Haptics: Perception, Devices, Mobility, and Communication (2012)
5. Iwata, H.: Pen-based haptic virtual environment. In: IEEE Virtual Reality Annual International Symposium Seattle, pp. 287–292 (1993)

Demo: The (Un)predictability of Visuo-Haptic and Haptic-Haptic Biases

Irene A. Kuling, Marieke C.W. van der Graaff,
Eli Brenner, and Jeroen B.J. Smeets

Faculty of Human Movement Sciences, MOVE Research Institute Amsterdam,
VU University, Amsterdam, The Netherlands
i.a.kuling@vu.nl

Abstract. Systematic biases have been found when matching haptic and visual locations. In this demo we can show two things; first we can show that these biases are similar when pointing at a visual target with the index finger or with a handle in a power grip. Second, we show that intermodal biases are not simply the result of a mismatch between the senses and that the transformations of the position information between modalities (and hands) are not simply reversible.

Keywords: Visuo-haptic biases · Proprioception · Hand localization

1   Introduction

Moving one's hand to a visually presented target on a surface under conditions that prevent one from seeing one's hand generally results in idiosyncratic errors [e.g. 1, 2]. Changing the visual target for a haptic one (the other hand on the other side of the surface) results in completely different, in general smaller, biases [e.g. 3]. As movements in these experiments are without timing constraints and subjects have to indicate explicitly that the moving hand is at the targets position, one might expect that these intermodal biases reflect a mismatch between the senses. Is this indeed the case?

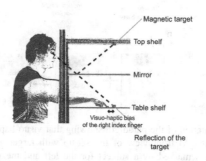

Fig. 1. Set-up of the demo. The subjects could not see their hand, so they had to visually judge the position of (the reflection of) the target and use that information to move their hand to this target. A structural difference between the physical and indicated position is called a visuo-haptic bias.

© Springer-Verlag Berlin Heidelberg 2014
M. Auvray and C. Duriez (Eds.): EuroHaptics 2014, Part II, LNCS 8619, pp. 435–437, 2014.
DOI: 10.1007/978-3-662-44196-1

In this demo we show that intermodal biases are not simply the result of a mismatch between the senses and that the transformations of the position information between modalities (and hands) are not reversible.

2 Demonstration

The demo uses a three-shelf metal construction with a mirror on the middle shelf. On the top shelf, magnets can be placed to indicate the target positions (Fig. 1). Subjects were asked to place a magnetic marker at the mirrored position of the targets on the table shelf with their unseen hand.

In this set-up different paradigms can be used to reveal various (in)consistencies between intermodal biases. Two examples:

1. by first pointing to a visual target with the fist (and place a magnetic marker) and afterwards with the index finger we can show that there is hardly any difference in visuo-haptic bias between effector (consistent)
2. by first pointing to a visual target with the right index finger on top of the board (and place a magnetic marker) and then point to the same target with the left index finger below the board (and place a magnetic marker) we can show that visuo-haptic biases for the different hands do not sum up to the haptic-haptic biases between hands (inconsistent). An schematic example of this paradigm can be seen in Fig. 2.

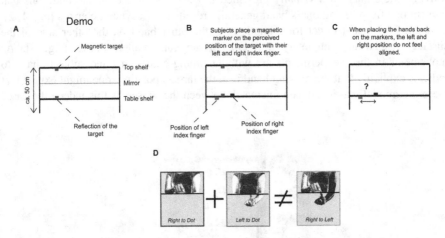

Fig. 2. Schematic representation of the paradigm showing that visuo-haptic biases do not sum up to the haptic-haptic equivalent. (A) front view of the set-up with target and reflection of the target. (B) example of the positions marked by a subject for the left and the right hand. (C) the marked positions of both hands do not feel aligned. (D) symbolic representation of the inconsistency.

References

1. Rincon-Gonzalez, L., Buneo, C.A., Helms Tillery S.I.: The proprioceptive map of the arm is systematic and stable, but idiosyncratic. PLoS One **6**: e25214 (2011)
2. Kuling, I.A., Brenner, E., Smeets, J.B.J.: Proprioception is robust under external Forces. PLoS One **8**: e74236 (2013)
3. Haggard, P., Newman, C., Blundell, J., Andrew, H.: The perceived position of the hand in space. Percept. Psychophys. **68**, 363–377 (2000)

Haptic Rendering of Tissue Stiffness by the Haptic Enhanced Reality Method

Yoshihide Otsuru, Toshio Tsuji, and Yuichi Kurita

Hiroshima University,
1-4-1 Kagamiyama Higashihiroshima, Hiroshima 739-8527, Japan
{y-otsuru,tsuji,kurita}@bsys.hiroshima-u.ac.jp
http://www.bsys.hiroshima-u.ac.jp/

Abstract. We have developed a prototype medical simulator that uses the haptic enhanced reality (HER) method. In this method, the force from a haptic device overlaps the reaction force from a base object. The key idea is to use a base object that has a material property similar to that of the target and to combine the virtual force produced by the haptic device with the reaction force from the base object. To display a realistic stiffness based on color information in the image, we defined the stiffness parameter in terms of the luminance of the image.

Keywords: Haptic display · Surgical training simulator · Haptic enhanced reality

1   Introduction

Our research group has proposed the use of force rendering by augmentation to produce a realistic force response even when using a low-performance haptic device [1]. The key idea is to use an object that has a material property similar to that of the target object and to overlap the force produced by the haptic device onto the force of the base object. The haptic sensations produced by the proposed haptic enhanced reality (HER) method are improved because the base object compensates for a force response that is not perfectly modeled or that the device cannot completely produce [2].

In this demonstration, we will show a training simulator system for a minimally invasive surgery that utilizes the proposed HER method. To develop a surgical simulator with haptic feedback, it is necessary to display the force response of elastic tissue. We propose to use an elastic rubber sheet to generate the base stiffness, and enhance the force response of the elastic sheet using a haptic device based on color information from the target tissue.

2   Demonstration

Figure 1 shows an overview of the demonstration. A prototype surgical training system will be used for the demonstration. The system is composed of a haptic device, an image projector, an elastic rubber sheet, and a box training system with a camera.

© Springer-Verlag Berlin Heidelberg 2014
M. Auvray and C. Duriez (Eds.): EuroHaptics 2014, Part II, LNCS 8619, pp. 438–439, 2014.
DOI: 10.1007/978-3-662-44196-1

Surgical forceps for a minimally invasive surgery were attached to the end of the manipulator of the haptic device (Geomagic Touch, 3D Co., Ltd.). To monitor the force response, a force sensor was attached to the forceps. The mobile projector displays an image of the target object on an elastic rubber sheet. The elastic rubber sheet was placed on the box training system for a minimally invasive surgery. A web camera captured the workspace of the forceps and displayed the image on a screen placed in front of the user.

In the HER method, the force generated by the haptic device F_{dev} is augmented by the reaction force of the base object F_{base}, and the total force $F_{\mathrm{user}} = F_{\mathrm{dev}} + F_{\mathrm{base}}$ is displayed to the user. In this study, the reaction force of the elastic sheet was modeled by $F_{\mathrm{base}} = K_{\mathrm{sheet}}\,x$, where K_{sheet} is the stiffness constant of the elastic sheet and x is the penetration depth. The force generated by the haptic force was modeled by $F_{\mathrm{dev}} = K_{\mathrm{dev}}\,x$, where K_{dev} is the stiffness constant that changes depending on the endpoint position of the forceps. The penetration depth was determined by monitoring the endpoint position of the forceps, which was calculated by a coordinate transformation from the endpoint of the haptic device. And to display a realistic stiffness based on color information in the image, we defined the stiffness parameter K_{target} in terms of the luminance of the image.

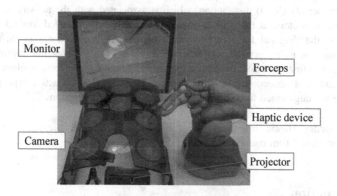

Fig. 1. Overview of the haptic display system.

References

1. Ikeda, A., Kurita, Y., Tamaki, T., Nagata, K., Ogasawara, T.: Creating virtual stiffness by modifying force profile of base object. In: Astrid M.L., Jan B.F., Wouter M., Frans C.T. (eds.) Euro-Haptics 2010. LNCS, vol. 6191, pp. 111–116. Springer, Heidelberg (2010)
2. Kurita, Y., Ikeda, A., Tamaki, T., Nagata, K., Ogasawara, T.: Haptic Augmented Reality Interface using the Real Force Response of an Object. In: Proceedings of the 16th ACM Symposium on Virtual Reality Software and Technology, pp. 83–86 (2009)

A Multi-DOF Haptic Representation
Using Suction Pressure Stimuli on Finger Pads

Daiki Maemori, Lope Ben Porquis,
Masashi Konyo, and Satoshi Tadokoro

Graduate School of Information Science, Tohoku University,
6-6-01 Aramaki Aza Aoba, Aoba-ku, Sendai Miyagi, 739-8527, Japan
http://www.rm.is.tohoku.ac.jp
{maemori,lopeben,konyo,tadokoro}@rm.is.tohoku.ac.jp

Abstract. Humans can perceive external forces applied on a grasping tool based on skin pressure distribution at multiple contact areas during grasp. We had tried to represent external forces and torques by controlling the skin pressure distributions using suction stimuli and confirmed the potential but in a heuristic manner. In this time, we improve the heuristic method by combining psychophysical experiments and mechanical simulation of skin deformations. Especially, we focus on a simplification method to represent the complex strain energy density (SED) distribution, which is associated with the activity of the mechanoreceptors, at the contact areas. As a result, the improved method can express the diagonal force in between a pair of the orthogonal axes. In this demonstrations, we prepare two types of demonstration to show the improved effect. The first is a passive type that expresses virtual external force applying to the multi-DoF direction in a virtual space. The second is an active type that expresses augmented force on the pen during physical interactions.

Keywords: Haptic interfaces · Force illusion · Suction pressure · Skin deformation · Tool manipulation

1 Introduction

Humans can perceive external forces applied on a grasping tool even in indirect touch. We may feel that whatever action we did on the tool appears to be felt direct by our fingertips. This transparency of haptic information from indirect contact is an interesting topic for research. A possible cue of such capability is skin pressure distributions at multiple contact areas during grasp. For example, cutaneous sense has contributions to force perception. However, the force extracting procedure from multiple contact points is still unclear.

The authors have tried to represent external forces and torques by controlling the skin pressure distributions using suction pressure stimuli at multiple contact points. Our previously developed suction pressure interface called the TAKO–Pen [1] is shown in Fig. 1. The TAKO–Pen is in short for Tactile Augmented Kinesthetic illusiOn Pen. The interface is a combination of a tactile display and a six-DoF force sensor. It uses

M. Auvray and C. Duriez (Eds.): EuroHaptics 2014, Part II, LNCS 8619, pp. 440–442, 2014.
DOI: 10.1007/978-3-662-44196-1

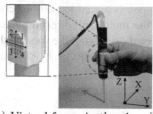 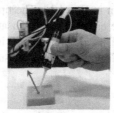

(a) Virtual forces in the air.   (b) Augmented forces against soft objects.

Fig. 1. Demonstrations representing multi-DoF virtual forces with the TAKO–Pen.

multipoint tactile stimuli for stimulating the fingerpads. Up to the present, a total of eight individually controllable pressure chambers allows a combination of pressure distribution to evoke a sense of force and torque up to six DoF. However, the conventional control method of the suction pressure was based on heuristics, and the quality of the induced force was limited. In addition, we could not represent the force direction between a pair of the orthogonal axes.

In this time, we optimize the method by combining psychophysical experiments and mechanical simulation of skin deformations. Especially, we focus on a simplification method to represent the complex strain energy density (SED) distribution, which is associated with the activity of the mechanoreceptors, at the contact areas [2]. The relationship between suction pressure and SED is achieved by connecting the experiment and the mechanical simulation. Consequently, we could control the on-target amount of perceived force and directions. In evaluation experiments, we confirmed the linearity between the applied force and the perceived force and capability of force direction between the orthogonal axes.

2 Demonstrations

In the previous study [1], the TAKO–Pen could express the virtual force on the three coordinate axes (X-axis, Y-axis, and Z-axis). However it could not express the diagonal force in between a pair of the orthogonal axes, which was critical for practical applications. The present demonstration is advanced from the previous study. We proposed a new representation method of multi-DoF forces by associating the psychophysical experiments with the FEA. As a result, TAKO–Pen could represent force vectors between orthogonal axes by using the proposed method.

In this demonstration, we prepare two types of demonstration, one is representing virtual force and the other is representing augmented force applying to the pen tip. The first is a passive type that expresses virtual external force applying to the multi-DoF direction in a virtual space as shown in Fig. 1(a). The operator can confirm the virtual external forces on the pen according to haptic interaction with visual cues in the virtual space. This demonstration will show that the TAKO–Pen has high portability. The second is an active type that expresses augmented force on the pen during physical interactions as shown in Fig. 1(b). The tip of the pen is placed to soft objects and the operator can feel the enhance force sensation in the multi-DoF direction gained from the force sensor. This demonstration is expected to show the potential of the TAKO–Pen to practical applications for supporting human skills such as surgical knife or sculpturing.

References

1. Porquis, L.B., Maemori, D., Nagaya, N., Konyo, M., Tadokoro, S.: Presenting virtual stiffness by modulating the perceived force Profile with suction pressure. In: 2014 IEEE Haptics Symposium, pp. 289–294 (2014)
2. Srinivasan, M.A., Dandekar, K.: An investigation of the mechanics of tactile sense using two-dimensional models of the primate fingertip, Trans. ASME J. Biomech. Eng. 118, pp.48–55 (1996)

High-Fidelity Haptic Device

Guillaume Millet, Abdenbi Mohand Ousaid, Antoine Weill-Duflos,
and Stéphane Régnier

ISIR, UMR 7222, Sorbonne Universités, UPMC Univ Paris, 75005, Paris, France
{millet,mohand_ousaid,weill,regnier}@isir.upmc.fr

Abstract. This demonstration presents our one degree-of-freedom high-fidelity haptic device. Electromagnetic drives are subjected to an inherent inertia–torque tradeoff that fundamentally limits transparency: the higher the torque, the higher the inertia. Based on a dual-stage design, our actuator is not subjected to this tradeoff and is able to approach perfect transparency for human users, combining very low inertia and high dynamic range. It comprises a large, proximal motor and a small, distal motor to reproduce the transients. The two stages are coupled by a viscous clutch based on eddy currents that, without contact, accurately transforms slip velocity into torque. A first demonstration evaluates the participant ability to detect small haptic details and shows that the high-level degree of transparency of the dual-stage drive allows users to detect details that are ten times smaller in magnitude than when using a conventional design. A second demonstration illustrates an application for microteleoperation, where forces to be rendered are highly dynamic.

Keywords: Haptic device · Transparency · Low inertia

1 Introduction

For all electromagnetic motors, a larger output torque always corresponds to a larger rotor inertia. This constraint is of little consequence when a motor is meant to operate at a constant or nearly constant speed. However, many applications of electromagnetic motors require fast, dynamic operation, in which case the rotor inertia plays a dominant role.

Our device, as shown on Fig. 1, relies on coupling to actuators of different characteristics, one designed to provide the bulk of the torque and the second meant to provide the transitory torques only. Since the main motor is speed controlled, its inertia is not transmitted to the load. In addition, accuracy is ensured by the auxiliary motor which is very fast due to its low inertia.

This work was supported by the ANR (Agence Nationale de la Recherche, France), project PACMAN 'perception haptique des échelles micro et nanoscopiques'. Additional funding was from the European Research Council, Advanced Grant PATCH (agreement number 247300 to VH), as well as from the SATT Lutech (Sociétés d'Accélération du Transfert de Technologies) through the project TACTOM, http://tactom.isir.upmc.fr.

M. Auvray and C. Duriez (Eds.): EuroHaptics 2014, Part II, LNCS 8619, pp. 443–444, 2014.
DOI: 10.1007/978-3-662-44196-1

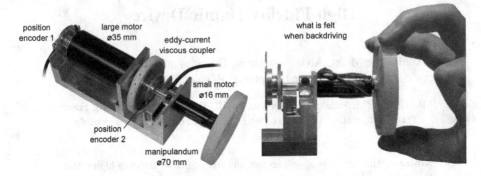

Fig. 1. High-fidelity haptic device, such as described in [2].

The main advantage of this architecture is to provide torques within a very large dynamic range (3 to 4 orders of magnitude) with exquisite precision, which surclasses the performance of any other electromagnetic actuators. For more details about the design and the control of the device, see references [1–3].

2 Demonstration

Psychophysics Experiment. Visitors will be asked to detect the presence of weak, high-frequency force perturbations superposed onto a slowly varying background force at random locations in the workspace. The stimuli will be administered through two identical handles, one connected to the high-fidelity device, and the other to a conventional single-motor device. The same experiment published in [2] showed that our device allowed users to detect details that were ten times smaller in magnitude than when using a conventional design.

Nanoscale Forces. One of the potential applications of our high-fidelity haptic device is to support delicate teleoperated force-based procedures such as manual sorting based on cells' mechanical properties, or manual positioning of microscopic parts under friction constraints. This demonstration will illustrate the transparency of the device to render a nanoscale interaction.

References

1. Millet, G., Haliyo, S., Régnier, S., Hayward, V.: The ultimate haptic device: first step. In: World Haptics 2009, pp. 273–278. IEEE Press, New York (2009)
2. Mohand Ousaid, A., Millet, G., Régnier, S., Haliyo, S., Hayward, V.: Haptic inter-face transparency achieved through viscous coupling. Int. J. Robot. Res. **31**(3), 319–329 (2012)
3. Millet, G., Hayward, V., Haliyo, S., Régnier, S.: Device for quicky generating a torque on an extended dynamic range with low inertia. PCT PatentWO2 010 102 998, WIPO patent application (2010)

A Tactile Display Using Pneumatic Membrane Actuators

Alexander Russomanno[1], R. Brent Gillespie[1], Sile O'Modhrain[2],
and James Barber[1]

[1] Mechanical Engineering, University of Michigan, Ann Arbor MI, USA
{arussoma, brentg, jbarber}@umich.edu
[2] School of Music, Theatre, and Dance, Performing Arts Technology,
University of Michigan, Ann Arbor MI, USA
sileo@umich.edu

Abstract. In this paper, we present a tactile display that uses pneumatics to actuate a 7×8 array of pins. The pin spacing is 2.5 mm with a pin diameter of 1.2 mm. The pins deflect 0.75 mm under an actuation pressure of 100 kPag and a measuring force of 0.1 N. The display supports two lines of braille text and a tactile graphic with 56 pixels.

Keywords: Pneumatic actuators · Tactile graphics · Refreshable brailledisplay

1 Introduction

Tactile displays provide a way of transmitting programmable haptic information to a user. They have been widely applied for teletaction and rendering virtual environments, but also hold promise in providing haptically-encoded information to visually impaired users (e.g. braille and tactile graphics). We have built a dense-array shape display that uses pneumatically driven pins to modulate skin deformations within the finger contact patch. Unlike tactile displays that rely on friction force modulation [1], our display can present spatially distributed and differentiable tactile information within the contact area (Fig. 1).

Other tactile displays that use an array of pins to modulate skin deformation have been built using piezoelectric bimorphs (Metec "Hyperbraille"[1]), shape memory alloys [2], radio-control servomotors [3] and pneumatics [4]. The advantage of using pneumatics is that the power source is divorced from the actuator. Power, in the form of pressurized air, is routed via small pipes and readily converted into the motion of a sliding pin. Separating the power source and means of modulating the power (e.g. valves) from the actuation point allows for many pins to be tightly packed together to form a large-area dense array shape display. The disadvantage of using pneumatics is the complexity associated with an independently controlled valve and pneumatic line for each tactile feature.

---

[1] http://web.metec-ag.de/

© Springer-Verlag Berlin Heidelberg 2014
M. Auvray and C. Duriez (Eds.): EuroHaptics 2014, Part II, LNCS 8619, pp. 445–447, 2014.
DOI: 10.1007/978-3-662-44196-1

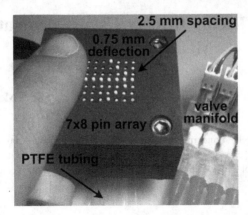

Fig. 1. The 7 × 8 tactile display showing a right-pointing arrow.

2   Demonstration

The display, shown in Fig. 1, uses the deflection of a thin-film elastic membrane (5.1 mils Microflex Latex glove) above pressurized cavities to drive a 7 × 8 array of mechanical pins. The array meets the standard spacing and deflection specifications for refreshable braille [5]; the pins are spaced 2.5 mm apart and can displace 0.75 mm vertically. The display supports two lines of braille text, each consisting of three six-dot letters. Each character is separated vertically and horizontally by a single row and column of inactive pins, respectively. A tactile graphic with 56 pixels can also be rendered. A braille pin sits in the top plate and slides freely up and down based on the deflection of the membrane under pressure. The pin returns to an inactive state under the action of gravity if the membrane is depressurized. The membrane acts as the actuator element, converting pressure into mechanical force and displacement, and provides a seal for the system. The pressure to each pneumatic actuator is controlled by a 3-way, 24 V solenoid valve (LHD Series, The Lee Company). Each valve is fixed to a common manifold that is maintained at a constant pressure from the source and connected to a single cavity by 0.02" ID EVA tubing (1883T1, McMaster-Carr). The valves are controlled using an Arduino microprocessor coupled with a 24 V transistor array.

We plan to use the display to conduct perceptual tests to quantify the limits of human perception in distinguishing pins at different sizes and spacing. We are particularly interested in achieving perceptually continuous features with discrete stimulators. The design of the device allows for it to be easily scaled to carry out these studies. Early prototypes are able to render braille characters that can be read without difficulty by blind braille readers.

References

1. Winfield, L., Glassmire, J., Colgate, J.E., Peshkin, M.: TPaD: Tactile Pattern Display through variable friction reduction. In: Eurohaptics Conference, 2007, pp. 421–426. IEEE March 2007
2. Howe, R,D.: The shape of things to come: pin-based tactile shape displays. In: Proceedings of the 4th International Conference Eurohaptics, pp. 2–11 (2004)
3. Wagner, C., Lederman, S., Howe, R.: A tactile shape display using RC servomotors. In: Proceedings 10th Symposium on Haptic Interfaces for Virtual Environment and Teleoperator Systems, HAPTICS 2002, pp. 354–355. IEEE Computer Society (2002)
4. Moy, G., Wagner, C., Fearing, R.: A compliant tactile display for teletaction. In: Proceedings 2000 ICRA. Millennium Conference, IEEE International Conference on Robotics and Automation, Symposia Proceedings (Cat. No. 00CH37065), vol. 4, pp. 3409–3415. IEEE (2000)
5. Runyan, R.H., Blazie, D.B.: The continuing quest for the 'Holy Braille' of tactile displays. In: Esteve, J., Terentjev, E.M., Campo, E.M. (eds.) SPIE NanoScience + Engineering, International Society for Optics and Photonics, pp. 81 070G–81 070G–17, September 2011

Several Discrete Stimuli to Whole Fingers Provide Surface Undulation Perception

Yoshihiro Tanaka, Yuki Goto, Masayoshi Hashimoto,
Tomohiro Fukuda, Koji Watanabe, Nagomi Tsuboi,
Nguyen Duy Phuong, and Akihito Sano

Nagoya Institute of Technology,
Gokiso-cho, Showa-ku Nagoya, 466-8555, Japan
tanaka.yoshihiro@nitech.ac.jp, y.goto.532@nitech.jp,
{26416576,26416585,cix13192,cix18002,
22113212}@stn.nitech.ac.jp,
sano@nitech.ac.jp

Abstract. This demonstration presents a wearable haptic display that presents wide and small surface undulation, which is hundreds micrometers in height and hundreds millimeters in width. Our proposed device is composed of nine independent stimulator units that control heights of nine finger pads of the index finger, the middle finger, and the ring finger (3 on each finger) according to the virtual surface. Users scan the surface with their hands having the display and perceive a single smooth surface undulation, not discrete surface undulation. The display could be available to a curved surface as well as a flat surface.

Keywords: Surface undulation · Haptic display · Whole finger · Wearabledevice

1 Introduction

Humans cannot perceive wide and small surface undulation, which is hundreds micrometers in height and hundreds millimeters in width, with their fingertips, whereas they can perceive it by scanning the surface with their whole fingers including the palm to the direction of a long side of the finger. Surface undulation is an important factor to design 3D shape of products in tactual aspect as well as in visual aspect. Haptic display of surface undulation might be available to design and evaluate the shape of products. Bordegoni and Cugini proposed a design-assistance system using a robot arm-type force display [1].

We developed a wearable haptic display that presents wide and small surface undulation [2]. We assumed that finger pads and palm make contacts with the surface undulation during scanning it. Whole area of the hand could not completely make contacts with the surface. Hence, we assembled nine stimulator units that be mounted separately on nine finger pads of the index finger, the middle finger, and the ring finger (3 on each finger) and control the height of each finger pad. Each finger pad makes contact with a flat surface of a movable part of the stimulator unit. The palm makes

© Springer-Verlag Berlin Heidelberg 2014
M. Auvray and C. Duriez (Eds.): EuroHaptics 2014, Part II, LNCS 8619, pp. 448–450, 2014.
DOI: 10.1007/978-3-662-44196-1

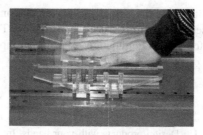

Fig. 1. Basic mechanical model of the haptic display.

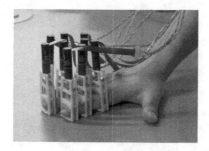

Fig. 2. Haptic display.

contact with the object surface as a base. The preliminary experiment showed that users scanned the flat surface with their hands having the display and perceived a single smooth surface undulation. The details of the haptic display are described in [2]. This demonstration presents the haptic display and its basic mechanical model.

2 Demonstration

First, we will demonstrate a basic mechanical model of the haptic display. Figure 1 shows the overview of the basic model. A plate with a real surface undulation is set on the bottom of the device. Cam followers with vertical linear guides trace the real surface undulation while a user moves the top surface of the device with his/her hand as shown in Fig. 1. User's finger pads make contacts with the base parts attached on the top of the liner guides. Hence, user's finger pads are moved vertically according to the real surface undulation. The user can perceive a similar surface undulation to the real surface undulation.

Then, we will demonstrate the haptic display [2], which is shown in Fig. 2. The haptic display is composed of nine independent stimulator units. A user mounts the nine stimulators on his/her nine finger pads of the index finger, the middle finger, and the ring finger. The servomotor and the ball screw mechanism allow the stimulator to move up and down within the stroke of ± 3 mm. An optical position sensor monitors the position of the haptic display and each stimulator controls the height of each finger pad according to the position and the virtual surface undulation. In this demonstration, a cosine waveform is used as the virtual surface undulation. The user can change the dimension of the presented surface undulation by using an input device.

References

1. Bordegoni, M., Cugini, U.: Design products with your hands. In: Virtual Concept (2005)
2. Tanaka, Y., Goto, Y. Sano, A.: Presentation of surface Uudulation to hand by several discrete stimuli. In: Proceedings of the EuroHaptics 2014 Conference (2014)

Motors and Music: Teaching Haptics and Sound for Product Design

Bill Verplank, David Gauthier, and Jakob Bak

Copenhagen Institute of Interaction Design,
Toldbodgade 37b, 1253, København Ø, Denmark
verplank@ccrma.stanford.edu
{d.gauthier,j.bak}@ciid.dk
http://ciid.dk

Abstract. We have developed a one-week workshop over the last four years teaching active force-feedback and simple sound synthesis as part of a one-year course in Interaction Design at CiiD.

1 Introduction

Copenhagen Institute of Interaction Design offers a one-year program of intensive hands-on workshops, projects and thesis work for post-graduate artists and engineers. We teach methods and tools related to tangible/product interaction, graphical/screen interaction and service design.

2 Motors and Music Workshop

Our one-week workshop on "Motors and Music" covers simple haptics and "hands-on" learning. The week starts with close observation of what we (and others) like; and how we use our hands to explore and manipulate objects. Basic dynamics (mass, spring, damping) are explored and programmed. We provide simple motors, sensors and software controlled computers and microprocessors. Arduino-based boards handle the haptics and simple audio applications are introduced. Simple exercises are followed by invention and implementation of working devices. The themes have evolved every year: from "artistic" to "two-person" to "practical product" to "public service".

Bill Verplank will be doing the demos, David and Jakob designed the custom PCB and software.

M. Auvray and C. Duriez (Eds.): EuroHaptics 2014, Part II, LNCS 8619, pp. 451–453, 2014.
DOI: 10.1007/978-3-662-44196-1

2.1   Exercises

The students are asked to bring in objects they "like the feel of". They watch others (blind-folded) explore the objects. Lederman and Klatzky [1] have a useful categorization of "Exploratory Procedures" or "EPs" which we introduce. We find it necessary to distinguish "static" objects which can be explored with the six EPs. "Dynamic" objects are the things we are more likely to interact with: push a button, manipulate a handle. What are the "Dynamic EPs": turn, bend, twist, open, close? Simple active-haptic examples include: spring (linear and non-linear), friction (viscous and static), mass, spring-mass, spring-mass damper. Stiff and soft walls.

Fig. 1. Student Projects "Super Angry Birds: shoot and explode" and "Hapticket: feel and hear".

2.2   Projects

http://ciid.dk/research/explorations/motors-music/
    During the first year, the projects were open ended or "artistic": flying a kite, Two-Person, Product, Skill.

3   Simple Devices

3.1   Devices and Hardware

"The Plank" is built from discarded disk drives by throwing away all but the head-positioner (a voice-coil between two rare-earth magnets). It is driven by an H-bridge and has Hall-effect sensor added for position feedback (A/D). It was developed at Stanford's CCRMA and presented at NIME05. [2] (Fig. 2 shows an example).

Fig. 2. The Plank and CiiD MandM Board controlling a Plank and Fader.

3.2 CiiD Motors and Music Board

David Gauthier and Jakob Back, at CiiD, developed an Arduino-compatible board: an AVR with H-bridge motor controller and a 12-bit D/A for audio out. After being programmed from Arduino environment, the board can be powered by a battery, and embedded in a portable prototype.

References

1. Lederman, S.J., Klatzky, R.L.: Hand movements: a window into haptic object recognition. Cogn. Psychol. **19**(3), 342–368 (1987)
2. Verplank, B., Gurevich, M., Mathews, M.: THE PLANK: designing a simple haptic controller. In: Proceedings of the Conference on New Instruments for Musical Expression (NIME-02), Dublin, Ireland, May 24-26 2002
3. Verplank, B.: Haptic music exercises. In: Proceedings of the 2005 International Conference on New Interfaces for Musical Expression (NIME05), Vancouver, BC, Canada (2005)
4. CiiD Labs: Motors and Music Platform, http://labs.ciid.dk/physical/motors-music-platform/
5. Gauthier, D., Verplank, B., Bak, J.: Studio 8: motors and music. In: TEI13, Seventh International Conference on Tangible, Embedded and Embodied Interaction (2013). http://www.tei-conf.org/13/studios:

Demonstration: A High-Fidelity Surface-Haptic Device for Texture Rendering on Bare Finger

Michaël Wiertlewski[1], Daniele Leonardis[1,2], David J. Meyer[1], Michael A. Peshkin[1], and J. Edward Colgate[1]

[1] Department of Mechanical Engineering,
Northwestern University, Evanston IL, 60208, USA
{wiertlewski,peshkin,colgate}@northwestern.edu
meyerdj@u.northwestern.edu
d.leonardis@ssup.it
[2] PERCRO Laboratory, Scuola Superiore SantAnna, 56127, Pisa, Italy

Abstract. In this demonstration, we present a device able to control the friction force that a bare finger experiences when exploring the workspace. Special attention has been given to the rendering fidelity of the force that the finger experiences. Participants will explore the glass plate freely with their bare finger and will able to feel any texture programmed onto the controller with a high level of reproduction accuracy.

Keywords: Surface-haptics · Texture rendering · High delity haptics

1 Introduction

Friction between a bare finger and a glass surface can be controlled via the modulation of the amplitude of an ultrasonic transverse wave applied to the glass plate [1–3]. The previous implementations of tactile interfaces that exploit this principle of actuation were, for the most part, ineffective at updating the friction level at a rate higher than 100 Hz. This limit stems from three major causes: the inability of capturing the finger position at high sampling rate and high spatial resolution; the high-latency in the rendering scheme; and the attenuation of the modulation of the friction force caused by the dynamic of the resonant system. To circumvent this limitation we implemented three key components: a high-speed high-resolution non-contact optical sensor for tracking the finger location; a realtime controller with 5 kHz refresh rate; and a feedforward filter for correcting the attenuation of the mechanics yielding at frequency response. The design of this device allows for high-fidelity rendering of texture on a glass plate.

© Springer-Verlag Berlin Heidelberg 2014
M. Auvray and C. Duriez (Eds.): EuroHaptics 2014, Part II, LNCS 8619, pp. 454–455, 2014.
DOI: 10.1007/978-3-662-44196-1

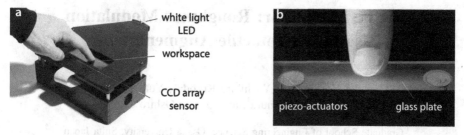

Fig. 1. (a.) Overview of the texture rendering apparatus. (b.) Close up of the finger. The light from the white LED is reflected off the fingertip and casts a shadow onto the photodiode array in the back.

2 Demonstration

The demonstration consists of a single apparatus comprising an ultrasonic tactile surface (TPaD), the optical position sensor, the texture rendering controller and the necessary amplifiers (see Fig. 1). The texture displayed can be sent to the controller as a waveform representing the level of friction for each of the 15,000 position quanta of the 120 mm long TPaD. As the participant's finger explores the surface, its position is measured using linear photodiode array (TSL1412s, AMS-TAOS Inc, TX, USA). A white-light LED constantly illuminates the array and the presence of the finger casts a shadow that is detected by a blob detection circuit. The position is then sent to a microcontroller (PIC32MX250, Microchip Inc., Itasca, IL, USA) that updates a low frequency modulation signal according to a spatially encoded texture stored onboard. The modulation signal is filtered then multiplied by the ultrasonic carrier signal using an analog multiplier (AD633, Analog Devices Inc., Northwood, MA, USA). The amplitude-modulated signal is then amplified (PDm200, PiezoDrive, Pty Ltd, Callaghan, Australia) and fed to the piezoelectric actuator glued onto the tactile surface. A complete technical description of the inner workings of the apparatus can be found in [4].

During the demonstration, the participants will be able to feel artificial textures such as square wave gratings, sine wave, and gaussian bumps with pitches ranging from 10 mm to 100 μm. Natural textures such as sandpaper and fabric will also be demonstrated.

References

1. Watanabe, T., Fukui, S.: A method for controlling tactile sensation of surface roughness using ultrasonic vibration. In: IEEE ICRA, pp. 1134–1139, May 1995
2. Winfield, L., Glassmire, J., Colgate, J.E., Peshkin, M.: T-pad: Tactile pattern display through variable friction reduction. In: World Haptics Conference, pp. 421–426. IEEE (2007)
3. Biet, M., Giraud, F., Lemaire-Semail, B.: Squeeze film effect for the design of an ultrasonic tactile plate. IEEE Trans. Ultrason. Ferroelectr. Freq. Control, **54**(12), 2678–2688 (2007)
4. Wiertlewski, M., Leonardis, D., Meyer, D.J., Peshkin, M.A., Colgate, J.E.: A high-fidelity surface-haptic device for texture rendering on bare finger. In Eurohaptics (2014). (In Press)

Tactile Modulator: Roughness Modulation Using Electrotactile Augmentation

Shunsuke Yoshimoto[1], Yoshihiro Kuroda[2], Yuki Uranishi[3],
Masataka Imura[1], and Osamu Oshiro[1]

[1] Graduate School of Engineering Science, Osaka University, Suita Japan
yoshimoto@bpe.es.osaka-u.ac.jp
[2] Cybermedia Center, Osaka University, Suita Japan
[3] Graduate School of Informatics, Kyoto University, Kyoto Japan

Abstract. We present a roughness modulation technique that employs electrotactile augmentation to alter material texture perception, which is conducted through mechanically unconstrained touch. The system detects user touch action and renders the electrical stimulus that induces the modulating nerve activities at the middle phalanx of a finger to control the roughness perception. The users perceive fused sensation of the virtual sensation from the artificial electrical stimulus and the real sensation from the natural mechanical stimulus. With the proposed system, users can explore the surface of real materials with their bare fingertip and feel the altered roughness.

Keywords: Haptic AR · Roughness modulation · Electrotactile displays

1 Introduction

Haptic augmented reality (AR), particularly modulation of real haptic perception has a potential to provide realistic sensation by fusing inadequate virtual haptic sensation with rich real haptic sensation. Previous studies about haptic AR have reported excellent results in terms of user perception [1, 2]. However, it is difficult to eliminate mechanical constraints of materials and a finger because of size, location and actuation of the stimulator. To this end, we have developed a compact electrotactile display that allows users to augment virtual tactile sensation at their fingertip by stimulating nerves at the base of the finger instead of at the fingertip [3]. In this demonstration, we present a texture modulation system that enables users to feel the altered roughness of real materials via electrotactile augmentation.

2 Demonstration

With the proposed system, users can have experience of the roughness modulation of real materials such as sand-paper, urethane, wood and so on. Moreover, the system allows users to touch freely a 3D printed object and feel altered roughness of the

© Springer-Verlag Berlin Heidelberg 2014
M. Auvray and C. Duriez (Eds.): EuroHaptics 2014, Part II, LNCS 8619, pp. 456–457, 2014.
DOI: 10.1007/978-3-662-44196-1

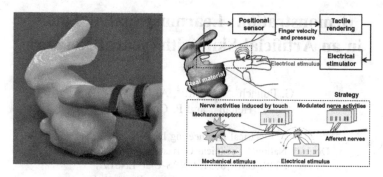

Fig. 1. The system overview: Users feel the altered texture of a real material (left). Modulating nerve activity is superimposed onto the afferent nerve (right).

surface. The system consists of a positional sensor, a computer, and the electrotactile display, and does not impose any mechanical constraints of materials and users as shown in Fig. 1. The system detects user touch action and renders the electrical stimulus that induces the modulating nerve activities at the middle phalanx of a finger to control the roughness perception. The users perceive fused sensation of the virtual sensation from the artificial electrical stimulus and the real sensation from the natural mechanical stimulus. We designed electrical stimulus to fuse the virtual electrotactile sensation with the real texture sensation naturally. The electrical stimulus is controlled according to the velocity and pressure of the finger. Specifically, we control the frequency of the vibrotactile sensation by changing the pulse density of the electrical stimulus according to finger velocity. We also control the pulse amplitude according to finger pressure to equalize virtual and real sensation intensities. Then, the calculated stimulus pattern is presented at each cathode.

With the proposed technology, haptic AR system without mechanical limitation of the touch action has been achieved. Although it is known that electrical stimulus causes unpleasant sensation, we succeeded to alleviate the unpleasant sensation by combining with the real sensation from the natural mechanical stimulus. Moreover, the proposed system is compact, low cost, and durable compared to the previous haptic AR using artificial mechanical stimulus.

References

1. Jeon, S., Choi, S.: Haptic augmented reality: taxonomy and an example of stiffness modulation. Presence: Teleoperators and Virtual Environ. **18**(5), 387–408 (2009)
2. Asano, S., Okamoto, S., Matsuura, Y., Nagano, H., Yamada, Y.: Vibrotactile display approach that modifies roughness sensations of real textures. In: Proceedings of IEEE RO-MAN, pp. 1001–1006 (2012)
3. Yoshimoto, S., Kuroda, Y., Imura, M., Oshiro, O.: Development of a spatially transparent electrotactile display and its performance in grip force control. In: Proceedings of IEEE EMBC, pp. 3463–3466 (2011)

Demonstration: Learning Spatial Touch in an Artificial Skin with Neural Network

G. Pugach[1,2], A. Pitti[2], A. Melnyk[1,2],
P. Henaff[3], and P. Gaussier[2]

[1] Electrical Engineering Department,
Donetsk National Technical University, Donetsk, Ukraine
[2] ETIS, UMR 8051, CNRS-UCP-ENSEA,
University of Cergy-Pontoise, Cergy-Pontoise, France
{ganna.pugach,alexandre.pitti,melnyk.artem}@ensea.fr,
patrick.henaff@loria.fr
[3] LORIA UMR 7503, University of Lorraine-INRIA-CNRS, Kyoto, Japan
gaussier@ensea.fr

Abstract. Sense of touch is considered as an essential feature for robots in order to improve the quality of their physical and social interactions. The development of a tactile device similar to human skin could give to robots the capabilities to function efficiently in real environment. In this demonstration, we present a new tactile sensor based on Electrical Impedance Tomography (EIT). The sensor is able to cover large surface areas and have high resolution nearest to the structure of the human skin. We propose a bio-inspired reconstruction algorithm for EIT using neural network technique and its advantages are simple mathematical formulation and online running. The participants can touch on the tactile sensor surface at any point of contact by a given object and can observe the Kohonen's neural network activity to recognize the presence of this point of contact with the surface.

Keywords: Touch sensor · Conductive fabric · Electrical Impedance Tomography · Neural network · Self-organizing network

1 Introduction

Different prototypes of artificial skin based on tactile sensors, various strategies used to build the interface between the tactile surface and the transduction mechanism have been presented [1–2]. Most of them use isolated unitary devices that cover the specified surface, where each to a small receptive field [3–4]. In scientific research, an artificial sensitive skin is usually considered as flexible and stretchable array of sensors or a tactile sheet that completely covers the body of a humanoid robot. We deal with a study of touch perception inherent in humans and its implementation using neural network to reconstruct human nervous system in the future works. Learning algorithm provides great robustness and great adaptivity to spatial localization and faster response for estimating the resistance distribution on the tissue's surface.

© Springer-Verlag Berlin Heidelberg 2014
M. Auvray and C. Duriez (Eds.): EuroHaptics 2014, Part II, LNCS 8619, pp. 458–460, 2014.
DOI: 10.1007/978-3-662-44196-1

We present the device to define the points of contact. Our motivation is to cover a humanoid robot the skin. This skin is able to provide the information about the point of the physical contact in a robot coordinate frame. We applied the EIT method and inverse problem analysis to sensitive skin: by injecting currents and measuring voltages from connected electrodes on the borders of a rubberized conductive fabric (Velostat® film), we reconstructed the local resistivity changes response from any applied pressure on the material.

2   Demonstration

In this demonstration, the participants asked to put and to move the conductive object on Velostat® sheet. For our basic setup, a rectangular flat conductive material of 200 × 250 mm with 16 electrodes are used around its boundary. The small constant current of 200 µA is applied and the voltages are measured while using of EIT technique (the electronic hardware is detailed in [5]). Kohonen's map has been used to solve the inverse problem of EIT. It works in a way to reconstruct the resistance distribution of a conductive tissue based on a limited number of electric potential samplings. The dataset of 208 boundary's voltages (the principle of data collection is detailed in [5]) was used as input data to train the neural network before the presentation. Trained neural network is stored in a computer memory for next usages. Finally, the same dataset on boundary's voltage in real-time operational mode is used to provide the solution of the inverse problem of EIT. The Fig. 1 presents a schematic diagram to reconstruct the spatial location of the conductive object. The participants will be convinced that Kohonen's map can produce a highly accurate image of touch sensing in a real time with the relative error which does not exceed 4.5 %.

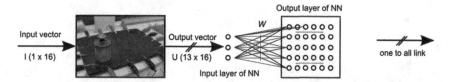

Fig. 1. Schematic diagram to estimate the resistivity distribution on the tactile sheet. Left: experimental setup. Right : Kohonen map.

References

1. Dahiya, R.S., Metta, G., Valle, M., Sandini, G.: Tactile sensing—from humans to humanoids. IEEE Trans. Robot. **26**(1), 1–20 (2010)
2. Lee, M.H., Nicholls, H.R.: Tactile sensing for mechatronics—a state of the art survey. Mechatronics **9**, 1–31 (1999)

3. Lee, H.-K. Chang, S.-Il, Yoon, E.: A flexible polymer tactile sensor: fabrication and modular expandability for large area deployment. IEEE J. MEMS Sys. **6**, 1681–1686 (2006)
4. Kato, Y., Mukai, T., Hayakawa, T., Shibata, T.: Tactile sensor without wire and sensing element in the tactile region based on EIT Method. IEEE Sensors, **2**, 792–795 (2007)
5. Pugach, G., Khomenko, V., Melnyk, A., Pitti, A., Henaff, P., Gaussier, Ph.: Electronic hardware design of a low cost tactile sensor device for physical Human-Robot Interactions. In: IEEE International Conference on Electronics and Nanotechnology (ELNANO), pp. 445–449 (2013)

Facilitating Planning: Tangible Objects with Multimodal Feedback Mitigate Cognitive Workload

Werner de Valk, Jouke Rypkema, and Jan B.F. van Erp

TNO Perceptual and Cognitive Systems, Soesterberg, The Netherlands
wdevalk@gmail.com, jouke.rypkema@tno.nl,
melnyk.artem@ensea.fr

Abstract. Complex planning tasks require substantial cognitive resources. Supporting planning tasks through enabling embodied interaction and providing multisensory feedback may reduce the cognitive load. We developed Sensators: interactive tangible objects to be used on multi-touch tables which provide both. In our demonstration, the user can experience the effect of these Sensators in planning a route through a virtual supermarket using touch-screen and passive Sensators (no feedback) or active Sensators providing multisensory feedback.

Keywords: Planning · Multisensory feedback · Embodied cognition

1 Introduction

Planning could be facilitated by enhancing working memory capacity [1]. Ways to do this are to use multiple modalities [2], or to support the embodiment of cognition [3] and therewith off-loading information into the environment [4]. 'Sensators' are tangibles that implement both approaches: they provide multisensory (visual, auditory and vibrotactile) feedback [5] and their haptic nature supports the embodiment of cognition. We demonstrate these Sensators in a planning task, i.e. the 'supermarket game'.

2 Demonstration

The 'supermarket game' is displayed on the Samsung Surface 40 touch-screen table [6] and is a complex planning game, see Fig. 1. Users control one fast basket (able to carry 5 products) and one slow cart (carrying up to 10 products) to gather products in a supermarket. The order in which these products are placed in the cart and basket determines the route of the lines running from entrance to exit; changing the location of one of these products causes the route to be updated instantly. Heavy products are not allowed to be placed on top of vulnerable ones. Products provide feedback about their location and intactness. The goal is to find a combination of routes which results in the shortest time the basket and cart take to finish their route (adding up the time of the two).

© Springer-Verlag Berlin Heidelberg 2014
M. Auvray and C. Duriez (Eds.): EuroHaptics 2014, Part II, LNCS 8619, pp. 461–462, 2014.
DOI: 10.1007/978-3-662-44196-1

The game can be performed using touch-screen, or by placing either passive or active Sensators on top of the screen. When using passive Sensators feedback originates from the screen, while active ones provide feedback themselves (they change color, play sounds and vibrate). Active Sensators represent both embodied cognition support (because they have to be picked up by hand) as well as multimodal feedback, whereas passive Sensators provide embodied cognition support only. This allows us to investigate the potential planning supporting abilities of Sensators.

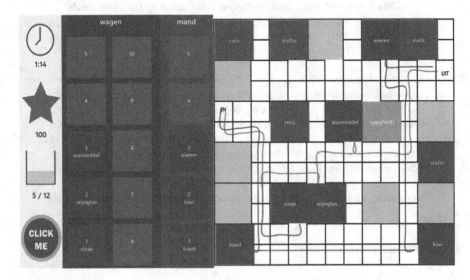

Fig. 1. Screen shot of the application (in Dutch). Three products are placed in basket and in cart; spaghetti is just picked up. 'Wagen' means cart, 'mand' means basket.

References

1. Newman, S.D., Carpenter, P.A., Varma, S., Just, M.A.: Frontal and parietal participation in problem solving in the tower of London: fMRI and computational modeling of planning and high-level perception. Neuropsychologia, **41**(12), 1668–1682 (2003)
2. Werkhoven, P, Van Erp, J.B.F., Philippi, T.P.: Navigating virtual mazes: the benefits of audiovisual landmarks. Displays (2014). doi:10.1016/j.displa.2014.04.001
3. Wilson, M.: Six views of embodied cognition. Psychon. Bull. Rev. **9**(4), 625–636 (2002)
4. Mayer, R.E., Moreno, R.: Nine ways to reduce cognitive load in multimedia learning. Educ. Psychol. **38**(1), 43–52 (2003)
5. Van Erp, J.B.F., Toet, A., Janssen, J.: Uni-, bi- and tri-modal warning signals: effects of temporal parameters and sensory modality on perceived urgency. Safety Science (submitted)
6. Samsung, Samsung SUR40 (2014). Retrieved from http://www.samsung.com/nl/business/business-products/large-format-display/specialized-display/LH40SFWTGC/EN-spec

Under-actuated Hand Exoskeleton with Novel Kinematics for Haptic Interaction with Virtual Objects

Nadia Garcia-Hernandez, Ioannis Sarakoglou, Nikos Tsagarakis,
and Darwin Caldwell

Italian Institute of Technology, Via Morego 30, 16163, Genova, Italy
{nadia.garcia, oannis.sarakoglou, nikos.tsagarakis,
darwin.caldwell}@iit.it

Abstract. In this demonstration, we present an under-actuated hand exoskeleton with novel kinematics for hand tracking and haptic interaction with virtual objects. The exoskeleton is a three-fingered device and it is connected to a grounded haptic interface. Users can grasp and manipulate objects within a virtual scene through a virtual hand which reflects their hand and fingers position, orientation and motions.

Keywords: Hand Exoskeleton · Virtual reality · Under-actuation

1 Introduction

Most of the existing hand exoskeletons used in VR (Virtual Reality) and teleoperation applications lack portability, wearability and ergonomy. They are bulky, difficult to wear, adjust and carry, and limit the range of motion of the users' fingers [1, 2]. In addition, due to the nature of the joints most of these systems are bound to suffer from misalignment at some location within their workspace [3]. Joint misalignment can be a severe problem due the complexity of the finger kinematics and due to the sensitivity of the fingers in perceiving even minute loads generated from misalignment. In this demonstration, we present a three-fingered hand exoskeleton that overcomes these limitations (Fig. 1). The device is wearable and ergonomic, and its design is based on a highly under-actuated mechanism which provides bidirectional force feedback to the extension and flexion of the fingers. The feedback forces are transmitted to the distal phalanges of the users' fingers through serial kinematic chains.

2 Demonstration

In this demonstration, users can grasp and manipulate objects within a virtual scene by using a hand exoskeleton attached to a grounded haptic interface (Haption Virtuose 6DTM), see Fig. 1. The Haption Virtuose 6DTM provides tracking of the users' hand

M. Auvray and C. Duriez (Eds.): EuroHaptics 2014, Part II, LNCS 8619, pp. 463–465, 2014.
DOI: 10.1007/978-3-662-44196-1

and grounded force feedback from the virtual interactions. The exoskeleton's serial linkages have 6 DOF (5 passive and 1 active revolute joints), they are grounded on one side and at the base are attached to the distal phalanges of the fingers through interchangeable thimbles. This single point of attachment of the links to the fingers allows for fast and easy donning and removal of the device and keeps the palm, the phalanges and joints free of mechanical obstructions. The linkage kinematics provides 6 DOF (rotations and translations) to the fingertips and allows unobstructed motion of the fingers in their entire workspace. The kinematics of the system support variable hand sizes without having to modify or adapt the linkage lengths, furthermore the thimbles are easily interchangeable with a snap-on mechanism for accommodating different finger sizes. Bidirectional actuation is provided by backdrivability low gearing motors at the first revolute joint of each linkage. The actuation system provides approximately 2N at the fingertips when the finger is fully extended. The exoskeleton integrates its own tracking system through rotary magnetic position encoders embedded in the linkage joints which allows measurement of the position and orientation of the fingertips.

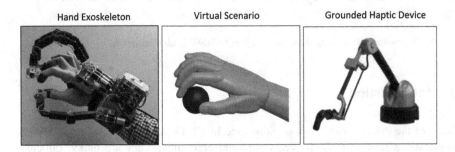

Fig. 1. Three-fingered hand exoskeleton for grasping/manipulating virtual objects

The virtual scenario consists of a virtual hand reflecting the position, orientation and motions of the users' hand and fingers, and virtual objects which can be grasped and manipulated. A multi-point haptic rendering method is implemented in order to detect the collision between the virtual fingertips and objects and calculate the forces to be conveyed to the users' fingers. The collision detection was performed by implementing an AABB collision detection algorithm, whereas the estimation of the magnitude and the direction of the force feedback at each finger were accomplished by a proxy-based force rendering algorithm. The libraries of the open source platform CHAI3d were used to render the graphic scenario, detect collisions and render the force feedback when the object was encountered by the users' virtual fingers.

References

1. Fang, H., Xie, Z., Liu, H.: An exoskeleton master hand for controlling DLR/HIT hand. In: IEEE/RSJ International Conference on Intelligent Robots and Systems (IROS), pp. 3703–3708 (2009)
2. Nishino, Y., Kunii, Y., Hashimono, H.: 20 DOF haptic device for the interaction with virtual environments. In: International Conference on Artificial Reality and Telexistence (ICAT), pp. 85–92 (1997)
3. Chiri, A., Vitiello, N., Giovacchini, F., Roccella, S., Vecchi, F., Carrozza, M.C.: Mechatronic design and characterization of the index finger module of a hand exoskeleton for post-stroke rehabilitation. IEEE/ASME Trans. Mechatron. **17**(5), 884–894 (2012)

Haptic Broadcasting

- *System of Transmitting the Experience in Badminton* -

Yusuke Mizushina, Charith Lasantha Fernando, Kouta Minamizawa,
and Susumu Tachi

Graduate School of Media Design, Keio University,
4-1-1 Hiyoshi, Kohoku-ku, Yokohama Kanagawa, 223-8526, Japan
{mizushina,charith}@kmd.keio.ac.jp
{kouta,tachi}@tachilab.org
http://tachilab.org

Abstract. We propose a Haptic Broadcasting system that allows the television audience to have realistic badminton game play experience with transmitted haptic sensation together with audiovisual content with existing broadcasting infrastructures. In this system, audio signals are being used as haptic content carrier so that the existing broadcasting infrastructures can be utilize to deliver realistic game play experience to worldwide television audience. In this paper, we describe the construction of real-time haptic capture system, embedded haptic display on a badminton racket and the effects of haptic slow motion in interactive game play.

Keywords: Haptic broadcast · Sports broadcast · Augmented sports

1   Introduction

In 2020, Olympics will be held in Tokyo. Not just Japanese audience, but also people all over the world will be watching the great Olympics in real-time via TV (Television) Broadcasting. In this context, apart from traditional audio-visual content, what kind of immersive experience we could provide to the audience around the world? During action sports viewing through broadcasted media, if haptic contents could be delivered in real-time synchronized with audio-visual content, it would be a new sports viewing experience. Next generation broadcast technologies [1] by Yamauchi et al. [2] allow transmitting haptic information (roughness, friction, and softness) over 300 km distance using Internet. However, it's not practical for a greater audience such as subscribers of a large TV channel because new infrastructures have to be implemented for haptic content delivery. The method proposed in TECHTILE toolkit [3] shows that haptic information can be carried as audio signals. Therefore, our approach is to use conventional audio-visual transmission channels used in broadcasting infrastructures to distribute haptic content to home audience.

Haptic Broadcast system consists of a badminton racket that captures the impact of a shuttle hitting the racket; haptic transmission via audio carrier to ordinary television

© Springer-Verlag Berlin Heidelberg 2014
M. Auvray and C. Duriez (Eds.): EuroHaptics 2014, Part II, LNCS 8619, pp. 466–468, 2014.
DOI: 10.1007/978-3-662-44196-1

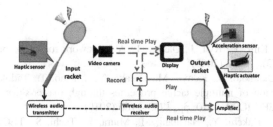

Fig. 1. Haptic broadcast system

Fig. 2. Interactive haptic slow motion

audience; and a simple receiver badminton racket to feel the badminton play experience at home. As shown in Fig. 1, a tactile microphone (Primo: MX-E4758) is used as the haptic sensor that can capture low frequencies up to 100 Hz or less vibration generated during shuttle impact. A wearable wireless audio transmitter (SHURE: SVX14/ PGA31) is attached to the player to transmit haptic content between the input racket and an amplifier (case of live) or a computer (case of recording). A Haptic actuator (Tactile Labs: Haptuator Mark II) and an amplifier is used as the display. In addition, to achieve a haptic slow motion effect proposed by Hashimoto and Kajimoto [4] into interactive gameplay, an accelerometer is attached to the racket. The sensor data is used to change the playback speed of the recorded haptic content. Thus, audience can feel entire play experience as they were playing at a slow motion manner by swinging the racket slowly at their own speed and also to feel the difference of hitting the sweet spot of racket or not.

2   Demonstration

In Eurohaptics 2014, we demonstrate our system in three configurations. The Audience is able to (1) experience the impact of the shuttle in a real time play scenario; (2) experience what the player felt during play with recorded haptics; (3) experience interactive haptic slow motion (Fig. 2) that can feel entire play experience as they were playing at a slow motion manner by swinging the racket slowly at their own speed.

References

1. Cha, J., Ho, Y., Kim, Y., Ryu, J., Oakley, I.: A framework for haptic broadcasting. IEEE MultiMedia, **16**(3), 16–27 (2009)
2. Yamauchi, T., Okamoto, S., Konyo, M., Hidaka, Y., Maeno, T., Tadokoro, S.: Realtime remote transmission of multiple tactile properties through master-slave robot system. In: Proceeding of IEEE ICRA 2010, pp. 1753–1760 (2010)
3. Minamizawa, K., Kakehi, Y., Nakatani, M., Miura, S., Tachi, S.: TECHTILE toolkit: A prototyping tool for designing haptic media. In: Proceeding of ACM SIGGRAPH 2012 Emerging Technologies, Article No. 22 (2012)
4. Hashimoto, Y., Kajimoto, H.: Slow motion replay of tactile sensation. In: Proceeding of IEEE ICAT 2010, pp. 51–56 (2010)

Tactile Vision Substitution System for Palm Using Electro-Tactile Display and Smartphone

Hiroyuki Kajimoto[1,2], Masaki Suzuki[3], and Yonezo Kanno[3]

[1] The University of Electro-Communications, Chofu, Tokyo, Japan
Kajimoto@kaji-lab.jp
[2] Japan Science and Technology Agency, Chofu, Tokyo, Japan
[3] EyePlusPlus Inc., Kapolei, HI, USA
{suzuki,kanno}@eyeplus2.com

Abstract. We developed a tactile vision substitution system, which is composed of an electro-tactile display, optical sensors beneath each electrode, and a smartphone with a camera and an LCD. The smartphone acquires the surrounding view, conducts image processing and displays the image on the LCD. The image is captured by the optical sensors and converted to a tactile image by the electro-tactile display. Combining the commonly available mobile device and electro-tactile display enables a low cost yet powerful and compact system.

Keywords: Electro-tactile display · Reading aid · Smartphone · Tactile vision substitution system · Visually impaired

1 Introduction

There have been numerous attempts to present surrounding visual information to a tactile channel for the people with visual impairments [1]. The system consists of a camera and tactile display. However, the developed systems have not prevailed in the blind community to date, and one aspect of the reason is cost.

We developed a TVSS named HamsaTouch (Figs.1 and 2), which is based on the authors' prior works [2, 3] and tries to resolve the cost problem with the following three frameworks. The first is to use a commonly available smartphone as a camera and image processor, the second is to use simple optical data transmission using an LCD and phototransistors, and the third is to use an electro-tactile display.

2 Demonstration

We will show two scenarios at the demo (Fig. 3). One is to use with smartphone camera to feel the surrounding scene. The other is to use with tablet PC to directly touch displayed image.

© Springer-Verlag Berlin Heidelberg 2014
M. Auvray and C. Duriez (Eds.): EuroHaptics 2014, Part II, LNCS 8619, pp. 469–471, 2014.
DOI: 10.1007/978-3-662-44196-1

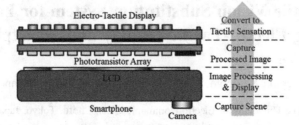

Fig. 1. System structure and process of HamsaTouch.

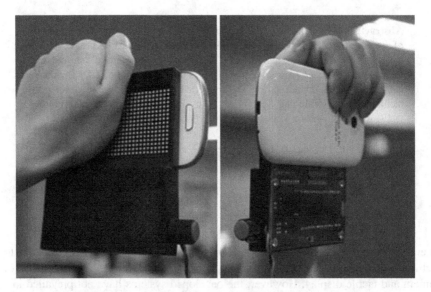

Fig. 2. (Left) rear view and (right) front view of HamsaTouch.

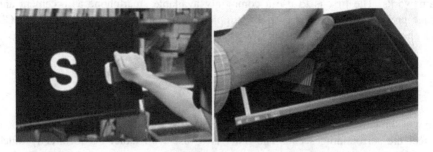

Fig. 3. Demo scenarios (left) with smartphone and (right) with tablet PC.

References

1. Bach-y Rita, P., Collins, C.C., Saunders, F., White, B., Scadden, L.: Vision substitution by tactile image projection. Nature , **221**, 963–64 (1969)
2. Kajimoto, H., Kanno, Y., Tachi, S. Forehead electro-tactile display for vision substitution. In: Proceedings of EuroHaptics (2006)
3. Kajimoto, H., Inami, M., Kawakami, N., Tachi, S.:SmartTouch: electric skin to touch the untouchable. IEEE Comput. Graphics Appl. Mag. **24**(1), 36–43 (2004)

Developing Immersive Virtual Worlds through Realistic Contact Rendering and Improved Transparency

Arash Mohtat, Colin Gallacher, and Jozsef Kovecses

Department of Mechanical Engineering and Centre for Intelligent Machines,
McGill University, Montreal QC, Canada
{amohtat, crgallac}@cim.mcgill.ca,
jozsef.kovecses@mcgill.ca

Abstract. This demonstration presents a virtual billiard game using a five degree of freedom haptic device. Realistic contact forces and torques are rendered through the use of a generalized haptic controller that couples the virtual environment to the physical tool by transitioning between penalty and impulse based approaches depending on the nature of the contact event. Participants can expect to experience an immersive virtual environment where force feedback haptics can be explored through a fun and familiar billiard setting.

Keywords: Force-feedback · Contact rendering · Workspace drift · Transparency

1 Introduction

A haptic interface enables users to interact with virtual environments through the sensation of touch. In a force feedback device, the forces that arise from this interaction are relayed to the human user. These forces must accurately emulate a real interaction. Many different factors can influence the perceived haptic experience, and make realistic rendering a challenge. The work presented here realizes an immersive virtual world through combining rigid body rendering techniques, improving device transparency via path specific orientation, and by implementing extrasensory stimuli to engage the user. The above concepts are demonstrated by way of a virtual billiard game. This demo employs the W5D device by Entact Robotics, S-functions using the W5D API, Simulink Real-Time Workshop and the VRML Blockset.

2 Demonstration

A critical component of a force feedback haptic display is the rendering of contact between a virtual object and the virtual tool, and the subsequent coupling of the virtual tool to the physical device. There are various combinations of coupling techniques and contact modeling methods [1] to accomplish this task. The current demo showcases the

© Springer-Verlag Berlin Heidelberg 2014
M. Auvray and C. Duriez (Eds.): EuroHaptics 2014, Part II, LNCS 8619, pp. 472–474, 2014.
DOI: 10.1007/978-3-662-44196-1

ongoing work of our research group in exploring these techniques within a unified framework. This framework builds upon previous developments on energy-consistent rendering [2], and, it facilitates comparison and combined utilization of different methods using a generalized formulation that allows for adaptation according to the nature of contact events. Here we use the five actuated degrees of freedom of the Entact W5D to implement our unified contact framework within a billiards simulation. Users can expect to compare varying sensations that arise from transitioning between the use of penalty and impulse based techniques (Fig. 1).

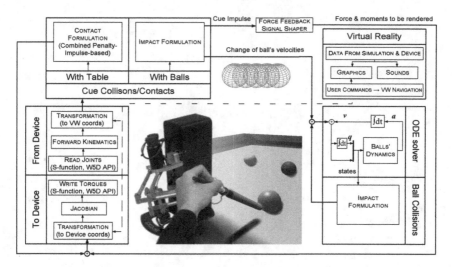

Fig. 1. A block diagram representation of the billiard demonstration's modular components: device communication, simulation and contact model, and graphical display.

Navigating a large virtual environment using a small workspaced device also poses a challenge for haptic simulation. Large translations outside of optimum workspace regions can lead to undesirable changes in perceived weight and perceived inertia forces. Along with the billiards demo we will showcase a software, developed by our research group at McGill, used to perform dynamic analysis of the Entact W5D along prescribed trajectories. This software enables us to visualize inertia properties of the device at varying locations in the workspace. Using this analysis we divided the workspace into two regions: one suitable for haptic interaction and the other for workspace drift control [3]. These techniques, combined with additional auditory and visual input, lead to a highly engaging virtual reality for the user.

References

1. Constantinescu, D., Salcudean, S.E., Croft, E.A.: Haptic rendering of rigid contacts using impulsive and penalty forces. IEEE Tran. Rob. **21**(3), 309–323 (2005)
2. Mohtat, A., Kovecses, J.: Energy-consistent force feedback laws for virtual environments. J. Comput. Inf. Sci. Eng. **13**(3) 031003 (2013)
3. Conti, F., Khatib,. O., Spanning large workspaces using small haptic devices. In: Eurohaptics Conference, pp. 183–188 (2005)

Localization Ability and Polarity Effect of Underwater Electro-Tactile Stimulation

Taira Nakamura[1], Manami Katoh[1], Taku Hachisu[1,2],
Ryuta Okazaki[1,2], Michi Sato[1,2], and Hiroyuki Kajimoto[1,3]

[1] The University of Electro-Communications,
1-5-1 Chofugaoka, Chofu Tokyo, 182-8585, Japan
{n.taira,katoh,hachisu,okazaki,
mich,kajimoto}@kaji-lab.jp
[2] JSPS, 1-5-1 Chofugaoka, Chofu Tokyo, 182-8585, Japan
[3] Japan Science and Technology Agency,
1-5-1 Chofugaoka, Chofu Tokyo, 182-8585, Japan

Abstract. In this paper, we describe a method for presenting underwater tactile electrical stimulation for in-bath entertainment. We investigated the localization abilities of participants and the polarity effect of the stimulation, and found that underwater electro-tactile anodic stimulation produced a stronger sensation than did cathodic stimulation. Furthermore, we found that the participants were able to successfully identify the direction of the tactile stimulation and the direction of rotation during anodic stimulation.

Keywords: Electrical stimulation · Haptic device · Human interface · Underwater stimulation

1 Introduction

In this demonstration, you can experience a method of presenting underwater tactile electrical stimulation. Electro-tactile displays are small and thin, affordable, energy efficient, and durable, making them useful for work in various fields [1, 2, 3]. Underwater electrical stimulation was developed mainly for massage [4], and it is well known that tactile sensations can be elicited in an electric-bath. To the best of our knowledge, no researchers have attempted to use underwater electro-tactile stimulation for entertainment. Thus, the potential of a whole-body tactile interface has not been fully explored.

As a first step in investigating the possibilities of underwater electro-tactile stimulation for in-bath entertainment, we investigated the ability of participants to localize the stimulation and identify the polarity effect of the stimulation. For safety, the electro-tactile stimulation was conducted using the forearm so that the current could not pass through the heart.

We fabricated an underwater electrical stimulation device (Fig. 1). The device comprised a water tank, current controlled electrical stimulator circuit and eight electrodes. The electrodes were independently current-controlled. A voltage pulse wave

© Springer-Verlag Berlin Heidelberg 2014
M. Auvray and C. Duriez (Eds.): EuroHaptics 2014, Part II, LNCS 8619, pp. 475–477, 2014.
DOI: 10.1007/978-3-662-44196-1

is generated by a microcontroller (mbed, NCP LPC 1768, NXP Semiconductors) and offset circuit. The voltage waveform is converted to a current waveform of ± 50 mA by a volt-age-current converter using high-voltage op-amps (OPA552, Texas Instruments), and emitted to the water by the electrodes.

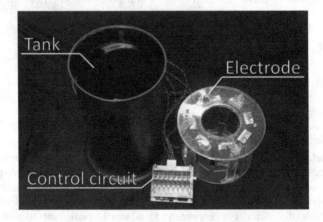

Fig. 1. Prototype system

2   Demonstration

As a first investigation of the potential use of underwater electro-tactile stimulation for in-bath entertainment, we made some demos. In this demo, you can feel flutter sensation like fish poke (Fig. 2).

Fig. 2. Applications to entertainment

References

1. Bach-y-Rita, P., Kaczmarek, K.A., Tyler, M.E., Garcia-Lara, J.: From perception with a 49-point electrotactile stimulus array on the tongue. J. Rehabil. Res. Dev. (A Technical Note), **35**, 427–430 (1998)
2. Kajimoto, H.: Skeletouch: transparent electro-tactile display for mobile surfaces. In: SIGGRAPH Asia 2012 Emerging Technologies, pp. 1–21. ACM (2012)
3. Collins, C.C.: Tactile television-mechanical and electrical image projection. In: Man-Machine Systems. IEEE Trans. Man Mach. Syst. **11**(1), 65–71 (1970)
4. Howard, M.: Electric bath. US1193018A (1916. 08. 01)

Diminished Haptics: Towards Digital Transformation
of Real World Textures

Yoichi Ochiai[1,2], Takayuki Hoshi[3],
Jun Rekimoto[1,4], and Masaya Takasaki[5]

[1] Graduate School of Interdisciplinary Information Studies,
The University of Tokyo, 7-3-1 Hongo, Bunkyo-ku Tokyo, 113-0033, Japan
yoichi.ochiai@me.com, rekimoto@acm.org
[2] Japan Society for the Promotion of Science,
6 Ichiban-cho, Chiyoda-ku Tokyo, 102-8471, Japan
[3] Nagoya Institute of Technology,
Gokisocho, Showa-ku, Nagoyashi, Nagoya Aichi, 466-855, Japan
star@nitech.ac.jp
[4] Sony CSL, 3-14-13 Higashigotanda, Shinagawa-ku Tokyo, 141-0022, Japan
[5] Saitama University, 255 Shimo-Okubo, Sakura-ku
Saitama, 338-8570, Japan
masaya@mech.saitama-u.ac.jp

Keywords: Diminished haptics · Real-world texture · Texture transformation · Ultrasonic

1 Introduction and Related Work

The representation of texture is a major concern during fabrication and manufacture in many industries. Thus, the manner of fabricating everyday objects and the digital expression of their textures have become a popular research area [1]. In the present study, we aim to transform the textures of real-world objects. Two steps are required to transform real-world textures. The first step is to reduce the original texture and the second is to rewrite the texture. In the present study, we focus on the first step and we introduce a technique named "Diminished Haptics" (Fig. 1(a)). This technique reduces the degrees of real-world haptic textures using ultrasonic vibration based on a squeeze film effect.

There are several related studies on haptic texture representation. One approach is wearable devices to provide additional vibration to users' fingers. The other is haptic displays add haptic feedback on their smooth surfaces. The technologies employed in the latter approach include ultrasonic vibrations [2, 3] and electrostatic forces [4]. The ultrasonic technology utilizes a squeeze film effect to reduce the friction of a flat surface and reproduces the texture by modulating the ultrasonic vibration. The electrostatic technology also adds textures to smooth surfaces. In the present study, we aim to achieve the opposite effect, i.e., we reduce the texture of a real material using a squeeze film effect. We focus on the transformation of real textures and we employ a real material as the surface of haptic display (Figure 1(b)). We consider that the reduction process has an important role as a preprocessing step in the transformation of real-world textures.

© Springer-Verlag Berlin Heidelberg 2014
M. Auvray and C. Duriez (Eds.): EuroHaptics 2014, Part II, LNCS 8619, pp. 478–479, 2014.
DOI: 10.1007/978-3-662-44196-1

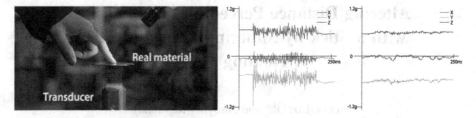

Fig. 1. (Left) System overview. (Right) Output of 3-axis accelerometer on nail (rough paper).

2 Demonstration

In the demonstration, the visitors will experience the haptic transformation of real textures that is obtained by following implementation. Our method transforms real textures by utilizing ultrasonic vibration. We employ ultrasonic vibration to reduce and erase the haptic textures of real-world objects based on the squeeze film effect. Using our system, the texture obtained is inherently high resolution and the altered textures are felt without lateral movement of fingers because real material has its own texture (Fig. 1(a)). Figure 1(c) shows a diagram of our system, which has four components: The host computer, the resonance controller, the ultrasonic transducer, and real material textures. Users can touch the real material with their bare fingers. The height of levitation by the squeeze film effect is controlled to transform the textures. The process operates as follows. The computer sends a start signal to the controller, which adjusts the resonance frequency. Next, the controller generates the input signal to the transducer. The amplitude of the input signal determines the levitation height of the finger relative to the material surface based on the squeeze effect. We paste papers of various real textures (Fig. 1(a)) onto a metallic plate that is acoustically coupled to the 28 kHz transducer. Resonance control (adjusting the frequency of the input signal) is necessary for this use because the resonance of transducer changes when user touches the transducer (Fig. 1(d)). The visitors experience the several haptic contents material pasted on the transducer. The analysis of haptic content that visitor will experience is shown in Fig. 1(e). It is measured by a three-axis accelerometer on a nail and it indicates the reduction of the textures.

References

1. Hullin, M.B., et al.: State of the art in computational fabrication and display of material appearance. In: EUROGRAPHICS 2013, State of-the-Art Report (2013)
2. Biet, M., et al.: Discrimination of virtual square gratings by dynamic touch on friction based tactile displays. In: Proceedings of Haptics Symposium 2008, pp. 41–48 (2008)
3. Winfield, L., et al.: T-PaD: tactile pattern display through variable friction reduction. In: Proceedings of World Haptics Conference 2007, pp. 421–426 (2007)
4. Bau, O., et al.: TeslaTouch: electrovibration for touch surfaces. In: Proceedings of ACM UIST 2010, pp. 283–292 (2010)

Altering Distance Perception from Hitting with a Stick by Superimposing Vibration to Holding Hand

Ryuta Okazaki[1,2] and Hiroyuki Kajimoto[1,3]

[1] The University of Electro-Communications,
1-5-1 Chofugaoka, Chofu Tokyo, 182-8585, Japan
{okazaki,kajimoto}@kaji-lab.jp
[2] JSPS, 1-5-1 Chofugaoka, Chofu Tokyo, 182-8585, Japan
[3] Japan Science and Technology Agency,
1-5-1 Chofugaoka, Chofu Tokyo, 182-8585, Japan

Abstract. Distance perception by hitting with a holding stick is quite important cue for the people with visual impairments who daily use white cane. In our previous paper, we have found that adding vibration to the thumb side may shorten the perceived collision distance than adding vibration to the little-finger side, which partly agrees with our hypothetical model. In this paper, we conducted similar experiment with changing the real distance between the palm and the object, to see the robustness of our hypothetical model. The experimental results showed that perceived collision distance shortened regardless on the real distance but may be easily induced when the object is placed far from the palm.

Keywords: Distance perception · Hitting · Stick · Vibrotactile

1 Introduction

Most people have experience of perceiving distance by hitting objects with a stick. This perception is quite important, especially for the visually impaired who use white canes to guide them in daily life. Therefore, understanding the perception mechanism underlying this phenomenon might help in the development of supporting devices, such as an electric white cane that consists of a range sensor and a haptic display [1].

Yao and Hayward [2] found that "rolling" a small object inside the rod can be expressed by simple vibration, but they did not directly deal with distance perception from hitting an object. The contribution of the rotational moment was considered but not fully explored [3]. Sreng et al. proposed that transient frequency components after hitting with a stick may play a role in perception [4]. However, the vibration frequency is easily affected by the material and length of the stick, which leads to frequency cues not being robust. We presume therefore that simpler yet more robust cutaneous cues play a role in this perception.

In our previous study [5], we advanced the hypothesis that the distance information obtained from hitting with a stick can be retrieved by the "center of gravity" of

© Springer-Verlag Berlin Heidelberg 2014
M. Auvray and C. Duriez (Eds.): EuroHaptics 2014, Part II, LNCS 8619, pp. 480–482, 2014.
DOI: 10.1007/978-3-662-44196-1

vibration in the palm, and experimental results showed that perceived collision distance shortened by adding vibration to the thumb side of the palm. Our demonstration introduces this phenomenon.

2 Demonstration

We developed a stick-type device that can superimpose vibrations generated by actuators to the real vibration induced by percussion. The device comprises an aluminum pipe, an acrylic grip, a single-axis accelerometer, two vibrotactile actuators on the grip, a pre-amplifier circuit, and an audio amplifier.

The accelerometer was placed at the tip of the aluminum pipe to record the real contact. Each actuator was connected to the right and left channels of the audio amplifier; the amplitude ratio of the two actuators could be controlled by the balance control knob of the audio amplifier.

We have a simple demonstration to show that the distance perception from hitting with a stick is altered by the artificial vibration to the palm. In this demo, the amplitude rate of artificial vibration from two actuators is gradually changed by controlling the balance control knob of the audio amplifier while the user repeatedly hit the object in a same position. The user will perceive that the subjective position of collision getting closer to the palm when presenting stronger vibration to the thumb side (Fig. 1).

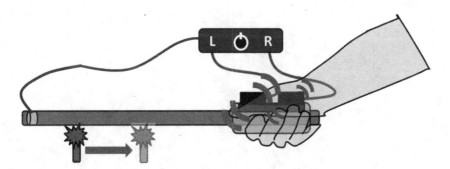

Fig. 1. Perceived distance shortens when the rate of artificial vibration from actuators become stronger at the thump side.

References

1. Vera, P., Zenteno, D., Salas, J.: A smartphone-based virtual white cane. Pattern Anal. Appl. **16**, 1–10 (2014)
2. Yao, H.-Y., Hayward, V.: An experiment on length perception with a virtual rolling stone. In: Proceedings of Eurohaptics, pp. 325–330 (2006)

3. Felicia, W., Zelek, J.S.: Tactile & inertial patterns from a long white cane. In: Proceedings of Biomedical Robotics and Biomechatronics, pp. 51–524 (2006)
4. Sreng, J. et al.: Spatialized haptic rendering: providing impact position information in 6DOF haptic simulations using vibrations. In: Proceedings of Virtual Reality Conference, pp. 3–9 (2009)
5. Okazaki, R., Kajimoto, H.: Perceived distance from hitting with a stick is altered by overlapping vibration to holding hand. In: Proceedings of ACM CHI 2014 (in press)

Surface Haptic Interaction

Semin Ryu, Dongbum Pyo, Seung-Chan Kim, and Dong-Soo Kwon

Department of Mechanical Engineering, KAIST, Daejeon, Republic of Korea
{ryusm,pyodb,kimsc}@robot.kaist.ac.kr,
kwonds@kaist.ac.kr

Abstract. This paper presents a new transparent surface haptic display that can generate both electrovibration and mechanical vibration simultaneously. It can provide not only effective vibrotactile feedback from uniform mechanical vibration on an entire touch surface, but also programmable friction force from electrovibration that enables to simulate the kinesthetic sensation of 3D geometric feature. Also, complicated texture information can be conveyed to users when they are rendered simultaneously.

Keywords: Electrovibration · Mechanical vibration · Haptic rendering

1 Introduction

2D texture information can be represented by using tactile patterns generated by mechanical vibration [1], and 3D feature information can be represented by adjusting lateral friction forces using the electrovibration [2]. This paper introduces a new transparent surface haptic display that can generate both electrovibration and mechanical vibration simultaneously as shown in the Fig. 1.

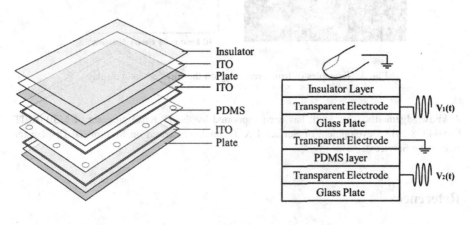

(a) disassembled schematic   (b) cross-sectional schematic

Fig. 1. Overall structure of the surface haptic display

M. Auvray and C. Duriez (Eds.): EuroHaptics 2014, Part II, LNCS 8619, pp. 483–484, 2014.
DOI: 10.1007/978-3-662-44196-1

The system consists of the surface haptic display prototype, a control board (myCortex-LM8962), high voltage amplifier modules (AS-3B1, Matsusada Precision Inc.), and a desktop PC as shown in Fig. 2.

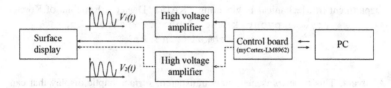

Fig. 2. Schematic representation of system configuration

2   Demonstration

For demonstration, we simulate various kinds of haptic information on the developed surface haptic display. As shown in Fig. 3, more realistic haptic sensations can be represented by adding both 2D texture information generated by mechanical vibration and 3D feature information generated by electrovibration in conjunction with visual information.

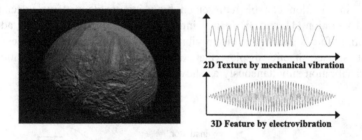

Fig. 3. Examples of haptic rendering on the surface haptic display

Acknowledgements. This work has been supported by the IT R&D program of MSIP/KEIT (10044308-2013-Development of Surface UX Technologies based on Multimodal Display for Interactive Services).

References

1. Jones, L.A., Sarter, N.B.: Tactile displays: guidance for their design and application. Hum. Factors: J. Hum. Factors Ergon. Soc. **50**(1), 90–111 (2008)
2. Kim, S.-C., Israr, A., Poupyrev, I.: Tactile rendering of 3D features on touch surfaces. In: Proceedings of UIST 2013, pp. 531–538. ACM, St. Andrews, UK (2013)

Sensators: Active Multisensory Tangible User Interfaces

Jan B.F. van Erp, Christian J.A.M. Willemse, Joris B. Janssen, and Alexander Toet

TNO Perceptual and Cognitive Systems, Soesterberg, The Netherlands
{jan.vanerp, christian.willemse,
joris.janssen, lex.toet}@tno.nl

Abstract. Although Tangible User Interfaces are considered an intuitive means of human-computer interaction, they oftentimes lack the option to provide active feedback. We developed 'Sensators': generic shaped active tangibles to be used on a multi-touch table. Sensators can represent digital information by means of 'Sensicons': multimodal messages consisting of visual, auditory, and vibrotactile cues. In our demonstration, we will present Sensators as suitable tools for research on multimodal perception in different tangible HCI tasks.

Keywords: Tangible user interface, Active tangibles, Multimodal feedback

1 Introduction

In the quest for innovative forms of HCI, the research area of Tangible User Interfaces (TUIs) has received a fair amount of attention. TUIs can physically represent the underlying digital connection and as a consequence, the user can grab and feel the digital bits (See [1] for a recent overview). Since a TUI draws upon our skill to physically interact with the world, it is expected to enhance the intuitiveness of the interaction; an example is interacting by placing and manipulating objects on a multi-touch table. However, TUIs typically only take orientation and location as input, whereas our sense of touch offers many other means of communication: e.g., stroking, tapping, and squeezing. Moreover, whereas the digital world is highly dynamic and subject to change, TUIs are generally rigid and passive, not capable of representing these changes in information appropriately. For instance, objects placed on a multi-touch table usually cannot actively convey underlying information. Although TUIs enable intuitive tactile input (to a certain extent), they lack informative tactile feedback. This reduces the intuitiveness of the interaction as a whole and led to several investigations on ways to provide active feedback in TUIs. Self rearranging tangibles [2] can overcome a discrepancy between digital and physical information and can also provide force feedback (e.g., 'Tangible Bots' [3]). Moreover, system feedback can be provided in different modalities (e.g., 'SmartPuck' [4]). This trend in TUI research motivated us to enrich tangible objects with active feedback capabilities to be used in combination with multi-user multi-touch devices or as standalone devices.

© Springer-Verlag Berlin Heidelberg 2014
M. Auvray and C. Duriez (Eds.): EuroHaptics 2014, Part II, LNCS 8619, pp. 485–487, 2014.
DOI: 10.1007/978-3-662-44196-1

We developed several generations of generic shaped active TUIs: 'Sensators'. Sensators (Fig. 1) can serve as tangible input devices by means of translation and rotation, but also through multiple conductive touch-sensitive areas which sense whether and where the Sensator is touched. As means of output, the Sensators can provide multisensory messages: 'Sensicons' (analogous to icons and earcons). Sensicons consist of visual information through color patterns, auditory information through pre-recorded audio-samples, and/or vibro-tactile information by means of varying frequencies and amplitudes of two vibration motors [5].

Fig. 1. Sensators (A) with markers for recognition (B) and touch-sensitive input areas (C) applied as research tools in a tangible interaction task on a multi-touch device (D).

We discern five goals for Sensator interaction on digital tabletops: (1) provide system feedback, (2) strengthen the interaction and collaboration between users, (3) display additional abstract and/or personalized information, (4) display touch properties of objects, and (5) support interaction styles and techniques.

2 Demonstration

We will demonstrate our latest generation of Sensators and provide insights in how Sensators have been applied as research tools in different user studies. Visitors can experience Sensators in different (multihanded) tasks. We would also like to present our ideas on possible extensions of the Sensators (e.g., heat as a form of communication, or sensing physiological data as means of system input), as well as on possible future application areas of active tangible objects (e.g., research on social interaction or higher level cognitive aspects of multi-sensory information).

References

1. Shaer, O., Hornecker, E.: Tangible user interfaces: past, present and future directions. Found. Trends Hum. Comput. Interact. **3**(1–2), 1–137 (2010)
2. Poupyrev, I., Nashida, T., Okabe, M.: Actuation and tangible user interfaces: The Vaucanson duck, robots and shape displays. In: Proceedings of TEI'07, pp.205–212 (2007)

3. Pedersen, E.W., Hornbæk, K.: Tangible bots: interaction with active tangibles in table top interfaces. In: Proceedings of CHI'11, pp. 2975–2984 (2011)
4. Kim,L.,Cho, H., Park, S., Han, M.: A tangible user interface with multimodal feedback. In: Jacko, J.A. (ed.) Human-Computer Interaction, Part III, HCII 2007. LNCS, vol. 4552, pp. 94–103. Springer, Heidelberg (2007)
5. Van Erp, J.B.F., Toet, A., Janssen, J.: Uni-, bi- and tri-modal warning signals: effects of temporal parameters and sensory modality on perceived urgency. Safety Science (submitted)

Haptic Technical Aids for Environmental Perception, Time Perception and Mobility (in a Riding Arena) for Persons with Deafblindness

Parivash Ranjbar[1,2,3], Dag Stranneby[3,4],
Cheryl Akner-Koler[5], and Erik Borg[1]

[1] Audiological Research Centre, Örebro University Hospital, Örebro, Sweden
parivash.ranjbar@oru.se,
borg.skrekarhyttan@gmail.com,
[2] School of Health and Medical Sciences, Örebro University, Örebro, Sweden
[3] Campus Alfred Nobel, Örebro University, Karlskoga, Sweden
dag.stranneby@oru.se
[4] School of Science and Technology, Örebro University, Örebro, Sweden
[5] Konstfack, University College of Arts, Crafts and Design,
Stockholm, Sweden
cheryl.akner.koler@konstfack.se

Abstract. This demonstration presents three vibrotactile aids to support persons with deafblindness. One aid, Monitor, consists of a microphone that detects sounds from events which are then processed as a signal that is adapted to the sensitivity range of the skin. The signal is sent as vibrations to the user with deafblindness, who can interpret the pattern of the vibrations in order to identify the type and position of the event/source that produced the sounds. Another aid, Distime, uses a smart phone app that informs the user with cognitive impairment and deafblindness about a planned activity through; audio, visual or tactile interaction that is adapted to the abilities of each individual. The last aid, Ready-ride, uses two smart phones and up to 11 vibrators that help the horse back rider with deafblindness to communicate with the instructor from a distance via vibrators placed on different parts of the riders body e.g. wrist, thigh, back, ankle.

Keywords: Haptic · Vibrotactile · Deafness · Blindness · Horse back riding · Sound

1   Introduction

There are approximately 1300 individuals/persons with deafblindness (severe combined visual and hearing impairment) in Sweden. About one hundred are persons with complete deafness and blindness [1]. The number will reach about 30000 if also persons older than 65 with severe visual and hearing impairment are included, several millions worldwide. Many people with deafblindness have also mental, cognitive and physical impairments. Difficulties in environmental perception, spatial

© Springer-Verlag Berlin Heidelberg 2014
M. Auvray and C. Duriez (Eds.): EuroHaptics 2014, Part II, LNCS 8619, pp. 488–490, 2014.
DOI: 10.1007/978-3-662-44196-1

awareness, time perception, social participation and music experience are examples of frequent problems [2]. To experience independence, participation and control, adequate processing of sensory information is important. The demonstration will involve three aids adapted to the individuals level of haptic sensitivity to inform persons with deafblindness about ongoing events producing sound, the time of a planned activity, and information concerning the users position and activity in a space (e.g. riding arena). The three demonstrations described below, use a combination of: microphone, processor/smart phones and vibrators to transfer signals to the user via haptic interaction. During the demonstration we intend to engage the participants in operating of the controls and taking part in the haptic experience. Our interest is to get feedback about modulating the interactive experience to improve the quality of the signal and discuss possible suggestions for advancing our technology.

2   Demonstration

2.1   Monitor

The user will be asked to put the bracelet with the vibrator placed on the palmar side of the wrist and microphone/processor placed on the backside of the wrist. The presenter will produce some sounds and the user can sense the vibrations representing the event, sound.

2.2   Distime

The user will be asked to keep the smart phone in her/his hand or pocket. The presenter will plan an activity (via the Calendar in the smart phone or the website Distime.dk), and choose when and in what way the person should be reminded of the event, choosing the appropriate interactive modality: audio, visual, tactile.

2.3   Ready-ride

The blindfolded user will be asked to put four vibrators on his/her right-, left wrist, back and in front of their body. The presenter and user will agree about the meaning of different vibrations as left, right front, stop or sit. The presenter will lead the user along a path with two chairs and lead the user to sit in a chair.

References

1. Ranjbar, P.: Sensing the environment: development of monitoring Aids for Persons with Profound Deafness or Deafblindness, in The School of Science and Technology. Örebro University, Örebro, pp. 1–185 (2009)
2. Ranjbar, P., Stenstrm, I.: Monitor, a vibrotactile aid for environmental perception; a field evaluation by four people with severe hearing and vision impairment. Sci. World J. (2013)
3. Remes, J., Ranjbar, P.: Time Understanding for Deafblind People, (Bachelor). Örebro University, Örebro (2010).
4. Stranneby, D., Ranjbar, P., Akner-Koler, C., Borg, E.: Ready-Ride: a positioning and communication system to increase the autonomy of riders with visual impairment. In: ADBN 2012, Lund (2012)

Author Index

Printed in the United States
By Bookmasters